TRANSFORMATIONS OF FREEDOM IN THE LAND OF THE MAROONS

■ CREOLIZATION IN THE COCKPITS, JAMAICA ■

TRANSFORMATIONS OF FREEDOM IN THE LAND OF THE MAROONS
■ CREOLIZATION IN THE COCKPITS, JAMAICA ■

Jean Besson

IAN RANDLE PUBLISHERS
Kingston • Miami

First published in Jamaica, 2016 by
Ian Randle Publishers
16 Herb McKenley Drive
Box 686
Kingston 6
www.ianrandlepublishers.com

© Jean Besson 2016

NATIONAL LIBRARY OF JAMAICA CATALOGUING-IN-PUBLICATION DATA
Besson, Jean
Transformations of freedom in the land of the Maroons : creolization in the Cockpits, Jamaica / Jean Besson.

pages : illustrations, maps ; cm. Bibliography : pages
ISBN 978-976-637-408-2 (pbk)

1. Maroons – Jamaica 2. Ethnohistory – Jamaica
3. Jamaica – History
I.   Title

972.9203   dc 23

All rights reserved. No part of this publication may be reproduced, stored in a retrieval system or transmitted in any form or by any means electronic, photocopying, recording or otherwise, without the prior permission of the publisher and author.

Cover image of Cockpit Country © Jeremy Francis
Cover and Book Design by Ian Randle Publishers
Printed and bound in the United States

In memory of my mother,
'Meggie' McFarlane (née Myers) of St Elizabeth

and

'Charlie' Dobson of St James

and

for the Jamaican people of
Accompong, Maroon Town and Aberdeen

Contents

List of Figures	... viii
List of Diagrams	... xiii
List of Genealogies	... xiv
List of Maps	... xv
Foreword by Karen Fog Olwig	... xvii
1. Introduction	... 1
2. The Roots of Creolization in the Cockpits	... 31
3. The Creolization of the Commons	... 59
4. Myal, Kinship and the Ancestors	... 99
5. Reinterpreting Accompong Maroon Society	... 127
6. Accompong, Aberdeen and Maroon Town: The Maroon/Non-Maroon Interface	... 146
7. Non-Maroon Maroon Town	... 176
8. 'Slave Master' Pickni': Meso-Creole Ethnicities and Narrative Transformations of Trelawny Town	... 203
9. Maroon Town Narratives of Maroon Descent and Marronage	... 239
10. The McGhie Maroons and the Maroon Town McGhies	... 269
11. Maroon Town and Accompong: Ritual, Tourism and Nationhood	... 304
12. Creolization at the Maroon/Non-Maroon Interface	... 335
References	... 349
Index	... 363

List of Figures

Figure 1.1	A view of the Cockpit Country.	...	xxi
Figure 1.2a	Monument to the Zong at the Estuary of the Black River, St Elizabeth, 2007.	...	5
Figure 1.2b	Inscription on the Zong monument, Black River, St Elizabeth.	...	5
Figure 1.3a	The Court House, recently restored, in Sam Sharpe Square, Montego Bay.	...	9
Figure 1.3b	Sculpture (by Kay Sullivan) of Sam Sharpe preaching to slaves, Sam Sharpe Square.	...	9
Figure 1.4	Flame trees (Spathodia) in the Cockpits.	...	10
Figure 1.5	Monument at Kensington, near Maroon Town, commemorating the 1831–32 slave rebellion.	...	11
Figure 1.6a	Asking the way to Accompong at Honour Rock, 1979.	...	13
Figure 1.6b	The author's first visit to Accompong, 1979.	...	14
Figure 1.7a	Melvin Currie and Dolphie Rowe (two sisters' children) clearing a sacred site near Old Town, Accompong, 1989.	...	23
Figure 1.7b	Maroon cousins Melvin Currie and Dolphie Rowe, Accompong, 2009.	...	24
Figure 1.8	Mrs Beryl Delgado (right), the author and Barbara Delgado (left), Maroon Town.	...	26
Figure 2.1	A maroon warrior, Leonard Parkinson, 1795. From Edwards 1796.	...	46
Figure 2.2	Salter's Hill Baptist Church, at John's Hall between Maroon Town and Montego Bay.	...	50
Figure 2.3a	Monument to the Emancipation War (1831–32), veiled in a combination of Jamaican national colours and Rastafarian colours, Montego Bay 2007.	...	51
Figure 2.3b	Monument to the Emancipation War (1831–32) unveiled August 1, 2007, Montego Bay.	...	52
Figure 2.3c	Monument to the Emancipation War (1831–32), Montego Bay.	...	52
Figure 2.3d	Names and punishments of some of the slaves who fought the Emancipation War, note Island Estate in St Elizabeth.	...	53
Figure 3.1a	The Accompong maroon commons and the Mountains of Aberdeen.	...	65

List of Figures

Figure 3.1b	The Leeward Maroon treaty kept by Mann O. Rowe, Secretary of State in Accompong.	67
Figure 3.1c	The text of the Leeward Maroon treaty in the Community Centre, Accompong.	68
Figure 3.1d	Colonel Martin Luther Wright (centre) and two of his Captains, early 1990s, Accompong (in front of a mural of Cudjoe and Nanny in the Community Centre).	68
Figure 3.1e	A mural of Captain Cudjoe in Ex-Colonel Harris Cawley's house, Accompong.	69
Figure 3.1f	A partial list of Accompong Maroon Colonels in the Community Centre.	69
Figure 3.2a	Looking up at the Accompong Cockpit forest from Appleton Estate.	72
Figure 3.2b	A provision ground in Accompong carved out of the forest.	73
Figure 3.2c	A house-yard in Accompong at the beginning of my fieldwork in 1979.	74
Figure 3.2d	The crossroads in Accompong at the beginning of my fieldwork in 1979.	74
Figure 3.2e	The crossroads in Accompong at the end of my fieldwork in 2009.	75
Figure 3.3a	The Kindah grove showing the reputed African graves in the bush, the grassland, cockpit rocks and the Kindah Tree.	76
Figure 3.3b	The Myal Play at Kindah, 2007.	77
Figure 3.3c	Cooking the Myal feast on the sacred rocks at Kindah, 1991.	77
Figure 3.3d	An entranced female Myal dancer at the Play, 1991.	78
Figure 3.3e	Male cooks at the Myal Play, 2006.	79
Figure 3.3f	The first sign, 'Kindah, We Are Family' on the Kindah Tree early in my fieldwork.	80
Figure 3.3g	The second sign, 'Kindah, The Family Tree'.	80
Figure 3.3h	The third sign, 'Kindah, One Family' later in my fieldwork.	80
Figure 3.3i	Lawrence Rowe sitting on the boulders at Cudjoe's reputed War Office under the Kindah Tree, 2009.	81
Figure 3.4a	Armed police officers at Kindah, 1991.	82
Figure 3.4b	The Myal pilgrimage returning from Old Town to Kindah in battle-camouflage.	82
Figure 3.4c	Weeding the lieutenants' reputed graves in the intermediate grove, December 1989.	84

Figure 3.4d	Weeding Cudjoe and Nanny's reputed graves at Old Town, December 1989.	...	84
Figure 3.5	The author and Melvin Currie at the symbolic Peace Cave, Accompong, January 1991.	...	86
Figure 3.6a	The Accompong Presbyterian/United Church cemetery, 1979.	...	88
Figure 3.6b	The Accompong Presbyterian/United Church cemetery, c. 2009.	...	88
Figure 3.6c	Recent house-yard vault burials, Accompong.	...	89
Figure 3.7a	The Civic Function at Cudjoe's monument, showing Jamaican flag, 1990s.	...	92
Figure 3.7b	Another Civic Function at the monument, showing the Jamaican flag with the maroon abeng.	...	92
Figure 3.7c	The Myal pilgrimage marching from Kindah to the Parade Ground, 2006.	...	93
Figure 3.7d	The national Civic Function at the Parade Ground.	...	93
Figure 4.1	Hansley Charles Reid in military uniform blowing the abeng at a Civic Function at Parade, 2006. (Inset: Gilbert Rowe, abeng-blower, 1979.)	...	106
Figure 4.2	Mann O. Rowe, Accompong Town's Secretary of State, checking a publication by the author, 1996.	...	114
Figure 4.3	Mann Rowe and his wife at their cottage in Accompong.	...	114
Figure 4.4	Mann Rowe's house-yard with his old cottage, the new villa and visitors' cars, 2006.	...	120
Figure 4.5	The author and Colonel Sydney Peddie at the Myal Play, 2006.	...	121
Figure 4.6	The author with Colonel Sydney Peddie (left) and Deputy Colonel Melvin Currie, Accompong, 2009.	...	122
Figure 6.1a	Ockbrook Moravian Church, Lower Aberdeen.	...	150
Figure 6.1b	The sign at the Ockbrook Moravian Church.	...	150
Figure 6.2	The Post Office in Lower Aberdeen.	...	151
Figure 6.3	Looking towards Island Mountain from the Ockbrook Moravian Church, Aberdeen.	...	155
Figure 6.4	Pastor Wint at his house in Upper Aberdeen.	...	157
Figure 6.5	Pastor Wint at the family-land burial ground of the African-Prince Maroon's descendants in Upper Aberdeen.	...	158
Figure 6.6	A family-land cemetery in Upper Aberdeen.	...	159

Figure 6.7	Mrs Bernetta Cawley of Maroon Town, wife and mother of Accompong maroon Colonels.	170
Figure 7.1	Trelawney Town, the Chief Residence of the Maroons.	180
Figure 7.2	The former Parade Ground, Flagstaff, Maroon Town.	180
Figure 7.3	The remains of the Barracks Well, Flagstaff.	181
Figure 7.4	The British colonial military cemetery at Flagstaff.	182
Figure 7.5	Maroons' Pride banana chip factory, Maroon Town.	185
Figure 7.6	The Maldon Baptist Church, Maroon Town.	189
Figure 7.7	Ex-Councillor Mortimer Reid and Pastor Cleopatra Jolly at the Pastor's Pentecostal Church at Browns' Town, Maroon Town.	196
Figure 7.8	Some of the children at Pastor Jolly's Basic School at Browns' Town.	197
Figure 8.1	A Cockpit Country landscape in Maroon Town.	206
Figure 8.2	A view of the Maldon Baptist Church from Mortimer Reid's house-yard in Vaughansfield, Maroon Town.	207
Figure 8.3	Mortimer Reid in his house-yard in Vaughansfield.	211
Figure 8.4	Mortimer Reid's house-yard cemetery including his tomb.	214
Figure 8.5	Bunny Johnson in the Harris family-land cemetery, Maroon Town.	230
Figure 9.1	Mrs Adeline Hall (née Walker), Maroon Town.	240
Figure 9.2	Charlie Dobson of Maroon Town and Montego Bay.	248
Figure 9.3	The Rockhead family land and cemetery, Browns' Town.	262
Figure 9.4	John Rockhead II's tombstone in the Rockhead family-land cemetery at Browns' Town.	263
Figure 9.5	The burial place of the mulatto Maroon John Rockhead I, Coote Bush, Maroon Town.	264
Figure 9.6	The Hedley family-land cemetery (below the mulatto Maroon's grave), Coote Bush.	264
Figure 10.1	Vincent McGhie's house-yard at Browns' Town.	278
Figure 10.2	Robert McGhie IV, Flagstaff.	284
Figure 10.3	Leonard Lambert McGhie (Papa Meggie, left), with friends by his Cessna plane, Montego Bay.	299
Figure 10.4	Leonard Lambert McGhie's saxophone.	299
Figure 11.1	Councillor Glendon Harris at the Emancipation Day festival, Flagstaff, 2000.	308

Figure 11.2a	A Rastafarian stall at the Emancipation Day festival, Flagstaff, 2002.	... 309
Figure 11.2b	Rastafarian tee-shirts at the Emancipation Day festival, Flagstaff, 2002.	... 309
Figure 11.3a	Jonkonnu masqueraders at Flagstaff, Emancipation Day festival, 2000.	... 310
Figure 11.3b	Jonkonnu Cow-Whip masquerader, Flagstaff, 2000.	... 310
Figure 11.4a	Sign to the tourist villas at the Bickle Village, Accompong.	... 315
Figure 11.4b	Tourist villa at the Bickle Village, Accompong.	... 316
Figure 11.5	A Rastafarian street stall at the Myal Play, Accompong, 2006.	... 323
Figure 11.6	The Overseas Maroons' Conference, Accompong, 2007.	... 324
Figure 11.7	Flagstaff Maroons United Youth Club sign at Ball Ground, Flagstaff, 2008.	... 326
Figure 11.8a	The Jamaica National Heritage Trust sign at Flagstaff Square, 2008.	... 327
Figure 11.8b	Maroon Trails on the Jamaica National Heritage Trust sign at Flagstaff Square, 2008.	... 327
Figure 11.9a	The Accompong Development Centre and Rastafarian craft shop, 2009.	... 328
Figure 11.9b	The Accompong Development Centre with the Maroon Trails sign, 2009.	... 329
Figure 11.9c	The Maroon Trails sign, Accompong Development Centre, 2009.	... 329
Figure 12.1	The author (left) and Ken Bilby discussing research at Kindah, Accompong, c. 2002.	... 339

List of Diagrams

Diagram 3.1	The Maroon Polity	...	64
Diagram 3.2	The Commons	...	72
Diagram 3.3	The Kindah Grove	...	75
Diagram 3.4	The Sacred Groves	...	81
Diagram 3.5	War Cemeteries	...	85
Diagram 3.6	Burial Grounds	...	86
Diagram 3.7	Accompong Town	...	90
Diagram 3.8	The Creolization of the Commons	...	94

List of Genealogies

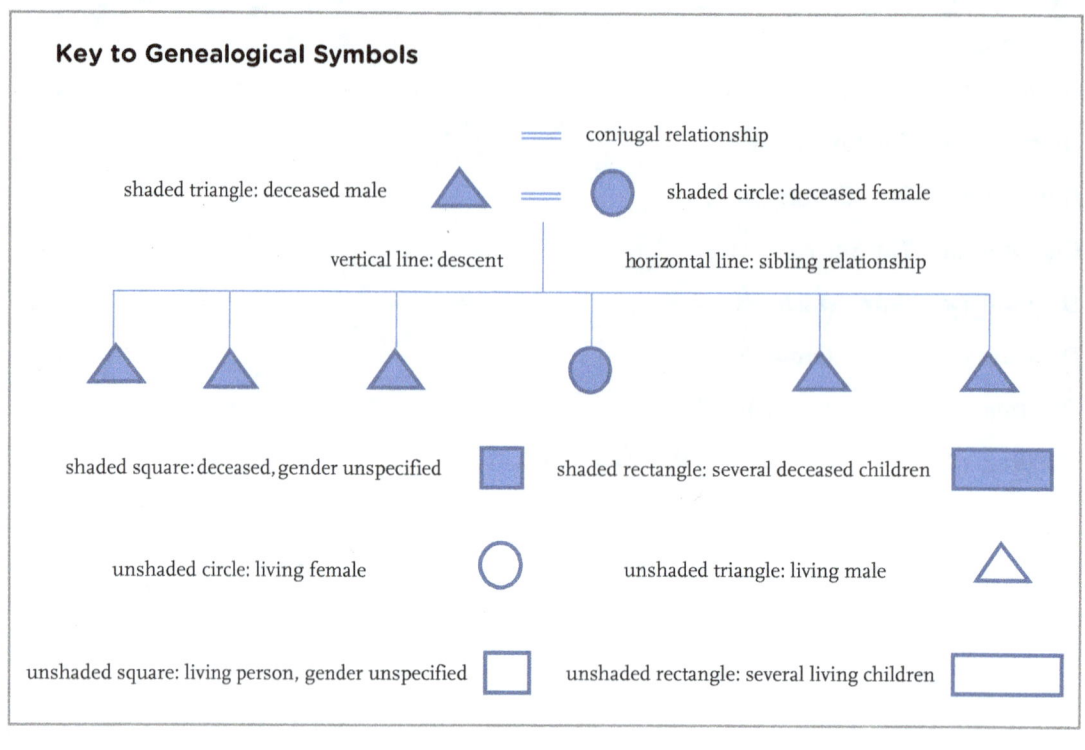

Genealogy 1.	Narrative Account of the Partial Genealogy of the Rowe Clan, Accompong	... 100
Genealogy 2.	Partial Genealogy of the Reid Clan, Maroon Town	... 210
Genealogy 3.	Partial Genealogy of the McIntyre, Stennett and Harris Clans, Maroon Town	... 222
Genealogy 4.	Partial Genealogy of Betsy Currie's ('Campong Nanny's) Descendants	... 241
Genealogy 5.	Partial Genealogy of the Hines Clan, Maroon Town	... 243
Genealogy 6.	Partial Genealogy of Charlie, a "Kongo Maroon"	... 247
Genealogy 7.	Partial Genealogy of the Felsenkopf Maroons and the Rockhead Clan	... 261
Genealogy 8.	The Early Afro-Scots McGhies of Maroon Town and their Descending Generations	... 270
Genealogy 9.	Partial Genealogy of the Descendants of Robert McGhie II	... 280
Genealogy 10.	Partial Genealogy of the Descendants of Jonathan McGhie III	... 288
Genealogy 11.	Partial Genealogy of the Descendants of Albert McGhie I	... 290

List of Maps

Map 1.	The Caribbean region.	... xxii
Map 2.	Jamaica and its parishes.	... xxii
Map 3.	The Cockpit Country and the Communities studied.	... xxii
Map 4.	Into the Cockpits (from Montego Bay to Maroon Town, Accompong and Aberdeen).	... 12
Map 5.	Trelawny Town Territory and the Second Maroon War August 9, 1795.	... 40
Map 6.	Sketch map of the Accompong commons.	... 71
Map 7.	Sketch map of the sacred sites on the commons.	... 87
Map 8.	Trelawny Town Territory August 9, 1795, with historic sites highlighted by the author.	... 132
Map 9.	Island Estate (including Island Mountain), St Elizabeth.	... 149
Map 10.	Island Mountain, St Elizabeth.	... 151
Map 11.	A Plan of the Parish of Trelawny ... performed AD 1800 (Estate Map Trelawny 496).	... 273

■ Foreword

The Caribbean, as we know it today, emerged through the large-scale transformations that were set in motion with the European colonization of the area. They began with the establishment of plantation systems and the almost complete eradication of the aboriginal Amerindian population and its replacement with Europeans, Africans and Asians, and continued with the long history of capitalist colonial class relations linked to a global economy and varying colonial and post-colonial regimes. The societies that arose through these massive changes were stratified in terms of race and class, culturally diverse and highly mobile. An important topic of interest in anthropological research on Caribbean culture and societies, therefore, has been the question of how Caribbean people have created meaningful and workable lives within the framework of such unequal, complex and fluid sociocultural systems.

Jean Besson's rich comparative study of creolization in Jamaica, as seen through the lens of the African-Caribbean history of three communities in the Cockpit Country, illuminates many of the broader central issues raised in anthropological studies of Caribbean culture. The Cockpit Country was the site of historical events that loom large in the imagination of Jamaicans. They include, most notably, the two Maroon Wars that were fought in the 1700s and resulted in the establishment of the Leeward Maroon polity, and a major slave rebellion that took place in 1831–32 and led to the abolition of slavery. The Emancipation Act sparked both the development of peasant villages where many of the freed settled and outmigration for better opportunities in urban centres and abroad. The Cockpit Country thus has been shaped by a long history of violent resistance as well as peaceful coexistence, continuity as well as change, mobility as well as rootedness.

Besson first describes this history with primary emphasis on the Maroon Wars and their aftermath. Then she presents how it is remembered and reflected upon in oral history narratives and cultural practice in Accompong, Aberdeen and Maroon Town, three communities that have had different historical trajectories in relation to the Wars and the post-emancipation history of Jamaica. Accompong became established as an independent maroon polity through the Maroon Wars of the 1700s; Maroon Town, which is located on the main site of the Maroon Wars, lost its original status as part of the maroon polity when local participants in the Second Maroon War were defeated through betrayal and essentially became a peasant community (claiming descent from planters, slaves and Maroons) after the abolition of slavery; Aberdeen did not emerge before the post-emancipation period when it was founded as a village of freed slaves bordering Accompong. The oral history narratives that Besson uncovers reflect these differences and reveal the disparate perspectives and associated interpretations and understandings of the past, that can be found in what for many Jamaicans represents the heart of the country – the rural communities that arose out of the oppressive slave-based plantation regime and claimed a place for themselves in Jamaican society.

This historical anthropological account is based on painstakingly detailed research entailing careful investigations into the historical records, oral history interviews with a large number of people in the three communities and participant-observation, focused on the ways in which people live with this history in their daily lives and commemorate their historical roots at special events. This methodological approach allows Besson to construct a micro-history account of the various events in the Wars and the circumstances leading up to them, the different sites where they took place, the main actors and their interrelations, as well as the later historical development of the communities and families, including the narrators' descriptions of the complicated genealogies that link them to various historical figures as well as fellow villagers.

By examining the specifics of the foundational events, and their continued social life in narratives, commemoration and local life, Besson is able to explore the particular character of creolization in these communities, understood as processes of localization or indigenization that give people a place of belonging in the world and a sense of purpose in life. In Accompong, a key framework of creolization is the land acquired by the Maroons through their treaty with the colonial authorities after the First Maroon War and held in common by all members of the polity. This land has come to constitute a vital social and religious foundation of the local community in the form of a sacred landscape where the various physical features of the land have been endowed with social and symbolic significance. This transformation of the land has involved a symbolic relocating of the main site of the Maroon Wars as well as continuous recognition and validation of the social and symbolic significance of the landscape through ritual. In Maroon Town and Aberdeen, on the other hand, creolization is grounded in the development of the peasant communities that first appeared as informal proto-peasant settlements during slavery and became formalized after the abolition of slavery with the establishment of free villages, located on land acquired by the emancipated. Some of this land was gradually turned into family land held in common by large cognatic kin groups, descendants of the original owner, and later sacralized through the burial of deceased family members on the land. While the communities have constituted an important source of identification, they clearly have not offered a secure livelihood for the ever-expanding groups of descendants of the original inhabitants of the area. Outmigration has long been of key importance in Maroon Town and Aberdeen, and it has been growing rapidly in Accompong in recent decades. Many of the individuals interviewed thus had either spent much of their life abroad – for example, as bus drivers in England or farm labourers in the US – or were part of local families that had been decimated by migration.

Throughout her analysis, Besson is primarily concerned with the places and relations that have had lasting importance in the three communities and the ways in which they have become redefined and reenacted through time in response to changing circumstances of life. She shows how oral history narratives, relations to the land, rituals and genealogical ties are redefined and re-created as the communities' position within Jamaica and in relation to the wider world has changed. Continuity through time and social coherence thus are maintained through ongoing reinterpretation of the physical and social landscape. Perhaps the most important contribution of Besson's account of these cultural transformations is her discovery that a 'tripartite structure of separation or rupture, transition or bridging of disjuncture, and incorporation or reparation' forms the basis of creolization processes in the three communities; a process that is most visible in the creolization of the Accompong commons. This leads her to conclude that creolization has entailed not only 'subaltern opposition and resistance to hegemonic power reflected in class conflict,' but also 'strategies of adaptation, negotiation, alliance, re-creation, culture-building and place-making', occurring both within and across local community and social class.

On the basis of this analysis, Besson discusses the ways in which her historical anthropological study clarifies central issues in research on creolization processes in the Caribbean, such as the significance of African elements in the development of African-Caribbean culture. I would suggest that Besson's work also has significant wider implications for our understanding of Caribbean culture, especially her uncovering of the tripartite structure of the cultural negotiations that have taken place since slavery within the framework of hegemonic sociocultural systems is groundbreaking. This is because it opens up for a new analytical framework that can shed light on the many different theoretical stances proffered in the extensive academic debate on the nature of Caribbean culture and society. The contradictions and challenges of life in the Caribbean, a key topic of interest among anthropologists, have been treated in a number of studies focused on Jamaica. They include Sidney Mintz's historical anthropology of peasant communities which led him to suggest the notion of resistant accommodation as a new way of conceptualizing cultural processes through time in African-Caribbean communities; Edith Clarke's ethnography of family land in rural communities that pointed to the significance of notions of kinship and land rights quite different from dominant (European) family structure and legal systems; R.T. Smith's mapping of extensive networks of family and kinship that demonstrated the complex and inclusive ways of reckoning family relations; Diane Austin-Broos' analysis of race and class in terms of divergent cultures existing within the context of dominant larger ideological schemata, which underscored the complicated relationship between cultural complexity and power in the Caribbean; Huon Wardle's fine grained study of urban life that has shown how radical differences between cultural notions may be negotiated through a process of mediation, or 'ambiguation' – just to mention some of the many important studies that have resulted from ethnographic research in Jamaica. Besson's analysis adds an in-depth historical dimension to these studies, which can give new life and depth to theory on Caribbean culture.

Besson ends her book by describing some of the recent changes taking place in the three communities and their possible impact on the historical consciousness and cultural heritage of the local people. For many years, Accompong, Maroon Town and Aberdeen led a rather quiet life in the margins of – if not in opposition to – mainstream Jamaican society. During the last decades, however, they have gained increasing prominence nationally and transnationally as key sites in the African-Caribbean history and culture of the independent state of Jamaica, as places of identification for migrants from the area, and as interesting cultural attractions in the Jamaican tourist industry. Rituals, commemorations of important events of the past and oral history narratives are, therefore, no longer primarily local concerns, but have become matters of staging Jamaican cultural heritage for the benefit of Jamaicans visiting from other parts of the island and from abroad, as well as foreigners vacationing in the nearby tourist areas.

If the cultural dynamics of the communities is based on a continuous movement involving rupture, bridging and transformation, one wonders how the communities will deal with this embracing of their heritage. As the Cockpit Country begins to become recognized as a key site of Jamaican cultural heritage, will there be a permanent bridging of the gap between the local communities and the wider Jamaican society as well as visitors from abroad, whether migrants or tourists? Besson's ethnography of the present-day celebrations of the cultural heritage of the three communities makes clear that the local communities have instituted some changes in the celebrations and added certain events to accommodate the presence of new participants in the historical commemorations, but they have also closed certain events to outsiders and refused to accept some of the attempted changes. This is exemplified by the failed introduction of Emancipation Day celebrations in Accompong. In recent decades, Emancipation Day celebrations have become an important way of demarcating the abolition of slavery and the rise of free peasant communities in Jamaica. Such celebrations have become popular in the communities of Maroon Town and Aberdeen. In Accompong, however, they are seen as inappropriate and rejected. In this community, the key celebration is the Myal Dance, commemorating the freedom that the maroon polity won for itself many years before the abolition of slavery. This suggests that cultural negotiation of the past – and thereby the present – is far from over.

Karen Fog Olwig
Department of Anthropology
University of Copenhagen

Figure 1.1. A view of the Cockpit Country.

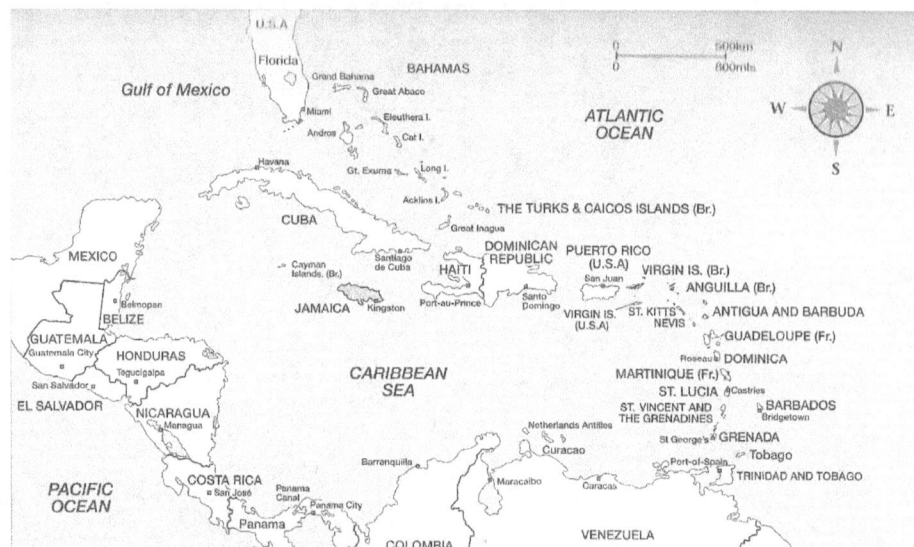

Map 1. The Caribbean region. From Besson 2005 p. 39.

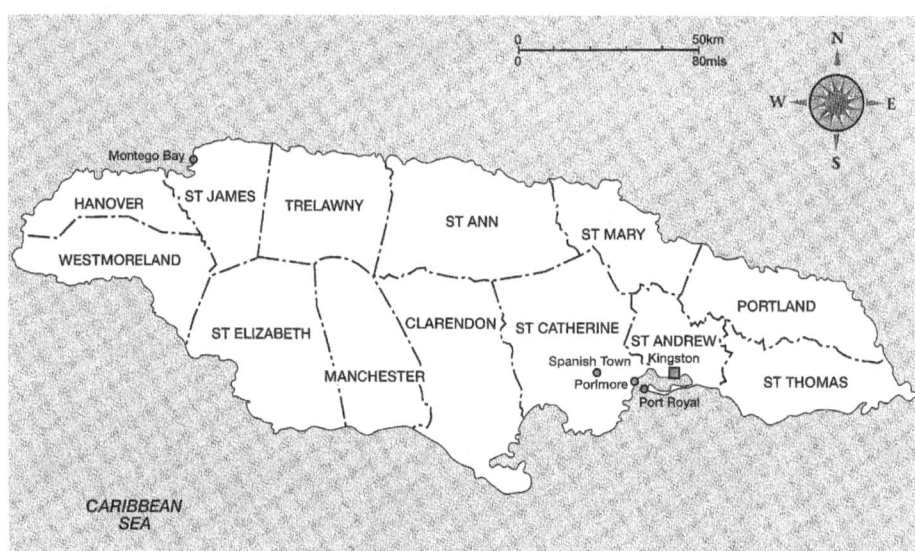

Map 2. Jamaica and its parishes. From Besson 2005 p. 40.

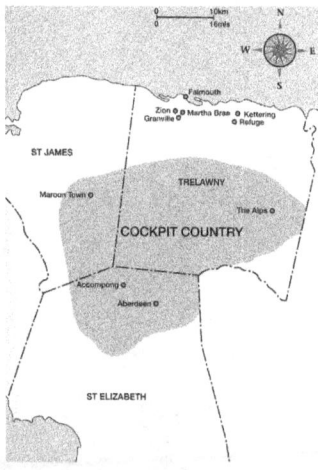

*Map 3. The Cockpit Country and the Communities studied.
From Besson 2005 p. 41.*

1 ▪ INTRODUCTION

The publication of the third edition of the classic book, *Maroon Societies: Rebel Slave Communities in the Americas* by Richard Price, in 1996, consolidated maroon studies in anthropology and history (see also R. Price 1990, 2002, 2008, 2011; S. Price 1993; Price and Price 1991). However, despite such groundbreaking work and other outstanding histories and ethnographies by maroon specialists (e.g. Bilby 1996, 2006; Campbell 1990; Carey 1997; Kopytoff 1979, 1987; Zips 1999, 2011), there has been little attempt to draw modern Maroons into a comparative perspective with the descendants of emancipated slaves who are the majority of African-Americans today. As a result, the comparative exploration of creolization (or indigenization in Europe's 'New World') in maroon and non-maroon derivations of African-American slave cultures, as called for by Raymond T. Smith's (1975) review of the first edition of *Maroon Societies* (R. Price 1973), remains neglected.[1]

This book rectifies that neglect through a comparative study of creolization in three communities at the maroon/non-maroon interface in the Jamaican Cockpit Country, at the heart of the Caribbean core of African-America, which I studied over a period of 30 years, from 1979 to 2009 (see also Besson 1995a, 1995d, 1997, 1998a, 1999a, 2000, 2001, 2005, 2009, 2011a, 2012a, 2012b). The Cockpit Country is an area of 446km² of virtually 'uninhabited roadless rain forest' (Eyre 1995, 259) that straddles the interior of the island's adjoining west-central parishes of St Elizabeth, Trelawny and St James (maps 1–3 and figure 1.1). It is one of the world's largest areas of limestone *karst* topography and is known locally as 'The Soul of Jamaica' and 'The Land of the Maroons'. In addition to historical research, I conducted anthropological fieldwork in the Accompong maroon society in St Elizabeth from 1979 to 2009 (and have kept in touch with the Maroons up to 2012), in Accompong's neighbouring free village of Aberdeen in St Elizabeth from 1991 to 1999 and in the non-maroon community of Maroon Town (named in memory of deported Maroons) in St James from 1999 to 2009. This research followed my earlier comparative study (1968–2001) of five non-maroon free villages in the plantation lowlands of my natal parish of Trelawny (see Besson 1974, 1984b, 2002) and has been concurrent with my on-going study of a Trelawny squatter settlement (Besson 2002, 2007, 2012a and map 3), and I sometimes draw on that work to illuminate my comparative study in the Cockpits.

This opening chapter outlines the contexts, contributions, structure and making of the book. I begin by expanding on what I mean by creolization, contextualizing this creative process within the scenario of globalization. I look first at globalization and creolization in the Caribbean core of African-America. I then focus more closely on the globalization of Jamaica and the Cockpits. I next situate Accompong, Aberdeen and Maroon Town (and my fieldwork there) in the Cockpit Country and introduce the variations in creolization that my research revealed in these communities. The structure and making of this comparative ethnography are then discussed, including the contributions of the book.

Globalization and Creolization in the Caribbean Core of African-America

European colonial expansion to the Americas (following Columbus's landfall on the Taino island of Guanahani[2] in 1492), the plantation system, European, African and Asian indentured labour and the transatlantic trade in enslaved Africans forged African-America and dragged it into a global capitalist economy from the late fifteenth century (Besson 2002, 37–47). In the Caribbean *oikoumenê* or societal area (Mintz 1996a),[3] the earliest site of western European overseas colonization, the gateway to Europe's 'New World' and the core of African-America, this early globalization almost completely wiped out the indigenous Caribs and Tainos and generated local capitalist class relations among imported populations from Europe, Africa and Asia and their New World descendants including planters, indentured labourers, slaves and Maroons.

Despite emancipation and decolonization, this globalization process, which may be defined as 'the tendency towards increasing global interconnections in culture, economy and social life' (Barnard and Spencer 2002, 607) and especially involves the penetration of the capitalist world system (Wallerstein 1974), has intensified into the twenty-first century in Caribbean societies with corporate plantations, urbanization, overseas migration and the bauxite mining, manufacturing and tourist industries. This escalating globalization has generated more complex Caribbean class systems including multinationals, elites, middle classes, farmers, post-slavery peasantries (Maroons, free villagers and squatters),[4] urban and rural proletarians and the unemployed and underemployed (compare Cross 1979, 115).

It is in these contexts of globalization that the dynamic process of creolization has occurred. Sidney Mintz (1996b, 43) defines creolization as a process of indigenization or localization forged by the descendants of Europeans, Africans and Asians born in the Americas. From this perspective, in the case of the Caribbean *oikoumenê*, where globalization started and the concept of creolization originated (Mintz 1996a; Sheller 2003), creolization refers to a process of Caribbeanization. As Mintz argued at the end of the twentieth century:

> Caribbean creolization began five centuries past, with migration and resettlement, forced transportation, the stripping of kinship and community, the growth of individuality on a new basis, and the appearance of the first true creoles – things of the Old World, born in the New... (Mintz 1996a, 301).

Kamau Brathwaite (1971) portrayed Caribbean creolization as a process of homogenization. In contrast, Nigel Bolland argued that creolization 'is not a homogenising process, but rather a process of *contention* between people who are members of social formations and carriers of cultures' (Bolland 2002, 38).

My view of Caribbean creolization is that it is a process of localization or rooting identities, kin groups and communities in post-conquest Caribbean societies, especially in Caribbean land, involving both cultural continuity and transformation, forged in the contexts of global and local capitalist class relations and social change. This approach, which draws on Mintz, also has similarities with Bolland's focus on contention. However, I suggest, in addition to subaltern opposition and resistance to hegemonic power reflected in class conflict,[5] creolization may involve the strategies of adaptation, negotiation, alliance, re-creation, culture-building and place-making both within class-based communities and across the boundaries of class (Besson 2002, 2005, 2011a, 2012b).

In the Cockpit Country communities that I studied, such strategies are embedded in a long history of creolization originating in the cultures of imported and local-born or Creole slaves and Maroons, and continuing among their descendants today in the face of escalating globalization. I now outline the contours of this globalization in Jamaica and the Cockpits, which are the immediate contexts of the creolization that has occurred in Accompong, Aberdeen and Maroon Town at the maroon/non-maroon interface.

The Globalization of Jamaica and the Cockpits[6]

The parishes of St Elizabeth, St James and Trelawny, in which the Cockpit Country is situated have a history of intensive colonial plantation slavery resulting from Columbus's encounter with the Taino island of Xaymaca ('land of wood and water') in 1494, Spain's colonization of the island by 1509 and the English capture of the colony (renamed Jamaica) in 1655. The Spanish introduced export-crop production to the island, including sugar-cane plantations, worked initially by the forced labour of the Tainos. However, colonization by Spain and Taino opposition to Spanish rule resulted in the almost complete eradication of the indigenous population.[7] There was little agricultural development under the Spaniards, who were primarily interested in gold. When the English seized Jamaica from Spain in 1655, some of the Africans enslaved by the Spanish escaped into the hills to join previous runaways and became early Maroons. Their successors would fight two maroon wars (in 1725–38/39 and 1795–96) against the British and much of this warfare would be in the Cockpits.

Following England's capture of Jamaica, including the creation of parishes, colonization of the island proceeded by land grants from the crown. The colony was administered from the metropolis 'by a governor, council, and representative assembly, with parish churches, vestrymen, and justices of the peace at the local level, and a militia for protection' (Dunn 2000, xxi). From the mid-eighteenth century, after the colonial treaties with the Leeward and Windward Maroons in March and June 1738/39 (in the Cockpits and the eastern mountains respectively), sugar plantations burgeoned and an English (and Scottish) slave-owning planter class was born, linked to the escalating slave trade (Besson 2002, 47–80).

In 1707, the Acts of Union had given Scotland permission to join the slave trade, and 65 per cent of the estimated 9,000–10,000 Scots who migrated to Jamaica and the Chesapeake, from 1750 to 1800, went to Jamaica. The parishes where Scottish settlement concentrated included St James, Trelawny and, to a lesser extent, St Elizabeth (Karras 63–66; Hamilton 2005; Palmer 2007).

By the 1750s, Jamaica was the leading British West Indian sugar-producing colony (Blackburn 1997, 404–405; Eltis 2000, 195–219). In the second half of the eighteenth century sugar plantations in Jamaica increased 'from 535 in 1750 to 900 in 1790, together with a doubling or trebling of the size of the average estate' and a threefold increase in sugar productivity (Blackburn 1997, 407 in Besson 2002, 48). The Jamaican sugar-and-slave economy reached its height between 1783 and 1815 and, after the overthrow of the slave-plantation system by the enslaved in neighbouring French Saint Domingue in the 1790s, Jamaica became the world's leading sugar producer.

With these developments, 'The slave trade to Jamaica was greatest, in both value and volume, between 1783 and 1808, the year Britain abolished the slave trade to its colonies, when 354,000 slaves – the island's largest-ever slave population – lived on Jamaica' (McDonald 1993, 2).[8] Many of the African slaves and their Creole descendants were enslaved in St James, Trelawny and St Elizabeth where Jamaican plantation slavery was most intense. The slave-trading ports of these parishes included Montego Bay, St James, Martha Brae in Trelawny (Besson 2002) and Black River in St Elizabeth. Black River was the site of the massacre of 133 enslaved Africans, mainly from the Gold Coast, on the slave ship, the *Zong*, in 1781 (Reid and Shepherd 2007). In 2007 (the bicentenary of the passage of the Abolition of the Slave Trade Act in the British Parliament in 1807, which came into effect after January 1, 1808), a monument commemorating this massacre was erected and unveiled in Black River by the Institute of Jamaica and the Jamaica National Bicentenary Committee[9] (figures 1.2a and 1.2b).

The personnel on the Jamaican slave plantations reflected the dichotomy of white masters and black and (over time) coloured slaves. Each group was, however, internally differentiated and stratified. The whites (English, Scots, Irish and Euro-Creoles) included planters, attorneys, overseers, bookkeepers and artisans. Among the enslaved, in addition to the ethnic differences between Africans and Creoles, socio-legal 'racial' distinctions ('blacks', 'sambos', 'mulattoes', 'quadroons', 'mustees', 'musteffinos' and 'whites') emerged among the Creoles, resulting from miscegenation especially between white men and black or coloured enslaved women (Besson 2002, 50–51). Such children (with the exception of 'white' children of musteffinos) remained enslaved. Narratives of such 'mixed' ancestry and social exclusion are a central theme in Maroon Town and Aberdeen today. There were also occupational distinctions among the slaves, some of which interrelated with colour, gender and age.

While slave status descended through females, transmission of plantations and slaves was generally based on primogeniture, as in Western Europe and elsewhere in the British West Indies (Higman 1998, 2; Besson 2002, 51). Primogeniture would, however, be modified by miscegenation and creolization including the culture-building of the slaves; for some planters left property to their enslaved mixed race children and the slaves also appropriated their customary land rights to house-yards and provision grounds, creating a customary cognatic land transmission system traced through both genders that reversed the colonial principles of primogeniture (Besson 2002, 28–30, 65–66, 88; Pet[1]

These themes would unfold in Accompong, Maroon Town and Aberdeen

My view of Caribbean creolization is that it is a process of localization or rooting identities, kin groups and communities in post-conquest Caribbean societies, especially in Caribbean land, involving both cultural continuity and transformation, forged in the contexts of global and local capitalist class relations and social change. This approach, which draws on Mintz, also has similarities with Bolland's focus on contention. However, I suggest, in addition to subaltern opposition and resistance to hegemonic power reflected in class conflict,[5] creolization may involve the strategies of adaptation, negotiation, alliance, re-creation, culture-building and place-making both within class-based communities and across the boundaries of class (Besson 2002, 2005, 2011a, 2012b).

In the Cockpit Country communities that I studied, such strategies are embedded in a long history of creolization originating in the cultures of imported and local-born or Creole slaves and Maroons, and continuing among their descendants today in the face of escalating globalization. I now outline the contours of this globalization in Jamaica and the Cockpits, which are the immediate contexts of the creolization that has occurred in Accompong, Aberdeen and Maroon Town at the maroon/non-maroon interface.

The Globalization of Jamaica and the Cockpits[6]

The parishes of St Elizabeth, St James and Trelawny, in which the Cockpit Country is situated have a history of intensive colonial plantation slavery resulting from Columbus's encounter with the Taino island of Xaymaca ('land of wood and water') in 1494, Spain's colonization of the island by 1509 and the English capture of the colony (renamed Jamaica) in 1655. The Spanish introduced export-crop production to the island, including sugar-cane plantations, worked initially by the forced labour of the Tainos. However, colonization by Spain and Taino opposition to Spanish rule resulted in the almost complete eradication of the indigenous population.[7] There was little agricultural development under the Spaniards, who were primarily interested in gold. When the English seized Jamaica from Spain in 1655, some of the Africans enslaved by the Spanish escaped into the hills to join previous runaways and became early Maroons. Their successors would fight two maroon wars (in 1725–38/39 and 1795–96) against the British and much of this warfare would be in the Cockpits.

Following England's capture of Jamaica, including the creation of parishes, colonization of the island proceeded by land grants from the crown. The colony was administered from the metropolis 'by a governor, council, and representative assembly, with parish churches, vestrymen, and justices of the peace at the local level, and a militia for protection' (Dunn 2000, xxi). From the mid-eighteenth century, after the colonial treaties with the Leeward and Windward Maroons in March and June 1738/39 (in the Cockpits and the eastern mountains respectively), sugar plantations burgeoned and an English (and Scottish) slave-owning planter class was born, linked to the escalating slave trade (Besson 2002, 47–80).

In 1707, the Acts of Union had given Scotland permission to join the slave trade, and 65 per cent of the estimated 9,000–10,000 Scots who migrated to Jamaica and the Chesapeake, from 1750 to 1800, went to Jamaica. The parishes where Scottish settlement was pronounced included St James, Trelawny and, to a lesser extent, St Elizabeth (Karras 1992; Besson 2002, 63–66; Hamilton 2005; Palmer 2007).

By the 1750s, Jamaica was the leading British West Indian sugar-producing colony (Blackburn 1997, 404–405; Eltis 2000, 195–219). In the second half of the eighteenth century sugar plantations in Jamaica increased 'from 535 in 1750 to 900 in 1790, together with a doubling or trebling of the size of the average estate' and a threefold increase in sugar productivity (Blackburn 1997, 407 in Besson 2002, 48). The Jamaican sugar-and-slave economy reached its height between 1783 and 1815 and, after the overthrow of the slave-plantation system by the enslaved in neighbouring French Saint Domingue in the 1790s, Jamaica became the world's leading sugar producer.

With these developments, 'The slave trade to Jamaica was greatest, in both value and volume, between 1783 and 1808, the year Britain abolished the slave trade to its colonies, when 354,000 slaves – the island's largest-ever slave population – lived on Jamaica' (McDonald 1993, 2).[8] Many of the African slaves and their Creole descendants were enslaved in St James, Trelawny and St Elizabeth where Jamaican plantation slavery was most intense. The slave-trading ports of these parishes included Montego Bay, St James, Martha Brae in Trelawny (Besson 2002) and Black River in St Elizabeth. Black River was the site of the massacre of 133 enslaved Africans, mainly from the Gold Coast, on the slave ship, the *Zong*, in 1781 (Reid and Shepherd 2007). In 2007 (the bicentenary of the passage of the Abolition of the Slave Trade Act in the British Parliament in 1807, which came into effect after January 1, 1808), a monument commemorating this massacre was erected and unveiled in Black River by the Institute of Jamaica and the Jamaica National Bicentenary Committee[9] (figures 1.2a and 1.2b).

The personnel on the Jamaican slave plantations reflected the dichotomy of white masters and black and (over time) coloured slaves. Each group was, however, internally differentiated and stratified. The whites (English, Scots, Irish and Euro-Creoles) included planters, attorneys, overseers, bookkeepers and artisans. Among the enslaved, in addition to the ethnic differences between Africans and Creoles, socio-legal 'racial' distinctions ('blacks', 'sambos', 'mulattoes', 'quadroons', 'mustees', 'musteffinos' and 'whites') emerged among the Creoles, resulting from miscegenation especially between white men and black or coloured enslaved women (Besson 2002, 50–51). Such children (with the exception of 'white' children of musteffinos) remained enslaved. Narratives of such 'mixed' ancestry and social exclusion are a central theme in Maroon Town and Aberdeen today. There were also occupational distinctions among the slaves, some of which interrelated with colour, gender and age.

While slave status descended through females, transmission of plantations and slaves was generally based on primogeniture, as in Western Europe and elsewhere in the British West Indies (Higman 1998, 2; Besson 2002, 51). Primogeniture would, however, be modified by miscegenation and creolization including the culture-building of the slaves; for some planters left property to their enslaved mixed race children and the slaves also appropriated their customary land rights to house-yards and provision grounds, creating a customary cognatic land transmission system traced through both genders that reversed the colonial principles of primogeniture (Besson 2002, 28–30, 65–66, 88; Petley 2005). These themes would unfold in Accompong, Maroon Town and Aberdeen (chapters 3–10).

Figure 1.2a. Monument to the Zong at the Estuary of the Black River, St Elizabeth, 2007.

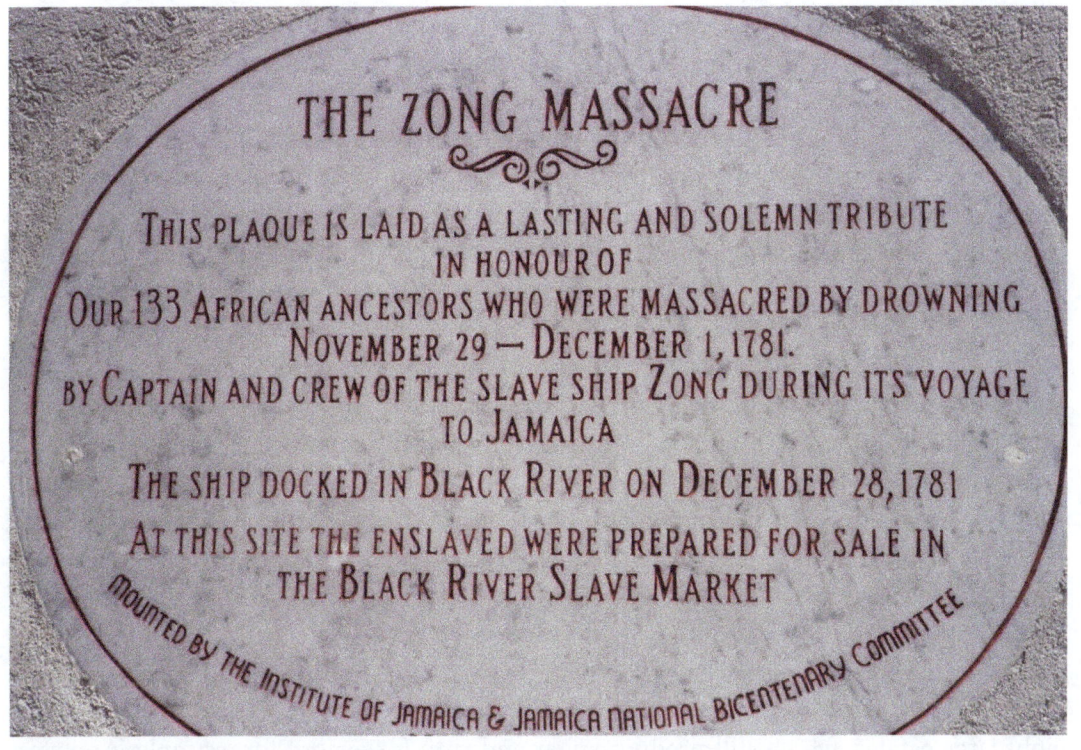

Figure 1.2b. Inscription on the Zong monument, Black River, St Elizabeth.

Within the wider context of Jamaican plantation slave society, slave plantations encompassed the Cockpits which, as early as the period of Spanish colonization and especially during the eighteenth-century maroon wars with the British, offered a refuge for runaway slaves, including the ancestors of the Accompong Maroons. From the time of Spanish colonization, this precipitous limestone landscape became known as the Cockpit Country, named after the cock-fighting pits introduced by Spain (Hall 1991). The Cockpits also provided a niche for plantation slaves to create 'proto-peasant' economies (Mintz 1989, 151–52) on their provision grounds and for post-slavery peasantries to establish free villages, such as Maldon (now part of Maroon Town) and Aberdeen, after the abolition of slavery in 1834 and emancipation in 1838 (chapter 2).

Despite emancipation, Jamaica's inequitable agrarian structure linked to the global economy has remained essentially the same. Under Crown Colony government (introduced in 1866), the state's 'land lease policy was not conducive to peasant development' (Satchell 1999, 60). The island's plantation economy (which had declined in the east and parts of the south of the island after emancipation) was re-established and invigorated in these areas by 1880–1900 through the export of bananas (Satchell 1990) and the livestock industry; while sugar estates persisted uninterrupted in many areas of the island such as the western parishes, including Trelawny and St James, and in south-central Clarendon (Besson 2002, 106–107). The south-western parish of St Elizabeth, with its post-slavery plantation economy based on sugar cane and bananas, and livestock pens, reflected a transitional area in time and space and the Aberdeen plantation changed from sugar cane to banana production in this context (chapter 6). By 1900, the plantation economy was re-established by the colonial state throughout Jamaica (Satchell 1999). In spite of plantation labour protests in 1938, government freehold land settlement schemes on marginal land in the 1930s and 1940s, universal suffrage in 1944, decolonization in the 1950s and 1960s (with political independence in 1962), and Project Land Lease in the 1970s, this inequitable agrarian structure has persisted into the new millennium, reinforced by corporate and state capitalism (Besson 2002, 132–35).

During my fieldwork in Jamaica (1968–2012), the corporate sugar plantations of Trelawny Sugar (formerly Long Pond Estates) in Trelawny, Hampden Estates on the boundary of St James and Trelawny, and J Wray and Nephew's three plantations, Appleton and Holland in St Elizabeth and New Yarmouth in Clarendon, were three of the island's eight large land-and-factory sugar estates. Trelawny Sugar comprises about 20,000 acres on a plateau, Hampden Estates is approximately 7,500 acres in the Queen of Spain's Valley and J Wray and Nephew's three plantations total 21,900 acres with the largest, Appleton Estate (below Accompong and bordering Aberdeen), comprising 11,000 acres in the Nassau Valley.[10] Appleton, which is watered by the Black River (whose estuary was the site of the slave massacre on the *Zong* in 1781), dates back to the English conquest of Jamaica in 1655, has been manufacturing rum since 1749 and is the island's oldest and most modern sugar estate and distillery.[11]

Many of Jamaica's other former slave plantations are now tributaries of the island's eight large estates, which still produce sugar and rum for export; for example, Appleton and Trelawny Gold rums.[12] Both the sugar and banana industries in Jamaica are, however, now in crisis due to the increasing globalization of agriculture and the trading crisis resulting from the World Trade Organization Agreement in 1999 (Clegg 2004; Ahmed 2004). These developments have constrained the peasant economies of Aberdeen, Accompong and Maroon Town, which all exported bananas and sugar cane.

Jamaica has been further impacted by globalization through urbanization, overseas labour migration, and the tourist and bauxite industries (Besson 2002, 135–37, 217–19) and all these trends have affected the communities that I studied in the Cockpits. Urbanization has resulted mainly from rural poverty and rural-urban migration and there is rising unemployment in the cities and towns (Hope 1989; Desai and Potter 2002, 241; Satterthwaite 2002, 243; Wardle 2011). Since emancipation, there has been overseas migration (to Central America, other parts of the Caribbean, the United States, Canada and Britain), including return- and circulatory-migration, and migrant remittances have become increasingly significant (Besson 2002, 217–26; Bauer and Thompson 2006), though remittances are being eroded by the global 'credit crunch'. Jamaica is one of the main tourist destinations for North America and Europe in the global South, based especially on the white-sand-beach North Coast (including St James) and tourism is now expanding on the island's southern coast (including St Elizabeth). Jamaica is also a leading producer of bauxite and alumina and during my fieldwork (up to 2009) the bauxite industry was pronounced in St Elizabeth, near Aberdeen and Accompong.[13] The impact of globalization is additionally manifested in Jamaica's financial crisis since the 1990s (Miller and Barker 2007), and this further constrains the peasant economies of Accompong, Maroon Town and Aberdeen.

In the new millennium, the Cockpit Country (which has been a Forest Reserve since the mid-twentieth century) therefore remains enmeshed in the global economy, hemmed in by persisting plantations, bauxite mines, a trans-island highway (Highway 2000), urban centres and luxury hotels. Despite environmental decline and in the context of global discourses on conservation and development, there are plans for a National Park (first proposed in 1970)[14] and a World Heritage Site for Jamaica's international tourist industry (Eyre 1995; Barker and Miller 1995; Miller and Barker 2007) – though these plans are constrained by a crisis of funding in the national economy (Miller and Barker 2007). There have also been plans to 'develop' the Cockpit Country for bauxite mining, including the individualization of maroon common land, and potential bauxite prospecting in the Cockpits has recently been the subject of debate in Accompong. Land disputes regarding the treaty boundaries of the commons continue and are a central theme in narratives in Accompong.[15]

In the face of these contentious issues, Accompong, Aberdeen and Maroon Town stand fast as transformations of African-American maroon and non-maroon slave cultures, forged through continuing creolization in response to persisting globalization and enmeshed in transnational social networks. However, there are significant differences as well as similarities among these three villages, including their community formation, ethnicities, kinship and land tenure systems, narratives, beliefs and rituals, and their relations with the Jamaican post-colonial state and its tourist industry. Before introducing these variations, I situate these three communities and my fieldwork there in the historic Cockpit Country landscape.

Into the Cockpits

As the sun rises over Jamaica, the splendour of the Cockpit Country begins to unfold. At dawn, damp from the night's dew and cool from the altitude, the precipitous limestone *karst* landscape of conical mountains and deep dells comes alive with colourful birds, wild flowers, tree-ferns and flame-trees – the fauna and flora of a potential National Park and World Heritage Site (Eyre 1995; Miller and Barker 2007). This spectacular landscape was the site of my long-term fieldwork in Accompong, Maroon Town and Aberdeen.[16]

My fieldwork often began with a journey into the Cockpits, at dawn, from my mother's home in Montego Bay, the capital of St James and the island's second city and primary tourist resort. I could then be in either Accompong or Aberdeen by 9:00 a.m. and in Maroon Town long before. I was always accompanied by my Guyanese husband, Dr John Besson, and often by our friend, Orville ('Charlie'/ 'Deacon') Dobson of Maroon Town and Montego Bay, who claimed descent from plantation slaves and Maroons. Our route would pass through Sam Sharpe Square in the centre of the city, with its statue of Sam Sharpe (the leader of the great 1831–32 slave rebellion that started near Maroon Town) and Georgian courthouse in front of which Sharpe was hanged (in what was at that time named Charles Square) by the British plantation-military regime in 1832 (figures 1.3a and 1.3b, and chapter 2).[17]

From the southern outskirts of Montego Bay (with its Anglican St James Parish Church and Burchell Memorial Baptist Church, where Sam Sharpe was a Deacon), our journey would continue past the former slave plantations of Barnett Estates.[18] We would then turn inland and southwards towards the magnificent mountains through Fairfield Estates and the districts of Irwin and Tucker, now an upper-class housing enclave. This route passes the St John's Anglican Church in Grace Hill and by-passes the turning to Granville (St James), a stronghold of the Revival religion with a Revivalist network that includes the Trelawny free villages that I previously studied (Besson 2002).

After passing the empty land of Worcester and the turning to Hurlock, we would reach the first high Cockpit mountain and John's Hall (map 4). At this village, which includes a Pentecostal Church of God, the steep climb into the Cockpits begins. At John's Hall quarry, we would pass the old road inland that collapsed in a landslide during my fieldwork, resulting in temporary detours to Maroon Town via either precipitous Kemptshot or spectacular Mount Horeb. On a hill above John's Hall is the Salter's Hill Baptist Church, which was voluntarily constructed by slaves in 1825, burnt down by the planters' Colonial Church Union after the 1831–32 slave rebellion and subsequently rebuilt. The English Baptist missionaries, William Knibb and Walter Dendy, both served as pastors of this church and Sam Sharpe was a Deacon there (as well as at Thomas Burchell's Baptist Church in Montego Bay).[19] From here inland the route is dotted with Baptist churches, as St James (like Trelawny) was the heart of Baptist slave proselytizing in Anglican Jamaica (Besson 2002, and chapter 2).

Introduction ■ 9

Figure 1.3a. The Court House, recently restored, in Sam Sharpe Square, Montego Bay.

Figure 1.3b. Sculpture (by Kay Sullivan) of Sam Sharpe preaching to slaves, Sam Sharpe Square.

Figure 1.4. Flame trees (Spathodia) in the Cockpits.

Entering the Cockpits from John's Hall, the landscape is one of misty mountains and dells, wild red ginger lilies, orange spathodia blossoms, cream and apricot cascadura bellflowers, and green tree-ferns and giant bamboo (figure 1.4). There are provision grounds in the valleys and on the hillsides, cultivated (mainly by men) with bananas, breadfruit and yams, and female market traders or 'higglers' sit by the road-side selling such produce. Other women are washing clothes by standpipes in house-yards and hanging them in the rising sun to dry. There are also many family-land tombs. Along the more inhabited parts of the route are children going to school, walking or waiting for transport, their colourful uniforms indicating which school they attend. On Sundays, there are people walking to churches and on Saturdays, Seventh Day Adventists too.

As the road continues ascending, it reaches Spring Mount, with its police station, and passes the Sandyland Valley, shrouded in mist, where there is a road-side tourist 'lookout' and a particularly wet area named 'Wetty-Wetty'. The road then climbs onwards to Springfield, with its Baptist church and all-age school. Passing more family-land tombs, we would reach Welcome Hall with its Seventh Day Adventist Church. The drive continues through more steep mountains and deep valleys with graceful bamboo. At times, the climbing stops and the road runs over a plateau, as if crossing the roof of the world.

The route then reaches Kensington, where the 1831–32 slave rebellion, led by Sam Sharpe, began on December 27, 1831 on the Kensington sugar estate (chapter 2). A roadside plaque marks this site and a replica of the plantation 'trash-house' that was torched

Figure 1.5. Monument at Kensington, near Maroon Town, commemorating the 1831–32 slave rebellion.

to start the rebellion can be seen higher up on the hill. Above the trash-house stands a new cell phone mast. Around the corner, at the entrance to the village of Kensington, is a monument recently erected by the Jamaica National Heritage Trust commemorating the slave revolt (figure 1.5). High across the main road is a banner proclaiming the annual Vigil held here as part of the national Emancipation Day celebrations that have been reinstated throughout the island since 1997. At Kensington there is also a disused banana boxing station that was busy until a few years ago, when the banana industry began to decline due to the increasing globalization of agriculture.

After Kensington, the road climbs further through the Cockpits to the remote post office at Point. When going to Maroon Town, we would leave the main road (which continues on to Elderslie and Appleton Estate) at Point, on a subsidiary road forking south-east. The rough stony route to Maroon Town winds further into the Cockpits, past Summer Hill (with its Peoples' Cooperative Bank and the Maldon High School), Maldon (with its Baptist Church and primary school), and Dundee (which has a small shop, a banana walk and a Methodist Church). The road then passes 'Popkin' (where spring water comes out of a mountain and villagers draw water) and reaches Maroon Town Square, with its crossroads and shops.

Four country roads meet at Maroon Town Crossroads (map 4): the entry from Point from the north-west; a precipitous road leading north-east to Schaw Castle and the Spring Vale plantation; another steep road east to Flagstaff, in the heart of Maroon Town;

Map 4. Into the Cockpits (from Montego Bay to Maroon Town, Accompong and Aberdeen), *Jamaica Road Map*, Macmillan Education 1999.

and a valley-road going south-west to Vaughansfield (with its Seventh Day Adventist Church near the Pond Piece government land settlement), which then joins the main road near Flamstead. During my fieldwork, the road to Flagstaff was asphalted for the annual Emancipation Day celebrations, which have been held there since 1997. This road climbs steeply above Maroon Town Square, with a precipitous view of Pond Piece adjoining Vaughansfield below, on via John Crow Cliff and onwards and upwards through Browns' Town to Flagstaff. All the roads through Maroon Town are surrounded by steep mountains and deep valleys embroidered by provision grounds, house-yards, family-land cemeteries, banana walks and giant bamboo.

When going to Accompong, we either detoured through Maroon Town and rejoined the main road at Flamstead or continued directly on the main road from Point. Here, the road (now improved since my earlier years of fieldwork) continues, past the twin white-faced limestone mountains named 'Honour Rock' (figure 1.6a), through the districts of Tangle River (with its Baptist Church and family-land tombs), Flamstead (with a disused banana boxing station), Garlands, Mocho and frequently-flooded Niagara near the south-eastern edge of St James. The route then passes over the parish boundary to Elderslie in northern St Elizabeth and on to Jointwood and Retirement. At Retirement, a subsidiary road (more like a stony riverbed) forks and winds upwards to Accompong, deep in the southern Cockpit Country, with driving speed sometimes reduced to two miles an hour (figure 1.6b).

Figure 1.6a. Asking the way to Accompong at Honour Rock, 1979.

Figure 1.6b. The author's first visit to Accompong, 1979.

To reach Aberdeen, in the southern foothills of the Cockpits, the main road beyond Retirement descends through Dry River and Vauxhall to the lowlands and forks, left past Appleton Estate (the right fork goes to the market town of Maggotty). Towering above Appleton's cane fields and sugar factory is the majestic Cockpit Country (and from Accompong one looks down southwards on the Appleton plantation and the 'Mountains of Aberdeen'). The main road continues past Appleton to Siloah, with its police station, and on to Raheen and then at Union forks to the hill town of Balaclava in the north and the lowland market town of Santa Cruz in the south. Between Appleton and Raheen, through the sugar-cane fields just beyond Siloah, a subsidiary road climbs back into the foothills of the Cockpits and on to Aberdeen.

The similarities and differences in creolization that evolved in Accompong, Aberdeen and Maroon Town, rooted in maroon and non-maroon transformations of African-American slave cultures, were forged in this Cockpit Country landscape. I now introduce these variations in creolization in the Cockpits, focusing first on community formation.

Creolization in the Cockpits

Accompong Town (originally named Accompong's Town and now generally known as Accompong),[20] in the precipitous southern Cockpit Country of St Elizabeth, is the oldest corporate maroon society in African-America. It was initially the secondary village of the historic Jamaican Leeward Maroon polity established by rebel slaves who fought Jamaica's First Maroon War of 1725–38 in the Cockpits (led by Captain Cudjoe or Kojo,[21] an Afro-Creole born in marronage [chapter 2]), defeated the British and made a treaty with the colonists that was endorsed on March 1, 1738/39.[22] This treaty, forged between Cudjoe, based at Cudjoe's Town in St James (the primary Leeward Maroon village) and the British Governor of Jamaica, Edward Trelawny, granted the Leeward Maroons their freedom and legal rights to 1,500 acres of land in the Cockpits north-west of Cudjoe's Town (renamed Trelawny Town[23] after the treaty with Governor Trelawny). This land grant was subsequently increased to 2,559 acres to include Accompong's Town (which was under the leadership of Cudjoe's 'brother' and lieutenant, Captain Accompong) and its surrounding territory in St Elizabeth (Campbell 1990, 127, 181–83). However, after the colonial betrayal and deportation to Nova Scotia of the Maroons of Trelawny Town (the 'Trelawny Maroons') in St James, following the Second Maroon War of 1795–96 and the confiscation of their lands, Accompong's Town became the sole surviving village of the Leeward Maroon polity. In the twenty-first century, Accompong endures as a virtually autonomous creole maroon polity on tax-free common treaty land.

Accompong's neighbouring free village of Aberdeen in St Elizabeth (also named 'Ockbrook' by Moravian missionaries after a Moravian settlement in England) was established in the south-eastern foothills of the Cockpits in the 1840s, a few years after emancipation. The village was founded by emancipated slaves from the Aberdeen plantation (part of Island Estates) bordering the Accompong commons. These ex-slaves (augmented by some Maroons who 'came out' from Accompong) squatted on plantation-mountains south of the Aberdeen plantation nearer to the plains and later purchased land (and then created 'family lands') – consolidating the free village in association with the Ockbrook Moravian mission church.

Maroon Town, St James, evolved on the former site of Cudjoe's Town/Trelawny Town which had been the primary village of the Leeward Maroon polity. This transformation occurred following the colonial deportation of the Trelawny Maroons in 1796 and the confiscation of their 1,500 acres of treaty lands. These lands were subsequently subdivided and sold by the colonial state which retained 300 acres and established a barracks there (on the site that became known as Flagstaff) for their troops who remained there until around the 1850s, by which time the area was renamed Maroon Town (or Old Maroon Town) in memory of the deported Maroons (Aarons 1981; Campbell 1990, 243; Craton 1982, 303).[24] Written history is silent on the subsequent development of Maroon Town, but my research (combining historical records, anthropological fieldwork and oral tradition) indicates that these land sales were made to the descendants of foraging non-treaty mulatto Maroons, colonists and slaves – who subsequently created family lands and whose descendants still hold such lands today. Maroon Town has expanded to incorporate adjoining Maldon, which was the first Baptist free village in St James.

These maroon and non-maroon transformations of African-American slave cultures have generated various creole ethnicities. The Accompong community has a strong Afro-Creole maroon identity[25] rooted in its tax-free common treaty land and reinforced by an elected Maroon Council and Colonel whose authority derives from Captain Cudjoe.[26] This Afro-Creole maroon ethnicity is further reinforced by oral traditions and Myal beliefs and rituals deriving from the Myal slave religion (a Jamaican transformation of African religions), in which a morally neutral magical/spiritual power (Obeah) was believed to be accessed from the ancestors through spirit possession (Myal) to protect the slaves from the sorcery of slavery (Schuler 1980; Bilby 1993; Besson 2002). In the Cockpits, Myalism was transformed in marronage to focus on communication with the spirits of the First-Time Maroons (the Afro-Creoles who fought the war and won the peace, including Cudjoe [Kopytoff 1979, 52]), who are believed to protect the maroon community.[27] Afro-Creole maroon ethnicity is further strengthened by dense bilateral kinship networks,[28] endogamous cousin-conjugality[29] and overlapping cognatic clans[30] traced through both women and men and claiming descent from the First-Time Maroons, who are said to have bequeathed the commons to all their descendants.

The Accompong maroon commons are viewed by some scholars as an African continuity in a plural society (Barker and Spence 1988; Campbell 1990, 190; Zips 1996, 1999, 131, 2011). However, the commons derive from a colonial treaty designed to marginalize the rebel slaves (Kopytoff 1979). Moreover, my research reveals that the Maroons have transformed the colonial reservation into a sacred landscape that reflects the process of creolization or Caribbeanization from the African ethnic groups of the earliest Maroons to an Afro-Creole community. This creolization process is evident in burial grounds, narratives and rituals as well as in kinship and marriage – all of which interrelate with the commons.

Whereas Accompong is an Afro-Creole maroon society descended from rebel slaves, Aberdeen and Maroon Town are generally regarded as villages descended from black emancipated slaves – like the Trelawny free villages in the plantation heartlands that I previously studied (Besson 2002). However, despite similarities with the Afro-Creole Trelawny villages (such as integration into the national political system, taxed and parcelled lands, a core of Old Families or cognatic clans holding customary family lands, bilateral kinship networks and 'complex' exogamous conjugal systems),[31] there are significant differences in ethnic identification between Aberdeen and Maroon Town, on the one hand, and Trelawny's free villages on the other, as well as a contrast with the Accompong Maroons. For many Old Families in Aberdeen and Maroon Town claim 'slave master' pickni' descent from British (especially Scottish) or Euro-Creole colonists (generally slave masters) and African or Afro-Creole enslaved women. The parcelled family lands of these Meso-Creole clans (which contrast with the common land of the Accompong Maroons and coexist with more recently purchased and rented lands) tend to be larger than the miniscule plots of family land in the Trelawny free villages traced to former slaves, and are sometimes said to have originated from planters as well as emancipated slaves. These larger landholdings provide a basis for cash-cropping (especially in bananas), as well as kitchen gardens, in addition to being sites of identity with kin-based cemeteries.[32] Also, in Aberdeen and Maroon Town, some Old Families (both Meso-Creoles and Afro-Creoles) either assert Leeward Maroon ancestry or seem to be descended from Maroons.[33]

The themes of mulatto ancestry and maroon descent are especially pronounced in Maroon Town, with its core of Meso-Creole cognatic clans with Scottish titles such as the McIntyres, Sutherlands, Hamiltons, Harrises, Reids, Grants and McGhies. There, I also uncovered a link between the McGhie Old Family (Maroon Town's central clan, who claim 'slave master' pickni' ancestry) and the Afro-Scots 'McGhie Maroons' of Congo Town in the Cockpits of Trelawny Parish, who escaped from their father's Trelawny slave plantation in the late eighteenth century and whose history has not received the attention it deserves. I discovered links too between the Meso-Creole Rockhead clan and the mulatto Felsenkopf Maroons. In addition, in Maroon Town, I found widespread narratives of marronage and maroon descent among both Afro-Creoles and Meso-Creoles.

In Aberdeen, the central Old Family not only claims Afro-Scots ancestry from slave masters and slaves but also asserts descent from an African-Prince Maroon who is said to have been brought on a slave ship to Jamaica and to have escaped to Accompong from a lowland plantation. His descendants are said to have 'come out' from Acccompong and to have acquired land in Aberdeen. The family land and extensive burial ground of this lineage, traced several generations to the African-Prince Maroon, can still be identified in Aberdeen. In both Aberdeen and Accompong, there are also oral traditions of military and conjugal alliances between the First-Time Maroons and the slaves on the Aberdeen plantation, and some Aberdonians have voting and land rights in the Leeward Maroon polity and its commons.

Like community formation, kinship and land transmission, narratives and ethnicity, the religious beliefs and practices in the Cockpit communities are variations on a creolization theme. As with the Baptist/Revivalist/Rastafarian free villages of Trelawny (Besson 2002), the communities of Aberdeen and Maroon Town are embedded in the Revival worldview that appropriated and transformed Nonconformist Christianity (the Baptists in Trelawny and Maroon Town, the Moravians in Aberdeen) through the Myal slave religion; though both Aberdeen and Maroon Town have other prominent religions such as Seventh Day Adventism (Maroon Town) and Pentecostalism (Aberdeen and Maroon Town). In addition, Rastafarians are prominent at emancipation rituals in Maroon Town. In Accompong, despite the presence of the Presbyterian (now United) Church, established at the invitation of the Maroons in the late nineteenth century (Kopytoff 1987, 473), Myalism endures at the heart of the maroon polity – reflecting both continuity and continuing transformations. The Revival and Rastafarian religions, which evolved from Myalism (Besson and Chevannes 1996), are also significant in Accompong as variants of creolization.

Creole politics likewise varies among the three communities. Accompong is a virtually autonomous corporate maroon polity, while both Aberdeen and Maroon Town are integrated into the Jamaican political system. However, of these three communities, Accompong is the most significant focus of the Jamaican tourist industry, which (in negotiation with the Maroons) is appropriating maroon culture for national heritage tourism. Maroon Town is in the early stages of developing heritage tourism – drawing on its historic links with Trelawny Town. Aberdeen is more removed from tourism, though some Aberdonians are also Accompong Maroons.

In Aberdeen and Maroon Town (as in Trelawny's free villages), overseas migration has been significant since emancipation. Maroon Town especially is now intensely transnational, being directly inland from the international airport in Montego Bay and having participated very actively in the North American Farm Work Scheme. In Accompong, migration is now well-established but started later due to its isolation and only with the building of the rocky road to the village in the 1940s (Barker and Spence 1988). However, there is now an Overseas Association of Accompong Maroons, based in the United States and migrants from both North America and Britain return to participate in the annual Myal Play. Migrant savings and remittances and transnational mortuary ritual are important in all three villages but family-land memorials are particularly prominent in Maroon Town.

The Structure of the Book

Following this introductory chapter with its overview of the book, the chapters focus on: 'The Roots of Creolization in the Cockpits' (chapter 2); 'The Creolization of the Commons' (Chapter 3); 'Myal, Kinship and the Ancestors' (Chapter 4); 'Reinterpreting Accompong Maroon Society' (chapter 5); 'Accompong, Aberdeen and Maroon Town: The Maroon/Non-Maroon Interface' (Chapter 6); 'Non-Maroon Maroon Town' (Chapter 7); '"Slave Master" Pickni": Meso-Creole Ethnicities and Narrative Transformations of Trelawny Town' (Chapter 8); 'Maroon Town Narratives of Maroon Descent and Marronage' (Chapter 9); 'The McGhie Maroons and the Maroon Town McGhies' (Chapter 10); 'Maroon Town and Accompong: Ritual, Tourism and Nationhood' (Chapter 11); and 'Creolization at the Maroon/Non-Maroon Interface' (Chapter 12).

In chapter 2, 'The Roots of Creolization in the Cockpits', I discuss the major historical themes of marronage, rebellion and peasantization in the Cockpit Country that have been so significant in the creolization of Accompong, Maroon Town and Aberdeen. This chapter also highlights the historical relationship between the Nonconformist missionaries and the Cockpit villages and situates these communities within the Jamaican social system.

Chapters 3 to 5 focus on my ethnography of the Accompong maroon society. In chapter 3, 'The Creolization of the Commons', I show that, rather than an African cultural continuity as others contend (Barker and Spence 1988; Campbell 1990, 190; Zips 1996, 1999, 131; 2011), the Accompong commons reflect a process of creolization in the maroon polity that is a response to globalization. I argue that, in this process of Caribbean cultural rooting, the Accompong Maroons have created a still-evolving land tenure system that has transformed a colonial marginal reservation into a sacred landscape. I show how this landscape, with its sacred burial grounds and Myal rituals, reinforces the Leeward Maroon polity and reflects a transformation within the maroon society from early African ethnicities to an Afro-Creole maroon community. This chapter also indicates the ambiguous relationship between the Accompong Maroons and the neighbouring free village of Aberdeen.

Chapter 4, 'Myal, Kinship and the Ancestors', explores more fully the Myal worldview of the Accompong Maroons that reinforces the creolization of the commons. I contextualize and present a range of narratives from Accompong Maroons including political leaders and Myal specialists. These narratives also reflect the creole kinship system in Accompong and perceived relationships with the ancestors.

In chapter 5, 'Reinterpreting Accompong Maroon Society', I show that the creolization of the commons in Accompong (chapter 3), reinforced by the Myal worldview (chapter 4), is a variation on a wider theme of Caribbean land tenure and transmission systems rooted in kinship and community. My reinterpretation revises interpretations by Barbara Kopytoff (1987), Mavis Campbell (1990), E. Kofi Agorsah (1994) and Werner Zips (2011) regarding the Accompong maroon landscape. It also revises conclusions by Kopytoff (1987) on the demise of Myalism in Accompong, by Campbell (1990) on the so-called confusion among the Accompong Maroons regarding the ancestress Nanny and her burial place and by Barry Chevannes (1995a, 7) that there is no religion called Myalism in Jamaica today. I show too, that Zips's (2011, 2012) dismissal of creolization in Accompong does not stand up to closer scrutiny and that an understanding of this dynamic process of creolization is enhanced by a comparative perspective on the maroon/non-maroon interface in the Cockpits.

Chapter 6, 'Accompong, Aberdeen and Maroon Town: The Maroon/Non-Maroon Interface', explores some of the complex relations among these three communities. I first present the narrative of an Accompong Ex-Colonel that expands on the ambiguous relationship between Accompong and Aberdeen. I then discuss my historical and anthropological findings on the development of the free village of Aberdeen from the slave community on the Aberdeen plantation bordering the Accompong commons, and the continued evolution of the Aberdonian community descended from slaves, planters and Maroons. I also outline the ambiguous alliance between the Aberdonians and the Moravian missionaries. I then explore a range of narratives, contextualized in daily life, from Afro-Creole and Meso-Creole Aberdonians that highlight these ethnicities and conclude with narratives from Aberdeen and Accompong on Maroon Town. As with other narratives collected in my fieldwork, the narratives in this chapter have both similarities and differences with written historical records and highlight the complexities of relationships and identities at the maroon/non-maroon interface.

Chapters 7–10 present a detailed ethnography of Maroon Town, based on my historical and anthropological research. Chapter 7, 'Non-Maroon Maroon Town', focuses on the post-slavery community of Maroon Town that evolved on the site of Cudjoe's Town/ Trelawny Town, which was the primary village of the Leeward Maroon polity until the deportation of the Trelawny Maroons in 1796 and the confiscation of their lands. The written history of this historic site ends with those events of the Second Maroon War (e.g. Campbell 1990) and the general view of Maroon Town is of an Afro-Creole non-maroon community. However, my research uncovers a hidden history of Maroon Town as a community claiming descent from emancipated slaves, colonists and Maroons, with a creolization process evolving within the transformations of enslavement, marronage, miscegenation and post-slavery peasantization and with continuity as well discontinuity from Trelawny Town. This chapter also provides an overview of modern Maroon Town.

Chapter 8, '"Slave Master" Pickni": Meso-Creole Ethnicities and Narrative Transformations of Trelawny Town', explores narratives collected from many of Maroon Town's Old Families who claim mulatto ancestry from the children of colonists and slaves. These Meso-Creole clans hold much of the core of family lands in Maroon Town. Their stories of kinship, social exclusion and inclusion, ethnicity and land are embedded in wider narratives regarding the transformation of the maroon society of Trelawny Town to non-maroon Maroon Town. As in Accompong and Aberdeen, such narratives (which I did not anticipate when I began my fieldwork in Maroon Town) combine myth and history, transcending the ruptures or disjunctures of enslavement and marronage and creating sites of identity on the Cockpit Country landscape (see also Besson 2005).

Chapter 9, 'Maroon Town Narratives of Maroon Descent and Marronage', both reinforces and widens the perspectives in chapter 8 by exploring another unexpected finding in my research; namely, that some Maroon Town villagers claim to be descended from the Trelawny Maroons. Such claims are generally embedded in assertions of Afro-Creole maroon ethnicity including claims of descent from the maroon ancestress-heroine, 'Betsy Currie' or ' 'Campong Nanny' ('Accompong Nanny'). However, I also found that some Meso-Creoles in Maroon Town claim to be descended from mulatto Maroons (as well as from colonists and slaves). Yet other Maroon Town villagers (generally Afro-Creoles and including Newcomers or immigrants to the community), who claim neither maroon nor mulatto descent, likewise narrate stories of Trelawny Town marronage. As in chapter 8, these Maroon Town narratives have both similarities and differences with written historical records, and reflect both factual and symbolic transformations of freedom. The narratives likewise transcend the ruptures of the Second Maroon War and order the relationship between Maroon Town and Accompong (the two sacred sites of the Leeward Maroon treaty towns), accounting for the ascendancy of Accompong in the Leeward polity today.

Even more unexpected than the findings in Maroon Town of 'slave master' pickni' ethnicity, and of some Afro-Creoles and Meso-Creoles asserting maroon ancestry, was the discovery of a likely link between the mulatto 'McGhie Maroons' who resettled the foraging non-treaty maroon village of Congo Town (later renamed Highwindward/Me No Sen You No Come) in the Cockpits of Trelawny Parish near Trelawny Town in St James, around the time of the Second Maroon War of 1795–96 until 1824 (Patterson 1973, 264; Mullin 1994, 58–61) and the McGhies of Maroon Town (who paradoxically do not assert maroon descent), who are the village's most prominent Old Family. My research indicates that, after the colonial destruction of Me No Sen You No Come in 1824, the McGhie Maroons migrated to settle in Flagstaff (the heart of the former territory of Trelawny Town and now part of Maroon Town) where their descendants became Maroon Town's central clan. Chapter 10, 'The McGhie Maroons and the Maroon Town McGhies', reveals that connection through data on genealogies, oral traditions and landholdings. This link is a significant dimension of the hidden transformation of Trelawny Town to Maroon Town (and of the neglected post-1824 history of the Me No Sen community) and an important contribution to Jamaican national history, as well as to the comparative study of creolization in maroon and non-maroon transformations of African-American slave cultures.

Chapter 11, 'Maroon Town and Accompong: Ritual, Tourism and Nationhood', explores similarities and differences in ritual between Accompong and Maroon Town (the two sites of the eighteenth-century Leeward Maroon polity) and their contrasting political relations with the Jamaican nation state. The first part of this chapter focuses on another important finding in my research, namely, that in the Flagstaff area of Maroon Town, on the site of Cudjoe's Town/Trelawny Town, Emancipation Day rituals have been staged on August 1 since 1997, within the contexts of the national and regional revival of such celebrations in the Caribbean and Jamaica (e.g. Brereton 1996, 2010, 2011; Higman 1998; Van Stipriaan 2004). I examine the introduction of such celebrations at Flagstaff within these wider contexts and show that they represent a complex statement on the place of Maroon Town in the history and identity of the Jamaican nation, as well as in Rastafarian, African-American and global discourses on slavery and freedom. Flagstaff's emancipation celebrations also reflect the incorporation of the former site of the primary village of the Leeward Maroon polity into the political system of the post-colonial nation state.

Emancipation Day celebrations are not generally held in the Accompong maroon society as it secured its freedom following warfare and treaty (1725–38/39), a century before emancipation in Jamaica in 1838. Instead, the Accompong Maroons hold their Myal Plays on January 6 to celebrate both the treaty and Captain Cudjoe's birthday. However, during my fieldwork, emancipation celebrations were held in Accompong on August 1, 2003. The next section of the chapter illuminates this short-lived innovation, relating it to the internal factions of the maroon polity and their shifting relationships with the Jamaican nation state. The penultimate section of the chapter examines another (and more enduring) innovation in Accompong maroon ritual in the new millennium, namely the transformation of the annual Myal Play into a symbol of Jamaican nationhood and a mode of participation in the island's global tourist industry. The final section of the chapter outlines recent developments in Flagstaff/Maroon Town regarding the revival of the history of Trelawny Town in the context of Jamaican heritage tourism; a transformation that, I suggest, is also attempting to repair the fractured boundaries of the historic Leeward Maroon polity. This section also highlights the reciprocal involvement of the Accompong Maroons in this reparation process, culminating in their launching of reconstructed Leeward Maroon trails in October 2012.

Chapter 12, 'Creolization at the Maroon/Non-Maroon Interface', draws together the main arguments of the book showing how this ethnography of three Cockpit Country communities contributes to the comparative study of creolization in maroon and non-maroon derivations of African-American slave cultures. I also highlight the book's contributions to a wider range of issues in anthropology.

The Making of the Book

This comparative study of creolization in Accompong and Aberdeen in St Elizabeth and Maroon Town, in St James, at the maroon/non-maroon interface, is informed by my earlier study of five non-maroon villages in the adjoining parish of Trelawny (Besson 2002). That earlier research, in the Jamaican plantation heartlands, included the free villages of Martha Brae, Refuge/Wilberforce, Kettering, Granville, and New Birmingham/The Alps.[34] I also undertook a preliminary study (currently being expanded) of Martha Brae's satellite squatter settlement of Zion, which has appropriated and transformed the backlands of a former slave plantation (Besson 2002, 2007, 2012a). Within a comparative context of documenting the neglected study of 'the origins and history of [Caribbean] peasant subcultures and the similarities and differences among them' (Mintz 1989, 230 in Besson 2002, 8), I focused especially on the transformation of Martha Brae from a British West Indian slaving port and planter town to a post-emancipation village with a core of Old Families and family lands. That momentous transformation (and the transformation of legal-freehold Baptist land settlements to customary family lands in The Alps, Refuge, Kettering and Granville and the appropriation of plantation land in Zion) provided insights into the transformation of plantation lands into peasant communities with creole tenures and landholding kin groups that occurred in various ways in Accompong, Maroon Town and Aberdeen (see also Besson 1999a, 2000 and chapter 2).

In addition to being enriched by that Trelawny study, this book draws on my background as a Jamaican of mixed European and African ancestry rooted in both the planter class and peasantry of St James, Trelawny and St Elizabeth (cf. Besson 2002, xxiv–xxvii). I am descended on my father's paternal side from the Afro-Scots McFarlane planter family of these three west-central parishes[35] and on his mother's side from the Afro-Scottish Baxters of eastern Jamaica. Through my mother, I belong to the Afro-English Myers and Elliott clans of the villages of Top Hill and Ballard's Valley in St Elizabeth, near Accompong and Aberdeen (the Myers clan also being of partial German-Jewish descent and the Elliotts claiming some Arawak/Taino ancestry). Three of these clans (McFarlane, Elliott and Myers) descend from planters and slaves. In addition, a segment of the McFarlanes interweaves with Meso-Creoles in Maroon Town and another branch married into the Accompong Maroons; while the Baxters claim Scottish-Windward Maroon descent.

As with my earlier Trelawny study (Besson 2002), this ethnography of Accompong, Aberdeen and Maroon Town is my interpretation as 'a positioned subject' (Rosaldo 1993, 19) – influenced by my life experiences, insider/outsider status, gender, sexuality, age, ethnicity, culture and class. This positioned subjectivity includes being a Meso-Creole middle-class Jamaican woman, born (as Jean McFarlane) in 1944, as outlined above. I am described as 'high-colour brown' in the Cockpits, 'fair-coloured' on the Jamaican lowlands, 'African American' in the United States and 'white' (with a 'perm') in Britain. I grew up on former slave plantations in Trelawny and at Hartmont Hill in Montego Bay (St James) and attended an Anglican high school in the parish of St Ann. Contra to *Dead-Yard* (Thompson 2009, 153), I have not converted to Revivalism but remain an Anglican (who now appreciates Myal, Revival and Rastafari as a result of my research). I was further educated at Edinburgh University, where I obtained a general MA (1965) followed by an MA Honours (1967) and PhD (1974) in Social Anthropology. I taught Anthropology at the Universities of Edinburgh (1974–76) and Aberdeen (1976–90) in Scotland before teaching at Goldsmiths, University of London, England where I established courses on Caribbean social anthropology and ethnography (1991–2014). I have held visiting appointments at the University of the West Indies in Jamaica and Trinidad and Tobago, and at the Johns Hopkins University in the United States.

Many individuals and institutions have assisted my research for this ethnography. I thank the people of Accompong, Aberdeen and Maroon Town for all their help, though space permits me to mention just a few here. However, the knowledge of many others becomes evident throughout the book. In Accompong, the late Martin Luther Wright, Harris Cawley, Meredie Rowe and Sydney Peddie (all Leeward Maroon Colonels), Melvin Currie (a former Deputy Colonel and Minister of Tourism and Culture in Accompong) and the late Mann O. Rowe (Accompong's Secretary of State, who lived to the age of 102) particularly helped with my fieldwork. So did Mann Rowe's son Dolphie Rowe, who plays an important role at Myal Plays. Melvin and Dolphie, 'two sister' pickni' (two sisters' children), were the first Maroons whom I came to know well and they became enduring friends (figures 1.7a and 1.7b).

Figure 1.7a. Melvin Currie and Dolphie Rowe (two sisters' children) clearing a sacred site near Old Town, Accompong, 1989.

Figure 1.7b. Maroon cousins Melvin Currie and Dolphie Rowe, Accompong, 2009.

Although my husband and I did not take up Dolphie's kind offer of a house-spot in his yard on the common treaty land, we thank him for this gesture of acceptance in the Leeward Maroon polity. Lucal and Aubrey Williams, ritual cooks at the Myal Plays, further illuminated the Myal worldview. Hansley ('Rupie') Reid, who during my fieldwork, succeeded Gilbert Rowe as the official abeng-blower, likewise assisted my research. So did Rupie's sister, Caroline 'Ena' Wright Lawrence, and their late mother, Gladys Reid, both Myal dancers of the Rowe Family, Accompong's central clan.

In Aberdeen, the late Pastor Charles Wint, who claimed Afro-Scots descent from slaves, planters and an African-Prince Maroon, was especially helpful in my fieldwork. Lucien Taylor, Alan Williams and the Mundy family helped me greatly too. I also thank Dudley Hazel and Kenneth Watson of Montego Bay for assistance with transport to Accompong and Aberdeen.

In Maroon Town, I am grateful to the late Mrs Beryl Delgado ('Miss Lil') and her husband and children (of Maroon Town's Reid and McIntyre clans) for their kindness. Thanks, too, to Councillor Glendon Harris and the late Ex-Councillor Mortimer Reid, who were especially generous with their knowledge and time. The late Mrs Adeline Hall ('Miss Ade'), who claimed maroon descent and lived to the age of 103, likewise taught me much about Maroon Town as did her granddaughter Nerissa. I am also grateful to the many members of the McGhie Old Family, Maroon Town's central clan, who contributed to my research. Several members of the Rockhead clan, especially Willard Rockhead, were likewise very informative and Pauline Rockhead often provided me with a base in Maroon Town. Orville ('Charlie') Dobson (based in Montego Bay) introduced me to his relatives in Maroon Town including Mortimer, Adeline and Nerissa and provided practical help throughout my fieldwork there.

My late mother Megs ('Meggie') McFarlane (née Myers, 1914–2004), whose paternal lineage and family land are rooted in Top Hill in St Elizabeth, not far from Accompong and Aberdeen, helped me in so very many ways throughout my fieldwork including providing a home-base in Montego Bay. She also drew to my attention, on an early visit to Maroon Town, that references to the 'Meggie' surname in Jamaica are creolized pronunciations of the Scottish 'McGhie'. She knew this from my late father's friendship (as a young man in Montego Bay) with Leonard Lambert McGhie (1902–73), known as 'Meggie', of Maroon Town's McGhie clan. Without her observation, I might have missed the significance of the McGhie Old Family in Maroon Town and its links with the McGhie Maroons. For these reasons, and many more, this book is dedicated primarily to her.

The knowledge gained from my father, Kenneth ('Lawyer') McFarlane (1910–86, a planter and attorney-at-law in Trelawny, Hanover and Montego Bay), regarding his natal parish of St James and his kindness to many people there, bore fruit in several unexpected ways in my fieldwork; for example, when people helped me in Maroon Town because of my relationship to him.

My husband, Dr John Besson (of Guyana, Edinburgh and London), continued to adjust his professional life to help my Cockpit Country fieldwork and I thank him for his patience and support and for some of the photography in this book.[36]

In my earlier Trelawny ethnography, I used pseudonyms for people whom I interviewed, only retaining the names or nicknames of ancestor-heroes and the surnames of the Old Families that perpetuated those communities (Besson 2002, xxx–xxxi). In this later study, I use real names, reflecting my long-term relationship with many of the individuals who contributed to my research over 30 years and the on-going negotiation of their consent to use the information they provided for this book. Consideration of intellectual property rights reinforced my decision that those who contributed to my research should receive explicit credit for their knowledge, time and views.[37] In addition, several persons whom I interviewed are public figures such as Parish Councillors and maroon Colonels or Ex-Colonels who are not only used to being quoted but also expect to be so (compare Carey 1997, 275; Bilby 2005; Zips 1999, 2011).

Much of the fieldwork for this book was funded personally, with help from my family. However, periods of research leave and travel grants from Aberdeen University and Goldsmiths assisted my research. I also thank the British Academy, the Carnegie Trust and the Nuffield Foundation for small research grants. I am grateful too to the library staff at the Universities of Aberdeen, Edinburgh and London, the Institute of Jamaica, the National Library of Jamaica and to Jackie Ranston in Kingston for help with archival research.

Like my earlier study of Trelawny free villages on the plantation lowlands (Besson 2002), a central aim of this comparative ethnography in the Cockpits is to empower the hidden histories of these post-slavery communities, contribute to the cultural history of African-America, the Caribbean and Jamaica and advance the discipline of Social Anthropology which traditionally marginalized the Caribbean but has now moved it to centre stage (Mintz 1996a, 2010; Trouillot 1992; Martin 2012).

My research for this book has been a journey of personal as well as professional discovery. I discovered kinship ties through my paternal grandfather, the Meso-Creole planter George McFarlane of Reading, St James, with the Afro-Scots Reid Family of Maroon Town and my newfound paternal aunt there, Mrs Beryl Delgado (née McFarlane), and her children (figure 1.8). I learned that Lower Aberdeen was consolidated on Island Estate, a plantation established by the Scotsman, Alexander McFarlane, of my paternal McFarlane clan prior to his death in Jamaica in 1755.

I also learned that later McFarlane plantations, Castle Wemyss and Spring Vale (where I often visited relatives while growing up in Trelawny), had featured in the Second Maroon War and that Sam Sharpe, the Native Baptist leader of the 1831–32 Jamaican slave rebellion, had been educated at Hartmont Hill (then called Coopers Hill) where I lived as a child in Montego Bay.[38] In Balaclava, near Aberdeen, where the son of the African-Prince Maroon of Accompong is said to have acquired land and lived, I met a 'new' branch of my McFarlane clan. In Accompong, at Myal Plays under the Kindah Family Tree, I encountered other new kin: a journalist from my maternal Myers clan and a cousin in my paternal Baxter Family, both previously unknown to me. I also met a McFarlane cousin who is an Accompong 'bye-Maroon'.[39]

Figure 1.8.   Mrs Beryl Delgado (right), the author and Barbara Delgado (left), Maroon Town.

Towards the end of my fieldwork in the Cockpits, Charlie Dobson, who had introduced me to his relatives in Maroon Town and who had become like family to mine, died suddenly in 2008, aged 64, in Montego Bay. His untimely death deeply saddened me and my husband in London as by then we had known Charlie for 20 years, even before my fieldwork in Maroon Town. Through the shared grieving with Charlie's transnational kin, conducted by cell phone across the Atlantic Ocean and Caribbean Sea, I experienced most fully both the spiritual worldview and the harsh reality of life and death at the maroon/non-maroon interface. For all these reasons, including the help and friendship that Charlie showed us, this book is dedicated partly to him.

Notes

1. An important exception to this is Mintz and Price (1992). See also Bilby (1984b). As seen in chapter 12, this book draws on and modifies some of Mintz and Price's conclusions and also provides both complementary and contrasting perspectives to Bilby.
2. Renamed San Salvador (now Watling Island) by Columbus, in The Bahamas chain.
3. Mintz's use of the concept of *oikoumenê* refers to the Caribbean region as a *societal* area, (including the Antilles, The Bahamas, the Guianas and Belize), forged by the common historical processes of colonialism, the plantation system and slavery, producing across the region similar 'social frameworks created for culturally diverse migrant peoples' (Mintz 1996a, 297). Mintz's usage, which recognizes the cultural diversity of Caribbean societies, builds on but modifies Kreober's (1946) adaptation of the ancient Greek concept of *oikoumenê* ('the inhabited world as the Greeks defined it') that referred to a great historic unit and *culture* area (Mintz 1996a, 293).
4. See chapter 2 for a discussion of the concept of 'peasantry' in general and in the Caribbean context.
5. Following de Certeau (1980 in Burton 1997, 6), a distinction may be drawn between opposition from within a system and resistance from outside it. From this perspective, marronage and maroon wars were resistance, while the 'proto-peasant' adaptation on the slave plantations (Mintz 1989, 151–52) was opposition (see also Besson 2002 and chapter 2).
6. Parts of this section draw on and develop my general discussion of Jamaica in Besson (2002). I am grateful to the University of North Carolina Press for permission to draw on this earlier work.
7. Referring to a census of 1611, Fernando Henriques (1968, 23) states of the island's indigenous peoples that, 'in little more than a century the Indian population had declined from an estimated 60,000 to 74', who were replaced by African slaves. Carey Robinson (1969, 14) likewise notes that this census (which recorded an estimated population of '1,510 persons of all classes and conditions') included only '74 native Arawak Indians [Tainos]', the remainder comprising '523 Spaniards including men and women, 173 children, 107 free Negroes,... 558 slaves and 75 foreigners'.
8. By 1834, 'Jamaica had 670 sugar plantations with an average population of 223 slaves, accounting for one-half of the island's 312,000 slaves' at that time (Higman 1998, 2).
9. Paul H. Williams, 'Zong Massacre plaque unveiled', *Jamaica Gleaner*, December 31, 2007.
10. By the turn of the millennium, Trelawny Sugar and Hampden Estates were two of the six large state-owned sugar estates in Jamaica. Hampden went into government receivership (sending its cane to be processed at Trelawny Sugar) at the end of the twentieth century after centuries of private ownership since 1757 (Besson 2002, 64, 135). However, by 2012, Hampden was again being privately operated (through lease from the government, as is now also the case

with Trelawny Sugar). On J Wray and Nephew Ltd and Appleton Estate see Moses Jackson, 'Observer Business Leader nominee #14: J Wray and Nephew Ltd', *Jamaica Observer*, November 29, 2012 http://www.jamaicaobserver.com/news/Why-J-Wray---Nephew-Ltd_... and 'Appleton Rum Estate', http://www.jamaicatravelandculture.com/destinations/st_elizabeth/appleton..., 2008, accessed May 23, 2014. During my fieldwork the parent company of the J Wray and Nephew conglomerate (who owned Appleton, Holland and New Yarmouth) was Lascelles de Mercado & Co. Limited. In 2012, Lascelles de Mercado was sold to the Italian distillers Campari: 'In December 2012, Gruppo Campari, the sixth largest player in the global spirits industry, completed its acquisition of Lascelles de Mercado & Co. Limited, parent company of J. Wray and Nephew. Subsequent to this acquisition, J. Wray and Nephew Ltd. merged with sister company Lascelles Ltd.' http://www.jwrayandnephew.com.

11. 'Appleton Estate', http://en.wikipedia.org/wiki/Appleton_Estate, March 2, 2010; 'Appleton Rum Estate', 2008, http://www.jamaicatravelandculture.com/destinations/st_elizabeth/appleton-rum-estate.htm. The cane from Appleton, Holland and New Yarmouth is processed at Appleton.
12. In addition to persisting plantation agriculture, other large farms raise livestock (especially cattle), monocrop in fruit or sugar cane, or grow winter vegetables for export (Besson 2002, 132).
13. The first shipment of bauxite from Jamaica was in 1952 and by 1957 the island had become the world's leading bauxite producer. By 1974, Jamaica was 'the world's second largest producer of bauxite and the second largest exporter of alumina' after Australia ('Development of the Bauxite/Alumina Sector', Jamaica Bauxite Institute, http://jbi.org.jm/pages/industry). This was still the case in 1997 ('Caribbean Eye Exhibition', Commonwealth Institute, London, England, 1997). However, by 2008, 'the year preceding the global economic downturn which had a deep impact on the bauxite/alumina industry', Jamaica's bauxite production had 'fallen to sixth place in the world' and, 'With over one-half of the country's alumina capacity still closed in 2012, ... Jamaica's position in the world industry would have experienced further slippage' ('Development of the Bauxite/Alumina Sector', Jamaica Bauxite Institute, http://jbi.org.jm/pages/industry, accessed May 20, 2014). In 2009, the bauxite mining and alumina processing plant of Alumina Partners of Jamaica (ALPART) located at Nain in St Elizabeth was shut down ('Bauxite Industry', Jamaica Bauxite Institute, http://jbi.org.jm/pages/bauxite_alumina_plants) and is not expected to re-open before 2016.
14. The area considered for a National Park is 600km^2, 'which includes the contiguous forest' (Eyre 1995, 259).
15. In addition, the Cockpit Country forests 'are major sources of yam sticks, charcoal, and commercial hardwood timber' (Miller and Barker 2007, 127), there is encroachment into the Cockpits from small-farming on its fringes and also deforestation both at the fringes and in the core area (Ibid.; Barker and Miller 1995).
16. From a geographical perspective, Learie Miller and David Barker describe this environment well: 'This region's unique conical karstic landscape combines a tropical wet limestone broadleaf rainforest with high biodiversity and endemism. Species diversity among its plants and animals is exceptional, and the area is a refuge for endangered endemic parrots and the Giant Swallowtail butterfly' (Miller and Barker 2007, 127).
17. Charles Square was named after Sir Charles Knowles, the British Governor of Jamaica from 1752 to 1756 (Sibley 1978, 33). It was renamed Sam Sharpe Square in 1981.
18. Montego Bay was founded in the early eighteenth century by Captain Jonathan Barnett (1677–1744), a wealthy planter who led the defence of St James Parish against pirates and Maroons. During slavery, the Barnett Estates belonged to the Barnett planter family and are now owned

by an elite family with origins in the planter class of Trelawny and St James (Besson 2002, 55, 61, 66).
19. See, e.g., http://www.jnht.com/churches/salters.htm.
20. Throughout this book, I use the abbreviated name Accompong, except where it is necessary to distinguish Accompong Town from its founder, Captain Accompong.
21. In this book, I use the Jamaican-English spelling of 'Cudjoe' and 'Cudjoe's Town', as Captain Cudjoe was born in Jamaica and is reported as commanding his followers to speak Jamaican-English/Creole rather than their African languages (Campbell 1990, 46; Kopytoff 1976b, 41–42, 45).
22. Citing Richard Hart, Werner Zips notes that, 'According to the Julian calendar, New Year's Day fell on March 25. Before the Calendar Act of 1751, the "old" year was usually listed with dates between January 1 and March 25 (Hart 1985, 129). The old sources… therefore date the peace treaty as March 1, 1738, but most modern authors list it as March 1, 1739' (Zips 1999, 253 n89). The Windward Maroons in the eastern mountains of Jamaica subsequently made a similar treaty in June 1739 and endure in the parishes of Portland and St Mary (chapter 2; Bilby 2006).
23. At that time, sometimes spelt Trelawney Town.
24. The changing names of the villages of Cudjoe's Town/Trelawny Town/Maroon Town and Ockbrook/Aberdeen are part of a wider pattern of transformational naming practices in rural Jamaica that reflects the complex histories of such communities (see Besson 1984b, 2002).
25. My usage of the concepts Afro-Creole, Euro-Creole and Meso-Creole draw on Richard Burton's study of creolization, in which he coined the terms to refer to the cultures of locally born black (and coloured) slaves, white colonists and Free Coloureds in Jamaican slave society (1997, 14), before focusing on the Afro-Creole cultures of 'opposition' and 'play' in Jamaica, Trinidad and Haiti from slavery to the present. In a previous article, I have addressed the construction of Euro-Creole, Afro-Creole and Meso-Creole ethnic identifications in west-central Jamaica and identified variations on these themes (Besson 2003a). I draw on my earlier perspective in this book, which develops my analysis of Afro-Creole and Meso-Creole ethnicities in the communities that I studied. I do not use these terms to denote a plural society (see chapter 2).
26. In Accompong, the titles Colonel and Captains or Lieutenants are now used for their hierarchy of leaders today (see chapters 2–5).
27. As Kopytoff (1979, 52) notes, 'First-Time Maroons' refers to the Maroons who won the treaties rather than to the first runaway slaves.
28. Relatives of an individual, traced through both parental sides.
29. This refers to conjugal relations between cousins within the same community. In contrast to the Accompong Maroons, cousin-conjugality is prohibited in Jamaican non-maroon communities (Besson 2002, 283).
30. The anthropological term 'cognatic' denotes descent traced through both genders in contrast to unilineal descent through one gender only (see Besson 2002). The anthropological concept of 'clan', which is used by Jamaican Maroons themselves, refers to a large ancestor-focused kin group claiming common descent that may not be demonstrable. Clans are generally comprised of lineages, where descent may be actually traced. In this book, I use 'clan' as synonymous with large cognatic descent groups or 'Old Families' and 'lineages' for their smaller branches or segments.
31. Lévi-Strauss (1969) distinguished two types of exogamous or out-marrying systems: 'elementary' and 'complex'. In contrast to the prescribed or preferential marriage rules of elementary systems, complex systems specify only which relations one may not marry. For all the Jamaican communities that I studied, I use the term 'marriage' in the anthropological

sense to refer to institutionalized conjugal relations (Seymour-Smith 1986, 179–80). In Jamaica, 'marriage', therefore, includes 'extra-residential relations', 'consensual cohabitation' and 'legal marriage' and also 'serial monogamy' or 'serial polygamy' (see chapter 12 and also Besson 2002).

32. Such kin-based cemeteries are found in some of the Trelawny free villages where, as elsewhere in Jamaica, variations in family-land burial are partly due to Jamaican state burial legislation governed by the Burial Within Towns' Limits Act of 1875 that regulates yard burial in relation to the proximity of villages to urban settlements and their boundaries (Besson 2002, 140, 146). Family-land burial grounds are pronounced in the more isolated non-maroon villages of the Cockpit Country and are now emerging in the Accompong maroon society (chapter 3).

33. In this respect, Aberdeen and Maroon Town differ from The Alps/New Birmingham (Trelawny's first Baptist-founded free village) in the foothills of the north-eastern Cockpit Country, where there is an unambiguous non-maroon Afro-Creole ethnicity based on descent from plantation slaves on The Alps coffee estate (Besson 1984b, 2002, and note 34 below).

34. Unlike the other four Trelawny villages that I studied, which are on the coastal plains or plateaux, The Alps is in the north-eastern foothills of the Cockpit Country. However, in contrast to Aberdeen in St Elizabeth and Maroon Town, St James in the Cockpits, which have a diversity of ethnicities at the maroon/non-maroon interface, The Alps is an unambiguously Afro-Creole non-maroon community, being the first post-emancipation free village in Trelawny established by emancipated slaves (in association with the Baptist church). See also note 33 above.

35. The early MacFarlanes/McFarlanes in Jamaica included Alexander MacFarlane/McFarlane of St Elizabeth and Kingston, youngest son of John MacFarlane, 19th Chief of the Clan MacFarlane based at Arrochar, Scotland, who came to Jamaica around 1735 and became a planter, merchant and the first Postmaster General of the colony, and who died there in 1755 (Besson and McFarlane 1995, 2005, 2009). My subsequent research has uncovered the more extensive Scottish and Creole MacFarlane/McFarlane clan network that spread through the southern Jamaican parishes of Westmoreland, St Elizabeth, Manchester, St Catherine and St Andrew/Kingston from at least the eighteenth century and which still endures, including a branch based in Balaclava, St Elizabeth, three miles from Aberdeen. I am grateful to the late Anne Mills, John Fowler, Michael McFarlane, Andrew McFarlane, Burt McFarlane, Dr Tony MacFarlane, Ivan MacFarlane, Johnny McFarlane, Hilary Russell, Doug Gore and Lieutenant Commander John McFarlane (all Jamaican MacFarlane/McFarlane descendants, some of whom reside in Canada and the USA), Robert Barker and Stephen Porter (UK) and Dr Amitava Chowdhury (Canada) for help with this research.

36. Except where otherwise indicated, the photographs in this book were taken by either John Besson or me.

37. I thank Marcus Goffe, a Jamaican lawyer specializing in intellectual property rights who works with the Maroons, for his helpful discussion with me on this point.

38. I am grateful to Geoffrey deSola Pinto, who married into the Hart family of Hartmont Hill, for this information: 'Hartmont prior to 1914 was called Coopers Hill which in earlier years belonged to the Sharpes – a lawyer. His slave Sam was educated with his own son who was about the same age and the relationship appears to have been a close one with the family' (personal communication from deSola Pinto 12/4/2009).

39. See chapter 6 for a fuller explanation of the concept of bye-maroon in Accompong, indicating the incorporation of a non-maroon spouse into the maroon polity.

2 ■ THE ROOTS OF CREOLIZATION IN THE COCKPITS

As outlined in chapter 1, creolization (the creative process of indigenization or localization) in maroon and non-maroon transformations of African-American slave cultures occurred in response to the globalization that began with the European Conquest of the Americas and the forging of the Caribbean *oikoumenê* after 1492 (Mintz 1996a, 1996b). This chapter explores more fully the roots of creolization at the maroon/non-maroon interface in the Jamaican Cockpit Country, at the heart of the Caribbean core of African-America that laid the foundations for Accompong, Maroon Town and Aberdeen.

I first highlight the responses of African-American slaves to slavery including rebellions, marronage and the 'proto-peasant' adaptation (Mintz 1989, 146–56), all of which were highly developed in the Caribbean, Jamaica and the Cockpits. Against that background, I focus in more detail on the Jamaican maroon wars with the British colonists that directly shaped creolization in the Cockpit Country, especially Accompong. I then indicate the role of the Nonconformist missionaries, who were variously involved in the villages that I studied in the Cockpits: Baptists in Maroon Town, Presbyterians in Accompong and Moravians in Aberdeen. Plantation and rebel slaves and their descendants had an ambiguous alliance with such missionaries and often appropriated and transformed their European religions to create creole worldviews that still endure. In addition, the Jamaican slave rebellion in 1831–32 that started near Maroon Town was initially named the 'Baptist War'. I also consider Caribbean post-slavery peasantization and the Jamaican free-village system, which were significant for the transformations that occurred in Maroon Town and Aberdeen.[1] In conclusion, I situate the Cockpit communities that I studied within the Jamaican social system.

Slave Rebellion, Marronage and Proto-Peasantization

From the beginning of colonial plantation slavery in African-America, enslaved Africans and Creoles sought to re-establish their freedom. This quest was manifested in resistance from beyond the plantations, opposition from within the plantation system and negotiation with the planter class. These responses included rebellion, revolution, marronage and the establishment of maroon treaty towns, as well as 'proto-peasant' adaptations by plantation slaves (Besson 2002, 85–90).

Long, continuous histories of slave rebellion typified the Caribbean, Brazil, and, to a lesser extent, the southern United States. Slave rebellion especially characterized the non-Hispanic Caribbean where plantation slavery was most pronounced. Such revolts included the Saint-Domingue revolution (1791–

1804) and the great Jamaican slave rebellion of 1831–32, which started at Kensington near Maroon Town. Despite being crushed in the short-term, this rebellion (led by the Creole slave Sam Sharpe) not only resulted in the abolition of slavery throughout the British Empire in 1834, but (like other slave revolts in the later slavery era) also reflected the process of creolization in its goal of African-American freedom rather than the restoration of African lifeways (Genovese 1981).

Marronage (escaping slavery and founding autonomous communities) likewise typified the entire span and scope of New World slavery (R. Price 1996; Heuman 1985) and, as Richard Price (1996, 25–30) has argued, in contrast to Roger Bastide (1972), such maroon communities reflected African-American creolization rather than 'mosaic cultures' (Price 1996, 27) from the African past. Maroon societies lived under constant threat of war from plantation-military regimes, and were therefore established in almost inaccessible areas such as mountains, forests, and ravines. Such topography enabled guerilla warfare and the 'capturing' of land, as occurred with the Jamaican Leeward Maroons in the Cockpits and the Windward Maroons in the island's eastern mountains.

Some maroon communities were wiped out in war, while others won freedom and legal land rights through treaties with colonial governments forced to sue for peace. Such treaties were forged in Brazil, Colombia, Cuba, Dutch Guiana, Ecuador, Hispaniola, Jamaica and Mexico (Price 1996, 3). Following treaties in Colombia between Maroons and the Spanish in the late seventeenth and early eighteenth centuries (de Friedemann and Arocha 1995; McFarlane 1985), the Jamaican Leeward and Windward Maroon treaties of March and June 1738/39 with the British provided a model for the treaties of the 1760s between the Dutch and the Maroons in Dutch Guiana, now Suriname. With the exception of the maroon *palenque* of San Basilio in Colombia, consolidated by a royal injunction of 1691 (de Friedemann and Arocha 1995, 54–55), the longest lasting post-treaty maroon communities are in Suriname and Jamaica. Suriname has the largest African-American maroon societies and the Jamaican Maroons are the oldest corporate maroon polities in African-America enduring on common land, San Basilio having been deprived of its common pastureland (54–55).

'Proto-peasant' adaptations were created by plantation slaves appropriating customary land rights, especially in the non-Hispanic Caribbean (particularly the British West Indies and French Saint-Domingue) from the eighteenth century (Mintz 1989; Trouillot 1998; Besson 2002, 86–88). Here, planters allocated marginal plantation land as provision grounds (in addition to house-yards) for the slaves to grow their own crops. The enslaved, however, developed the provision-ground system beyond the planters' intentions of ensuring a self-sustaining labour force, producing surpluses for sale in public marketplaces. This proto-peasant adaptation was most pronounced in Jamaica, with its hilly plantation backlands and separate estate 'mountains'[2] and flourishing Sunday markets. Such proto-peasantization, whereby the enslaved re-created economies, identities, families and communities, was highly developed in the west-central parishes, including Aberdeen Estate in St Elizabeth, and laid the foundations for the free village of Aberdeen.

A major dimension of such Caribbean proto-peasant culture-building was the transmission of customary land rights by male and female slaves to their descendants of both genders creating cognatic landholding lineages traced through both women and men (Besson 1992a, 1995b, 2002, 88). Jamaica provides clear evidence of slaves transmitting, through such a cognatic descent system, customary rights to plantation provision grounds and house-yards with family burial grounds (Besson 2002, 28–30, 88). This Afro-Creole system transformed the principles of both European plantation primogeniture and West and Central African unilineal descent to maximize forbidden family lines and scarce land rights among Caribbean chattel slaves, who were not only legally kinless and landless, but also property themselves. This cognatic system also provided the foundation of the Caribbean post-slavery institution of family land, as occurred in Trelawny's free villages (Besson 2002) and Aberdeen and Maroon Town (chapters 6–10). This cognatic system would also re-emerge in the Accompong maroon society as the basis for transmitting the common treaty land (Besson 1997, 2005 and chapter 3). In both maroon and non-maroon derivations of such slave cultures, cognatic lineages burgeoned into cognatic clans.

As well as being transformed by the slaves' creole institution-building, the Jamaican planters' primogeniture would be modified by the masters themselves, with some planters leaving property in wills for their enslaved children by slave women who were sometimes then also freed (Besson 2002, 65–66; Petley 2005). My research suggests that such property transfers from planters to their mixed-race children were significant in the evolution of Maroon Town, where such transfers seem to be the origin of some family lands. The application, by Meso-Creoles in Maroon Town, of the Afro-Creole cognatic system to create customary family land from property transferred from planters through the Euro-Creole legal system, reflects creolization not only through 'a process of *contention*' (Bolland 2002, 38) but also through negotiation across the boundaries of class (chapter 1).

The next section focuses on the Jamaican Maroon Wars, with particular reference to marronage in the Cockpits. These wars are central to the creole histories and ethnicities of Accompong, Maroon Town and Aberdeen.

The Jamaican Maroon Wars and Cockpit Country Marronage

The Jamaican Maroon Wars have been documented in detail from various historical perspectives (e.g. Long 1774; Dallas 1803; Robinson 1969; Craton 1982; Campbell 1990; Carey 1997).[3] My purpose here is not to duplicate those accounts but rather to outline these events in relation to the Leeward Maroon polity as a background to my ethnography of Accompong, Maroon Town and Aberdeen. I also highlight and assess points that link directly with the ethnography of these communities.

In western Jamaica, the Cockpit Country landscape was a crucial factor in the maroon wars (Eyre 1980),[4] and the sites and events of the wars in the Cockpits are recurrent themes in the oral traditions of the three communities that I studied there. In addition, there are continuities and transformations from the maroon wars embedded in these communities and their lands, clans and narratives. Both maroon wars are relevant to all three Cockpit villages where I conducted research. However, the First Maroon War (1725–38/39) is especially significant for Accompong and Aberdeen (chapters 3–6), while the Second Maroon War (1795–96) is particularly important for the transformation of Trelawny Town to Maroon Town, as well as for the transformation of Accompong from the secondary to the sole surviving Leeward Maroon village (chapters 3–10). A focus on the maroon wars also reveals the emergence of multi-stranded relations among Maroons, slaves and colonists that illuminate the complex relations among their descendants at the maroon/non-maroon interface in the Cockpits today.

The First Maroon War and the Consolidation of the Leeward Maroon Polity

The early backdrop to the First Jamaican Maroon War with the British, from 1725 to 1738/39, was the seventeenth-century marronage of runaway slaves belonging to the Spanish colonizers of the island, which escalated with the English invasion of the colony in 1655 as more slaves of the Spaniards escaped into the hills (Robinson 1969, 18–27; Campbell 1990, 14–43; Carey 1997, 96–144). The most numerous of these Maroons (as they would come to be named)[5] were a group in the south-central highlands of what would become the parish of Clarendon, under English rule. The leader of this group was Juan Lubolo, later known as Juan de Bolas. For a time, this group formed an alliance with the Spanish resistance leader, Don Christoval Arnaldo de Ysassi, who was made Governor of the colony in 1656 by the King of Spain. However, in February 1660, Bolas and his followers defected to the English; this greatly undermined Ysassi's Spanish resistance movement which ended with his departure from Jamaica in May of that year. The Juan de Bolas Maroons were granted freedom and land by the English and in 1663 Bolas 'was appointed Colonel of a black regiment of militia' and 'also made a magistrate over the Negroes with the power to decide all cases except those of life and death' (Robinson 1969, 27). Other Spanish Maroons, however, remained at large, despite offers from the English of freedom and land on surrender. The English, therefore, sought to defeat the Maroons, using Bolas and his men, but they were ambushed and Bolas was killed (27–29).

By the end of the seventeenth century, there had been no conclusive victory by the English over the Maroons. Marronage and related guerrilla warfare in the colony escalated into the eighteenth century, triggered by the rebellion of slaves from Colonel Sutton's plantation in Clarendon in 1690 to join the Spanish Maroons. This warfare, in response to continued attacks by the British, intensified from 1725 in both the west and east of the colony and would become known as the First Jamaican Maroon War (Patterson 1973, 269–70; Eyre 1980, 6–13; Robinson 1969, 30–62; Campbell 1990, 42–125; Carey 1997, 145–314). In 1690, the rebels established themselves in the Clarendon hills, kept in touch with the slaves on Sutton's estate and raided plantations as well as engaging in guerrilla warfare. In this context, the great maroon leader, Captain Cudjoe (who is central to narratives in the Cockpits), emerged sometime during the period 1690–1720.

There are diverse views on Cudjoe's birthplace and age. Robinson (1969, 46) states that, at the time of the Leeward Maroon treaty (in 1738/39), Cudjoe was 'more than 60 years old'. Robinson also writes that:

> We do not know when Cudjoe died, but [Edward] Long says that when Governor Lyttleton visited St James in 1764, the Trelawny Maroons went down to Montego Bay to greet him. They were led by Cudjoe who made a speech on the occasion. He must have been well over 80 years old at the time (Robinson 1969, 52; Long 1774 [2002] II, 348–49).

Consistent with these views regarding Cudjoe's age, Robinson (1969, 32) suggests that Cudjoe was 'a young Coromantee slave' who escaped from Sutton's plantation in 1690 ('Coromantee' being a British name for enslaved Africans shipped to the Americas from Fort Kormantine on the Gold Coast, many of whom were from the Akan peoples [Campbell 1990, 44; Zips 2011, xxxvi]). Carey (1997, 148) likewise argues that the generalissimo selected by these rebels was 'one Cudjoe, a new African in Jamaica' and equates him with the Leeward Maroon leader Cudjoe who 'died about 1765' as recorded by Thistlewood (Hall 1989, 134).

However, Kopytoff notes that Cudjoe (who had an Akan day-name meaning 'a male born on a Monday' [Campbell 1990, 46]), was local-born to a 'Coromantee' father who 'led the rebellion of Coromantees at Sutton's plantation in 1690' – 50 years before Cudjoe was 'a vigorous leader' of the Leeward Maroons (Kopytoff 1976b, 38, 40, 41, 42, 49 n36 in Besson 1997, 221 n69). Consistent with this, Campbell (1990, 44, 46) critiques Robinson's views and draws on a historical source[6] that states that the Leeward Maroon, Captain Cudjoe, was the son of the Akan rebel leader from Sutton's plantation. Like Kopytoff, Campbell therefore convincingly argues that Captain Cudjoe was born in Jamaica and probably in marronage:

> Cudjoe was probably born in the rebel camp and therefore would not have experienced slavery – or he may have escaped as a young man with his father, who probably trained his son to succeed him. We have no way of knowing Cudjoe's age... (Campbell 1990, 46).

Campbell goes on to point out that, although 'some of Colonel Sutton's slaves were still active guerrillas during the late 1720s', two of these being among those Maroons discovered and shot by colonists in 1729 and identified by Sutton's initials and symbol (T.S. and a heart) that had been branded on them as slaves, 'As far as we know, Cudjoe had no such marks' (46). This Cudjoe was a courageous and powerful maroon leader in the Clarendon hills by 1720. By then, he had defeated a group of Madagascan Maroons from Lacovia in St Elizabeth who then joined him to become the core of what would become known as the 'Leeward Maroons' – so-named by the colonists, who distinguished them from the eastern 'Windward Maroons' (Campbell 1990, 45–46; Carey 1997, 152).

By 1730, the Maroons were formidable in both the eastern and western mountains. The colony was regarded as a 'Maroon-infested land' (Campbell 1990, 84), there was a bounty of £10 on the head of every Maroon (Robinson 1969, 36) and Jamaica was in crisis due to the impact of marronage on its plantations. The Scottish governor of the island, Robert Hunter (from 1729 to 1734), intensified the campaign against the runaways and established more plantations to hem in the Windward Maroons who were under frequent attack (Campbell 1990, 49). In July 1733, the Council of Jamaica and the Jamaica Assembly planned to send 'the "strongest force" yet against the rebels', which set out in August of that year (75, 76). However, the counter-attacks and defeats by the Maroons continued though there were fatalities on both sides. In October 1733, the colony was divided into 'two military and administrative sections, the Eastern and Western Divisions, each having its own barracks' (83). Most of the inadequate militia at that time were Irish Catholic indentured servants (85) and Hunter sent for reinforcements from England, intensifying the attacks against both the Windward Maroons (who were strengthened by runaway slaves from Colonel Nedhams's plantation near Port Antonio)[7] and the Leeward Maroons.

Nanny Town in the Blue Mountains, the Windward Maroons' stronghold, named after their great freedom fighter, 'Grandy Nanny', was attacked many times and eventually destroyed by the colonists in 1735. Of Nanny, who also features in Cockpit Country narratives (chapters 3–9), Campbell (1990, 50) states that there is 'such an intricate network of myth and legend' woven around 'the redoubtable Nanny' that 'it is impossible to get at the real facts about her'. Nanny's reputation as warrior and obeah woman with magical powers included her reputed ability to catch the colonists' bullets between her buttocks and fire them back (51; Bilby 2006, 204).[8]

From 1732 to 1735, in the face of continued attacks in the east, there were several great marches by some Windward Maroons (of Spanish-African descent known as Katta-a-Woods) across the mountains to join Cudjoe's Leeward rebels, though at least some of the Katta-a-Woods later returned to the east as appears to have been instigated by Cudjoe (Robinson 1969, 38–39; Campbell 1990, 92–94; Carey 1997, 189–314, 385). These marches, as well as transformations of Cudjoe and Nanny, feature in narratives in both Accompong and Maroon Town. However, despite oral traditions in these two communities regarding Nanny's reputed presence there, Carey (1997, 287) states that, 'Nanny, of course, would not go west' and instead 'led her people away from the John Crow Mountains ..., to a new site, fairly low in the Blue Mountains, which later acquired the name of Pumpkin Hill'. There, Windward Maroon oral traditions state, Nanny 'called on the powers of Nyankypon (Yankypon), the Creator God, to save her people from sure extinction' and, following advice in a vision, planted pumpkin seeds that miraculously burgeoned to sustain her people (288; see also Bilby 2006, 133). Nevertheless, in Accompong today, Nanny, whose real name is said there to have been 'Matilda Rowe', is referred to as Cudjoe's 'sister' and the ancestress of the village's central Rowe clan and is reputedly buried beside Cudjoe at the 'Old Town' grove in Accompong. In Maroon Town, Nanny is portrayed as ''Campong Nanny' (and as a local ancestress 'Betsy Currie') and there are narratives of her miraculous 'pumpkin vine'. I discuss these narratives, their contexts and meanings in chapters 3–9.

Meanwhile, as Nanny stayed east, Cudjoe was consolidating his leadership of the Leeward Maroons in the west. By the mid-1730s, he had shifted his base from the hills of Clarendon (then the colony's main sugar-producing parish) in the south-centre of the island, north-westwards into the more remote Cockpit Country, from which he conducted guerrilla warfare against the colonists in the adjoining western parishes of St James, Hanover, Westmoreland and St Elizabeth (Robinson 1969, 43–44; Campbell 1990, 68–70). Initially moving into the Cockpits through the Hector's River area in what would later become Trelawny Parish (at that time the eastern part of Old St James), Cudjoe then moved even further north-west into the present parish of St James. There, he established Cudjoe's Town, with surrounding provision grounds, in what Eyre (1980, 10) described as a 'bowl-shaped feature, 27 square kilometres in area, with its interior drainage' in the limestone *karst* landscape. This village would be renamed Trelawny Town after the treaty with Governor Edward Trelawny and would be referred to as Cudjoe's Old Town after the internal subdivision of Trelawny Town.

As the First Maroon War intensified, including the reinforcement of the colonial troops by the 'Black Shots' (confidential armed plantation slaves), Cudjoe and his followers withdrew into Petty River Bottom to the immediate south-east of Cudjoe's Town. This seven-acre labyrinth of cockpit-dells with its water spring (Petty River) served as Cudjoe's military base, as it could be defended by a narrow entrance-defile from which the colonists could be attacked with rocks (Robinson 1969, 43–44; Eyre 1980, 9–12). In Maroon Town today, there is frequent reference to 'Cudjoe's River' and Petty River Bottom features in narratives in both Accompong and Maroon Town.

While Cudjoe's Town and its satellite Petty River Bottom were established in St James as the primary Leeward Maroon community, Accompong's Town was founded in St Elizabeth as the secondary Leeward village. Robinson states that as the First Maroon War escalated, Cudjoe, who 'had earlier placed a strong detachment under the command of his brother Accompong', subsequently

> increased the size of this group and sent it to Northern St. Elizabeth to establish a camp. Accompong chose a place above the Nassau Mountains. There he built a camp which later grew into a town and which was named Accompong after him. Accompong Town still stands to-day on the site chosen by its founder (Robinson 1969, 45).[9]

Campbell (1990, 46) writes that Cudjoe 'divided his gang into politico-military companies under the loyal command of two of his "brothers", Accompong, a name of Akan derivation, and Johnny – which may have been another Akan name, *Gyani*, having suffered from Anglo-Saxon orthography'. However, Campbell suggests that this brotherhood may have been based on African concepts of clanship rather than fraternal blood (47). Carey throws further light on the relationship between Accompong and Cudjoe, noting that Accompong was one of the Windward Maroon Katta-a-Woods who marched westward to join Cudjoe. However, she adds that 'some records say that he [Accompong] left Portland to join one "Cuffee" in St Elizabeth', that 'There is a Cuffee's Maroon Camp shown on some maps and there is the probability that Acccompong resided in the St Elizabeth cockpits as early as 1733' (Carey 1997, 385). Quoting from Dallas (1803, I, 28–29), Campbell (1990, 43) states that Cudjoe "'appointed his brothers Accompong and Johnny leaders under him, and Cuffee and Quao [sic] subordinate Captains'". The Accompong Maroons today refer to Accompong, Johnny, Cuffee and Quaco as Cudjoe's Lieutenants or Captains and claim to identify their graves on the commons (chapters 3–4).

On the British side, after Hunter's death in 1734, other governors (Ayscough, Gregory and Cunningham, who all died in quick succession) continued the offensive against the Maroons until the arrival of Governor Edward Trelawny in April 1738 (Campbell 1990, 87–97). During this First Maroon War, the British headquarters were at Vaughansfield Estate near Cudjoe's Town, with another base on the Aberdeen plantation bordering Accompong (Eyre 1980, 7; Agorsah 1994, 172).

Carey (1997, 298) notes that during Ayscough's introduction of martial law 'A warrior party of about 200–300 [Maroons] attacked a military barracks located at the Island Estate', which (despite indications that Island was in the west near the Leeward Maroons), she argues, was in the east near the Windward Maroons:

> Ayscough suggests that this estate was located in the west, but the author has not been able to trace such a site....
>
> Such an attack was hardly likely to have been carried out by Cudjoe's forces. It was more in the tradition of the Eastern Maroons. However, were there so many of them located in the west at that time? The possibility exists that the estate attacked was not in the west but in the east and could be identified as Island Head Estate on the upper levels of the southeastern Blue Mountains, where scores of the new [British] soldiers were barracked (298–99).

However, my research reveals that the Aberdeen plantation which served as a British base bordering Accompong was part of Island Estate – established by the Scotsman, Alexander McFarlane (of my paternal clan), who lived in Jamaica from around 1735 until his death there in 1755 (Besson and McFarlane 1995, 2005, 2009; and chapters 1 and 6). The attack on Island Estate may therefore indeed have been made by Leeward Maroons (from Accompong's Town) in the west, as Ayscough indicated and as oral tradition in Accompong suggests (chapter 4). Moreover, the inscriptions of names and punishments of slaves from St Elizabeth who took part in the Emancipation War of 1831–32 include slaves from Island Estate (see figure 2.3d later in this chapter).

After Governor Trelawny arrived in Jamaica in April 1738, influenced by the plantocracy, he sued for peace with the Maroons pursuing the idea of treaties that had been conceived by Hunter, Ayscough and Gregory. Trelawny sent Colonel Guthrie, a planter in St James, and Captain Sadler to negotiate the Leeward Maroon treaty with Cudjoe. But Guthrie first had to locate Cudjoe's Town and only did so by obtaining information from maroon traitors. On locating it, he wrote to Trelawny in February 1738/39 from a deserted Cudjoe's Town, informing the Governor that he had renamed the maroon village, which he had burned, Trelawny Town, in his honour. Meanwhile, Cudjoe and his Leeward Maroons were in their Petty River Bottom stronghold. From Trelawny Town, Guthrie sent a Dr Russell to negotiate with Cudjoe and on March 1, 1738/39 the peace treaty was concluded between Guthrie, Sadler and Cudjoe at the entrance to Petty River Bottom in what became known as 'Guthrie's Defile' (Eyre 1980; Robinson 1969, 45–50; Campbell 1990, 98, 105–117; Carey 1997, 315–41).

Around the time of the Leeward treaty, Governor Trelawny made attempts to either defeat or make a similar treaty with the Windward Maroons (Robinson 1969, 53–62; Campbell 1990, 119–24; Carey 1997, 343–50). These attempts included sending a party led by Lieutenants Concannon and Thicknesse against the Windwards but this was ambushed by Maroons now led by Quao, who is described by Carey (1997, 287) as 'Nanny's protégé'. Thicknesse reported seeing an old obeah woman among them, who may have been Nanny (referred to by her descendants as a 'scientist'). Another group of militia led by Colonel Guthrie, was assisted by some of Cudjoe's men, including a Leeward Maroon captain. However, Guthrie died en route, apparently poisoned by slaves. The final march to the Windwards was led by Captain Adair, accompanied by Thicknesse, and the Windward Maroon treaty was concluded with Quao (a Creole and former plantation slave) in late June 1739.[10] At that time, the population of the Windward Maroons was about 470 and the Leeward Maroons were about the same (Campbell 1990, 119).

The colonial treaties of March 1738/39 and June 1739 with the Leeward and Windward Maroons, respectively granted the Maroons their freedom, legal land rights and access to marketplaces. However, the treaties also regulated relations between the colonists and Maroons in favour of the planters, requiring the Maroons to cut roads and return future runaways (for which they would be rewarded), designating colonial Superintendents to oversee maroon affairs, confining the Maroons to mountainous reservations and enabling the expansion of the slave plantation system (Kopytoff 1976a, 1979; Campbell 1990, 126–63).

The Leeward treaty granted the Maroons in the two Cockpit towns 1,500 acres of land north-west of Cudjoe's Town in St James (map 5). This land grant was subsequently increased to 2,559 acres in 1756–58 to include Accompong's Town and its surrounding territory in St Elizabeth (Campbell 1990, 127, 181–83). Robinson states that, with the treaty, Cudjoe 'was made Chief of his community for life' and consolidated his headquarters at Trelawny Town where the village 'stood on an uneven ridge and the houses were built on little heights with gullies running between them in various directions' (1969, 51, 66). Edward Long (who records that he 'conversed with' Cudjoe 'many years' after the treaty) writes that: 'The command of Trelawny Town was limited to Cudjoe during life; and, after his decease, to Accompong, Johnny, Cuffee and Quaco; and, in remainder, to such person as the governor for the time being may think fit to appoint' (1774, II, 344, 345). Robinson tells us that:

> Cudjoe and his immediate successors managed to maintain the prestige of their office for about 30 years,... by the sheer force of personality, by a despotic exercise of power and by a tradition of respect founded on the memory of great deeds.

He added that, 'The last of the chiefs to wield this kind of strong influence and authority was a man named Furry...' (1969, 63).

After Cudjoe's death, Trelawny Town became divided by political factions disputing the succession to Chief. Furry was the leader of one of these factions, which split off from Cudjoe's Old Town and established a new settlement half a mile away which was initially called Furry's Town and then came to be known as the New Town (64; Long 1774 [2002] II, 346; Campbell 1990, 183–85; map 5). The two Trelawny Town settlements were linked 'by a steep narrow path running for half a mile through a wood' (Robinson 1969, 66).

Map 5. Trelawny Town Territory and the Second Maroon War August 9, 1795. The National Archives, Kew.

This precipitous path would feature significantly in the Second Maroon War, with the maroon ambush of Colonel Sandford's Dragoons, and is today, one of the sacred sites (known as 'Dragoon Hole') in the landscape of Maroon Town and a recurring theme in their narratives (chapters 7–8).

Meanwhile, Accompong's Town became consolidated as the secondary Leeward Maroon community with its treaty lands bordering the Aberdeen plantation. Unlike the Trelawny Town settlements situated on the slopes of the cockpits, Accompong was initially located in a large cockpit dell, around 1,000 feet below its present site, 'where it was surrounded by hard rocky outgrowths, typical of karst geology and easy to defend' but with poor drainage and 'deep bauxite mud' in the heavy rains (Carey 1997, 529). The village was still in that location in 1805 but was moved to its present site later in the nineteenth century (528, 616). However, while historical and archaeological evidence substantiates this original location of 'Accompong Old Town' (616; Agorsah 1994), my anthropological research reveals that the annual pilgrimages by Accompong Maroons to this sacred 'Old Town' grove include symbolic transformations that refer to Cudjoe's 'Old Town' in St James and which modify the interpretations of Campbell (1990), Agorsah (1994), Carey (1997) and Zips (2011). These symbolic transformations seek to repair the Leeward Maroon polity (chapters 3–5), which was fractured in the Second Maroon War.

The Second Maroon War and the Fracturing of the Leeward Maroon Polity

Three issues triggered the Second Maroon War of 1795–96 between the Trelawny Maroons (the largest Jamaican maroon community) and the British colonial state: land scarcity, discontent concerning the post of the colonial Superintendent and the whipping of two Maroons in Montego Bay for the theft of two domesticated pigs. These issues were fuelled by the uncompromising attitude towards the Maroons by the Scotsman, Alexander Lindsay, who became Earl Balcarres and the Governor of Jamaica in 1795 (Dallas 1803; Robinson 1969; Craton 1982; Campbell 1990; Carey 1997). Were it not for Balcarres's attitude, the Second Maroon War is unlikely to have occurred, as by this time, there were multi-stranded relations among the planters, Maroons and slaves who became players in the war (Dallas 1803, 156–57; Craton 1982, 213–14; Campbell 1990, 225; Carey 1997, 458, 465). For example, there were amicable relations (sometimes based on kinship) as well as hostility between Maroons and planters, both planters and Maroons fathered enslaved children, and slaves and Maroons had relationships of interdependence as well as conflict. In addition, the Leeward Maroons had internal conflicts; these would escalate in the war, with the Accompongs siding with the colonial state. These complex relations that evolved through creolization, continued to unfold in the three communities that I studied, among the descendants of Maroons, planters and slaves (chapters 3–11).

Since the early post-treaty years (from around 1741), land scarcity had been an issue for the Trelawny Maroons, whom Carey (1997, 395) states should have received 15,000 acres in the treaty rather than 1,500 and were, therefore, possibly cheated of 13,500 acres of land (a view reflected in Accompong narratives today, [chapters 3–6]). By 1790, three generations of Trelawnys were hemmed in on mountainous land by three surrounding plantations owned by magistrates in St James: David Schaw's Schaw Castle, Crew Estate (owner unspecified) and Vaughansfield (a coffee plantation, one and a half miles from Trelawny Town) owned by Samuel Vaughan (461). Vaughansfield had been the British military headquarters in the First Maroon War and would play this role again in the Second Maroon War. Today, both Schaw Castle and Vaughansfield are part of Maroon Town. In 1792, Trelawny Town unsuccessfully petitioned the Jamaica Assembly for more land (460–62).

The British treaties with the Jamaican Maroons in 1738/39 had specified that a colonial Superintendent should reside in and oversee the maroon towns. An Act of 1791 gave these Superintendents more powers to regulate maroon affairs but also provided for the punishment of Superintendents. Major John James had been appointed Superintendent of Trelawny Town in 1767. In 1779, he was promoted to the role of Major-Commandant of all the maroon towns and was succeeded as Superintendent in Trelawny Town by his son, Captain John Montague James. Both were popular with the Trelawnys (and supported their land petition) but both stopped residing in Trelawny Town and the Trelawnys complained about the non-residence of John Montague James. As a result, he was removed from his post in 1792 and replaced by Thomas Craskell, an unpopular Superintendent, who in 1795 would be driven out to Vaughansfield by the Trelawnys (who detained Craskell's white assistant, John Merody),[11] who petitioned unsuccessfully for James's return. By this time, the last strong Trelawny Maroon Chief, Furry, had died and 'Old Montague' (Montague James, so named after John Montague James) was Chief of Trelawny Town. Old Montague, elderly and weak, would be the last Chief of the Trelawnys (Campbell 1990, 211–14; Carey 1997, 457–67).

The catalyst for the Trelawnys' expulsion of Craskell was the flogging of two of their men in Montego Bay following the theft of two domesticated pigs. The pigs belonged to planters, who ordered the whipping to be carried out, in the presence of slaves, by a runaway slave whom the Trelawnys had captured and returned. The humiliation of the Maroons by these planters was therefore calculated and inflammatory (Robinson 1969, 82; Campbell 1990, 211; Carey 1997, 465). Following these events in July 1795, discontent escalated among the Trelawnys, Craskell advised magistrates in St James of his expulsion, the magistrates informed Governor Balcarres, inaccurate rumours spread concerning a unified uprising by the Leeward Maroons and Balcarres assumed revolutionary influences from Saint Domingue and France (Robinson 1969, 83; Campbell 1990, 214; Carey 1997, 466).

However, a unified front by the Leeward Maroons could not be assumed as Trelawny Town and Accompong's Town were competing for land. There was also a dispute between them regarding which community should hold the treaty. When Samuel Vaughan, the proprietor of Vaughansfield, contacted Alexander Forbes, the Superintendent in Accompong, to ascertain the Accompongs' intentions, they assured him that they would support the colonists and, to underline this alliance, had their younger Maroons baptized (Robinson 1969, 83; Craton 1982, 214; Carey 1997, 469–70).

Initially, the planter-magistrates of St James and Trelawny tried to persuade Balcarres to negotiate with the Trelawnys and meetings between the magistrates and the Maroons took place. For example, Thomas Reid (of the St James Militia, whose land was near Trelawny Town and who had 'close relations with the Maroons' [Campbell 1990, 225]), John Tharp (Custos of Trelawny Parish), and John James (former Superintendent of Trelawny Town) went to Trelawny Town (as the Trelawnys would not go to Vaughansfield) to attempt a compromise with the Maroons (Robinson 1969, 84–85; Campbell 1990, 212–14; Carey 1997, 422, 466–67). In Maroon Town, I would find villagers who claimed 'slave master' pickni' descent from a planter, Charles Reid, and his mulatto son, Thomas Reid (chapter 8).

Some compromise between the magistrates and Maroons was reached at Trelawny Town but Tharp's departure for England soon after jeopardized this tenuous peace and relations deteriorated between the Trelawnys and Balcarres. The arrest of six Trelawnys at Llandovery in St Ann, on their way to Spanish Town to meet Balcarres, deepened the Maroons' mistrust. On August 3, 1795, Balcarres declared martial law, established military headquarters at Vaughansfield under Colonel Fitch and received the promise of support from the Accompongs who provided knowledge of the Cockpits. In addition to Balcarres and Fitch at Vaughansfield, Colonel Sandford led other troops to Spring Vale, Castle Wemyss, Parnassus and Blue Hole on the borders of Trelawny Town and Colonel Walpole and 150 dragoons were sent to Black River. Balcarres's force included 1,500 British troops and several thousand militia and, having surrounded maroon territory, on August 8, he demanded the Trelawnys' surrender by August 12 (map 5).

The Trelawny Maroons, who numbered around 600, including women, children and the elderly, received advice and reinforcements from Trelawnys who had moved to Westmoreland, including Captains Johnson and Smith. There was disagreement among the young and old Trelawnys as to whether they should fight or surrender. Old Montague, along with 37 of his followers, including James Palmer and Leonard Parkinson, went to Vaughansfield to surrender but were arrested and shackled. Palmer and Parkinson were, however, allowed to return to Trelawny Town, with the mission of persuading the Trelawnys to surrender. However, the betrayal and arrest of the Maroons at Vaughansfield catalyzed Trelawny Maroon resistance. On August 11, the Trelawnys burnt their Old and New Towns and withdrew to Schaw Castle (near the New Town) to oppose the colonists, sending their women and children to secluded provision grounds. On August 12, the Maroons fired on approaching troops near Schaw Castle and Vaughansfield. Two of these colonists were killed and others wounded. Balcarres offered a bounty for the killing or apprehension of Parkinson and Palmer and these two Maroons would become outstanding warriors in the war (Robinson 1968, 86–90; Craton 1982, 214–15; Campbell 1990, 215–17; Carey 1997, 467–73).

Balcarres then 'sent a strong company of mulattos from the St James Regiment' against the Trelawnys, 'who sustained considerable loss' – the only maroon fatalities recorded for the Second Maroon War, as their subsequent guerrilla warfare was virtually invincible (Campbell 1990, 217) and they would only be eventually defeated through Balcarres's treachery. On August 12, Balcarres ordered Sandford and his Light Dragoons to take the New Town and its provision grounds. Sandford took the New Town and advanced on the Old Town with 45 dragoons, aiming to trap the Maroons in the defile between their New and Old Towns. However, Sandford was ambushed in this ravine by the Maroons, who killed him and about 37 dragoons, several of whom bled to death. The surviving soldiers fled to Vaughansfield, while the Maroons celebrated at Old Town and Petty River Bottom (Robinson 1969, 92–95; Craton 1982, 215; Campbell 1990, 217–18; Carey 1997, 473–75). Today, 'Sandford's Defile', known locally as 'Dragoon Hole', is a sacred site near Flagstaff where I was shown the red flowers that grow there, which are said to mark the places where the bleeding dragoons died (chapter 8).

On 13 August (1795), in revenge for the ambush of Sandford and his dragoons, Balcarres sent the 35 Trelawnys still held at Vaughansfield to be imprisoned in Montego Bay. The Accompongs attempted to persuade the Maroons at Trelawny Town not to fight, but the Accompongs' emissary, Chambers was beheaded on the orders of Captain James Palmer of the Trelawnys. This incident consolidated the alliance between the Accompongs and Balcarres. The Trelawnys retreated to Guthrie's Defile from which they continued guerrilla warfare, communicating military information across the landscape with the musical alphabet of their cow-horn 'abengs'. Balcarres attacked both the Old and New Towns, found them empty and buried the bodies of Sandford and 18 dragoons. Returning to Montego Bay, where he transferred the 35 maroon captives to a ship, Balcarres now aimed to encircle the Trelawnys in the Cockpits and destroy their provision grounds. He stationed Colonel Fitch at Old Town, with General Reid in overall command at Vaughansfield. These troops were assisted by the Accompongs and the Black Shots (Robinson 1969, 95–98; Carey 1997, 475–76; Campbell 1990, 218–19, 222).

While Balcarres was in Montego Bay, the former Trelawny Town Superintendent, Major James, led a party of 'young black hog hunters who customarily ran in the bush with the Maroons', but who now offered their services to hunt them, to the Trelawnys at Guthrie's Defile (Carey 1997, 476). However, when the Maroons called out to James, he and the hog hunters fled. Meanwhile, a potential peace was being negotiated between Fitch and the Trelawnys. However, this was aborted when the Trelawnys heard of Balcarres's imprisonment of the Maroons on the ship in Montego Bay. This imprisonment at sea, reminiscent of the slave trade, fuelled the war as the Maroons resolved to continue fighting. Fitch therefore continued to lay ambushes and deforest the defile with slave-gang labour, and troops from Kensington Estate were sent to reinforce those at Vaughansfield. In one of the attacks on Guthrie's Defile, Fitch, two Accompongs (for which Accompong Town would receive compensation) and at least 18 members of the militia were killed by the Trelawnys on September 12 without a Trelawny Maroon casualty (476–80; Robinson 1969, 102–103, 105; Craton 1982, 215; Campbell 1990, 219).

Fitch was replaced by Colonel Walpole (who was promoted to Major-General) who on September 15, rode from Accompong to Trelawny Town where most of Balcarres's troops were based. Walpole continued Fitch's strategy of aiming to drive the Trelawnys (whose command was delegated to Captain Charlie Shaw by Captain Johnson who raided the countryside) from Petty River Bottom through deforestation. Walpole also cordoned off the Maroons with a military road encircling Trelawny Town's territory (map 5). Walpole's attacks on the Maroons were initially unsuccessful. However, he eventually dispersed them by gunfire into Petty River Bottom from a howitzer dragged to a hill above the maroon citadel (Robinson 1969, 103–109; Eyre 1980; Carey 1997, 481–82). Today this hill, named 'Gun Hill', is a sacred site that features in Maroon Town narratives.

On dispersing, the Trelawnys, led by Johnson, divided into bands raiding the plantations in the western parishes and on October 10 Leonard Parkinson burned Amity Hall Estate near Trelawny Town. In that same month, Colonel Quarrell of the Legislature suggested the use of Cuban bloodhounds against the Trelawnys. At the end of October, after consultation with Walpole and Balcarres, Quarrell sailed from Bluefields in Westmoreland to Cuba to procure the dogs. In mid-December, he returned to Montego Bay with about 100 hounds and 40 dog-handlers or chasseurs. The dogs spread terror in Montego Bay and Vaughansfield and among the Trelawnys to whom Walpole, accompanied to Pond River by General Reid, proposed a treaty – giving them his word that they would not be deported. Old Montague played for time by signing this treaty (which included terms for the Maroons' surrender) on December 21. Balcarres, who ratified the treaty at Castle Wemyss on December 28, 1795, set January 1, 1796 as the deadline for surrender and, as he anticipated, the logistics proved impossible for the Maroons. However, by January 15, 326 Trelawnys had surrendered including 91 men, 111 women and 124 children. Balcarres accused them of breaking the treaty and would deport them to Nova Scotia along with others who surrendered later (Campbell 1990, 224–33; Robinson 1969, 108–134; Craton 1982, 220; Carey 1997, 483–88).

Meanwhile, James Palmer and Leonard Parkinson remained at large and leaving a white flag at Pond River, they retreated into the Cockpits of Aberdeen. On February 16, 1796, Walpole set out from Trelawny Old Town with Colonel Skinner, about 80 dragoons and infantry, bloodhounds and chasseurs, two Trelawny Maroon Captains (Johnson and Smith), the surveyor James Robertson and Accompong guides to find Palmer and Parkinson. Walpole and his party 'passed through Elderslie, Accompong and Aberdeen and on 29th February were guided to a hill about a mile and a half north of Aberdeen where smoke had recently been seen' (Robinson 1969, 136). Eventually, some of the colonists spoke to Parkinson, and Johnson and Smith persuaded him to surrender to Walpole with 36 other Trelawnys on March 21. Leonard Parkinson, the 'last Jamaican maroon rebel' (Craton 1982, 221), would become the outstanding symbol of Trelawny Maroon resistance and his engraving, commissioned by the planter-historian Bryan Edwards, has remained the classic illustration of the Second Maroon War (figure 2.1).

However, Parkinson, along with all those Trelawnys who surrendered on the assurance that they would not be deported, were betrayed by Balcarres with the backing of the Legislature who deported 568 Trelawnys to Nova Scotia on June 6, 1796. Balcarres was rewarded by the Assembly with 700 Guineas for a sword. Walpole was offered 500 Guineas for a sword but, furious that his oath to the Maroons had not been honoured by Balcarres and that his evidence to the Assembly was refused, declined the offer, resigned and returned to England to oppose the slave trade (Craton 1982, 221–23; Robinson 1969, 13–42; Eyre 1980, 17; Campbell 1990, 234–42).

In addition to a significant loss of lives, the cost to the colonists of the war to eradicate the threat of 167 armed Maroons was around £500,000 plus damage to plantations (Campbell 1990, 243–44). However, the colonial state claimed some compensation; for, after deporting the Trelawnys, their 1,500 acres of treaty land, which included fertile provision-ground land suitable for plantations, were confiscated. As Campbell records:

> The land was to be sold either as a whole or in lots not exceeding 100 acres each. But 'at least' 300 acres were to be reserved for the use of the troops. By [the] mid-nineteenth century, barracks were built on the site, and the area was designated Maroon Town, and is still so identified on the maps (243).

The barracks were built at the site that became known as Flagstaff, near Gun Hill, and the British military base remained there until around the 1850s (Eyre 1980, 9, 17; Aarons 1981; Carey 1997, 493).[12] Today, the site of the barracks with its military hospital and water tank can be identified, adjoining the colonial troops' parade ground (levelled by slaves) and the British military cemetery endures (Eyre 1980, 18; chapter 8). At the time of Eyre's geographical study, Flagstaff was 'under banana monoculture for export to Britain' (1980, 10). During my fieldwork, Flagstaff (which is part of Maroon Town) was still intensively cultivated in bananas though exports had declined (chapters 7 and 10).[13]

Robinson (1969, 155) states that 'Trelawny Town has been a ghost town ever since the defeat of the Trelawnys'. However, my research reveals the hidden history of the transformation of this historic site to non-maroon Maroon Town. This transformation includes the subdivision and sale of some of the Trelawny Town lands to the ancestors of Maroon Town villagers in the context of both persisting

Figure 2.1. A maroon warrior, Leonard Parkinson, 1795. From Edwards 1796. Courtesy of National Library of Jamaica.

plantations and post-slavery peasantization. Today, Flagstaff is a 'history place' (as the late Mortimer Reid who took me there put it [chapter 8]) for the Maroon Town villagers and their narratives tell of the transmission of their ancestral lands and the sacred sites of the Cockpit Country landscape. In addition, in all three communities that I studied in the Cockpits, narratives both transmit and transform the memories of events of the Second Maroon War (chapters 6–10). Towards the end of my fieldwork, the re-creation of some of these sacred sites and historic maroon trails would become a focus for local development projects and national heritage tourism (chapter 11).

Campbell points to 'the apparent lack of deserters' from among the Jamaican slaves in the Second Maroon War compared to the First Maroon War and notes that:

> What appears to have happened is that those who did desert went on their own and established their own communities, independent of the Maroon groups. All this is suggested by the number of runaways in the woods, who became a source of great irritation to the authorities soon after the Trelawnys were deported (Campbell 1990, 223).

Campbell also refers to Jamaican communities of runaways discovered in the early nineteenth century, including the village of Me No Sen You No Come in Trelawny Parish 'said to have been formed around 1812' and to have persisted until its destruction in 1824 (159; see also Patterson 1973, 264). Mullin (1994, 58–61), however, indicates that this maroon community was established earlier, from the 1770s, and was originally named Congo Town and renamed Highwindward before it became known by its creole name, Me No Sen You No Come[14] and that some 200 plantation slaves joined the Second Maroon War as fighters or foragers, including the foragers of this non-treaty village (293–94, 297). These sources do not link Congo Town/Highwindward/Me No Sen You No Come to Trelawny Town. However, my research indicates that the Maroons of that non-treaty community, which was just a few miles from the site of Trelawny Town/Flagstaff, became highly significant in the subsequent development of Maroon Town (chapter 10).

Enabled by an Act of 1791, some Trelawnys appealed to change their status from Maroons at the end of the Second Maroon War, to avoid deportation; those successful included 'fourteen women and one man' (Campbell 1990, 247). Narratives in Maroon Town today concerning villagers who claim descent from the Trelawnys, especially from a Trelawny Maroon woman (chapter 9), may, therefore, be consistent with historical records.

The tragic saga of the deportation of the Trelawny Maroons to Nova Scotia by the colonial state, including their resistance to acculturation and the eventual departure (partly through their own efforts) of 551 Maroons on August 6, 1800 to Sierra Leone where they became ancestors of today's Freetown Creoles, is recorded in several sources (Robinson 1969, 143–54; Craton 1982, 222; Campbell 1993; Hinds 2002).[15] Some decades later, in the 1830s and 1840s, some Trelawnys – at least 64 – returned from Freetown to Jamaican maroon villages (Bilby 1984a, 26 n14).

In the immediate aftermath of the deportation, the Windward Maroons were traumatized by the fate of the Trelawnys (Bilby 1984a; Campbell 1990, 247–48). The Accompongs, however, were rewarded by the Assembly for their part in the war against Trelawny Town with the passing of an Act in 1798 'authorising the Government to "employ the Maroon Negroes of Accompong Town, for the Internal Defence and Security of the island"' (Carey 1997, 496). This role continues today; for example, during my research, two Accompong Colonels were in the Jamaican police force and an Aberdonian Maroon was a retired policeman. In addition, the status of Accompong Town became transformed from the secondary Leeward community to the sole surviving village of the Leeward Maroon polity.

By 1836 (during Apprenticeship), the population of Accompong numbered 409 under 12 officers of the Maroon Council including Captains, Lieutenants and a Major James Rowe, aged 66 (Carey 1997, 551–52). Carey notes that the population of Accompong also included 12 ex-slaves who had had their apprenticeship annulled. There were also:

> two people from other towns living among them but these were not strangers. One, Jean Harris, came from Island Estate, which would be the Blue Mountain estate in St. Thomas in the East (attacked by the Maroons in the 1730 decade), supporting the contention that Maroon communities resided in the mountains as an identifiable and distinct community (Carey 1997, 552).

However, as mentioned earlier, my research reveals that the Aberdeen plantation bordering Accompong was part of Island Estate in St Elizabeth (chapter 6). Jean Harris is, therefore, more likely to have been from St Elizabeth's Island slave plantation adjoining Accompong. Today, there are social networks between the Accompong Maroons and the Aberdonians and narratives in both communities link these networks to ties forged between Maroons and slaves (chapters 3–6).

Despite the Maroons Land Allotment Act of 1842 (four years after emancipation) and subsequent related legislation in the mid-nineteenth century, the Accompongs resisted the attempts from the colonial state to undermine their maroon status and subdivide their common treaty land though there was some informal allocation of house-plots (Kopytoff 1979; Carey 1997, 559–63). In 1857, the Superintendents were discontinued in the Jamaican maroon communities (Carey 1997, 560). From 1870 to 1920, the Accompong Maroons 'developed close bonds with white (mainly Scottish) pastors residing and working in their community' (613).

In my fieldwork (1979–2009) in Accompong, around 200 years after the Second Maroon War, I would find that the shrunken Leeward Maroon polity and its remaining common treaty land had endured and that the Rowe Family (with a surname dating back to at least 1770, between the two maroon wars) is the village's central clan (chapters 3–4).

Slaves, Missionaries and the 'Emancipation War'

Despite the 1738/39 Jamaican maroon treaties, most Africans and their descendants in the colony remained enslaved on plantations. The planters' established Anglican Church had little impact on these slaves, who created their own Afro-Creole Myal worldview by transforming African religions in the Jamaican slavery context (chapter 1). In the later eighteenth and early nineteenth centuries, however, English Nonconformist (Moravian, Methodist, Baptist) and Scottish Presbyterian missionaries had more influence on the non-white population (Besson 2002, 98–103). The Moravians were the first British missionaries to arrive in Jamaica, in 1754 in St Elizabeth, followed by the Methodists in 1789, the English Baptists in 1813 and the Presbyterians in 1824.

The Anglican Church and most planters were opposed to this missionary activity. However, the Moravians and Presbyterians were invited to the colony by slave-owning families. The Moravians, who came at the invitation of the Barham-Foster family who had plantations near Aberdeen Estate, would become significant in the free village of Aberdeen where the Moravian church coexists today with North American Pentecostalism and the Jamaican Revival religion (chapter 6). In 1823, the Stirling family of the Hampden plantation, on the boundary of Trelawny and St James, along with their Scottish friend, William Stehart, owner of Trelawny's nearby Dundee Estate, invited the Scottish Missionary Society to that area where Jamaica's first Presbyterian Church was founded in 1827 (Besson 2002, 65). Later in the nineteenth century, the Maroons would invite the Presbyterians to establish a church in Accompong (Kopytoff 1987), where it still exists (as the United Church in Jamaica and The Cayman Islands) in tandem with the Myal, Revival and Rastafarian religions (Besson 2009, and chapters 3–4).

The Moravians had the least impact on the non-white population, while the Methodists became the stronghold of the free coloureds and free blacks (and would become significant in Maroon Town, along with the Baptist church). The Baptists, who were especially active in St James and Trelawny (which were also the heart of Myalism), were the most successful in 'converting' the slaves, as the Baptist faith had been introduced by black preachers. The most important of these were George Lisle (or Liele), an ex-slave from Virginia and Georgia, who came to Jamaica in 1784, and Moses Baker, another American ex-slave, who was baptized by Lisle in 1787. In 1788, Baker began preaching in St James and Trelawny.

In 1813, the Baptist Missionary Society (BMS) in England sent out its first missionary to Jamaica, John Rowe, after Lisle called on the BMS to respond to the appropriation of the Baptist faith by Myalism. After examining Baker's congregation (founded in 1791) at Crooked Spring, St James, Rowe took up residence in Falmouth, Trelawny, in 1814. The Crooked Spring Baptist Church was later moved to Salter's Hill (where it can still be seen en route from Montego Bay to Maroon Town [chapter 1 and figure 2.2]). Following Rowe's death in 1816, other Baptist missionaries established churches in Jamaica. In 1824, Thomas Burchell founded the Baptist Church in Montego Bay and, in 1827, formed the Falmouth Baptist Church. Burchell's assistant, James Mann, became the first pastor of this Falmouth church. In 1830, Mann was replaced in Falmouth by William Knibb (Besson 2002, 99).

However, the work of Burchell and Knibb was interrupted by the Christmas Rebellion of 1831–32, which started a few miles from Maroon Town (which was developing on the former site of Trelawny Town). This rebellion (also known as the Baptist War) was the largest slave uprising in the British West Indies and the most spectacular slave revolt in Anglo-America (Craton 1982, 291–93; Mullin 1994, 254; Besson 2002, 100–101). It was based on an ambiguous alliance between the slaves and the Baptist missionaries, who opposed slavery (but not colonialism) and whose class-leader system opened up positions of leadership among the slaves, facilitating the continuity of Myalism in the 'Native Baptist' variant.

The revolt was widely thought to have been led by slave headmen (who were usually class-leaders) from estates in the hinterland of Montego Bay and by 'Daddy' Sam Sharpe, a domestic slave who was a Native Baptist class-leader in Burchell's congregation (chapter 1). The revolt started 'with the firing of Kensington estate, high above Montego Bay, on the night of Tuesday, December 27, 1831' (Craton 1982, 293), which was 'symbolically close to Old Maroon Town' (303), spreading swiftly throughout the western parishes including St James, Trelawny and St Elizabeth with a large number of slaves (estimates vary from 20,000 to 60,000) escaping and burning over 150 estates. Martial law was declared, the rebellion lasted for two weeks before it was put down and martial law was lifted on February 5, 1832. Only 14 whites were killed, but several hundred slaves were either killed in action or executed and a hundred more were flogged. Sam Sharpe was tried on 19 April and hanged on May 23, 1832 in front of the courthouse in Montego Bay (chapter 1 and figures 1.3a and 1.3b). In 2007 (the bicentenary of the abolition of the British transatlantic slave trade), a marble monument with the names of several hundred slaves who fought and died in this rebellion, including Sam Sharpe, was erected by the Jamaica National Bicentenary Committee in what is now named Sam Sharpe Square.[16]

Figure 2.2.   Salter's Hill Baptist Church, at John's Hall between Maroon Town and Montego Bay.

The monument was unveiled at a national ceremony that I attended on August 1, 2007, Emancipation Day, and the rebellion was renamed the 'Emancipation War' (figures 2.3a, 2.3b, 2.3c and 2.3d).

The planters also took revenge on the missionaries, imprisoning William Knibb. On Knibb's release, he found that the Falmouth Baptist Chapel, along with 13 others (including the Salter's Hill Baptist Church, where Sam Sharpe had been a Deacon and which was subsequently rebuilt), had been destroyed by the Colonial Church Union (a planter-based organization), following the lifting of martial law.

However, in the aftermath of this Emancipation War, slavery was abolished throughout the British Empire in 1834 (to be followed by a period of Apprenticeship until 1840) and, two years earlier than planned, on August 1, 1838, the slaves were fully freed. Following emancipation, the membership of the Baptist Church in Jamaica rapidly increased and would consolidate in the contexts of the free village movement and post-slavery peasantization (Besson 2002, 102–107). These developments would be significant for the evolution of Maroon Town and Aberdeen.

Figure 2.3a. Monument to the Emancipation War (1831–32), veiled in a combination of Jamaican national colours and Rastafarian colours, Montego Bay 2007.

Figure 2.3b. Monument to the Emancipation War (1831–32) unveiled August 1, 2007, Montego Bay.

Figure 2.3c. Monument to the Emancipation War (1831–32), Montego Bay.

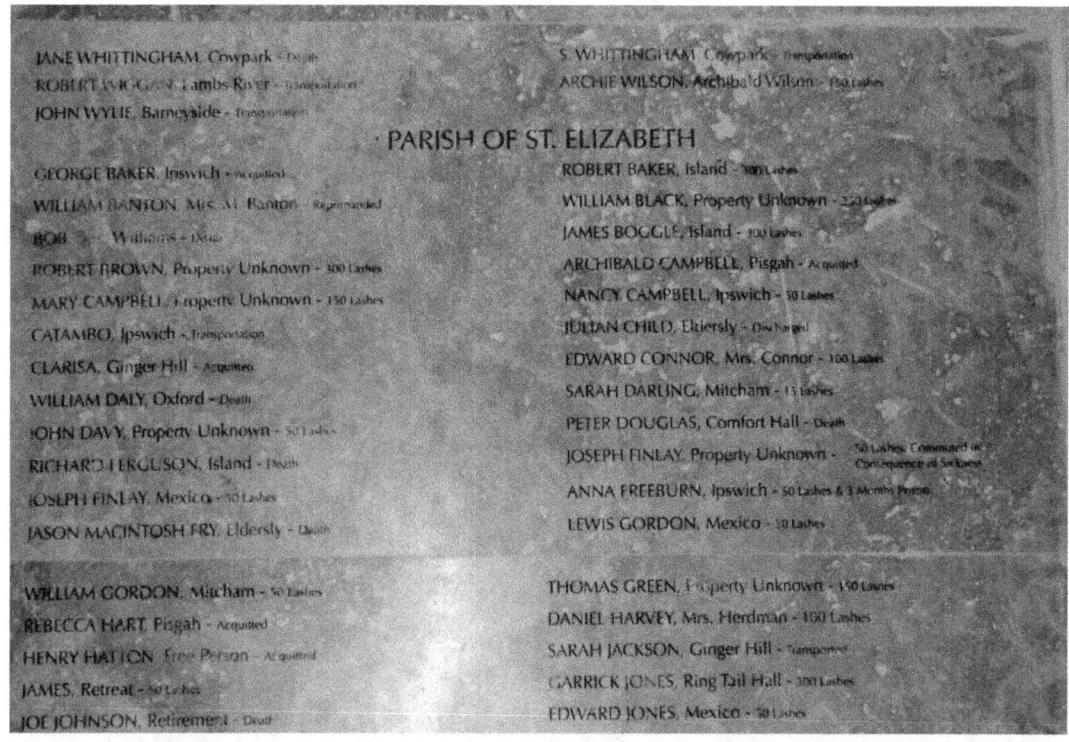

Figure 2.3d. Names and punishments of some of the slaves who fought the Emancipation War, note Island Estate in St Elizabeth.

Jamaican Free Villages and Caribbean Post-Slavery Peasantization

Like Trelawny's free villages (Besson 2002), Aberdeen in St Elizabeth and Maldon (now part of Maroon Town) in St James were established as free villages by emancipated slaves in their flight from the plantations (chapters 6–7). The transformation of Trelawny Town into Maroon Town likewise took place partly within this context (chapters 7–10). These developments were part of a wider process of Caribbean post-slavery peasantization, which was pronounced in Jamaica where the peasant-plantation competition was acute in the west-central parishes. The flight of ex-slaves from the Caribbean estates was rooted in a tradition of slave resistance (rebellion and marronage) and opposition from within the plantation system itself (including proto-peasantization) and was both triggered and constrained by planter policy and colonial-state legislation (Besson 1992a, 2002, 81–132).

The flight of ex-slaves from the Caribbean estates sometimes occurred in alliance with Nonconformist missionaries (Besson 2011b, 325). In Jamaica, the Baptist missionaries William Knibb and James Phillippo initiated the church-founded free village system in the parishes of St Catherine and Trelawny (Paget 1964; Mintz 1989, 157–79; Besson 2002, 102–25; Davis-Palmer 2005, 2010). The Baptist missionaries, Thomas Burchell and Walter Dendy, were likewise active in the free village movement in St James with Dendy founding Maldon, the first Baptist free village in St James (which became part of

Maroon Town). In St Elizabeth, the Moravians established an outstation, a schoolhouse and a church in the free village of Aberdeen.

Jamaican post-slavery peasantization occurred mainly in the years immediately following full freedom (Besson 1992a, 192, 2002, 106–107). At emancipation in 1838, there were only 2,014 freeholders in the island. In 1840, just two years later, this figure had risen to nearly 8,000 (Paget 1964, 49, 50). Freeholders holding under 40 acres rose between 1838 and 1840 from 146 to 916 in St Elizabeth, from 71 to 406 in Trelawny, and from 94 to 332 in St James (50). On September 21, 1840, the Honourable D. Robertson, Custos of St Elizabeth, wrote to the Governor of Jamaica, Sir Charles Metcalfe, outlining the exodus of freed slaves from the estates in that parish to small freeholds on 'very poor unproductive savanna lands, too distant from the large estates to enable them to labour thereon' and urging the establishment of free villages, each around a chapel and school, in the 'healthy and productive' interior of the parish 'in the vicinity of large estates' to provide continued plantation labour (cited in Paget 1964, 45). The establishment of the free village of Aberdeen in the foothills of the Cockpit Country and bordering the Aberdeen plantation was consistent with this recommendation.

By 1860, there were 50,000 landholders with fewer than 50 acres in Jamaica (Marshall 1985, 6); these included ex-slave ancestors of villagers in Maroon Town and Aberdeen. From 1860, the peasantry produced cash crops (especially coffee and bananas) for export, in addition to cultivation for subsistence and internal markets, and both Aberdeen and Maroon Town developed banana peasantries. At a later stage,[17] Accompong maroon banana production became a variation on this theme (chapter 3).

However, the Morant Bay Rebellion of 1865 in south-eastern Jamaica underlined the continuing land scarcity among the former slaves (Heuman 1994) and this was reinforced by the re-establishment of the plantation system, including the expansion of banana plantations. Since the 1880s, the Jamaican peasantry has been severely constrained, due to corporate plantations and (after the Second World War) the bauxite mining and tourist industries (chapter 1). This escalating land monopolization continues to constrain the peasant economies of Accompong, Maroon Town and Aberdeen.

Post-emancipation peasantization in Jamaica had parallels elsewhere in the British West Indies and in the Danish, French and Dutch Caribbean (Besson 1992a, 1995b, 2002, 94–98). Likewise, as with the maroon polities in the mountains of Jamaica that persisted after emancipation including Accompong in the Cockpits, Maroons consolidated in the forested interiors of French Guiana and Dutch Guiana (now Suriname). In such maroon societies and post-emancipation villages, maroon and non-maroon transformations of African-American slave cultures endure as variations on a Caribbean peasantization theme.

The Cockpit Country Communities in the Jamaican Social System

Although Accompong, Aberdeen and Maroon Town have varying political relations with the Jamaican post-colonial state (chapter 1), they are all embedded in the island's social system where inequalities of 'race' and class persist, despite political and social change. This racialized class stratification derives from early globalization and colonial plantation slavery and is perpetuated by the neo-colonial world economy, as elsewhere in African-America. However, Caribbean race-class relations are more complex than the black/white dichotomy in the United States and the interpretation of this complexity has been the subject of debate (Besson 2002, 10–34, 2011a).

The functionalist view posited a 'white bias' integrating different 'colour-classes' in Caribbean societies (Braithwaite 1953; Henriques 1968; Rodman 1971; R.T. Smith 1956, 1988, 1996). Meso-Creole narratives of 'slave master' pickni' descent and 'bastardy' in Maroon Town partly reflect this theme (chapters 7–10). However, the functionalists did not adequately address power, capitalist class relations, the Rastafarian movement, or Afro-Creole maroon and non-maroon ethnicities.

Challenging the functionalists, M.G. Smith (1965a, 1965b, 1998) advanced his plural society theory of racialized 'social and cultural sections' with plural institutions held together only through the domination of colonial/post-colonial elites. Smith's discussion of Jamaica highlighted the importance of plantations for the elite and family land for the peasantry (1965a, 169). His theory influenced other pluralist interpretations of family land in Jamaican villages (Comitas 1962, 1973; Davenport 1961a, 1961b) and common land in Accompong (Barker and Spence 1988; Zips 1996, 1998, 1999, 2011). However, Smith did not fully recognize the process of creolization in Caribbean customary land tenures and their complex interplay with legal codes. He also oversimplified the family system of the peasantry and overlooked the cognatic principles of family land (Besson 1999a, 2002, 2011a; and chapters 3–10).

Some scholars synthesized the functionalist-pluralist debate (Beckford 1972; Lowenthal 1972, 76–212; Wilson 1973; Hoetink 1985). However, these syntheses did not adequately address either capitalist class relations or creolization. In addition, Wilson's theory slighted the role of Afro-Creole women in Caribbean culture-building (Besson 1993).

I advanced an alternative interpretation of capitalist race-class relations in Jamaica as the wider context for the Trelawny peasant communities in the island's plantation heartlands, where Afro-Creole women as well as men have been at the vanguard of Caribbean culture-building since slavery days (Besson 1993, 2002). It is, likewise, within this context of a post-colonial race-class stratified society embedded in the world economy that Accompong, Aberdeen and Maroon Town have evolved as Caribbean 'reconstituted peasantries' (Mintz 1989, 132) in the Cockpits at the maroon/non-maroon interface.

My view of these Cockpit Country villages as Caribbean peasant communities draws on Sidney Mintz's (1989, 132) view of peasantry as:

> a class (or classes) of rural landowners producing a large part of the products they consume, but also selling to (and buying from) wider markets, and dependent in various ways upon wider political and economic spheres of control.

Mintz qualified the criterion of land ownership by noting that peasants are 'small-scale cultivators who own or have access to land' (141). I, likewise, draw on Mintz's argument that 'Caribbean peasantries are, in this view, *reconstituted* peasantries, having begun other than as peasants – in slavery, as deserters or runaways, as plantation laborers, or whatever – and becoming peasants in some kind of resistant response to an externally imposed regimen' (132; see also Besson 2002, 6–8). Mintz's modes of Caribbean peasantization include various sixteenth-century 'squatters', seventeenth-century European 'yeomen', 'proto-peasant' plantation slaves from the eighteenth century, 'runaway peasantries' or Maroons during the entire slavery period and post-slavery peasantries (1989, 146–56).[18]

From these perspectives, Accompong is an Afro-Creole maroon-peasant community forged by rebel slaves or 'runaway peasantries'. The post-slavery peasantries of Maroon Town and Aberdeen derive partly from proto-peasant adaptations of plantation slaves but are more complex, with some Afro-Creoles asserting both slave and maroon ancestry and Meso-Creoles claiming descent from colonists as well as slaves and Maroons.

Accompong, Aberdeen and Maroon Town, therefore, reflect variations of gendered Caribbean oppositional peasantization and creative creolization, rooted in maroon and non-maroon transformations of African-American slave cultures, in the face of globalization. This interpretation is directly relevant to the understanding of the Accompong maroon society and its commons, which reflect Caribbean creolization in response to global and local capitalist race-class relations (Besson 1997, 2011a and chapter 3), rather than pre-capitalist African continuities in a plural society as others contend (Barker and Spence 1988; Campbell 1990; Alleyne 1996; Warner-Lewis 2003; Zips 1996, 1998, 1999, 2011, 2012).

Notes

1. The opening section of this chapter on African-American slave responses and the later sections on the Nonconformist missionaries and Caribbean peasantization, including Jamaican free villages draw on and expand parts of Besson 2002, chapter 3. I am grateful to the University of North Carolina Press for permission to use this earlier work.
2. In Jamaica, as in many other Caribbean colonies, the slaves' provision grounds were usually on the marginal hilly backlands of plantations. However, in some western parishes, including St James, Trelawny and St Elizabeth, such land was sometimes on separate 'mountains' in the interior (Besson 2002, 48–49).
3. The main historical sources used in the sections on the maroon wars, written from varying perspectives, are largely complementary but they do sometimes conflict in both interpretation and fact. Contemporary accounts are provided by Edward Long (1774) and R.C. Dallas (1803) from the viewpoint of the planter class. The account by Carey Robinson (1969), then Director of the Jamaica Information Service, which draws in part on these sources, is highly readable and sympathetic to the Maroons but is not well documented. Mavis Campbell's (1990) history, covering the period 1655–1796, though dry, is documented well. *The Maroon Story* by Bev Carey (1997), a descendant of the Windward Maroons, which covers the years 1490–1880, is likewise well documented and more readable. However, I question Carey's identification of the Island

slave plantation as being in the east of the island near the Windward Maroons (298–99), as my research reveals that Island Estate bordered the Leeward Maroon Accompong commons in St Elizabeth. Carey is critical of Campbell; some of these criticisms are that Campbell's account includes 'misconceptions' that maroon oral traditions are 'a mere legend' and that 'Throughout Campbell's book, the secondary references, persons interviewed in field work among the Maroons, are never named and dates and places are not recorded' (Carey 1997, 274, 275). In my ethnography (chapters 3–5), I question Campbell's (1990, 178) assumption that the Accompong Maroons are confused about Nanny and her burial place, showing instead the symbolic meanings in their cosmology and classification of the sacred landscape. Both Campbell and Carey are critical of Robinson. Carey (1997, 275) argues that his accounts 'do not consider the circumstances and historic events of the period, or the difficulties of Maroon decision making'. Campbell's (1990, 46) questioning of Robinson's (1969, 46) description of the Leeward Maroon leader Cudjoe's age (and therefore his related assertion that Cudjoe was African-born [32], an argument adopted by Carey, 148) is important for my ethnography, which focuses on creolization and as Kopytoff (1976b, 41) like Campbell indicates that Cudjoe was a Jamaican-born Creole.

4. The geographer, Alan Eyre, remarks that the eighteenth-century Jamaican Maroon Wars 'were the only significant British colonial wars to be fought in the humid tropical forest environment'; for 'Not until World War II was the British army again called on to plan and execute a serious military conflict in such conditions' (Eyre 1980, 5).

5. Werner Zips (2011, xxvi n2) translates the word 'Maroons' as derived from the Spanish term for 'runaway pets'. However, the name 'Maroons' derived from the notion of escaped livestock (and the escape of slaves was sometimes advertised by their masters on the same notice as escaped plantation livestock [Besson 1997, 211]). As Richard Price states: 'The English word "maroon", like the French *marron*, derives from Spanish *cimarrón*. As used in the New World, *cimarrón* originally referred to domestic cattle that had taken to the hills in Hispaniola...and soon after to Indian slaves who had escaped from the Spaniards as well... By the end of the 1530s, it was already beginning to refer primarily to Afro-American runaways..., and had strong connotations of "fierceness", of being "wild" and "unbroken" ....' (Price 1996, 1–2 n1; Besson 1997, 211 n45).

6. James Knight, 'The Naturall, Morall and Political History of Jamaica...From the Earlist [sic] Account of Time to the Year 1742', in Campbell (1990, 46, 264 n31, 267 n9) B.M. Ms.12415.

7. Despite several references by Campbell (1990, 67, 71, 73, 74, 80) to Colonel Nedham of Port Antonio and his plantation in the north-east (near Titchfield), his Christian name is not provided and neither is the name of his plantation. Information kindly provided to me by Mrs Helen Nedham from the family papers researched by her late husband, Andrew Nedham, both of whom I met in England, indicates that there were many members of the colonial Nedham family in Jamaica during plantation slavery, following George Nedham (born c. 1635) fleeing there after the Royalists were defeated at the Battle of Worcester in England (1651). George Nedham received several large land grants in Jamaica and the Nedham plantations included Williamsfield in St Thomas in the Vale and Mount Olive in St Catherine. The parishes of St George and St Mary were named after George Nedham and his wife Mary. The Colonel Nedham of Port Antonio (originally in St Thomas in the East and later in Portland)

referred to by Campbell was probably William Nedham (1669–1746), Speaker of the House of Assembly (personal communication from Mrs Helen Nedham, April 25, 2010). The colonial Nedham family intermarried with the Ellis family of Montpelier Estate in St James (personal communication from Andrew Nedham, c. 2003; see also Higman 1998).

8. See Kenneth Bilby's (2006) ethnography of the Windward Maroons for more extensive discussions of Grandy Nanny, who was made a National Hero in post-colonial Jamaica and whose reputed image adorns the nation's $500 bill. See also Zips (2011, 133–83) for a detailed exploration of Nanny, whom he argues was a military commander paralleling the queen mother in the dual leadership structure of chief and queen mother among the Akan.

9. However, as discussed later, in the nineteenth century Accompong's Town was shifted from its original site in a cockpit dell to a higher location nearby (Carey 1997, 529, 616; Agorsah 1994).

10. Zips (2011, 149) argues that, paralleling the Akan dual leadership structure of queen mother and chief, Nanny was the authority behind Quao's conclusion of the Windward Maroon treaty.

11. The name Merody (or Meredie) would later become the name of one of the Accompong Maroons, Meredie Rowe, who was a Colonel during the period of my fieldwork (chapters 3–4 and 11).

12. John Aarons (1981, 29–30) provides a detailed description of the military settlement around the barracks.

13. Flagstaff is reached by a steep road that ascends east for about a mile from Maroon Town Crossroads or Square (chapters 1 and 6). Apart from the recent tarmac, this road, which continues the precipitous road from Montego Bay in the north-west, through Johns Hall and Kensington, is not unlike the mule track that R.C. Dallas described in 1803. As Dallas noted, Trelawny Town could also be reached from Falmouth in the north-east by an even more precipitous route through the Spring Vale plantation, which still rises sharply into the Cockpits and would have passed through Furry's New Town (1968 [1803], 79–81).

14. The creole name (meaning 'I haven't sent for you, don't come after me' – my translation) conveys a defiant message from the Maroons to the planters from whom they have escaped.

15. At Goldsmiths in London, I have met (and taught) some of these Creole descendants from Sierra Leone who still treasured their Trelawny Maroon heritage and talked of landmarks in Freetown commemorating this maroon history and identity.

16. See chapter 1 note 17.

17. Facilitated by the building of the rocky road to Accompong in the 1940s (Barker and Spence 1988).

18. Mintz (1989, 147) concludes that squatter-peasantries were wiped out by the escalating plantation system. However, squatting was significant in the establishment of Accompong, Maroon Town and Aberdeen (chapters 3–7), as well as the Trelawny post-slavery village of Martha Brae and is the basis of Martha Brae's satellite squatter settlement of Zion (Besson 2002, 2007, 2012a).

3 ■ THE CREOLIZATION OF THE COMMONS

African Continuities or Caribbean Creolization?

Accompong (or 'Campong in Jamaican Creole), where I conducted fieldwork over a period of 30 years, from 1979 to 2009, among the descendants of rebel slaves, is the oldest corporate maroon society in African-America enduring on common land. Situated in northern St Elizabeth, the village is in the deep-forested southern area of the precipitous Cockpit Country that straddles the west-central parishes of St Elizabeth, Trelawny and St James (maps 2–4).

Historical, linguistic, anthropological and geographical studies have argued that the Accompong maroon society and its commons are a result of African cultural continuities (Alleyne 1996; Barker and Spence 1988; Campbell 1990; Warner-Lewis 2003; Zips 1996, 1999, 2011, 2012). For example, the sociolinguist, Mervyn Alleyne (1996), includes the Accompong Maroons in his study of African retentions in Jamaica and his related critique of Mintz and Price's thesis of *The Birth of African-American Culture* (1992). Maureen Warner-Lewis, a Professor of African-Caribbean Language and Orature, focuses on Central African continuities when mentioning the burial grounds of the Accompong Maroons (2003, 133–34). The legal anthropologist, Werner Zips, argues that the value system of the Accompong Maroons reflects 'socio-legal African traditions', including 'collective or communal landownership (in Maroon law)' (Zips 1996, 281, 297, see also 1999, 131, 2011, 2012). Likewise, Mavis Campbell, in her history of the Jamaican Maroons from 1655 to 1796, which includes Accompong Town, states of the Maroons that:

> Their allotted land, then as now, was held in common, and no Maroon might alienate any portion of it to an outsider, following African practice. Again, in line with African custom, they cleared their land by the 'slash and burn' method – a very effective means of clearing among preindustrial peoples (Campbell 1990, 190).

In a geographical study of Accompong maroon agriculture, David Barker and Balfour Spence (1988), too, advanced a thesis of African retentions of form in relation to Accompong's land tenure system, arguing that this is quite different from other Jamaican and Caribbean customary tenures. Drawing on my own work on family land in Caribbean non-maroon communities (Besson 1984a), and on Harvey Blustain's (1981) related Jamaican study, they observed that:

> In Jamaica, land rights have both a legal dimension, derived from Europe and defined in Jamaica's Legal Code, and a traditional dimension, a customary system of freehold tenure called 'family land' (Besson, 1984). Family land, which is widespread throughout the Caribbean, is a form of joint tenure, for all... children, legal and illegal [sic, i.e., non-legal], of a particular farmer

(Blustain 1981). Both systems coexist, and rural squatting is of some significance. *In Accompong the system of land tenure is quite different from the rest of Jamaica, and even from other Maroon groups on the island. Historically, Accompong Maroons acquired a tract of communal land on which they have maintained elements of a system of communal tenure which has more in common with African than Caribbean tenure systems* (Barker and Spence 1988, 200–201) (my emphasis).

However, while not denying the significance of African cultural influences (such as landholding kin groups and beliefs in ancestral spirits), my research questions the interpretation of the Accompong maroon society and its common land primarily in terms of pre-capitalist African retentions. Instead, my fieldwork reveals that the Accompong maroon community and its commons reflect Caribbean creolization or 'indigenization'/localization (cf. Mintz 1996b, 43) and place-making in response to globalization. This interpretation (which includes Caribbean transformations of underlying African 'cognitive orientations' in new social contexts [Mintz and Price 1992, 10]) also illuminates the links between the Accompong maroon society and the non-maroon villages of Aberdeen in St Elizabeth and Maroon Town, St James. It, likewise, shows the relationship between Accompong and other maroon and non-maroon derivations of African-American slave cultures, revealing that the Accompong maroon society and its commons are a variation on wider Caribbean creolization and peasantization themes (see also Besson 1997, 2005, 2012a). By uncovering such dynamic Caribbean culture-building and its sustainable land development, my conclusions also challenge Garrett Hardin's (1968) classic theory on 'the tragedy of the commons' with its argument of inherent underdevelopment in common land.

Building on chapters 1 and 2, this chapter first highlights the origins of the commons in the contexts of globalization and creolization. Utilizing anthropological perspectives on symbolic classification, rituals, sacred space and narratives as well as Accompong maroon ethnohistory, I then show how the still ongoing creolization process, reflected in a transformation from African ethnicities to an Afro-Creole maroon identity, is embedded in the sacred landscape of the commons, with its related political organization, kinship system, peasant economy, narratives and rituals. These rituals include the symbolic re-creation of Cudjoe's Old Town through the annual Myal Play,[1] which is a transformation of the Jamaican Afro-Creole Myal slave religion that transformed African religions in the new Caribbean context (Schuler 1979, 1980; Besson 2002, 2009).

Chapter 4 will explore more fully the Myal worldview in Accompong that reinforces the creolization of the commons. In chapter 5, I discuss further my reinterpretation of Accompong maroon society: uncovering the relationship between Accompong maroon common tenure and other Caribbean creole land transmission systems; revising Kopytoff's (1987) conclusion on the demise of Myalism in Accompong, as well as Campbell's (1990, 178) view of so-called confusion in Accompong regarding the ancestress, Nanny, and Chevannes's (1995a, 7) conclusion that there is no religion named Myal in Jamaica today. I also show that Zips's (2011, 9, 2012) dismissal of creolization in Accompong does not stand up to closer scrutiny.[2]

The Caribbean Origin of the Commons

The roots of the Accompong maroon community and its commons are grounded in their enslaved ancestors' resistance to the early globalization that followed Columbus's landfall in the Caribbean in 1492, his encounter with Jamaica in 1494, the colonization of the island by Spain in 1509 and the seizure of the colony by the English, from the Spanish, in 1655. This globalization included the enslavement of Africans on New World plantations in the context of European colonial expansion and the related creation of the capitalist world-system. Plantation slavery on the Jamaican lowlands and intermontane valleys escalated under the British and so did marronage into the mountainous interior. Much of Jamaica's First Maroon War (1725–38/39) was fought in the Cockpit Country, though Maroons also waged guerrilla warfare against the colonists in the island's eastern mountains (chapters 1–2).

After the First Maroon War, the treaty of March 1738/39 between the victorious maroon leader Captain Cudjoe and Edward Trelawny (the British governor of Jamaica) consolidated the Leeward Maroon polity in the Cockpits. The Leeward polity initially comprised the primary village of Cudjoe's Town (renamed Trelawny Town after the treaty) in St James and the secondary community of Accompong's Town (under the leadership of Cudjoe's 'brother' or Lieutenant, Captain Accompong) in St Elizabeth. This treaty, forged at Cudjoe's Town/Trelawny Town, granted the Maroons in the two Cockpit towns their freedom and legal rights to 1,500 acres of land north-west of Cudjoe's Town (map 5). This land grant was subsequently increased to 2,559 acres in 1756–58 to include Accompong's Town and its surrounding territory in St Elizabeth (chapter 2).

The Second Maroon War of 1795–96 was fought between the Trelawny Town Maroons in St James (assisted by the foragers of the non-treaty maroon village of Congo Town, later renamed Highwindward/Me No Sen You No Come, in the Cockpits of Trelawny Parish) and the British colonists. In the aftermath of the Second Maroon War, the Trelawny Maroons were betrayed by the British and deported to Nova Scotia in 1796 and Accompong Town became the sole surviving Leeward Maroon village. After the deportation of the Trelawnys, their 1,500 acres of treaty land were confiscated by the colonial state (chapter 2). However, the 1,059 acres of Accompong Town's treaty lands have endured as common land and are now the prime basis of the fractured and shrunken Leeward Maroon polity.

However, the threat to the Leeward Maroon polity did not cease with either the 1738/39 treaty or the disbanding of Trelawny Town in 1796; for external pressure (from the British colonial government and the post-colonial Jamaican state) to undermine the commons, and therefore maroon society and corporate identity, has continued since the post-emancipation era into the twenty-first century. Barbara Kopytoff's (1979) ethnohistorical study of the Jamaican Leeward and Windward maroon polities up to the 1970s showed that (with the important exception of the Second Maroon War of 1795–96) the post-treaty pre-emancipation period (1739–1834) saw relative peace between the Jamaican Maroons and the British colonists. However, with the Maroons Land Allotment Act of 1842 (four years after emancipation in 1838), the colonial government nullified the maroon treaties, abolished the special rights and duties of Maroons, and revested 'the Maroon common lands in the Crown, to be reallocated to individual Maroons' (53).

The firmest resistance to this legislation came from Accompong Town and in 1868, 1870 and around 1880, the Accompong Maroons were again involved in border and tax disputes (Kopytoff 1979, 54, 57). Such disputes continued into the twentieth century and were documented by Kopytoff up to the 1970s (despite Jamaican Independence in 1962). Throughout this time, Accompong was 'the most aggressive in asserting its rights' (58) and during my fieldwork from 1979 to 2009 land disputes were still occurring. For example, in 1993, a Jamaican government minister visiting Accompong 'spoke of the need for the government to aid the maroons, particularly in the matter of providing land titles to property, as this was necessary to raise funds from the financial institutions for further development'.[3] This reflected the persisting attempts by the Jamaican state to individualize this spatial manifestation of the Leeward Maroon polity and its corporate identity, attempts reinforced by the realization that the commons could be rich in bauxite ore. In the first decade of the new millennium, the issue of potential bauxite mining in the Cockpits escalated. In 2006, debates on potential bauxite prospecting in the Cockpits intensified, fuelled by the involvement of foreign capitalists in discussion with the Jamaican state. These discussions were challenged by the Accompong Maroons in collaboration with their Council of Overseas Maroons from North America and Britain, reinforced by the concern of Jamaican environmentalists and by the use of the national media and the World Wide Web (chapter 1).[4] This issue was the main focus of the Homecoming and International Conference held by the Council of Overseas Maroons, in Accompong, on January 4, 2007, though several members of the Jamaican government listed on the conference programme did not attend (chapter 11).

At the present time, Accompong, a transnational Afro-Creole maroon community with a dispersed adult voting population of around 3,500 persons (some of whom reside elsewhere in Jamaica and in the United States, Canada and England),[5] is surrounded by Appleton Estate and other plantations. These sugar-cane estates, on the fertile plains of St Elizabeth, produce sugar and rum for the world economy and this land monopolization is reinforced by further capitalist land engrossment through the bauxite and tourism industries (chapter 1). In St Elizabeth, during my fieldwork (up to 2009), Alpart was one of four companies in the island mining bauxite for export. In addition, Accompong is directly inland from Jamaica's north coast tourist capital, Montego Bay. From the later years of my research, Accompong itself has become a tourist attraction, facilitated by the rocky road to the village built in the 1940s (which also enabled overseas labour migration) and the global expansion of tourism. Other impacts of globalization include the consideration of the Cockpits as a National Park and World Heritage Site (while simultaneously being impacted by environmental decline), the proposed Cockpit Country Conservation project, and the construction of Highway 2000, which are all perceived by the Maroons as attempts to encroach on their common treaty land. In 2006, investors from the United States proposed building a casino, a guest house and a hotel on the tax-free Accompong commons and these issues continued into the later years of my research.[6]

In the face of these continuing inroads from the global economy, the Accompong Maroons have forged a creole land tenure and transmission system that is still evolving. In the rest of this chapter, I outline these continuing elaborations on the common land of the Maroons, revealing two seemingly contradictory but related processes of incorporation and creolization repairing and preserving the corporate Leeward Maroon polity. At the heart of these processes is the symbolic shifting and ritualization of Cudjoe's Old Town, which became Trelawny Town after the treaty of 1738/39 and whose population was deported following the Second Maroon War of 1795–96. Cudjoe's Old Town/Trelawny Town (Jamaica's largest maroon village [Kopytoff 1979, 62 n2]) was in the parish of St James and its former site is now the basis of the non-maroon village of Maroon Town (chapters 2 and 6–11). However, my research shows that the Accompong Maroons have symbolically 'shifted' (through narratives and rituals) this historic site of Cudjoe's Old Town to the 'Old Town' grove at the edge of Accompong, in St Elizabeth, in the context of the creolization of the commons (see also Besson 2005). This 'shifting' of Cudjoe's Old Town, likewise, involves the symbolic relocation of the 'Peace Cave' (where the Leeward treaty was signed) from the Petty River Bottom cockpit-dell near Cudjoe's Town (Eyre 1980; Besson 2005; and chapter 2) to Accompong. The shifting of these sacred sites incorporates the shrunken Leeward Maroon polity. As discussed in chapter 5, my interpretation revises some of the conclusions of maroon specialists (Agorsah 1994; Campbell 1990; Carey 1997; Zips 2011) regarding the sacred landscape and its rituals.

The Creation of the Sacred Landscape of the Commons

Pursuing Emile Durkheim and Marcel Mauss's (1963) anthropological theory of symbolic classification, Claude Lévi-Strauss (1964, 1966) argued that the main feature distinguishing humans from animals is intellect, manifested in the construction of meaning through classification, concept-building and ordering the universe well beyond practical need. Arnold Van Gennep (1960) showed that it is especially through ritual, such as rites of passage, that human beings construct meanings and classify their cosmos; suggesting that all such rituals involving changes in condition share a common tripartite structure of separation, transition and incorporation. Victor Turner (1962, 1966) further elucidated how this threefold pattern may focus on sacred natural symbols, such as trees, and can construct categories of sacred space upon the landscape (cf. Pocock 1975, 166–85).

This elaborate ordering of the cosmos can be clearly seen among the Accompong Maroons, whose ancestors' marronage (which transformed their status from enslaved to free) was advertised by their masters along with the escape of plantation livestock.[7] This elaboration of meaning focuses on the landscape, with its symbolic graves and groves, and several interlocking tripartite schemes chart the commons as sacred space. These symbolic classifications, reinforced by Myal rituals (deriving from the Jamaican Myal slave religion and transformed in marronage), reflect processes of separation, transition and incorporation preserving the Leeward Maroon polity and its land in the face of threat and change. Such incorporation, distinguishing the Accompong maroon community from the wider Jamaican society, paradoxically also reveals on-going Caribbean creolization or indigenization/localization in adaptation, negotiation and resistance to the external constraints of the capitalist world system (see also Besson 1997, 2005, 2011a).

These classifications, symbols and rituals are reinforced by maroon narratives. Nigel Rapport (2000, 74) has argued that, 'Narratives embody a perceived order, and in their telling they maintain this order despite seeming temporal, spatial, experiential disjunctures', and 'provide for the world-traveller a place to continue to be'. In the case of Accompong, maroon narratives reflect the disjunctures of enslavement, marronage and the rupturing of the Leeward Maroon polity in contexts of globalization. However, their narratives also repair these ruptures by ordering the landscape and constructing a sense of locality and belonging by anchoring maroon identity in the groves, trees, boulders, mountains, valleys, forests and graveyards of the common treaty land. These place-making narratives, which reinforce the tripartite structure of separation or rupture, transition or bridging of disjuncture, and incorporation or reparation, reflect a process of creolization providing a place in the 'new' Caribbean homeland for both maroon residents and world-travellers 'to continue to be' (see also Besson 2005).

From these perspectives, seven interlocking tripartite classifications embroidering the commons and reinforced by narratives and rituals can be identified. I first outline the widest of these classifications, namely, the continuing segregation and incorporation of the maroon polity and its common land in the face of globalization and Jamaican non-maroon society, including the disputed maroon treaty boundaries and the border zone of Aberdeen (diagram 3.1 and maps 3, 4 and 6).

1. The Maroon Polity: Disputed Boundaries, Aberdeen, and the Commons

Diagram 3.1: The Maroon Polity

Separation/Rupture	Transition/Bridging Disjuncture	Incorporation/ Reparation
Disputed Boundaries	Aberdeen	Accompong Commons

With the Leeward Maroon treaty of March 1738/39 following the First Maroon War, the land grant of 1,500 acres to Cudjoe's Town/Trelawny Town and the additional land grant of 1,059 acres to Accompong's Town in 1756–58, the British colonial government confined the Leeward Maroons to marginal mountainous reservations, which enabled the colonists to expand their slave plantation system (chapters 1–2). However, from the maroon perspective, the treaty became a sacred charter of corporate identity reflected in their common lands (Kopytoff 1979). While the Trelawny Town treaty lands were confiscated by the colonial state in 1796 after the deportation of the Trelawnys following the Second Maroon War, the treaty land of the Accompong Maroons endures.

Today, this common land reflects the widest context of Leeward Maroon incorporation from the world economy, the surrounding plantations, bauxite mines and luxury hotels and the Jamaican post-colonial state.

The still ongoing boundary disputes with the Jamaican government, reinforced by the Maroons' continuing and controversial exemption from land taxes, are the most powerful rituals of separation and are reflected in Accompong maroon narratives concerning the boundaries of the treaty land. During my fieldwork (1979–2009), the view remained in Accompong that the Jamaican state has deprived Accompong Town of some of its treaty lands by a falsely imposed boundary. Such claims vary: some Maroons say that the Leeward Maroons were allocated land 'from coast to coast' (chapters 4 and 6); that is, from the southern seaport of St Elizabeth to the northern port of Falmouth in Trelawny[8] and includes extensive lowland plantations that are, but should not be, in the hands of non-Maroons. Consistent with this perspective, I was told that the new trans-island highway (Highway 2000) invades Accompong territory.

However, other Maroons state that the treaty land extends just beyond the boundary in the Cockpit Country imposed by the Jamaican state, with the disputed lands including Bethsalem, Cooke's Bottom, Elderslie, Jointwood, Retirement, Thornton, Quick Step, Whitehall and especially the land of Aberdeen in the southern foothills of the Cockpits bordering both the maroon commons and Appleton Estate (figure 3.1a). For example, in 1991, Ex-Colonel Harris Cawley (who estimated the population of Accompong to be 'about 2,000 including children' in 160 households), observed more generally of the Accompong maroon population and their lands:

Figure 3.1a. The Accompong maroon commons and the Mountains of Aberdeen.

> On the outskirts now, Aberdeen, Thornton, Elderslie, Jointwood, Retirement, Bethsalem, Whitehall – all those are maroon areas but they are living on lands that they bought that were maroon lands. So you have another six to seven thousand [Maroons] on the outskirts.[9]

Likewise, in 2000, Caroline 'Ena' Wright Lawrence, a leading Myal dancer in Accompong explained to me that:

> We don't pay tax to the Jamaican government for our land. They have taken away a lot of it. We are trying to get it back. Even now they are taking a bit by Elderslie and Cooke's Bottom.

In similar vein in March 2009, in an interview with the Maroon Colonel Sydney Peddie and his Deputy, Melvin Currie, I was told that:

> The Cockpit Country is maroon country. We [the treaty stipulates] should cut open, wide and convenient roads to Trelawny, St James, Westmoreland, and if possible to St Elizabeth. But they [the Jamaican government] are telling us we are living in St Elizabeth. But we are living in the Cockpit Country apart from the other part of the country. 'Maroon' means 'wild', untamed. We were marooned in the Cockpit Country. The Cockpit Country belongs to the Maroons. Problem areas are the [bauxite] mining, but Maroons say mustn't mine. Aberdeen, Cooke's Bottom and Quick Step are disputed areas with the [Jamaican] government.

Aberdeen is therefore perceived by Accompong Maroons as a transitional zone between their commons and the wider Jamaican society, and maroon narratives concerning the ambivalent status of the Aberdonians bridge the disjuncture between the maroon polity and Jamaican non-Maroons (see also chapter 6). Some of these narratives concern the various historical and contemporary links between the two communities; others focus on the mixed descent of many Aberdonians (from planters, slaves and Maroons); yet others relate to Aberdonian landholders being taxed by the Jamaican state.

During slavery, the Mountains of Aberdeen, on Accompong's southern horizon, were the backlands of the Aberdeen sugar estate, established by Alexander Forbes of Scotland's Aberdeen (chapters 2 and 6). On these backlands, plantation slaves cultivated provision grounds and Accompong Maroons narrate that their warrior-ancestors forged alliances with these (proto-peasant) slaves to assist maroon livestock-raids on Aberdeen Estate. Conjugal relations between male Maroons and Aberdonian slave women are also said to have been established; an oral tradition reinforced by the historical fact that the Leeward polity suffered from a shortage of women during marronage (Kopytoff 1978, 301–304).

In the Aberdeen post-slavery community, established on taxed and parcelled land on plantation-mountains south of Aberdeen estate, oral tradition complements Accompong's oral history as a ritual of transition at the maroon/non-maroon interface. Aberdonians, many of whom are of maroon descent or have ties of marriage, kinship and affinity with Accompong Maroons, support Leeward treaty claims, asserting that some of their ancestors were Maroons who 'came out' from Accompong after emancipation to live on former maroon land nearer to the plains. Such oral tradition (which is paralleled by a history of post-emancipation squatting and Jamaican government land retrieval, registration, land sale and taxation) is exemplified by the Aberdonian ancestor-hero of Aberdeen's central family line, who is said to have been an African Prince, brought on a slave ship to Jamaica, who escaped to Accompong from a plantation on the plains. His descendants are said to have 'come out' from Accompong and to have acquired land in Aberdeen (chapter 6).

In Accompong, the continuing incorporation of the maroon commons is symbolized by the preservation of the colonial treaty, which was kept during my fieldwork by the maroon Secretary of State, the late Mann O. Rowe (who died aged 102 in 2006), who led land-protest marches in his prime and defined his role as the guardian of his peoples' land (figure 3.1b and chapter 4). In the later years of my research, the text of the treaty was inscribed on the wall of the Community Centre in Accompong in the context of escalating heritage tourism (figure 3.1c and chapter 11). The corporate identity of the Leeward Maroon polity, reflected in the treaty and the commons, is reinforced by maroon political organization, religious ritual, kinship, marriage and descent, oral history and the maroon-peasant economy.

Figure 3.1b. The Leeward Maroon treaty kept by Mann O. Rowe, Secretary of State in Accompong.

A Maroon Council, led by an elected Colonel, oversees community affairs and settles internal disputes including those concerning common land. In 1991, Ex-Colonel Harris Cawley (whose late father Tom Cawley had likewise been a Colonel in Accompong), explained the Council's composition to me:

> About 30 people on the Council: the Colonel, the Deputy Colonel, the Mayor, the Captains and below that the different people that have their different offices, like the cultural leader, and the one who is responsible for community planning. And then you have the general members. (See figure 3.1d.)

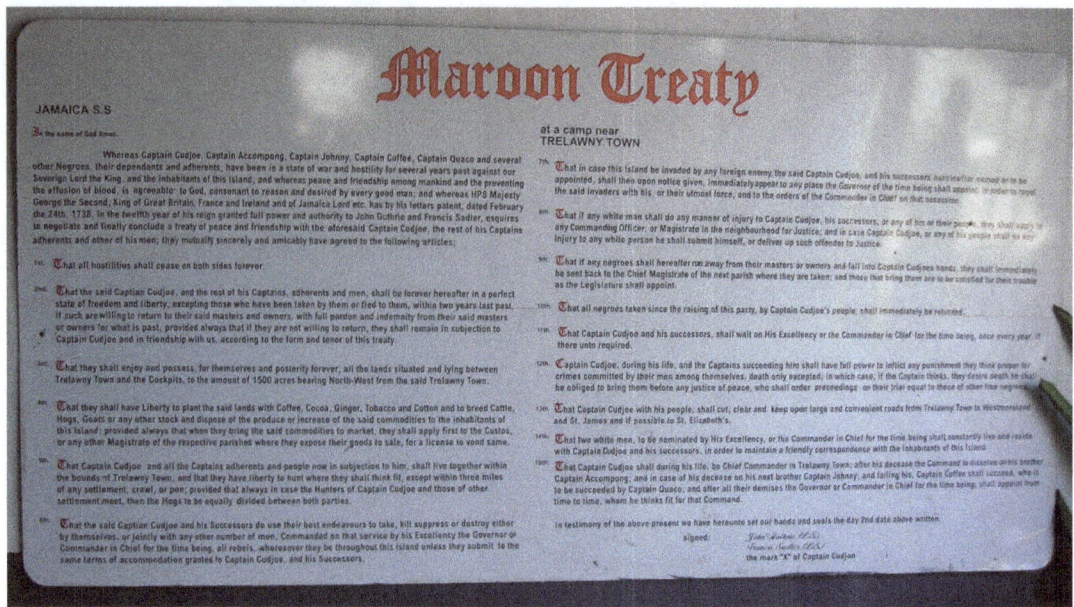

Figure 3.1c. The text of the Leeward Maroon treaty in the Community Centre, Accompong. Photo by Johnny McFarlane, 2007.

Figure 3.1d. Colonel Martin Luther Wright (centre) and two of his Captains, early 1990s, Accompong (in front of a mural of Cudjoe and Nanny in the Community Centre).

 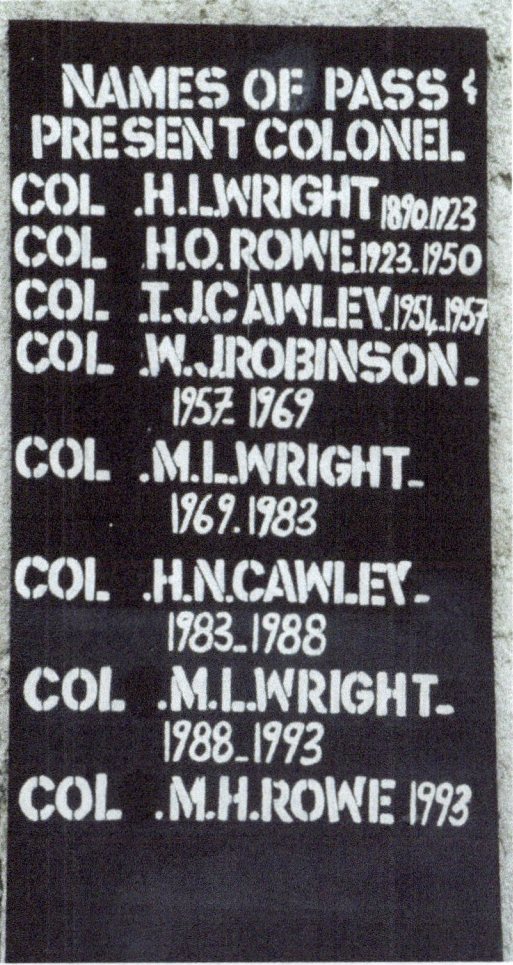

Figure 3.1e. A mural of Captain Cudjoe in Ex-Colonel Harris Cawley's house, Accompong.

Figure 3.1f. A partial list of Accompong Maroon Colonels in the Community Centre.

The Council comprises seven ministerial offices, each with its own committee. Decisions by the Colonel and the Council may be scrutinized and ratified by the Elders, 11 Maroons over the age of 50, chosen to give guidance to the community.

Regarding the office of Colonel, Ex-Colonel Cawley explained how this derives from the historic Leeward Maroon leader, Captain Cudjoe, and how the method of electing the Colonels reflects both continuity and change (figures 3.1e and 3.1f). This includes a transformation from a lifetime office to a five-year term (a change that occurred in 1945, one year after Universal Suffrage was introduced to Jamaica), a shift from an informal to a formal electoral process, and the assistance of the Jamaican government in recent elections, at the invitation of the Maroons:

> Goes right back to Cudjoe. Cudjoe was a Captain. Somewhere along the line they became Colonels. And then coming down we had 13 Colonels. But why it is so long is because

they used to serve for life. When one died another one would be elected. It was just in 1945 that they started to change to five-year terms. In days gone by, they were elected by showing of hands. A special meeting would be called at the Parade Ground, where the school is, that was their general meeting ground, where they had their Council. And the Council meet and people would show hands to favour a certain individual to be Colonel, after they had given their speeches.

But today they have to do it by popular vote, democratic system, ballot boxes would have to be used and candidates nominated. We have a nomination day and we ask the [Jamaican government's] Electoral Office to assist us since they have the machinery already, so that we do not put ourselves in extra expenses. And then the day of the nominations would be announced and the election would be announced and you would go out on a campaign programme. The Maroons in Kingston would be on the [voting] list, the Maroons in Aberdeen, the Maroons in Windsor, Thornton, Elderslie, Retreat and Montego Bay. Those are the main areas. And all those areas would have a polling station that is set up...So during that time of the campaign, you have to hire transport and you go out with your people and go to these areas and keep your public meetings and persuade the people to give you their support.

During the remainder of my fieldwork in Accompong, from 1991 up to 2009, another three Colonels were elected and (as in the past) some Colonels or Ex-Colonels were re-elected to serve a second term (which accounts for the present Colonel, Inspector Ferron Williams elected in August 2009, being the 26th Colonel).[10] The Council is predominantly male and all Accompong Maroon Colonels have been men.[11] However, in 2009, when Colonel Ferron Williams was elected (succeeding Colonel Sydney Peddie), a maroon woman was elected Deputy Colonel for the first time (chapter 4).[12]

As well as perpetuating links with the Leeward Maroon leader Captain Cudjoe, through the Colonel and his Council, an annual Myal Play, rooted in the Afro-Creole Myal religion, forged by Jamaican plantation slaves (Schuler 1980; Besson 1995a, 2009), transformed in marronage and said to be handed down in Accompong for more than 270 years, is believed to regenerate relations with the 'First-Time Maroons', the rebel slaves who won the War and forged the Peace. This ritual of incorporation is centred around ancestral burial grounds at and beyond a sacred grove called 'Kindah', at the edge of the residential zone of the common land, where the 'Kindah Tree' (a fruitful mango tree) has a sign proclaiming: 'Kindah, One Family'.[13] This common kinship is manifested in overlapping cognatic clans,[14] claiming descent through both genders from the First-Time Maroons (especially Cudjoe and his reputed sister Nanny), articulating with personal bilateral kinship networks on both parental sides and with tendencies towards community endogamy and cousin-conjugality (Besson 1997, 2005). Such conjugal relations are said by the Maroons to originate with 'tribal' marriage exchange between 'Kongos' and 'Coromantees' or 'Ashantis' in the early maroon community.[15] These patterns of descent, kinship, marriage and affinity are reflected in the maroon sayings, 'We are all one family' and 'We are Royal Family'; the latter being a reference to parallels with both European royal cousin-marriage alliance and the Maroons' claim of royal African descent.

Oral history, transmitting the moral precepts of maroon society (cf. Bilby 1984a), provides a charter for land rights, political organization, Myal ritual, kinship and the maroon-peasant economy. Maroons narrate that the commons were left by Cudjoe 'for the born and unborn' and that any of his descendants traced through either gender (and also the cognatic descendants of his 'sister', Nanny, as discussed later) have rights to use the commons and voting rights in the polity. This kin-based community includes migrants overseas and many maroon world-travellers return to settle or visit, especially for the annual Myal rituals which focus on the ancestors and their links with the creole maroon community and its common land. Further narratives reinforce these rituals, ordering and protecting the commons.

The peasant economy, rooted in maroon common land, continues to underwrite Accompong's corporate identity. The traditional maroon economy was based on shifting cultivation in hidden provision grounds for subsistence and clandestine market trade, supplemented by hunting wild pigs, gathering giant bean pods from cacoon vines, and plantation-livestock raids. The contemporary maroon economy focuses on the cultivation and grazing of the commons for subsistence and for peasant marketing on the plains; supplemented by income from cash-cropping, lumber-felling, shop-keeping, migration and the tourist industry. This expanding peasant economy elaborates the commons in a further tripartite scheme; namely, the deep forest, the provision grounds, and the village or residential zone (see also Besson 1997, 2005; Barker and Spence 1988).

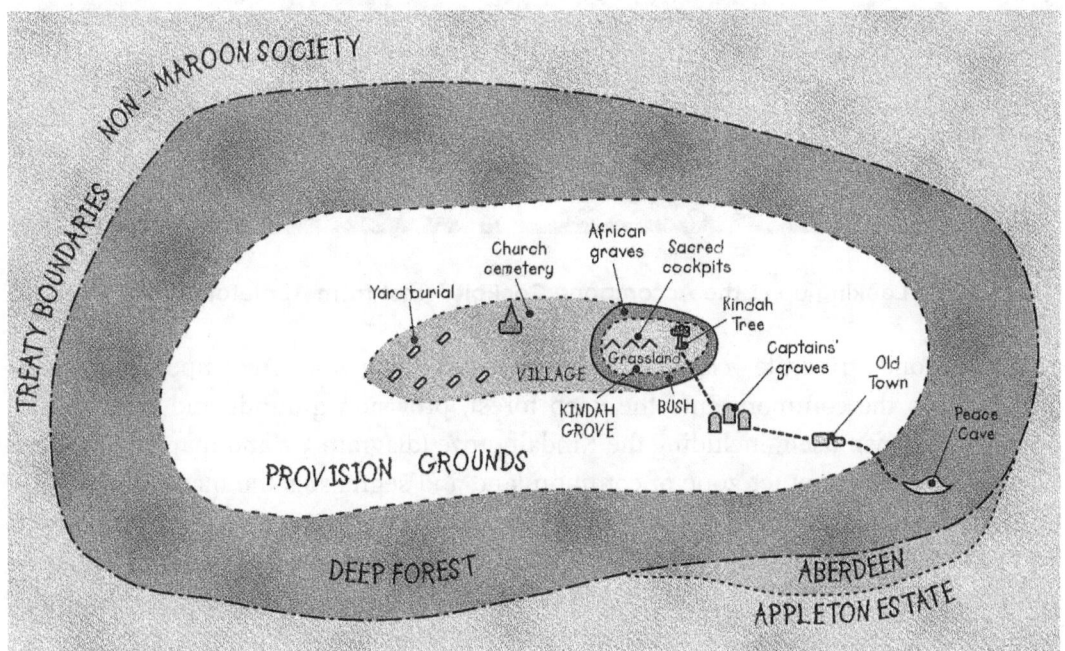

Map 6. Sketch map of the Accompong commons (Besson 2005, 42).

2. The Commons: Deep Forest, Provision Grounds and Village

Diagram 3.2:   The Commons

Separation/Rupture	Transition/Bridging Disjuncture	Incorporation/Reparation
Deep Forest	Provision Grounds/ Pasture	Village/Kindah

Figure 3.2a.   Looking up at the Accompong Cockpit forest from Appleton Estate.

The second tripartite classification constructed by the Accompong Maroons differentiates the commons into the deep forest, provision grounds and pasture, and Accompong Town itself, including the Kindah grove (diagram 3.2 and map 6). The deep forest comprises the outer zone of common land and segregates the maroon commons from the surrounding plantations, such as Appleton Estate (figure 3.2a). The forest was the scene of warfare with the plantation-military regime and the hunting and gathering grounds of the fighting Maroons. Today, common rights especially typify deep-forest land, which is the source of sacred medicines and timber.

Provision grounds, likewise, hold a special place in Accompong oral traditions and ethnohistory. Shifting cultivation provided subsistence and clandestine market trade during the First Maroon War, and provision grounds were a focus of destruction by the colonial regime. Today, an intermediate zone of provision grounds, surrounded by pasture and cash-cropped land, has been carved out of the deep forest (figure 3.2b; cf. Barker and Spence 1988). Cash-crops are mainly bananas and sugar cane, and more recently yams, developed for the world economy; for example, sugar cane is sold to Appleton Estate for processing and export. However, both bananas and sugar cane have been impacted by further globalization, resulting in a decline in these industries. Provision grounds continue to provide 'pot food', which is more highly prized than the 'shop food' now encroaching on the maroon economy (Besson 1997, 215). Individual Maroons who clear such grounds for cultivation have usufructuary rights, which may be transmitted to all of their descendants. Land cleared for cash-crops (especially bananas) and for grazing livestock is a variation on this theme, as are economic trees planted on provision grounds or on other land. A cognatic landholding and tree-holding transmission system (traced from ancestors through both genders) is therefore emerging, within the wider framework of the commons, in relation to the intermediate zone.

At the heart of the commons is the inner residential area, which most fully incorporates the creole maroon polity. This is Accompong Town itself, with its house-yards and crossroads (figures 3.2c, 3.2d and 3.2e). The yards are not only residential sites, but also the nucleii of the maroon-peasant economy. Here, food forests are cultivated (see also Barker and Spence 1988), small livestock raised, and fruit and shade trees grown.

Figure 3.2b. A provision ground in Accompong carved out of the forest.

Figure 3.2c. A house-yard in Accompong at the beginning of my fieldwork in 1979.

Figure 3.2d. The crossroads in Accompong at the beginning of my fieldwork in 1979.

Figure 3.2e. The crossroads in Accompong at the end of my fieldwork in 2009.

Cognatic transmission is likewise evolving here, in relation to yards and fruit trees, at this core of common land (Besson 1997, 2005). Narratives relate the founding of the village and the transmission of usufructuary rights to its house-yards through the cognatic clans and lineages that claim descent from the First-Time Maroons, especially Cudjoe and his reputed siblings. This cognatic system creolized the unilineal landholding systems derived from the West and Central African societies from which the imported slaves came (chapter 2). Narratives also highlight the Kindah grove at the edge of the village, said to be the place where the disjunctures of enslavement and marronage were transcended to forge the creole maroon community. As discussed below, the Kindah Tree (at the heart of the Kindah grove) is the supreme symbol of this kin-based community. The secular incorporation of the commons, reflected in the residential zone, is reinforced by the annual Myal Play at the Kindah grove commemorating the heroes of the First Maroon War and the founders of the Accompong community.

3. The Kindah Grove: African Graves, Sacred Cockpits and the Kindah Tree

Diagram 3.3: The Kindah Grove

Separation/Rupture	*Transition/Bridging Disjuncture*	*Incorporation/ Reparation*
African Graves	Sacred Cockpits	Kindah Tree

The sacred Kindah grove itself, which is also the meeting-place, at the Myal Play, between the Leeward Maroon polity and representatives of the Jamaican post-colonial state, is perceived in a further tripartite classification of rupture/segregation, transition or bridging of disjuncture and incorporation/reparation reflected in reputed African graves, the sacred cockpits and the Kindah Tree (diagram 3.3). This threefold classification repairs the disjunctures experienced by the enslaved African ancestors transported across the Atlantic and highlights the making of a Caribbean place for their Creole descendants, including voluntary world-travellers, 'to continue to be' (Rapport 2000, 74, quoted in Besson 2005, 17).

The Kindah grove is a sloping hillside of grassland with limestone rocks around a fruitful mango tree,[16] surrounded by bush and stones – a microcosm of the Jamaican Cockpit Country *karst* topography of the commons (figure 3.3a). In the bush, reputed ancestral African ethnic burial grounds, marked by cairns and boulders, segregate the Kindah grove from the village yards and crossroads creating a capsule of sacred space. Maroons say that these cairns and boulders mark the African 'tribal' burial grounds of enslaved 'Kongos' and 'Coromantees'/'Ashantis' who escaped from the plantations into the forest through marronage.[17] These narratives underline not only the rupture experienced by the Africans taken from their homelands but also the ethnic divisions that existed among them.

Figure 3.3a. The Kindah grove showing the reputed African graves in the bush, the grassland, cockpit rocks and the Kindah Tree.

Figure 3.3b. The Myal Play at Kindah, 2007.

Figure 3.3c. Cooking the Myal feast on the sacred rocks at Kindah, 1991.

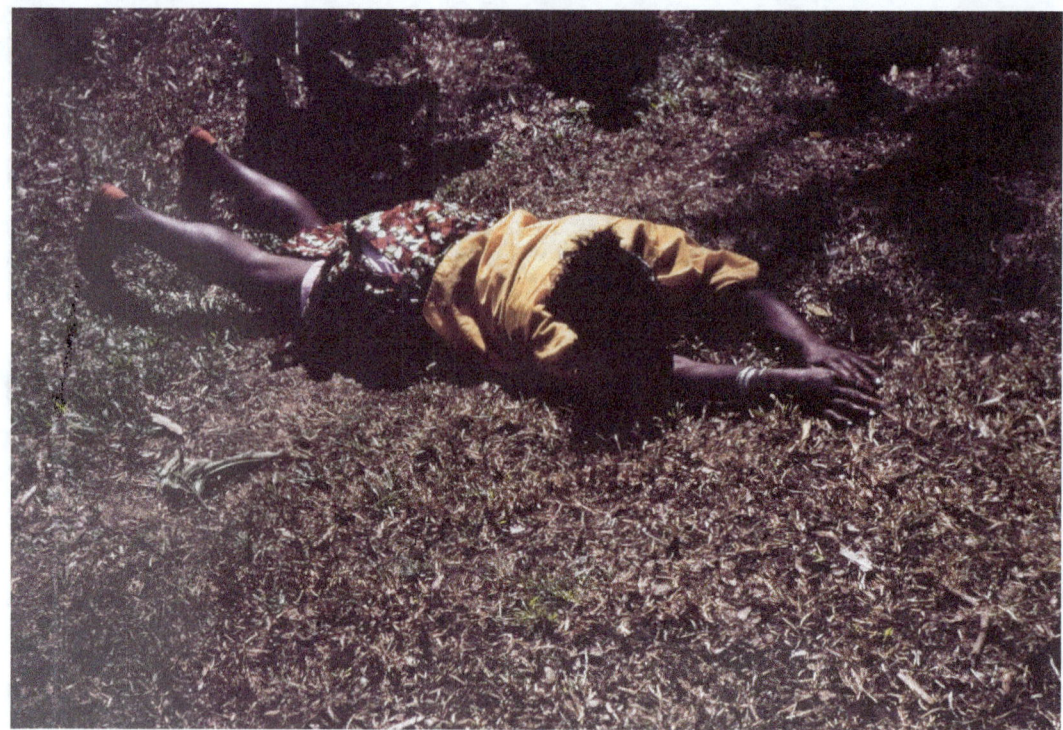

Figure 3.3d. An entranced female Myal dancer at the Play, 1991.

Encapsulated within these bushy 'African' burial grounds is an intermediate zone of grassland and jutting cockpits. Here, the annual Myal Dance or Play is held on January 6 (figure 3.3b).[18] This creole ritual is said to mark both the birthday of Captain Cudjoe – who was an Afro-Creole, born of a 'Coromantee' father in marronage (Kopytoff 1976b, 41–42; chapter 2) – and the ending of the First Maroon War, and is hedged by taboos and rules ordering communication with the Afro-Creole First-Time Maroons who won the war and forged the peace. The Myal Play includes rituals rooted in oral traditions concerning the sacred feast cooked on the limestone rocks (figure 3.3c); the pilgrimage from Kindah to other sacred sites; the dancing to the music of the abeng (a cow-horn replicating those used to communicate in maroon guerrilla warfare) and drums; and the perceived possession by the spirits of the First-Time warrior Maroons. Such 'spirit possession'[19] which I witnessed at Myal Plays, was traditionally of maroon women by the spirits of male ancestor-heroes (Besson 1997, 2001 and figure 3.3d). However, in recent years men have occasionally experienced such reputed spirit possession, though it is generally still women who become possessed.

At the feast, pigs and fowls are sacrificed, 'pot food' is cooked, representing the traditional maroon economy and 'shop food' is tabooed. The gender and colour of the animals and ground provisions are also specified (Besson 1997). Male pigs and male fowls are sacrificed, and even the yams are male; while the hogs and cocks are black or brown. This gender-specific and colour-coded food symbolizes the predominantly male warrior Maroons, within the wider context of the racialized class conflict of the First Maroon War. The ritual cooks are likewise male (figure 3.3e), and their role is reinforced by ritual sanctions and narratives (see also chapter 4).[20]

At the heart of the Kindah grove is the Kindah Tree, with its sign, 'Kindah, One Family', which during my fieldwork, replaced earlier signs of 'Kindah, We Are Family' and 'Kindah, The Family Tree' (figures 3.3f, 3.3g and 3.3h). Maroons narrate that, in the First Maroon War, the 'Kongos' and 'Coromantees' or 'Ashantis' stood under this tree and forged an alliance, through intermarriage, against the plantation-military regime (thereby repairing the disjunctures of African ethnicities).[21] This alliance (the narratives continue) is reflected in the Maroons' practice of cousin-marriage (which contrasts with Jamaican non-maroon communities [Besson 1997, 2002]). Narratives further relate that the Kindah Tree was Captain Cudjoe's 'War Office', where he sat on the boulders beneath the branches planning guerrilla tactics with his 'brothers' or 'lieutenants', Captains Quaco, Cuffee, Johnny, and Accompong (figure 3.3i).

As other narratives state (and rituals portray), it is directly under the Kindah Tree that maroon women are perceived to be possessed, through dance (to the music of male Maroons) and trance, by the spirits of the male ancestor-heroes, highlighting the historical role of scarce and precious females in reproducing the maroon polity (Kopytoff 1976b, 44; figure 3.3d). As mentioned earlier, this polity (fractured and shrunken since the Second Maroon War) has been incorporated and repaired through a creolization process that includes not only ritual, narratives and cousin-conjugality, but also the creation of overlapping cognatic clans and interweaving bilateral kinship networks. The fruitful mango tree, with its sign proclaiming common kinship, is a powerful incorporating symbol of this kin-based creole community. In addition, the symbol of the Kindah Tree incorporates both the generational links and the complementary male and female principles perpetuating the corporate community and embedded in its enduring system of descent, kinship, marriage and affinity (Besson 1997, 217, 1998a, 2005).

Figure 3.3e.   Male cooks at the Myal Play, 2006.

Figure 3.3f. The first sign, 'Kindah, We Are Family' on the Kindah Tree early in my fieldwork.

Figure 3.3g. The second sign, 'Kindah, The Family Tree'.

Figure 3.3h. The third sign, 'Kindah, One Family' later in my fieldwork.

Figure 3.3i. Lawrence Rowe sitting on the boulders at Cudjoe's reputed War Office under the Kindah Tree, 2009.

4. The Sacred Groves: Kindah, The Captains' Graves and Old Town

Diagram 3.4: The Sacred Groves

Separation/ Rupture	Transition/Bridging Disjuncture	Incorporation/ Reparation
Kindah Grove (African Graves)	The Captains' Graves: (Quaco, Cuffee, Johnny, and Accompong)	Old Town (Cudjoe and Nanny's Graves)

The Kindah grove is itself linked in another threefold classification with two other sacred groves among the provision grounds and pastures: the Captains' reputed burial ground and Cudjoe and Nanny's reputed graves at 'Old Town' (diagram 3.4). At the Myal Play, Kindah segregates Maroons from non-Maroons. Increasingly, visitors, including tourists and invited Jamaican government ministers, are being welcomed at the Play, which (as I discuss more fully later in this chapter), has now become both a tourist attraction and a symbol of Jamaican nationhood. However, such visitors to the Play are not allowed beyond the Kindah grove; while the Maroons themselves proceed on a pilgrimage to the other sacred groves. As the Myal Play is in part a celebration of the treaty, Kindah is also the meeting place of allies and former enemies. Early in my fieldwork, the separation between these categories of participants was further underlined by the presence of armed police officers accompanying the representatives of the Jamaican post-colonial state (figure 3.4a). This separation continues to be highlighted by the return of the Maroons from their pilgrimage armed with sticks and battle-camouflaged with cacoon vines (figure 3.4b).

Figure 3.4a. Armed police officers at Kindah, 1991.

Figure 3.4b. The Myal pilgrimage returning from Old Town to Kindah in battle-camouflage.

Along with other non-Maroons at the Myal Plays that I attended in 1991, 1996, 2002, 2006 and 2007, I was not allowed to proceed beyond the Kindah grove on those ritual days. However, I have twice been taken by Maroons along the route of the pilgrimage: the first time was in December 1989 during the preparations preceding the Myal Play on January 6, 1990; the second being in the immediate aftermath of the Play in 1991. These journeys enabled me to reconstruct the tripartite scheme, which represents another dimension in the creolization process that repairs the disjunctures of Leeward Maroon history.

While the graves at Kindah are reputedly those of unnamed Africans, the other two groves are said to be the burial grounds of more recent, named ancestors who won the First Maroon War (1725–38/39) in the Cockpits. After a precipitous descent from Kindah, reached by climbing down mountainsides and a rocky riverbed, the second grove becomes apparent in a grassy clearing under shade trees. This intermediate grove is said to be the burial ground of Colonel Cudjoe's 'brothers' and lieutenants, Captains Quaco, Cuffee, Johnny and Accompong, who had a mixture of African and Creole names (chapter 2). Their reputed graves are marked by stones and weeded for the pilgrimage (figures 3.4c and 1.7a).

Further on, about a mile from Kindah, is 'Old Town', the third and most sacred grove of all. Old Town is situated where a valley adjoins a precipitous cockpit-mountain covered with cacoon vines. Maroons say that this grove was the military camp at Cudjoe's Old Town during the First Maroon War, the mountain being Cudjoe's 'lookout' for miles around;[22] that the cacoon vines, with their giant bean pods, provided camouflage and food during this maroon war; and that Cudjoe himself is buried here in a stone-marked grave. Nanny, the ritual-heroine of the Windward Maroon polity, who is claimed by Leeward Maroons to have been Cudjoe's 'sister' and is said to have been Matilda Rowe, the ancestress of the Rowe Family, Accompong's central clan (chapter 4), is likewise said to be buried here. These graves are weeded for the pilgrimage and an altar is built of branches for a sacrificial meal (figure 3.4d).

However, Cudjoe's Old Town (renamed Trelawny Town after the treaty, renamed again as the Old Town after Trelawny Town split into the Old Town and the New Town, and renamed yet again as Old Maroon Town after the deportation of the Trelawny Maroons), was in the parish of St James, about 14 miles from Accompong in St Elizabeth (chapter 2). The symbolic relocation of Cudjoe's Town/Trelawny Town/Old Town/Old Maroon Town to the edge of Accompong therefore tightens the boundary of Leeward Maroon society around the surviving Accompong community.[23] The Old Town grove in Accompong can, therefore, be seen to symbolize the continuing incorporation of Leeward Maroon society, and the redrawing of the corporate boundary of the fractured and shrunken Leeward polity. Paradoxically, the contentious claim (challenged by Windward Maroons) regarding Nanny's grave at Old Town simultaneously expands the corporate boundary to include the Windward Maroon polity, which makes an annual pilgrimage to Accompong and its Old Town grove at the Myal Play. The symbolic relocation of Nanny's grave, from the Windward polity to Old Town in Accompong, also underlines the complementary male and female principles at the heart of Leeward Maroon society; for the reputed Nanny-Cudjoe sister-brother bond represents the sacred origin of the cognatic descent system, with its overlapping clans traced from either ancestor-sibling through both women and men, which continues to incorporate and perpetuate the creole maroon community.

The three sacred groves at Kindah, Old Town and in between, therefore, order the disjunctures of transportation from Africa, marronage in Jamaica, and the deportation of the Trelawny Maroons to Canada following the Second Maroon War, thereby repairing the corporate boundary of the ruptured Leeward polity in a continuing process of creolization.[24]

Figure 3.4c. Weeding the lieutenants' reputed graves in the intermediate grove, December 1989.

Figure 3.4d. Weeding Cudjoe and Nanny's reputed graves at Old Town, December 1989.

5. War Cemeteries: Kindah, the Heroes' Graves and the Peace Cave

Diagram 3.5: War Cemeteries

Separation/Rupture	Transition/Bridging Disjuncture	Incorporation/ Reparation
Kindah Grove (African Graves)	Heroes' Graves (Afro-Creole Warriors)	The Peace Cave (white Soldiers and black Maroons)

The African burial grounds at Kindah in the village, the graves of all the Afro-Creole maroon heroes (Captain Cudjoe, his 'brothers' and 'sister') among provision grounds and pastures, and the 'Peace Cave' in the forest, form a fifth tripartite scheme (diagram3.5). This symbolic classification reconstructs a journey back in time, as well as a pilgrimage through sacred space. I have been taken by Maroons on this entire ritual journey.

The Kindah grove, with its reputed graves of the early 'Kongos' and 'Coromantees' or 'Ashantis' ruptured from Africa, segregates the distant ancestors from contemporary Maroons. The reputed burial grounds of the 'First-Time' Afro-Creole warrior-heroes (Cudjoe and his 'sister', Nanny, at Old Town and their 'brothers', Quaco, Cuffee, Johnny and Accompong in the intermediate grove), who led the First Maroon War and forged the Peace, together represent a transitional zone between Kindah and the Peace Cave. Cudjoe and Nanny are also regarded as the originators of the creole cognatic clans in Accompong. Our transit through these burial grounds was marked by intercessions and libations of white rum (which I provided as a condition of being taken on the journey) by my maroon guides to their ancestors, especially to Cudjoe (including reasoned arguments explaining my presence there).

These prayers and libations intensified when we reached the reputed Peace Cave (figure 3.5), about three miles from Kindah, where Cudjoe was again addressed and the rum bottle was placed inside the cave. Narratives relate that the cave is the site of both the victorious maroon ambush of British soldiers, which concluded the First Maroon War, and the signing of the treaty between Cudjoe and the colonial regime. Graves of British and Euro-Creole soldiers and Afro-Creole maroon warriors who fell in battle are said to be scattered around the cave, marked by stones and boulders. The maroon graves are said to be those nearest to the Peace Cave, with the colonists' graves being a bit further from the cave, in the direction of Aberdeen. The ambush and the treaty are regarded as effecting the legal incorporation of the creole Leeward Maroon polity, and the pilgrimage to the Peace Cave in the annual Myal Play re-enacts this incorporation.

However, like 'Old Town', the 'Peace Cave' has been symbolically shifted on the landscape – from Petty River Bottom near Cudjoe's Town/Trelawny Town/Old Town/Old Maroon Town in St James to Accompong territory in St Elizabeth (chapter 2). The symbolic shiftings of these sacred sites are part of the creolization process whereby the Accompong Maroons have re-incorporated the fractured and shrunken Leeward Maroon polity on their remaining treaty land (Besson 1997, 2005).

Figure 3.5. The author and Melvin Currie at the symbolic Peace Cave, Accompong, January 1991.

6. Burial Grounds: Warriors' Graves, the Church Cemetery and Yard Burial

Diagram 3.6: Burial Grounds

Separation/Rupture	Transition/Bridging Disjuncture	Incorporation/Reparation
Warriors' Graves (Kindah/Old Town/Peace Cave)	Church Cemetery (The Afro-Creole Community)	Yard burial (Afro-Creole Cognatic Lineages)

The Maroon warriors' graves (at Kindah, Old Town, the Peace Cave and in between), the Presbyterian/United Church cemetery, and house-yard burials comprise a sixth symbolic classification of the commons ordering and repairing all the ruptures of Leeward Maroon ethnohistory by embedding them in the sacred landscape (diagram 3.6 and map 7). This classification again reflects a tripartite process of creolization (separation, transition and incorporation).

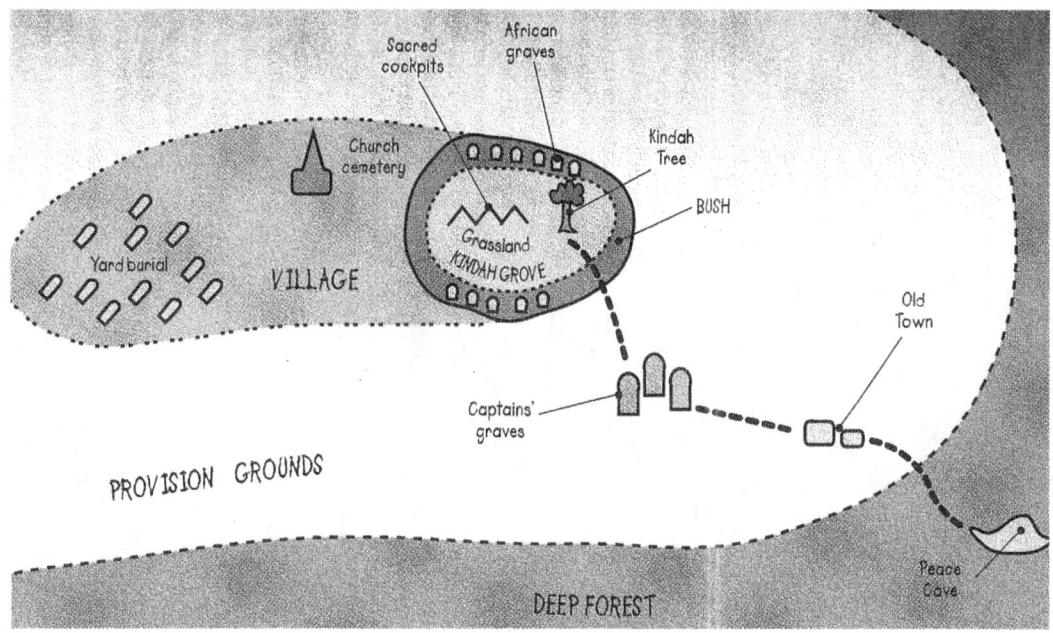

Map 7. Sketch map of the sacred sites on the commons (Besson 2005, 43).

The Maroon warriors' reputed graves segregate living Maroons from their ancestor-heroes, who established Leeward Maroon society. These ancestors are set apart through rituals, taboos, sacrifice, narratives, intercessions and libations. Their symbolic burial grounds order the disjunctures experienced by the ancestors in enslavement and marronage, which severed them from Africa. Central themes relating to these graves are African ethnicities, the Afro-Creole First-Time Maroons and the First Jamaican Maroon War, all in the distant past.

More recent Afro-Creole ancestors are buried in the cemetery of the Presbyterian (now United) church, established in Accompong in 1882 (Kopytoff 1987, 473; Besson 1997, 2001, 2005; figures 3.6a and 3.6b). This cemetery interment, still ongoing, highlights a significant intermediate stage of maroon ethnohistory; namely, the transformation from marronage, African ethnic groups and Afro-Creole warriors to a post-treaty Caribbean maroon community. The village cemetery is a symbol of this corporate creole community and its common land, and the tombs, vaults and sepulchres in this cemetery order the more recent ruptures of death within the polity. In this transitional context, Afro-Creole Myalism became coexistent with Scottish-mission Christianity, reflecting further creolization.

Most recently, during my fieldwork in Accompong (1979–2009), a further process of incorporation has been evolving, reflected in yard burial. House-yards comprise the major area of the village and yard-rights (as well as rights to provision grounds and trees) may be transmitted through both genders within the wider context of the commons. In the yards, such gendered land transmission is further consolidating through the emergent practice of burial in the yard; a practice that simultaneously marks and effects incorporation within creole cognatic landholding lineages (figure 3.6c).

Figure 3.6a. The Accompong Presbyterian/United Church cemetery, 1979.

Figure 3.6b. The Accompong Presbyterian/United Church cemetery, c. 2009.

The significance of this new burial pattern is underlined by the indignation it has aroused among some conservative Maroons, who regard this practice as typifying plantation-slave communities and non-maroon free villages (such as Aberdeen, Maroon Town and the Trelawny villages, where family-land cemeteries are symbols of cognatic family lines [chapters 6–10; Besson 2002]), and as undermining the corporate identity of the maroon community and its common land. For such Maroons, the recent introduction of yard burial in Accompong is, therefore, regarded as rupturing their traditions of community burial grounds.

Figure 3.6c. Recent house-yard vault burials, Accompong.

However, as other Maroons indicate, since usufructuary rights to house-yards were allocated by the Maroon Council (which has yet to vote on the contentious issue of yard-burial), and as their transmission through generations is endorsed by the Council, yard burial may be seen as embedding the clans and lineages that claim descent from Cudjoe and Nanny in the sacred treaty land. This is especially so in the face of external attempts by foreign interests and the Jamaican state to 'develop' a land market for the commons, which would rupture maroon corporate identity.

Therefore, it is this emerging incorporation in cognatic landholding descent groups that most clearly reveals the creolization process that has enabled Leeward Maroon society to survive. These survival strategies of incorporation and creolization are variants on a wider Caribbean theme; for, as I show later, peasantries throughout the region have created overlapping and ever-expanding cognatic landholding clans and lineages, maximizing kinship and scarce and precious rights to land (chapter 5; see also Besson 1997, 2000). This has been especially so in the case of the descendants of chattel slaves, who were not only legally denied both kinship and land rights, but were also property themselves. From this perspective, the emergent overlapping cognatic corporations in Accompong can be seen to be strengthening (not undermining) maroon corporate identity. This kin-based process of incorporation, culminating in yard burial, is nowhere more clearly legitimized than in the central maroon symbol of the Kindah Tree with its sign, 'Kindah, One Family'.

Moreover, historical sources show that the creolization strategy was endorsed by Captain Cudjoe who was an Afro-Creole rebel slave (chapter 2). Cudjoe stipulated that his followers should set aside their African languages and speak Jamaican Creole English (Kopytoff 1976b, 45). He also forged an early treaty between the British colonial government and their Caribbean rebel chattel slaves, who were factors of production in the capitalist regime. In addition, oral history suggests that Cudjoe himself personified the process of creolization at the Afro-Scots interface, by adopting the alias 'Alfred McPherson' in addition to his Akan day-name (Besson 1997, 222).[25]

However, the issue of yard burial reflects current contentions/disjunctures in the creolization process, not only between the Leeward polity and the post-colonial Jamaican state, but also within the maroon polity. The ongoing debate on yard burial therefore shows that creolization varies even within the Accompong maroon society itself (which is differentiated by political factions, gender, age and migration). But the two contrasting views among Maroons both highlight the continuing incorporation of the commons as a place for Cudjoe's descendants ('born and unborn', residents and migrants) to 'continue to be'. In both these contexts of yard burial and church cemetery interment, the savings and remittances of maroon world-travellers are contributing to the construction of modern concrete vaults and sepulchres that complement the traditional cairns and tombs on the sacred landscape. This changing architecture of death and burial embedded in the treaty land is a further dimension of creolization.

7. Accompong Town: Ancestors, Community and Nation

Diagram 3.7: Accompong Town

Separation/Rupture	*Transition/Bridging Disjuncture*	*Incorporation/ Reparation*
Ancestral Graves ('Traditional Ceremony', Kindah to Peace Cave)	Community and Kin Groups (Church Cemetery and House-Yards)	A Symbol of the Nation ('Civic Function' at Monument and Parade)

In the new millennium, a seventh symbolic tripartite scheme has emerged, reflecting yet further creolization of the commons (diagram 3.7). Together, the reputed ancestral graves (at Kindah, at and near Old Town and at the Peace Cave) set apart the ancestral past with its disjunctures of enslavement, marronage and war. This tumultuous past is highlighted by the Myal Play, which is now referred to (on programmes printed for the January 6 festival) as the 'Traditional Ceremony' that takes place at Kindah and through the Myal pilgrimage to Old Town and the Peace Cave.

The community of recently deceased and living Maroons is symbolized by the Presbyterian/United Church, with its communal cemetery and in the emergent pattern of yard burial, reflecting the evolving cognatic clans and lineages and their house-yards within the maroon community. This community and its kin groups includes migrants in North America and Britain, many of whom return for the Myal Play. In the twenty-first century, this transnational kin-based community bridges the disjuncture between the First Maroon War and the Jamaican post-colonial state.

By the 1990s, after the Myal pilgrimage returned from the Peace Cave through Old Town and the lieutenants' graves to Kindah, it proceeded for a 'Civic Function' (attended by representatives of the Jamaican government and other visitors) to a national monument (erected during my fieldwork) near the village crossroads that valorizes Cudjoe's defeat of the colonial plantation-military regime (figures 3.7a and 3.7b).[26] Since 2002, this Civic Function has become so large that it has shifted from the Monument to the more spacious flat area outside the school referred to as both the 'playing field' and the 'Parade Ground' (figures 3.7c and 3.7d). The Parade Ground, portrayed as the drilling ground of the Maroons in the First Maroon War, has parallels not only with the Windward Maroon *Asafo* Ground (Bilby 2006, Zips 2011), but also with the drilling ground of the British colonial soldiers established at Flagstaff on the former site of Trelawny Town after the Second Maroon War; a flattened area now referred to as 'Ball Ground' in Maroon Town and used for emancipation festivals and sport (chapters 2, 7 and 11). This Civic Function at Parade, in which maroon leaders and Jamaican government officials participate and which is now organized in alliance with the Tourism Product Development Co. Ltd (TPDCo), an Agency of the Jamaican government's Ministry of Tourism and Entertainment, highlights the new role of the Accompong maroon community as a symbol of the Jamaican nation state within a creolization process of incorporation and reparation in the context of Jamaican nationhood. The role of Accompong Town as a symbol of the nation is underlined by the flags flown at the Civic Functions, which include the Jamaican flag and a banner combining both the national flag and the maroon abeng.

This role of the Accompong maroon community as a symbol of the Jamaican nation state intensified in 2012, the year marking 50 years of Jamaican Independence (Besson 2012a, 2012b). At the Civic Function in Accompong on January 6, 2012, which was attended by then Director of Culture (Sydney Bartley) in the Jamaican government's Ministry of Youth and Culture, the role of Accompong Town as a national symbol was highlighted explicitly through the portrayal (by the Jamaican government, the national media and the Maroons themselves) of the maroon ceremony as the start of the celebrations of the 50th Anniversary of Jamaican Independence. The prominent participation of the Jamaican government in the Civic Function was marked by its Ministry of Youth and Culture providing 'facilities for the event, including the Jamaica 50 backdrop, stage and lighting', as an article in the *Gleaner* highlighted.[27] The *Gleaner* article added that this event, as well as marking 'the 274th [anniversary of the] signing of the treaty of peace and friendship between Captain Cudjoe and the British…was also part of Jamaica 50 celebrations'. In his speech in Accompong, Mr Bartley observed that, 'As the ministry which has responsibility for Jamaica 50, it is very good and strategic that we start Jamaica 50 here in the first part of the year'.[28] Bartley went on to point out that 'the movement for Independence 50 years ago started with the resistance of Africans who were captured in their homeland and shipped to the region as slaves';[29] thereby underlining the role of the Maroons as a symbol of the Jamaican nation state. I explore this recent transformation of the Myal Play in relation to the Jamaican nation state and its global tourist industry more fully in chapter 11.

Figure 3.7a. The Civic Function at Cudjoe's monument, showing Jamaican flag, 1990s.

Figure 3.7b. Another Civic Function at the monument, showing the Jamaican flag with the maroon abeng.

Figure 3.7c. The Myal pilgrimage marching from Kindah to the Parade Ground, 2006.

Figure 3.7d. The national Civic Function at the Parade Ground.

The Creolization of the Commons

In sum, the seven interlocking tripartite symbolic classifications outlined above chart the commons as sacred space and embed the 'localization' process in the landscape (diagram 3.8), reflecting a continuing process of creolization from African/Afro-Creole enslavement and resistance onwards to Caribbean freedom and transnational Jamaican nationhood.[30] This creolization of the commons has created a sacred place where the transnational maroon community can 'continue to be' (Rapport 2000, 74, quoted in Besson 2005, 17).

Diagram 3.8: The Creolization of the Commons

Sacred Sites	Separation (Rupture)	Transition (Bridging Disjuncture)	Incorporation (Reparation)
1. Maroon Polity	Disputed Boundaries	Aberdeen	Accompong Commons
2. Commons	Deep Forest	Provision Grounds	Village/Kindah
3. Kindah	African Graves	Sacred Cockpits	Kindah Tree
4. Sacred Groves	Kindah	Captains' Graves	Old Town
5. War Cemeteries	Kindah	Heroes' Graves	Peace Cave
6. Burial Grounds	Warriors' Graves	Church Cemetery	Yard Burial
7. Accompong Town	Ancestors	Community and Kin Groups	National Symbol

In chapter 5, I discuss, more fully, the implications of my conclusions on the creolization of the commons for the reinterpretation of Accompong maroon society. However, I first further explore, in chapter 4, the Myal worldview of the Accompong Maroons that reinforces the creolization of the commons.

Notes

1. The concept of Play derives from the dances and rituals of the enslaved that formed 'the spiritual heart of Jamaican slave culture' (Burton 1997, 18; see also Mintz and Price 1992, 39). Warner-Lewis (2002, 105) notes that 'play' is 'a danced religion, typical of all African and African-Caribbean religions'.
2. This chapter and chapter 5 draw partly on and expand my earlier analysis of Accompong maroon common tenure (Besson 1997). I am grateful to the editor of the journal, *Plantation Society in the Americas*, for permission to draw on that article. A later version of this analysis was presented in Besson 2005 and the diagrams and sketch maps in this chapter build on and develop the illustrations in that publication. See also Besson 1995a, 1995d, 1999a, 2000, 2001, 2003c, 2011a, 2012b
3. *Jamaica Gleaner* (Western Bureau), 'Maroons Urged to Unite', January 8, 1993, 2.
4. With the change of the Jamaican government from the People's National Party to the Jamaica Labour Party in 2007 (who lost the next election in December 2011), the issue of bauxite mining in the Cockpits was put on hold. However, Esther Figueroa's YouTube video 'Cockpit Country is Our Home', http://jamlink.com/index.php?option=com_k2&view=item&amp (Windsor Research Centre, Jamaica), last modified on July 2, 2013, highlights continuing concerns about the potential threat of bauxite mining in the Cockpits.
5. This estimate was provided by the Maroons early in my fieldwork. See note 9 below on other population estimates for the Accompong Maroons.
6. See, e.g., 'Former Maroon colonel lashes out on casino facility discussions', *Jamaica Observer*, January 8, 2009.
7. See chapter 2 note 5.
8. This claim is made even though the treaty was made several decades before the founding and consolidation of Falmouth from 1769–90 (Besson 2002; Conolley and Parrent 2005).
9. See also chapter 6 for a more detailed narrative by the Ex-Colonel saying that the lands of Aberdeen were 'robbed' from the Accompong Maroons by the colonial state. The Ex-Colonel's population estimates of 2,000 including children resident in Accompong with another 6,000–7,000 on the outskirts of Accompong complements the estimate given earlier in this chapter of approximately 3,500 adults for the transnational Accompong community.
10. 'New maroon colonel sworn in', September 27, 2009, http://www.radiojamaica.com/content/view/21889/26/. Colonel Ferron Williams is a police inspector in the Westmoreland Police Division (ibid). During my fieldwork in Accompong, another Colonel, Meredie Rowe (who resided during the week in Montego Bay), was likewise a member of the Jamaican police force. This paradox of Maroons serving in the Jamaican police force goes back to an act passed by the Jamaican Assembly in 1798 to reward the Accompong Maroons for their assistance against the Trelawny Town Maroons in the Second Maroon War of 1795–96 (Carey 1997, 496; and chapter 2).
11. As in the Windward Maroon communities in eastern Jamaica.
12. 'New maroon colonel sworn in', September 27, 2009, http://www.radiojamaica.com/content/view/21889/26/; Horace Hines, 'I'm in charge of everything – maroon colonel', *Jamaica Observer*, October 15, 2009. In 2008, the Maroon Indigenous Women's Circle, founded in 2007 and directed by Gloria Simms (said to be 'from the Trelawny Town Maroons in St James'

[sic, Flagstaff?]), was formalized, comprising approximately 100 members from all the maroon communities in Jamaica, including some who work or live outside these villages (Kimesha Walters, 'Women's group give female Maroons voice', *Jamaica Gleaner*, November 23, 2009). This article further notes that Simms said, 'I sat for a while with all the colonels from all the villages and I realize from sitting in those meetings that the women did not have a voice', and that 'Simms said it could be the group's influence that resulted in the election of the first woman deputy colonel, in Accompong, St Elizabeth this year'.

13. See chapter 5 for a fuller discussion of the meaning of the term 'Kindah'.
14. These clans and lineages traced through both women and men include non-resident migrants as well as residents. In anthropological terms, they are therefore 'unrestricted' cognatic descent groups; that is, there is no restriction in membership based on either gender or residence.
15. According to Kopytoff (1976b, 38, 40) 'Coromantees and their descendants' dominated the Leeward Maroons in the eighteenth century and '"Congo"' runaways settled 'deep in the western woods' after the treaty. In addition to referring to 'Kongos' and 'Coromantees', Accompong Maroons sometimes mention a third ancestral 'tribe', 'Ashanti', and then qualify this by stating that Ashanti and Coromantee coincide: 'is the same thing' (compare Patterson 1973, 119, 135, 138). Such statements and the related oral tradition of tribal marriage alliance portray a symbolic system of 'elementary' or 'direct' marriage exchange (or 'symmetrical alliance') between two social groups as the basis of society as described by Claude Lévi-Strauss (1969) for some cultures. Such a system contrasts with the 'complex' or 'indirect' marriage exchange of non-maroon Jamaican communities (see Lévi-Strauss 1969; Besson 2002, 282–88). Today, there are attenuated 'Coromantee'/'Ashanti' and 'Kongo' ethnicities among some Afro-Creole Maroons in Accompong, expressed in terms of stereotypes of phenotype and speech. For example, in December 1996, an Accompong Maroon (with parents and land rights in Accompong) working in the tourist industry in Montego Bay told me that he is a 'Kongo' descended from three overlapping 'breeds' (named unrestricted cognatic descent groups). He contrasted the 'Kongos' and 'Coromantees', in Accompong, in terms of phenotype and speech: 'The Kongos are shorter, blacker, and their eyes are red. Coromantees are taller and speak [Jamaican Creole] slightly differently'. He further asserted that Kongos are descended from Nanny, and Coromantees from Cudjoe, though 'some say they [Cudjoe and Nanny] are brother and sister'. Thus, African ethnicities in contemporary Accompong are symbols of an African past within the contexts of creolization; for example, the fact that my informant was a tall 'Kongo' who claimed descent in three overlapping descent groups and spoke like non-Maroons did not seem to invalidate his symbolic ethnic stereotypes. Werner Zips (2011, 54) clarifies that, 'Coromantees' was a British name for enslaved Africans departing to the Americas from Fort Kormantine on the Gold Coast.
16. Sacred trees among the Jamaican peasantry are usually cotton trees; a belief dating back to slavery and undoubtedly originating in African beliefs regarding the religious meaning of trees, jungles and wilderness (Patterson 1973, 205; Hennessy 1993, 4; Besson 1995b, 93). For example, Orlando Patterson (1973, 205–206) notes that, 'In 1832 Knibb told a Parliamentary Committee that he had not "heard of any act of superstitious reverence to trees for the last four years: they used to worship the cotton tree but I have not heard of that for some time".... By the 1920s, as Beckwith [1929, 145] observed, the cottonwood tree was more venerated and feared

because it was felt to be the habitation of ghosts than because of any belief in its intrinsic spiritual qualities.' However (as my late mother, Meggie McFarlane of St Elizabeth pointed out to me), cotton trees would be unlikely to grow at the high altitude of Accompong which is why a mango tree may have been chosen as the Kindah Tree. Calabash trees are also sacred in Jamaica and some mark reputed African graves at the edge of Kindah. Both the cotton tree (with its exceptionally large wooden roots above the ground) and the calabash tree (with fruit growing along the branches) are anomalous, which may account for their sacred role (compare Leach 1965; Douglas 1966). The exceptional fruitfulness of the mango tree at Kindah, as a symbol of fertility to a community preoccupied with reproducing a maroon polity historically typified by a shortage of women, may be a similar reason contributing to its sacred role in Accompong as a symbol for the proliferation of Cudjoe and Nanny's reputed descendants in the kin-based Afro-Creole community.

17. See note 15 above.
18. January 6 is the date of Epiphany. Given the presence of a Presbyterian church in Accompong since 1882 established at the invitation (in 1875) of the Maroons (Kopytoff 1987, 473), the choice of January 6 to symbolize Cudjoe's birthday and the ending of the War may represent an appropriation of this Christian festival (compare Karasch 1979). As discussed in chapter 5 (see also Besson 1997, 216–17 n60), the focus on Cudjoe at the Myal ritual has replaced an emphasis on Captain Accompong as 'Town Master'. Kopytoff (1987, 476) reports that the annual celebration of Accompong's birthday in the early 1930s was likewise in early January. In addition, January 6 is said by some Rastafarians to be the birthday of Jesus Christ (with January 7 being Christmas Day), a tradition which, in view of the growing presence of Rastafari in Accompong, may have reinforced this date of the Myal ritual.
19. Werner Zips (2011, 121) disagrees with the use of the concept of 'possession' for Myal in Accompong as an oversimplification, referring instead to 'a reciprocal communicative process that involves a larger community of the living and the dead'. However, Kenneth Bilby indicates that Myal is perceived spirit possession that is believed to enable access to the morally neutral magical/spiritual power of Obeah that could be used for protection and healing (Bilby 1993 in Besson 2002, 31; see also Handler and Bilby 2001). I find 'spirit possession' a useful concept for Myal as perceived as a means of accessing the ancestors and ancestral power as it is wider than 'communication' and also includes connection, interaction, and access to protection and healing, all of which are conveyed in varying discussions of Myal by Maroons in my interviews (chapters 3–4).
20. The ritual cooking by men portrays the predominance of men in marronage (Besson 1998a, 147; cf Price 1996). However, women were also significant in marronage and played an important role in the maroon economy, including the cultivation of provision grounds. Cultivation by maroon women did not simply reflect African tradition as Campbell (1990, 47) contends, but was related to the fact that maroon men were often engaged in guerrilla warfare (Craton 1982, 219; Price 1996, 6–7) and hunting.
21. See note 15 above.
22. Carey Robinson (1969, 96) refers to 'a high rock overlooking the Town' (Cudjoe's Old Town/ the Old Town, Trelawny Town having split due to factionalism into the Old Town and the New Town built by Furry [63–64, 91]) and used by 'a small scouting party of about a dozen

Maroons' (96) as a lookout observing Governor Balcarres's troops during the Second Maroon War. The Accompong Maroons, in their appropriation of Cudjoe's Old Town, claim that the cockpit cliff under which Cudjoe is reputedly buried at the Old Town grove in Accompong was this lookout from which Cudjoe surveyed the Cockpits for miles around during the First Maroon War.

23. This symbolic relocation of Trelawny Town is also manifested in the sign painted on the cottage of Accompong Town's Secretary of State, the late Mann O. Rowe (chapter 4): 'Trelawny Town 1738–39', the date of the endorsement of the treaty.

24. As will be discussed in chapter 5, the narrative shifting of Cudjoe's life and death from Cudjoe's Town/Trelawny Town in St James to Accompong Town in St Elizabeth also repairs the internal disjuncture within Accompong itself, resulting from religious change (the eclipse of the ancestors by the Christian God) between the 1930s and the 1970s, reported by Kopytoff (1987), reinstating the ascendance of Myalism in an ongoing process of creolization (cf. Besson 1997, 216–17 n60, 2001, 96–97 n36).

25. This oral tradition and my interpretation of it find some support from Mavis Campbell's general historical account of naming among the Jamaican Maroons. She states that 'by the time of the Trelawny War [1795–96], most of the Maroons had chosen Anglo-Saxon names – elitist, too – for they adopted the names of men of the first rank in the society, men of substance and influence – all slave masters' (1990, 255). She further notes that, 'Like Trelawny Town, all the officers of Accompong Town...had assumed Anglo-Saxon names' – a pattern that may have emerged by the early 1770s (255). Campbell also refers to a 'Dougald or Dugall McPherson' recommended as a surveyor by the Moore Town Windward Maroons around 1782, but this is likely to have been after Cudjoe's death in the Leeward polity (173) (chapter 2). However, the western area of Jamaica, including the parishes of St Elizabeth and St James, were areas of pronounced Scottish settlement, and this further underwrites the oral account of Cudjoe's nickname, Alfred McPherson. Campbell reviews a number of possible reasons, including creolization, for the maroon naming system but is inconclusive on this point (255).

26. This monument was initially erected on the plantation lowlands by the Jamaica National Trust Commission during my fieldwork. The Maroons sent a telegram to the then Prime Minister instructing him to move the monument to Accompong. It was duly moved.

27. 'Maroons Celebrate – Mark 274th Anniversary Signing', *Jamaica Gleaner*, Saturday, January 14, 2012.

28. 'Maroon celebrations kick starts "Jamaica 50"', *Jamaica Observer*, Thursday, January 19, 2012.

29. Ibid.

30. The Jamaica 50 celebrations in London highlighted the Jamaican Diaspora's link to the Jamaican nation state. At home, the Jamaican government is proposing that this nation state becomes a republic. I raised this potentially controversial issue for Accompong (a state within a state) with an Ex-Colonel in a phone conversation from London, on May 12, 2012, who advised that from the Maroons' perspective while this republican 'argument is around' in Jamaica it is 'not a serious argument' for Accompong. It remains to be seen how this potential issue will develop.

4 ■ MYAL, KINSHIP AND THE ANCESTORS

This chapter explores more fully the Myal worldview of the Accompong Maroons that reinforces the creolization of the commons. As well as learning about the sacred landscape with its Myal burial grounds, from 1979 to 2009, and attending Myal Plays in 1991, 1996, 2002, 2006 and 2007, the Myal worldview and its relationship to the ancestors and the common treaty land was explained to me by many Maroons during my long-term fieldwork. In this chapter, I present and contextualize some of these narratives on the Myal worldview, its rituals, the ancestors and the commons by maroon leaders, Myal dancers, the abeng-blower and ritual cooks for the Myal Play. Some of these narratives also illuminate distinctions between Myal, Revival, Obeah and Science.

In addition, these narratives illustrate the kinship ties that weave through the maroon community and are perceived to link it with the ancestral spirits. The narratives also reflect both the endurance and the continuing creolization of Myalism in Accompong. In the narratives, there are frequent references to Captain Cudjoe, his 'sister', Nanny, Cudjoe's Old Town, Petty River Bottom and the Peace Cave (usually symbolically relocated from St James to Accompong in St Elizabeth). I begin with the narrative of a Myal dancer who had migrated to London and returned to Accompong, had seen a 'vision' of Cudjoe and experienced spiritual healing through Myal and who claims descent from 'Accompong Nanny'.

The Narrative of a Migrant Myal Dancer

In August 2000, Mrs Caroline 'Ena' Wright Lawrence, a returned migrant from London and a leading dancer at Myal Plays, taught me about the Myal worldview and told me about her ancestress, 'Accompong Nanny'. Ena is a member of the overlapping Wright and Rowe Old Families, two of Accompong's central cognatic clans (traced through both women and men). Her father's paternal uncle was the father of the late maroon Ex-Colonel, Martin Luther Wright (who was Colonel when I began my fieldwork [figure 3.1d]) and her mother was from the Rowe Family.

Ena's mother was the late Gladys Reid who, as Ena (Gladys's eldest daughter) explained, had been 'one of the old-time dancers' in the Myal Plays. Gladys died in 1994 and is buried in 'a marked grave' (Ena narrated) in the Accompong Presbyterian/United Church cemetery. Gladys was also the mother of Hansley Charles Reid (also known as 'Rupie' and 'Ralston'), the abeng-blower during most of the period of my research. Gladys's mother was Louisa Rowe, first cousin to Mann O. Rowe, Accompong Town's Secretary of State. Louisa's

Genealogy 1. Narrative Account of the Partial Genealogy of the Rowe Clan, Accompong

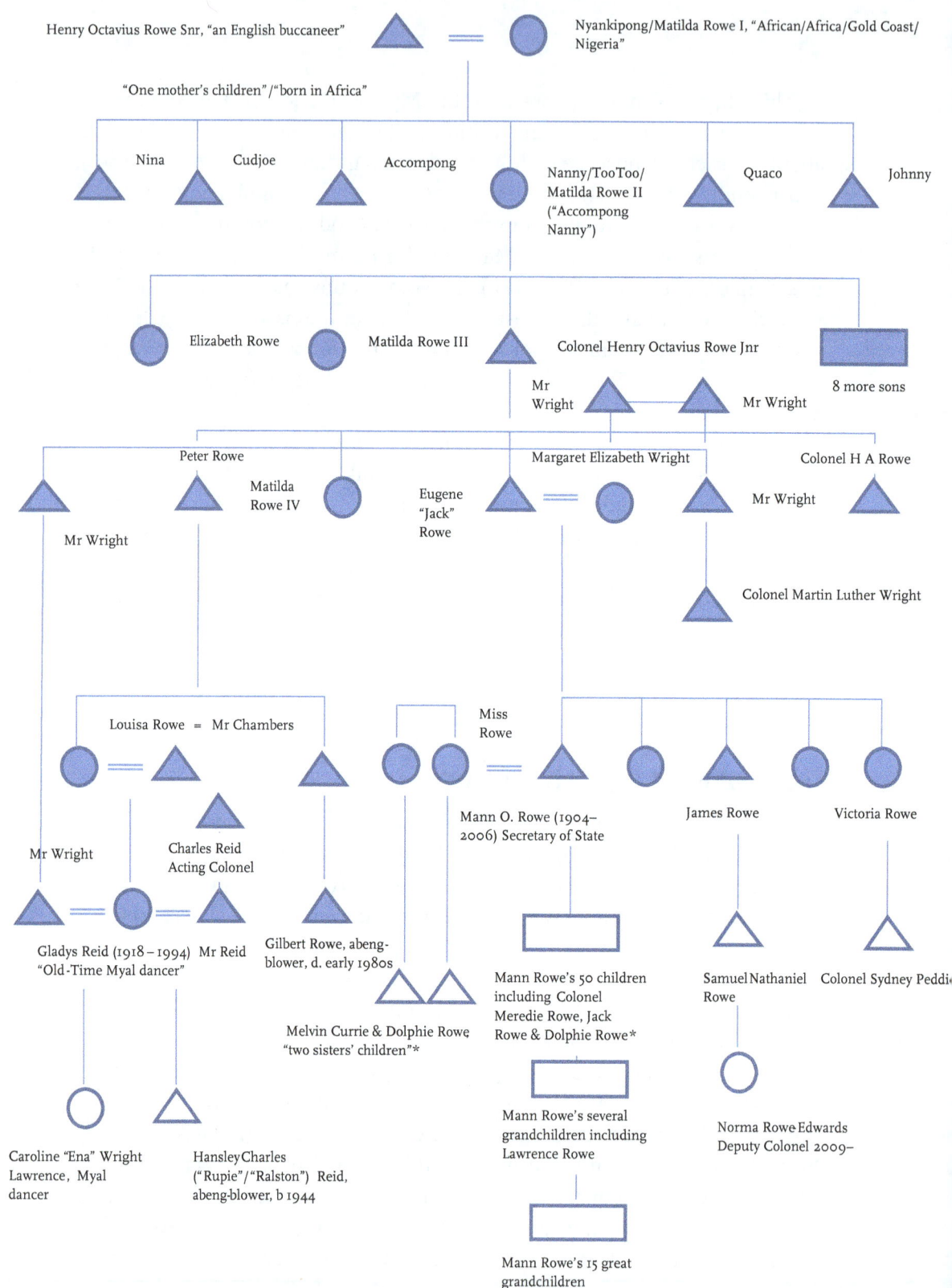

father, Peter Rowe, and Mann's father, Eugene 'Jack' Rowe, were brothers and Ena narrated that 'they are descendants of Nanny' (Genealogy 1). Ena added that, 'Nanny was born in Accompong, "Accompong Nanny"' and had lived at Petty River Bottom:

> Her home was in River Bottom, called Petty, that's where Nanny lived, up to the Resistance [First Maroon War]. My great-grandmother usually tell us the tales of what happened there. How they hide in the bushes and move from place to place. And they hide the children in the bushes. And they grow up there and the fighting still going on.

Ena's maternal grandmother, Louisa Rowe, had been a returned migrant from Cuba who came back to Accompong 'in her teens with ideas of making lace'. Louisa died in 1960 of 'a broken heart' when Ena migrated to England. Ena narrated that she 'had a vision' of her grandmother before she died, explaining that she had visions from she was a child, including a vision of 'Town Massa/Captain Cudjoe riding his horse'. This parallels the visions reported by Kopytoff regarding Captain Accompong, who as Town Master up to the 1930s, it was said, 'frequently rode through the village on his big white horse' (Kopytoff 1987, 475). Ena's vision also reflects the transformation of the Town Massa's identity from Captain Accompong to his leader, Captain Cudjoe. Ena continued:

> It was four brothers: Cudjoe, Quaco, Cuffee and a fourth [Accompong] and one sister, [who] was Nanny. My great-grandmother always tell us about her ancestors and about walking bundles of grass [camouflage]. But no specific tracing [to Nanny], because it was so mixed up. But Nanny was the mother of all the people. And she'd move and go to Maroon Town in St James [where Ena says there are still some Maroons, including some of her relatives]. That was one of the focal point of fighting. The English was present and fighting with the maroon people.

> Accompong [Town] now – all the descendants of Cudjoe, Nanny, Quaco all over the world now, England, Canada and America. But we come back 6th of January, anywhere we are, to celebrate [at the Play]. That's when the freedom come and the treaty.

Ena herself had lived and worked in London from 1960 to 1997, with visits to Accompong in between, until she returned to settle there – though even in 2000 she was 'not quite home' as she was 'going and coming' between London and Accompong. But her 'home is here' in Accompong and she was looking after her father there. When I interviewed her, she was wearing a tee-shirt of the London Underground.

Ena began her narrative of the Myal worldview by recounting how she had been healed by an ancestral spirit on a visit from London for the Myal Play on January 6, 1995. It was a Monday, she recalled, 'Monday was the Play' and she went to Kindah with a bad foot that she washed in rum. She was then able to dance the whole day and came back dancing from Kindah to Cudjoe's monument. When she went home, although she was alone, 'someone was there' and 'fingled' her at the foot of the bed. She stood on her foot and 'nothing wrong'. She woke up the next day, Tuesday, 'all OK'. On the Wednesday, her foot was scratching and she felt a string tied to her toe. She cut the string, bloody water ran out and from then she could walk on her foot. She summed up her healing: 'It's not perfect, but it's miraculous. It was spirit, it was Nanny or one of the spirits'.

Ena went on to elaborate on Myal possession by the ancestors and the potential dangers of unprotected spirit possession:

> Myal: when we are dancing, like last night [at a Vigil on the night of Saturday, August 12] and start Accompong songs, you get into a Myal and the spirits come. And if you don't have rum, you fall on the ground and you flutter or stumble and get into trouble until somebody get you right – wash you down with rum and walk you down till you get out of it. It's not detrimental but you can fall into difficulty if someone who understands is not there to help you.

I had previously seen (in January 1991) the entranced Myal dancers being revived by their attendants and I would witness this again at the Myal Play in 2007. Ena continued her narrative, explaining that when one is in Myal:

> You can speak the Kromanti language. You speak to the dead. They talk to you and then you speak back to the people. Not anybody [can do this]. Like February 25 gone [Black History Day 2000] a young lad [aged 19] from Siloah [a nearby village on the lowlands], part of maroon people, he was carrying on antics and he got into trouble. That was the last time someone got into trouble [with the spirits].

Three little girls who were sitting with us took up the story about the teenage lad: 'He started to dance, run like he was mad and he never got out of it until they wet him with rum and blow the abeng.'

Ena continued: 'Myal is when you interact with the spirits of our ancestors. You can feel their presence and they talking to you and you talking to the people and telling them what's happening.' I asked which spirits? Ena explained there are a variety of ancestral spirits including the First-Time Maroons and more recent ancestors:

> Sometimes you don't know who's moving around. But we have quite a few: Cudjoe, Quaco, Nanny. Plus some of our younger ones – elder people like Edgar Rowe, he's one of the most recent. He died around 20-odd years ago. And Auntie Queen, Queen Wright. They would give names of our ancestors to people. Married name Wright and 'Queen' was the name of one of the ancestors. They call me 'Ena' [as a 'pet name'] – is one of our ancestor's names.

Ena distinguished the community Myal ritual from Obeah as a negative individual activity:

> Obeah – far from that [Myal]. An Obeahman uses oils and goes to the grave and take the spirit up if you want to harm somebody and can send the spirit anywhere they want. They deal with the dead.

This view of Obeah contrasts with its original meaning of a neutral magical/spiritual power to be accessed through spirit possession or Myal (Bilby 1993; Handler and Bilby 2001), a transformation that is likely to have occurred as a result of contact with Presbyterian mission Christianity and a Eurocentric view of Obeah – as happened in Trelawny's Baptist free villages (Besson 2002).

Ena also distinguished Myal from Revival:

> Revival people – we have a Revival Church here – they use drums, wrap their heads and sing and clap and get into spirits – a different thing from Myal. Myal is originated from our ancestors. It's handed down the generations. You are chosen to get into Myal, by the spirits. And yes [in answer to my question on gender], Myal can pass through men and women.

Ena went on to explain her role as the main representative of the Cultural Group that has been formed from the Myal dancers and which not only performs at the Myal Play but also networks with non-maroon communities elsewhere in St Elizabeth as well as going to Kingston:

> I am the elected one for the Cultural Group. Miss Cons [whom I met] is the second representative of the Cultural Group. If you want dancing, anywhere you want entertainment you get in touch with either myself or Miss Cons. At the 6th of January or go to Kingston. We were at Santa Cruz at the Emancipation this year, we were at Lacovia at the [Community] Centre and the groups from Accompong and all over St Elizabeth met at Lacovia and we had a whale of a time. Lacovia adjoining Santa Cruz. We have about 24 in the Group. Men as drummers and two male dancers. On the 6th of January, we have all 24 dancers but otherwise perhaps only 12.

However, Ena explained, that year she had been unable to dance due to her bad foot. But she 'co-ordinates and oversees' the Group and plays the musical 'rattle' for the dancing. Ena concluded her narrative with observations on the common treaty land including the contentious issues of land tax, boundaries and development.

An 'Old-Time' Myal Dancer and Her Son

Before meeting Ena in 2000, I had interviewed her late mother Gladys Reid (1918–94, the daughter of Louisa Rowe) and Ena's maternal half-brother, 'Rupie' Reid (born 1944), Gladys's son, several years before, in January 1991, two days after the Myal Play that I attended that year. As seen above, Ena would later describe her mother Gladys as 'one of the old-time dancers' in the Play. At the time of my interview with Rupie and Gladys, Rupie had recently succeeded to the position of the main abeng-blower of Accompong. I would come to know him well and he would make me an abeng (which, as he predicted, I am unable to blow as that skill is said to be a gift from the ancestors).

I interviewed Gladys and Rupie in the latter's house-yard, where Gladys was visiting. Gladys began their joint narrative, explaining that she was born a Maroon in Accompong in 1918 (and was therefore then aged about 73) and had 'spent all my time here'. Gladys was a member, on her mother's side, of Accompong's central clan, the Rowes, whom she described as 'a big Family, stretch far and near'. She was 'One Family' to Mann O. Rowe (Accompong's Secretary of State) and had a brother from the Rowe family living in neighbouring Aberdeen. She was also closely related to two other Accompong clans: 'My mother is Rowe but me father is Chambers and I married name Reid' (Genealogy 1).

By then widowed, Gladys lived alone (except when Ena visited), in another yard near the Presbyterian/United Church. She had been a cultivator all her adult life but now only cultivated a kitchen-garden in her yard. However, Rupie cultivated several pieces of land in the 'outskirts' of the commons in addition to working as a mechanic in Santa Cruz. They both explained that their house-yards are 'family land' and that the land that Rupie works in the outskirts is also 'generation land'. Rupie further narrated that, as he belongs to various maroon clans through his four grandparents, his land rights have been transmitted down several overlapping (cognatic) lineages and that all these lands are on 'Cudjoe's land, the Maroons' land, which is not to be sold, [as] the land is for the born and unborn'.

Gladys, who had been at the Myal Play at Kindah two days before, remarked on the change in this now-public ritual and recalled how it used to be a private celebration: 'It wasn't so like this before. First it was only the Maroons' alone celebration. But it widespread now that it call in all [Jamaican] citizens.' At the Play that year (1991), Gladys had gone on the pilgrimage to Cudjoe's reputed grave at Old Town. I asked her why I had not been allowed to go to Old Town that day (as I had been taken there by Maroons in December 1989) and she explained:

> It is a tradition, just a rule that no strangers are not to pay the visit down there on that celebration day...Is from the inheritance come down. From Cudjoe's time, them don't accept any strangers. Is down where him bury. Old Town.

Likewise Rupie narrated that Old Town is the site of Cudjoe's Old Town:

> It [Old Town] was the first town for the Maroons. There Captain Cudjoe' house were. And you have the soldiers them who die after the war. And they are buried down there. So on the 6th of January, while we have a certain amount of entertainment for Captain Cudjoe, we don't accept of no-one that is not a Maroon to go on that scene.

Rupie, who had helped to build the altar for the sacrificial meal that I had seen at Old Town before the Play of the previous year, had again helped to erect the altar this year.

On this recent pilgrimage, Gladys had carried 'roast yellow yam' and 'meat' on her head from Kindah to Old Town. She narrated that, en route to Old Town, the pilgrims had stopped at the Captains' graves and 'sprinkled rum and fired explosions, gun'. Rupie added: '[We] use our old white rum and speak to the spirits and fire the gun'. Gladys continued that the gun (licensed to a Maroon who is a market inspector outside of Accompong) was also fired at 'Cudjoe's house and at the sport ground at Kindah'. Then, from the Captains' graves, 'you sing and march up to Cudjoe's [grave] where the spirits congregate. Eat and leave food for them [the spirits] to partake of.'

Rupie explained how the spirits of the maroon-warrior ancestors (said to be invisible to some but visible to others) had assembled at Old Town two days before:

> They all assemble at Cudjoe's house. Johnny, Quaco, Benji, Nanny, Dunde and all the other rest of soldiers that Cudjoe have. Some people don't see them but some see. Spirit. See them through the spirit.

Rupie narrated that he himself had 'seen them through the spirit'. As he explained, they looked:

Just like a natural person, like any one of us. Because they were person before they die, so they come back in the same shape. Having on garments, just like any other live person.

He clarified that: 'Benji is one of Captain Cudjoe's soldiers. There are lots of our soldiers for Cudjoe. Many of the people don't know their names.' Rupie continued:

Sprinkle rum and speak to them in certain words. The words are secret, kept by the Maroons. That's why they don't want the visitors to go. Can be spoken in Kromanti or English but we don't expose it because it is a secret.

I asked about the meaning of the vines and sticks used by the Maroons on their return from Old Town to Kindah. Rupie explained:

The sticks proving they had guns to fight the war. And the cacoon bush shows the way the Maroons were dressed [camouflaged] when they fighting the war.

I recalled that he had given me a cacoon bean as a gift at Old Town the year before.

Rupie narrated that the spirits who had possessed the women dancing under the Kindah Tree at the Myal Play two days before were 'the spirits of Captain Cudjoe'. He also explained why the food at the Play was gendered male: 'In Captain Cudjoe's days they did not eat no female flesh – they say they [females] are the mother'. Hence, the pig and fowl sacrificed at Kindah in the morning of the Play had been male (a hog and a rooster). The hog was black, Rupie added, because 'In the forest where Captain Cudjoe used to go and hunt wild pigs, they were pure black'. His explanation complemented my own interpretation that the colour and gender of the food used for the Play symbolizes a racialized class war and the predominant black masculinity of marronage (chapter 3).

In answer to my queries, Rupie explained that the late abeng-blower, Gilbert Rowe, was his maternal grandmother's brother's son (Gladys's first cousin [Genealogy 1]):

Same family, by [Gilbert's] father's side. The Maroons are Royal Family. So is one set of family just rise up. So when you work it out they all are Maroons' family.

Rupie again referred to the Maroons as 'Royal Family' (paralleling the inter-marriage of European Royalty) when he explained that rights to one of the pieces of 'generation land' that he works in the outskirts of the commons had been transmitted through both his mother and father: 'The Maroons are Royal Family and my mother's mother's father and my father's father is somehow relatives.'

Blowing the Abeng: A Gift from the Ancestors

In my interview with Rupie and Gladys Reid, Rupie discussed his role as the main abeng-blower in Accompong. The abeng, or cow-horn that was used in maroon guerrilla warfare in the Cockpits, is blown at the Myal Play (and certain other events) and Rupie would continue this role (dressed in military uniform for Plays) throughout my fieldwork (figure 4.1). The status of abeng-blower (who is male) is an important office in Accompong and his ability to blow the abeng is believed to be a gift from the ancestors. At the Play, as well as blowing the abeng, the abeng-blower spews white rum to the spirits of the maroon warriors.

Of the skill to blow the abeng, Rupie explained that: 'I get it as a gift. I just see the first abeng-blower, Gilbert Rowe. Captain Cudjoe choice [chose] me, why I got it. Says I should blow it.' Rupie narrated that this is why he could pick up the abeng and blow it and yet other Maroons could not. He found he could blow it at the cemetery at a burial when he was talking to the late Gilbert Rowe and had asked Gilbert to let him blow it. Rupie explained how Gilbert had trained him as his successor:

> He [Gilbert] didn't hesitate and he hand it to me and I tek it and blow it. And after when I blow it, he seh 'you want to blow it better than that'. Me seh, 'likkle by likkle I will blow it'. From that day whenever he blowing it and I go around, he give me to blow. And so I blow and do better blowing [until he perfected the skill].

I had met the elderly abeng-blower, Gilbert Rowe, on my first visit to Accompong in 1979 (figure 4.1) and when Gilbert died in the early 1980s, Rupie succeeded him. In 1991, Rupie explained the occasions on which he blows the abeng:

> I blow it because of Captain Cudjoe's celebration [the Play]. I blow it to call the people to come to the graves [in the Accompong cemetery] of community people who die. And when the Colonel needs the people to speak to, I blow it to call them together...And when tourists come into Accompong, I blow it for them to let them hear it and know something about the history of the Maroons.

Figure 4.1. Hansley Charles Reid in military uniform blowing the abeng at a Civic Function at Parade, 2006. (Inset: Gilbert Rowe, abeng-blower, 1979.)

Rupie narrated that at the Play two days before, he had 'oiled' the abeng with white rum: 'to get the inside of the bugle more sleezy so you have less pressure to blow the abeng and get a clearer sound'. He blows 'different [tunes] according to the occasion'. He learned these tunes from Gilbert and other Maroons who passed them on.

As we spoke in Rupie's house, he showed me a collection of abengs that he had made, hanging on the wall, some of which he planned to sell to tourists. I asked him which of the abengs was his. He pointed out one that was painted green and narrated that it had been inherited down the generations from Cudjoe:

> The green one [abeng] there is for Captain Cudjoe. Is that Cudjoe use to fight the war. That same one. Sure. Captain Cudjoe use it. Him give it down to who leave into his batch while he deceased. They use it and hand it down to keep up the celebration and all those former activities that the Maroons start. Well, we are doing the very said thing, so it come right down to we. And our generation coming up will come and come have it. The said one [the same abeng from Cudjoe]. Yes, it's a cow-horn but it is not our local cows them out here. The Indian cows. Those come down from, Captain Cudjoe carry them away down from Africa with him. Is when he come on the plantation here now in Jamaica and he having the struggling [maroon war] they all get to know the great use of it…because them did want us to be some slaves. So Captain Cudjoe and his followers don't believe in having slavery business. So they fight for that occasion. Say they want to be free.

I asked Rupie who was Accompong and he narrated the following account of Cudjoe and his siblings: '[Accompong was] Captain Cudjoe' brother. Three brothers and one sister. Captain Cudjoe's brothers: Quaco, Johnny, and Accompong.' I enquired who was the sister? Rupie replied: 'Nanny'. I expressed surprise and said I thought she had lived in the east of the island. Rupie chided:

> You have a whole lot of false rumour. She did not live in the east. Even some of our said Maroons here are saying it but not true. She did live right here. But being as they are fighting the war, they have several place which they stop to fight and move again and fight. So the lands now shared up and Nanny get that piece, Captain Cudjoe get that piece and is so it share. But they all were lived together at Old Town.

I checked again where Old Town was and Rupie explained: 'Just couple furlongs from here ... right there is the yard, where we put up the barbie [altar for the barbecue]', where Cudjoe is said to be buried and where I had met Rupie, in 1989, in my visit with Maroons to the Old Town grove. I would be taken there soon again.

Seeking further clarification of the Accompong Maroons' perception of Cudjoe's Old Town, I asked Rupie to clarify whether Old Town had not been on the site of Maroon Town/Flagstaff in St James (which at that time I had not yet researched). Rupie patiently continued his narrative, which portrays a contrast between the Accompong maroon society and the non-maroon community of Maroon Town and which has similarities and differences with written records (chapter 2):

> Different. You have Maroon Town in St James, leading into Flagstaff. That is St James, Maroon Town…Those lands are completely sold out, so the maroon traditions are

not there. Those people sold out their complete rights and privileges...They believe in support the whites' cause. So they were taken from there by a ship, say they are going back to Sierra Leone. While they dumped them. Because from they leave to Sierra Leone, there is no returnal of any letters to say that those Maroons reached there from that ancience until now...They dumped them in the sea. They blindfold them telling them that they are carrying them back down to Sierra Leone in Africa. But when they take the ship in Montego Bay Freeport,[1] and going, one man who is named Al Fowler him seh, 'Let the crew get off the ship because this is not justified for we to leave, we are not going nowhere good'. And he jumped off the ship and swim back to shore. The only Maroon which was saved from down there.

I enquired again from Rupie who had therefore lived at Old Town. He reiterated:

Just Cudjoe and his followers lived there. But after the death of Cudjoe, and his followers, no one lived there because of the rough, rugged way to get out to see the doctor or to go to the hospital. Because our treaty say we should cut intersection roads wide and long from this said St Elizabeth Accompong to the said Trelawny Accompong. Trelawny Maroon Town. History show you that, it is well known, that the Maroons are Trelawny Maroons by treaty and history.

Rupie searched to see if he had a copy of the treaty to reinforce his point but could not locate it. He then explained that his relative and neighbour, 'Mr Mann O. Rowe', has the original treaty 'but he don't showing it to no one'.

Concluding his narrative, Rupie clarified his full name, residence and Leeward Maroon status:

My name is Hansley Charles Reid from this said Accompong, Trelawny. We take some postal address in St Elizabeth Parish but we are the Trelawny Maroons.

Rupie and others would introduce me to Mann O. Rowe, Accompong Town's Secretary of State, and I would come to know him well and see the treaty that he held. A later section of this chapter draws on some of the narratives that I collected from Mann Rowe up to a few years before his death in 2006, when he was over 100 years old. Before turning to Mann's narratives however, I present the accounts of two of the ritual cooks at the Myal feast as well as the narrative of an Ex-Colonel, both collected a few days after the Myal Play of 1991.

Ritual Cooks at the Myal Play

I interviewed two brothers, Aubrey and Lucal Williams, under the Kindah Tree, shortly after the Myal Play that I attended in January 1991, and explored their role as ritual cooks for the sacred Myal feast. I would find that their ritual role was inherited and perceived as sanctioned by the ancestors. They would also tell me about their land rights in both Accompong and Aberdeen.

Aubrey (born in 1939) narrated that he and his older brother, Lucal, 'born and grow Maroon' in Accompong, where their late father had a house-yard. Aubrey's and Lucal's mother was a non-Maroon from Aberdeen. The brothers' father's yard (about five acres) had been transmitted from *his* father and beyond: 'from generation to generation', as Aubrey explained, and had been passed on to his three children (Lucal, Aubrey and their sister) and 17 grandchildren.

Lucal interjected to narrate that 'unmolested' rights to the outlying areas of the commons were created through working the land, in contrast to family-land transmission of house-yards:

> Hold on, hold on, one second, let me butt in and tell you something. Maroons' land, you come and you work the land and you get it off a claim. You see you work it and from you work it nobody molest you again. You get it from the work, you claim that piece for yourself. So a how it go. When in the back-wood, in the Cockpit part, now no one don't have no owner. Everybody go and you use it according to what you want. The land is plenty and no man nuh claim in the Cockpits. You just go and you can work today and me go and work tomorrow on the same land. So it just work that way. [Whereas] out here now [in the village] one man claim a certain spot [yard] from generation to generation, both man and woman and all children.

Lucal and Aubrey explained that maroon migrants and their children can return to these yards and that no one can sell such land, only trees (whose purchase confers some rights to the land). Likewise, they added, houses can be sold.

Both brothers had been overseas once for Farm Work to the United States but returned to settle in Accompong. Lucal lived in their father's yard, Aubrey resided on other land where he had bought the banana cultivation but he also cultivated a piece of his father's yard. Their sister was living on her share of their father's land. Aubrey also cultivated food crops on his paternal uncle's land in Accompong and sold them to higglers who resold at marketplaces in Westmoreland. In addition, he raised cows and goats on a part of 30 acres of land, at Big Ground, near the Peace Cave that his father had cleared and cultivated. Aubrey explained that any Maroon can likewise raise livestock there, as all Maroons 'keep all of the Cockpits' as common land. Lucal and their sister also worked parts of that land. The brothers narrated that although they were not using their mother's family land in Aberdeen, they retain these land rights and their maternal family there 'live loving and if we go over there and want a breadfruit we can pick it, or want an orange we can pick it'.

While Aubrey and Lucal had kin buried on their maternal family land in Aberdeen, there were no graves on their paternal land in Accompong. Instead, many of their paternal kin are buried in the Kongo burial ground at Kindah, as Aubrey narrated:

> My father buried right over there so, in the Kongo burying ground. All of my people buried there. My grannie buried there, my sisters them buried there, my father buried there. So if I should die, I just say I want to bury there too. We prefer round there [rather than in the community cemetery near the United Church and school]. Over here [the Kongo cemetery] go like a family burying ground.

I asked about the kinship sign on the Kindah Tree and the brothers explained: 'Well the Maroons is family [kin]. All of us come from Africa and they run away and tek out a slave and come here and fight and win and they get their freedom and their land and everything. So all Maroons are family.'

Aubrey's and Lucal's father 'used to do the cooking' for the Myal feasts, as did their paternal grandfather. It is a practice they describe as 'coming right down from generations'. Aubrey and Lucal now cooked on the sacred rocks at Kindah for the Plays. Each generation of men had taught the next ones how to cook there and this tradition would continue to be passed on within the males of the family. Other men cook at the feast and one woman mixes a sugar and water drink under the Kindah Tree, a tradition passed on from her maternal grandmother, through many generations. Aubrey explained this gendered cooking for the Play: 'from I born and see, is just man do the cooking' at Kindah. This contrasts with everyday routine as 'women in the yard do the cooking'.

Aubrey and Lucal narrated that they had to cook at Kindah every year for (as they whispered) 'as long as we no sick, have to come or something wrong'. Mystified, I requested clarification. Aubrey illustrated what they meant by recounting an incident (which I recalled being discussed in Accompong) where Lucal was perceived to have experienced near-fatal punishment from the ancestors for neglecting cooking duties, mobilized by the Town Master Captain Cudjoe:

> My brother Lucal, one year he never come round here [at Kindah] and help us cook [on January 6]. On January 7 morning, right at Mr Egbert Wright's shop, he has dropped down right there. He nearly died. They have to tek him and bring him round here [to Kindah] and *beat* him and mek up some fire and they tek some green bush and beat him, say he's disobedient. Well a so they haffe come and beat him round here the morning and him get survive [revived].

When I asked why Lucal had collapsed, Aubrey explained: 'The old ghosts them, well he shoulda come and cook as usual and never come...The Town Master.' When I had enquired which ghosts Aubrey meant and was told 'The Town Master', I enquired again and Lucal took up the narrative:

> We have something like what you would call it '*duppy*' [ancestral spirits]. We don't know [exactly who]. Can be him [Cudjoe's] friend de deh [there]. All who usual to cook round here and deceased. It can come from that way. We don't know but it was something funny [odd]. Very, very funny...Greater man than me, who was in the town business [two men on the Maroon Council, now deceased] a long time, before me.

Due to this perceived spiritual sanction by the ancestors, Aubrey and Lucal explained they were duty-bound to cook at Kindah every year. Six men had cooked the Myal feast that year, but of these only Aubrey and Lucal had inherited this role.

We went on to discuss the meaning of the food cooked at the Myal Play. Aubrey had helped to kill the sacrificial hog early in the morning so that it could be cooked by noon. The hog had to be black, for 'Nothing white used down here. Is a culture [tradition] from the beginning'. They had also sacrificed three brown fowls at dawn and had cooked 'yellow yam, plantain, no white yam'. They explained that the sacrificial pig and fowls were male and the plantains were likewise 'actually male, for the horse plantains male, male...we never see them use any female at all – that is from the culture'. About 50 Maroons had taken some of this food to Old Town.

Lucal's 'lady' had led the dancing that I had seen at Kindah two days before, when some of the maroon women dancing had become entranced and rolled down the hillside. Lucal explained that the singing that accompanied the dancing had been 'necessary' as the 'spirit can't go on without the singing'. He narrated: 'First-time they usually dance Myal, have Myal, and so them say they have Myal this last time'. I enquired, 'What is Myal?' and Lucal explained: 'You dance with *duppy*'. I asked whether he meant the spirits of Cudjoe's people and he replied, 'something like that'. I would later learn that Lucal's lady was believed to resemble the ancestress Nanny.

Aubrey continued to cook for the Myal Plays up until at least 2010, by which time one of his 'second cousins', Ferron Williams, had been elected Colonel (in August 2009), but by then Lucal had died.

An Ex-Colonel's Narrative

Harris Cawley (aged 70 in 2009) was born in 1939 in Accompong, where he has lived all his life except for 'a few months of studies' elsewhere in Jamaica. He is a farmer and retired teacher from the Accompong all-age school and was Colonel of Accompong from 1983 to 1988. His late father, Tom Cawley, was Colonel in the 1950s. I interviewed Harris Cawley many times, including soon after the first Myal Play that I attended in 1991. He provided a comprehensive narrative on the Play, including its songs, feast, dancing, pilgrimage, reputed spirit possession, gendered performance and taboos, and its re-enactment of the activities of the First-Time Maroons. Here, I present some extracts from his 1991 narrative:

> That [the Myal Play] is a festival that the Maroons held for many years. After the war was concluded and the peace treaty was signed, this was a time that they celebrated. That they were out of a war and were now free to live, not in fear or in threat of being captured by the British. And so they come together and they started to celebrate. And they sing some of the songs that depict the warfare and they tell about their *freedom*, different kinds of songs that they have.

> And so the cooking of the food, they cook the food *fresh* [unsalted] because they [the First-Time Maroons] could not get salt in those days, because they had to be on the run and fighting a war. So they do not use salt, they cook it fresh to show this was the way they had it back there in those days.

I asked about the pig used at the feast and the Ex-Colonel explained:

> It is prepared in a different way from how you'd do it today. They [the First-Time Maroons] would boil the water and throw it on the pig and scrape it. They make up the fire and that was the original thing that they did…Generally a black pig. They do not use anything white, because they do not use any rice because rice is white. They do not use yam that is white, they use yellow yam. They use plantain, as you know the colour of plantain. They eat rice any other day but not on that day [and not at that place, Kindah], because a lot of rice is cooked on the street with the curry goat but over there [at Kindah], at that special ritual, they do not use anything that is white… And even the meat that they use, the rooster – they have to use a *rooster* and a male pig. They do not use any female

animals. Because even in some of the rituals, you notice they use very few women. And even the women who had to do the dancing down there, those women have to abstain from sex for a few days before they enter into that ritual.

I enquired about the apparent spirit possession of two female maroon dancers that I had witnessed at the Play and the Ex-Colonel explained: 'That is what they call Myalism. That is Myalism, when they get into that way'. I enquired who possessed them and he narrated: 'Well, they generally say the spirits of the old people [ancestors] like from Cudjoe, coming down. Cudjoe and all those *men* [my emphasis]. They say that these are the people who come'. He confirmed that these are believed to be generally male spirits because:

> Generally is the *male* they speak about, it is more masculine than feminine, the whole setting, the whole aspect of it. The feminine side is toned down very low. It's the women who are dancing and the women who sing but it is the men who do the cooking and especially men who go down the bottom [to Old Town]. And if a woman is there, she will go there just to do the singing.

Ex-Colonel Cawley narrated that he had been on such pilgrimages to Old Town when he was Colonel and that 'many people say' that the spirits of the First-Time Maroons meet at Old Town. Although he himself had not seen them, he commented, 'but there are spirits around that are still evident' and narrated an incident where a police raid in Accompong, when he was Colonel, had been disrupted by a maroon ritual that persuaded the police (who fled) that they were being attacked by the spirits of the warrior-ancestors.

Returning to the narrative of the recent Myal Play, the Ex-Colonel illuminated the symbolism of the pilgrims' return from Old Town carrying sticks and adorned in cacoon vines as representing the First Maroon War:

> That was depicting the way in which the warfare was carried out. The bush they wore was depicting the ambushing of the Maroons' fight against the English, because they [the Maroons] used to hide behind bushes. The bush that they wore there is cacoon bush. And they had some big beans [bean pods]. Because it [the vine] can wrap very easily and without breaking off, it is very flexible. And then the cacoon is a food that the Maroons used to use.

I asked why the Play was held on January 6 and the Ex-Colonel continued:

> That is the day, from ever since, that they say that they have chosen. It's Cudjoe's birthday, so it coincides with the maroon independence... Cudjoe died very old, think he was 81 or 91 when he died. After the treaty. Some people say it was 1790-something.

Ex-Colonel Cawley explained the meaning of the sprinkling of the rum at the Play as feeding and communing with the ancestors:

> Well, the people have their own beliefs that the spirits [are] around, to appease the spirits around by sprinkling the rum and drink some of it too. So by sprinkling the rum they are enjoying it too. They are coming to the communion of the whole thing too.

I asked about the sign, 'We are Family', on the Kindah Tree and the Ex-Colonel commented:

> That means it's a communal thing that they have. And the re-gathering of Maroons from everywhere coming back [e.g., from overseas] to *make* the family and to celebrate together. They feel they are all related.

He had previously explained about the dispersal of much of the maroon population due to 'the constant brain-drain, they find jobs out there and they stay out there'. However, many migrants return for the Play:

> When the 6th of January comes, that is the time that they really pull back themselves to make that family reunion. Some of them might not come for the year but they make that a point of duty to be here that day.

Ex-Colonel Cawley narrated that although he could not trace the direct descent of the maroon population from the First-Time Maroons, resemblances to the ancestors can be identified in the community, including the leading dancer for the Play:

> You can only see figures [features] of people who look like Cudjoe and even like Nanny. The lady who dances and sings [Lucal's 'lady'], the main one who dances and sings, Nanny was a wiry lady and she has that same characteristic. And you can look around and see people and you can figure them out that you could be coming from that line.

He added that the main clan in Accompong is the Rowe Family and estimated that 'about 35 per cent' of the community bear the surname, Rowe, through their fathers and that there are many others in the Rowe Family descended through women. I would learn more about the Rowes and their ancestors from Mann O. Rowe (1904–2006), Accompong Town's Secretary of State, holder of the Leeward Maroon treaty and guardian of the commons.

Narratives by the Maroon Secretary of State, Guardian of the Commons

The late Mann Octavius Rowe, Accompong Town's Secretary of State, was born on December 10, 1904. During my fieldwork, he was the oldest member of the Rowe Family, the central clan in Accompong, from which many maroon Colonels have been elected (figure 4.2). Mann O. Rowe, who described himself as a 'herbalist' or 'scientist' who dealt in 'recipes and spells', died in Accompong in December 2006, aged 102. His funeral was held there in January 2007, soon after the Myal Play (which I attended), which that year highlighted the bicentenary of the Parliamentary abolition of the British transatlantic slave trade. However, Mann Rowe's rebel ancestors had challenged slavery long before 1807 and won their freedom through the Leeward Maroon treaty of March 1738/39. Mann was guardian of the Maroons' copy of the treaty, which he kept in a plastic folder in a wooden box under his bed in his cottage, on which he had painted, 'Trelawny Town 1738–39' over the front porch (figures 3.1b and 4.3). He had been given the treaty by his paternal grandfather the late Henry Octavius Rowe (Colonel from 1923–1950), who conferred on

Figure 4.2. Mann O. Rowe, Accompong Town's Secretary of State, checking a publication by the author, 1996.

Figure 4.3. Mann Rowe and his wife at their cottage in Accompong.

Mann the life-long title of Secretary of State, in 1942 (a century after the Maroons Land Allotment Act of 1842), an office that Mann alone would hold, as he narrated in 1995:

> Since 1942, [Secretary of State] for the rest of my life, like a sovereign monarch. [I was] chosen by 32 officers of the Maroon government. Was not opposed by no one. According to my qualifications and my movements.

Mann's main task was to defend the common treaty land and he had done so vigorously in his prime. In 1995, he defined his role as follows:

> To do all the good I can to my people and to secure our lands. The situation is that we are cheated of our lands [by] the legislators, ranging from 1842 [the Maroons Land Allotment Act]...[In] 1939, I myself led a march to Cooke's Bottom...And in 1956 we, the late Colonel Rowe, H.A. Rowe, that's my uncle, hand over 57 of us rebels [the grounds] being that we intrude upon [the Jamaican] government's land, yet is our forefathers' land. H.O. Rowe was my grandfather, my father's father. And I had was to go against

Colonel [H.A.] Rowe. But the Colonels always reign like a sovereign monarch...This land Cooke's Bottom is strictly the maroon land and they [the Jamaican government] cutting up the land now and selling to a Chinaman and a white man. The treaty said all the land line off of this Trelawny Town, Cockpit Country....

Mann was very helpful in my research and I had many interviews with him, including in January 1991 (when he was 86 years old), June 1995 (when he was 90), December 1996 (when he was 92) and 1999 (when he was nearly 95). On all of these occasions, Mann narrated accounts of his reputed descent from Nanny, who he asserted was named 'Matilda Rowe' and was Captain Cudjoe's sister (Genealogy 1). Mann's accounts trace a Rowe cognatic lineage of eight generations, including four ascending generations (all deceased): his father Eugene, 'Jack' Rowe, his paternal grandfather, Colonel H. O. Rowe, his great-grandmother, Nanny/Matilda Rowe (said to be the Colonel's mother) and Mann's great-great-grandparents (identified as Nanny's parents), Henry Octavius Rowe Senior and 'Nyankipong' (also named Matilda Rowe).[2] In Mann's accounts (which have similarities and differences with historical records as well as with other maroon narratives [chapters 2–6]), such ancestors and their place in the Myal worldview are fleshed out in some detail.

In Mann's narratives, Nanny/Matilda Rowe Junior, whom he described as 'my great-grandmother', was born in Africa to her mother, Nyankipong (Matilda Rowe Senior) and was fathered by an 'English buccaneer', Henry Octavius Rowe Senior, who 'was taking slaves from Africa right down to Jamaica' and who spent 'three months in Africa and cross forty women'. (As the name Matilda Rowe continues down another two generations, I refer to the second, third and fourth ones as Matilda Rowe II, III and IV.) According to Mann, Nanny (Matilda Rowe II) had five brothers (by 'one modder [mother]': Nina, Cudjoe, Accompong, Quaco and Johnny, 'Nina was the oldest brother to Nanny. He was the head of it and he was a great scientist, like me!' Mann continued:

> She [Nanny/Matilda Rowe II] is my great-grandmother. We are from Gold Coast or Nigeria in Africa. 'Nanny' means 'warrior'. But her name was Matilda Rowe. So that's why I name – the family relation – is Rowe...We are from Nigeria in Africa.

I asked Mann where Nanny was born. He replied:

> In Africa. And Cudjoe, Cuffee, Quaco, Johnny, in Africa. They came on the slave ship, but they were not slaves. Cudjoe's chief reason is that he won't tolerate the British ruling, because it's too *tricky*. So what he fought for is *freedom*. Freedom. Want freedom in this country (Mann's emphases).

I commented that I had thought it was Cudjoe's father who had come from Africa (see chapter 2) but Mann retorted:

> No man! Cudjoe himself...Nanny, the great religious warrior, came out here at the age of 12...And that [12-year-old] child was the religious lady Queen Nanny. But her name was Matilda Rowe and her pet-name was Too-Too. Her mother was a Nigerian in Africa, Nyankipong, an African name. Then Accompong now was [derived from Nyankipong] an English name.

Mann said this information was passed down from his 'predecessors'. He went on to narrate that Nanny, 'who didn't marry', had 'nine sons and two daughters', Elizabeth and Matilda Rowe III, and that one of Nanny's sons was his paternal grandfather, the late maroon Colonel H.O. Rowe: 'Nanny was the mother of H.O. Rowe, I was told by my father and elders'. Mann's narrative continued that Colonel H. O. Rowe's children were Mann's father, Eugene 'Jack' Rowe (who married Margaret Elizabeth Wright), Eugene's brother, H.A. Rowe, and their sister, Matilda Rowe IV. Mann narrated that his parents, Eugene and Margaret, had five children: two sons and three daughters (one of whom was the mother of Sydney Peddie, Colonel in the later years of my fieldwork) and that all of his four siblings lived in Kingston. However, they all have inalienable rights to the commons: 'could be 99 years before they return and they would still have land'.

Mann added that 'the Rowe Family is the largest family' in Accompong and that they are a 'Royal Family' as they inter-marry like European royalty. For example, he explained, some of his children were by his 'first cousin Miss Rowe' who was the daughter of Mann's father's brother. (Her sister was the mother of the Deputy Colonel, Melvin Currie.) These children are, therefore, described as 'double Rowe, both mother and father is Rowe. We are all Royal Family, like the Royal family of England, cousins married to cousins'. Of this large Rowe clan, Mann further recounted:

> They are all children [descendants] from my predecessors [ancestors], namely Cuffee, Quaco, Johnny...Now Cudjoe did not marry. He say he prefer to sit in a corner than to marry a contentious woman, because a contentious woman is just like a nightingale sitting on a tree and whistling. He won't tolerate with any contentious woman.

According to Mann, Cudjoe (who Mann said 'could not read' but whose 'thoughts were promulgated by Jesus') 'had no children, not to my knowledge', so he (Mann) and the other members of the Rowe clan are descended from Cudjoe's sister Nanny/Matilda Rowe II. Other big clans in Accompong include the Fosters and the Wrights. Mann's mother Margaret Wright's father and the paternal grandfather of Ex-Colonel Martin Luther Wright (who was Colonel when I began my fieldwork), were brothers.

Mann narrated that he himself had 50 children, many of whom were born in Accompong and 45 of whom were still alive (in Accompong, elsewhere in Jamaica and overseas), by 'quite a few mothers' (for, as he explained, 'the Bible said go forth and multiply'), numerous grandchildren and 15 great-grandchildren. I came to know three of Mann's sons, including Colonel/Ex-Colonel Meredie Rowe, Dolphie Rowe (one of the first Maroons whom I got to know) and Jack, as well as Jack's son, Lawrence Rowe. Dolphie (a farmer and butcher) has been a migrant farm worker in the United States and Lawrence (who has taken a computer course on the lowlands) has likewise been to the USA but, like Dolphie, has returned to Accompong where I met them both again up to 2009 (figures 1.7b and 3.3i). Mann, himself, had only left Accompong occasionally for Kingston.

Soon after the Myal Play of 1991, Mann explained the meaning of the Play, including its rituals and taboos, that was held on January 6 to mark Cudjoe's birthday and treaty, and its relation to the sacred sites and shifting histories of the Leeward Maroon landscape. His narrative included the assertion that Accompong/Old Town is 'Anferry Town' renamed Trelawny Town,³ a claim underlined by the inscription, 'Trelawny Town 1738–39' on his cottage. Here are some extracts from his narrative:

> Accompong was a brother to Generalissimo Cudjoe. Cudjoe is a born-day's name. Cudjoe's name was Alfred McPherson, an English [Scottish] name. His father was an Englishman with an African girl...He [Cudjoe] was settled a mile from here, [at] Old Town. Here is not St Elizabeth. We are on the north side of St Elizabeth. Here is Anferry Town. First name given by Cudjoe. At that time [of the treaty] the then Governor of Jamaica was Sir Edward Trelawny. He said, 'Why not give the place name after me?' Cudjoe never hesitated. Cudjoe gave the place name (the second name) Trelawny Town. The House of Commons, the Privy Council, the House of Lords knew here as Trelawny Town. Accompong was a brother to Cudjoe. When the war was ended, then Cudjoe says to his brother Captain Accompong that you stay here in the east and I will go down to the west to prevent *abrono* (white people) get behind us.
>
> [The Myal Play] is a tradition...Going on before I was born, going on from 1738 [commemorating] the victory of Cudjoe with the English. The cooking and the feasting [at Kindah], in Cudjoe's day you could never eat no white yam, no white rice, because we fought the English. Nor sleep with your wife the night before. The hogs [eaten at the Play] have to be black. All black on this earth is Maroons. The most holy place on earth is Africa, as is written in the Bible.

The black hog sacrificed at the Play two days before had been killed by Mann's son, Dolphie.

Mann continued his narrative, explaining that the Play at Kindah involved:

> Having feasting in memory of Generalissimo Cudjoe and his brethren, namely, Nanny, a sister, Nina, a brother, Cuffee, Quaco, Johnny, Quanki, Fantaright and all those names...They sing the war dance and Kromanti language...The spirits now, we use rum and there should be gun-fire there at Old Town.

Mann explained that the pilgrimage from Kindah (where 'plenty First-Time Maroons, Miles and Fowler' and his son Jack's maternal grandfather are buried) to Old Town 'went to pay tribute to his [Cudjoe's] good works'. At the age of 86, Mann himself had been 'too busy' to attend the Play that year, but he had many times before danced at Kindah and been on the pilgrimage to Old Town where, he explained, 'some see the spirits'. He himself had never seen them in person, but:

> I saw it [the spirits] by smoke coming up from the graves. That supposed to be Cudjoe and the religious lady Queen Nanny. Some people say [she's buried] in Portland, but [she's] not in Portland. Nanny was coming down from MoBay and was attacked by heart failure and died at Elderslie [near Accompong]...So anyone at Moore Town or Scott's Hall [Windward Maroons who say Nanny is buried in Portland] is a big No. Cudjoe died in 1793 from old age. Then 1795, two years later, was the Cudjoe's Town rebellion in St James [the Second Maroon War].

I asked what happens at Old Town on the day of the Play and Mann continued:

> Well we go down there and we throw a little rum and water and scatter some of the food there in memory of Cudjoe (and at the other Captains' graves too). And share out the food. And every year they put a new flask of rum at the Peace Cave where the peace treaty was signed.

Mann, who held the treaty, said that every day people come to view the treaty and that he would pass it on to one of his sons. Meanwhile, as Secretary of State and guardian of the commons, he knew the treaty's context and contents by heart:

> We got it [the treaty] from 1738. This is the original treaty. The third clause say all the lands that line off from the said Trelawny Town. And Cudjoe and his people is to cut large, clear and convenient roads to Westmoreland, to St James and if possible to St Elizabeth. But those political tricksters [of the Jamaican colonial/post-colonial state] want to change it.

At this point in his narrative, Mann gave a detailed critique of the two main political parties in Jamaica, including Members of Parliament, regarding their reputed views challenging the Leeward Maroon treaty. He then continued with reference to the Maroons' original allies, the British colonial government:

> The treaty was signed in 1738 and in 1740 our gracious Majesty, I must say, King George the Second, King of Great Britain, France and Ireland, and of Jamaica, sent out the two Esquires, namely Colonel John Guthrie and Francis Sadler as you will see here [on the treaty] to negotiate and make a final conclusion of peace and friendship amongst us in the name of God, forever and ever, Amen.

Mann also expressed his view on the current situation of the Accompong maroon lands as transmitted from Cudjoe, with named areas of the commons, including the most disputed area of Aberdeen and also the lowlands of Trelawny Parish (where Mann knew I came from), including Martha Brae (Besson 2002) as well as the plains of St Elizabeth:

> This maroon land was given by Generalissimo Cudjoe. This land is fe the born and unborn. And Cudjoe name the land, the many sections and parts of the land. We have [for example], to begin with, Elderslie, we have Aberdeen... Aberdeen is maroon land but occupied by government...the maroon lands range right out, even to Martha Brae where you coming from...The capital of Trelawny [Falmouth] is supposed to be one of our treaty seaport town. Crane Wharf in Black River [the seaport capital of St Elizabeth] is another one.

> Aberdeen is on our [maroon] property, according to the boundary. The boundary was laid down by the King's engineer, the Right Honourable Sir James R.E. Thompson, and drawn up by Thomas Harrison. So Aberdeen is maroon land.

Mann narrated that the seaport of Black River in St Elizabeth 'was given to Quaco [Cudjoe's brother] during the reign of George II'. He added that in 1738, at the time of the treaty, when Edward Trelawny was Governor of Jamaica, the town of Falmouth also became the Maroons' seaport. When I remarked that Falmouth had not existed at that time (Besson 2002), Mann retorted: 'but the sea was there'. He then continued:

> This land [the commons] was never made to surveyor [be surveyed and subdivided]. Cudjoe say this land is fe the born and unborn. So like I live over that yard, I die and leave it for me sons and daughters.

Mann himself had been born in Acompong (which he reasserted is Trelawny Town, collapsing the two Leeward treaty towns into one), like his parents before him. In 1991, he narrated:

> I was born just about 7 miles from here in the interior part of this compound, in this same Trelawny Town, at a place call Thatch Bottom. You pass through Farland and go above it, call it Thatch Bottom. Part of the maroon land…My father and mother was born and grow right here in Accompong, in this said Trelawny Town, Cockpit Country. So me was here in the same Trelawny Town, Cockpit Country land. They used to go at crop time to reap them crops [which is why Mann was born at Thatch Bottom].

Eight years later, in 1999, Mann asserted that his birthplace in Accompong territory is 'Anferry's Town'[4]:

> I was born about 7 miles from here in Anferry's Town, Cockpit Country, in the deep woods. That was the name given by Cudjoe. Cudjoe says this place (Anferry's Town/ Farland in the bush) resembles Africa.

Mann had rights to use about ten acres of the treaty land transmitted from his parents through his father's side: 'They got it coming down from the Rowe Family. Four generations now.' The land, which stretches up to the school at the edge of the village and 'into the outskirts' of the commons and is cultivated is (as Mann narrated) 'a family land', passed down 'to several people', including Mann, his siblings and their children, numbering 'quite a few hundred'. However, only Mann, his wife, his son, Jack, and some of Mann's grandchildren resided on the land and many of the co-heirs are in 'England, Canada, Kingston, Montego Bay and elsewhere'.

Mann grew up on this family land in a yard near the school, where his father used to live. Jack now resides there in a house that he built near his grandfather's old house. Mann explained that he himself 'gave a portion of the land to build the school', which was donated by the Canadian government in discussion with the Jamaican Ministry of Education. Mann had built his own house (a stone cottage), in 1944, in a neighbouring yard and lived there until the last few years of his life, when he was moved next door into a modern villa built by one of his granddaughters who lives in Kingston (figure 4.4). When Mann's wife (mother of 11 of his children) died in the 1990s, he broke with maroon tradition and tombed her in his yard. However, in January 2007, he was interred in a sepulchre in the community church cemetery.

Mann's paternal Rowe lineage and its family land overlap with the maternal lineages and lands of some of his children's maroon mothers. For example, Mann's son, Dolphie, lives nearby on land passed down from Dolphie's maternal grandmother.

Figure 4.4. Mann Rowe's house-yard with his old cottage, the new villa and visitors' cars, 2006.

Likewise, Jack cultivates seven acres of bananas (selling them to 'local markets because we don't have lots of banana ships anymore') elsewhere on the commons, where he has usufructuary rights transmitted from his mother's maternal grandmother. Tracing back through this lineage, Jack explained that other members of his mother's family line likewise have rights to use that land but are 'in England, MoBay, Kingston and throughout the island'. I asked whether such land could be sold and he explained:

> No. Maroon land can't be sold. One of the easy ways you get piece [to use] is if you married to a maroon man or a maroon woman. We can't sell the land even among ourselves. We can sell *trees*; for example, to [the Jamaican] government when they are building roads or if someone is building a house and someone has fruit trees, can buy them, cut them down. But the land is not for sale.

Mann and his sons further explained that a Maroon may cultivate outlying land on the commons and it is only if the portion of the land is disputed that the Maroon Council is consulted.

Mann's narratives differed from historical records and geography in some respects, including his assertions that Accompong is Trelawny Town/Anferry's Town, that he lives in Trelawny Town (St James) not in St Elizabeth, and that Cudjoe was born in Africa to an African mother and an English buccaneer (and would, therefore, have been an African mulatto). History indicates that Cudjoe was born in marronage of a 'Coromantee' father in Jamaica and was therefore an Afro-Creole (chapter 2). Regarding Cudjoe's and Nanny's reputed mulatto descent, Mann's narratives raised a point that did not feature in other narratives in Accompong where a dominant theme is Afro-Creole maroon ethnicity. However, mulatto ancestry would emerge as a significant theme in Aberdeen and especially in Maroon Town, where a major motif is 'slave master' pickni' descent, including mulatto maroon ancestry (chapters 6–10).

The Narratives of a Maroon Colonel and his Deputy

In January 2006, after attending the Myal Play on January 6 that year, I discussed the Myal worldview with Colonel Sydney Peddie (who was in his second consecutive term as Colonel [figure 4.5]) and his kinsman, Melvin Currie (on whose family land the Kindah grove is situated). Colonel Peddie (who would become Ex-Colonel in August 2009) is a returned migrant from London, where he lived for over 30 years working as a bus driver, on the railways, at the Mint in Tower Bridge and as a porter and technician in a hospital.

Melvin Currie, who in 2006 was Accompong's Minister of Culture and Tourism, would later become Deputy Colonel for the second time. A farmer, Currie has lived all his life in Accompong except for a few years when he worked as a security guard in Kingston. However, five of his eight children are in Canada and England. I interviewed Peddie and Currie many times and, in January 2006 (and again in March 2009), we not only discussed the Myal worldview but also the difference between Myal, Revival, Obeah and Science, as well as the Rowe Family, whose ancestors are believed to be central to Myalism in Accompong (figure 4.6).

Both Peddie and Currie were born in Accompong in the 1930s and, by 2006, were in their 70s. Both had 'born come see' Revival Seal Grounds in Accompong; in other words, Seal Grounds had existed there ever since they

Figure 4.5. The author and Colonel Sydney Peddie at the Myal Play, 2006.
Photo by Collin Reid.

could remember. They explained that these sacred sites (which are sometimes moved) are created through libations at Revival meetings and are 'touched by the spirits' that reside there. Peddie recalled that when he was a boy in Accompong, they had Revival-Zionists from the parish of St Thomas 'knocking drum' who would go without directions to a Seal Ground – drawn there by the spirits. He observed that Revival 'was the black man's religion, came from Africa' and is 'still strong' as bus-loads of Revivalists had come to visit and stay in Accompong the previous week. In 2006, another Seal Ground was being planned by a Revival Mother who had built a tabernacle in Accompong. Peddie and Currie remarked that they both 'believe in' Revival and 'like it', even though they go to the Presbyterian/United Church, and they attend Revival meetings which are held at night.

However, Peddie explained in 2006, although Myal and Revival are both 'touched by spirits', they are touched by 'different spirits'. Revival concerns 'divine spirits, like Holy spirits from [Revival-]Zion or Pentecostal'. Myal, by contrast, primarily 'concerns the 6th of January – Kindah and Old Town', though some may 'get Myal' at other times. Myal involves 'ancestral spirits, who connect with' the Maroons. As Peddie reiterated: 'Myal now, that ghost isn't holy, it's an ancestor. Two different kinds of ghost there [in Myal and Revival]. Myal now, any ancestor', who does not need to be important or holy. In this respect, he explained, Myal in Accompong is similar to the Kumina Dance in Portland. In Myal (Peddie continued):

> You could find yourself in a trance on the ground and have to be revived by an experienced person, who rubs [you with] white rum. We haven't had any fatalities yet, but could lead to that.

Figure 4.6. The author with Colonel Sydney Peddie (left) and Deputy Colonel Melvin Currie, Accompong, 2009.

Peddie and Currie explained that people who 'are touched' by Myal can walk on broken bottles and that persons who 'get Myal' forget their experience afterwards. When touched by Myal, people can also administer medical herbs to the sick and heal them. Most often, they explained, it is women who get possessed by the ancestors but men can also be possessed. For example, they had seen a male drummer at the recent Myal Play become possessed: 'He just get into the spirit, get into Myal and fell to the ground and started to roll'. In such cases, they explained, 'Rum might bring them out [of the trance], but may need water. They believe a person is dancing with them – ancestral spirit.' They explained that most Myal ancestral connections occur at Kindah, due to the drumming and singing of the Play, rather than at Old Town: as 'sounds bring it out'; in other words, the music induces such connections. I had also observed that those portraying spirit possession at Kindah in recent years had included men as well as women. Indeed, at the Play in 2007, the most dramatic case that I witnessed was a (visiting) man.

In March 2009, I was told by Colonel Peddie and Currie (who was by then Deputy Colonel again) that at the Myal Play on January 6 that year, two Charles Town Maroons (from the Windward polity) who attended the Play had 'got possessed' and that one was a woman and the other a man. Peddie explained that the Charles Town Maroons are prone to spirit possession when they come to Accompong:

> Those from Charles Town always get into this [Myal], because of the songs they sing. Sing them here when they come, bring their own group and drums and use a lot of white rum, like us, because it is traditionally believed that white rum invokes the spirit of the ancestors. White rum [also] brings them round [revives them] when they are flat on the ground.

Discussing the Play on January 6, 2009 and the ancestral connections that were said by these maroon leaders to have occurred on that occasion, I asked naively which spirits had been involved. Currie (who by then had known me for 20 years), chided: 'What a stupid question that!' and indeed, I should have known better. However, Peddie patiently explained: 'All spirits are not the same, some are friendly, some warlike.' Currie interjected, 'Dance Myal' and continued:

> The spirits that we deal with at Kindah [are] our ancestors, Cudjoe, Nanny, Quaco, Cuffee, Johnny, Accompong, all alike. Their cultural activities we are carrying out. Hard to tell which ones [to differentiate among these spirits].

Peddie also explained the relationship between the commons and the ancestors: 'The land is passed down from Cudjoe and Nanny, so the people here is descendants from them'.

In sum then, as the narratives of Peddie and Currie (as well as other Maroons) portray, the Accompong Myal worldview, embedded in the commons, concerns the spirits of the maroon ancestors: especially, those who fought and won the First Maroon War and who manifest themselves particularly at Kindah in the Myal Plays. However, Maroons may be 'touched by Myal' at other times and the spirits involved can include more recent maroon ancestors.

Peddie and Currie, along with other Maroons, also helped me to understand the relationship between Myal and Obeah in Accompong and the transformation of this relationship since slavery days. In the Jamaican Myal-Obeah slave religion, Obeah was believed to be a morally neutral magical/spiritual power that could be accessed from the ancestors through spirit possession (Myal) for protection against the 'sorcery' of slavery (Bilby 1993; Handler and Bilby 2001; Schuler 1979, 1980; Besson 2002). However, as seen from Ena's narrative, in Accompong today, Obeah is distinguished from and contrasted with Myal as an individual negative activity; a transformation that is likely to have occurred due to contact with Presbyterian mission Christianity and Eurocentric views of Obeah (compare Besson 2002, 242–44). In 2006, this contrast between Obeah and Myal was likewise made by Peddie and Currie who explained that 'Obeah is bad mind, bad-minded people' whose activities include manipulating the spirits of the dead ('setting *duppy*') in the grave to harm others.[5]

However, Peddie and Currie continued: 'Some people can block the bad spirits in the grave. Not "block", but "subdue"'; for example, by planting burnt corn on the grave (I had come across this strategy in Trelawny [Besson 2002, 258]), or by making a cross over the grave. Then, as Peddie explained: 'the spirit is not effective, even if it leaves [the grave] and it seems to be working, as they are neutralized'. The 'proof that spirits are not working, are neutralized, [is that] they don't respond if you go to the grave, converse or throw rum, no response for help to harm or Obeah'. This 'power' to neutralize Obeah, they added, 'is passed down' or inherited.

I also discussed with Colonel Peddie, the Rowe Family, Accompong's central clan, to which he belongs through his mother, Victoria Rowe (Genealogy 1). As Victoria was the sister of the late Mann Rowe, Peddie is Mann's nephew and a first cousin to Mann's son, Meredie, these cousins having contested recent elections for Colonel. (Mann's son, Dolphie, whose mother is also a Rowe, and Currie are 'two sisters' children', so Currie is related to Mann and Peddie too.) In 2009, Peddie narrated that, 'The Rowes was one of the biggest Families in Cudjoe's time. They lived in a big house at the foot of the hill, it's now a ruin. From 1923, *that* house, but one before that, long before.'

Peddie explained that his maternal grandfather, Jack (Eugene) Rowe, was (like Mann) a 'scientist'. Jack couldn't read but he would ask his grandson, Peddie, to read his book of spells and recipes for his clients (who visited him 'wanting something done', such as having a stolen cow-chain returned) to 'get influence'; for example, advising them to 'buy oil and drop it on the doorstop'. Mann, who went to school and could read, inherited this book. (Mann had shown it to my husband, John, pointing out that John, a medical doctor, could grasp 'science' – unlike me.) Peddie further narrated that, many years ago, Mann had got the maroon treaty from Charles Reid (the paternal grandfather of the abeng-blower Rupie Reid), who was Acting Colonel.

Regarding the surname Rowe (and other British surnames in Accompong), Colonel Peddie explained that: 'Our names was changed by the British, when the Presbyterian Church came in after emancipation'. Peddie continued that the Church 'changed name from African names' to Christian names and would not record the Maroons' African names. The churches, he explained, were in charge of the schools as well, in Jamaica, and the Presbyterian Church started the school in Accompong. In contrast, he said, 'Myal is a part of the African culture, and [Revival-] Zion and Puku [Pukumina]'. However, these religions also reflect Caribbean creolization (chapters 2–5). In addition, the creolization of naming in Accompong goes back even further than the establishment of the Presbyterian Church there in 1882, at least to the Second Maroon War of 1795–96 and possibly to the early 1770s (chapter 3 n25; see also Besson 1997, 222 n71). Also, as part of their alliance with the colonists in the Second Maroon War, the Accompongs had their younger Maroons baptized (chapter 2).

Up to 2009, Colonel Peddie and Deputy Colonel Currie continued to be prominent leaders in Accompong and, although they both claim Ashanti descent, both continued to contribute to Caribbean creolization. Peddie did so as a returned migrant from London, whose leadership skilfully articulated the Myal worldview with the experience of more than 30 years abroad (see chapter 11). Currie is a pioneer of yard burial and has created elaborate vaults for his parents in their house-yard (where he now lives in a modern concrete house where he is visited by his overseas kin [figure 3.6c]), as well as tombs in the yard of his older house near Kindah. He is guardian of the Kindah grove as it is on his 'family land' (the co-heirs include his brothers, sisters, children, cousins, nephews and neices, many of whom are abroad). Currie traces this family land at least five ascending generations on his paternal grandmother's side: 'as far as we can remember' to his 'father's great-great-grandparents'. However, as Accompong's Minister of Culture and Tourism, Currie was also gatekeeper for the escalating impact of the global tourist industry (chapter 11).

In 2009, Peddie again stood in the elections for Colonel. One of his cousins, Norma Rowe-Edwards, a returned migrant from the United States and a member of the Rowe clan,[6] likewise stood for election to Colonel, being the first woman to stand for this office. Both she and Peddie lost the election and, in August 2009, Inspector Ferron Williams was elected as the 26th Colonel. However, in 2009, Norma Rowe-Edwards became the first female Deputy Colonel of Accompong – a momentous gender transformation in the Leeward Maroon polity. In August 2014 (after this book was completed), Ex-Colonel Peddie died (aged 81) and was buried in the Accompong community church cemetary.

Notes

1. The Freeport in Montego Bay was, however, only built in the mid-twentieth century, by dredging the seas around Bogue Islands, in the bay. It is now a main port of call for cruise ships.
2. Compare Werner Zips (2011, xxxviii), though in Mann Rowe's quotation given there Nanny/'Mathilda Rowe' is said to be his 'great-great-grandmother'. However, in Mann's account to me, he narrated detailed links of the generations that he perceived descended from 'Nyankipong' (who is portrayed as his great-great-grandmother, also named Matilda Rowe like Nanny). Zips (2011, 45) identifies 'Nyankipon' as 'the Asante god of creation'. Kenneth Bilby (2006, 248) translates 'Yankipong' as 'the Supreme God...in the esoteric Kromanti language' of the Windward Maroons.
3. Bilby's spelling (in a 1991 narrative from Colonel Martin-Luther Wright of Accompong) is 'Amferi Town' (2006, 174), though he notes that Mann Rowe spelt it for Laura Tanna (1984, 19) as 'Anferry Town', that Colonel Wright (1994, 66) spelt it as 'Amphrey Town', derived from 'Humphrey Town', but that other Maroons told him it is an 'African name' (Bilby 2006,

447 n41). Zips (2011, 97 n98), citing Mann Rowe, spells it '*Unferie Town* (or Anferry Town)' and claims that I 'render' this as 'Ann Ferry'. However, Zips cites no reference or supportive evidence for this alleged infelicity, and I spell it as Mann Rowe pronounced it to me and as recorded in my field notes: 'Anferry'. Bilby (2006, 447 n41) and Zips (2011, 97 n98) concur that it is a name used in Accompong as the former name of Old Town and a map of 'Accompong Town quarters' by the Ghanaian archaeologist, E. Kofi Agorsah (1994, 171), shows 'OLD TOWN (ANN FERRY)', which is presumably the real source of the misspelling that Zips misattributes to me. Bilby (2006, 447 n41) states that Old Town is 'the original site of Accompong', as does Agorsah (1994, 163, 170). Zips (2011, ix, 117), however, claims that Old Town was a key station in Cudjoe's life and is the site of Cudjoe's grave (see also Agorsah 1994, 171, 181). Cudjoe's Old Town was, however, in St James and as I have shown Old Town in Accompong (in St Elizabeth) is a *symbolization* of Cudjoe's Old Town in St James (Besson 1997, 2005, and chapter 3). Zips (2011, 97 n98), from his Africanist perspective, asserts a possible connection between '*Unferie Town*' and the Twi word *afrihyia*, meaning 'year' and 'a meeting' and refers the reader to Bilby (2006, 447 n41) 'for more sources on the African derived name ánféri'. However, in that note Bilby provides no sources for African derivation and it is interesting that the Ghanaian Agorsah's 'Ann Ferry' above asserts no African link. A possible Jamaican derivation (especially as Mann Rowe states that Anferry was a name for Trelawny Town) is from Furry's Town which was a part of Trelawny Town (Robinson 1969, 66; Campbell 1990, 165, 183, 217; and chapter 2).

4. See note 3 above.
5. This view of Obeah is consistent with the rationale for the Christian burning of the ritual hut at Old Town, in the 1930s, to prevent ancestral spirits being manipulated through Obeah (Kopytoff 1987, 477; see chapter 5).
6. Norma Rowe-Edwards is the grand-niece of the late Mann Rowe, Secretary of State. Her father was Samuel Nathaniel Rowe, whose father James Rowe was one of Mann's brothers (personal communications with Marcus Goffe and Norma Rowe-Edwards, September 13 2012 and September 24, 2012). She is, therefore, first cousin once removed to Mann's sons (e.g., Dolphie, Jack and Ex-Colonel Meredie Rowe) and to Ex-Colonel Peddie and third cousin to the abeng-blower, Hansley Reid, and the Myal dancer, Caroline 'Ena' Wright Lawrence (Genealogy 1).

5 ■ REINTERPRETING ACCOMPONG MAROON SOCIETY

In this chapter, I show that my interpretation in chapters 3 and 4 of the creolization of the commons and the related Myal worldview revises a number of conclusions on Accompong maroon society by anthropologists, archaeologists, geographers and historians. These conclusions by various scholars include the argument that the commons are an African continuity (Barker and Spence 1988; Campbell 1990, 190; Zips 1996, 281, 297; 1998; 1999, 131; 2011); the related dismissal of creolization in Accompong (Zips 2011, 9; 2012); the view that 'Old Town' is either simply the site of the original settlement of Accompong Town (Kopytoff 1987, 476; Carey 1997, 528–29, 616) or/and the actual site of Cudjoe's grave (Agorsah 1994, 163, 170–71, 181; Zips 2011, ix, 117); and the interpretation of the 'Peace Cave' on the commons as the site of the signing of the Leeward Maroon treaty (Agorsah 1994, 172; Zips 2011, x, 116–17). My analysis also revises Barbara Kopytoff's (1987) conclusion on the decline of Myalism in Accompong, Mavis Campbell's (1990, 178) opinion on the Accompong Maroons' so-called confusion regarding Nanny and her burial place and Barry Chevannes's (1995a, 7) observation that there is no longer a religion named Myal in Jamaica.

I first show that the creolization of the commons is a variation on a wider Caribbean theme of creole tenures, rooted in kinship and community, created in the New World social context in response to globalization. I next revise Kopytoff's (1987) conclusion on the decline of Myalism in Accompong, some interpretations of Old Town and the Peace Cave (Kopytoff 1987; Agorsah 1994; Carey 1997, 616), Campbell's (1990, 178) view of Accompong confusion regarding Nanny, and Chevannes's (1995a, 7) conclusion that there is no religion named Myal in Jamaica today. I then assess Werner Zips's (2011, 9; 2012) dismissal of creolization in Accompong and show that his argument does not stand up to closer scrutiny.

The Commons as a Variant of Caribbean Creole Tenures

As outlined in chapter 3, David Barker and Balfour Spence (1988, 201) argued that Accompong's tenurial system is 'quite different from the rest of Jamaica, and even from other Maroon groups on the island', and that it 'has more in common with African than Caribbean tenure systems'. Likewise, Campbell (1990, 190) and Zips (1996, 281, 297; 1998; 1999, 131; 2011) contend that Accompong land tenure is an African continuity.

Common tenure in Accompong does differ from both European-derived legal freehold and the kin-based institutions of 'family land', 'generation property' and 'children's property' widespread throughout the Caribbean region and Jamaica (Besson 1984a, 1997, 2002; Barker and Spence 1988, 200–201). The Accompong commons also reflect non-market principles similar to those of African pre-capitalist land tenures, and the Maroons may have drawn on African heritages to reinforce their common landholding. In addition, in contrast to other Jamaican maroon communities, Accompong common tenure was consolidated in the post-emancipation era (Kopytoff 1979).

However, the Accompong commons derive from Caribbean slave resistance and a colonial treaty, and differ from the unilineal landholding systems of West and Central Africa, including the Akan/Asanti matrilineal landholding kin group or *abusua* that Zips (2011, 165–67) argues is reproduced in Accompong. Moreover, Paul Bohannan (1967, 57) noted that while 'communal ownership' of land may exist in Western capitalist economies, it does not typify traditional African landholding.[1] Furthermore, Accompong's tenurial system shares non-market principles with customary tenures in non-African, as well as African societies, including those found elsewhere in the Caribbean and Jamaica. Accompong common tenure also parallels the commons of the Bahamian Out Islands and Barbuda, where isolated proto-peasantries bordered on marronage (Craton 1987; Berleant-Schiller 1987). Common tenure is likewise found on the coastlands of Guyana and Suriname, on the Carib reservations of Dominica and St Vincent, and among the Black Caribs of Belize (Besson 1995d, 1997, 2002). These examples cross-cut various types of Caribbean 'reconstituted peasantries' (Mintz 1989, 132), originating from dispossessed indigenous cultivators, proto-peasant plantation slaves, post-emancipation peasants and Maroons. The examples not only straddle maroon and non-maroon derivations of African-American slave cultures, but also include Native-Caribbean ethnicities, further questioning African continuity.

In addition, the Accompong commons encompass an emergent cognatic descent system similar to those of the Pacific region and a few East African societies (Goodenough 1955; Caplan 1969; Hanson 1971; Hoben 1973; Webster 1975) and to Caribbean tenures rooted in cognatic descent groups; namely, generation property, children's property and family land. As I have shown elsewhere (e.g., Besson 1984a, 1984b, 1995d, 1997, 2002), such kin-based tenures have been identified not only in non-maroon communities in Jamaica, such as Trelawny's free villages (and as will be seen to characterize Aberdeen and Maroon Town in the Cockpits [chapters 6–10]), but also in Haiti and Providencia; the Virgin Islands of Tortola and St John; the Leeward Islands of Antigua, Nevis, and Montserrat; the Windward Islands of Dominica, Martinique, St Lucia, St Vincent and Grenada; Carriacou and Bequia in the Grenadines; Barbados, Trinidad and Tobago; some Guyanese villages and in urban creole neighbourhoods in Suriname. Moreover, a cognatic descent system interweaves with common land on Barbuda, The Bahamas, the coastlands of Suriname and Guyana, and among the Windward Island Caribs and the Black Caribs of Belize – as in Accompong.

The parallel between Accompong and Barbuda's single village of Codrington is especially close, for both are corporate communities with common land. In both cases, too, common tenure rooted in slavery was consolidated in the face of external pressures after emancipation. In addition, in both Accompong and Codrington, individual rights to trees, which may be transmitted to all descendants, and the cognatic transmission of village yards exists within the context of common land (Besson 1995d, 1997, and chapters 3–4; Berleant-Schiller 1977, 1978, 1987). Riva Berleant-Schiller's (1987, 130) observation that 'true family land' may emerge from the Barbudan commons, due to encroachment by the tourist industry, suggests further parallels with Accompong's emergent cognatic land transmission system of house-yards (and some provision grounds) within the wider framework of the commons.

At the time of Barker and Spence's (1988) study of Accompong maroon agriculture, more work was needed on land and kinship among the Jamaican Windward Maroons. Even then, however, preliminary evidence suggested that cognatic descent had consolidated there, within the context of common land, as in Accompong. Kenneth Bilby had observed of Moore Town in the Windward polity, that:

> Membership in the Maroon community is automatically passed on (bilaterally) from parent to child, and according to traditional Maroon belief, all of the special attributes, knowledge, and powers connected with being a Maroon can only be passed on 'in the blood'. They are seen as being conferred by the original Maroon ancestors (and particularly Nanny) upon their descendants (Bilby 1984b, 14).

Kenneth Bilby's (1996) subsequent analysis illuminates more fully, the relationship between kinship and landholding in Moore Town. He draws a parallel between family land, rooted in an unrestricted cognatic descent system as described by me (Besson 1988a, 48) and Edith Clarke (1966, 48), elsewhere in Jamaica and 'a similar concept of sacred family land' in Moore Town based on common descent from the ancestress, Grandy Nanny, 'conceptualized as the original "owner" of the Maroon treaty lands' (Bilby 1996, 124–25).[2] Bilby rightly qualifies this parallel by noting that, 'in the [Moore Town] Maroon case, this family land extends beyond individual yards or plots to encompass the entire territory held by the community (i.e., the collectively held Maroon treaty lands)'; a landholding system reinforced by burial 'within a specially designated, centralized public cemetery', in contrast to family-land burial grounds (125, 124).

However, Bilby (1996, 139 n10) further notes that this common kin-based landholding system, rooted in descent from Nanny, is qualified by the assertion of some Moore Town Maroons that there are other family lines descended from 'the men and women who fought alongside this founding ancestress'; and that it coexists with 'a few Maroon individuals living on communal land...who have buried relatives in their own yards (for which they have been strongly criticized)'. This parallels the overlapping cognatic clans and lineages and the related and contentious yard-burial pattern emerging in Accompong. The parallels between Moore Town and Accompong are even closer than this evidence suggests, for some Leeward Maroons claim that their central clan is descended through both genders from the First-Time Maroon, Matilda Rowe (chapter 4), who is said to have been Nanny herself and Cudjoe's sister, buried in the Old Town grove in Accompong.

Accompong landholding, therefore, has parallels with customary tenures based on kinship and community among non-maroon peasantries elsewhere in the Caribbean and Jamaica, and with the tenurial system of the Jamaican Windward Maroons. However, Accompong land tenure, based on commonage and cognation through both genders, differs from the matrilineal systems (traced through women only) of the Maroons of Suriname and French Guiana (e.g., S. Price 1993), though it shares the 'cognitive orientations' (Mintz and Price 1992, 10) of these maroon societies, regarding corporate landholding rooted in kinship and community.

Land tenure in Accompong, therefore, straddles the maroon/non-maroon divide and is a variation on a Caribbean 'reconstituted' peasant theme (Mintz 1989, 132); namely, the creation of customary tenures through the process of creolization in response to global capitalist relations and colonially-derived agrarian legal codes (Besson 1984a, 1995d, 1997, 2002). Like Accompong's tenurial system, such Caribbean creole tenures also reflect processes of incorporation in kin groups and communities, preserving threatened environments and villages in contexts of escalating land monopolization by plantations, bauxite mines and tourism. In Accompong, where the symbolic landscape charts the hidden history of this oldest surviving African-American corporate maroon society, the incorporation process is most pronounced.

The dynamics of creolization and incorporation reflected in Caribbean creole tenures can, therefore, be seen as creative strategies appropriating and reversing colonially-derived agrarian-legal institutions, and preserving threatened peasant communities and their lands. These tenures are therefore not an obstacle to development as some scholars argue (e.g., Mathurin 1967; Espeut 1992; compare Hardin 1968 on the 'tragedy of the commons'), but are repositories of hidden history and bases of sustainable development in the face of globalization (see also Besson 1997, 2001, 2002, 2005; Olwig 1997; Lowenthal and Clarke 2007).[3]

Variations on this theme can also be related to Caribbean agrarian capitalist relations. Unrestricted cognatic family-land systems (traced through both genders and including migrants as well as residents), rooted in the proto-peasant adaptation of plantation slaves and maximizing scarce land rights and formerly forbidden kinship lines, have been forged in Antillean peasant communities at the heart of plantation-tourism society – as has occurred in the Jamaican non-maroon adaptations, such as Trelawny's free villages (Besson 2002) and Aberdeen and Maroon Town at the maroon/non-maroon interface (chapters 6–10). At the margins and frontiers of the Caribbean region, such cognatic transmission functions within the wider context of more extensive common land: as in Barbuda, coastal Suriname and Guyana, on the Carib reservations of Dominica and St Vincent, and among the Black Caribs of Belize.[4] Accompong's marginal mountainous reservation, surrounded by plantations, is a variation on this theme. Only in the vast mainland forested interiors of Suriname and French Guiana have rebel slaves and their descendants had the relative autonomy and sufficient land to retain, or forge anew, restricted African-type matrilineal landholding systems (Besson 1995b, 1995d, 1997, 2002). Moreover, such unilineal systems, forged in contexts further removed from capitalism, are more typical of West and Central African pre-capitalist societies with extensive land resources than either the cognatic landholding kin groups or the common tenures created throughout the rest of the Caribbean *oikoumenê*, in the face of globalization, including Accompong.

The Re-Ascendance and Continued Creolization of Myalism

In addition to showing that the sacred landscape of the Accompong Maroons is a variation on Caribbean creole tenures, my research reveals a continuing process of creolization in the Myal Play, reinforcing the creolization of the commons when compared with Kopytoff's (1987) earlier ethnohistorical study. Kopytoff described the ascendance of the Christian God over the 'Town Massa' (Town Master) in Accompong Town's traditional cosmology from the 1930s to the 1970s. At that time, the Town Massa was believed to be the spirit of Captain Accompong (one of Cudjoe's 'brothers' or lieutenants), who was said by the Maroons to often ride 'through the village on his big white horse' (Kopytoff 1987, 475), and the annual ritual was a celebration of his birthday. This celebration included dancing in front of a ritual hut built over Captain Accompong's reputed grave at Old Town, which Kopytoff (1987, 476) described as 'the site of the original settlement' of Accompong Town (a view reiterated by Agorsah [1994, 163, 170, 181] and Carey [1997, 616]). Kopytoff explored the confrontation of the traditional maroon ancestral spirit beliefs with Christianity, crystallized in the mid-1930s in the burning of the ritual hut at Old Town (an event recalled by an elderly Maroon in Aberdeen whom I interviewed, see chapter 6). Kopytoff also examined the related decline of the celebratory dancing and traditional beliefs, and the simultaneous ascendancy of the Christian God over the ancestors into the 1970s.

However, my research shows the re-emergence, strengthening and further creolization of Myalism in Accompong from the 1980s into the twenty-first century (chapters 3–4; see also Besson 1995a, 1995d, 1997, 2005, 2011a). This process of creolization includes the continued embedding of the Myal worldview in the common treaty land, a transformation in the Town Massa's identity and in the related meaning of Old Town and also the creation of the Kindah grove. During the 30-year period of my fieldwork in Accompong (1979–2009), Captain Cudjoe (whose status was superior to his lieutenant, Captain Accompong) has become the main focus of the Myal Play, which, since the 1980s, has commemorated both the signing of Cudjoe's treaty and his birthday (a shift reinforced by the establishment, during my fieldwork, of the monument to Cudjoe in Accompong and the murals of Captain Cudjoe [figures 3.1d and 3.1e]). Another change is that the Play is now held at the edge of the residential zone under the Kindah Tree, which is said to be Cudjoe's 'War Office' where he sat with his lieutenants on the boulders beneath the spreading branches planning guerrilla tactics (figure 3.3i), rather than at the Old Town grove, which is about a mile beyond the village among provision grounds and pastures.

With this transformational focus on Captain Cudjoe in Accompong Town's cosmology and the related re-ascendance of Myalism, Captain Accompong's reputed grave has been symbolically shifted and demoted from Old Town to the grove between Kindah and Old

Town, where Cudjoe's other 'brothers' (Quaco, Cuffee and Johnny) are said to be buried. In addition, the Old Town grove is now said to be the site of Cudjoe's Old Town, including his military 'lookout' (a cockpit mountain covered in cacoon vines) and his burial place (a view taken literally by Agorsah [1994, 171, 181] and Zips [2011, ix, 117]).

However, the actual site of Cudjoe's Town, renamed Trelawny Town after the treaty (which then split into Cudjoe's 'Old Town' and Furry's 'New Town'), and 'Old Maroon Town' after the deportation of the Trelawny Maroons, is 14 miles away in the parish of St James (chapters 2–3, 6–11 and map 8). Although the Accompong Maroons are aware of this former site of Trelawny Town (chapters 6 and 11), they have symbolically relocated Cudjoe's Old Town from St James to Accompong in St Elizabeth; a shift that encapsulates the continuities and disjunctures in Leeward Maroon history (see also Besson 1997, 2005, 2011a). The symbolic shift of Trelawny Town to Accompong Town, reflected in the sign, 'Trelawny Town 1738–39', on Mann Rowe's cottage (figure 4.3) and in Mann and Rupie Reid's narratives (chapter 4), is a variation on this theme. Therefore, while the references to Old Town as the original site of Accompong Old Town by Agorsah (1994, 163, 170, 181) and Carey (1997, 528–29, 616) following Kopytoff (1987, 476) may be correct, this perspective overlooks the symbolic transformation of the Old Town grove,

Map 8.   Trelawny Town Territory August 9, 1795 (The National Archives, Kew), with historic sites highlighted by the author.

since Kopytoff's study, from Captain Accompong's old village to represent Cudjoe's Old Town/Trelawny Town; a transformation that symbolically repairs the fracturing of the Leeward Maroon polity, which occurred with the colonial deportation of the Trelawnys, in 1796, after the Second Maroon War.[5]

As seen in chapter 3, during the now-strengthened Myal Play, the Maroons make a pilgrimage from the reputed African graves at Kindah, through the Afro-Creole First-Time maroon burial grounds (where a sacrificial meal is offered to Cudjoe on an altar at Old Town) and on to the reputed Peace Cave deep in the forest, with its maroon and slave-master war cemetery, where a bottle of rum is placed inside the cave for Cudjoe. The Ghanaian archaeologist, E. Kofi Agorsah (1994, 172), and the Austrian anthropologist, Werner Zips (2011, x, 116–17), take this location of the Peace Cave literally.[6] However, my research indicates that the Peace Cave, too, has been symbolically shifted from St James to Accompong in St Elizabeth; for the Leeward treaty was signed at Petty River Bottom, the satellite-citadel of Cudjoe's Town in St James (chapter 2 and map 8), a conclusion that illuminates Agorsah's (1994, 172) assumption that the shape of the 'Peace Cave' has changed.[7] This symbolic shift, like that of Cudjoe's Old Town, reinforces the continuity and identity of the fractured and shrunken but enduring Leeward Maroon polity.

The narrative shifting of Cudjoe's life and death, from Cudjoe's Town/Trelawny Town to Accompong, also repairs the internal disjuncture within Accompong Town itself, resulting from the religious change (the eclipse of the ancestors by the Christian God) between the 1930s and the 1970s, reported by Kopytoff (1987), reinstating the re-ascendance of Myalism in an ongoing process of creolization (see also Besson 1997, 216–17 n60; 2001, 96–97 n36). As discussed in chapter 3, since the 1990s, the Myal Play has been even further creolized, becoming a symbol of Jamaican nationhood and a mode of participation in the island's tourist industry, developments reflected in the Civic Function at Monument and Parade, as well as becoming a magnet for Maroons overseas (see also chapter 11). The whole sequence of sacred sites traversed by the Myal pilgrimage therefore reflects a continuing process of creolization from African/Afro-Creole enslavement and resistance to Caribbean freedom and transnational Jamaican nationhood.

As well as revising Kopytoff's (1987) conclusion on Myal's demise in Accompong and reinterpreting Old Town and the Peace Cave, my research clarifies the so-called confusion regarding the maroon ancestress, Nanny, and her burial place raised by Campbell (1990). Campbell notes that both the Windward Maroon community of Moore Town and the Leeward Maroons of Accompong 'have claimed Nanny, some holding that she was the "sister", others the "wife", of Cudjoe – which would shatter the generally held view that she was of the windward's' (178). Campbell states that, 'Equally confusing is the fact that both these communities have burial places for Nanny', and adds that in Accompong, Nanny's reputed burial place 'is so sacred, that, ironically, the author was not permitted a visit, on the grounds that no woman is allowed there' (178).

However, as mentioned earlier, I have twice been taken by Maroons on the route of the Myal pilgrimage, including Old Town, where Nanny as well as Cudjoe is said to be buried. These journeys enriched my understanding of the shifting sites of the sacred landscape and its transforming but enduring Myal rituals. The ritual relocation of Cudjoe's Old Town to Accompong Town and the symbolic shifting of Cudjoe's grave to Accompong's Old Town grove symbolically redraw and tighten the boundary of the Leeward Maroon polity around the surviving Accompong community. Simultaneously, the claim in Accompong that Nanny is buried there at Old Town symbolically expands the Leeward Maroon boundary to include the Windward Maroons, who attend the Myal Play in Accompong and participate in the pilgrimage to Old Town and the Peace Cave. This inclusion of the Windward Maroon polity in the Leeward Myal ritual strengthens Jamaican maroon ethnicity, which is rooted in the First Maroon War and the Leeward and Windward Maroon treaties of 1738/39 in which both Cudjoe and Nanny played central roles.

My revision of Campbell's view of maroon confusion may be taken further still. The symbolic relocation of the burial place of Nanny from the Windward polity to the Old Town grove in Accompong, where Cudjoe is likewise said to be buried, highlights the complementary male and female principles at the heart of Leeward Maroon society that have reinforced the enduring polity through gendered land transmission, marriage, descent, work and ritual. Throughout my research, Accompong Maroons stressed Nanny's status to be that of Cudjoe's sister. This reputed sister-brother sibling bond represents the sacred origin of the gendered creole cognatic system of descent and land transmission, traced through both women and men, which incorporates and perpetuates the Accompong community and its commons (chapter 3; see also Besson 1997, 1998a, 2001, 2005).

In some Accompong narratives Nanny is referred to as 'Accompong Nanny' or 'Campong Nanny, and identified as the ancestress, Matilda Rowe, of Accompong Town's central clan (chapter 4). 'Campong Nanny, likewise, features in Maroon Town narratives and is sometimes identified there as the ancestress, Betsy Currie; a transformation I explore in chapters 8–9.

My above conclusions also show that Chevannes's (1995a, 7) observation that, 'There is no religion in Jamaica today to which the name Myal applies' is not entirely accurate, as Myalism endures in Accompong. However, in Accompong, Myal coexists with both Revival and Rastafari, which are likewise transformations of the Afro-Creole Myal slave religion (Chevannes 1995b; Besson and Chevannes 1996; Besson 2002, 2009), reflecting yet further creolization.[8] There is a Revival tabernacle and at least three 'Seal Grounds' in Accompong and some Myalists attend Revival rituals. The Seal Grounds are sacred sites, where Revival meetings may be held, which are perceived to be associated with Revival spirits and with their spiritual protection and healing and that are believed to protect various areas of the village. In addition, the kin-based cemeteries emerging in house-yards within the wider framework of the commons with their symbolic Myal ancestral burial grounds, parallel Revival family-land cemeteries in non-maroon communities, including Trelawny's free villages (Besson 2002), Aberdeen and Maroon Town (chapters 6–10).

Likewise, some Accompong maroon men are Rastafarians as well as Myalists. These Rastafarians participate in the maroon economy through farming, raising livestock and making crafts such as gumbay drums for the tourist industry. As in the other Jamaican communities that I studied, their Rastafarian identity is reinforced by networking with Rastafari organizations elsewhere in the island such as The Twelve Tribes in Kingston (Besson 1995a, 1995c, 2002, 2009). This island-wide network of Rastafarians was highly visible at the Myal Plays that I attended in the new millennium (chapter 11).

In Accompong, Myalism also coexists with the Presbyterian/United Church,[9] established in Accompong at the invitation of the Maroons in the late nineteenth century (Kopytoff 1987); for, as Maroons explained to me, they 'practise' Christianity but 'Myal is a gift from the spirits'. The Myal Play, which is said by Maroons to have been performed in Accompong for more than 270 years (since the treaty of 1738/39), therefore endures at the heart of Accompong maroon society, facilitated by creolization.

However, Werner Zips, whose ethnography of Accompong (e.g., Zips 1996, 1998, 1999, 2011) complements my own (Besson 1995a, 1995d, 1997, 1998a, 1999a, 2000, 2001, 2003a, 2005, 2009, 2011a) in many ways, dismisses my interpretation of creolization in Accompong (Zips 2011, 2012). I next address Zips's critique and show that his dismissal of creolization does not stand up to closer scrutiny.

Assessing the Dismissal of Creolization in Accompong

Werner Zips's recent book, *Nanny's Asafo Warriors: The Jamaican Maroons' African Experience* (2011), represents the culmination of his research on Accompong (undertaken mainly in 1984–85, with later visits) and Ghana (from the 1990s). His central aim is to challenge Eurocentric colonial portrayals of the Maroons (which he does well) and to prove that the political and legal organization of Accompong is a continuity from West Africa and that there are, therefore, plural legal systems, based on European and African traditions, in Jamaica (see also Zips 1996, 1998, 1999). On these latter points, this erudite Austrian lawyer and legal anthropologist, in many ways, presents a persuasive argument, highlighting parallels in political and legal organization between the Accompong Maroons and the Akan peoples, especially the Asante kingdom, of the former slave-trading Gold Coast. These parallels focus particularly on his interpretation of 'Kromanti' as an overall politico-legal Jamaican maroon complex that stands for the point of African displacement (Fort Kormantine on the Gold Coast) and for common African experiences in Jamaica.

However, despite drawing on Sidney Mintz and Richard Price's (1976) theory of Caribbean 'culture-building' (Zips 2011, 39, 41), Zips (2011, 9) misinterprets as 'intermingling' and dismisses in a single sentence the powerful analytical concept of creolization central to Mintz and Price's approach (see also Zips 2012). Zips states (in the context of asserting that the Maroons illustrate the conflict of European and African traditions in Jamaican legal pluralism) that:

> the discrepancies between the two clashing cultures issue a warning not to be too quick to impose a concept of *intermingling* (syncretism, *creolisation* or hybridisation) on the 'African logic of praxis' (2011, 9, my emphases).

This outdated functionalist view of creolization (Brathwaite 1971) surprisingly ignores the substantial recent literature (since 1971) developing the concept of creolization anthropologically to focus on dynamic Caribbeanization or 'indigenization'/localization (Mintz 1996b, 43) and culture-building in contexts of class conflict or 'contention' (Bolland 2002, 38), and across the boundaries of class, in the unique experience of intense displacement and re-rooting that characterizes the Caribbean *oikoumenê* (e.g., Mintz and Price 1976, 1992; Mintz 1996a, 301; 2010; Sheller 2003; Romberg 2005; Trouillot 1998; Davis-Palmer 2005, 46; 2010; Besson 1995d, 1997, 2002, 2011a and chapter 1). For example, in my ethnography of Trelawny free villages, my use of the concept of creolization focused on the appropriation and transformation or reversal of European institutions through the agency of the enslaved and their descendants (Besson 2002). Zips also overlooks the central theme of creolization in the work of leading maroon specialists (e.g., Price 1996, 29–30; 2001; 2006; 2008, 395 n3; Bilby 2006, 28, 70). In addition, without fully considering my argument, Zips (2011, 2012) parodies and dismisses my creolization perspective on Accompong maroon society (Besson 1995a, 1995d, 1997, 1998b, 2011a), despite the fact that our ethnographies complement each other in many ways.

However, Zips's dismissal of creolization in Accompong leads, in turn, to at least eight further limitations in his own study. First, there is little sense of the wider Jamaican and Caribbean contexts in which Jamaican maroon society in general and the Leeward Maroon polity in particular evolved to the present during the some 300 years that separate the Maroons from Africa. For example, there is little insight into the multi-stranded relations that developed among Maroons, slaves and colonists and their descendants, or even between the two Leeward Maroon treaty towns. In addition, apart from passing references to Trelawny Town (formerly Cudjoe's Town, in St James), the primary Leeward Maroon community in the eighteenth century, Accompong Town (in St Elizabeth), is portrayed as the centre of the historic Leeward Maroon polity (like Agorsah 1994, 170). Yet, Accompong only became ascendant after the Second Maroon War (1795–96), the deportation of the Trelawny Maroons to Canada in 1796 and the colonial confiscation of Trelawny Town treaty land. Moreover, despite Zips's (1999, xi, 12, 249 n50; 2011, 249) indication that he conducted research in Maroon Town (which has evolved on the former site of Trelawny Town), I could find no evidence of his study of Maroon Town.[10] In addition, no comparisons are made between the maroon land tenure and kinship systems and those of other Jamaican and Caribbean rural communities, although such similarities exist (see, e.g., Besson 1995b, 1997, 2000, 2002, 2003c and this chapter). Also, Zips (2011) does not consider the maroon struggle as a variation on a wider theme that includes other Caribbean slave responses such as those of plantation slaves who opposed slavery in more subtle ways (a point likewise made in Mutabaruka's [2011] Epilogue to Zips's book) and whose descendants today have various relationships with the Maroons, as I show in this ethnography (see also Mintz 1989; Besson 1999a, 2002, 2005).

Second, complementing this virtual absence of wider Jamaican and Caribbean historical and social contexts, there is geographical confusion in Zips's study of Accompong. He states that, 'The Abeng is blown at the entrance of [the] Peace Cave – the same place it "sounded freedom" some 270 years ago for the Leeward Maroons' (2011, x) and that 'Going by the *oral traditions*, various battles were fought here [at the Peace Cave in Accompong] prior to the peace treaty and, ultimately, the treaty was concluded here as well' (116) (my emphasis). Likewise, Zips states that Old Town is 'the place of origin and site of Kojo's and other *first-time* Maroons' graves' (2011, ix, see also 117) and that Kindah, Old Town and the Peace Cave in Accompong were the '"key stations in his [Kojo's/Cudjoe's] life' (117).[11] However, the Leeward Maroon treaty was made near Cudjoe's Town/Trelawny Town (now Maroon Town) in St James, where Cudjoe was based (chapter 2), rather than in the secondary Leeward village of Accompong in St Elizabeth (which was under the leadership of Cudjoe's lieutenant, Captain Accompong).[12] As I have shown in chapter 3 and earlier in this chapter, the 'Peace Cave' in Accompong may, therefore, rather be understood as a symbolic site that has been shifted on the landscape. Likewise, 'Old Town' in Accompong is now a symbolization of Cudjoe's Town/Trelawny Town/Old Town/Old Maroon Town, in St James (see maps 5 and 8). These symbolizations are part of the creative creolization process, whereby the Accompong Maroons have re-incorporated the fractured and shrunken Leeward Maroon polity on their remaining common treaty land and have made, through narratives and rituals, for themselves and their world-travellers 'a place to continue to be' (Rapport 2000, 74 in Besson 2005, 17; see also Besson 1995a, 1995d, 1997, 1999a, 2000, 2001, 2009, 2011a).

Third, Zips does not address the evidence that the Cudjoe's Day festival reflects creolization. He notes that, in the 1930s, Archibald Cooper reported that the ghosts of four siblings 'Accompong, Nanny, Cuffee, Quankee', were believed to live under four cotton trees at Old Town, that 'until recently' a house was built over Accompong's grave at Old Town 'in which were kept all the sacred paraphernalia of the Accompong cult' and that 'It was in front of this house that the annual feast in honour of Accompong's birthday was held' (Cooper 1939, 4 in Zips 2011, 117). However, Zips plays this down in an endnote (130 n47), concluding that this former focus on Accompong rather than on Cudjoe is insignificant for his analysis. Zips also seems unaware of (and does not cite) Kopytoff's (1987) related article, noting that, from the 1930s to the 1970s, there had been a decline in Myalism in Accompong following the burning, by a Maroon Colonel, of the ritual hut over Accompong's grave at Old Town and a related ascendance of Christianity in Accompong maroon cosmology. As I discussed earlier, this indicates that the shifting focus to Cudjoe (who outranked Accompong) at Kindah has emerged since Kopytoff's fieldwork in the late 1960s and 1970s, resulting from a re-ascendance and strengthening of Myalism in the face of escalating external pressures from globalization (see also Besson 1997, 2005, 2009, 2011a).[13] This transformation from the focus on Captain Accompong at Old Town to Captain Cudjoe at Kindah (and at Old Town, the Peace Cave and the Monument), clearly indicates that Myalism in Accompong (which derives from the Jamaican creole Myal slave religion forged from African religions as a protection against enslavement and further transformed in marronage) has continued to evolve through creolization (Schuler 1979; Besson 1997, 2009, 2011a).[14]

This transformation from the focus on Captain Accompong at Old Town to Captain Cudjoe at Kindah (and, therefore, the recent creation of Kindah) also indicates that Zips's (2011, 104) interpretation of 'Kindah' as derived from the Twi word *kyinie* for the royal umbrellas (and *kyini* for their 'circling' or rotation) symbolizing the rituals of renewal of the political authority of the Asante high-ranking chiefs and king among the Akan of Ghana is not entirely 'obvious' (127 n24), as several centuries separate Kindah from Africa. Indeed, Zips himself concedes that the parallel between 'Kindah' and *kyinie* may be 'mere coincidence' (113).

Instead, the reference point for Kindah is the common creole *kinship* that is said by Accompong Maroons to have been forged (through 'tribal' intermarriage) to fight the First Jamaican Maroon War (1725–38/39) and that characterizes the maroon community, which is portrayed as cognatically descended through both males and females from Cudjoe and Nanny (Besson 1997, 2005 and chapters 3–4). The link between 'kin' and 'Kindah' was made explicit to me by Melvin Currie (then Deputy Colonel) in June 1995, as we sat under the Kindah Tree. It was also contextualized by Currie within the oral traditions of the Tree as Captain Cudjoe's 'War Office' in the First Maroon War and the uniting of the African 'tribes' under the Tree, through marriage alliance, to forge a vibrant kin-based community (symbolized by the fruitful 'common' or 'stringy' mango tree):[15]

> [The Kindah Tree] is a... stringy/common mango tree...hundreds, thousands of mangoes for this one, [on] all the limbs. As I said, the War was fought between 1655 and 1738. And all the battle plans for that War was made under this tree. These stones [large smooth boulders] that you see, they are stones that were placed for seating. This was where the people sit, the officers of the community, and makes their plans for the battle. In other countries, you'd call this the War Office. [It was] under this tree also that the different tribes unite. *That's why the tree is named 'Kindah'; [that means] 'kin', we are kin, we are family. All three tribes*[16] *join together make one family, one big family. So they call the tree 'Kindah'. All of us are kin and family, we are fighting for one cause. And that's how the intermarriage between the tribes began* (my emphasis).

The link between 'kin' and 'Kindah' was likewise made explicit by Currie to Kenneth Bilby when he visited Accompong in 1999:

> Now, for survival, they could not [have stayed divided] in their [different] groups, they could not have survived very long. So it was under that mango tree that Kojo calls all leaders of all tribes to sit under that mango tree. And under that mango tree now they form a pact, that we are one family, we are *kin*, so let us join together and put our resources together, and fight the British. Because we are from one place, we are the same people, we are *kin*, and we are free. So therefore let us put everything together and fight the British here, and see if we can win. *Hence the tree was known as 'Kindah': 'we are a family'* (Bilby 2006, 87) (my emphases).

Bilby adds, in an endnote:

> This oral tradition demonstrates with perfect clarity that, as Jean Besson points out, 'this fruitful mango tree, with its sign proclaiming common *kinship*, is a powerful incorporating symbol of the creole maroon community' (Besson 1997, 217). (Bilby 2006, 439 n18, my emphasis).

Moreover, Currie even highlighted to Zips, himself, the link between Kindah and kinship:

Kindah, the meaning of the word Kindah is that we all are *family*. Now when we say 'we all are *family*' it only means that the Maroons are different Africans from the tribes that came here into Accompong to unite themselves as one people to fight for a common cause (Zips 2011, 110) (my emphases).¹⁷

This role of the fruitful Kindah Tree in symbolizing the common creole kinship forged among the Accompong Maroons in marronage and freedom is a variation on a wider *Caribbean* theme as Mimi Sheller (2012) highlights in her work on power, resistance, oppositional culture, agency and freedom in Caribbean societies; for, as Sheller notes, 'Trees have long been at the center of social and political struggles in the Caribbean' (201). Summarizing her chapter on 'Arboreal Landscapes of Power and Resistance' (187–209), Sheller (2012) writes that this chapter:

> examines how trees in particular have been used to identify, symbolize, demarcate, and sustain various Caribbean places, meanings, and lives. ...I focus especially on the contestation of colonial arboreal landscapes of power by Afro-Caribbean agents who reclaim particular trees for their projects of survival and meaning-making – sacred ancestral trees, liberty trees, family land trees, gathering-place trees (15).

Discussing the caption of a recently-discovered photograph of 'The Cotton Tree at the Cross Roads near Morant Bay where the rebels assembled immediately before the attack on the Court House', in the Jamaican Morant Bay Rebellion of 1865 (139), and including reference (137) to 'the sacred Kindah tree of the Accompong Maroons in Jamaica (Besson 1997, 214)', along with a wide range of other examples, Sheller argues that, 'particular trees have special symbolic meanings and social functions within indigenous Caribbean, African Caribbean, and Indo-Caribbean cultures' (2012, 137). She further contends that:

> Through a study of trees and their relation to humans, I suggest, we can track the competing ordering, reordering, and *disordering* of the *Caribbean landscape* and *the social struggles that came to be materialized in that landscape* – a kind of citizenship from below the ground itself (Sheller 2012, 193) (emphases added).

Situated within this wider Caribbean societal context, Sheller's perspective underlines my argument that the Kindah Tree in Accompong is a powerful symbol of the common creole Leeward Maroon *kinship* forged through creative *Caribbean agency* in marronage and freedom in and after Jamaica's First Maroon War in the Cockpits to the present, rather than an 'obvious' continuity from the rituals of renewal of the political authority of the Asante high-ranking chiefs and king and a derivation of the Twi name *kyinie* for the royal umbrellas (and *kyini* for their 'circling' or rotation) symbolizing such authority, as Zips (2011, 127 n24, 104) contends.

Fourth, despite identifying the significance of the (possibly classificatory) sibling relationship between Cudjoe and Nanny and highlighting the parallel with the chief's and queenmother's roles in the Asante royal *abusua* or matrilineal kin group, Zips does not explore the creole descent system that has evolved in Accompong and which is at the heart of the 'Family Reunion' at Kindah. In matriliny, descent is traced through women *only* and the descendants of men are excluded, thereby restricting the size of the landholding kin group as in West African societies with their extensive land resources (as also occurs in the vast forested interiors of French Guiana and Suriname inhabited by their Maroons). However, in Accompong, descent is claimed from Cudjoe and/or Nanny, through *both women and men*, in a system of unrestricted cognatic descent (Besson 1995d, 1997, 2000, 2005 and chapter 3). As in many other parts of the Antilles, this creole cognatic transformation of African matriliny maximizes in the Caribbean context family lines and scarce kin-based land rights among the descendants of chattel slaves who were legally kinless and landless and property themselves. As discussed above, it is this creole cognatic descent system that provides a central basis for incorporating the Leeward Maroon polity in Accompong and that is symbolized by the sign, 'Kindah, One Family' (which during my fieldwork replaced earlier signs, 'Kindah, We are Family' and 'Kindah, The Family Tree') on the Kindah Tree. However, Zips (2011, 101 n127) dismisses my interpretation of cognatic descent, despite quoting Bilby's evidence of similar 'bilateral' descent traced through both genders among the Windward Maroons (Bilby 1996, 125, quoted in Zips 2011, 165–66) – interpreting this instead as evidence of Asante matriliny (165–66).[18]

Fifth, while Zips does not distinguish oral tradition from geography in relation to Old Town and the Peace Cave (as discussed above), he paradoxically dismisses my report of the Accompong oral tradition of an alliance among reputed African ethnic groups through inter-marriage made under the Kindah Tree to oppose the slave-plantation military regime because it does not support his view of *Kromanti* jural incorporation. In misrepresenting this maroon oral tradition as my personal assumption (Zips 2011, 101 n123), overlooking my references to this being 'said' or 'stated' by the Maroons, Zips inadvertently discards the *Maroons' own view* of the *Jamaican* origin of their creole maroon polity (Besson 1997, 1999a). Yet Zips himself refers to the oral tradition of African ethnic groups ('Kongo', 'Coromantee' and 'Ashanti') and their reputed 'tribal' burial grounds (2011, 77, 78, 79, 81, 96 n94, 102 n130, 109, 110, 125 n12). He also refers to the unity transcending various ethnicities in Accompong (80, 109) but does not explore the role of the oral tradition of 'tribal' inter-marriage in portraying this unity.

Sixth, although Zips draws repeatedly (69, 125, 128 n33 and sometimes unreferenced, 96 n90, 108) on my concept of the 'symbolic landscape' in Accompong (Besson 1997, 210 ff), he does not examine or contextualize the creolization perspective that generated this concept. This creolization process is reflected in the sequence of sacred sites that the Maroons have created on the commons: the reputed African ethnic burial grounds in the bush surrounding Kindah, the reputed graves of the Afro-Creoles Cuffee, Quaco, Johnny and Accompong (whose symbolic burial place has been demoted from Old Town) among provision grounds and pastures in a grove near Old Town, the reputed graves of the Afro-Creole Cudjoe and Nanny at Old Town, the reputed graves of Jamaican maroon warriors and British soldiers at the 'Peace Cave' near Aberdeen, the interment of Jamaican Maroons in the Presbyterian/United church cemetery, the emerging pattern of burial in house-yards and the recent procession to Monument and Parade. This sequence of sacred sites reflects a transformation through time and space, created and perceived by the Maroons, from African enslavement to Caribbean freedom and Jamaican maroon identity (Besson 1997, 2005, 2011a, 2012a, 2012b and chapter 3).

Zips (2011, 125–26 n14), likewise, decontextualizes my reference to the creolization process reflected in the changing signs on the Kindah Tree,[19] omitting the reason that I gave: namely, 'the new role of the Myal ritual and the Kindah grove in the contexts of Jamaican nationhood and the tourist industry' (Besson 1997, 214 n54). Indeed, there is no discussion in Zips's book of the growing relationship in Accompong between the Cudjoe's Day festival and the Jamaican post-colonial state and its international tourist industry (see Besson 1997, 2011a, 2012a, 2012b, and chapters 3 and 11).

Seventh, Zips's dismissal of creolization results in his arguing for some African derivations that are not entirely convincing. For example, in addition to his speculation that 'Kindah' is derived from the Asante Twi words *kyinie* for 'royal umbrella' and *kyini* for their 'circling' or rotation (Zips 2011, 104, 127 n24) – despite the recent creation of the Kindah grove and the Kindah Tree's link with both 'kinship' and the Caribbean symbolism of trees (discussed above) – he argues that cooking yams for the Cudjoe's Day festival is a continuity of West African yam festivals. However, the yams cooked at Kindah commemorate the role of provision ground cultivation in Jamaican marronage. Likewise, the use of pigs for the Myal feast highlights the hunting of wild boar in the fighting-maroon economy (Besson 1997, and chapters 3–4; cf. Zips 2011, 70). In addition, the use of male yams, male pigs and male fowls at Kindah, and the prescription that the hogs and cocks sacrificed for the feast should be black or brown symbolizes the Jamaican racialized class war fought in marronage. Similarly, the wearing of vines by the Maroons returning to Kindah from Old Town symbolizes the role of the cacoon vine (with its giant bean pods) as both food and battle camouflage in the First Maroon War (Besson 1997, 1998a, 2005 and chapters 3–4). This *Jamaican* war forms a central reference point for Accompong maroon society that is as powerful as ancestral African experiences.

Likewise, the 'Parade Ground' or 'playing field' in Accompong is portrayed by the Maroons as their ancestors' drilling ground in the First *Jamaican* Maroon War. Moreover, Parade has parallels not only with the drilling ground of the Akan *asafo* warriors (Zips 2011, 73) but also with the drilling ground of the British colonial soldiers established at Flagstaff on the former site of Cudjoe's Town/Trelawny Town after the Second Maroon War, a flattened area now referred to as 'Ball Ground' and used for Emancipation festivals in Maroon Town (chapters 2–3, 7–8 and 11). Therefore, as M.G. Smith (1960, 44) observed, we must be cautious in asserting African derivations for Caribbean practices that may simply be parallels. Richard and Sally Price have likewise pointed out, in relation to the Saramaka Maroons of Suriname, that African parallels do not necessarily denote African derivations (R. Price 1996, 29–30; S. Price 2006, 106, 111).

Eighth, while Zips's assertion of legal pluralism in Jamaica on the basis of his interpretation of Accompong's legal system as African-derived is central to his argument, he does not address the Caribbean plural society debate and the challenge to plural society theory from Caribbean creolization (e.g., M.G. Smith 1965a; Besson 2002, 2011a; Meeks 2011).[20] Furthermore, Caribbean creole tenures, including the Accompong commons, articulate with official legal systems in complex ways that go beyond the concept of legal pluralism (Besson 1997, 1999a, 2002, 2011a).

Therefore, while African cognitive orientations and symbols are undoubtedly significant in Accompong, and would have been especially so among the early Maroons, equal weight needs to be given to the process of Caribbean creolization, particularly in the more recent generations of this Jamaican Maroon community. As Richard Price observed, the process of creolization in African-American maroon societies has gone furthest among the Maroons of Jamaica who have had 'increasing contact with the rest of Jamaican society' (1996, 228). Price noted that this process of creolization could only be understood by carrying out 'sensitive in-depth field work...in the immediate future' (229), a task I address in this book. In addition to such fieldwork in Accompong itself (Besson 1995a, 1995d, 1997, 2005, and chapters 3–6 and 11), attention needs to be given to similarities and differences in creolization between the Accompong maroon society and Jamaican non-maroon communities – such as Trelawny's free villages in the plantation heartlands (Besson 2002) and Aberdeen and Maroon Town in the Cockpits (chapters 6–11).

Zips (1996, 1998, 1999 and 2011) does not explore the relationship between Accompong and such other Jamaican communities. Yet, Maroon Town evolved on the former site of Trelawny Town, the primary Leeward Maroon treaty town (and the largest Jamaican maroon community [Kopytoff 1979, 62 n2]), which features significantly in the history, narratives and symbolic landscape of the Accompong Maroons. Likewise Aberdeen (which Zips does not mention) is prominent in the Accompong Maroons' discussions of their treaty land (chapters 2–6). The remainder of this book addresses and develops these neglected themes, which also contribute to understanding comparative creolization in maroon and non-maroon derivations of African-American slave cultures (chapter 1), unravelling similarities and differences in creolization between Accompong, Maroon Town and Aberdeen such as their narratives, ethnicities and kinship and landholding systems. Chapter 6 begins this fuller exploration by focusing on the maroon/non-maroon interface between the three communities, including narratives collected on this theme in Accompong and Aberdeen – as well as my own historical and anthropological research on Aberdeen.

Notes

1. Paul Bohannan also stated that, 'in a fully developed, contractually oriented society like our own, communal ownership can and does exist. That is to say, the commune, whatever its nature, can be viewed as a jural person. As a corporation aggregate, it is capable of owning property under the law. The difficulty [misinterpretation of African landholding as "communal ownership"] arises because this fiction has been used by many Westerners to make sense out of most African land systems....' He adds that, 'The indigenous basis of grouping is kinship in some parts of Africa, while in others it is a village community...In *no* place in Africa did the basis of grouping depend indigenously on contract' (Bohannan 1967, 57, quoted in Besson 1997, 223 n75). Seen from this perspective, the Accompong commons clearly derive from the contract of a colonial treaty in the context of a Western capitalist market economy, rather than from pre-capitalist African retentions.

2. Both Kenneth Bilby (1984b, 14; 1996, 125) and Clarke (1966, 61–62) used the older term 'bilateral' to refer to descent and land transmission through both genders. In anthropological kinship theory, when referring to ancestor-focused descent, 'bilateral' has now generally been replaced by the term 'cognatic' (which also replaced the term 'non-unilineal' descent), with 'bilateral' being reserved for ego-focused personal kinship networks which (unlike descent groups) do not endure beyond the death of the focal individual (see, e.g., Goodenough 1955; Solien 1959; Fox 1967; Besson 1974, 1979, 1987b, 106–108, 2002).
3. David Barker and Balfour Spence's (1988) study of Accompong maroon agriculture, likewise, shows that the Accompong tenurial system is a basis of sustainable development in contexts of dependency and vulnerability generated by the world economy.
4. In the Leeward Island of Nevis, where the stranglehold of the plantation system virtually stifled the emergence of free villages, the principles of commonage and unrestricted descent are emerging within imposed leasehold land settlements in a situation of constraint with continuities from the proto-peasant past (Momsen 1987; Besson and Momsen 1987; Besson 1992a, 1995d, 201). However, Karen Olwig (1993, 130–131; 1995, 112) has identified family land even in Nevis; this is consistent with my hypothesis regarding regional variations.
5. This symbolic shift of Trelawny Town to Accompong is likewise taken literally in a recent article in the main Jamaican newspaper advertising the screening of Roy T. Anderson's film *Akwantu: The Journey*, in Accompong. The article included the statement that: 'This year is the 275th independence anniversary of the victory of *the Trelawny Town Maroons of the Sovereign State of Accompong*' (Paul H. Williams, 'Overseas Maroons screen film this weekend', *Jamaica Gleaner*, Saturday, January 5, 2013, my emphasis).
6. E. Kofi Agorsah's (1994) analysis of the 'Archaeology of Maroon Settlements in Jamaica' seems to contain some incorrect factual information on Accompong Town due to (1) the fact that, as he states, 'The Accompong excavation was too small and limited' (183); (2) his discussion contains inaccuracies regarding the geographical location of some Leeward Maroon sites; and (3) he conflates oral traditions with historical facts. For example, in addition to mislocating the Peace Cave (and Cudjoe's likely burial place) in St Elizabeth, rather than at Cudjoe's Town/Trelawny Town in St James, Agorsah states that, 'Accompong was granted some 1,500 acres of land, 1,000 of which was for Accompong itself. Trelawny Town was another such settlement near Accompong' (1994. 170). However, in addition to misinterpreting the relative importance of the two Leeward Maroon treaty towns and portraying Accompong as the primary rather than the secondary Leeward village, Agorsah misinterprets the Leeward Maroon land grant. As noted in chapter 2 and earlier in this chapter, the initial Leeward treaty grant of 1,500 acres was land north-west of Trelawny Town in St James; this land grant was increased to 2,559 acres in 1756–58 to include Accompong's Town and its surrounding territory in St Elizabeth (Campbell 1990, 127, 181–83). I assess Werner Zips's interpretations of Accompong more fully later in this chapter.
7. E. Kofi Agorsah, in asserting that the actual 'Peace Cave site is located almost on the eastern border of the Accompong Maroon lands', and that the actual 'Peace Cave' was 'referred to as Pettee River Bottom', concludes that, 'The physical appearance of the cave appears to have changed over time and no longer fits the description in reported documents and photographs' (Agorsah 1994, 172). Agorsah (1994, 172) cites Alan Eyre (1980) as his reference for the location

of the Peace Cave/Pettee River Bottom on Accompong territory in St Elizabeth. However, the geographer, Alan Eyre (9–13) clearly indicates that the Peace Cave/Pettee River Bottom were on the outskirts of Cudjoe's Town/Trelawny Town in St James. This mis-location of the actual Peace Cave by Agorsah undoubtedly accounts for his assumption that the shape of the cave has changed.

8. Some Accompong Maroons are also Pentecostalists.
9. A sign outside the church in Accompong states that in 1965 'the Presbyterian Church in Jamaica and the Cayman Islands combined with the Congregational Union to form the United Church of Jamaica and the Cayman Islands'.
10. In Werner Zips's (2011) book, Maroon Town does not even feature in the index and he cites only one acknowledgement and lists only one interview for Maroon Town (249). Indeed, in an earlier work, Zips seems unsure that Maroon Town is the site of Trelawny Town, stating in a footnote that, 'Kojo's Town was renamed Trelawney [sic] Town after the peace treaty. *It was most probably* where Maroon Town is located today' (Zips 1998, 97 n11) (my emphasis).
11. Consistent with his Africanist perspective, Werner Zips (2011) uses the African spelling 'Kojo'. However, consistent with my focus on creolization, I use the Jamaican spelling 'Cudjoe'.
12. Similar geographical conflations to those found in Werner Zips (2011) regarding the sacred sites of the Leeward Maroons, based on the conflation of oral tradition and historical records, are included in the otherwise excellent documentary film, *Akwantu: The Journey* (2012) produced by Roy T. Anderson on the Jamaican Maroons.
13. In addition to Barbara Kopytoff (1987), I could find no reference to Kindah in Kopytoff's (1973) study.
14. Some of the main maroon experts in Accompong for both Werner Zips's study and my own, including the leaders Sydney Peddie, Harris Cawley and Melvin Currie, were born in the 1930s (the decade of the burning of the ritual hut over Captain Accompong's reputed grave at Old Town) and would, therefore, not have participated in the Myal rituals at Old Town focused on Captain Accompong. However, as mentioned, the burning of this hut at Old Town was recalled to me by an elderly Maroon in Aberdeen (the late Pastor Charles Wint, born in 1914, who had been a Deputy Colonel of the Accompong Maroons, chapter 6). According to Barbara Kopytoff (1987, 477), the 'earnest young Christian Maroon' who in the mid-1930s courageously 'one night...crept down to Old Town, set fire to the ritual hut and burned it down' was 'Thomas J. Cawley'. This is likely to have been Harris Cawley's father Tom Cawley, who became Colonel in the 1950s, and this may be another reason why the burning of the hut is unlikely to be discussed in Accompong with the re-ascendance of Myalism.
15. See chapter 3 note 16 on the symbolism of the fruitful mango tree.
16. See chapter 3 note 15 on the three 'tribal' ethnic groups.
17. Werner Zips (2011, 127 n24) dismisses, on the grounds that, 'eighteenth century plantation colonies did not feature any "kindergartens"', my tentative suggestion (Besson 1997, 214 n54) that the word Kindah might derive from the German *kinder* for children. The reasons for my speculation included my conclusion that the focus on Kindah (where the 'children' or reputed descendants of Cudjoe and Nanny gather) has occurred since Barbara Kopytoff's (1987) study and that there was a German-speaking Dutch anthropologist in Accompong around that time. There are also communities of German descendants in western Jamaica, including

St Elizabeth. However, whether or not there has been any German linguistic input in the concept, the Maroons' own link between 'kin' and 'Kindah' is explicit.

18. See note 2 above on Bilby's (1984b, 14; 1996, 125) and Clarke's (1966, 61–62) usage of the older term 'bilateral' to indicate cognatic descent and land transmission through both genders.
19. As noted previously, the sign changed from 'Kindah, We Are Family' to 'Kindah, The Family Tree' and has since changed again to 'Kindah, One Family'.
20. Werner Zips (2012) in his review of Brian Meeks (2011), a volume focusing on the work of M.G. Smith, again overlooks the parallels between his own view of legal pluralism in Jamaica (Zips 1996, 1998, 2011) and Smith's plural society theory. In that review, which devotes disproportionate space (a third of his commentary on 15 chapters) to my essay on the challenge to Smith's plural society theory from a creolization perspective (Besson 2011a), Zips continues his parody of my use of the creolization concept in relation to Accompong (see also Zips 2011). Overlooking his own Afrocentric ideology and positioned subjectivity (Rosaldo 1993, 19) as well as that of Don Robotham (1980; Smith 1983) and Mervyn Alleyne (1988), who he cites in an attempt to dismember my argument, and also invoking Rastafarian '"fire bun" rhetoric' against me (903), Zips bases his unconvincing critique on outdated functionalist and nationalist meanings of creolization (e.g., Brathwaite 1971) and the watering down of the concept beyond the New World context (see Sheller 2003). As discussed earlier in this section of the chapter, Zips (2011, 2012) therefore fails to update his understanding of creolization as an anthropological concept and overlooks his own explicit use of Sidney Mintz and Richard Price's (1976) creolization perspective, as well as this central theme in the work of leading maroon specialists. In so doing, he inadvertently slights the 'subaltern agency' (Sheller 2003, 287) of Afro-Caribbean peoples, including Rastafarians (see Mataburaka 2011) and the Accompong Maroons. Moreover, as Barry Chevannes and I showed, while Alleyne's Africanist perspective could find no cultural continuity between Rastafari and Africa (Alleyne 1988, 103), our creolization approach identified that link: showing that Rastafari is a transformation of Revival which transformed Native Baptist Christianity and Myalism, creole religions that in turn not only drew on but also transformed African religions (Besson and Chevannes 1996, 210–11).

6 ■ ACCOMPONG, ABERDEEN AND MAROON TOWN: THE MAROON/NON-MAROON INTERFACE

Previous chapters have touched on the relationship between the Accompong maroon society and the non-maroon villages of Aberdeen and Maroon Town in the Cockpits. This chapter looks more closely at this maroon/non-maroon interface and also provides a more detailed view of Aberdeen. This is done, in part, through narratives collected in Accompong and Aberdeen and partly through other aspects of my fieldwork combined with historical research. Like my ethnography of Accompong (chapters 3–5), this chapter therefore draws on a methodology combining anthropology, history and oral tradition in which narratives may convey symbolic perspectives as well as alternative views of history complementing, modifying or challenging Eurocentric historical records (see also Besson 2002, 159; Price 1983, 1990; Higman 1998, 1999; Bilby 1984a, 2006).

I begin with an Accompong maroon narrative on Aberdeen, highlighting it as a disputed area between the maroon polity and the Jamaican colonial/post-colonial state (see also chapter 3). I then present my historical and anthropological research on the evolution of Aberdeen, the role of the Moravian missionaries in Aberdeen, and Aberdonian maroon and non-maroon ethnicities. I conclude with narratives from Aberdeen and Accompong (in St Elizabeth) about Maroon Town (in St James), which evolved on the historic site of Trelawny Town (the primary Leeward Maroon village) after the deportation of the Trelawny Maroons following the Second Maroon War of 1795–96 (chapter 2). My own detailed historical and anthropological research on Maroon Town (1999–2009), including Maroon Town narratives on Accompong, is presented in chapters 7–10. Chapter 11 will explore further comparisons and contrasts between Maroon Town and Accompong.

An Accompong Maroon Narrative on Aberdeen

Harris Cawley was Colonel of the Accompong Maroons from 1983 to 1988 (chapters 3–4). His house often provided a base for my fieldwork and I interviewed him many times throughout my research in Accompong from 1979 to 2009. His narratives included detailed outlines about the disputes between the Accompong Maroons and the Jamaican government regarding the boundaries of 'the Accompong property or state' (as he put it), which he estimated 'to be about six square miles and 640 acres to a square mile'[1] but were being eroded on the 'outskirts' while 'the Maroons were living here in peace'. He explained that when he was Colonel, he wrote many articles to the Jamaican national newspaper on this issue, some unpublished. In 1991, as I was about to begin my Aberdonian fieldwork, I recorded the following narrative from the

Ex-Colonel on the disputed lands of Aberdeen (a recurring theme in Accompong). As the Ex-Colonel's late father, Tom Cawley, who had likewise been a Colonel in Accompong (in the 1950s), had been actively involved in the issue of the Aberdonian lands, the narrative provides a two-generational perspective. It also takes us back a century earlier to the 1850s, soon after emancipation in 1838 and the Maroons Land Allotment Act of 1842.

Following a query from me (in 1991) about the lands of Aberdeen, Ex-Colonel Cawley narrated:

> Those are part of the maroon lands but they were robbed from the Maroons many years ago. My father used to tell me about the Aberdeen plantation and about the lands. And he used to even show me the map and show me how the government had robbed the lands by turning an angle by a few degrees. By running a mile up there, hundreds of acres of land fall on the government's side. And that was how they robbed the lands. And the boundary lines are very *crooked* and not straight. So even until today, there's a lot of the land to be straightened out with the Jamaican government. When I was Colonel, I call upon them but they did not respond. Because I discovered that the lands are...to assess where the boundaries are, I need to have straight lines. So after writing to them, to the Commission of Lands and other people, they did not respond. So I wrote to a place in Montego Bay, where they have a Forest Department, and made claims to the land in Cooke's Bottom, that's a part of the maroon lands to the west [towards Maroon Town]. Aberdeen is in the east. So between Aberdeen and Accompong you find the Peace Cave, where the peace treaty was signed. You'd have to walk about 45 minutes from the [Accompong] school. You have Kindah, where they do the dancing and cooking [at the Myal Play] and then beyond that you have Old Town where Cudjoe's grave is and beyond that now you have Peace Cave, about a mile [beyond Old Town] as the crow flies.

I enquired further about the Jamaican government and the land of Aberdeen and the Ex-Colonel explained:

> They'd come here, say they are running the line for the Maroons, turn the angle a few degrees in. By rob a mile they rob off several acres of land. Back in the 1850s coming down. The government out there, they were more sensitive to the value of land than the Maroons. They were living here and had sufficient land and not too concerned about lands out there [at that time], while the government was out there robbing off [gradually encroaching on] the lands. When they discover that was what was taking place, a lot of the lands were robbed.

I asked the Ex-Colonel what his father had told him about the Aberdeen plantation and he continued:

> He told me they had robbed the lands and there was a Great House on the property that belonged to the Maroons. And [as Colonel] he put up a lot of resistance against the government for the lands. And when they discovered that the lands were going to be on the maroon property, I heard that they went there and they scrap the house. It had a lot of valuable lumber, mahogany and so forth. And they took down the whole house and carry it away to Kingston.

This account of the dismantling of the Aberdeen Great House coincided with narratives that I later collected in Aberdeen.

The Ex-Colonel went on to explain that many Aberdonians are Accompong Maroons: 'We have about 80 per cent of the people [in Aberdeen] are Maroons, and it's a large community, born from Accompong'. I asked why these Maroons had moved and he explained:

> Perhaps because they want different areas to go. They had to buy the lands from the government and that is what the government do all the while. They take off the land and after a while they offer it for sale!

So on this view, Accompong Maroons in Aberdeen had to buy maroon treaty land. Complementing this account and other similar narratives about Aberdeen that I heard from Accompong Maroons from 1979 to 2009, is my historical research on Aberdeen and my anthropological fieldwork there from 1991 to 1999. The next three sections of this chapter outline this research.

The Land of Aberdeen

In addition to oral traditions in Accompong and Aberdeen, my archival research confirms the existence of Aberdeen Estate in the parish of St Elizabeth, during slavery, and indicates the presence of a slave community on the plantation, which bordered the Accompong maroon commons.[2] As in St James and Trelawny, the fertile lowlands and the foothills of the Cockpits in St Elizabeth attracted much Scottish and some English colonial settlement as Jamaica's slave plantations burgeoned in the eighteenth century (Patterson 1973, 45; Sibley 1978, 13–14, 40, 47, 50, 115; Sheridan 1977, 99–100; Karras 1992; Besson 2002; and chapter 2). The establishment of Aberdeen Estate by an Alexander Forbes of Scotland's Aberdeen, who built a Great House there (Sibley 1978, 4), occurred within this context and Aberdeen's plantation history interweaves with that of other colonizing families in St Elizabeth such as the MacFarlanes/McFarlanes with whom the Forbes family intermarried.[3]

The archives establish that, during the period 1736–55 (around the time of the Leeward Maroon treaty of 1738/39), 120 acres of Alexander Forbes's Aberdeen Estate were included in 'Island Estates', the incorporated plantations of Alexander McFarlane (which totalled 3,290 acres) that also comprised Large Island, Windsor (just south of Aberdeen) and other estates in the Thatchfield district. Alexander McFarlane (c. 1705–55), the youngest son of the 19th chief, John MacFarlane, of Scotland's Clan MacFarlane of Arrochar and a graduate (with a Masters degree in Science) of Glasgow University in 1728, was a merchant who settled in Jamaica around 1735 where he became a planter and traded in land and slaves in St Elizabeth and St Catherine from about 1736 until his death in Jamaica in 1755 (Besson and McFarlane 1995, 2005, 2009; Besson 2013; and chapter 1).[4]

In 1772, the Aberdeen plantation still belonged to an Alexander Forbes and was a sugar-and-slave estate.[5] A map of 1794 shows the Aberdeen plantation as comprising 1,063 acres, and the records state that by 1806/1807 (when the slave trade was abolished) the estate was under the direction of Phillip Levy, sole trustee and mortgagee, who had been in possession from January 1, 1806. By 1809 the proprietor of Aberdeen Estate was James Rowe, deceased. The records also confirm that, in 1845, seven years after emancipation in 1838, A. Dewar was the owner; by 1886, Aberdeen Estate (still 1,063 acres) was owned by John Calder Earle; and in 1894, Dr J.A.L. Calder, attorney for Marian Calder, ran a 60-acre banana business at Aberdeen Estate.[6] Oral history in the contemporary Aberdonian peasant community locates the transformation of Aberdeen estate-production from sugar cane to bananas (and some cattle-raising) within the period of ownership by John Calder Earle. This transformation reflected wider trends of continuity and change throughout Jamaica (chapter 1).

In the wider context of the freehold land settlement schemes of the 1930s and 1940s in Jamaica, the Aberdeen plantation was subdivided by John Calder Earle and sold to small settlers, expanding the older settlement of 'Upper Aberdeen' (founded on Island Mountain south of Aberdeen Estate, as discussed below) through the establishment of 'Higher Aberdeen'; while 'Lower Aberdeen', on the plains adjoining Appleton Estate, is on land more recently bought from 'Large Island' or Island Estate (map 9).[7] Together, these three districts of contemporary Aberdeen comprise some 16,000 adults in a dispersed community extending over an estimated 3,500 acres of mainly mountain land.[8] 'The Square' in Lower Aberdeen is now the formal centre of this community: with the Moravian Church (figures 6.1a and 6.1b), a post office (figure 6.2) and an all-age school. There are also Adventist, Baptist and Pentecostal churches in Lower Aberdeen.

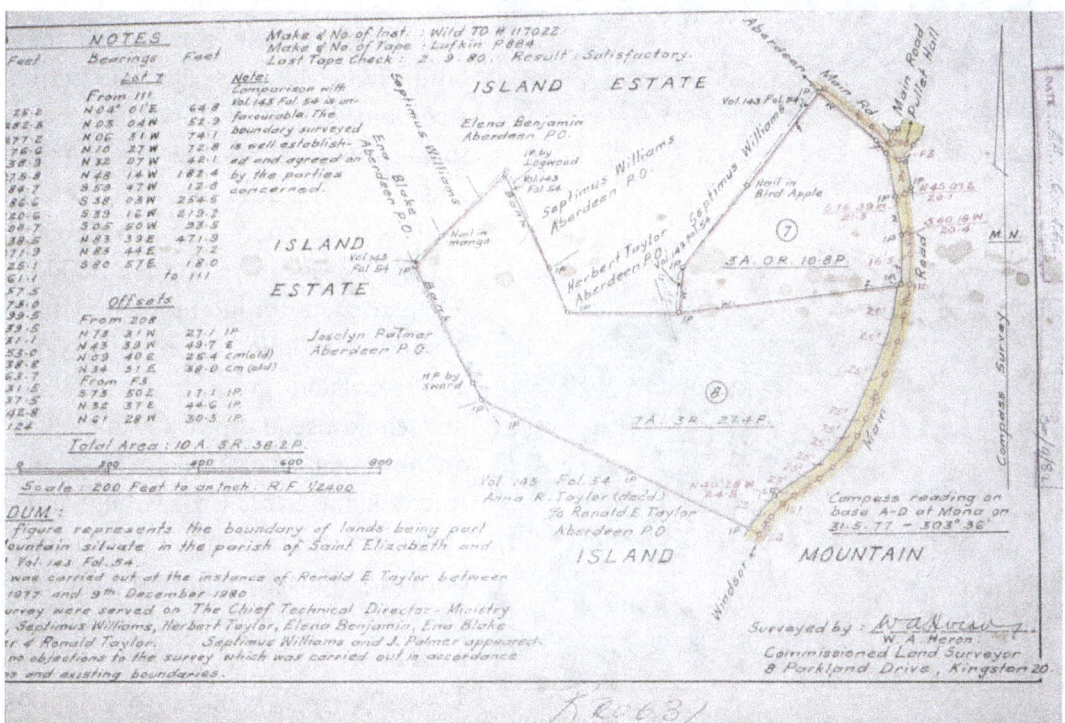

Map 9.   Island Estate (including Island Mountain), St Elizabeth. Courtesy of Lucien Taylor, Aberdeen.

Figure 6.1a. Ockbrook Moravian Church, Lower Aberdeen.

Figure 6.1b. The sign at the Ockbrook Moravian Church.

Fieldwork and oral tradition indicate links between Upper Aberdeen and the slave community that the archives show existed on Aberdeen Estate. The ruins of the Aberdeen Great House and sugar works are less than two miles from Upper Aberdeen, near the boundary of the Leeward Maroon commons. This suggests that the Aberdeen slave village was in that interior vicinity.[9] This conclusion is consistent with oral tradition in Accompong regarding alliances between the First-Time Maroons and Aberdonian plantation slaves, established through provision grounds on the backlands of Aberdeen Estate bordering the maroon commons (chapter 3). Reports among Upper Aberdeen villagers of an old burial ground on the former Aberdeen plantation further indicate the proto-peasant adaptation from which their family-land burial patterns derive. Aberdonian oral history also states that slaves cultivated in the interior; and the yard-ground-marketing-land transmission complex, rooted in proto-peasant institution-building (chapter 2), is pronounced in Upper Aberdeen. Production on house-yards and provision grounds is for both household use and peasant marketing on the plains, for example, at Maggotty, Junction and Santa Cruz; while family land is transmitted within unrestricted cognatic lineages (traced through both women and men, and including migrants and residents), as in Trelawny's free villages (Besson 2002) and Maroon Town (chapters 7–10), and as is emerging in Accompong within the commons (chapters 3–5).

Figure 6.2. The Post Office in Lower Aberdeen.

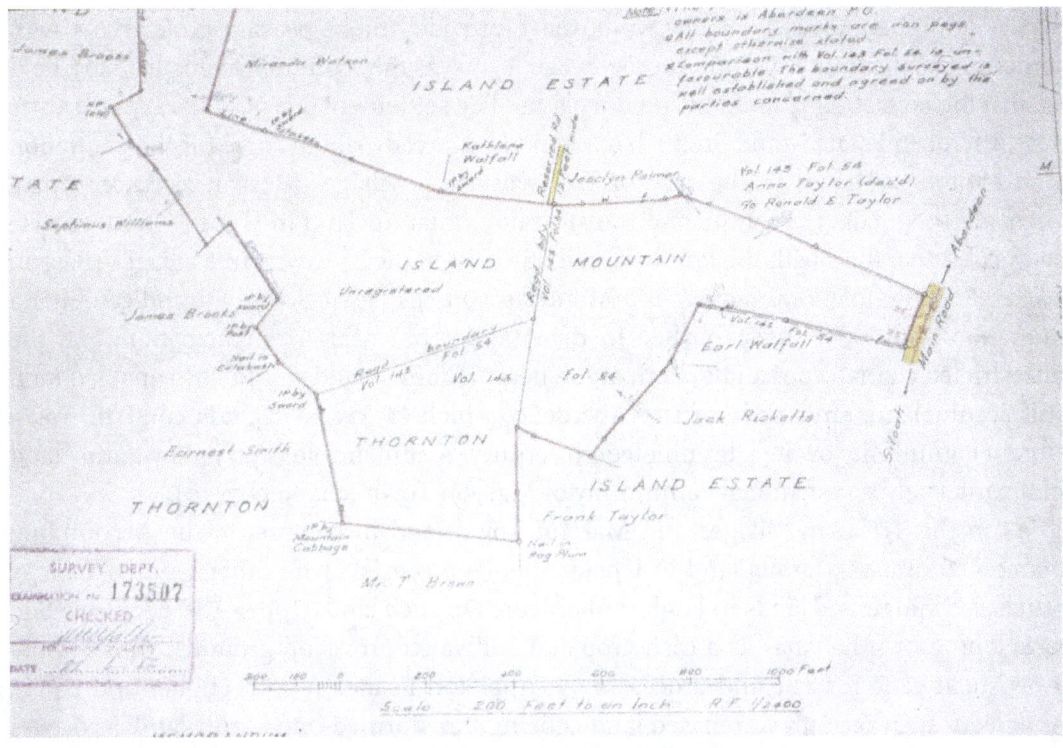

Map 10. *Island Mountain, St Elizabeth. Courtesy of Lucien Taylor.*

The combined evidence from archives, fieldwork and oral tradition indicates that Upper Aberdeen was established within a few years of emancipation by ex-slaves from Aberdeen Estate and other nearby plantations such as Large Island, augmented by some Accompong Maroons and their descendants, who squatted on plantation mountain backlands south of Aberdeen Estate; for example, on Island Mountain, the backlands of Island Estate (maps 9 and 10). Oral history recounts that such land was then surveyed and subdivided for sale, enabling the squatters to purchase land and the government to impose taxation. This oral tradition is consistent with historical accounts of government land retrieval, registration, land sale and taxation that took place in Jamaica, especially in the 1860s and 1870s, under Crown Colony government, in the aftermath of the 1865 Morant Bay Rebellion (Satchell 1990; Young 1993, 203 n2; Besson 1992b). This process in Aberdeen parallels the transformation of Martha Brae in Trelawny after emancipation, the current consolidation of Martha Brae's satellite squatter settlement of Zion and the development of Maroon Town in St James (Besson 2002, 2007 and chapters 7–10).

The Accompong Maroons' claim (supported by Aberdonians) that the lands on which Aberdeen is located are maroon treaty lands, would have provided a powerful rationale to post-emancipation squatting by ex-slaves and Maroons on the lands that became Upper Aberdeen. Moreover, the ancestors of the Upper Aberdonians continued to work on the Aberdeen plantation for about a century after emancipation; that is, until the subdivision and sale of the estate around 1949. The creation and transmission of the family lands that persist in Upper Aberdeen today would have provided those peasant-proletarians with some degree of autonomy from Aberdeen Estate, just as they continue to ensure a foothold against the persisting plantations on the plains. The settlement of a post-slavery peasantry near Aberdeen Estate would, in turn, have ensured a ready labour force for the plantation after emancipation (as in the case of Trelawny's free villages [Besson 2002; compare Carnegie 1987, ix]). The tenure and transmission of family land in Upper Aberdeen also shows clear parallels with the family-land institution in the Trelawny free villages (Besson 2002). For example, oral history and Moravian sources (see below) both indicate that a migration tradition was established in the Aberdeen area after emancipation; and the unrestricted cognatic descent system at the heart of family land would have enabled (and still permits) migrants to return to Aberdeen, which Moravian records confirm was a vibrant community by the later nineteenth century. A similar role is played by family land in the intensely transnational community of Maroon Town (chapters 7–10).

As in the Trelawny villages and Maroon Town (and in contrast to the Accompong maroon commons), family land in Upper Aberdeen coexists with other tenures such as purchased and rented lands in Higher Aberdeen. On such land, Upper Aberdeen villagers have long grown bananas as a cash crop and cultivated provision grounds; while others grow sugar cane for sale and processing at Appleton Estate. In both Higher and Lower Aberdeen, such recently purchased land is being transformed into family land, as occurs in other Jamaican free villages. However, family-land holdings in Upper Aberdeen tend to be more extensive than in Trelawny's nucleated villages on the plantation lowlands, where land is still measured in square chains. These more extensive family lands in Aberdeen have parallels with those of Maroon Town and both these communities evolved as post-slavery banana peasantries.

In addition to the links with Aberdonian proto-peasants and the parallels with Trelawny's free villages and Maroon Town, Upper Aberdeen villagers stress their links with the Accompong Maroons who likewise acknowledge this relationship (chapters 3–6), which includes ties of conjugality, affinity, bilateral kinship and cognatic descent. In Upper Aberdeen such common descent is a basis for Accompong maroon status, which is underwritten by the rights to reside on and cultivate the commons and to vote in elections for the Colonel of Accompong. The links between the two communities are facilitated by a precipitous 'shortcut' footpath of about two miles between Accompong and Upper Aberdeen and these villages refer to each other in Jamaican Creole as 'Campong and 'Badeen. (However, when 'Aberdeen' is pronounced in Upper Aberdeen, it is with a Scottish-Aberdeenshire drawl.)

Aberdeen, therefore, represents a dynamic interface between Jamaican maroon and non-maroon post-slavery peasantries. To some extent, this interface (which is likewise pronounced in Maroon Town) extends, by networking and migration, throughout the island to other non-maroon villages as well as to urban areas and overseas. Aberdonians observe that, in a symbolic sense, all black Jamaicans are Maroons by virtue of their common African descent and history of enslavement; a view that highlights the significance of the tradition of slave resistance in generating free villages as well as marronage. Among the proto-peasantry and in the post-emancipation villages, these themes articulated with Nonconformist missionary activity as with the Baptists in Trelawny and St James (Besson 2002, and chapter 2). In Aberdeen, this link was with the Moravians, Jamaica's first slave missionaries.

The Moravian Missionaries and Aberdeen

Aberdonian proto-peasant slaves and post-slavery peasants became linked with the Moravians through the northern St Elizabeth plantation network. Moravian missionising in the island was initiated by two slave-owning planter brothers, Joseph Foster-Barham and William Foster, and from their estates, Moravian missions spread throughout St Elizabeth and into the neighbouring parishes of Westmoreland and Manchester (Patterson 1973, 209; Hastings and MacLeavy 1979, 16–19 and the map opposite 210). By 1753, the Foster brothers had been converted to the Moravian Church in England, at which time they already had plantations and slaves in St Elizabeth. On being converted, they 'became uneasy' and were anxious to missionize their slaves (Hastings and MacLeavy 1979, 17). At the brothers' request, three Moravian missionaries landed at Black River, the coastal capital of St Elizabeth, on December 9, 1754.

The Fosters' St Elizabeth plantations at that time (Lancaster, Elim, Two-Mile-Wood and Bogue), just south of Aberdeen and Windsor estates, became the headquarters of these Moravian missionaries, 'and on the 300 acres of land given to them they began to establish their work'; there being 'about 900 slaves on these estates'(Hastings and MacLeavy 1979, 17).[10] By 'the beginning of 1756 there were 77 baptized members and 400 under instruction'[11] and Caries[12] had also preached 'periodically at Windsor and Islands [McFarlane plantations in St Elizabeth], near Siloah and Balaclava, and made trips to faraway Mesopotamia' in Westmoreland (19).[13]

Although the Moravians were the first slave missionaries in Jamaica, they were the least successful. Nevertheless, by emancipation the Moravians had provided 'eighty-four years of continuous and unbroken service to the slaves' in St Elizabeth and neighbouring parishes (Hastings and MacLeavy 1979, 54); though their conversion rate was low (Patterson 1973, 209). In this scenario, and in the more immediate context of the plantation network of northern St Elizabeth, Aberdeen became an outpost of the Moravian station at New Eden (established in 1816 near Bogue on land belonging to the Fosters).

A Moravian publication records the founding of a Moravian outstation at 'Aberdeen (Ockbrook)' during the period of Moravian growth and expansion in Jamaica, from the 1860s to around 1900; especially during the period from the 1880s to 1904 (Hastings and MacLeavy 1979, 76–90, especially 89). In 1891, another Moravian source comments on the 'populous district of Aberdeen and its likely development into a "separate station"':

> There is one out-station about ten miles distant [from New Eden] called Aberdeen, where day-school is kept, and regular services are held by the preacher. The minister goes once a month to keep services, and give 'speaking,' but the members attend New Eden for the Holy Communion, and are recognized as members of that congregation. Aberdeen is in a populous district. The work appears to prosper, and under the Lord's blessing this place is likely to develop into a separate station (*Periodical Accounts*, 2nd Series, vol. 1, 1891, 577).

A further Moravian record notes that, '[T]he new school-house at Aberdeen was opened on November 24th'; that is, on November 24, 1884 (*Periodical Accounts* vol 33, 1885, 288). This same source also illuminates the situation of post-slavery peasants and plantation labourers in the Aberdeen area at the time. This included the continuity of the provision ground-marketing system from the proto-peasant past. Another theme was the declining sugar industry, which contributed to the migration of ex-slaves and their descendants to other parishes and to and from Colon in Panama and the effect this had on low church membership and subscriptions.

Moravian records, likewise, provide insight into a further reason for the slow increase in Moravian Church membership in Aberdeen in the late nineteenth century: '[M]any think its discipline too strict. "Your Church", some say, "does not allow dancing..."' (*Periodical Accounts*, 2nd series, vol 1, 1891, 93). Dancing was integral to Myalism among the Jamaican slaves, and has remained central to Revivalism (which evolved from Myal and Native Baptist Christianity) as in Trelawny villages (Besson 2002), Accompong and Maroon Town, and to Myalism itself as at the annual Myal Play among the Accompong Maroons which is also attended by Aberdonians.

Nevertheless, from the late nineteenth century to the present, the Moravian Church has maintained a significant presence in 'Ockbrook (Aberdeen)' (Hastings and MacLeavy 1979, 190, 198, 214, 235, 256, 262), and Mr and Mrs Jack Earle are recorded as being 'Godparents to the Troop of Scouts' at Ockbrook in 1936 (197–98). In Upper Aberdeen, an elderly Aberdonian explained that Moravian church services were held in the schoolhouse (established in 1884), until the present Ockbrook Moravian Church was built in Lower Aberdeen. The notice by the church, which is on the former Island Estate looking up to Island Mountain, confirms that it was built in 1927 (figures 6.1b and 6.3).

The involvement of the Moravians in Aberdeen has both similarities and differences with the role of the Baptists among the slaves and free villages in Trelawny (Besson 2002) and St James (chapters 2 and 7). Similarities include, first, the dual naming system of some peasant communities associated with the Nonconformist churches. 'Ockbrook' was named after a Moravian settlement in Derbyshire, England, and the names 'Aberdeen (Ockbrook)' parallel the dual naming system of some Trelawny Baptist free villages such as New Birmingham/The Alps, Wilberforce/Refuge, and Granville/Grumble Pen (Besson 2002). Second, the satellite relationship of Aberdeen as a Moravian outstation to New Eden was similar to that of some Baptist free villages in Trelawny; such as Granville and Martha Brae, with their Prayer Houses, in relation to the Baptist church in Falmouth. Third, Moravian records as well as fieldwork reveal the coexistence of Nonconformist Christianity with creole religions (such as Pentecostalism[14] and the Revival worldview embedded in family land) in Aberdeen. This parallels the coexistence of the Baptist church, Revival worldview and Rastafarian movement in Trelawny free villages (Besson 2002); the articulation of the Presbyterian/United church, Myalism, Revival and Rastafarianism in Accompong (chapters 3–5), and the interweaving of Revivalism, Adventism, Pentecostalism and Baptist Christianity in Maroon Town (chapter 7).

Figure 6.3. Looking towards Island Mountain from the Ockbrook Moravian Church, Aberdeen.

Differences include, firstly, the contrasting impact of the Moravians and the Baptists on the slaves, ex-slaves and their descendants. As seen above, Moravian records refer to low membership in the mission church in Aberdeen; while the Baptists had a strong impact, especially in St James and Trelawny. This success of the Baptists was due, in part, to the role of black preachers and class-leaders, and partly to the forceful missionizing of preachers such as Thomas Burchell and William Knibb (chapter 2). Secondly, the Baptists played a major role in establishing church-founded villages, especially in Trelawny and St James; whereas I could find no evidence of Moravian involvement in peasantization in Aberdeen (St Elizabeth).

However, the independent but related processes of land acquisition and Nonconformist church activity in Aberdeen provide a parallel with the transformation of Trelawny's planter town of Martha Brae, where Baptist ex-slaves initiated peasant settlement through squatting and then by land purchase after government land retrieval (Besson 2002). In this respect, the establishment of the free villages of Aberdeen and Martha Brae contrasted with the imposed land settlements of other free villages (including the Baptist land settlements of New Birmingham, Wilberforce, Kettering and Granville in Trelawny [Besson 2002] and Maldon, the first Baptist free village in St James, which is now a part of Maroon Town). Aberdeen and Martha Brae also provide a parallel for the transformation of the primary Leeward Maroon village of Cudjoe's Town/Trelawny Town into non-maroon Maroon Town (chapters 7–10). The next section of this chapter explores the present-day life and ethnicities of the Aberdonians, including their relationship with the Accompong Maroons.

Aberdonian Maroon and Non-Maroon Ethnicities

The villagers of Aberdeen variously claim descent from slaves, planters and Maroons and Aberdonians have constructed varying Jamaican maroon and non-maroon ethnicities. These include Afro-Creole identities relating to maroon and slave ancestry, as well as Meso-Creole ethnicities based on descent from planters and slaves. This section presents a selection from a range of narratives that I collected on these themes, from 1991 to 1999, in Aberdeen, contextualized in my wider fieldwork there.

Afro-Scots Descent and the African-Prince Maroon

The late Charles Wint, a Pentecostal Pastor who claimed Afro-Scots descent from Maroons, slaves and planters and whom I interviewed at various times in Aberdeen (and who died there aged 95, in 2009), exemplifies the relationship between Aberdeen and Accompong as well as the complexities of ethnic identification and the process of creolization at the maroon/non-maroon interface. Pastor Wint (who explained that 'Wint' was his 'slave name') was born in 1914 in Upper Aberdeen. In 1999, when he was 85 years old, he still walked two miles each day between his house-yard in Upper Aberdeen and the provision ground that he cultivated in Higher Aberdeen (figure 6.4). His overlapping cognatic lineages include two of particular significance, both traced five ascending generations (through both genders) to his great-great-great grandparents. As he had children and grandchildren, his accounts (in the 1990s) provided eight-generational family histories. One of these lineages, on his maternal side, reflects Afro-Scots miscegenation and creolization (a significant theme in Aberdeen): his mother's great-great-grandfather was a Scotsman, surnamed Berry, whose descendants are widespread in Jamaica's Aberdeen.

Overlapping with this Meso-Creole non-maroon lineage is another, on Pastor Wint's paternal side, of Afro-Creole maroon descent that interweaves between Accompong, Balaclava (a mountain village a few miles south-east), and Upper Aberdeen. This maroon lineage is traced to one of Pastor Wint's great-great-great-grandfathers (his father's mother's father's father), who is said to have been an African Prince brought on a slave ship to Jamaica and to have escaped into Accompong from a plantation on the plains.[15]

The descendants of this African-Prince Maroon are said to have 'come out' from Accompong, and to have acquired land in the non-maroon communities of Balaclava and Upper Aberdeen. These descendants, including Pastor Wint and his children and grandchildren, retain their maroon status (which he also conferred on his non-maroon wife, born in Upper Aberdeen, according to the custom of 'bye-maroon', whereby outsider spouses are incorporated into the maroon polity).[16] Pastor Wint was involved in Leeward Maroon politics throughout his life: he had been Chairman of the Maroon Council,

Figure 6.4. Pastor Wint at his house in Upper Aberdeen.

Second Deputy Colonel of Accompong, Adviser to another Colonel, and his house-yard served as a voting station for Maroons in Upper Aberdeen. He had also pursued a typical maroon career, combining farming with an occupation in the Jamaican police force, and was entitled to reside on and cultivate the commons. In addition, he had played a central role in the annual Myal Play and even recalled the Christian burning of the ritual hut at Old Town in the 1930s (reported by Kopytoff 1987, 477). With other Aberdonians of maroon descent, he had also participated in the re-ordering of the Myal Play and the ritual transformation of Old Town (chapters 3–5).

Pastor Wint narrated that his great-great-grandfather, the son of the African-Prince Maroon, acquired land in Mount Pleasant, Balaclava, before emancipation, about 180 years previously, around 1815. This ancestor subsequently obtained, through squatting and purchase, about 16 acres of mountain land in Upper Aberdeen, around 1845, seven years after emancipation. His house-yard was at Mount Pleasant and his provision ground was in Upper Aberdeen and, as the journey between his yard and ground was arduous, he had a cottage in Upper Aberdeen, where he and his family sometimes stayed. This land in Upper Aberdeen (as well as the Balaclava land) was orally transmitted to the African-Prince Maroon's son's daughter and two sons, and has been passed on as family land to all their descendants within a dispersed and ever-increasing cognatic lineage. Such transmission includes the family-land burial ground, where 23 old tombs and cairns could still be seen (figure 6.5). Pastor Wint stressed that many of those buried there are Maroons and that any member of the landholding lineage (including himself and his descendants) descended from the son of the African-Prince Maroon through male or female links may be buried on that land, whether or not they reside in Upper Aberdeen. Absentees who retained such rights included kin in New York (USA) and Bradford, England. In addition to Pastor Wint's rights to the family land, where he lived and cultivated a food-forest on a three-quarter acre yard, he bought 17 acres of land, in 1949, from the government's subdivision of John Calder Earle's Aberdeen plantation. This is where Pastor Wint farmed a one-acre provision ground, one mile from his yard, for household use and sale to higglers for marketing on the plains. In his younger days, he

Figure 6.5. Pastor Wint at the family-land burial ground of the African-Prince Maroon's descendants in Upper Aberdeen.

Figure 6.6. A family-land cemetery in Upper Aberdeen.

also cultivated sugar cane on this land and on another ten acres of leased land nearby, producing 200 tons of cane a year for sale to Appleton Estate. His purchased land supplemented the land rights that he transmitted to his descendants. In Accompong, in March 2009, I learned that Pastor Wint had died two months before and been interred in a sepulchre on his family land in Aberdeen.

Afro-Creole Maroon and Non-Maroon Ethnicities

Like Pastor Wint, Alan Williams illustrates the rooting of Old Families in Aberdeen and the kinship ties and interweaving identities that link Aberdeen and Accompong: in Alan's case, the overlapping of Afro-Creole maroon and non-maroon ethnicities. I interviewed Alan in 1991, in Upper Aberdeen, where the family lands and burial grounds of Aberdeen's Old Families or clans and their lineages embroider the landscape (figure 6.6). Alan belongs to the overlapping Williams and Welch clans on his father's and mother's side, respectively and has many relatives in Aberdeen; for, as he put it, 'most of Aberdeen is one family' with different branches having their family lands and cemeteries 'all through the district [village]', especially in Upper Aberdeen. He also has kinship ties through his paternal Williams clan with the Accompong Maroons.

Alan was living in Upper Aberdeen in an old house built by his late mother on half an acre of land that she bought and transmitted to her children. Alan (then aged 62) said that he was born in 1928, 'right here in this said yard', where he had lived all his life. He explained that he was the only one of his siblings to have remained on this land and that his four adult children and 13 grandchildren had likewise migrated, including to St James and England. Nevertheless, the land was being transformed into family land: any of his siblings could return ('no objection because it's mother's land') and it would remain for future generations: 'gran-pickni, gran, gran, gran, gran'. The yard is fruitful with mango, breadfruit and coconut trees and he cultivates bananas there which he sells to higglers in southern St Elizabeth.

Alan's mother is interred in a vault in the family-land cemetery of her maternal grandparents' land nearby, which belongs to a branch of the Welch clan, as Alan narrated: 'Right up there, against the road-side deh in a piece a bush. It don't weed up yet. Is a *big* piece a burying ground, for family'. We crossed the road into a cane field and he showed me this burial ground, where I saw his mother's vault and the tombs of many of her kin, for as Alan continued: 'A whole heap a people buried here, umpteen. See them all up there so, the whole of it. Same one family, several generations back'. He recounted what he had learned from his mother about this family cemetery where his ancestors, including his maternal grandmother and great-grandparents, are buried:

> The First-Time people...to me now, I have to tek what my mother say. Because I don't know what going on in olden times. What going on now is new things. Him seh [she said] is the old family plot. The old-time come on to fe we little children buried there. My grandmother, gran-gran-grandfather, gran-gran-grandmother buried there. From far [up his genealogy]. That's why I said the old-time people buried there.

He traced this non-maroon maternal lineage at least six generations.

Alan explained that, in contrast to the family lands of Upper Aberdeen, the lands of Higher Aberdeen are more recently bought, as that land was purchased from the subdivision of Aberdeen Estate in the mid-twentieth century. He said that there had been successive owners of the Aberdeen plantation (the Dewars, Calders and Earles) before it was subdivided and sold as a land settlement (around 1949) 'to the people and everybody purchase what they need'. Alan himself had bought an acre there from Jack Earle where, as he explained, 'me work me ground up 'Badeen property, cultivating cocos, breadfruit and bananas'.

Alan remarked that there are ancient graves of 'old-time black people' on the former Aberdeen slave plantation:

> But they don't tomb. You get some old-time people who is dead so long, so long [ago] and they just bury them and some people will know where them bury. Through on the property [estate] them live and on the property them dead, a there them just bury them same place.

These unmarked graves of 'invisible' women and men contrast with the tombs and vaults on the post-slavery family-land cemeteries in Upper Aberdeen (as in Trelawny's free villages [Besson 1984b]). Alan narrated that the lands of Lower Aberdeen by the Post Office and 'The Square' or crossroads are even more recently bought (from Island Estate) than the land from the Aberdeen plantation. He himself had also purchased half an acre in Lower Aberdeen that he sometimes cultivated.

In contrast to his maternal non-maroon ethnicity, Alan claims maroon descent through his late father, whose ancestors came from "Campong Town' (Accompong), though he remarked that, in a more general sense, 'Everyone in Aberdeen is Maroon, attached to Maroon. Because you have Maroon deh [in Accompong], Maroon here, and everybody go, everybody come [interacts]'. His father, who had been born in the neighbouring parish of Manchester, had returned to live in Accompong. Alan narrated that he himself has land rights in Accompong and had practised shifting cultivation on the commons:

> Well, according to 'Campong [Accompong Town], anybody attached to the family [can] go to 'Campong and work. And you go and they say, 'work yeh so'. And from you work yeh so, you just work until you die. Me work over there, whole heap a times already. But

me old now and me can't stand the walking. It's about two miles from here to go to 'Campong, you know.

I asked Alan which part of the commons he had cultivated. He explained:

Just when you pass the big ground at Peace Cave and go long out a the common. So we turn on the right and work over the hillside. When my mother was along with a maroon man [his father], so he work there and we go and work. And nobody molest [trouble] us. Well every year you cut a different, you cut a two-square [chains] of bush and work. The other year, you cut two and a half square and work, and so on.

Alan said that, even after his father died, he was allowed to continue working maroon land undisturbed. In response to my query as to how his father had acquired land rights in Accompong, he explained that Maroons don't individually own land and that this has been the case 'from ancient time, because they don't pay no taxes fe land'.

On his father's side, Alan is related to the Williams clan in Accompong, including the two Williams brothers whom I interviewed regarding their role as ritual cooks for the Myal Plays (chapter 4), and Alan remarked that he had 'been a whole heap a times' to the Play. Likewise, Alan explained, his other Williams relatives in Aberdeen belong to Accompong's Williams clan: 'we are all one family'. In August 2009, one of Alan's maroon cousins Inspector Ferron Williams, was elected Colonel of Accompong.

Meso-Creole Non-Maroon Ethnicities

The Mundy Old Family of Upper Aberdeen claims mixed British and African ancestry – a recurring theme among many Meso-Creole Aberdonians. I first interviewed William Mundy, who was nearly 78 when I met him in 1991, then his sister Adella (aged 80) and their brother Reginald ('Reggie', aged 71). William lived on his own bought land 'on the Mountains of Aberdeen', as he described it. His view looked upwards to Accompong and he remarked that there are some Accompong Maroons who live 'out here' in Aberdeen. His bought land in Upper Aberdeen is cultivated and his late wife and one of his daughters are buried here. He explained, with a chuckle and referring to his striking blue eyes, that his ancestors included English and Scots: 'My father's father was from England, my mother's father was from Scotland'. William and Adella narrated that their Scottish maternal grandfather, surnamed McTaggart, had purchased land in Trelawny, Westmoreland and St Elizabeth. William added that the McTaggart family land, with its burial ground, is 'over at Bagdel Mountain, a good walk across to that land'.

However, William's paternal Mundy family land, which is about five acres, is near his yard in Upper Aberdeen. Reggie and Adella resided on that land. I spoke with all three siblings about this family land, which was purchased by their late father who built a house there. William narrated that he was born (in 1913) and raised on that land and that, 'My father's father had a burying ground on that property'. Adella showed me this family cemetery, which is high on a hillside behind the house. There were at least nine tombs there, including those of her parents, two sisters, two brothers, an uncle and a cousin. The inscriptions dated back to a Gilbert Mundy, born in 1898, and the most recent burial had been just a few months ago. The father's descendants, including William, Adella, Reggie, their other siblings and their children and grandchildren all have rights to this land.

William explained the relationship between the village of Aberdeen and the former Aberdeen plantation:

> As far as I know, I heard my father say that this Aberdeen property [plantation], the owner of it was from England [Scotland?] and those people was Dewar. Calder supposed to buy it from them. And Calder sold it to Earle. Earle, supposed he mortgage it and the government took it over and sell it out to the people [as a land settlement]. When them selling out the property, them pull down the Great House. It was a banana plantation, over 800 acres, a mountainous plantation. Aberdeen [village] is from down at the Square, down by the clinic [Lower Aberdeen]. We call up here 'Upper Aberdeen'. The plantation was further up [now Higher Aberdeen]. The district [village] of Aberdeen called after the plantation.

Another Aberdonian, Lucien Taylor, who likewise claims some Scottish ancestry and who is related to the Earle family that had owned the Aberdeen plantation and who lives in Lower Aberdeen, told me more about the development of Lower Aberdeen where his paternal family was involved in its transformation from a part of Island Estate. Lucien narrated that when he was a child, his paternal grandfather (who had 'some connection' to the Scots) and other families bought land here from the subdivision of the part of Island that became Lower Aberdeen. Lucien grew up in a big house further up the hill but now resided in the house nearer to the Square where his grandfather lived when Lucien was a boy. Lucien's father subsequently sold some of this land (the Raheen plantation) to Appleton Estate as Lucien narrated:

> Island Estate boundaries [borders] on Aberdeen, Lower Aberdeen. It goes as far into [as] Ben Lomond, through the mountain ranges that would at one time encompass Raheen Estates, which was later sold to Appleton by my father Ronald Taylor. Over there on the flats where it used to go to the head of the Black River. Black River came here, on the property or close by the property. If you go to Ben Lomond now, when you get there somebody will show you the real Island Mountain chain because it goes into Balaclava. When you go further north into the hills you start to get into the Cockpit Country. And then this would be Island Mountain...They have a district Marlborough and if you go to Ben Lomond, you could walk across the hills in and around and you'd get back into Balaclava [three miles from Lower Aberdeen].

Lucien showed me maps of his family's land purchased from Island Estate (maps 9 and 10) and explained: 'I saw it on the map that this is Island Estate. But I grew up [knowing it] as Aberdeen. Ben Lomond, people would say Island Mountain, where you going, to Island Mountain.'[17] I asked what is at Island Mountain and he replied: 'Just the [extensive mountain] range, just the valleys'; for example, Pullet Hall is flat. He explained that, 'Some of my relatives were related to the Earle property people', including Jack Earle who had owned the Aberdeen plantation and lived in the Great House. Lucien also recalled the extensive cultivation of bananas in the area when he was a boy. I would later discover from my McFarlane relatives in Balaclava and Black River that the Taylors are also related through marriage to that branch of the Afro-Scots McFarlanes.

An Aberdonian Narrative on Maroon Town

During my research in Accompong and Aberdeen, I collected narratives in both communities regarding Maroon Town – the non-maroon village that evolved on the historic site of Cudjoe's Town/Trelawny Town (the primary Leeward Maroon village) after the deportation of the Trelawny Maroons in 1796, following the Second Maroon War. The remaining sections of this chapter present and contextualize some of these accounts, before I discuss my own research in Maroon Town (chapters 7–11). I begin with an Aberdonian narrative on Maroon Town from the late Pastor Wint (1914–2009), who claimed descent from planters, slaves and Maroons.

In Upper Aberdeen, in 1999, Pastor Wint narrated the following account of Maroon Town as I began to extend my fieldwork there from Accompong and Aberdeen. This narrative (which combines oral tradition with documented history) also ranges over the Cockpit Country and discusses three maroon ancestor-heroes: Cudjoe, Nanny and Accompong. In addition, the narrative portrays both continuity and change in Jamaican maroon society including the transformation of Trelawny Town to Maroon Town and the relationship between Trelawny Town/Maroon Town and Accompong Town. It also reflects the earlier view of the Accompong Maroons up to the mid-twentieth century that the Old Town grove was the burial place of Captain Accompong (Kopytoff 1987), rather than the current view that Old Town is Captain Cudjoe's burial place. However, the narrative simultaneously portrays the Accompong maroon view that the Peace Cave (which was near Cudjoe's Old Town in St James) is located on the Accompong commons in St Elizabeth. The narrative of this elderly Aberdonian, who claimed partial maroon descent, and held land and voting rights in Accompong (and who remembered the ritual burning of the hut at Captain Accompong's reputed grave at Old Town in the 1930s), is therefore especially valuable as it reflects an important stage in the process of the creolization of the commons and its Myal rituals (chapters 3–5).

Pastor Wint began his narrative on Maroon Town modestly:

> I know a little bit. When you leave the Maroon Town Square you go up eastward and that was the maroon headquarters. That is Flagstaff. They had a springing well. I went there in the maroon camp and I drank some of the water. That place is a level camp ground.

> Cudjoe and Nanny, brother and sister, both go up and down visiting one another. But Nanny have a place in Quick Step in Trelawny and Cudjoe in Maroon Town. Here [nearby] is Accompong Town and [Captain] Accompong live here in St Elizabeth and Cudjoe live in St James. Up there, they call it Flagstaff. Accompong (one of the brothers of Cudjoe and Nanny) buried in Old Town at Accompong. I could not tell where Nanny and Cudjoe is buried. The Peace Cave at the edge of Accompong is where the war was fought.

Pastor Wint reflected on the transformation of the maroon settlement of Trelawny Town to non-maroon Maroon Town, including its integration into the Jamaican political system which contrasts with autonomous Accompong (and touched on land boundary disputes there):

[The Jamaican] government occupy that St James Maroon Town. You see this Accompong Town is the head, responsible for all the Maroons in Jamaica. Maroon Town, now, it is mixed up with the outside Jamaicans – those people that government is responsible for – so you can't really tell who are the Maroons.

Those lands in Maroon Town, they are not now occupied by the Accompong Maroons, but occupied by the government of Jamaica [who] take over that town now. Can't tell when, but Mann O. Rowe [Accompong Town's Secretary of State] has the history of all these things. Even some of the Accompong lands occupied by government. And there's a treaty sent by King George...

The [Maroon Town] land was given [sic] to these people by the government of Jamaica...I know when the people of Maroon Town given land but can't remember ... After the treaty, the war...They [the original inhabitants of Maroon Town] are mixed up with the other government people now.

Pastor Wint also said that the Jamaican government has occupied the Leeward treaty seaport towns (Falmouth in Trelawny and Black River in St Elizabeth): 'The Accompong seaport towns are occupied by the Jamaican government'. This view of Jamaican government occupation of Leeward seaports is a recurring theme in the narratives of many Accompong Maroons (chapters 3–4).[18]

Accompong Maroon Narratives on Maroon Town

I collected several narratives in Accompong regarding Maroon Town and the relationship between Accompong and Maroon Town – the two original sites of the Leeward Maroon treaty towns. These narratives (collected mainly in the 1990s and especially around the time that I began my fieldwork in Maroon Town in 1999) reflect varying views on the fractured Leeward Maroon polity, the transformation of the primary Leeward Maroon village of Cudjoe's Town/Trelawny Town to non-maroon Maroon Town, and the relationship between Accompong (originally the secondary community of the Leeward polity) and Maroon Town today.

The narratives reflect some knowledge of the historical relationship between Trelawny Town and Accompong as Leeward Maroon treaty towns, the Second Maroon War and the subsequent deportation of the Trelawny Maroons to Canada (chapter 2); a theme that I would later find largely elided from the narratives of the villagers of Maroon Town itself, who also have different views of the relationship between Maroon Town and Accompong (chapters 8–10). There is also some awareness in Accompong narratives of the colonial confiscation of the Trelawny Town treaty lands.

Other themes that emerge in Accompong narratives on Maroon Town include the view (which differs from historical records) that Accompong was the primary Leeward Maroon village; a view reinforced by the Accompong Maroons' reordering of their Old Town grove to represent Cudjoe's residence and burial place (rather than Captain Accompong's village and grave), reflecting a symbolic shifting of Cudjoe's Old Town from St James to St Elizabeth (chapters 3–5). Differences regarding the populations and landholding systems of Accompong Town and Maroon Town are likewise recurring themes, including a focus on the diverse demography of Maroon Town's population and their payment of land tax in contrast to the tax-free status of the Accompong Maroons.

The absence of Myalism in Maroon Town and the attendance of Maroon Town villagers at Accompong Town's Myal Play also feature in the narratives, as well as commentaries on the relationship between Nanny and Cudjoe. Warfare between the Maroons and the British is another theme. The ongoing issue of Leeward Maroon treaty boundaries likewise recurs. These Accompong narratives combine contemporary knowledge with oral tradition and fragments of documented history, sometimes compressing historical time; for example, by collapsing the two maroon wars into one.

I begin with a narrative by Melvin Currie, who was twice elected Deputy Colonel during my fieldwork in Accompong.

The Narrative of a Deputy Colonel

I interviewed Melvin Currie many times in Accompong, up to 2009. In 1999, as I began to extend my fieldwork from Accompong and Aberdeen to Maroon Town, he narrated an account of the relationship between Maroon Town and Accompong Town. The narrative portrays Maroon Town as being on the site of the secondary Leeward Maroon community, with Accompong being the primary Leeward village, thereby symbolically reordering the two historic Leeward treaty towns. It also includes an account of the deportation of the Trelawny Maroons to Canada and Africa:

> It [Maroon Town] is relating to Accompong [Town] in several ways. That was one of Cudjoe's outposts. Here [Accompong] was his ancient dwelling, where he operated from. It [Maroon Town] was also the maroon village that the Maroons were transported from to Nova Scotia and then to Sierra Leone, where I think they are still in existence. And the sequence leading up to their removal was the Second Maroon War, 1740 [sic] or somewhere around that.[19] It all cause through a pig that was slaughtered by a Maroon on the Maroons' hunting grounds in St James. That pig was eventually claimed by one of the planters. And there's a clause within the treaty that says if one of us should wrong a white man he should be brought to justice. So they tried to take this man from the community. The people rebelled because the pig was caught on their hunting ground. The Superintendent in Maroon Town, St James, sent for troops to invade and it turn out into a full-scale maroon war again.
>
> And it was in this war that the Mosquito Indians and the dogs were brought from Cuba to hunt them down. The war still continue until the intervention of the Accompong Maroons. It was there that they entered into an agreement for peace with the British. An arrangement was made for them to meet on a boat in Montego Bay, including representation from this maroon community, Accompong. So while they met on this boat, they realize the boat is drifting to sea carrying them all away. After the departure of the boat, the leader of the Maroons in Accompong made representation to the British. The morning they sent back representation for the return of these men, especially their own men from Accompong that were part of the peace arrangement. After a time, a man from this community came back from Nova Scotia to Jamaica and was reunited with his family in Accompong – a man by the name of Fowler.[20] A girl...[descended from him] living round here. Another in St James.

I asked Currie whether there were any Maroons in Maroon Town today. He replied:

> I believe so, I'm not too certain because of the disturbances and the government of the day added 2,000 acres from that area and handed it over to the Accompong Maroons.[21] The lands are adjoining. Today it's developed to a far extent [Maroon Town], but these people pay taxes for land and licences for businesses like any other part of Jamaica. I feel they [the Trelawny Maroons] left some relatives there. They would most take the men [for deportation].

Having highlighted the tax-paying status of the inhabitants of Maroon Town, Currie continued his narrative, focusing on Cudjoe's reputed base at the Old Town grove in Accompong and the taboo on non-Maroons (including those from Maroon Town) visiting this sacred site at the Myal Play:

> Cudjoe was the overall leader of the Maroons. There is some contradiction that there was Cudjoe's Town. But according to the oral history of Maroons, Cudjoe's headquarters were at Old Town just down there [about a mile from Kindah, which is on Currie's family land], where he is buried. Nanny is buried same place.
>
> People from Maroon Town and across the island come [to the Play] as visitors, not as Maroons. [Whereas] The Colonel of Scots Hall and Moore Town [of the Windward Maroons] can travel with us to Old Town.

Currie's narrative reflects the symbolic shifting of the sacred sites of the maroon wars on the Cockpit Country landscape and both the clear and ambiguous boundaries between Maroons and non-Maroons today.

Three-Generational Narratives from Accompong's Central Rowe Clan

In 1999, I collected three-generational narratives on Maroon Town from the late Mann O Rowe, Accompong Town's Secretary of State, one of his sons Dolphie and one of Mann's grandsons, Lawrence of Accompong Town's central Rowe clan. In addition to contributing Accompong Maroon perspectives on Maroon Town, the narratives illustrate the transmission of oral history down the generations of Accompong's largest clan.

Mann's account (narrated at the age of 94) was the most elaborate. His narrative presents his view of both the First and Second Maroon Wars (collapsing these into one[22] and including his paternal grandfather's involvement by compressing historical time) and the still ongoing land-boundary disputes between the Leeward Maroon polity and the Jamaican state. Like Currie's narrative, Mann also shifts the locations of Cudjoe's Town/Trelawny Town on the Cockpit Country landscape and highlights the tax-paying status of the Maroon Town population (portrayed as mainly Maroons):

> Maroon Town in St James belonged to the Maroons. Water works [the well at Flagstaff] in St James belonged to the Maroons. Cudjoe died 1786. The treaty was signed 1738. It was a rebellion, a fellow by the name of Montague stole a pig from one Jack Vaughans, a white man. Montague was a Maroon down in St James and they court-martial him and put on the cat-o-nine [whip] 'pon him and he got indignant and start to put fire to

houses and cane fields in St James. And [the colonists] sent a couple of soldiers from Falmouth [in Trelawny] to Vaughansfield in St James. That was war. When the first batch of soldiers leave Falmouth, they coupled them two by two. And when the first two reached Vaughansfield the last batch was just leaving Falmouth. Falmouth is *our* seaport town in [the treaty of] 1738.

The treaty was burnt up down there [Trelawny Town/Maroon Town], by the fire. My grandfather, H. O. Rowe [Colonel from 1923 to 1950], applied to the Reverend Basset [Brisset?]. Basset and King George was two first cousins and six months time they sent a copy of the treaty and the first bearer from King George the Second, from Great Britain, sent one Dr Kent to make peace with the Accompong Maroons. My grandfather, H. O. Rowe, sent two of his Captains to suppress the rebellion. One James Bryan and James Fowler to suppress the rebellion at Maroon Town in St James, a place called Vaughansfield.[23] And, as I said, he [King George] sent one Dr Kent. And Cudjoe says he ready to return back his blows, to stop fighting. The Maroon named Generalissimo Cudjoe.

The Accompong Maroons fought the English 57 years, fight and stop and Cudjoe killed 6,000 of the British soldiers right there in Cudjoe's Town. Here [Accompong Town] is the place in Trelawny [Trelawny Town, St James], *not* [we are not in] St Elizabeth.[24] King George the Second said, 'Lord my God, I cannot afford to let so much of my people dieing for lands' and Dr Kent folded his left hand round the back of his body and stretched forth his right hand and called for peace. And he granted £250,000 as war indemnity to Generalissimo Cudjoe. It went to the Jamaican government (at that time the [British] Governor was Sir Edward Trelawny) and up to now we don't get a cent.

Edward Trelawny sent a message to George the Second to send troops immediately, otherwise...Cudjoe would be killing all the soldiers. Falmouth town belonging to the Maroons – it wasn't a town at the time but the land was ours. That was in 1738.

Returning to the theme of the maroon wars (in whose aftermath he contextualized the origin of his Rowe clan [see also chapter 4]), Mann continued:

The Trelawny Town/Vaughansfield Maroons was invited to a dinner and dancing by the British soldiers and when they went down there to Montego Bay, they [the colonists] tell them they going to have the dance at sea. And them put them into an upstairs house on the ship and barricade it and then took the Maroons from Montego Bay in the ship to Cuba and from there to Nova Scotia [in Canada] and Sierra Leone in Africa....[25]

Then now, the ship captain was an Englishman, so we the Rowe family is from Africa and from England. That captain was carrying soldiers and slaves, so that's how we [the Rowes] are descendants of David and Solomon.

Maroon Town, now. The legislators in the House [of Assembly], they raped and seized and captured our lands at Maroon Town. So the Maroons in St James be tax-payers now on their own lands. But still Maroons. And [there are] some people in Maroon Town, St James who are not Maroons. But most [are] Maroons.

One of Mann's sons, Dolphie Rowe (born in Accompong in 1942 and a returned migrant from the United States), also gave his account of Maroon Town which he presented as knowledge that had been passed down to him. His narrative outlines a historical link between the two Leeward Maroon communities, with Maroon Town (implicitly identified with Trelawny Town) becoming integrated into the political system of the Jamaican state in contrast to Accompong:

> What I understand about Maroon Town: it was another brother or sister – this maroon town [Accompong] and that Maroon Town, from what I was told, was neighbouring brother and sister. That section [Maroon Town] was slightly different, they were more ruled by the outer government quicker than us...At one stage, our treaty used to be kept by one of the older heads down in St James. Some fire burn and when one section of the treaty was burnt, they could get the copy from the other [colonial] side.
>
> Even now some Maroons still live in St James's Maroon Town [but he added there are also non-Maroons there]. The connection [between Accompong and Maroon Town] was some brother and sister, I don't positive but they were relative. But ask my old man [Mann Rowe] that, he's the best person to tell you.
>
> What I did know – the Maroons was spread out from here to St James. The Maroons in St James was part of the maroon settlement. Even now they keep it that way. Some in Maroon Town will say they have relatives here and vice versa.

In the next generation, Mann's grandson, Lawrence Rowe (son of Mann's son Jack), narrated the following account of Maroon Town (in 1999) when he was 23 years old. At that time, he had taken a computer course on the lowlands and he would later migrate to, and return from the US, to Accompong, where I would meet him again many times up to 2009. Lawrence's narrative, which reflects the continued transmission of oral history down the generations, highlights a historical link between the two communities of Accompong and Maroon Town but contrasts the present populations and their status in relation to land tax. The narrative also portrays a contrast in the roles of Nanny and Cudjoe, situates Cudjoe's residence in Accompong, which is identified with Trelawny Town, and represents his great-great-grandfather (Mann's paternal grandfather, Colonel H.O. Rowe) as collecting taxes from Maroon Town:

> What I know 'bout down there [Maroon Town]: Maroon Town, St James and Accompong Town did have a tie in my [great] great-grandfather's days – 'Pa Coolie' Rowe, he was Henry Octavius Rowe, go down there and collect tax from the Maroons living down in St James. But after his time no one never collect taxes from the maroon villages to show they control it. So the people don't know that their land is self-governing. So they start paying land taxes to the [Jamaican] government. So they are not really free like we are.
>
> In Maroon Town, most of the people got repatriated to Canada and to Africa. Just like how Mann Rowe said. So all the people in Maroon Town mix up now with outsiders.
>
> Nanny is more revolutionary than Cudjoe (brother and sister). So she tried to set up camps all over Jamaica, for example [in the] Blue Mountains and Moore Town and Scots Hall [in the east of the island] and burn down plantations and Great Houses, so she do more travelling than Cudjoe. But Nanny died when she was coming from St James. Cudjoe was more of a hide-and-seek person, he like to stay in the Cockpits and the British never see him till the day of peace. All over the island, the people know more of Nanny than Cudjoe.

> We [the Accompongs in the past] were having our celebrations [Myal Play] and there were two African Maroons down there in St James who got flogging for stealing white man pig to bring to the celebration in Accompong – Trelawny Town, same place. So the British broke the law as there shouldn't be no flogging after the treaty. And because of that, the St James Maroons started a next rebellion. They wanted Cudjoe to come down from Accompong to settle the dispute but Cudjoe didn't want to go during the time of the 6th of January celebration. So they decided to settle the dispute themselves. That's how I hear the history over and over again. So it go.

While Lawrence narrated, his grandfather, Mann, sat with us and occasionally interjected, thereby highlighting the active transmission of oral tradition down the generations of Accompong's central clan.

An Ex-Colonel's Narrative

The several interviews that I had throughout my fieldwork in Accompong, from 1979 to 2009, with Harris Cawley (including his narrative on Aberdeen earlier in this chapter), who was Colonel of Accompong, from 1983 to 1988, and whose late father, Tom Cawley, had been Colonel in the 1950s, included accounts of Maroon Town. In 1991, Ex-Colonel Cawley told me that his mother, Mrs Tom Cawley (Bernetta Cawley/'Auntie B', then aged 90), was from Vaughansfield in Maroon Town. By then, I knew Auntie B quite well, as she resided with Harris when she was not travelling (with her bundle of medicinal plants) to stay with her daughter in the United States (figure 6.7). However, regarding my research, she sometimes referred me to her son. So I asked the Ex-Colonel whether his mother was a Maroon (as she was from Vaughansfield)[26] and he assured me that she was, contextualizing this in a narrative on Maroon Town, including the issue of disputed Leeward Maroon lands:

> Yes, but the Maroons, they were there [in Maroon Town] too. Because Maroon Town, that was a lot of Maroons' outpost too, that was robbed from the Maroons. When you go up the hill to where the graves are, Flagstaff, all those places were where the Maroons fought for their lands. So after the peace treaty was signed, those lands were under the Maroons' jurisdiction. Straight back to Elderslie. Thousands of acres of land. But they had been robbed from the Maroons. And so the Maroons, that's why when it comes to land, them jealously guard what they have. Because the [colonial] government had mistreated them about their lands.

Some years later, in 1999 as I was about to commence my research in Maroon Town (where I would meet relatives of Auntie B, by then aged 97), Ex-Colonel Cawley narrated a fuller account of the relationship between Accompong Town (which he portrayed as historically the primary Leeward Maroon village, including Cudjoe's Old Town) and Maroon Town:

> In the early days when the Maroons got this portion of land [in the Cockpits] it was extended beyond Elderslie, Niagara, Horse Guard, into Maroon Town. Cudjoe felt that the land was too extended for proper control under his administration. He thought it wise to install and reinforce a camp in Maroon Town. He was here in Accompong, then in Maroon Town. He then left [Captain] Accompong here and that was for the protection

of his whole company. He went to be the leader in Maroon Town to safeguard the maroon lands so that there could be no surprising attack on the Maroons. He then left Accompong in charge here and that was how this portion of maroon territory got its name, Accompong Town.

After some years, Cudjoe left Maroon Town and came back and lived at Old Town [the Old Town grove in Accompong]. Old Town is the first settlement where the Maroons lived. I think you have been to Old Town, down beyond Kindah. He came and lived at Old Town, where he later died at about the age of 83 or 85. So Maroon Town was left in the hands of other Maroons.

Flagstaff [at Maroon Town] was an outpost of the British, where a British regiment was stationed to fight against the Maroons. The Maroons captured Flagstaff and took control of the whole operation. The British then left and went elsewhere (they were scattered at Horse Guard at one time) to continue their warfare against the Maroons. It was after that Cudjoe and his men installed the Maroon Town settlement.

After the peace treaty was signed, there was no great need to fear the British and so eventually the Maroon Town establishment was not well protected. And after many years, it was actually dissolved, that means not many Maroons were living there. Most of them returned, little by little, over the years. More activities were being done here [in Accompong]. Even today, Maroons come up to the [Myal] celebration from Maroon Town and other places.

Figure 6.7.   Mrs Bernetta Cawley of Maroon Town, wife and mother of Accompong maroon Colonels.

There were other Africans who were Jamaicans, they were not identified as Maroons and some of these lands [at Maroon Town] were sold by the Jamaican government on which people settled until today. It would have been after the abolition of slavery in 1838, because at that time they [ex-slaves] wanted land and were scattered all over. Some of them in Maroon Town are Maroons and still claim their identity. Some Maroons are living elsewhere too and still claim their maroon heritage...

My father, Thomas Cawley, was from here, Accompong, and got in contact with maroon relatives in St James in the German Town area, the Maldon and Vaughansfield area (a little extended out from Maroon Town) and there were Maroons living in that area and got in contact with Mr and Mrs Daniel Morris and married one of their daughters [Auntie B] and brought her back here to the community. I was born right here in Accompong and when we were little boys we used to travel to and from Accompong to Vaughansfield in the Maroon Town area to my mother's relatives....

After the Maroons left the land the government took back the Maroon Town land, after it was left and it wasn't properly surveyed. The government posing on the land and it's not theirs and after many years the government start to sell the land and the same Maroons would start to buy their own lands. There's still right now a lot of problems with the Jamaican government on the land issue with the Maroons and over the years with my father, he had to answer many questions in court on behalf of the Maroons when he was Colonel. And he called for the lands to be properly surveyed – in the Cookes' Bottom area (adjoining the Accompong lands) bordering Elderslie, Cedar Spring, Retirement and the Appleton Estate, it was formerly the Maroons' territories. They generally go there for part of their festivities each year, play the gumbay [drum] and sing, because they didn't want that land to be lost like the Maroon Town lands. But not for some years now, stopped about 30 or 40 years ago.

Ex-Colonel Cawley then gave an overview of the diversity of religions in Maroon Town and Accompong but highlighted the focus on Myalism in Accompong in contrast to its absence in Maroon Town:

Different Christian churches [in Maroon Town]. Same up here. But the most African is the Zion-Revivalist, they wrap their heads, play their drums and sing Christian songs. And they've other religions in the community.

Myal is being demonstrated mainly at the [January 6] celebration [in Accompong]. They induce the spirit and Myalism takes over. They do curious things then, even run up the roof and come down. The old people used to tell us they in 'high Myal' then. No Myalism in Maroon Town.

The Ex-Colonel then resumed his account of the history of Maroon Town and the role of Nanny and Cudjoe:

Nanny used to go with Cudjoe. His sister. Nanny used to be all over the island helping Cudjoe to protect his soldiers and his territory. She used to give Cudjoe certain instructions, how to get his soldiers prepared – must abstain from sexual operations for some days before they go to the war. Nanny was buried near Elderslie, a place they call Nanny, and Cudjoe was buried at Old Town...

> The estimate of the Maroon Town land is not known. It goes beyond Maroon Town [Square], to the Flagstaff area and coming to the Horse Guard area. Because in days gone by, I know Colonel Rowe and he used to go to Leavendon to collect taxes on behalf of the Maroons. Maroon land that was rented to other people: through Horse Guard, Leavendon, Niagara and Elderslie. Part of Accompong territory.

However, as he added:

> No common lands at Maroon Town now. All the lands are dominated by the [Jamaican] government. They possessed the lands and sold to other people. But in those days there was lands that the Maroons had...Not a clear-cut boundary [for Maroon Town]. Check at the Electoral Office, Kingston. They have a housing scheme and a banana chip factory and sometimes Accompong farmers ask me to carry [transport] bananas there.

In my research in Maroon Town (from 1999 to 2009), I would hear narratives on the relationship between Accompong Town and Maroon Town that contrasted with those collected in Accompong and Aberdeen. I would also discover, through my anthropological fieldwork and historical research, unexpected findings on the transformation of the former maroon site of Trelawny Town to non-maroon Maroon Town (chapters 7–10).

Notes

1. This would total 3,840 acres, much more than the historical figure of the additional land grant of 1,059 acres for Accompong Town (Campbell 1990, 181–83).
2. In the Jamaica Archives, Spanish Town, the Annual Crop Accounts of May 9, 1788 for Aberdeen plantation mention hiring out Negroes (slaves) to Island Estate (Ref: 1B/11/4/15, f.35); while in the National Library of Jamaica, Kingston, in-givings taken from poll tax returns as recorded in the Jamaica Almanacks for the years 1809 and 1811, include 37 slaves and 50 slaves, respectively, for Aberdeen. I am grateful to Jackie Ranston for her assistance with this archival research.
3. Alexander McFarlane's half-first cousin, James McFarlane, was married to Jean Forbes, daughter of Sir Alexander Forbes of Foveran in Aberdeenshire, Scotland. James McFarlane's brother, Duncan, had settled in Jamaica prior to 1764 (Besson and McFarlane 1995, 2005, 2009).
4. While documents regarding these transactions 'are clearly inscribed as relating to Alexander MacFarlane, he signed them "*Alex McFarlane*"' (Besson and McFarlane 2005, 5). In addition to my own collaborative research on my paternal MacFarlane/McFarlane family in Jamaica (Besson and McFarlane 1995, 2005, 2009; Besson 2013; and chapter 1), whose origins there begin with the migration to the colony of Alexander McFarlane around 1735, Robert B. Barker's research has further illuminated the life of Alexander McFarlane in Jamaica by uncovering its urban dimension: Alexander McFarlane (a keen astronomer), who initiated postal services in Jamaica and was appointed the first Post Master General of the island in 1735, had a substantial Georgian townhouse in Kingston with an observatory where he kept his astronomer's instruments (Barker 2000; Cundall 1937, 158, including Michael Hay's illustration). These instruments were left to the University of Glasgow in Alexander's will of 1755 (Besson and McFarlane 1995, 2005, 2009; personal communications from John Fowler 2009).

5. The records in the Jamaica Archives, Spanish Town, show details of sugar and rum shipped from Aberdeen Estate to London and Bristol and delivered to Alexander Forbes in 1772 (Crop Accounts 1B/11/4/6, f.79). The records also show at least three Alexander Forbes, in Jamaica, in the eighteenth and early nineteenth centuries, one of whom died in Jamaica as early as 1729 (ibid; Wills in the Archives; and in-givings taken from poll tax returns as recorded in the 1809 Jamaica Almanack, National Library of Jamaica). In 1775, an Alexander Forbes 'found the lands in the neighbourhood of Accompong fertile and well suited for coffee pens or penns, and provisions -- areas which "formerly [were] the haunts of runaway and rebellious Negroes"' (Campbell 1990, 182). The Annual Crop Accounts for Aberdeen in the Spanish Town Archives follow the same format as those for 1772 until 9 May 1788, by which date the estate was in the possession of Wn. Mitchell, Esq. (Ref: 1B/11/4/15, f.35). As mentioned in note 2 above, also recorded is the hiring out of Negro slaves from Aberdeen plantation to Island Estate, which by then was owned by Joseph Foster-Barham of Bedford, England, who had owned Island plantation since 1762. Prior to acquiring Island Estate, Joseph Foster-Barham (who claimed kinship with an officer in Cromwell's conquering army) and his brother, William Foster, already had Jamaican estates in St Elizabeth and in Westmoreland (Sibley 1978, 93; Hastings and MacLeavy 1979, 17; and later in this chapter).

6. After 1809, Aberdeen Estate disappears from the available records until 1845, with a further period of archival silence up to 1886.

7. I am grateful to Lucien Taylor of Lower Aberdeen, whose grandfather purchased land from the subdivision of the Island plantation (see later this chapter), for information and maps on the recent history of Island Estate and the two related Island Mountains.

8. I am grateful to the late Pastor Charles Wint of Upper Aberdeen for providing this estimate in 1999.

9. The slave village would have been located near the Great House for surveillance.

10. In the twenty-first century, descendants of the Foster family reside in Montego Bay where an eighteenth-century tomb of a Captain Foster may be seen in the yard, and retain the Great House at Elim in St Elizabeth.

11. This was only a few months after the death of Alexander McFarlane, who died in Jamaica in August 1755.

12. Zacharias George Caries, with two associates, was sent (at the request of the Foster/Barham brothers) by the Elders of the Moravian Church in Britain to St Elizabeth to missionise the slaves in 1754 (Hastings and MacLeavy 1979, 17).

13. As Moravians tended to preach in Jamaica by the invitation of the planters, it is likely that Alexander McFarlane of Island Estates (including Windsor) had extended such an invitation to the Moravian missionaries on the neighbouring Foster estates. (Evidence of a connection between the Fosters and the McFarlane/Forbes plantation families is underlined by the acquisition of Island plantation by Joseph Foster-Barham in 1762). At around this time, there was an unsuccessful attempt by the Moravians to missionize the Accompong Maroons (Hastings and MacLeavy 1979, 19).

14. See Diane Austin Broos (1997) and Yvonne Davis-Palmer (2010, 148–53) on the 'indigenization' of Pentecostalism in Jamaica.

15. This account is consistent with Price's (1996, 20, 24) observations that early Maroons in the Americas were often recently enslaved Africans, and that the first maroon leaders tended to claim African royal descent (before the adoption of a military model of leadership, as had occurred by the time of the Leeward Maroon treaty).
16. Compare R.T. Smith (1988, 40), who notes of West Indian kinship that, 'Those who have "come into the family" may also be called "bye family", a term derived, apparently, from the old English meaning of "bye" as secondary or subsidiary'.
17. The Island Mountain range extends from Ben Lomond and stretches to Balaclava, three miles from Lower Aberdeen. The family seat of the Scottish Mac/McFarlane clan, to which Alexander McFarlane who established Island Estates in the eighteenth century belonged, was at Arrochar near Loch Lomond; the Clan McFarlane burial ground (which I have visited) being in the village of Luss on the banks of Loch Lomond.
18. Though, as I had pointed out to Mann Rowe, Falmouth (founded around the 1770s [Besson 2002]) did not exist at the time of the treaty in 1738/39. However, as Mann retorted 'But the sea was there' (chapter 4).
19. The narrative compresses historical time, shifting the events of the Second Maroon War to around the time of the First Maroon War.
20. The escape and return from deportation of this Trelawny Maroon surnamed Fowler was likewise referred to by the Accompong abeng-blower, Rupie Reid, who gave this Maroon's full name as Al Fowler (chapter 4). Later in this chapter, Mann Rowe refers to an Accompong Maroon Captain named James Fowler who was sent to 'Maroon Town' (Trelawny Town) 'to suppress the rebellion' (see also note 23 below). These Leeward Maroons may have appropriated the surname Fowler from an officer or officers in the colonial army (which made incursions into Trelawny Town territory in the Second Maroon War), as was the maroon custom at that time (chapters 2 and 4). There were three Scottish Fowler planter brothers in the Trelawny militia that participated in the Second Maroon War: John, Andrew and James Fowler. John and Andrew were officers in the mounted militia (the 'Trelawny Light Horse') and their younger brother James was a lieutenant in the regular infantry militia. I am grateful to a McFarlane/Fowler descendant John Fowler for this information (personal communications October 3, 2012 and October 9, 2012). Of Andrew Fowler, John Fowler further writes: 'Andrew's cavalry troop was one of the units that were ambushed and suffered heavy losses in the initial engagement in the campaign. The commanding officer of the troop was killed in the ambush, so I assume that, as second in command, Andrew would have led the survivors in their escape' (personal communication, October 3, 2012).
21. These figures differ from the historical account of the treaty granting 1,500 acres of land to Cudjoe's Town, with the land grant subsequently increased to 2,559 acres with the additional 1,059 acres to the Accompong community (Campbell 1990, 127, 181–83).
22. Mann's references to the incident of the stolen pig and the colonial soldiers coming from Falmouth to Vaughansfield concern the Second Maroon War, while his references to Cudjoe relate to the First Maroon War.
23. Despite the compression of historical time, Mann Rowe's oral history has close parallels on this point with Robinson's historical account of a colonial scouting party sent to Trelawny Town on September 12, 1795 commanded by Colonel Fitch that included a Captain Brisset and two unnamed Accompong Maroons (Robinson 1969, 101–102; and see chapter 2).

24. As mentioned in chapter 4, Mann Rowe's claim that Accompong Town is the former Trelawny Town was underlined by the sign, 'Trelawny Town 1738–39' painted above the verandah of his cottage (see figure 4.3).
25. Compare Kenneth Bilby (1984a) on the Windward Maroon oral tradition of the 'treacherous feast'.
26. As I later realized, Auntie B would in any case have maroon status through her marriage to an Accompong Maroon (chapters 4 and 6).

7 ■ NON-MAROON MAROON TOWN

Maroon Town, in the Cockpits of the parish of St James, where I conducted fieldwork over a period of ten years, from 1999 to 2009, evolved as a non-maroon community on the historic site of Cudjoe's Town/Trelawny Town, which was the primary village of the eighteenth-century Leeward Maroon polity and the largest Jamaican maroon community. Cudjoe's Town was established by Captain Cudjoe, the most prominent African-American maroon leader, during the First Jamaican Maroon War (1725–38) and was consolidated by the Leeward Maroon treaty of March 1738/39. Cudjoe's Town was renamed Trelawny Town after the treaty between Cudjoe and Edward Trelawny, the British Governor of Jamaica, and endured until the Second Jamaican Maroon War of 1795–96. However, following the Second Maroon War, the Trelawny Maroons were betrayed and deported to Nova Scotia, in 1796, by the British colonists and the Trelawny Town treaty lands were confiscated by the colonial state. The deportation of the Trelawnys to Canada left Accompong Town, in St Elizabeth, which had sided with the colonists in the Second Maroon War, as the sole surviving village of the Leeward Maroon polity (chapters 2–5). The written history of Trelawny Town ends with those disastrous events and Carey Robinson (1969, 155) stated that 'Trelawny Town has been a ghost town ever since the defeat of the Trelawnys.'

However, like the 'ghost town' of Martha Brae in the adjoining parish of Trelawny, where my earlier research uncovered a hidden history of transformation from a British West Indian planter town to an Afro-Creole peasant village (Besson 2002), my research reveals that the ghost town of Trelawny Town was, likewise, transformed through the development of the non-maroon village of Maroon Town (chapters 7–10).

The renaming of the historic site of Trelawny Town as Maroon Town (initially 'Old Maroon Town' [Craton 1982, 303]), in memory of the deported maroons has previously been recognized. For example, as noted in chapter 2, Mavis Campbell (1990, 243) states that, after the deportation of the Trelawny Maroons, 'the area was designated Maroon Town, and is still so identified on the maps'. Bev Carey (1997, 385) notes that, 'That old village [Cudjoe's village] was destroyed in 1796 (after the Second Maroon War) and can be identified by the district of Maroon Town in St James' (see also Sibley 1978, 106). Werner Zips tentatively concludes that 'Kojo's Town was renamed Trelawney [sic] Town after the peace treaty. It was *most probably* where Maroon Town is located today' (1998, 97 n11) (my emphasis).

However, the process of transformation from Trelawny Town to Maroon Town and the significance of Maroon Town in Jamaican nation-building,

Caribbean peasantization and the comparative study of creolization in maroon and non-maroon derivations of African-American slave cultures has not been given the attention it deserves. A central aim of this book is to highlight the importance of Maroon Town in these contexts and to uncover its hidden history of transformation and creolization at the maroon/non-maroon interface, including continuities and discontinuities with Trelawny Town.

As will be unravelled in this and the following chapters (7–11), this history has involved the transformation of the common treaty land of Trelawny Town into the parcelled lands of Maroon Town, in the contexts of Caribbean post-slavery peasantization and the Jamaican export-oriented banana industry (chapter 1). This transformation has included the creation and transmission of family lands, which not only provide a basis for agriculture but also serve as sites of identity for transnational Old Families or clans traced through both genders and including migrants as well as residents. The transformation from Trelawny Town to Maroon Town has also included the creation of new ethnicities among villagers who claim descent from planters, colonial soldiers, slaves and Maroons.

This chapter provides an overview of Maroon Town, including its boundaries and political integration within the Jamaican post-colonial nation state; the transformation from Trelawny Town; the gendered and class-differentiated peasant economy; post-maroon mobilities (the transport industry, migration and tourism); its mosaic of religions, including the significance of the Baptist Church and the Revival worldview; the integration and differentiation of the community through education, youth and age; and the main patterns of kinship and ethnicity.

Subsequent chapters develop and elaborate some of these themes, including the rich oral traditions that highlight various Meso-Creole and Afro-Creole ethnicities within the wider context of the transformation from Trelawny Town to Maroon Town (chapters 8–9); the links between the 'McGhie Maroons' of Trelawny Parish and the McGhie Old Family, Maroon Town's central clan (chapter 10); the role of Maroon Town's Emancipation Day commemorations (which have both similarities and differences with Accompong maroon rituals) in the Jamaican nation state and the Maroon Town heritage-tourism projects that symbolically repair the fractured Leeward Maroon polity (chapter 11).

Maroon Town's Boundaries and Political Integration in the Nation State

In contrast to the Accompong maroon society, which, as the sole enduring Leeward Maroon village is virtually independent of the Jamaican nation state, Maroon Town is integrated into the island's political system. This political integration, which also internally differentiates the community, through varying political party affiliations, is effected through voting in a national electoral division and in parochial elections for the Parish Council of St James. The integration of Maroon Town in the Jamaican nation state is also reflected in the community's Emancipation Day commemorations, organized by Maroon Town's Parish Councillor, that have been held annually, since 1997, in the Flagstaff area of the village, as part of the national revival of these secular rituals.

In Maroon Town, political affiliations reflect the Jamaican two-party system: the Peoples' National Party (PNP) and the Jamaica Labour Party (JLP), which formed the government and opposition, respectively throughout much of my fieldwork in St James, until the victory of the JLP in 2007. The PNP, however, was returned to power in 2011. Maroon Town's Parish Councillor, throughout my fieldwork (1999–2009), Glendon Harris, is a member of the PNP and of several overlapping Old Families in Maroon Town where he was born in 1957 (chapter 8). The Councillor now resides in the parish capital, Montego Bay, where (in addition to his public service) he keeps a guesthouse and runs tourist tours to his main family-land home in Maroon Town where he also farms bananas, coffee and cocoa and oversees various family lands.[1]

The Councillor, who is qualified in Agricultural Economics and is a graduate in Education from the University of the West Indies (Mona), used to be a teacher at the Maldon Primary and Secondary Schools in Maroon Town and also worked in the Jamaican government's Ministry of Agriculture in St James. Now 'retired' (with children at school in Jamaica and university in the United States, and siblings scattered in Jamaica, Canada, the USA and England), he has extensive responsibilities, not only as Parish Councillor, but also as a member and/or Chairman/Director of numerous national associations, boards and committees, including the Jamaica Agricultural Society.[2] In addition, he serves as Chairman of the Maldon High School Board. He has represented Maroon Town on the Parish Council since 1983, when he succeeded a former PNP Councillor from another Maroon Town Old Family. This Ex-Councillor, the late Mortimer Reid, a returned migrant labourer from the United States who became a sugar cane and banana farmer and tailor in Maroon Town, remained (until his death in 2007, aged 96) a highly respected man both locally and nationally. This was reflected in the national award to the Ex-Councillor from the Jamaican government on National Heroes' Day in 2002 (the 40th Anniversary of Jamaican Independence) for his services to the Maroon Town community (chapter 8).[3]

Both Councillor Harris (who since my fieldwork has become Chairman of the St James Parish Council and, in 2012, Mayor of Montego Bay)[4] and Ex-Councillor Reid were very helpful in my research. The Councillor provided useful definitions of the boundaries of Maroon Town and informed estimates of its population. He identified three different but interrelated boundaries of Maroon Town: as a national political electoral division, the general non-political definition of Maroon Town and the core of Maroon Town. The national political electoral division of Maroon Town is the widest boundary, covering an area of around 60 square miles, much of which is uninhabited, with a population of about 24,000, as the Councillor explained:

> From Spring Garden near Kensington northerly to Brown Hill, Burkes Mountain, encompassing Content Mountain, taking an imaginary line to the Trelawny border at Wemyss and to the Cockpits encompassing Hope Mountain, Chatsworth, Georges Valley, Flagstaff, Silver Grove to Garlands, Cold Spring, taking the right side of the road from Cold Spring to Garlands Square, right side of the main road to Point encompassing Cold Spring, Jackson Road, German Town, Flamstead Gardens, Tangle River, Maldon, Summer Hill (see map 4).

The general non-political definition of Maroon Town includes about six square miles, as the Councillor outlined: 'places like Flagstaff, Browns' Town, Schaw Castle, Woodlands, the greater section of Vaughansfield, including Pond Piece, Dundee, Maldon and Maroon Town Square'. This area has around 630 households comprising a total population of roughly 16,000, including a voting population of about 2,800. Within these 'districts' of Maroon Town, one can narrow to a third boundary of about one-quarter of a square mile, comprising 'Maroon Town Square' or 'Maroon Town Crossroads' as 'Maroon Town proper', with a total population of a little under 3,000. As I found in my fieldwork, the Community Centre and main grocery stores and rum shop are at or near the Crossroads. There is also a Health Centre, on land donated by a member of the McGhie Old Family (Maroon Town's central clan), on a hillside overlooking the Square.

In my research, I worked mainly with the second and third non-political definitions of the community, reinforcing participant observation with interviews and the collection of genealogies and narratives especially in Maroon Town Square, Flagstaff (and beyond, in Georges Valley), Browns' Town (between the Square and Flagstaff), Maldon, Woodlands and Vaughansfield. All of these areas are significant in the history and transformation of Trelawny Town to Maroon Town.

The Transformation from Trelawny Town to Maroon Town

In addition to Maroon Town's political integration into the Jamaican nation state, which contrasts with the political autonomy of the Accompong maroon society, the taxed and parcelled lands of Maroon Town distinguish it from Accompong's tax-free common treaty land.[5] This is an intriguing contrast, since Accompong was the secondary community of the Leeward Maroon polity, while Maroon Town evolved on the site of Cudjoe's Town/Trelawny Town, which was the primary village of the Leeward polity and the community that received the main grant of Leeward Maroon treaty land. My anthropological fieldwork, combined with my historical research, reveals the contours of this transformation of the Trelawny Town treaty lands to the parcelled lands of the Maroon Town community.

As noted in chapter 2, following the deportation of the Trelawny Maroons to Nova Scotia in 1796, the 1,500 acres of Trelawny Town treaty land were confiscated by the colonial state and designated to be sold 'either as a whole or in lots not exceeding 100 acres each', with '"at least" 300 acres...reserved for the use of the troops' (Campbell 1990, 243). Barracks were built on the land reserved for the troops, on the former site of Trelawny Town/Cudjoe's Old Town and this core site of Maroon Town became known as Flagstaff (243; Eyre 1980, 9, 17; Aarons 1981, 29, 31). The colonial military settlement there with its hospital and water tank included the flat parade ground levelled by slaves, now known as 'Ball Ground', where sports are played and Maroon Town's annual Emancipation Day rituals have been held since 1997 (figures 7.1, 7.2 and 7.3).

Historical sources (e.g., Aarons 1981; Brathwaite 1982, 18, 27, see also 15, 21, 29) indicate that Maroon Town was still a colonial military settlement at the time of the great 1831–32 slave rebellion that started at nearby Kensington and that the barracks endured until the time of the Crimean War (1854–56). John Aarons (a former government Archivist) states that:

Figure 7.1. 'Trelawney Town, the Chief Residence of the Maroons'. From Edwards 1801. Courtesy of National Library of Jamaica.

Figure 7.2. The former Parade Ground, Flagstaff, Maroon Town.

Figure 7.3. The remains of the Barracks Well, Flagstaff. Courtesy of Councillor Glendon Harris 2003.

> We do not know the exact date when Maroon Town was abandoned by the British troops. Frank Cundall (1915) says that the regiments were maintained there until the middle of the nineteenth century when they were withdrawn at the time of the Crimean War. He also said that in 1839 the town was made into the site of a sanatorium for troops, and huts were erected there for the purpose. From the information contained on the 1847 Plan,...the camp was not operating at full capacity at that time...and only 161 men were in residence in the Barracks.

According to the government *Blue Book* in 1862, 'only two soldiers, both privates, are listed under Maroon Town, in the section on the distribution of the troops...' (Aarons 1981, 31).

The Maroon Town Councillor's oral history (chapter 8) likewise mentioned that Maroon Town became an 'English' military base, including Flagstaff (where a flag was hoisted to guide British ships into the harbour at Falmouth, which could be seen from Gun Hill at Flagstaff) and remained an 'English' settlement (which spread to the 'township' of Maroon Town Crossroads/Square, where various routes meet) until cholera and typhoid outbreaks in the mid-nineteenth century,[6] when the barracks became deserted. These historical and oral history accounts are reinforced by the mid-nineteenth century tombstone inscriptions of the British military cemetery that can still be seen at Flagstaff (figure 7.4 and chapter 8).

Figure 7.4. The British colonial military cemetery at Flagstaff.

While Mavis Campbell's (1990) historical account of the Second Maroon War of 1795–96 gives useful information on the colonial confiscation of the Trelawny Town treaty lands and the building of the barracks, her periodization (1655–1796) provides no insight into the subsequent transformation of Maroon Town, where the core of parcelled lands are now family lands (coexisting with bought and rented lands) held by Old Families or clans who claim descent from colonists, slaves and Maroons.

However, my research indicates that the ancestors of these Old Families bought the lands that are now family lands through the colonial government's subdivision of Trelawny Town's treaty land in the wider context of Caribbean post-slavery peasantization and the Jamaican free village movement in the mid-nineteenth century (chapter 2). This peasantization was catalyzed or reinforced, in the case of Maroon Town by the desertion of the barracks at Flagstaff and the disbanding of the military settlement, around the 1850s, after which time, land sales were made to individuals, including those from the colonial militia and other local people. This post-emancipation peasantization, which included the acquisition of lands around what is now Maroon Town Square or Crossroads, also included the establishment of the Baptist free village of Maldon (the first free village in St James established by English Baptist missionaries soon after emancipation) that has become a part of Maroon Town.

My research also indicates that such land purchases at Maroon Town Crossroads and Flagstaff followed an earlier stage of 'squatting' on Crown Land, which was the former

Trelawny Town treaty land confiscated by the colonial state after the Second Maroon War. My fieldwork, combined with historical research, further indicates that such 'squatters' included the mulatto 'McGhie Maroons' from the foraging non-treaty maroon village of Congo Town/Highwindward/Me No Sen You No Come (which was destroyed by a military attack in 1824 [Patterson 1973, 264]) in the Cockpits of Trelawny Parish, near Flagstaff, who subsequently purchased land near Flagstaff in the mid-nineteenth century and whose descendants became Maroon Town's central clan (chapter 10). Oral tradition indicates that squatting also included cultivation by some ancestors of Maroon Town's Old Families (who had already purchased former Trelawny Town land from the colonial government at the Crossroads and were resident there) of the area around the military settlement at Flagstaff from the mid-1800s and that such informal occupation went on for nearly a century. Such squatters went in daily to cultivate, including cash-cropping in bananas and sugar cane, sometimes with the help of imported labour from other parishes such as Westmoreland. These migrants to Maroon Town and their descendants are now referred to, in the village, as 'Newcomers' and form an important part of the community.

From 1929, the colonial government made further land sales of the former Trelawny Town treaty lands, through purchase from a large-scale landowner and subdivision of over 200 acres at Flagstaff (including the area immediately around the former military settlement), which then became residentially developed. These land purchases (including land for banana cultivation), made by members of the Old Families and Newcomers, usually ranged from three to ten acres, though some were more. An important stage in the post-military development of Flagstaff was the establishment of the Flagstaff Bakery by an ancestor of one of Maroon Town's Old Families (the Youngs), who started by cultivating ginger and subsequently imported labour for the bakery. The bakery has now been relocated to Montego Bay and is said to be the distributor of the best 'hard dough' bread throughout the island.

More recent land purchases in Maroon Town include those made in the late twentieth century through the Jamaican government's land settlement schemes. This includes the land settlement at Pond Piece (where some land is also rented from the government's Lands Department), which originally comprised an area of about 1,000 acres of bush and swamp that was part of Vaughansfield (which was a British military base during both the First and Second Maroon Wars). The Pond Piece land was purchased by the government from a large-scale land owner in the 1970s. The government allocated some of this bought land for housing and some for farmsteads. The government also purchased and subdivided around 400 acres at Georges Valley, beyond Flagstaff, and sold this for both houses and farms.

There were still further land purchases at the turn of the millennium through the development of an additional area of Vaughansfield by the Greater Maroon Town Development Trust, a community-based organization, established by Councillor Harris to develop Maroon Town in liaison with the government's Operation Pride land settlement scheme. In this additional section, 77 lots were developed, inclusive of the Vaughansfield cemetery. The Trust carried out the survey and subdivision and installed roads, water and electricity, with individual owners contributing to the Trust and helping to finance the development. The project was started around 1999, with the land sales agreement consolidated in 2002.

It was against this background of the transformation of the lands in and around the site of Trelawny Town – including land transformed from land captured through 'squatting' in marronage (1725–38) to legal treaty land (1738/39–95), to confiscated land (1796), to captured land again and then to purchased land and family land – that the Maroon Town community developed into a dynamic banana peasantry descended from ex-slaves, colonists and Maroons.

This historic transformation took place within the wider contexts of Caribbean post-slavery peasantization combined with the burgeoning banana industry in the Caribbean and Jamaica, which was tied to the world economy in the late nineteenth and twentieth centuries (chapters 1 and 2). This globalization reflected in the banana industry not only invigorated the Caribbean plantation system but was also appropriated by the region's peasantries, who established cash-cropping for global markets (Marshall 1985; Trouillot 1988; Horowitz 1992). This development was evident in Accompong and Aberdeen (chapters 3 and 6) but was even more pronounced in Maroon Town, where banana cultivation for export flourished among the post-slavery peasantry.

The Gendered and Class-Differentiated Peasant Economy

The mainstay of Maroon Town's peasant economy has been the production and distribution of bananas for internal markets and export in various contexts of globalization. From the later nineteenth century, banana production became established in Maroon Town and consolidated into the twentieth century. Many of Maroon Town's banana farmers produced for export, for example, to England from Montego Bay. Farmers could sell to global markets through intermediaries such as the All Island Banana Growers Association and, later, to the Western Banana Development Co. (West Ban), a company set up in 1991 by the Jamaican government and private investors to reinforce banana cultivation in the western part of the island, through the Agricultural Credit Bank. Bananas were transported by truck to boxing stations, including those at nearby Kensington and Flamstead. However, due to the further globalization of agriculture in the later 1990s, the Caribbean banana industry declined (Clegg 2004; Ahmed 2004; and chapter 1); this is evident in all three of the Cockpit Country communities that I studied but especially impacted Maroon Town, and the boxing stations are now deserted.

Banana production in Maroon Town is now mainly for sale at marketplaces in Montego Bay (St James), Wakefield and Falmouth in Trelawny, and Savanna-la-Mar in Westmoreland, to hotels in Montego Bay and to the locally owned banana chip factory, named 'Maroons' Pride', between Maroon Town Square and Vaughansfield (figure 7.5). The factory provides employment for washing, peeling and slicing the bananas, then frying and packing the chips. Women peel and wash the fruit (drums of water are brought by truck from the 'Popkin' area of Maroon Town), men fry the chips and women pack them. The packaged chips are either sold at the factory or trucked to Montego Bay for sale, for example, to schools and the Donald Sangster's International Airport where they are served on departing flights.

Variations in banana production in Maroon Town have reflected, and still reflect, the internal class differentiation of the banana peasantry (cf. Mintz 1973), with banana farms ranging from a few acres to about 60 acres. The farms are often fragmented, with scattered landholdings and varying forms of tenure, and banana production is often combined with cultivation of other food crops, cash-cropping in coffee, cocoa, sugar cane and yams, and raising cows and goats.

Like the sale of bananas, the marketing of other cash crops in Maroon Town has been tied to the world economy, often by selling through corporate intermediaries. Sugar cane was generally sold to Hampden Estates (chapter 1), on the parish boundary of Trelawny and St James, for processing into sugar and rum for export. However, Hampden now sends its cane to Trelawny Sugar's factory for grinding. Coffee is sold to the Catadupa Coffee Growers Co-operative, cocoa to the St James Cocoa Growers Co-operative, and yams to licensed export-higglers. Livestock are sold to butchers in Maroon Town. In the past, wet sugar or 'sugar head' was sold in internal markets such as Wakefield or Falmouth.

Some farmers sell their produce themselves, in local markets, but higglers from Maroon Town play an important role in the distribution of bananas and other food crops in the island's internal marketing system. While farmers are mainly men, women are prominent in higglering – though some females farm and some higglers are male (compare Mintz 1989; Besson 2002, 2003b). Most men in Maroon Town are farmers and some male cultivators also work as agricultural labourers for the more prosperous farmers: 'carrying bananas' or chopping grass.

Figure 7.5.   Maroons' Pride banana chip factory, Maroon Town.

While most men in Maroon Town are farmers, some have additional or other occupations such as teachers, carpenters and masons, and there are several taxi-drivers with their own cars for transporting passengers, especially between Maroon Town and Montego Bay (a journey of 14 miles each way). Women's occupations, in addition to being cultivators, housewives, marketers and higglers, include domestic workers, nurses, teachers, dressmakers and garment-factory workers (who, like some nurses, teachers and domestic workers, commute to Montego Bay). Therefore, in addition to a gendered and class-differentiated peasant economy incorporating 'occupational multiplicity' (Comitas 1973), skilled working-class, clerical and middle-class occupations are embedded in Maroon Town's peasant-farming households (compare Mintz 1973; Besson 2002, 214–17).

My analysis of Maroon Town's economy is reinforced by villagers' narratives and the rise and decline of the banana industry were recurring narrative themes. For example, at the turn of the millennium, Clinton McBean, a Newcomer who had lived in the community for many years and keeps a bar and grocery shop at Maroon Town Crossroads, narrated that:

> Most of the people in Maroon Town, once upon a time used to be farmers. Bananas were [the] main source [of livelihood], but bananas took a nose dive. It's coming back a little but don't have any government subsidies now. Bananas were involved with West Ban, a foreign-based company which provided boxes and transport, spray and fertilizers and shipped to England. Died out now. Long ago, there were government subsidies for fertilizer, etcetera, and people paid in small instalments. Now [there are] still some small farms and bananas are sold, for example, to the market, hotels and supermarkets in MoBay and to markets in Sav-la-Mar, Santa Cruz and Falmouth.

About a decade later, in 2009, Councillor Harris explained the impact of globalization (combined with environmental disasters) on the decline of the Jamaican and Maroon Town banana industry:

> Under the World Trade Agreement we don't have that preferential agreement again. So it has become very competitive, small farmers and larger estates. We were touched as far back as Hurricane Gilbert [in 1988] and other hurricanes which wiped out bananas. The main thing now is the World Trade Organisation (WTO) Agreement. We are not competitive again due to the cost of production here and we are not subsidized, whereas other countries are. So farmers can't afford to produce high quality or the quantity to compete in the market, even though ours tastes much better and is preferred. Can't produce the quantity to make it viable for ships to come here.

I asked him about the significance of Fair Trade for Jamaican banana farmers and he continued:

> Fair Trade? That is working against us. Fair Trade and WTO is asking for competition. So this has wiped out our preferential treatment. And you have to be HACCP-certified on an international agreement about chemicals used, etcetera, but pretty costly and hurricanes cut into getting back the returns. [7]

In 2009, I would learn more about the impact of globalization on the decline of the banana industry from Robert McGhie of Maroon Town's central clan, who succeeded his grandfather Leonard McGhie (1904–74) as one of the most successful banana farmers in the community (chapter 10).

Narratives, likewise, highlighted the development of the transport industry in Maroon Town, which is an important aspect of the economy of this very mountainous village – facilitating not only the trucking of bananas and commuting for work (and education) in Montego Bay but also the intense overseas and circulatory migration typifying Maroon Town and the village's emerging tourist industry. These trends in geographical mobility in the nineteenth and twentieth centuries, and into the new millennium, have replaced the earlier population movements of marronage and deportation that marked the rise and fall of Trelawny Town in the eighteenth century.

Post-Maroon Mobilities: Transport, Migration and Tourism

In 1999, at the beginning of my fieldwork in Maroon Town, the late Jonathan Dunstan (1908–2004), who was the oldest man in the Maldon area of Maroon Town (who had lived there all his life except for a trip to the United States on the Farm Work Scheme in 1943) and whose grandparents were emancipated slaves, recalled how his parents used to travel to market by 'beast'. Nowadays, there is a motor-transport industry in the community, including several resident taxi-drivers and a public bus service. Marketers and higglers from Maroon Town travel by car, taxi, mini-bus or bus to marketplaces in the lowlands of Trelawny, St James and Westmoreland, and blue- and white-collar workers and some schoolchildren and college students commute to Montego Bay (approximately an hour each way). Some villagers had also owned trucks for transporting bananas.

Mobility in Maroon Town is even more highly developed in relation to global labour migration, via the cities and ports of Montego Bay or Kingston. Emigration and return migration were initially by ship, but are now through the island's international airports, and overseas migration has been a central theme elaborating the peasant economy since emancipation. These migrations, facilitated by access to land in the community and proximity to Montego Bay, have occurred in the wider contexts of Jamaican post-slavery migrations, shaped by global labour demands, combined with the quest for economic and social improvement and related views of personhood.

In Maroon Town, narratives tell of early migrations to Central America and Cuba, followed by movements to North America and Britain. The Ex-Councillor Mortimer Reid was prominent in establishing, in Maroon Town, the Jamaican government's post-war Farm Work Scheme to the United States (and later to Canada) and several Maroon Town villagers have participated in this Scheme. The village is now intensely transnational with Old Families and Newcomers enmeshed in global networks, linking Maroon Town to various parts of the Americas and Britain. In addition to providing a channel for remittances, such social networks include return- and circulatory-migration; for example, returning to settle on family land or purchased land and visiting for funerals and other mortuary rituals.

Globalization and geographical mobility are further reflected in the impact on Maroon Town of Jamaica's international tourist industry. During my fieldwork, this was evident in the tourist tours organized by the Maroon Town Councillor (and advertised in Montego Bay hotels) to his family-land home near Maroon Town Square from his guesthouse in Montego Bay. Such tours (which sometimes operate three times a week) are by mini-bus, with a driver from Maroon Town assisted by a local tour guide. The mini-bus brings tourists and a picnic to the Councillor's family-land house-yard near the Square, which now includes a large thatch-roofed hut, where lunch is served while local musicians entertain. There is also a small museum in the house on the maroon wars. The tours sometimes continue on to Flagstaff or Accompong, for example, for the annual Myal Play. The Councillor's tourism development plans include improving the domestic water supply and attracting cruise-ship passengers from Montego Bay. In the later years of my fieldwork, Maroon Town attracted support from the Jamaica National Heritage Trust (JNHT) and foreign organizations for its heritage-tourism industry (chapter 11).

The Religious Mosaic of Maroon Town

Like politics, class, gender and migration, religion both integrates and differentiates the Maroon Town community. There are a range of Protestant churches in Maroon Town and these are significant sites for social activities and socialization. The two oldest and most prominent churches are the Baptist Church at Maldon and the Mount Edmonson Methodist Church at Dundee, both originating in colonial missionary activity during and after slavery (chapter 2), and many Maroon Town villagers attend them. The Mount Edmonson Methodist Church was originally situated at Browns' Town between Maroon Town Square and Flagstaff. However, it was re-established at Dundee in 1914 and its foundation stone commemorates the men of Maroon Town who fought in the First World War for Britain. The Baptist Church was central in the founding of Maldon as the first free village in St James, after emancipation in 1838.

There are also three Seventh Day Adventist churches (near the Crossroads on the way to Schaw Castle, at Vaughansfield and at Bottom Pasture River), Pentecostal churches at Browns' Town, Flagstaff and Tangle River, and a Pentecostal New Testament Gospel Hall, Mount Ararat, near Maroon Town Square. In addition, there is a large Revival yard in Maldon.

The Maldon area of Maroon Town, with its Baptist Church and Revival tabernacle, illustrates well the role of religion in the consolidation of Maroon Town and the links between its churches and those elsewhere in Jamaica. I look first at these two complementary churches in Maroon Town and then briefly at Adventists, Pentecostalists and Methodists.

The Maldon Baptist Church

Maldon was established (as the first free village in St James) by English Baptist missionaries, the Reverends T.C. Hutchins and Walter Dendy, who purchased the mountainous land (now the Maldon Hills) on behalf of the church with financial support from Baptists in Maldon, Essex, England (Sibley 1978, 101). These missionaries established the Maldon Baptist Church (one of the first five built in Jamaica after the enactment of Apprenticeship in 1833), which overlooks Maroon Town Crossroads in the distance (figure 7.6). They also subdivided the Maldon land for sale to ex-slave members of the church, who worshipped, for example, at the Crooked Spring/Salter's Hill Church where Sam Sharpe (who led the 1831–32 slave rebellion that started at Kensington) had been a deacon (chapter 2 and figure 2.2).

In 1999, the late Jonathan Dunstan, an Afro-Creole born in Maldon in 1908 (mentioned previously as the oldest man in Maldon), who was a grandson of emancipated slaves and who was described by the Revival leader, who sent me to him, as 'the oldest man in Maldon for history', provided an illuminating narrative regarding the Baptist missionaries and his Old Families at Maldon. Jonathan's paternal grandfather, an ex-slave, had (like Sam Sharpe) been a deacon in the Baptist Church. Jonathan's father, born in Maldon, had likewise been a Baptist deacon. Jonathan, too, became a deacon of the Maldon Baptist Church. Jonathan's ex-slave maternal grandparents purchased ten acres of the land that had been subdivided at Maldon by the Baptist missionaries, Hutchins and Dendy. This land, which is next to the Baptist Church, and has a family cemetery with eight graves, has been orally transmitted as family land for the ex-slaves' descendants. At the turn of the millennium, these descendants numbered at least six generations, including Jonathan and his siblings and their many children, grandchildren, great-

Figure 7.6. The Maldon Baptist Church, Maroon Town.

grandchildren and great-great-grandchildren traced through both males and females. These cognatic descendants of the emancipated slaves are partly dispersed through migration to Canada, the United States and England, but Jonathan said that all of them retain rights to use the land as is 'customary'.

Both of Jonathan's parents, who are buried in the family-land cemetery, farmed in Maldon cultivating food crops which they sold at marketplaces in Wakefield and Deeside in Trelawny, travelling by donkey or mule. His parents had also cash-cropped in bananas and sugar cane, selling cane to Hampden Estates and producing bananas for export as 'later bananas became a product and they ship bananas from I have sense'; that is, from Jonathan could remember. In addition, his parents milled cane for 'sugar head', which they wrapped in banana leaves to sell at market.

Jonathan's parents knew both Hutchins and Dendy as pastors of the Maldon Baptist Church. Jonathan's mother (who was born in Maldon and whose first child was born there around 1900) had told him how the slaves had worshipped secretly at the Salter's Hill Baptist Church, as Jonathan narrated:

> Of course they [Hutchins and Dendy] were Baptists. They sold the land to the so-called members. They [the members] came up out of the slave trade. Me mother used to tell us a story. She said that the head church was Salter's Hill and the people went on beast-back – donkey, mule and horse – they would have to leave before day-break to worship. Because if the Massas [slave masters] hear the beast foot [beasts' feet] coming they would shoot. So they [the slaves] would have to tie trash under the horse shoe [horses' shoes] so they don't hear the tramp of the feet. Imagine, you have to do that even to worship.

Jonathan's mother also passed on to him a firsthand oral account of river-baptism and of Revd Hutchins's death in 1906 and his burial in the Maldon Baptist churchyard, where his tomb can be seen.

Jonathan (whose wife was a shopkeeper in Maldon and who had children, grandchildren and great-grandchildren) was, like his parents, a farmer who had cash-cropped in bananas and sugar cane. He used to sell cane to Hampden Estates and also to Green Park Estate in Trelawny and Barnett Estates in St James. In the past, he had sold bananas for export through the (American) United Fruit Company and then later through West Ban. In 1999, he still cultivated bananas and yams. At that time, he was living on his own bought land near the Baptist church and had two other pieces of purchased land that he was cultivating in Maldon, one of which adjoined his family land. He described Maldon as 'an old Baptist community', with Old Families and family lands originating in the subdivision of lands by the Baptist missionaries and where some land still belongs to the Baptist church. He had been a Baptist all his life, though he had recently become a member of the Mount Edmonson Methodist Church as well (where he was buried in the churchyard when he died, aged 96, in 2004).

Jonathan explained that Maldon and Maroon Town are one community and outlined the relationship between them (portraying Maroon Town as becoming a part of Maldon, despite the earlier origin of Maroon Town):

> Maroon Town is part of Maldon. Because Maroon Town was capital for Maldon. The post office used to be at Maroon Town. The school used to be Maldon School – until today. More schools born out of Maldon. Maroon Town was here before Maldon but the activities in Maldon become big and swallow up Maroon Town.

Jonathan's oral history included a narrative of the Flagstaff area of Maroon Town, where, he said both Maroons and white soldiers had 'camped' and where there are 'plenty of tombs'. He then stated: 'But there is something peculiar about this Maroon Town now' as there are no longer Maroons there and instead the Maroons now celebrate their annual 'Anniversary' at Accompong. I would find this view of a migration of Maroons from Flagstaff (the former site of Trelawny Town) to Accompong to be a recurring theme in Maroon Town narratives, which tend to conflate the First and Second Maroon Wars, thereby not only compressing historical time but also transforming the outcome of the Second Maroon War. This transformation, which elides the deportation of the Trelawny Maroons (replacing it with a migration to Accompong), symbolically repairs the fracturing of the Leeward Maroon polity and provides an explanation for the relationship between Maroon Town and Accompong today (Besson 2005, and chapters 8–10). As we spoke, Jonathan was visited by a friend from Aberdeen in St Elizabeth. This Afro-Aberdonian reinforced Jonathan's account by explaining: 'They keep up Maroon Town in 'Campong Town [Accompong]' (compare chapter 6).

The Revival Worldview in Maldon/Maroon Town

Maldon's Revival leader, Bishop Drummond, was 64 years old when I met him at the beginning of my fieldwork in Maroon Town in 1999. He was still leading his Revival congregation there ten years later, at the age of 74, in 2009. Born in Summer Hill, near the Maldon High School, he settled in Maldon in 1977 to acquire land of his own. He first lived on leased land then bought land on a mountain-top, where his Revival yard can be seen from miles around. His mother had been a Revivalist ('I born come see her as a Revivalist') in the Trelawny village of Sherwood Content[8] and the Bishop narrated that he was 'called by the Spirit' when he was eight years old. When I met him in Maldon, he had been a Revival Pastor for 40 years before becoming a Bishop two years previously. His tabernacle, the Mount Zion Revival Church of God, is fully recognized by and registered with the Jamaican government. This reflects the acknowledgement by the nation state that Afro-Protestant Revival, which evolved through creolization from the Myal slave religion (Schuler 1979, 1980; and chapters 2–4), is an integral part of Jamaican nationhood (Besson 1995c, 2002, 239–75, 2007, 2009; Besson and Chevannes 1996).[9]

At Maldon, the Bishop first built a bamboo tabernacle but, after this was destroyed by Hurricane Gilbert in 1988, he built a stronger structure with a corrugated iron roof and concrete floor. This tabernacle is set within a spacious yard, which is being transformed from purchased land to family land and there is already a family grave there. The Bishop also built two houses here for himself and his extended family. The Bishop is a farmer who was cultivating bananas, plantains and yams. His wife is a dressmaker and frequent traveller to the United States, where one of their daughters lives. Their grandchildren attend various schools in or near Maroon Town. All the adults in the yard are involved in the Bishop's church and the children are being socialized into the Revival worldview. As seen below, this worldview pervades the Maroon Town community despite its mosaic of religions.

The Bishop's Revival church has a core of about 30 members, who attend services every Sunday for a 'full day, morning and night', as he explained. Several members of his family, including his wife and daughters, are Revival officers and his son-in-law (who builds and repairs churches) is an Elder in the church. Baptisms are sometimes performed early on Sunday mornings, at Bottom Pasture River near the Baptist Church. In addition, prayer meetings are held on Monday evenings, a regular service is conducted on Wednesday nights, women's missionary meetings are held on Thursday evenings and a Young Peoples' Association (YPA) of about 18 boys and girls is convened on Friday nights.

The core members of the Revival church are from Maldon, Maroon Town Square, Tangle River and Flamstead. However, in addition to this core, there is community-wide participation in Maroon Town in Revivalist mortuary rituals as the Bishop narrated:

> After you have a dead [death], you have wakes first, every night for about one to two weeks before the burial. Then [if] going to bury tomorrow, you have the Nine Night. Simply means all the people gather together to sing from hymnals and read from the Bible, and prayers and choruses, then burial the next day. Eating and drinking, a feast, at the close of the funeral. They used to have Forty Nights but not any more. Used to have Gerreh [a traditional celebratory dance symbolizing rebirth at death] like using graters, playing fork and bamboos during the wakes, but now use sound system.
>
> People in the area from other churches do these practices. They have to adopt the Revival way, as that is the basis of Africanism. The Revival way is coming straight from Africa. Revival is coming straight from the Bible. Revival from dead works, truly repent, born again.

This community-wide participation was reflected in the wakes held for Baron McGhie, a prominent banana farmer from the McGhie Old Family (Maroon Town's central clan), who resided on bought land in Maldon and died there at the beginning of my fieldwork in 1999. Yet he was a member of the Maldon Baptist Church and was buried in its churchyard (chapter 10). Revival rituals also pervade the many burials in Maroon Town, including Maldon, that take place in house-yards especially on family land – as in Trelawny's Baptist villages (Besson 1984b, 2002). In Maroon Town, community involvement in Revivalism is likewise reflected in participation in annual conventions held by the Bishop for eight days in July. As the Bishop explained, 'all the district people support it, a whole lot, full church'.

From an anthropological perspective, Revival may indeed be understood as evolving from the African religions of the enslaved, as the Bishop asserted, but through a process of Caribbean creolization, as his reference to the Bible indicates (Besson 1995c, 2002, 239–63, 2009; Besson and Chevannes 1996). The Jamaican slaves forged, from their

African religions, the creole Myal slave religion in which a morally neutral magical/spiritual power (Obeah) was believed to be accessed through spirit possession (Myal) to protect the slaves from the 'sorcery' of enslavement (Schuler 1979, 1980; Bilby 1993; Handler and Bilby 2001). While Myalism was retained and transformed in marronage and endures in Accompong (chapters 3–4), among the enslaved population in the later slavery period, Myalism (which was especially pronounced in Trelawny and St James) appropriated Baptist Christianity to form the Native Baptist variant (chapter 2). After emancipation, Myalism appropriated and transformed the Euro-Protestant Great Revival into two variants of Afro-Creole Revivalism in 1860 and 1861: Revival-Zion (known as 'the '60') and Pukumina ('the '61'). Zionism was regarded as closer to Baptist Christianity and opposed to Obeah in the Eurocentric sense of 'sorcery' and Pukumina was seen as more like the Myal-Obeah complex.

Both variants of Revivalism share a worldview of an integrated world of living persons and spiritual beings, which include God (especially the Holy Spirit) and the dead. The Revival spirit pantheon is perceived as having three dimensions: Heavenly spirits (the Triune Christian God, archangels, angels, and saints), Earthbound spirits (fallen angels or satanic powers, biblical prophets and apostles), and the spirits of the known human dead (Seaga 1982, 10; Chevannes 1978, 5; Besson 2002, 244–45). However, as Edward Seaga noted in a pioneering study of Revivalism:

> *Zionists* deal primarily with Heavenly spirits and with Apostles and Prophets of the 'Earthbound' group. They believe in the existence of other powers of the pantheon, but consider them evil, and therefore useful only for evil purposes...On the other hand, *Pukkumina* [sic] followers work primarily with 'Ground' spirits and 'Fallen Angels,' who in their value system are not considered evil. They maintain that these spirits are more useful than those used by Zion, since they are nearer to them and more easily contacted (Seaga 1982, 10–11, quoted in Besson 2002, 245).

Seaga's (1982) delineation of the different emphases on the various categories of spirits in Revival-Zion and Pukumina is mirrored in the Revival congregations or *bands* that I studied in Trelawny (Besson 2002, 245–50), where all Revival leaders claimed their churches to be Revival-Zion rather than Pukumina (which was, however, believed to be practised elsewhere in the island). Barry Chevannes, likewise, found this in Kingston in the 1990s (Besson and Chevannes 1996). I further discovered this to be the case in the Bishop's church in Maldon,[10] where he explained the worldview of his Zion church in contrast to Pukumina:

> We are *not* Pukumina! Those are the people that visit grave. They get a lot of wood and build fire and jump over it. Kill goat and drink the blood. Go in the cemetery and call up spirits. That is Pukumina. *No*, we don't have this here in this district. Those are in [the eastern parishes of] St Mary and St Thomas and Portland – out of our parish [St James] completely. Those are a wicked set of people, dressed all in red. They are *demonic* people. They hurt people. We are spiritual Revival-Zion. We are led by the Spirit, do nothing of self, through the Holy Ghost. The main spirit is the Holy Ghost, power of God. Several types of spirits, [for example] spirit of the devil, that's what the Puku people use. The scripture saying 'Behold my beloved Son and the heavens open and the spirit descend

like a dove' and that's the same spirit we worship today. (Compare Besson 2002, 245–48 on Trelawny parish.)

This biblical emphasis on the Holy Ghost descending like a dove is reinforced by the doves reared in the Bishop's Revival yard.

However, my research in both Trelawny (Besson 2002) and Maroon Town reveals that the distinction between the two variants of Revivalism is blurred; for the belief in the morally neutral magical/spiritual power of Obeah is retained and cocooned at the heart of the Revival-Zion worldview. This enduring belief has some parallels with the endurance of Myalism in Accompong (chapter 3–4).

The Bishop explained that he performs spiritual healing ('give bush medicine to the sick, pray for the sick, anoint in olive oil') and that numerous people visit his tabernacle on an individual basis for healing (compare Besson 2002, 248–51). These visitors come not only from 'the district, including Maroon Town' and various parts of Jamaica and the Caribbean, but also from the United States, Canada and England.

In addition to the core members of the tabernacle, the participation in Revival rituals by the wider Maroon Town community and the numerous visitors to the Revival yard, the Bishop's church is enmeshed in a far-flung Revival travelling network that extends throughout Jamaica (compare Besson 2002, 245–51). He travels, for services and conventions:

> all over Jamaica, St Elizabeth, Westmoreland, Trelawny (Clark's Town, Martha Brae, Zion, Freeman's Hall, Sherwood, Spring Garden, Rock Spring), Hanover, St James (Cambridge, Dumfries, Limer near Adelphi), St Thomas, St Ann (Watt Town), Kingston.

'On invitation', the Bishop also goes to other churches including Baptist, Adventist and Pentecostal, such as the Pentecostal church in Tangle River. His travels to Trelawny within the Revival network linked up with many people that I knew there from my earlier research in Martha Brae and Zion (Besson 1993, 2002, 2007, 2009). In addition, when I revisited Zion in 2011, I was told that Bishop Drummond from Maldon was still involved with the Revivalists there.

Adventists, Pentecostalists and Methodists

While the Baptist and Revival religions are rooted in the slavery era and reflect cultural influences from Europe and Africa, as well as Caribbean creolization, the Seventh Day Adventist and Pentecostal sects have a more recent history in Jamaica (and Maroon Town) where they have spread from the United States in the twentieth century and been creolized by Revival (Chevannes 1995a, 2–3; Austin-Broos 1997; Davis-Palmer 2010, 148–55, 276–83).

The late Asta Williams, an elderly Afro-Creole who lived near Maroon Town Square and attended the Seventh Day Adventist Church at Vaughansfield, provides an illustration of the Adventist religion in the Jamaican context and an example of some of the factors influencing the choice of membership in the mosaic of religions in Maroon Town, as he narrated at the turn of the millennium:

Join Adventist now. The first church I went to, I baptize in the river, Adventist. Fe me sin wash me [it washed away my sins]. Down a Bottom Pasture River in Maroon Town. [However,] me backslide [but] me go back now [to the Adventist church at Vaughansfield], but me naah baptise again.

Asta drew a contrast between the river-baptism of the Seventh Day Adventists (whose Sabbath is on a Saturday) and Sunday baptism in a tank at the Mount Ararat Pentecostal New Testament Gospel Hall, near Maroon Town Square, and a further contrast between their communion practices, highlighting the emphasis on health in the Adventist church:

> Mount Ararat baptize too, in the tank, but me no love the tank business. A Sunday they keep it. But what beat me, every Sunday they take communion and everybody drink out a the *one* glass. Me no like it. Me no like the baptism inna de tank or drink out de *one* glass. Have communion at Adventist, but everybody have dem *own* glass.

The late Cleopatra Jolly, an Afro-Creole Pentecostal Pastor and Infant School Teacher who was born in the neighbouring parish of Hanover in 1911, provided a different perspective on Pentecostalism in Maroon Town. She was nearly 88 years old when I interviewed her in 1999 in her Pentecostal Church at Browns' Town, between Maroon Town Square and Flagstaff, where she also lived and had a basic school (and where she died around 2006). Miss Jolly described how she had moved to Browns' Town and become a Pentecostal Pastor following a 'vision' that she had when she was doing 'evangelical work' in Montego Bay:

> One night, I was in my sleep when I heard a voice say 'Bebe, get up'. So I got up. When I looked up the street, I saw a white man in a big ball of fire. He said I should leave MoBay at once: 'I am going to take you to a place and hide you'. He said, 'Come at once and take nothing with you, because this place [Montego Bay] will be set on fire'. That is a vision. The fire and the man went down Barnett Lane [in Montego Bay]. The man was in the fire just the same. The other Sister before me stopped, afraid of the fire. When me get up to old Barnett Estate [an old sugar plantation at the edge of Montego Bay] I woke up out a the sleep. The other Sister told me the dream I had was prophesying.

As a result of the vision (which reflects the Pentecostalists' emphasis on spiritual empowerment and the direct personal experience of God through baptism with the Holy Spirit), Miss Jolly moved to Browns' Town and continued 'doing my evangelistic work, I work among the people here'. She first lived as a tenant and held meetings in a little booth, but then moved to her present location on land gifted by a philanthropist in Montego Bay. Here, she started with a booth, then built a house and Pentecostal Church in 1969 and the basic school. She was holding Pentecostal meetings in her church, though her congregation had declined due to her church's strict way of life as she narrated:

> We baptize in Jesus' name as all Pentecosts do and we live a special life for the Lord. So for that reason I don't have much link-up with the other churches. Because they don't see to the depth I see. And no man is going to break me off it...Used to have the church full, about 100 of us. Now young people like to follow around other churches and our gospel is strict. We preach the old time Pentecostal message.

Figure 7.7. Ex-Councillor Mortimer Reid and Pastor Cleopatra Jolly at the Pastor's Pentecostal Church at Browns' Town, Maroon Town.

In contrast to this Pentecostal message, the late Ex-Councillor, Mortimer Reid, who took me to meet Pastor Jolly in 1999 (figure 7.7) and who was a member of the Mount Edmonson Methodist Church at Dundee, explained that: 'Methodists preach the conversion of John Wesley and celebrated his 261 years of conversion two weeks ago.' Like the Baptists, the history of the English Methodists in Jamaica goes back to slavery. However, while the Baptist missionaries were the most successful with the enslaved, the Methodists were significant among the free coloured and free black population (chapter 2). In Maroon Town, with its core of Meso-Creole Old Families, the Mount Edmonson Methodist Church (which was originally situated at *Browns'* Town, an area associated with mulattos, chapter 10) is prominent and many funerals and memorials are held there.

Education, Youth and Age

Like churches, schools in and near Maroon Town are important places for social relations and socialization and (like religion) education, youth and age both differentiate and reinforce the community. Education also integrates the village with the Jamaican nation state, whose Ministry of Education oversees the island's schools. There are several schools in Maroon Town, ranging from basic schools to primary and secondary. Some children from Maroon Town also attend secondary schools in Montego Bay.

During my fieldwork, there were three basic schools in Maroon Town: one near Maroon Town Square, another linked to the Baptist Church in Maldon and the Pentecostal Pastor's school at Browns' Town. About 50 boys and girls, between the ages of three and six years old, attend the basic school near Maroon Town Square. The school has a blackboard, pictures of 'Living in Our Community', and illustrations on the walls, of numbers, poems and days of the week. The children are educated with stiff discipline. When I visited, they were first instructed by their teacher to be silent ('everybody lock your mouth') and then, with fingers obediently on mouths, to 'unlock mouths' and sing 'Jesus Loves Me'. These young children also learn to write and count. Their education continues informally after school and they told me what they do to help at home. There is not much gender differentiation in tasks, which include fetching water and sweeping the house and yard. At the end of my visit, the teacher told the children how proud she was of them.

The Browns' Town Basic School was situated next to Pastor Jolly's Pentecostal church, under bamboo-covered cockpit mountains, and was taught by the Pastor (who used to teach at the Maroon Town Basic School). The children were divided into two classes, aged three to four and five to six (figure 7.8). The younger children sang 'Jesus Loves Me' and a song about the Cockpit Country landscape. They also learned to write and to use the recently-installed landline telephones (initiated in Maroon Town by Councillor Harris, in 1997, to receive calls from overseas kin). After school, the children played, carried water, cleaned the house and swept the yard.

Figure 7.8. Some of the children at Pastor Jolly's Basic School at Browns' Town.

The older children at the Pastor's school did similar tasks at home. However, at school they spoke of what they wished to do when they grew up, showing awareness of gender and kinship roles: the girls wanted to be 'doctor, nurse, teacher, mother and sister', the boys 'bredda [brother], uncle and driver'. These older children also had some knowledge of Jamaican national history, reinforced by participation in National Heroes Week and emancipation commemorations at Kensington and Flagstaff, including the role of Sam Sharpe and 'Nanny of the Maroons', both of whom (as the children explained) 'are on the money'; that is, their pictures are on Jamaican dollar notes. At school, these children learned poems, the names of the days of the week and the months, that 'God made the flowers' and about honesty and courtesy. My husband and I were introduced to them by the Pastor as 'our guests' and they were told that 'J is for Jeanie and John'.

Approximately 60 boys and girls up to 12 years old, after basic school, attend the Maldon Primary School. Students at Maldon Primary come from Maroon Town Square, Flagstaff, Woodlands, Browns' Town, Vaughansfield, Maldon Road, Summer Hill, Point, Kensington, Tangle River and German Town. In addition to more advanced schoolwork (and some awareness of oral traditions regarding Nanny and Cudjoe), these children are more experienced and articulate regarding their extra-curricular activities (academic homework, sports, helping in the house-yard and watching TV) and occupational aspirations than the children at the basic schools. Girls have more varied (and often higher) occupational ambitions than boys such as lawyer, doctor, nurse, scientist, teacher, university student, business woman, firefighter, air hostess, actress and singer, as well as working in the fields. Occupations mentioned by boys include teacher, mason, cricketer, footballer, biologist, scientist, and working in arts and crafts. In addition, the boys are interested in agriculture and invited me to see the school garden, cultivated with cabbages, melons, sugar cane, tomatoes and dasheen. The produce is sold to the school canteen and to the 4-H Club.[11] Some of the boys also helped cultivate their households' provision grounds. As my visit to the school concluded, the children went to 'Devotion' and bible-reading, singing to the accompaniment of tambourines.

After passing their exams at Maldon Primary, students progress to a secondary school (from age 12 until 17 or 18), either Maldon Junior and Comprehensive High School at Summer Hill in Maroon Town, or in Montego Bay.[12] Maldon High School, which has links with the Baptist and Methodist Churches, marks the culmination of the educational system in Maroon Town and I was told that 'everyone [there] is from Maroon Town'. When I visited the school, I spoke with 16 students, of both genders, in Grade 10 (the penultimate grade). At this level, the range of subjects that may be studied include Caribbean History, Biology, Accounts, Principles of Business, Agricultural Science, Integrated Science, Computing, Social Studies (including Tourism), English, Maths, Food and Nutrition, and Clothing and Textiles. The students were taking the Caribbean Examinations Council's (CXC) Caribbean Secondary Education Certification Examinations (CSEC) the following year. This exam, equivalent to Ordinary/'O' Level exams in the United Kingdom, is taken by children 16-plus and provides an employment qualification.

Looking ahead, these Maldon High students explained that, depending on how many subjects they passed, 'We'll go on to other schools, university or college' and may take part-time jobs (for example, at Burger King, supermarkets or clothing stores in Montego Bay) to help finance their further education. Such education may include attending the Montego Bay Community College, whose extensive range of programmes includes short certificate courses training girls as dressmakers and boys as tailors, electricians, carpenters, masons and mechanics. Some school-leavers from Maroon Town progress to the University of the West Indies (Mona Campus), in Kingston, after passing the Caribbean Advanced Proficiency Exam (CAPE), the equivalent of A-Levels in the UK.

Students at Maldon High School participated in partly gendered extra-curricular activities: the girls do housework and look after younger children and the boys herd livestock. Both genders do academic homework, shop and carry water. As at primary school, students at Maldon High are aware of some of Maroon Town's oral traditions of marronage (chapters 8–10).

In addition to interviews at schools, I spoke with many children at their homes in Maroon Town where the role of children and young people in their households and families and in the village economy could be clearly seen. Both formal and informal education reinforces the significance of agriculture in this banana-farming community, where some boys learn to farm and girls acquire the skills to look after the house-yard. However, formal education opens up a wider range of occupations and the possibility of social mobility.

Whereas formal education and social mobility through education are especially the preserve of the young in Maroon Town, the older generations (some of whom achieved social mobility through banana farming and/or migration) are the repositories and transmitters of the rich oral traditions of the clans and family lands that form the core of the community (chapters 8–10). These clans overlap and are further linked through inter-marriage and personal networks of kinship and affinity. Such relationships interweave with varying Afro-Creole and Meso-Creole ethnicities relating to assertions of slave, maroon and colonial/planter ancestry. The concluding section of this chapter outlines the main contours of such kinship and ethnicity.

Kinship and Ethnicity

The core of the Maroon Town population are the Old Families, cognatic clans that claim descent from a particular ancestor or ancestress through both males and females and including migrants as well as those living in the community. These gendered transnational clans and their component lineages generally have family lands with kin-based cemeteries, as in the free villages of Trelawny Parish (Besson 2002) and Aberdeen, in St Elizabeth (chapter 6), in contrast to the common land of the Accompong Maroons (chapter 3).[13]

However, there is a significant difference of identification among many of Maroon Town's Old Families in contrast to the Afro-Creole ethnicity of the Trelawny communities descended from emancipated slaves and also to Afro-Creole maroon identity in Accompong; for several Old Families in Maroon Town claim to be 'slave master' pickni', descended from British (especially Scottish) or Euro-Creole slave masters or other colonists and African or Afro-Creole enslaved women. This theme of Meso-Creole descent (which exists to a lesser extent in Aberdeen [chapter 6]), is the dominant motif in Maroon Town, where it is linked to oral traditions regarding the transformation from Trelawny Town to Maroon Town (chapters 8–10). A number of factors lend credence to this claim of 'slave master' pickni' ancestry in Maroon Town, including the Scottish titles of many Old Families, their detailed genealogies tracing descent from colonists and slaves, their brown-skinned phenotype and/or light-coloured eyes and wavy hair, and their larger landholdings (compared to the smaller family lands in Trelawny's villages).

This mixed ancestry is ambivalently recounted, for it is underlined by both a pride in descent from the colonists and a poignant awareness of the rape or seduction of enslaved women and the 'outsider status' of their mulatto slave children (some of whom became Maroons). This outsider status, which was one of the defining criteria of slavery (Watson 1980; compare Green 2006), was transmitted to other descendants and is still felt by Maroon Town's Meso-Creole Old Families today.

However, there are some Afro-Creole clans in Maroon Town and some of these claim maroon descent. In addition, some Meso-Creole clans assert maroon ancestry as well as descent from colonists and slaves – thereby claiming both mulatto maroon and 'slave master' pickni' ethnicities (chapter 9). Moreover, although the village's central clan, the Meso-Creole McGhies (who claim slave master pickni descent) do not assert maroon ancestry, my research indicates that they are descended from the mulatto 'McGhie Maroons' of Congo Town/Highwindward/Me No Sen You No Come of Trelawny Parish near the Flagstaff area of Maroon Town (chapter 10).

Embedded in the narratives of these various Old Families (and also of some Newcomers), are interweaving dichotomies of whiteness and blackness, colonists and slaves, and slaves and Maroons. These dichotomies are further elaborated by references to the transmission of varying degrees of European and African ancestry and the use of the biological concepts of 'blood', 'breed', 'half-breed' and 'half-caste' to refer to the cultural constructs of descent groups and ethnicities. These themes of miscegenation and creolization are often situated in narrative accounts of the transformation of Trelawny Town to Maroon Town (chapters 8-10).

Maroon Town's overlapping transnational Old Families and their individual members' personal kinship networks interrelate with a marriage system based on multiple conjugal unions and various marital forms (extra-residential visiting unions and legal and non-legal co-residential relationships), as in the other Jamaican communities that I studied (Besson 2002, and chapters 3–10). However, in Maroon Town (St James), unlike those other communities in St Elizabeth and Trelawny, there is an explicit distinction between 'lawful' and 'bastard' children or kin. This dichotomy interrelates with the themes of 'insider' and 'outsider' kinship embedded in the dominant motif of slave master' pickni' descent. Another difference is the explicit recognition, in Maroon Town, of multiple *simultaneous* conjugal unions by some men, paralleling the polygyny of the Trelawny Maroons (see, e.g., Dallas 1803; Robinson 1969, 70). This differs from the pattern of *sequential* unions (by both women and men) in the other communities that I studied, though such serial monogamy is likewise widespread in Maroon Town. Like Aberdeen and Trelawny's free villages, Maroon Town villagers prohibit conjugality with close kin, in contrast to the cousin-conjugality among some Accompong Maroons. Such intricate patterns of descent, kinship and marriage in these maroon and non-maroon derivations of African-American slave cultures are variations on a Caribbean creolization theme.

The next three chapters explore, more fully, kinship and ethnicity in Maroon Town to further illuminate the transformation from Trelawny Town to Maroon Town and creolization at the maroon/non-maroon interface. I focus on narratives from a diverse range of Maroon Town villagers, who situate their reflections on kinship and ethnicity within wider oral traditions of the transformation from Trelawny Town to Maroon Town. I combine these narratives with other dimensions of my research, including historical sources and fieldwork findings on genealogies and landholding and contextualize the narratives in the villagers' daily lives. After an introductory discussion of history, myth and creolization in Maroon Town oral traditions, the chapters focus on the themes of 'slave master' pickni' descent from colonists and slaves (chapter 8), stories of maroon ancestry and marronage (chapter 9) and accounts from many members of the McGhie Old Family, Maroon Town's central clan, who assert slave master pickni descent and who my research indicates are also descended from the mulatto 'McGhie Maroons' (chapter 10).

Notes

1. In addition to my fieldwork in Maroon Town, I am grateful to Councillor Harris for much of the general information in this chapter on politics, land sales, agriculture and tourism in Maroon Town, given in interviews graciously granted over a period of ten years (1999–2009), in his office, in Montego Bay.
2. The Jamaica Agricultural Society was formed in 1895 and initially promoted the interests of the planter class. In the 1930s, it became a middle-class institution focused on rural development among the peasantry and was subsequently also linked to nationalism (Crichlow 2005, 69–71).
3. This national honour in the new millennium has some parallels with the creation of Sam Sharpe and Nanny as National Heroes in the late twentieth century.
4. Sheena Gayle 'Harris to Be Montego Bay's Next Mayor', *Jamaica Gleaner*, Thursday March 29, 2012; www.localgovjamaica.gov.jm/mayors.aspx.
5. In these respects of national political integration and taxed and parcelled lands, Maroon Town has similarities with Aberdeen in St Elizabeth (chapter 6) and Trelawny's free villages (Besson 2002).
6. Oral traditions in both The Alps/New Birmingham in the Cockpits of Trelawny Parish and the Trelawny free village of Refuge, likewise, tell of a cholera outbreak around the mid-nineteenth century (Besson 1984b, 2002).
7. HACCP refers to the Hazard Analysis Critical Control Points system in international food safety inspection management.

8. The natal village of the Olympic and World gold medallist, Usain Bolt (who went to school in Martha Brae). At the time of writing in 2014, Bolt is a double individual gold medallist (100m and 200m) and is widely considered the fastest sprinter ever.
9. This conclusion revises Barry Chevannes's (1978, 16) assumption that Revivalism was a 'disappearing religion' that was 'virtually dead' and 'buried under the forces of change'.
10. However, at Maroon Town Square, a Newcomer described the Revival-Zion church at Maldon as 'Pukumina', remarking that: 'We have a Pukumina in Maldon – get in spirit, wrap them heads, beat drum. Same thing as Revival.'
11. An international non-profit organization devoted to youth and community development.
12. Secondary schools in Montego Bay include Montego Bay High School (for girls), Cornwall College (for boys), the Herbert Morrison Technical High School (named after an Edinburgh-trained doctor from Montego Bay) and Mount Alvernia (a Catholic school for girls).
13. However, family lands and cemeteries are emerging in Accompong house-yards within the commons (chapters 3–5).

8 ■ 'SLAVE MASTER' PICKNI': MESO-CREOLE ETHNICITIES AND NARRATIVE TRANSFORMATIONS OF TRELAWNY TOWN

History, Myth and Creolization in Maroon Town Oral Traditions

Narratives of kinship and ethnicity in Maroon Town are often embedded in wider oral traditions regarding the transformation of Cudjoe's Town/Trelawny Town to Maroon Town. Such oral traditions include both parallels and contrasts to written historical records, especially those regarding the First and Second Maroon Wars in the Cockpits (1725–38 and 1795–96, chapter 2). These oral traditions, which combine myth[1] and history, often reflect a symbolic ordering and repairing of the ruptures of the past and the present resulting from globalization, colonization, the plantation system, slavery, marronage, emancipation and migration. The narratives also anchor these shifting histories in sacred sites on the Cockpit Country landscape. As in Accompong and Aberdeen, these narratives in intensely transnational Maroon Town, therefore, reinforce Nigel Rapport's observation that, 'Narratives embody a perceived order, and in their telling they maintain this order despite seeming temporal, spatial, experiential disjunctures', and 'provide for the world-traveller…a place to continue to be' (Rapport 2000, 74, quoted in Besson 2005, 17). In this way, narratives in Maroon Town, likewise, serve as a vehicle for creolization and place-making. This interpretation does not mean that the symbolic order embodied in Maroon Town oral traditions is not sometimes varied and contested. However, this variation and contestation are themselves a part of the rich diversity within the community with its different generations and Meso-Creole and Afro-Creole ethnicities, asserting varying degrees of descent from slaves, colonists and Maroons.

Parallels between Maroon Town oral traditions and historical records include a focus on the defeat of the British colonial plantation-military regime by Cudjoe's and Nanny's Maroons in the First Jamaican Maroon War (1725–38); the related treaties and land grants (1738/39); the colonists' use of Cuban bloodhounds to rout the Trelawny Maroons, the ambush of Colonel Sandford and 45 of his 20th Dragoons and the killing of Sandford by the Trelawny Maroons in the Second Maroon War (1795–96); and the occasional reference to the subsequent colonial deportation of the Trelawnys in 1796. There is also more frequent reference to the colonial confiscation and sale of most of the Trelawny Town lands and the establishment of the barracks at Flagstaff in the early nineteenth century (until the mid-nineteenth century), on land retained by the colonial state until the early twentieth century. In addition, the accounts of the sale of the Flagstaff lands in the 1930s and the establishment of the Pond Piece land settlement near Vaughansfield in the late twentieth century, are consistent with written records on Jamaican land settlements (chapter 1).

The main discontinuities between Maroon Town oral traditions and historical records include the recurring narrative relocation of the victories of Cudjoe and Nanny from the First Maroon War to the Second Maroon War and the omission of the outcome of the Second Maroon War, namely, the deportation of the Trelawny Maroons to Canada; the portrayal and exaggeration in some narratives of Sandford's debacle as part of a conclusive maroon victory in that war; and the assertion in many narratives of an exchange, between the British colonists and the Trelawnys, of Trelawny Town territory for the lands of Accompong Town (whose African name has been creolized to 'Campong Town) and of a related maroon migration from Trelawny Town to Accompong.

In addition, these narratives provide a context for the assertion by some of the Maroon Town population of direct descent from the Trelawny Maroons, in contrast to the historical record of the eradication of these Maroons (though written history indicates that some Trelawnys evaded deportation by renouncing their maroon status [chapter 2]). Some narratives also refer to a partly historical, partly mythical ancestor-hero 'Campong Nanny ('Accompong Nanny'). Such narratives draw on the historical existence of Nanny, the Windward Maroon ritual leader, but mythically relocate her among the Leeward Maroons and, in this context, elevate her significance in Trelawny Town above that of the Leeward leader, Captain Cudjoe. This transformation of the relative significance of Cudjoe and Nanny in the Leeward Maroon polity departs not only from written history (and from the oral tradition of the Windward Maroons, see, e.g., Bilby 2006) but also from narratives in Accompong, where Nanny is portrayed in a secondary role to Cudjoe (chapters 3–6). There is also a further difference between oral traditions in Maroon Town and Accompong: in Accompong, Nanny is sometimes identified as 'Matilda Rowe', an ancestress of the Rowe Old Family, Accompong Town's central clan (chapter 4); whereas in Maroon Town, 'Campong Nanny is sometimes said to have been 'Betsy Currie', an ancestress of the overlapping Currie, Clarke, Walker and Hines Old Families of Maroon Town (chapter 9). In addition, a variation on the Maroon Town narrative theme of Nanny is a gender transformation, with 'Campong Nanny portrayed as a man and 'different from Moore Town Nanny' of the Windwards.

These differences between Maroon Town narratives and written history (and between the oral traditions of Maroon Town and Accompong), which include the narrative collapsing and editing of events between the First and Second Maroon Wars, could potentially be explained with reference to the limited historical knowledge of the narrators. However, a more illuminating interpretation is that the narratives order the ruptures of the Second Maroon War. These ruptures occurred not only between the British colonists and the Trelawny Maroons, but also between the primary Leeward Maroon village of Trelawny Town and the secondary Accompong community which supported the colonists in the Second Maroon War that led to the fracturing of the Leeward polity. The narratives likewise symbolically order the related transformation from Trelawny Town maroon society to non-maroon Maroon Town, as well as the shifting boundaries and power relations within the Leeward polity, reflected in the ascendancy of Accompong from the secondary to the primary and sole surviving Leeward Maroon village. The narratives further address the disjuncture, on the one hand, between the Leeward polity and the colonial/post-colonial Jamaican state, and, on the other, between virtually autonomous Accompong and Maroon Town, which is incorporated into the Jamaican nation state.

In addition to symbolically repairing ruptures and creating sites of identity, these narratives when combined with historical and anthropological research, can illuminate the past and the present, including the process of creolization – as in Accompong and Aberdeen (chapters 3–6; see also Besson 2002). From these perspectives (and combined with chapter 7), this chapter and the following two unravel the transformation from the Trelawny Town maroon society to non-maroon Maroon Town. This chapter focuses on the narratives of Meso-Creole Old Families in Maroon Town who claim 'slave master' pickni' descent from European or Euro-Creole male colonists (especially slave masters) and African or Afro-Creole slave women; a dominant theme being Afro-Scots ethnicity. Chapter 9 highlights the narratives of Old Families in Maroon Town who assert Afro-Creole maroon ethnicity, as well as presenting stories by other Afro-Creoles about black marronage and narratives by some Meso-Creoles who claim mulatto maroon ancestry. Chapter 10 focuses on the McGhie Old Family, Maroon Town's central clan. As I show there, although the McGhies (who assert 'slave master' pickni' descent) do not claim maroon ancestry, my research indicates that they are descended from the 'McGhie Maroons' – mulatto foraging maroons whose history has not received the attention it deserves. The narratives (narrated from various points of the Jamaican linguistic continuum) are combined with my historical and anthropological research and contextualized within the narrators' daily lives, where themes such as banana farming, migration, transnational kinship and mortuary ritual intertwine.

In this chapter, I present the narratives of three groupings of Meso-Creole Old Families who claim 'slave master' pickni' descent. I group these clans in this way because of the dense interrelations among them. I look first at the oral traditions of the interrelated Reid, Grant and Hamilton clans, then at the narratives of the McIntyres, Stennetts and Harrises, and conclude with the Peterkins, Fennels and Andersons. In addition to the overlapping membership within these three groups of Old Families, there are further links among the three groupings of clans and between them and other Maroon Town clans.

The Reids, Grants and Hamiltons: Sacred Sites and Meso-Creole Ethnicities

I begin the presentation of Meso-Creole ethnicities as portrayed through the 'slave master' pickni' oral traditions of the interrelated Reid, Grant and Hamilton clans, of mainly Afro-Scots descent, with the narratives of the late Mortimer Reid, the distinguished Ex-Councillor of Maroon Town (chapter 7).

The Ex-Councillor's Narratives

Mortimer Reid (1910–2007) was a Justice of the Peace (since 1974) and a former Parish Councillor for Maroon Town who, in 2002, received an honour from the Jamaican government for his services to the St James Parish Council and the Maroon Town community. As a Councillor (from the Peoples National Party, for 15 years, from 1966), Mortimer had administered the migrations from Maroon Town to North America on the Farm Work Scheme. He had been a migrant labourer to the United States during the Second World War, where he did Farm Work in 1943 and then worked in the Manpower Scheme. In 1945, Mortimer returned to his father's paternal family land, where he was born, in Vaughansfield. This land, originally 130 acres, known as the Calder Property,[2] had been purchased by Mortimer's paternal grandfather, Tommy Reid, and became family land for Tommy's descendants. In 1946, Mortimer bought his own land, eight acres, adjoining this family land. Here, he built a house and settled as a tailor and farmer, cash-cropping in sugar cane, bananas and yams.

I first met Mortimer in 1999, when (aged 89 and retired) he had just returned from visiting relatives overseas – which he had often done since his wife's death in 1983. Mortimer's hill-top house-yard offered a panoramic view of the Cockpits, with mountains encompassing the slopes, valleys and glades of his bought land and family land and his neighbours' land below. Such breathtaking vistas would become a routine enchantment of my fieldwork in Maroon Town (figure 8.1). From Mortimer's yard could also be seen the two oldest churches serving the community: the Maldon Baptist Church and the Mount Edmonson Methodist Church at Dundee (figure 8.2). Mortimer was a member of Mount Edmonson, like his late mother and other members of his maternal Old Family (the Simms). I revisited Mortimer several times up to January 2007, by which time he was 96 and settled at home. He died the following month, in February 2007. He knew I would write his story in this book, with which he had helped me so much.

Figure 8.1.   A Cockpit Country landscape in Maroon Town.

Figure 8.2. A view of the Maldon Baptist Church from Mortimer Reid's house-yard in Vaughansfield, Maroon Town.

Mortimer provided a detailed account of his paternal clan, the Reid Old Family, which is one of the central Meso-Creole clans in Maroon Town who claim Afro-Scots 'slave master' pickni' descent. He situated this family history in a wider narrative of sacred sites of the Second Maroon War and the related transformation of the black maroon village of Trelawny Town and the white colonial military settlement at Flagstaff into the mainly brown non-maroon community of Maroon Town. Although he did not explicitly identify the Second Maroon War (in contrast to the First Maroon War), Mortimer's narrative has a number of parallels with the documented history of this war (chapter 2). In addition to the widespread local knowledge that the site of Maroon Town was once occupied by Maroons, and of maroon guerrilla warfare and battle camouflage, his account reflects the knowledge (widespread locally) of the maroon ambush at Sandford's Defile. There is also the reference (seldom made in Maroon Town narratives) that the Maroons, nevertheless, lost out after the Second Maroon War due to betrayal by the British colonists. Mortimer also recounted the historical facts that the colonists settled at Flagstaff after this war and that the Accompong Town land was granted by the colonial state.

However, Mortimer's account diverges from written historical sources in omitting any reference to the deportation of the Trelawny Maroons, asserting instead a migration of these Maroons to Accompong after the Second Maroon War – a common theme in Maroon Town narratives. There is also the speculation that the Flagstaff cemetery might contain white victims of the war (which is unlikely as the British base was established there after the war), and an implicit relocation of Cudjoe from the First to the Second Maroon War.

Yet, in addition to reflecting the symbolic ordering of 'temporal, spatial, experiential disjunctures' and providing 'for the world-traveller...a place to continue to be' (Rapport 2000, 74, quoted in Besson 2005, 17) through these departures from documented history, Mortimer's narratives add to the historical record through his account of the creolization of the colonial Reid Family (who are referred to in written history) and their role in the transformation of Trelawny Town to Maroon Town. In her history of the Jamaican Maroons, Bev Carey noted that the land of Trelawny Town bordered, in the south-west, 'on or near land patented by Thomas Reid, esquire' (1997, 22). Vaughansfield (where Mortimer Reid was born on the land of his grandfather, Tommy Reid) is in the south-western area of Maroon Town and it seems likely that Mortimer's grandfather was descended from or related to Thomas Reid, as Mortimer was of partial European descent. There are also historical references to a General Reid, who owned Belvedere Estate in St James, who was Commander of the Great River Post and Second Major-General of the colonial militia during the Second Maroon War of 1795–96, who accompanied Major-General Walpole to visit the Trelawny Maroons (Robinson 1969, 123, 129; Campbell 1990, 213, 225) and had 'close relations with the Maroons' (Campbell 1990, 225). Robinson (1969, 84) refers to a 'Colonel Thomas Reed [sic] of the St James Militia' who headed a colonial party that visited Trelawny Town in 1795 and Campbell notes that Balcarres 'sent a strong company of *mulattos* from the St James Regiment' against the Trelawnys in 1795 (Campbell 1990, 217, my emphasis; see also chapter 2). As seen later in this section, Mortimer's elderly cousin, Melvin Pearson, identified Tommy Reid as the mulatto son of a planter, Charles Reid. It is, therefore, likely that Mortimer's white and mulatto Reid ancestors, including the mulatto, Tommy Reid, belonged to the planter class of St James around the time of the Maroon Wars.[3]

Mortimer's narratives also reflect factual knowledge of the Accompong Maroons, the Afro-Scots Old Families of Maroon Town (including his paternal clan, the Reids) who made early land purchases there in the nineteenth century and more recent settlers from other parishes, as well as members of Maroon Town clans who purchased the Flagstaff lands in the 1930s. His narratives, likewise, show detailed knowledge of the history of the British settlement at Flagstaff and the role of the barracks there in the colonial defence of the island. In addition, Mortimer's narratives illustrate the elaborate mortuary rituals that link the village's transnational clans and embed their identity in Maroon Town.

Mortimer's narratives, presented below, began with an outline of the Second Maroon War and its aftermath (though he did not explicitly distinguish the Second from the First Maroon War), combining both historical and mythical elements, and a view that the Maroon Town population is now non-maroon, including Old Families of mixed African and European ancestry:

> Maroon Town was once occupied by the Maroons. Jamaica was belonging to England. The Maroons and the British soldiers went to war at Flagstaff in Maroon Town. Cudjoe

was a Maroon. The Maroons lost the War and they migrated to Accompong Town in St Elizabeth, where they occupy until today. Every year the people at Accompong have celebration 6th of January. At that time, the Maroons went to Accompong. Those lands given to them by the government. People from Maroon Town and all over the country go to the celebration.

Most of the lands were belonging to the English people, the Maroons didn't have any land. A portion of it, at Flagstaff, was sold to people already in Maroon Town by the colonial government in the 1930s. There are no Maroons in Maroon Town now. This was a farming area, so people from different parishes came in and never left, especially in the Flagstaff area. Flagstaff is a history place; that is where much of the history lies.

Mortimer explained that there are, however, many Old Families in Maroon Town, including his own paternal and maternal clans:

The Reids [his paternal clan] are among the oldest. And the Fennels, McGhie, McIntyre, Rockhead, Walker, Peterkin, Harris, Hamilton and a lot more.

He confirmed that these clans include women's children with different surnames and explained that these Old Families are primarily of mixed descent:

During the time of the Maroons, there were people like myself here who weren't Maroons and not British – born here, *mixed* by the coloured people and the white people.

Elaborating this point, Mortimer explained that both his parents were born in Maroon Town and belonged to Old Families who had been there for at least two to three generations before him. His mother was a Simms and his father was a Reid. His paternal grandfather, Tommy Reid, 'came from Scotland'. To underline his assertion of Scottish ancestry, Mortimer showed me a picture-framed history in his living room of 'The Ancient History of the Distinguished Surname Reid', a Scots Border Clan.

Mortimer recounted that the 130-acre Calder property bought by his grandfather, Tommy Reid, stretched from Vaughansfield to Maroon Town Square. Mortimer narrated that Tommy had five children: two daughters and three sons, the youngest of whom was Mortimer's father, William, who, in turn, had nine children, of whom Mortimer was the only one still alive. As an illustration of Tommy's ever-increasing family line, Mortimer had eight children, numerous grandchildren and 16 great-grandchildren. Another of Tommy's sons, Edgar, was the father of Mary Reid, who was the mother of the late Beryl ('Lil') Delgado (née McFarlane) in Maroon Town (figure 1.8), who had nine children as well as grandchildren and great-grandchildren. Including Tommy, the Reid clan in Maroon Town, therefore, numbered at least seven generations. (Mortimer's cousin, Melvin Pearson, would take the genealogy one further ascending generation [Genealogy 2].)

Genealogy 2. Partial Genealogy of the Reid Clan, Maroon Town

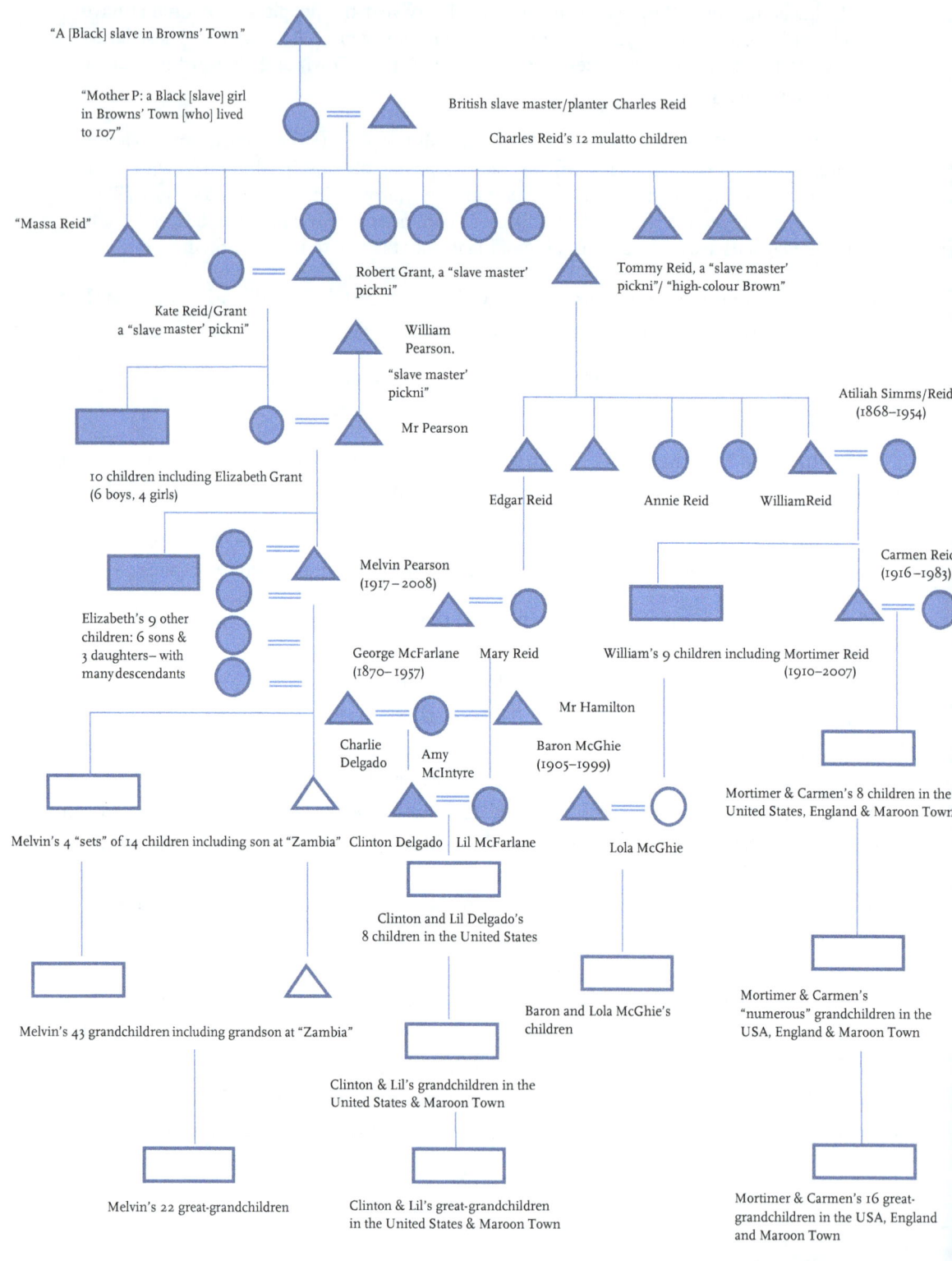

Mortimer narrated that all of Tommy's five children received portions of the Calder property (the 'Reid family land'), but only William (Mortimer's father) and his sister, Annie, retained theirs – the rest was sold. Tommy's son, Edgar's, alienated portion included a large upstairs building at Maroon Town Square. Mortimer further illuminated that the lands and buildings at Maroon Town Square used to be owned by three overlapping Old Families, all of mixed Afro-Scots descent: the Reids, McIntyres and McGhies. Despite some land sales, there is some continuity in such landholdings: McGhies and McIntyres still reside there and some of Edgar Reid's descendants still live on land overlooking the Square.

As Mortimer recounted, there are Reid family tombs on the Calder property. However, Mortimer's cemetery (where his mother, his wife and one of their grandsons are buried) is on his own bought land – from which he had created family land (figure 8.3). Mortimer's children are co-heirs to both this new family land and his share of the older family land from his grandfather, Tommy Reid.

Like many of Tommy's other living descendants, most of Mortimer's children were abroad (in the United States and England), with only one remaining in Maroon Town (a son who lived with him). However, Mortimer's land serves as a base for their return- and circulatory-migration as he narrated:

> It will be family land. The children will return and will live here. They talk about coming home. I always teach them: 'There is one part of the earth that is more dearer than all beside – no gold could measure its worth, that place where love abides. However far my feet may roam, my heart remains at home sweet home'.

Figure 8.3. Mortimer Reid in his house-yard in Vaughansfield.

Mortimer explained that his children could all return to the family land, but that two of his sons in the United States have bought their own house-lots with modern houses from the government's National Housing Trust at Pond Piece in Vaughansfield.

The following week, Mortimer took us on a tour of the historic landscape in and around Flagstaff, which is reached by a road ascending eastwards above Pond Piece and Maroon Town Square. Below is his account of Flagstaff, based on oral traditions of events 'before my [his] time'. Mortimer's Flagstaff narrative focused on four main historical/symbolic sites central to the Second Maroon War and its aftermath: the Ball Ground or flattened drilling field at the colonial military barracks, established after the Second Maroon War; the Flagstaff cemetery of the white soldiers stationed at the barracks; Gun Hill, where a large cannon was situated by the colonists after the Second Maroon War; and Dragoon Hole, the reputed site of the maroon ambush of Sandford's colonial troops during this war (chapter 2). Mortimer also introduced us to the present-day settlement at Flagstaff, illuminating its roots in the sale of land by the colonial government in the 1930s.

On our journey to Flagstaff with Mortimer, we first stopped at Ball Ground, the flat drilling field of the former barracks that is surrounded by bamboo-covered mountains and house-yards established on land bought from the government (figure 7.2). Ball Ground is reached by a turning off the recently-asphalted road from Maroon Town Square to Flagstaff. At Ball Ground, Mortimer explained the historical significance of this site where the colonial troops were stationed after the Second Maroon War:

> This is 'Ball Ground'. This was the drilling ground for the white soldiers and the playfield. It was a settlement here [on the surrounding slopes]. It was a lot of buildings, dwelling houses. The police station [also] used to be here, [it's now] moved to Spring Mount [between Maroon Town and Montego Bay]. There was a well down there too [figure 7.3]. After the Maroons ran away, the white soldiers came and settled here.

A little further on, to the left of the still-ascending main road, is Flagstaff cemetery where 24 tombs surround a calabash tree, which is associated with the Revival spirit-pantheon (figure 7.4). Mortimer observed of this site: 'White soldiers are buried here, but there is no history of who are buried here. The Maroons wanted to capture this piece of land, because they didn't have anywhere.'

These older tombs have no names, inscriptions or dates. However, two other tombs are inscribed and dated in the 1840s.[4] When Mortimer was Councillor he used to oversee the cleaning of this cemetery.

A short way further on is the majestic mountain known as Gun Hill, where is said to be a cannon (overgrown by bush) used by the colonists. As Councillor, Mortimer also used to oversee the cleaning of this site:

> That gun came to shoot across to [the Trelawny seaport of] Falmouth [at enemy ships]. They [the British] were attempting to shoot at Falmouth and the fire-ball land[ed] at Green Park [Estate] and burn the cane field. The gun is still up there, but trees grow on it. A tank [water-well] down there that they used to use to get drinking-water. The hospital was over there [to the right of Gun Hill, by a bamboo tree]; *this place* called 'Hospital'. When the people started to work the land [after land sales in the 1930s], the amount of [cannon] *shots* they find!

Mortimer's narrative of finding gun-shots from the cannon is reinforced by the six musket shots and a larger 'grape' shot from a cannon-ball found at Flagstaff that are displayed in the small museum in the present Councillor's Old Family's house near Maroon Town Square.

Further up the main road from Ball Ground and the barracks cemetery a few houses, some shops and a Church of God Pentecostal Church surrounded by 'banana walks' comprise Flagstaff Square – which on a clear day offers a view of Falmouth harbour on Trelawny's north coast. Further on, along a rocky road leading north-west from Flagstaff Square, we stopped with Mortimer at Dragoon Hole, where the road is flanked on one side by a steep cliff and on the other by a precipitous valley (which has close parallels with the site of the ambush of Colonel Sandford at Sandford's Defile). Here Mortimer continued his narrative:

> In those days it [the road] was only a track. So the British soldiers were coming from Falmouth this way [from the north]. The Maroons were dressed [camouflaged] in trees, branches for guerrilla warfare up there and they wait until – there were two angles, right and left [both ways/directions] – and they wait until the soldiers came. And see the condition [deep 'dragoon hole' on the left side, cockpit cliff to the right when coming from Falmouth]. And the British soldiers lose the battle here. They had to get reinforcements and the Maroons fled some days after that. Some of the tombs (at Flagstaff) *might* be the [white] victims.

Returning to Maroon Town Square, Mortimer pointed out that the cultivated lands, houses and tombs in the yards along the way were on Flagstaff lands that had belonged to the government. He showed us the boundary of the Flagstaff lands, going towards Browns' Town, as we drove back to his house-yard in Vaughansfield.

In 2002, Mortimer (then 92) described some of the mortuary rituals that reflect the interweaving and transnational kinship relations of Maroon Town. He focused on two of the memorials that had been held for his mother and his wife who were buried in two of the four tombs in his yard. Mortimer's mother, Atiliah Reid (born in 1868), died in 1954 aged 86 – a mother, grandmother and great-grandmother (for example, she was the great-grandmother of some of Baron McGhie's children of Maroon Town's central clan [chapter 10]). Mortimer's wife, Carmen Reid (born in 1916), died in 1983. One of the joint memorials for Atiliah and Carmen had been held in 1990, when 21 relatives came in the same plane from the United States to join other kin in Maroon Town.

Another of the memorials for Atiliah and Carmen was in 2001, when several relatives and members of the Reid Old Family had, likewise, returned from the United States. One of Mortimer's granddaughters from Los Angeles had re-tiled their tombs, where many people gathered to eat and drink. The next day, a memorial was held at the Mount Edmonson Methodist Church, followed by a reception at the house of Atiliah's granddaughter Lola McGhie (Baron McGhie's widow), near her uncle Mortimer's yard.

In 2002, Mortimer told me that he had missed the transnational memorial in 2000 held for Baron McGhie (a prominent Maroon Town villager), as he had been visiting his relatives overseas. Mortimer then showed me where he planned to be buried: in his yard, between his wife and his mother. When I visited him again in 2006, he was frail, had given up his travels and was settled on his verandah, secure in the knowledge that his plans were in place and that, in the future, his numerous transnational descendants would gather in his memory there.

Soon after I visited Mortimer again in January 2007, I heard, in London, that he had died the following month (aged 96), that a large transnational funeral had been held at the Mount Edmonson Methodist Church and that he had been buried behind his house. Six of his children and more than ten grandchildren from the United States came for the funeral. When I revisited Mortimer's yard in August 2007 (with my husband and Charlie Dobson who had 'grown' with Mortimer there), his nephew (who lives in another house in the yard) showed us Mortimer's tomb. This was situated exactly where Mortimer had planned, between his wife and his mother. Mortimer's large white-washed tomb, which he himself had designed, dominated the cemetery and portrayed a staircase going upwards – leaving no doubt of where he had gone and of who was still in charge (figure 8.4).

It was planned that Mortimer's tombstone would be laid on the first anniversary of his death, in February 2008, when numerous descendants would come from the United States. However, in March 2009, his son explained that the memorial had been postponed due to another memorial marking the 25th anniversary of the death of Mortimer's wife that had been held by some of her children and grandchildren, in America, in October 2008. He showed me the memorial tee-shirt they had sent him, with the inscription, '25th Year Anniversary of our Beloved Carmen Reid'.

Figure 8.4. Mortimer Reid's house-yard cemetery including his tomb.

The mortuary rituals for Mortimer, his mother, his wife and his affine, Baron McGhie, are part of a wider pattern of such rituals that not only continue Revival practices but have also evolved to both reinforce and reflect the transnational kinship that draws migrant 'world-travellers' back to Maroon Town where their roots 'continue to be' (compare Rapport 2004, 74, quoted in Besson 2005, 17). For example, in August 2003, a large transnational memorial was held at the Mount Edmonson Church for Mortimer's cousin, Lil Delgado, who had died in January that year while visiting her daughters in Los Angeles. Lil's late mother was a Reid and Lil's late husband's mother was a McIntyre who had married into the Hamilton clan (Genealogies 2 and 3). Lil's memorial, which drew relatives from the United States, was therefore embedded in the Maroon Town community, including its Meso-Creole Reid, McIntyre and Hamilton transnational clans.

Melvin Pearson's Narrative

Soon after our visit to Flagstaff with Mortimer, I returned there to meet his elderly second cousin, Melvin Pearson, who lived just beyond Flagstaff at the Georges Valley land settlement nicknamed 'Zambia'. Melvin, a Seventh Day Adventist, was born in 1917, in the Coote Bush section of Browns' Town where, as he explained, 'A *breed* of people [a clan] living there called Cootes'. He was aged 81 when I first interviewed him in 1999. I met him again at the Emancipation Day celebrations at Ball Ground in 2001 and 2002, by which time he was 84.

Like his cousin Mortimer, Melvin had been a farmer producing bananas for export and yams (on family land at Browns' Town). He had also been a butcher and a migrant labourer in 'the first batch of Farm Workers' that went from Jamaica to the United States in 1943. After working there for six months, Melvin returned to Jamaica and then went back to the US in 1944, returning to Maroon Town that year. In the 1970s, he migrated again for Farm Work, then returned to Maroon Town. He then purchased his own 'house lot' at Georges Valley from the government.

Melvin died in 2008, aged 91. After his death, his elderly maternal half-brother described Melvin as 'a history man' – as indeed I had found. In his narrative, Melvin traced the genealogy of the Reid Old Family one ascending generation further than Mortimer, who had traced the Old Family back to his paternal grandfather, Tommy Reid. Melvin traced the genealogy to their great-grandfather, Charles Reid (Melvin's mother's maternal grandfather), whose children included Tommy Reid. Melvin's ancestry also includes two other overlapping Meso-Creole Old Families in Maroon Town, the Pearsons and the Grants (Genealogy 2). Below are some extracts from his narrative in relation to Maroon Town 'slave master' pickni' ancestry, including his Reid clan (which he portrays as originating 'from Ireland in England' but which Mortimer had stated originated from Scotland), and regarding the distinction between such Old Families and Newcomers:

> Most of these lands in Maroon Town, they belong to the Englishman [British men] and the Englishman came and go to the slave girl and give them pickni [children]. So most of the people at Maroon Town, they are slave masters' children: Pearson and Reid. So my old great-grandfather name Charles Reid, coming from England. And they are European

children. And Brown and Stennett – *high colour* [high-status fair-skinned] people. And 'Son' Reid [Mortimer] coming from same way. Son Reid' father *high colour*...

The people [in Maroon Town today] are not Maroons...All who born a' Maroon Town is 'slave master' pickni'...And some are from the parishes of Westmoreland, Hanover, St Elizabeth, Trelawny and Manchester. At Flagstaff, not one born here, me alone, my foreparents from Browns' Town. They all come in and have children. You have Reid, Harris, born here Maroon Town, St James, but others come in.

Melvin moved on to a detailed account of his Old Families and their family lands:

My great-grandmother [his mother's maternal grandmother] 'Mother P' lived to 107. And when she was 106 she walked from Maroon Town Crossroads to Point[5] for a letter. Go and come. She was a black girl. Her father was a slave in Browns' Town – the whole place was plantation. My great-grandfather [his mother's maternal grandfather] Charles Reid was from Ireland in England. The slave master's child [children] lived at Browns' Town.

The British slave master, Charles Reid, is said to have had 12 mulatto children by the Afro-Creole slave girl 'Mother P': six daughters and six sons. 'Massa Reid' was the eldest; Tommy Reid was another. The daughters included Melvin's maternal grandmother, Kate Reid, who married Robert Grant. Kate and Robert had ten children: six boys and four girls, including Melvin's mother, Elizabeth Grant. She likewise had ten children: three daughters and seven sons, including Melvin, the eldest. He had 'about 14 children' (four 'sets' of paternal half-siblings), who are scattered in Maroon Town, Montego Bay and the United States, 43 grandchildren and 22 great-grandchildren. His brothers and sisters also have many descendants, thereby contributing to an ever-expanding cognatic clan (Genealogy 2).

Melvin used to live on the family land of his maternal grandfather Robert Grant at Coote Bush, Browns' Town. Melvin did not know the exact origin of his grandfather's land, 'but I [born] come see him 'pon it and *I know he was a slave master's pickni'*. There is a graveyard on that land in which the grandfather, Robert Grant, Melvin's grandmother Kate (Reid) Grant and his mother, Elizabeth Grant, are buried. (Melvin himself was buried here in 2008, by which time no one lived there and it was just a family burying ground.) Melvin's paternal grandfather, William Pearson, was likewise 'a slave master's pickni – all who born a Maroon Town is slave master' pickni'. Melvin went on to refer to other clans in Maroon Town: 'Same Massa' [slave master's] children'.

Like Mortimer, Melvin situated his account of the Reids (and his other clans) within a wider narrative of the transformation from Trelawny Town to Maroon Town and of sacred sites on the Cockpit Country landscape (see also Besson 2005, 32–34). Melvin's narrative partly reflects and partly transforms the actual history of the Second Maroon War, ordering and repairing the disjunctures of globalization, slavery and the disastrous Second Maroon War by collapsing the First and Second Maroon Wars into one maroon victory with a subsequent local maroon migration from Trelawny Town to Accompong, thereby eclipsing the 1796 deportation of the Trelawnys to Canada by the maroon victory of 1738/39.

Melvin's narrative also orders the disjuncture between Leeward and Windward Maroons by transforming the Windward heroine, Nanny, into a Leeward Maroon hero named 'Campong Nanny, and even addresses the ruptures of the Spanish and English conquests of Jamaica. The narrative includes references to sacred sites in the Cockpits such as Flagstaff, Garrison, Ball Ground, Gun Hill, Dragoon Hole, Malloney Hole, Hines Mountain and Cudjoe River, as well as to Maroon Town in general as a non-maroon community. Like Mortimer, Melvin narrated that Flagstaff was the site of the colonial barracks after the Second Maroon War. Garrison and Ball Ground were part of these barracks (which had a cemetery). Gun Hill overlooked the barracks. Dragoon Hole bears a close resemblance to the defile where Sandford's colonial Dragoons were defeated in a battle in this War (chapter 2). Malloney Hole, Hines Mountain and Cudjoe River are sites said to mark the journey of Cudjoe and 'Campong Nanny (and I would hear more about the Hines Old Family and Cudjoe River from members of the Hines clan [chapter 9]). Also mentioned in Melvin's narrative are the slave plantations of Green Park, Hampden and Rose Hall in Trelawny and St James and various villages in Trelawny, St James and St Elizabeth:

> The Arawak Indians were living here [in Jamaica]. The Cubans [Spanish] came and beat them out. The English come and run the Cubans. A big hill up there called Gun Hill and can see Falmouth in Trelawny. After the English take over they get slave from Africa and they work...
>
> After, they get the slaves and a batch of the slaves was down Trelawny at Green Park and a batch was at Hampden and a next batch in St James at Rose Hall. So the slaves rebel from Green Park...Cudjoe – and Nanny was up Maroon Town, up here. And they [the runaway slaves] come through Green Park, Wakesfield and Deeside, and up Long Hill and a shortcut to Flagstaff called Pembroke. And when they come, they fight a battle at Dragoon Hole.
>
> But Nanny and Cudjoe [portrayed as slaves], they escape and they come to the same Garrison at Ball Ground. *So this place get the name Maroon Town, that's where they live.* And they leave from there and go Hines Mountain and Malloney Hole and a place name Packitik where water came out a the rock, and they go a place name Cudjoe River where Cudjoe put him foot and mark it out. Then they go a place name Phelan Bush and Whitehall in St Elizabeth and they leave from there to Accompong Town. *So this Maroon Town is the original Maroon Town and they leave here go to Accompong Town and they live there now.* And they worship, every 6th of January, Nanny. Nanny was killed at Hines Mountain (at/near Flagstaff) by the white soldiers. But him tek him batty [buttocks] catch the bullets. And after, they kill him. *And the Maroons carry him to Accompong Town and bury him up there.* Cudjoe was there. I don't have a history where Cudjoe died. *'Campong Nanny was a man, but they call him Nanny – different from Moore Town Nanny.* So the cemetery – see the names there. *The Maroons tek a piece of land up 'Campong Town, St Elizabeth, and they don't pay tax...*When I was a boy, I go up Gun Hill and see the Great Gun – it mash up, but see the place where the gun was on...
>
> When the Maroons fight a battle round Dragoon Hole, they fight and hide in the bush – cut the green bush and put around them [as camouflage]. When they [the colonial enemy] turn back, they [the Maroons] run down and kill them. A great battle fight there, 99 persons/white soldiers died there and the Maroons stay away now from there and

came to Flagstaff (at the crossroads/square) and they walk and get to where the burial ground is and to the Garrison and go through Hines Mountain to Malloney Hole where the water sink to Packitik – and that water cramp you' teeth [is icy cold] and come out a big rock – *and they go to Cudjoe River and from there to Phelan Bush and then to Whitehall and then to Accompong Town where they are living now. The 99 white soldiers buried in Dragoon Hole* – a spot there, nobody works [cultivates] it. A few Maroons were also killed in the battle (my emphases).

Such narratives are passed down the generations of the Maroon Town community and its expanding cognatic clans, repairing the disjunctures of the maroon/non-maroon interface.

In addition to Melvin's oral history, I collected narratives from his son and grandson. His son, who was born in 1942 in Coote Bush, was also now living at Zambia, having likewise purchased a house-lot there in the 1970s. This son's son, aged 29 in 1999, was born at Zambia and was still residing there. Together, their oral accounts illuminated generational discourses regarding the control of sacred knowledge and the transmission of oral tradition down the generations, with both its continuities and divergences. Parts of Melvin's narrative were reiterated and elaborated by his son and contested by his grandson, illustrating both the inter-generational transmission and the editing of oral tradition. For example, reflecting on the name Maroon Town, Melvin's son reiterated an abbreviated version of his elderly father's oral history on the Second Maroon War and added an account of the great 1831–32 slave rebellion, at the Tulloch Plantation, at Kensington, that he had learned from older people there. He also remarked (in 1999) on the annual emancipation celebrations at Flagstaff, introduced in 1997 (and which would continue into the new millennium):

The only reason it call Maroon Town – out by Maroon Town was the barracks. So they store the ammunition there for the white soldiers. Maroons was living here. They have a fight. The soldiers came from Falmouth to Dragoon Hole. The Maroons dress in bush and ambush the soldiers. And kill 99 of them. Buried in Dragoon Hole. They [the Maroons] leave from there to a place called Likkle Petty [Petty River] Bottom and from there to Accompong Town in St Elizabeth. They took up their residence there. Those born in 'Campong Town is Maroons. The people in Maroon Town are not Maroons.

Cudjoe was a fighter. Nanny also was a great fighter, great warrior. I heard that a rebellion from Kessington [1831–32, Kensington], have a strike, start burn cane down. It was a slavery attitude. The treatment was not right. I heard that from elder people at Kessington. Have some a the building where the slaves was living out there...

From Maroon Town Square to Flagstaff, we have a lot of history. Where the soldiers built the building, hospital, prison and all like that. So we have a general Emancipation Day on August 1 and we'd like some of the foreign[ers] from England to come as we are inviting a lot of people. A national Emancipation we want to have this year. We're inviting the Prime Minister, the Opposition Leader and the Governor-General. The Prime Minister has been in Maroon Town Square – two time.

Melvin's son explained that the road to Flagstaff was being asphalted for the Emancipation Day celebration and 'to get our crops out'. He compared this Emancipation celebration (which I would attend in 2000, 2001 and 2002) to Accompong's Myal Play:

'Have a band, quadrille, dancing and singing, speech, performers, people/bands from here and from Trelawny and Cambridge and Kensington'.

Melvin's grandson added to his father's and grandfather's narratives, contributing a variant that he said he had heard on the radio and asserting the right of the younger generation to be bearers of oral tradition. In this version, influenced by the media, notions of science and the theme of African renaissance, Nanny once again becomes female (in contrast to being male in his grandfather's narrative) and she and Cudjoe are portrayed as coming from Africa:

> Nanny wasn't a slave. She come on the ship from West Africa with Cudjoe and the others. Cudjoe, Quaco and the rest a them. She own a piece a land same way like the rest a them. When she start work the land, the Spaniard want them to work fe them and cut down them farm. So Nanny decide they going to *teef* [steal] them cow a night-time. Chop the cow in two and gone with it. Quaco – why them call him Quaco, him use a bush and when him get a cut him use it and heal himself.

> Our right name not 'Maroon'. Is the British give us that name. 'Maroon' mean 'wild', if you look it up in the dictionary. We black people in Jamaica is the mighty Coromantee people from West Africa.

Melvin interjected, at this point, and stated that his grandson's narrative was 'rubbish'. Melvin's grandson, however, continued, retorting (with reference to his grandfather) that, 'He might be older than we, but we know *facts* too' and attributing the next part of his knowledge to an elderly farmer (known as 'Farmer') in the community, who specialized in the cultivation of cabbages for sale:

> This [story] is from an old man ['Farmer']. When Nanny go fight the War in Dragoon Hole him [she] plant a pumpkin vine and [she said] if the pumpkin vine grow she will win the battle, if it don't grow she will lose it. And the pumpkin vine did grow and she win it. Them used to dress in *leaves* when they going to fight war so look like *trees*. Them have a bush in the area at those times name 'Spirit Weed'. Them seh it speed up them cells in the body and mek them invisible.

'Farmer', himself, would provide a more detailed narrative of 'Campong Nanny and the pumpkin vine (chapter 9).

The Reid Old Family, in addition to overlapping with other clans of mixed ancestry such as the Pearsons, Grants and McGhies, is also interrelated with the Hamiltons, another Meso-Creole Maroon Town clan. I next present the narrative of a member of the Hamilton Old Family, Mrs Roberta Brown.

Roberta Brown's Narrative

Mrs Roberta Brown's house-yard (inherited from her maternal aunt) is opposite the Maroons' Pride banana chip factory and looks across to the Pond Piece land settlement and the road ascending from Maroon Town Square to Flagstaff. I interviewed her there in 1999, when she was nearly 70 years old, and she was still living there in 2009. She was born, in 1930, on her mother's adjoining family land, which had been 'passed down by our [maternal] old parents' and whose co-heirs include all of Roberta's mother's descendants including Roberta's five siblings and their descendants, Roberta's 12 children (daughters and sons) and her numerous grandchildren who are scattered in Jamaica and the United States.

Roberta 'grew up in the Mount Edmonson Methodist Church' but had become a Baptist after she met her late husband, who was a deacon in the Maldon Baptist Church. He had farmed land at Parkin/Pond Piece and sold bananas to the United Fruit Company and cane to Hampden Estates. Roberta used to sell yams to higglers in Maroon Town and at the Montego Bay marketplace. She now cultivated bananas in her yard, which she sold to the chip factory.

Roberta narrated an account of her maternal Meso-Creole Hamilton Old Family to which she, her siblings and their descendants belong. She recounted that her great-grandfather (her mother's paternal grandfather), John Hamilton, known as 'Country John', was 'from Scotland, a white man, but came to Jamaica and reside in Maroon Town. My great-grandfather came to Maroon Town and met with a black lady, my grandfather's mother'. Roberta explained that their son, her maternal grandfather, Philip Hamilton, a light-skinned mulatto, 'was a Fair man like you [me]' and that 'my mother's hair could not plait, so lively [it was so straight] but she have the darkness from my great-grandmother'. She said that Country John was 'a big plantation owner', who owned 'that land up the hill by the Chinaman shop, from the topside land right down to Popkin'. She added that her granduncle, Philip Hamilton's brother, married Amy McIntyre, the mother of Clinton Delgado (who married Lil McFarlane, whose mother was a Reid), and was Clinton's 'stepfather'. Clinton and Lil (now both deceased, but with eight children in the United States and descendants in Maroon Town) bought Country John's land, which is therefore owned by members of the McIntyre and Reid clans (Genealogy 2).

Roberta situated this family narrative within a wider narrative of the transformation of the Trelawny Town maroon community to non-maroon Maroon Town, which she contrasted to the Accompong Maroon society:

> It's called Maroon Town because from the ancient days the Maroons were here, at Flagstaff and Cudjoe River. Maroon Town is different from Accompong Town – they govern themselves and do their own thing. Here is Maroon Town. The old people in those days was from different parishes, poor people, farmers, and live here. Some were so ambitious, they bought lands, make houses, have children.

> They are not Maroons [in Maroon Town] anymore. They come from different parishes and live here. All the way over there [Pond Piece] was a big bush and swamp. A Chinaman...have a shop at Maroon Town and he lease the lands from the owner of this big property...His grandson sold it out, hundreds of acres.

> Cudjoe and Nanny – Nanny was from Accompong Town, but Cudjoe came here and he had a place named Cudjoe River at Vaughansfield. Those people were from down in Africa and develop this place. They have a lot of history at Flagstaff. That was part of Maroon Town. There [Flagstaff] was where the white soldiers camp out there. I understand they going to keep Emancipation Day this August up there.

Emancipation Day was indeed celebrated at Flagstaff that year and in subsequent years.

The McIntyres, Stennetts and Harrises: More Afro-Scots Landholding Clans

In this section, I present narratives from the overlapping Afro-Scots McIntyre, Stennett and Harris Old Families, set within their wider accounts of the transformation from Trelawny Town to Maroon Town. The themes of mixed descent and sacred sites continue through these narratives. I begin with a narrative of the McIntyre clan (that is also linked to the Hamiltons and Reids), which additionally illustrates that the British colonial population in the Maroon Town area, during and after slavery, was internally differentiated and included poor whites as well as the planter class.

Gaby McIntyre's Narrative

Gaby McIntyre, a Mount Edmonson Methodist, who was born in Maroon Town in 1939, used to cultivate bananas for export to England until 'it went on the rocks'. He lived on a portion of his paternal family land near Maroon Town Square, above the Schaw Castle road, where I interviewed him in 1999. He was still there in 2009. The land belongs to his father's 12 children (now mainly in the United States and England, though some return for funerals) and to their children and grandchildren. I also interviewed Gaby's paternal aunt who lived in the adjoining yard. The family land, with its three burial grounds, is situated on a steep hillside in an exquisite setting of Cockpit mountains covered with bamboo. Gaby was born in a family house further up the hill.

Gaby traced the family land, about 50 acres in all 'right in this area hitting back to Flagstaff', back through his father (who was born in Maroon Town and is tombed in Gaby's front yard) and his father's seven siblings, to their father, Benjamin McIntyre (also buried on the land) and Benjamin's siblings (Genealogy 3). Gaby described his grandfather Benjamin, whom he knew, as a poor white Scotsman and remarked that, 'how my father's older ancestors get it [the land] I don't know, maybe from the Maroons'.

However, Gaby narrated that the present-day population of Maroon Town are not Maroons but mixed – in contrast to the Accompong Maroons:

> A mixed population [in Maroon Town]. If you look at the Maroons in Accompong Town you see full-blooded Maroons. Some of the population, when they touch with the Maroons you can know those with maroon blood, they are not quiet if they get upstir...
>
> My father – his descendants [ancestors] not really from Jamaica, mostly some touch of the Scottish descendants. Even the name [McIntyre] could tell you that...My grandfather is not from Jamaica, he is from Scottish descendant. Long hair, fair colour, like you [me], long, long, white hair. I know him. As little children we call him 'Bada Ben', a pet-name or nick-name, a pet-name.[6] He smoked a curved pipe. A pipe man. He wasn't from Jamaica. He was cultivating, no [sugar] factory, poor.

Gaby remarked that others in Maroon Town likewise have 'a touch' of Scottish ancestry, in contrast to 'full-blooded Maroons' and that, 'if you see the Maroons, you'd definitely know them'. Such other mixed descent groups include the McGhie Old Family (chapter 10), who overlap with the McIntyres and who, as Gaby explained, are the dominant clan in Flagstaff: 'One set of Family controls Flagstaff – the McGhies, a few of them call my father granduncle'.[7]

Genealogy 3. Partial Genealogy of the McIntyre, Stennett and Harris Clans, Maroon Town

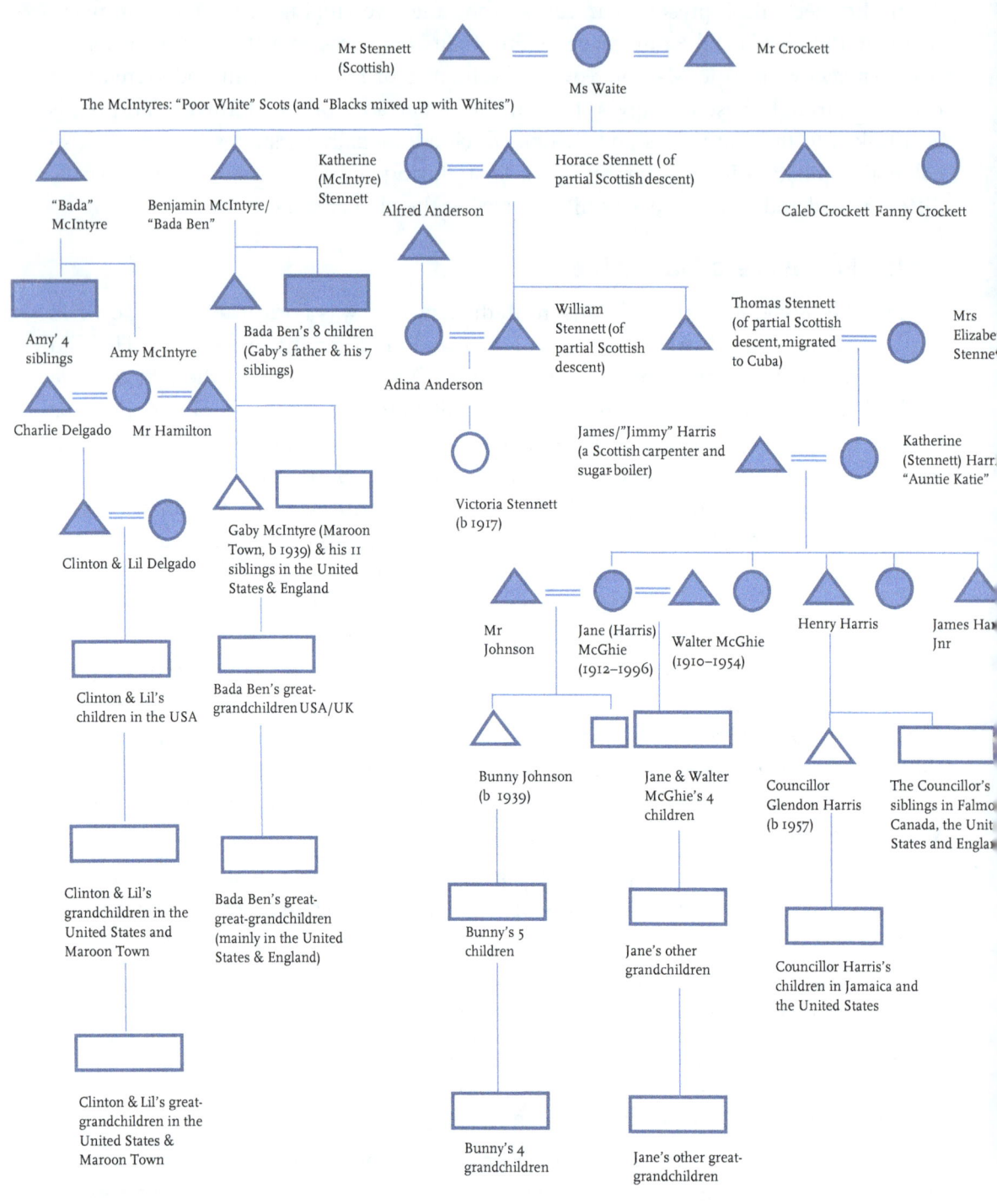

Gaby narrated a detailed account, combining myth and history, of maroon warfare (collapsing the First and Second Maroon Wars into one) and the related landscape, the transformation of the maroon settlement (Trelawny Town) to Maroon Town and the role of Nanny and Cudjoe:

> This Maroon Town, the Maroons were here, all about, at a place called Flagstaff and there was one of those Maroons by the name of Jago, Cudjoe was there too. There's also a little village by that said name, 'Jago Hole'/'Dragoon Hole'. You have the original hospital and camping ground [of the colonial troops]. You have a slight remain of the structure to prove it's really true. Their lookout was the highest point at Flagstaff, name Gun Hill. That's where they used to stay and see the soldiers coming from Trelawny. Dragoon Hole, they had a fight there, the English and the Maroons.
>
> JB: When was this?
>
> Up more in the fourteenth [sic] century. Plenty life was lost. There's a mark there to prove where those that might be hurt and couldn't move [British and Maroons] were buried there. (Accompong slaves were taken from West Ghana.) Those who couldn't move, they died and were buried at Dragoon Hole. Jazarus, a man from England or Scotland, was buried at Flagstaff, his monument is there with his name on it.
>
> JB: Who won the war?
>
> It was settled. They say the Maroons could settle in Flagstaff, they like the hills, caves and mountains.
>
> JB: How does Maroon Town fit in?
>
> They were Maroons, they were the first inhabitants [of Maroon Town], so they just give it the name 'Maroon Town'. There was a lady, she was the leader, that's Nanny, [s]he was really the leader for the maroon troops – just machetes, they didn't have guns, machete was the really supply for warring.
>
> I shouldn't think Nanny was buried. We didn't have road like this. Travel through mountain and reach Accompong Town. The Maroons were very tricky and use green leaves to cover their body and you walk right into them...
>
> A next fighter [another warrior was], Cudjoe. He was back on the other side, Vaughansfield. Also have a river there, Cudjoe River, plenty life was lost there. Tracing a person [trying to track-down a Maroon] – oops into the water, no way out!
>
> Nanny have her set [of troops], Jago have their set, Cudjoe have his set, so they separate into the hills and they were all looking to see the slave boss, the English slave masters, the Maroons wouldn't have any sympathy. They [the Maroons] hide, they know the mountains. They [the colonists] use dogs and the Maroons use arrows to stop the dogs and the English, and the machete for close contacts.

In addition to his narrative of maroon warriors at Flagstaff, Gaby indicated that Maroons had also inhabited the area where he lived near Maroon Town Square; for, as we walked together on the road, he remarked: 'We may be walking on dead people, Maroons [right here].' And of the road behind his mountainous yard, which leads to Flagstaff, he remarked that it is named 'Campersdown, Maroons used to camp there' (a point that recurred in other Maroon Town narratives such as that of Jonathan Dunstan, the oldest man in Maldon [chapter 7]).

Gaby's oral history of the McIntyre Old Family was reinforced and extended by the narratives of Victoria Stennett and Councillor Glendon Harris, whose Stennett and Harris clans overlap with the McIntyres.

Vicky Stennett's Story

Victoria Stennett ('Miss Vicky') was born in Maroon Town in 1917, on the Stennett family land near Maroon Town Square where she was living when I interviewed her, aged 82, in 1999. She still resided there in 2009, by then 92. Vicky belongs to at least four of Maroon Town's overlapping Old Families – the Stennetts, Waites and McIntyres (on her father's side) and Andersons (her mother's Old Family) – and has further kinship and affinal connections through members of these clans with the Harrises, Peterkins and McGhies.

Vicky narrated that the land on which she lives was transmitted from her paternal grandfather Horace Stennett (whose wife was Vicky's grandmother, Katherine McIntyre, the sister of Gaby McIntyre's grandfather, Benjamin McIntyre), who got the land from his maternal half-siblings, Caleb and Fanny Crockett, who 'get the land in slavery'. The mother of these three siblings, Vicky's great-grandmother, was a member of the Waite clan. The land was 'willed' and Vicky's grandfather, Horace Stennett, shared it among his children (to be passed on to grandchildren), including Vicky's father, William, and his brother, Thomas, who migrated to Cuba (Genealogy 3). William's share was two acres and he sold two square-chains at Maroon Town Square to other villagers, including Richard McGhie (who had a shop there), Edgar Fennel and a 'Chinese shopkeeper'. Vicky has a wooden house on half an acre of the family land.

Nearer to the road, the old Stennett family home where Vicky was born and the rest of the surrounding family land are overseen by Councillor Glendon Harris (one of Horace Stennett's great-great-grandsons and the great-grandson of Vicky's paternal uncle Thomas Stennett) who acts as the family-land trustee. Thomas was the father of Councillor Harris's paternal grandmother, Katherine Stennett ('Auntie Katie') who 'had children with Jimmy Harris' (said to have come from Scotland as a sugar boiler and carpenter), whose family land is also near Maroon Town Square and for which the Councillor is likewise trustee (Genealogy 3). Vicky's paternal grandparents, Horace Stennett and his wife, Katherine McIntyre, and Vicky's maternal half-sister, Ethel McGhie, are buried on the Stennett family land, as is Vicky's sister's baby. Also buried there are Thomas Stennett and his wife, Elizabeth, and their daughter, Katherine Stennett/Harris, the Councillor's great-grandparents and paternal grandmother.

The Councillor uses the old Stennett family home as a base for tourist tours from his guesthouse in Montego Bay. In addition, in 2006, a large transnational Harris/Stennett Family Reunion, involving about 200 attendees from Europe, Canada and the United States and organized through the Internet 'for the descendants of Arabel, Jimmy, and

Charlotte Harris of Maroon Town and their relatives and friends',[8] was held here. This followed an earlier transnational Harris/Stennett Reunion of about 150 people in 2004, when it was decided to hold such a Reunion every two years. Reunions were held in 2006, 2008 and scheduled for 2010.

Vicky lived in Kingston for most of her life, working in domestic service and a button factory. She retired, in 1970, to the family land and two young women and two children, 'friends and family', resided with her there. Surrounded by these friends and family, including a young man who lived next door, Vicky began her narrative on Maroon Town stating that: 'We are not Maroons, though we are descended from Maroons.' The young man from next door interjected to contradict: 'We *are* Maroons, I *know* we are Maroons!' Unperturbed, Vicky continued her narrative:

> The Maroons – me old people used to talk about the Maroons, my [paternal] grandfather [Horace Stennett] had a [Peterkin] cousin used to tell me about Maroons, but me grandfather never tell me. Hear the Maroons were living at Flagstaff Garrison. My [maternal] grandfather [Alfred Anderson] used to tell me he was working with the Maroons. Is him, when them [the Maroons] dead, is him carry them 'pon the mule-dray to Falmouth to the Maroons' burying ground. Don't know what part of Falmouth.

Vicky's maternal grandfather, Alfred Anderson, lived in Browns' Town. He had six children, one of whom (Annie) 'had children with Jacob McGhie', the father of Baron McGhie (chapter 10). Baron and Vicky are, therefore, 'two sisters' children', as Vicky's mother was Annie's sister, Adina Anderson.

Vicky resumed her account, which touched on the role of Cudjoe and Nanny, and the now-familiar narrative themes of collapsing the First and Second Maroon Wars and the mythical migration of the Trelawny Maroons to Accompong:

> Cudjoe and Nanny (him sister) were the [maroon] leaders and they take rocks and fight them [the colonial troops]. That's why, after they [the Maroons] win the war with the Spaniard, they capture Accompong and get that land there.

Vicky then narrated an account of the McIntyre Old Family, of which she is a member, through her paternal grandmother, Katherine McIntyre. Katherine had two brothers, 'Bada' McIntyre and 'Bada Ben' (Benjamin) McIntyre. These siblings, Vicky explained, were 'black mixed up with whites'; that is, Meso-Creoles (though Gaby McIntyre, Vicky's second cousin, had narrated that Bada Ben, his grandfather, was a white Scotsman). Katherine married Horace Stennett and lived with him on his Waite/Stennett family land, where Vicky now lives. Katherine's brothers (Vicky's paternal granduncles), Bada and Bada Ben, each had their own share of land near Maroon Town Square.

Bada McIntyre's land was shared among his five children (four daughters and a son) in a will. The land of one of Bada's daughters, Amy McIntyre (who married one of 'Country John' Hamilton's mulatto sons), passed to her son, the late Clinton Delgado (Country John's step-grandson), who married Lil McFarlane who belonged, through her mother, to the Reid clan. Amy's share of the McIntyre family land, on a hillside above Maroon Town Square, still belongs to her descendants, Clinton and Lil's children, who are members of the overlapping McIntyre and Reid clans.

Bada Ben's land, on the hillside overlooking the Schaw Castle road, is now with his son's son, Gaby McIntyre (Vicky's second cousin), whose narrative was given above. Vicky's narrative was reinforced, not only by Gaby's oral history, but also by the accounts of Councillor Glendon Harris, Horace Stennett's great-great-grandson.

The Councillor's Narratives

Councillor Glendon Harris was born in 1957 at the Stennett family-land home at Maroon Town Square. As the St James Parish Councillor for Maroon Town, he now resides in Montego Bay where he also keeps a guesthouse and runs tourist tours to the Cockpits using his Stennett family-land home as a base.[9] Despite his busy schedule, he helped me throughout my research. Here is an extract from one of his narratives, regarding the overlapping Meso-Creole Old Families of Maroon Town, including his Afro-Scots Stennett, Harris and McIntyre clans and the Stennett family land where he was born and where Vicky, his elderly first cousin twice removed, was living:

> That land used to be owned by my great-grandfather, Thomas Stennett [his father's maternal grandfather and Vicky's paternal uncle]. I think he was one of the descendants of those that came from Scotland. There were five [McIntyre] sisters that came to Maroon Town and that is where you get all the mix coming from the McIntyres: the McGhies, the Thompsons, the Reids, the Stennetts and the Harrises, the Delgados, all had children with one of those five McIntyre sisters. Can't tell you exactly where they came from, I think they were a generation after Scottish...[for example] Miss Biddy, Miss Amy, these were some of five. These ladies have died. Thomas Stennett's daughter was Katie and Jimmy Harris had children with Katie, that's how the Harris/Stennett come in and link back to McIntyre. The Harris property is where Bunny [whom I had visited on the Schaw Castle road] is. I have the papers for both sides of the road.

The Councillor is the only one of eight full siblings who is still based in Maroon Town, most of the others having migrated to Canada, the United States and England. However, they all retain rights to their paternal Stennett family land. The Councillor narrated that the graves there include those of Thomas Stennett and his wife, Elizabeth, and their daughter, 'Auntie Katie', his great-grandparents and paternal grandmother (Genealogy 3).

Councillor Harris also provided an eloquent narrative of marronage in the history of the transformation from Trelawny Town to Maroon Town. His main account, collected early in my fieldwork, reflects the dominant Maroon Town narrative themes of conflating the First and Second Maroon Wars and deleting the deportation of the Trelawny Maroons, replacing it with a migration to Accompong.[10] Nanny and Cudjoe also feature in the narrative:

> Flagstaff was where Cudjoe was and most of the lands there are known as the Maroon Town property, if you have a title. Our land up at Flagstaff has 'Maroon Town property'. It became an English settlement after the Maroons retreated further into the hills. The Dragoon Hole battle – there was 100-man troops of English soldiers and the Maroons ambushed them at a place that's now known as Dragoon Hole and they killed 99 and sent back Captain Schaw to the then Governor [to say] that they are there ready and

waiting for battle. So I'm trying to establish the exact date for that battle. The burial site for that battle, there's no mark or tombstone. Eventually, the Maroons retreated and later on the signing of the treaty between Colonel Cudjoe and Colonel Guthrie [took place in] 1738.

Flagstaff being located in the hills was used as a military base for the English. They established their barracks, armoury, hospital and their cemetery is there and a military pool that was the first in Jamaica. Remnants of the pool is still there, the armoury where they store the gun, the cemetery is still there. The now 'playfield' was the site of the barracks, which underneath the soil, at the top, was ballast without stones. They [the colonial troops] signed off with the Maroons, but they still had problems with the runaway slaves and the Cuban problem – some war with the Spanish and establishing bases around Vernon Field in Clarendon. The Spanish control Jamaica before the English took over Jamaica through pirating.

The Maroons went further into the hills and subsequently the signing of the treaty relocated them to Accompong Town. Most of the battles were fought in the Maroon Town area, no battles fought in Accompong. So Maroon Town is really more significant historically. There is a river we call Cudjoe's River, there's a little spring which is the last place where Cudjoe drank water before he went to Accompong. I don't know which year exactly, but they signed up officially 1738. Nanny? Not to my knowledge. She came across the hills two times, three walks. She was told by Cudjoe to go back and control her village, Moore Town, Maroons in the east. She went back. In the battle with the English in the east, she got shot eventually and she travelled back to Accompong with the bullet in her bottom. She didn't live long after that. She's buried in Accompong. Somewhere in the hills between Maroon Town and Accompong. I think its down at Old Town [see chapter 3]. That is where they used to have the village firstly, halfway between the Kindah Tree and the Peace Cave.

As the name suggests – Flagstaff – it was used to hoist the flag to indicate to the British ships coming into Falmouth harbour that they should head in that direction. When you [are] in Flagstaff, you looking out [to] Falmouth harbour [which, he explained, is 15 miles as the crow flies].

In reply to my query on the relationship between Nanny and Cudjoe, the Councillor explained that they were 'sister and brother' and continued with his narrative to reflect on the role of Maroon Town Square as a colonial civilian settlement:

In all of that the Crossroads used to be the township where merry-making used to go on. And in travelling you'd use that as your pick-up point, whether to the north or south. Maroon Town Square became an English non-military settlement, so most of the people there are 'Jamaica White' or 'mulatto'.

In response to my query about the population of Maroon Town today, the Councillor emphasized that the population is now non-maroon, being of mixed descent from colonists, Maroons and slaves as people started to move into this fertile area to farm (especially bananas) and as the more established Old Families imported agricultural labour from other parishes, especially Westmoreland:

No they *aren't* of maroon descent. With the English non-military settlement and the mixing with the Jamaican population – both the slaves and the Maroons – you have that cross [mix] coming.

It became attractive for farming because the area was never enslaved. No stone-walls [Scottish dry-stone dykes] like on the slave plantations. In the early nineteenth century, they – the persons living in the Maroon Town Square area – they started to go into the Flagstaff area to open up lands to farm. That went on for nearly a century. About 90 years ago the English moved out. After the cholera and a major typhoid outbreak, people started to live back in the Flagstaff area. All the houses in the Flagstaff area are under 90 years old. Most of the people used to go into the area to farm and go back out in the evening. It became attractive for persons from outside the area and the parish.

So Flagstaff was developed around cultivation. Peterkin, McGhie, Reid, Young – they [these Old Families] imported labour; most of those people are from Westmoreland. All the elderly people who are not Peterkin, McGhie, Reid or Young came from Westmoreland to work with either the Flagstaff Bakery or in banana cultivation or sugar cane...People came to the area for work. Banana was king and the area was thriving... They were known as the 'S19' banana and after the [banana] disease, [farmers] moved into the Gros Michel banana, and after that into sugar cane. Wilson Young imported most of the labour. He owned Flagstaff Bakery. He started with ginger. The Flagstaff belt was known as Trelawny Town.

When I asked what had happened to the Trelawny Town lands, the Councillor touched on one of the dominant Maroon Town narrative themes of an exchange of land between the colonists and the Maroons that resulted in a maroon migration from Trelawny Town to Accompong:

It was a swop. They [the colonists] gave them [the Maroons] the 1,800-odd acres in Accompong Town and retained the state land [at Flagstaff/Maroon Town Crossroads].

He then returned to the history of the Maroon Town clans, explaining that the Peterkins and other Old Families were working on Crown Land at Flagstaff and the government subdivided and sold it. The McIntyres, however, were at Maroon Town Square rather than Flagstaff and their family land is still at the Square. The Councillor remarked on the names and background of the British ancestors of these clans and his account (like Gaby McIntyre's) suggests the internal differentiation of the white colonists, including planters, poor whites, soldiers and missionaries:

With the English settlement, even the Harrises [his paternal Old Family] are Scottish. It was a swop for leaving jail in Europe. They gave them the lands at Maroon Town in the early 1800s.[11]

The English missionaries were here and they did some work in the area and established the Maldon Baptist Church...The Maldon free village was *bought*...[it was] the first Baptist free village in St James, [established by] Walter Dendy. He got the money in Maldon, Essex, England and bought the land at 'Maldon'...

There was the English sub-settlement in Maroon Town. The plantations up to Kensington would have been the Tulloch Estates, he [Tulloch] owned the Kensington Estate. So the *mix* between there. ... Because you have the dissidents [dissenting/Nonconformist missionaries] to the English. Samuel Vaughan[12] and Rodriquez, they were the plantation owners but were not as anti-black, [they] were accepted by the slaves...It's my belief the mix [occurred] between the slave plantations, the dissidents and the runaways [Maroons].

I asked about the relationship between Maroon Town and Maldon and the Councillor explained that Maldon is now part of Maroon Town:

> They are the same community. The school is Maldon, the Baptist Church is Maldon. Maldon Primary [School] was established by the Methodists at Dundee, with government assistance, used to be joint between both churches, Baptist and Methodist...[Maroon Town is] traditional Baptist...Methodist, Baptist and Anglican.

Councillor Harris concluded his narrative by remarking on the changes in Maroon Town since his childhood, with many members of the Old Families, including the McGhies (the central clan) migrating overseas and the population becoming more diverse due to in-migration.

Bunny Johnson's Narrative

Bunny Johnson and Councillor Harris are 'sister and brother's children' (first cousins): Bunny's mother, Jane (Harris) McGhie, was one of the sisters of the Councillor's father, Henry Harris. Both Jane and Henry were the children of Jimmy Harris, and Bunny described Jimmy (his maternal grandfather) as coming 'from Scotland', explaining that 'he wasn't a soldier, he was a carpenter and a sugar boiler on this land' (Genealogy 3). The land that Bunny referred to is the Harris family land on the Schaw Castle road, extending up to Maroon Town Square, where he was born in 1939 and was still living when I met him in 1999.

Bunny narrated a history of the land that complemented the narratives of the Councillor (above), whom I would meet later and who is trustee for this family land. Bunny explained that:

> What I know, is my grandfather' land, James ['Jimmy'] Harris. The land name Russell Hill. Twelve and a half acres: hillside [across the road] and down here. One of my mother's sisters sell two squares [square chains] of it for the Church of God [across the road].

Bunny thinks that his grandfather, who came to Maroon Town with his mother from St Ann 'to look a better living', bought the land from the government. As Bunny continued, Jimmy Harris had five children, three daughters (including Bunny's mother) and two sons (Henry and James Junior). Jimmy left the land as family land for his five children, now deceased. As Bunny described, 'only grandchildren now occupy the land' and 'the land don't divided, any family can come and build but can't sell it'.

Jimmy Harris has numerous descendants, as four of his children had several children. For example, as both the Councillor and Bunny narrated, Henry had several children and, as Bunny described, his mother, Jane, had six. Four were by her husband, Walter McGhie, of Maroon Town's central clan; for, as Bunny said, 'everybody mix up here in Maroon Town'. Of Jane's six children, five have children and three have grandchildren, including Bunny who has five children and four grandchildren. Many of these descendants of Jimmy Harris have migrated from Maroon Town and/or live elsewhere in Jamaica or in the United States and England. However, many return to Maroon Town for transnational Family Reunions, funerals and memorials.

Bunny had never migrated. A skilled craftsman, he worked as a cabinet-maker, farmed and used to cultivate bananas for sale to a 'boxing house at Baron McGhie's place, first-time'. However (as Bunny continued), 'Banana not selling now, they buy in England and Europe' as he hears 'on TV all the while'. However, he remarked, they are 'fighting to get banana back on track'.

When I interviewed Bunny, there were four houses on the land. Bunny lived in one, his paternal uncle, James's widow lived in a second, the Councillor's stepmother resided in a third and a tenant lived in the fourth. The family cemetery is on this land and Bunny showed me eight tombs there (figure 8.5), including those of his wife (who died in 1988), his mother, Jane (1912–96), and Jane's husband, Walter McGhie (1910–54).

Bunny's mother, Jane, in addition to belonging to the Harris clan and marrying into the McGhie clan, was also a member of the Stennett Old Family. Jane's mother (Jimmy's wife, Kate Stennett/Harris) was the daughter of Thomas Stennett and granddaughter of Horace Stennett (above). All three of these clans (Harris, McGhie and Stennett) claim some Scottish ancestry.

In addition to his narrative of these Old Families and the Harris family land, Bunny reflected on the evolution of Maroon Town from a maroon village (Trelawny Town) to a non-maroon community, in contrast to the Accompong maroon society (where, as a young man, he used to play cricket):

Figure 8.5. Bunny Johnson in the Harris family-land cemetery, Maroon Town.

People who live here now are not Maroons. The people who was before was Maroons. Like the big battle up at Garrison at Flagstaff. They kill off one another. You see the soldiers' tombs. They must have dumped the Maroons and buried them over the gully. Don't know that year. Hear about Cudjoe and Nanny ina the eighteenth century. If you go a 'Campong [Accompong] you find the younger generations of Maroons.

When I asked Bunny how the non-Maroons of Maroon Town originally acquired land there, he remarked:

The higher authorities sent them from England and Scotland to go and get land here. When they get the land, the government came in and mark their boundary and they start to pay tax for the land. In those days, land was cheap: five pounds (£5) for 100 acres, so bought lands.

As seen above, Bunny thought his Scottish grandfather, Jimmy Harris, had acquired the family land in this way.

The Peterkins, Fennels and Andersons: African, English, Irish and Scots

Other overlapping Old Families in Maroon Town claiming mixed African and European ancestry, including some Scottish, English or Irish descent, are the Peterkins, Fennels and Andersons. These Meso-Creole clans also overlap and interweave with other Maroon Town Old Families. This section begins with the narrative of the late Caleb Finnigan, whose mother was a Peterkin. His oral history is followed by that of his first cousin, Walter Peterkin. Walter also belongs to the Anderson, McIntyre, Young and Rockhead Old Families. We then move on to the narrative of the late Rudyard Kipling McGhie who, in addition to being a member of Maroon Town's central McGhie clan, belongs to the Anderson and Fennel Old Families. Rudyard's oral history of the Fennels is reinforced by observations from the late Edgar Fennel. As in the previous sections, these oral histories of Old Families are set within wider narratives on the transformation of Trelawny Town to Maroon Town, including recurring themes such as the conflation of the First and Second Maroon Wars into one war focused on the battle at Trelawny Town (now Flagstaff) and a reputed subsequent maroon migration to Accompong.

Caleb Finnigan's Narrative

The late Caleb Finnigan ('Mas Cay') was born in 1911 and was 87 years old when I interviewed him, in 1999, in his house-yard near Maroon Town Square. He died in his mid-90s, around 2007, and was buried in his yard. Caleb was a 'Wesleyan Methodist' and was, at first, irate when my husband and I approached his yard, as he thought we were Jehovah's Witnesses who (as he put it) 'no preach the right gospel about Gaad [God]'. However, once that confusion was clarified, he welcomed us warmly and we were mutually pleased to learn that he had known my paternal grandfather, the planter and pen-keeper George ('Mas Georgie') McFarlane of the Spring Garden plantation near Montego Bay who had a daughter in Maroon Town. By the time the interview was concluded, Caleb observed that we had made him 'feel good' and he ordered 'two to three photos' from us for his funeral programme. This initially puzzled me until I saw other elaborate funeral programmes with photographs.

Caleb was born in this same yard and had always lived in Maroon Town. This yard had been purchased by his parents, who bought the land from a member of the Reid Old Family (Mortimer's paternal uncle) and willed it to their three children (whose children may also use this family land, including Caleb's son, in England, and daughter in Kingston). Caleb's father was from Westmoreland but Caleb's mother (Eveleena Peterkin, who lived to 103) was from Maroon Town and belonged to the Peterkin Old Family, who claim mixed ancestry and whom he described as 'a big breed, whole heap a family, most people in the area are my relatives'. Caleb's mother had paternal family land in Maroon Town, near the Square, which remains in her Peterkin clan, but she is buried 'in the [Mount Edmonson] Wesleyan churchyard'. His father is 'tombed' in Caleb's yard and there are three other members of the family buried there.

Caleb was a retired farmer, who used to raise cows and cultivate bananas and yams. When I interviewed him, he was preoccupied with the coming of the Millennium, when 'things will be getting sterner' or perhaps the world would end with 'the coming of the Lord'. Meanwhile, however, he enthusiastically provided a narrative on marronage and the history of Maroon Town reaching back to the European Conquest. His account highlights the battle (in the Second Maroon War) at the site now named Flagstaff, which he identifies as the 'right Maroon Town' (Trelawny Town), commenting on its transformation from a maroon to a non-maroon community, in contrast to the autonomous Accompong maroon society (portrayed as established after a maroon migration from Trelawny Town to Accompong). Cudjoe and Nanny also feature in his narrative, though no distinction is drawn between the First and Second Maroon Wars:

> Yes man! When after Columbus come and find out the West Indies, England come in and tek charge. And the Maroons was against them. The English tek certain amount of English, African, Indian and bring them here. The English start to plant cane, open up estate and get land. And treat the black people so rough, so 'nough of them left the estates and go away into the hills and fight the white man. So when the boat left England and come to Falmouth, the Africans have a hill up at Flagstaff, Gun Hill and look. And they kill a whole heap of white people at Dragoon Hole. See a whole heap a red roses, Dragoon plant[s], mark the place where them bury. [Mortimer Reid had shown us these plants.] So up at Flagstaff the Maroons keep them capital and call down here Maroon Town Crossroads and up the hill [at Flagstaff] is Maroon Town. Go up the cemetery and you see big official from England that them kill...Flagstaff is the *right* Maroon Town, down here they call Maroon Town Crossroads.

> *JB: Are the people here Maroons?*

> No. The Maroons evacuate here and they go to St Elizabeth, 'Campong Town. You go to 'Campong Town, St Elizabeth, you find blood Maroons.

> *JB: What about Cudjoe and Nanny?*

> I hear sey dem a head of affairs. They were the head a the set-up of the Maroons in a the War. They all were one-blood people.

JB: So who are the people in Maroon Town now?

Everybody call themselves Jamaican and can live where them want. But don't have a right one seh *dis* one Maroon. [And he later expressed scepticism about those in Maroon Town who claim maroon ancestry.] But go to St Elizabeth now, catch up to Elderslie, go right down can stop a 'Campong Town, Maggoty and Santa Cruz. They have *one* capital of the Maroons – 'Campong Town, St Elizabeth. Every 6th of January a big memorial [the Myal Play] – day and night. Anywhere the Maroon deh, they come up. A memorial fe dem time, when they get freedom [by treaty]. Them coulda do anything fe themselves and the English no trouble them. Deh 'pon dem own run [on their own territory].

Walter Peterkin's Story

Caleb Finnigan and Walter Peterkin are, as Caleb explained, 'two first cousins, Walter' father and my mother is brother and sister'. Walter was born in Browns' Town, in 1920, and was 79 when I interviewed him, in 1999, at a beautiful old house on his paternal family land near Maroon Town Square (though he lived on his wife's land at Browns' Town). This is the family land (six acres) that Caleb also told me about that was transmitted from his and Walter's grandfather, Caleb Peterkin (from Maldon), who had purchased the land. Walter, who is trustee for this land, planted bananas here for sale to higglers. Walter explained that both his father and paternal aunt (Caleb Finnigan's mother, Eveleena) are buried in the Mount Edmonson churchyard, but that his paternal grandparents (Caleb Peterkin and Margaret Young) are buried on the family land, as are two of Walter's siblings. While Eveleena had lived on her husband's land (now Finnigan family land), Walter's parents had raised their ten children on the Peterkin family land. Most of these (now elderly) children are in Canada and the United States, but they all return to Maroon Town for funerals.

Walter had lived and worked abroad for many years. He first lived in Panama to work on the Panama Canal (1941–44) and then in Birmingham, England (1954–73). In between, he returned to Maroon Town and worked as a truck driver transporting bananas and cane. Now, home again, he was doing 'ups and down agriculture, banana fail first, then cow!' He has six children in England and Canada, and grandchildren. All his dispersed descendants, as well as his siblings and their descendants, retain rights to the undivided family land.

In addition to his paternal Peterkin clan, Walter's mother came from Maroon Town: her father was from the Anderson clan and her mother belonged to the Rockhead Old Family, all of whom claim mixed ancestry. Her father owned 'a big property by Camperdown', along with his brothers and 'another family of theirs' (the McIntyres), though this land had since been sold. Walter is, therefore, a member of several overlapping Meso-Creole Old Families, including the Peterkins, Rockheads, Andersons and McIntyres, as well as his paternal grandmother's father's Afro-Creole clan, the Youngs.

Walter provided the following narrative of marronage and maroon warfare, 'Campong Nanny, Cudjoe, the transformation of Trelawny Town to Maroon Town (with a non-maroon 'half-caste' population descended from slave masters and enslaved women) and a maroon migration from Maroon Town to Accompong:

The Maroons were pushed out from the Trelawny area. They stop by this Dragoon Hole where 'Campong Nanny could catch the bullet the soldier fire. Accompong just over that hill there, on 6th of January you can hear their music [from the Myal Play]. Cudjoe end up over 'Campong same place. Nanny – I never remember how she end up. [But] not much people [in Maroon Town] have any trace of Maroons. Couldn't tell you a single one!

JB: So how did Maroon Town get its name?

This was the first [maroon] settlement. They [the Maroons] go through here, it was all woodland. They were settling up that area, Flagstaff area. That's where the battle was. And they end up over that hill in Accompong. No settlement between here and there, all woodland and they used to have a lot of wild boar in there...If you go over there in my olden days hunting wild boar and pigeon, like me father, they would meet people from Accompong doing same thing. But people don't do that again...We're going into a *rough millennium*...

Up at Garrison [at Flagstaff] where the soldiers used to live, they have a cricket ground, playfield, football, everything – they have sport [Emancipation Day rituals] there every year at August time...

The people in Maroon Town now, they purchase the land, they have title and legal document for it. Maybe they were the children of slave masters – slave masters' kids with slave women. The people don't have maroon looks, it's 'half-caste', maybe some of their parents white and some are slave women, that's why they have lighter skin and that's why some of these people get these inheritance and Irish, English and Scottish names, like Reid and Peterkin.

Walter described his mother's side as 'light-skinned' but said he was not sure where the 'fairness' comes from. Likewise, he explained that, 'Some a the Peterkin fair but my father mother [Margaret Young] more on the maroon side, more look like Maroon'.

In addition to Walter's oral history, Vicky Stennett's narrative above included information on the Anderson clan (her mother's Old Family), who had also married into the Stennett and McGhie clans. I would learn more about the Andersons from Rudyard Kipling McGhie.

Rudyard McGhie's Narrative

I interviewed the late Rudyard Kipling 'Baba' McGhie in December 2006, in Vaughansfield, when he was 81 years old.[13] He would tell me not only of his place in Maroon Town's central McGhie clan (see also chapter 10) but also about his Fennel and Anderson Old Families. I found him, a contented returned migrant from the United States, Britain and Canada, sitting on his verandah where he welcomed me. Born in Maldon around 1925, he explained that he was the son of Rose-Ann Fennel and Albert 'Bertie' McGhie (1901–95) of the Woodlands area of Maroon Town. Baba grew up in 'Bottom Pasture, near Duppy Hole, near Pond Piece' with his maternal grandmother, Rozanne Fennel.[14]

Baba narrated that Rose-Ann's father (Baba's maternal grandfather) was Edmund Fennel, whose brother was George Fennel, and that Edmund and George's father (Baba's great-grandfather) and his brother were plantation owners who came to Jamaica from Ireland and lived in Westmoreland. Baba further narrated that the two slave-owning brothers were killed in the 'last slave revolt' (the 1831–32 slave rebellion) but that the life of his great-grandmother had been spared:

> Two Fennel, two slave masters, came from Ireland and was living in Westmoreland. One married had two children, Georgie and Edmund. During the slave revolt, the last one, slave kill both of them, [the] two slave masters and going to kill the wife but her slaves said 'Don't touch her, she's very nice'. Edmund is me grandfather by me mother' side.

Baba continued that his mother, Rose-Ann Fennel, 'tie up in the McGhie Family' (she had children with Albert McGhie) and that his paternal grandmother (Albert's mother) was an Anderson 'and way before that were Andersons'. In addition, Albert's first cousin, Jacob McGhie, had children with Annie Anderson. The Anderson Old Family, who likewise trace descent from white ancestors, were based in Browns' Town.

Baba's life had been eventful. During the Second World War, he had migrated to the United States for Farm Work, from 1943 to 1944. He came back and lived with his maternal uncle, a mechanic in Montego Bay, and became an apprentice there. He then worked with the Public Works Department for six years, then as Third Mechanic with Pan American Airways (who also looked after Avianca planes) at the Montego Bay International Airport.

As Third Mechanic for PanAm, Baba was on duty at the Airport on the night of the Avianca plane crash on January 21, 1960 and witnessed the crash. (I too remembered this tragedy, in which my neighbour's nephew died, when I was a teenager in Trelawny.) Baba's eyewitness account included the information that the plane was flying from New York, via Atlanta, Miami and Montego Bay to Colombia and Venezuela. It was raining and Baba was to signal in the plane but, he explained, the altimeter was wrong due to pilot fatigue and the plane 'dropped down': 'The plane came in, crashed, went in the swamp, turn over, went on fire. Turned hose on it…It was gruesome, you no want hear that part of it'.

Soon after, in 1960, Baba migrated again. This time, he went to Birmingham, England, where he made gear-boxes for cars. He next went to London, where he worked as a mechanic. He then migrated to Canada where he worked, in Toronto, as a diesel mechanic on trains. After that, he spent 21 years in Connecticut working for a diesel electric phone company until his retirement in 1989, when he moved to Florida. He subsequently came to Jamaica regularly, as his nephews persuaded him to look after this house on his late sister's land. His sister is buried in the front yard and one of her sons raises cows on the land. Five years previously, Baba had finally settled in Maroon Town on this land, to be near his 'favourite uncle', his mother's brother, the late Edgar Fennel, whom I had met and interviewed in 1999 (below). Baba's own land, from his late father, Albert McGhie, is in Woodlands.

Baba had five children, three daughters and two sons, all in the United States. As his three daughters each have two children, he had six grandchildren. He also had great-grandchildren. All of these descendants are members of the overlapping transnational Meso-Creole McGhie, Anderson and Fennel clans.

Edgar Fennel's Story

I had interviewed Baba McGhie's maternal uncle, the late Edgar Fennel, at his home near Maroon Town Square in June 1999. Edgar told me that he was 'exactly 94', having been born in June 1905. He was born in Maldon on his father's family land, which has since been sold. Edgar's account of the Fennel Old Family complemented that of his nephew Baba McGhie. Edgar narrated that his father, the late Edmund Fennel (Baba's maternal grandfather) came from Westmoreland and was 'a carpenter, came down this side [to Maroon Town] to work and start to buy up land down here and never go back'. Edgar continued that his father, Edmund, had told him that *his* father (Edgar's paternal grandfather, Baba's great-grandfather) was an Irish slave master:

> Me father always tell me his father was fair, an Irishman. They have some fuss over the other side of the world [Ireland] and some leave out [emigrated]. Was big [high status] men in Jamaica. Them come here as slave owner.

Edgar said his father, Edmund, went to Montego Bay but bought four different pieces of land in Maroon Town: at Maldon, Vaughansfield, Schaw Castle and near Maroon Town Square where Edgar was living. Edmund had bought this land near the Square, in 1927, from William Stennett and had moved there from Maldon.

Edgar, who was one of his father's ten children, had been a bus driver for 19 years (from 1940). He also used to farm, growing bananas for export on the Vaughansfield land. He had never migrated. Some of his siblings, however, went to Canada and England and died there. Only Edgar and a sister in Kingston were still alive.

Light-skinned Edgar stressed the European ancestry of himself and his siblings in contrast to 'Africans' and 'Maroons'. Explaining his father's Irish descent and stating that, 'We are not African', he added that his own mother, Rozanne Fennel (who lived to 103 and was from Aberdeen, in St Elizabeth, where she had family land), was 'a bit darker than my father, but don't black'.

Edgar situated this family history within a wider narrative of the transformation of the maroon society of Trelawny Town (identified with Flagstaff) to the non-maroon community of Maroon Town, including the recurring narrative theme that the Trelawny Maroons had migrated to Accompong following an exchange of land from the colonial government after a battle at Flagstaff:

> I'm not a Maroon, don't touch my blood at all! The Maroons were living up that side at Flagstaff. It was there the black Maroons was living. A big settlement there. And it was there the white soldiers live too. But there was confrontation and them fight, the black and the white fight up there and the black disarm the white, hide in the bushes. The Maroon them leave out and go to St Elizabeth at a place name 'Campong Town.

That's where they are now, they still there now. None of the Maroons down this side [in Maroon Town]. The government take over the property, many years ago, couldn't tell you when. The government swop out the land in St Elizabeth for here. Send them up there and divide all the land down here for small settlers. Sold it to plenty a small settlers. None a them [Maroons] came back down this side.

When I asked Edgar how Maroon Town got its name, he explained: 'Because the Maroon them was here – *once*. That place up there name Flagstaff but is a part of Maroon Town'.

As this chapter has shown, many of the overlapping transnational clans of Maroon Town – like the Reids, Grants, Hamiltons, McIntyres, Stennetts, Harrises, Peterkins, Andersons and Fennels – assert Meso-Creole non-maroon ethnicities based on mixed European and African ancestry, a central theme being 'slave master' pickni' descent. Such oral histories are set within wider narratives, regarding the transformation from Trelawny Town maroon society to non-maroon Maroon Town.

However, my research reveals that another significant theme in Maroon Town is the assertion by some villagers of maroon ancestry. Such claims are generally embedded in Afro-Creole ethnicities. Some Afro-Creoles who do not claim maroon ancestry, likewise, transmit narratives of marronage. In addition, some Meso-Creoles assert descent from Maroons as well as from slave masters and slaves. The next chapter uncovers these themes.

Notes

1. I use 'myth' in an anthropological sense to refer to issues of origin and creation in a social context (see Besson 2000, 130 n2).
2. The property may have been named after, and/or previously owned by, the Calder plantation family (chapter 6).
3. Mortimer's ancestors may have included the planter, Thomas Reid, and his son, Thomas Reid the younger, who founded Falmouth in the eastern part of Old St James around 1769 (Connolley and Parrent 2005). Thomas Reid the younger, who sold his Falmouth lands in 1795, was later indebted to John Tharp, Custos of Trelawny, who was involved in the Second Maroon War (Connolley, personal communication February 12, 2012). Moreover, the colonial party headed by Thomas Reid that visited Trelawny Town, in 1795, included John Tharp (chapter 2).
4. The earlier of the two has a Free Mason's symbol and reads: 'Sacred to the memory of Charles Ross Late Color Sergeant of her Majesty's…[illegible] Durham Regiment of Light Infantry who departed this life on the…[illegible] Day of January 1840 [illegible inscription]'. The second tombstone reads: 'Harriet, wife of James Wilbill 38th Regiment Died 15th November 1846, Aged 32'.
5. Point is the site of the post office serving Maroon Town, several miles away.
6. Orlando Patterson (1973, 170) indicates the use of 'Boda' for brother in the contexts of both actual and fictive kinship among Jamaican slaves. Frederic Cassidy (1971, 183) refers to 'Baba' as a pet name for brother. In Maroon Town, where the pet name 'Baba' is used to mean 'the father has come back in his son' (see note 13 of this chapter), 'Bada' seems to be a combination of 'Boda' and 'Baba'.

7. This narrative of the dominance of the McGhies at Flagstaff is consistent with my research, which indicates a link between the McGhie Maroons, near Flagstaff, and the Maroon Town McGhies whose ancestors settled in Flagstaff (chapter 10).
8. This web reference (http://www.gingeration.com/index.html) was kindly given to me by Councillor Harris in his account of the Reunion to me, by phone, in London, in 2006. The website, rich in visual illustration and musical background, includes photos of the Reunion in Maroon Town, lists of attendees and projects, hotel information in Montego Bay and sightseeing excursions associated with the Reunion. The photos on the website include a picture of the tombstone of a member of the Crockett Old Family of Maroon Town, which overlaps with the Waites, Stennetts and Harrises.
9. As noted in chapter 7, Councillor Harris subsequently became Mayor of Montego Bay (in 2012).
10. In 2009, however, the Councillor distinguished between the First and Second Maroon Wars (see note 11 below).
11. In 2009, the Councillor explained that the land at Maroon Town Crossroads was bought around the early 1800s. In this later account, he distinguishes between the First and Second Maroon Wars, including the outcome of the second war and the confiscation of the Trelawny Town lands: 'After the treaty and the Second Maroon War, when they [the Maroons] lost in 1798, the government took back the lands, set up the military base there. And after some time, they abandon it and individuals (from the military settlement and other locals) got it to purchase'.
12. Compare Mary Turner (1982, 22), who states that, 'Samuel Vaughan, longstanding protector of the Black Baptist preacher, Moses Baker, proved a firm friend to the Baptist missionaries on the north coast'. Samuel Vaughan was the owner of Vaughansfield coffee plantation on the border of Trelawny Town and a magistrate for St James, around the time of the Second Maroon War (Carey 1997, 461; and chapter 2). Vaughansfield is now a part of Maroon Town (chapters 7–9).
13. In Maroon Town, the nickname 'Baba' means 'Father' in the sense of 'the father has come back in his son'. Cassidy, likewise, identifies this term as a pet name but states that *baba* means brother (1971, 183). See also note 6 above.
14. Baba explained that although his mother and maternal grandmother's Christian names were pronounced the same, they were spelt differently and that 'Actually me grandmother is me mother, my grandmother and grandfather tek the first one of each'; that is, his maternal grandparents had raised the oldest grandchild born to each of their children.

9 ■ MAROON TOWN NARRATIVES OF MAROON DESCENT AND MARRONAGE

The previous chapter focused on the dominant narrative theme of Meso-Creole non-maroon ethnicities among many of Maroon Town's Old Families, especially 'slave master' pickni' descent. As we saw, those narratives are situated within wider oral traditions regarding the transformation from the historic Leeward Maroon village of Trelawny Town to non-maroon Maroon Town.

This chapter explores other important findings from my research in Maroon Town, including the discovery that some villagers claim to be descended from Trelawny Town Maroons. Such claims are generally embedded in Afro-Creole maroon ethnicity, with any references to black/white miscegenation underplayed. Some other Afro-Creoles, including Newcomers, who do not claim maroon descent, likewise narrate stories of Trelawny Town black marronage. In addition, however, some Meso-Creoles who stress 'slave master' pickni' descent also assert mulatto maroon ancestry.

As in chapter 8, these narratives combine myth and history, including symbolic elements, which order the ruptures that occurred among colonists, plantation slaves and rebel slaves and root Maroon Town's transnational clans in the Cockpit Country landscape. Some of these narratives include a focus on the partly historical, partly mythical ancestor-hero, 'Campong Nanny (Accompong Nanny), who is accorded a central role in the transformations of freedom that evolved in the Cockpits. The tales of 'Campong Nanny are set within the mythical context of a maroon migration from Flagstaff (the former core area of Trelawny Town) to Accompong. As seen in chapter 8, this narrative theme repairs the rupture that occurred within the Leeward Maroon polity following the Second Maroon War (1795–96), in which the Accompongs sided with the colonists against the Trelawny Maroons (chapter 2). It also reorders the disjuncture between Trelawny Town (the primary Leeward Maroon village that was disbanded with the deportation of the Trelawnys in 1796) and Accompong (the secondary and sole surviving village of the Leeward Maroon polity) – as done through different narratives in Accompong (chapters 3–6).

The first part of this chapter explores narratives from Maroon Town Old Families who claim Afro-Creole maroon descent from Trelawny Maroons, including 'Campong Nanny. The second section focuses on the narratives of some other Maroon Town villagers, generally Afro-Creoles and including Newcomers, who do not assert maroon ancestry but who nevertheless transmit oral traditions of Trelawny Town black marronage. The third part presents the narratives of yet others in Maroon Town who claim mulatto maroon ancestry from planters, slaves and Maroons. As in chapter 8, these accounts are combined with other dimensions of my research and contextualized in the narrators' daily lives; and, as in that chapter, this combination of oral tradition, anthropological fieldwork and documentary research not only extends the exploration of creolization at the maroon/non-maroon interface but also adds to Jamaican national history.

Narratives of Afro-Creole Maroon Descent

The assertion of Afro-Creole Trelawny Town maroon descent is especially prominent among the overlapping Currie, Clarke, Walker and Hines Old Families of Maroon Town (though it exists in some other clans too). While these claims contrast with the historical record of the deportation of the Trelawny Maroons, they are consistent with written history indicating that some Trelawnys evaded deportation by renouncing their maroon status (Campbell 1990, 247). Whether factual or mythical, these narratives symbolically repair the disjunctures of the maroon wars in the Cockpits and the fracturing of the Leeward Maroon polity. I begin with narratives claiming descent from the partly historical/partly mythical ancestress-heroine, 'Campong Nanny.

The Descendants of 'Campong Nanny

Some Maroon Town villagers claim descent from 'Campong Nanny, who is said to have been a woman named Betsy Currie (her married surname),[1] whose descendants are traced seven generations in Maroon Town (Genealogy 4), initially through Betsy's daughter Frances Currie (who had children with Robert Clarke) and Betsy's granddaughter, Frances Clarke (who died in 1973). Their descendants in the Clarke clan include the late Mrs Adeline Hall (née Walker, 1903–2007), who was the daughter of Frances Clarke (and Betsy's great-granddaughter), as well as Adeline's daughter, Laurel Hines (who married Ronald McKenzie) and Laurel's daughter, Nerissa McKenzie (born in 1953). I came to know Adeline ('Miss Ade') and Nerissa well and often visited them in Vaughansfield. Ade was a 'Maldon Baptist', as was her mother Frances Clarke. Nerissa had visited Brixton, England, with a Rastafarian Federation, twice, but is also a Seventh Day Adventist 'through the Hines'. As well as caring for her grandmother, Ade,

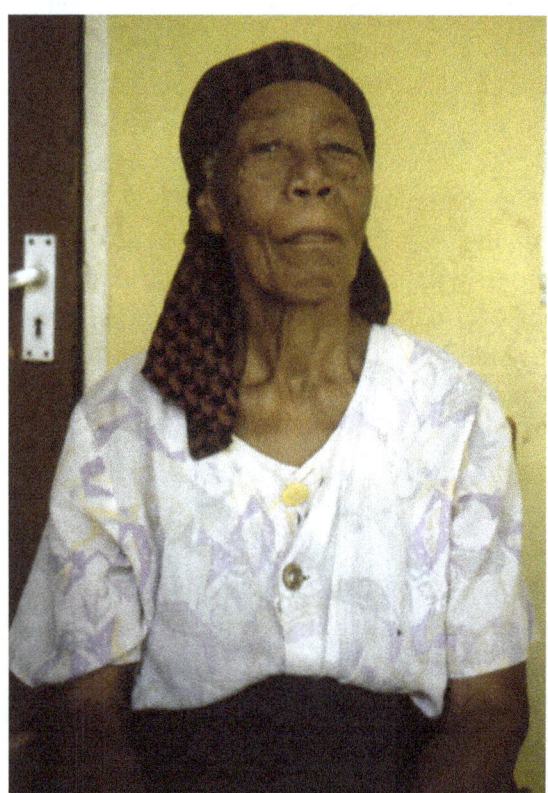

Figure 9.1. Mrs Adeline Hall (née Walker), Maroon Town.

Genealogy 4. Partial Genealogy of Betsy Currie's ('Campong Nanny's) Descendants

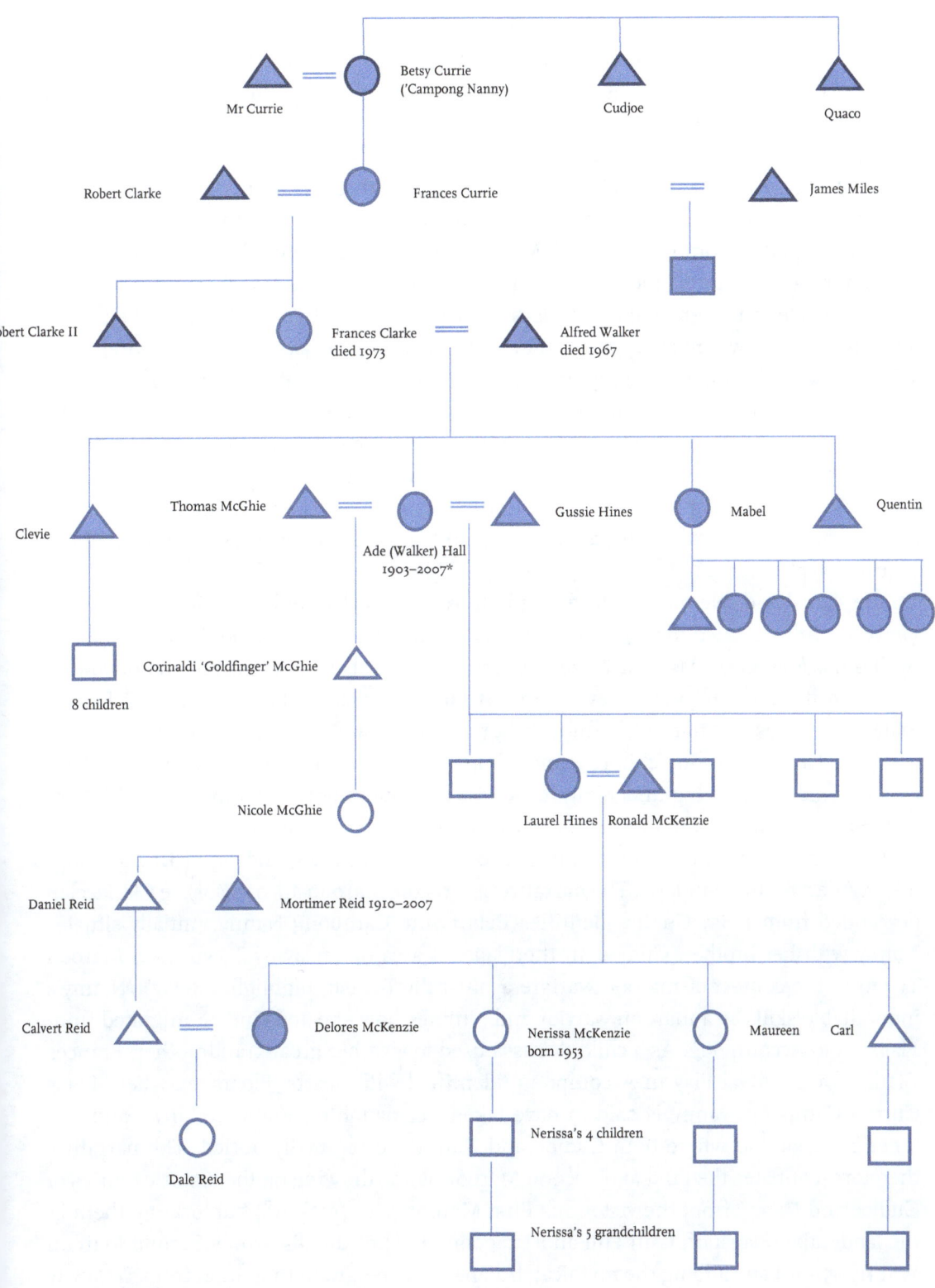

*Adeline (Walker) Hall has at least 15 grandchildren
(in Maroon Town, St James, Kingston, England & the USA),
plus great-grandchildren and great-great-grandchildren

until her death in 2007, Nerissa farms and makes hammocks for sale. Ade was 94 years old when I first interviewed her in 1999 (figure 9.1) and 103 when I last visited her early in 2007, shortly before her death in October that year (by which time she was the oldest woman in Maroon Town).

In addition to overlapping with the Currie Old Family, the Clarke clan overlaps with the Walker and Hines clans (all of which are traced through both women and men). Nerissa belongs to all of these cognatic clans and claims descent (in the sixth generation of the Currie clan) from the Trelawny Maroons through 'Campong Nanny/Betsy Currie, as did her mother Laurel, and grandmother, Ade (Genealogies 4 and 5).

Ade narrated that her mother, Frances Clarke, married Alfred Walker ('Old Fed', who died in 1967) and was the daughter of Frances Currie, one of Betsy Currie's children. Ade said that Betsy ('Campong Nanny) had many other children but these were unknown to Ade. Frances Currie, too, is said to have had 'plenty children': one 'set' by Robert Clarke I (including Frances and her brother Robert Clarke II) and another set by her husband, James Miles. Frances Clarke and Alfred Walker had four children: two daughters (Ade and her sister in Maldon) and two sons (deceased) and at least 20 grandchildren scattered in Maroon Town, elsewhere in Jamaica, England and the United States, some of whom return to visit.

Ade's husband, Nemiah Hall, died many years ago. He and Ade had no children. However, Ade narrated that she had five children by Augustus 'Gussie' Hines and a son by Thomas McGhie of Maroon Town's central clan. She also had at least 15 grandchildren (scattered in Maroon Town, elsewhere in St James, Kingston, England and the United States) as well as great-grandchildren and great-great-grandchildren. For example, Ade's daughter Laurel had four children (including Nerissa and her sister, Delores), all with children and some with grandchildren. Nerissa has four children and five grandchildren.

Below are extracts from the joint narrative of Ade (narrated in her 90s), Nerissa and one of their relatives from the Hines clan, Ralston McLoughlin (a grandson of David Hines, one of Ade's brothers-in-law). The narrative asserts the maroon ancestry of the Clarke clan descended from Betsy Currie, identifies Betsy with 'Campong Nanny, initially situates Nanny with her brother, Cudjoe, in the Flagstaff area of Trelawny Town (now Maroon Town) in the context of maroon warfare against the British, highlights Betsy's/Nanny's indomitable skills as a maroon warrior and outlines how she and Cudjoe migrated from Flagstaff to Accompong. As a child, Nerissa used to visit her great-grandmother, Frances Clarke, for the Myal Play in Accompong (identified with nearby Elderslie), where Betsy Currie/'Campong Nanny is said to have taken her daughter, Frances Currie, and had other children and where both Cudjoe and Nanny are reputedly buried. The narrative, therefore, conflates the First and Second Maroon Wars, drawing on the historic figures of Cudjoe and Nanny from the victorious First Maroon War (1725–38) but locating them in the landscape (Flagstaff, Gun Hill and Dragoon Hole) of the disastrous Second Maroon War (1795–96) and adding the mythical dimension of a maroon migration from Trelawny Town/Flagstaff to Accompong, resulting from a reputed exchange of lands between the colonial government and the Maroons (as in chapter 8). The narrative, therefore reorders

Genealogy 5. Partial Genealogy of the Hines Clan, Maroon Town

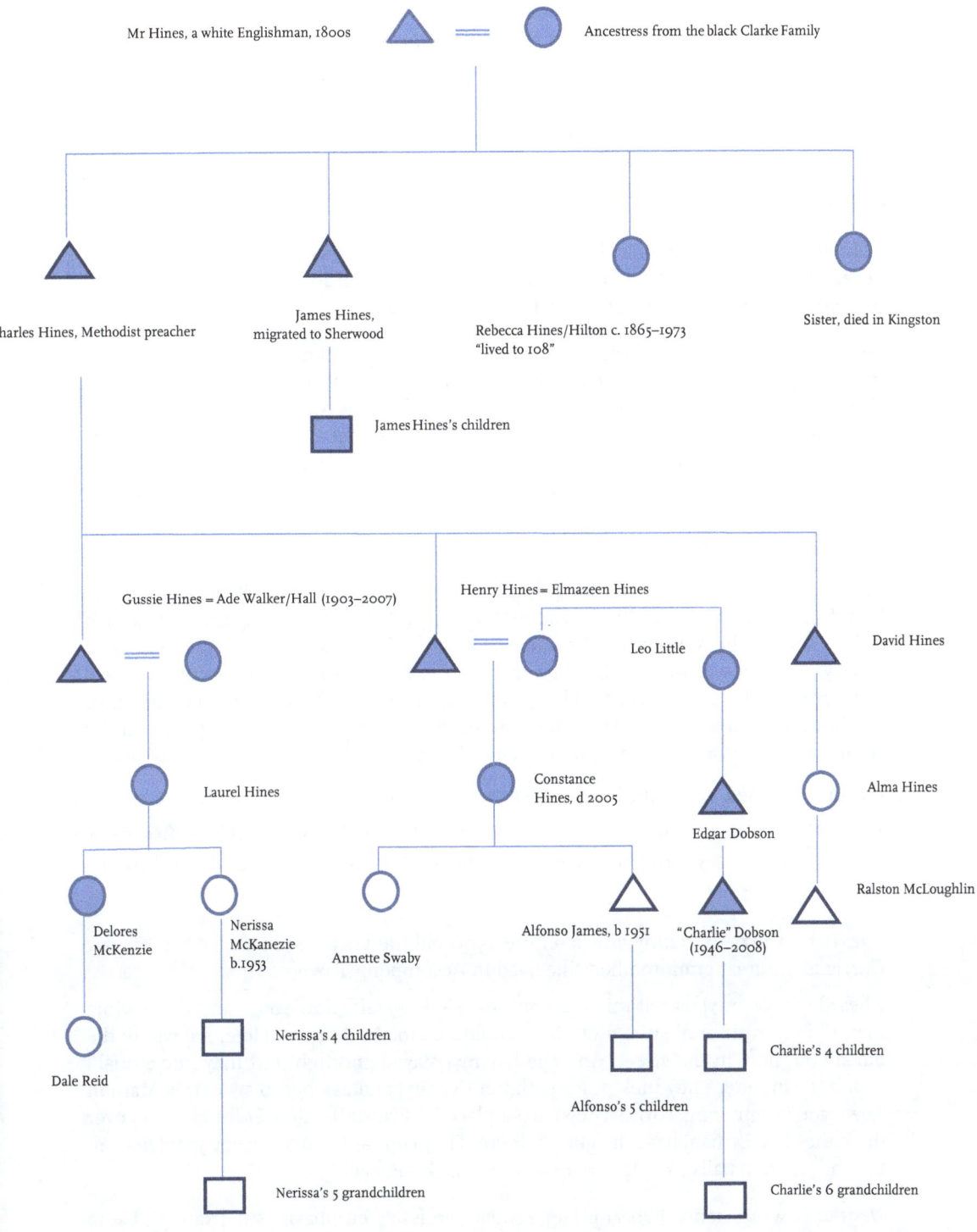

the disbanding of Trelawny Town and the ascendancy of Accompong Town that followed the deportation of the Trelawnys after the Second Maroon War, repairing the rupture of the Leeward Maroon polity.

Ralston opens the narrative, which is continued by Nerissa with Ralston joining in. Ade (who knew most about Betsy Currie) then takes up the story and her account is occasionally edited by Nerissa.

> *Ralston:* This land [Maroon Town] was a captured land by the Maroons, but...the government get it in a settlement and sold them [the lands] about 1920s. The people in Maroon Town is Maroons, especially the Clarke breed.
>
> *Nerissa:* My great-grandmother, Frances Clarke [later Frances Walker], is the granddaughter of the Accompong Nanny who supposed to name Betsy Currie. The Family of Clarke is from Elderslie. My great-grandmother was born at Elderslie, she was taken here by Nanny, she and her mother [Frances (née Currie) Miles] and sisters, when she [Nanny] was in hiding. Accompong is a secret place in Elderslie. I used to go to Accompong when I was a kid, because of my great-grandmother. She was old and asked my grandmother [Ade] to send us to Accompong for 6th of January, maroon celebration of freedom.
>
> *Ralston:* Nanny was living at Flagstaff, Maroon Town. So when the British came here to fight against the slaves, that's where Maroons and Cudjoe fight against the British army. So they [the Maroons] kill some [at Flagstaff, Gun Hill and Dragoon Hole] and Nanny and Cudjoe run away through the bush to Accompong Town. So that's where Nanny start to have children. And his [Cudjoe's] sister's [Nanny's] children come down to Hines, McGhies and all. The father Hines was a white man from England but he come here and have children with the Clarke Family and they [the Clarkes] were black.

Ralston explained that Cudjoe was Nanny's brother. Ralston did not claim to know exactly where Cudjoe and Nanny are buried, but asserted that their graves are at Accompong where there are 'many graves, that's why they have the 6th of January and they have feast there'.

> *Ade:* Betsy Currie is Nanny. She's on the $500 bill [Jamaica's $500 dollar note]. Betsy Currie is my great-grandmother. She lived in Accompong Town.
>
> I heard she [Nanny] was at this Maroon Town – Flagstaff, Garrison – and them white men fight a battle and white men them couldn't win. At Dragoon Hole, see where the blood still there in the street. And she [Nanny] stayed and fight but they [the British] couldn't win here. They mek peace with her [Nanny] and ask her to swop this Maroon Town for Accompong Town. They have a place [at Flagstaff], Gun Point Hill – is over there they [the British] have the gun up there. They couldn't manage [cope with] her. All the ball [cannon balls], she take her back and catch the ball.
>
> *Nerissa:* It was Science [Obeah]. Her *bottom* [Nerissa's emphasis] she [Nanny] use to catch the gun shot, but Mammy [Ade] don't want to say that. They are warrior, you know.
>
> *Ade:* Nanny stayed behind the rock and took her back[side] to catch the balls.

When I conducted interviews at schools in Maroon Town, a similar oral tradition regarding the Trelawny Maroon ancestry of the Clarke clan was referred to by a schoolgirl in the youngest generation of the Clarkes, reflecting the transmission of sacred knowledge down the generations.

In addition to the Clarke clan's claim of Leeward Maroon descent from Betsy Currie/'Campong Nanny, through Ade's mother, Frances (Clarke) Walker, and maternal grandmother, Frances (Currie) Miles, Ade's father, Alfred Walker, is said to have 'belonged to the Moore Town Maroons' of the Windward polity in Portland, though his father was from Paisley in St James. Alfred purchased land in Maroon Town and is described as having a 'long gun and cartridge' and hunting 'bird and wild goat and hog'. His land (about three acres) in Vaughansfield became the Walker family land and burial ground and is described as going down from 'generation to generation'. Ade and her granddaughters Nerissa and Delores and a grandnephew of Ade were living in three houses in a yard (near the burial ground), where Ade was born that is a part of the Walker family land. After the deaths of Delores (2006) and Ade (2007), Nerissa continued to live in this yard. Alfred (who died in 1967) is buried in the Walker family-land cemetery, which Nerissa showed me in 1999. At that time, there were seven graves there, including those of Alfred's parents, himself, his wife, Frances (Clarke) Walker, and some of his descendants. In 2007, Ade too was interred in this Walker cemetery.

Nerissa's mother, Laurel (Hines) McKenzie, who was the daughter of Ade and Gussie Hines and one of Alfred Walker's grandchildren, is, however, buried on the nearby Hines family land along with other members of the Hines clan – to which Nerissa, her children and grandchildren likewise belong. Like these descendants of Betsy Currie/'Campong Nanny, members of the Hines clan assert maroon ancestry. The next two narratives by Nerissa's cousins, Alfonso James and Orville ('Charlie') Dobson, take up this story: Alfonso discussing the Hines clan and Charlie providing more detail on its Afro-Creole maroon identity.

The Hines Clan

In addition to Ade's children and descendants by Gussie Hines, other members of the Hines clan in Maroon Town include Annette Swaby, who keeps a small shop there, and Annette's maternal half-brother, Alfonso James (Genealogies 4 and 5). Annette's and Alfonso's mother, Constance Hines ('Miss Consie') and Nerissa's mother, Laurel Hines (Ade's daughter) were 'two brother's children' (first cousins): Consie's father being Henry Hines, the brother of Gussie Hines (Laurel's father). Ralston McLoughlin, whose maternal grandfather was David Hines (brother of Gussie and Henry), is another member of the Hines clan through his mother, Alma Hines. Ralston, Nerissa, Annette and Alfonso are, therefore, second-cousin descendants of the three brothers: Gussie, Henry and David Hines. These three brothers are said to have been the sons of Charles Hines, a preacher in the Methodist church, who was one of the children of a Mr Hines who is said to have been a white Englishman who lived in 'the 1800s or 1700s' and 'had children with the black Clarke family' (who claim Trelawny Maroon descent). Charles's great-grandson, Alfonso, narrated some of the history of the Hines clan, now in its seventh generation (Genealogy 5), and its family lands.

Alfonso (who was born in 1951 in Vaughansfield, where he was still living in 2009) narrated that he had been raised by his 'grandmother', Rebecca Hilton (née Hines). Rebecca was actually Alfonso's great-aunt, being the paternal aunt of his maternal grandfather, Henry Hines and the sister of Alfonso's great-grandfather, Charles Hines. Rebecca is said to have 'raised seven children', several of whom were not her own. Alfonso explained that his house-yard in Vaughansfield derives 'from generations – "grandmother" [great-aunt Rebecca Hines/Hilton] that raised me was the head of this land. Rebecca got the land from his [her] father. Is a long time [ago]. Rebecca live to 108 when she die' in 1973. Rebecca was, therefore, born around 1865 – in the year of the Morant Bay Rebellion (chapter 2). Alfonso did not know the first name of Rebecca's father, nor how he obtained the land, but he knew a fairly detailed history of the family land transmitted from this great-great-grandfather, Mr Hines.

Alfonso said that Rebecca had a sister (who died in Kingston) and two brothers, Charles (Alfonso's great-grandfather) and James. These siblings shared their father's 'good size' land, some of which was later sold. Rebecca, however, retained her half-acre share. There she farmed and was also supported by remittances sent from England by some of the children whom she 'grew'. Alfonso further narrated that a 'good time before Rebecca died she bust the land in two' (subdivided it) and left it for some of her nephew Henry's children and descendants whom she raised, including Alfonso. Alfonso lives on a quarter-acre of this land with his wife and children. Other co-heirs lived next door, including Alfonso's mother Consie, until her death around 2005. Alfonso explained that these yards will pass on as family land to all the co-heirs' descendants, including migrants who can return. There are tombs on this family land transmitted from Rebecca, including her own. Consie, however, is buried on another piece of Hines family land, deriving from her father, Henry. In 2009 there were five tombs on that family land and two empty 'sepulchres', built to await other kin. Alfonso, likewise, has rights to this other Hines family land through his mother, Consie, as well as to paternal family land nearby where his siblings and his father live.

Alfonso and his wife are farmers, as was Consie. Alfonso farms two plots of land beyond his yard, cultivating ground provisions and four acres of bananas. He sells bananas to higglers and the chip factory and used to sell to West Ban for export before it closed down in 1999. He also makes furniture for sale in Montego Bay and had been a migrant farm labourer, several times, to the United States.

Alfonso explained that he has 'the Seventh Day Adventist mind'. He also asserted maroon ancestry: 'I must be a Maroon. I think we all related'. However, he added that, 'the right Maroon is in St Elizabeth [Accompong] – according to me 'grannie' [his great-aunt, Rebecca Hines]. I've been there'. He had been to Accompong, many years previously, to the Myal Play. Alfonso's cousin, Charlie Dobson, would tell me more about the links between the Hines clan and the Maroons.

Charlie's Story: The 'Kongo Maroons'

Like Alfonso, Charlie Dobson and his father, Edgar Dobson, were raised by Rebecca Hilton (née Hines) in Maroon Town. Like Alfonso (but more strongly), Charlie also asserted maroon descent (and 'the Seventh Day Adventist mind'). Edgar and Charlie were

Genealogy 6. Partial Genealogy of Charlie, a "Kongo Maroon"

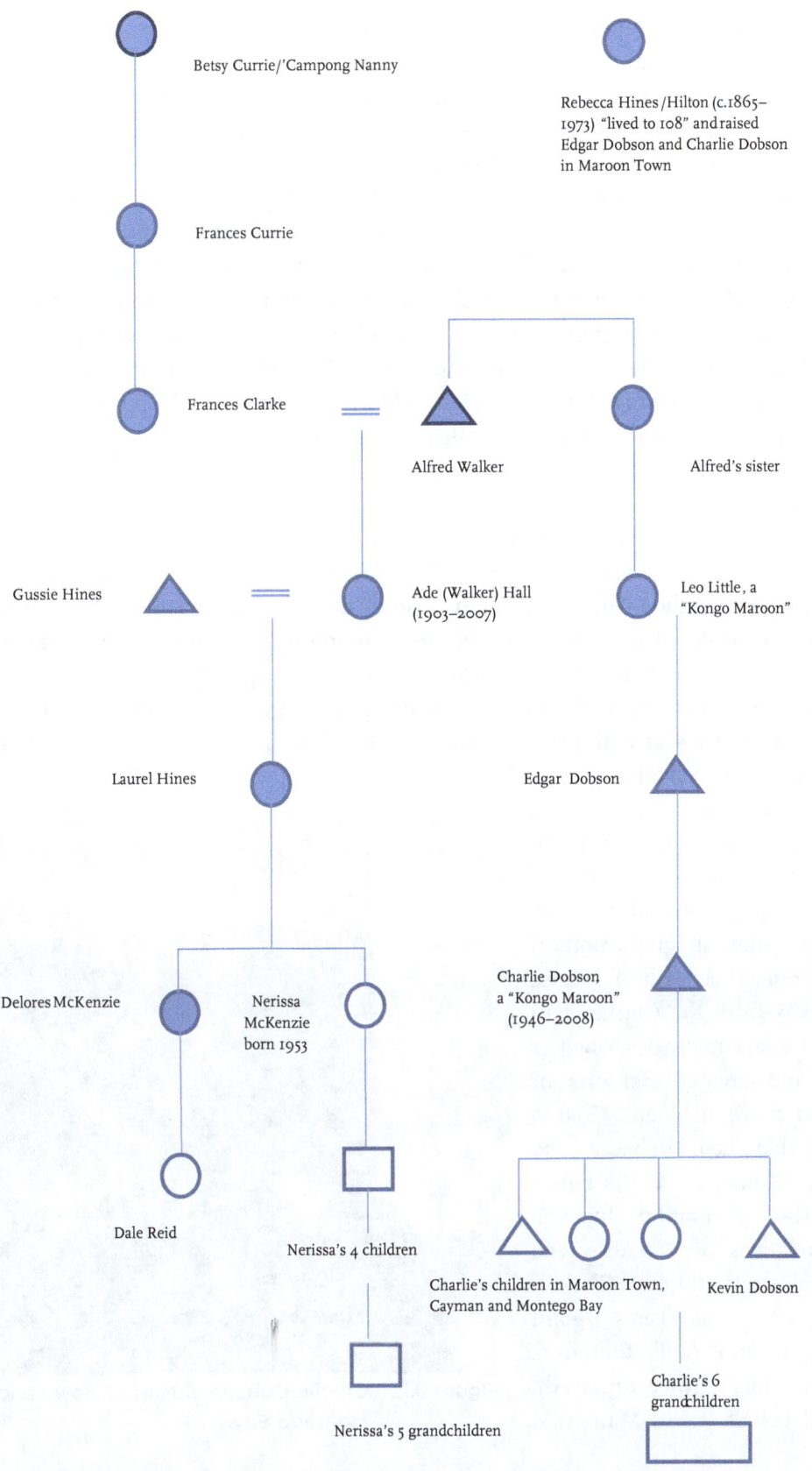

the son and grandson of Henry Hines's sister-in-law, Leonora Little ('Miss Leo'), the sister of Henry Hines's wife, Elmazeen Hines, who was Consie Hines's mother and Annette and Alfonso's maternal grandmother (Genealogy 5). Charlie was, therefore, second cousin to Annette and Alfonso. Miss Leo was also the neice (sister's daughter) of Alfred Walker and, therefore, first cousin to Ade (Walker) Hall, who had children by Gussie Hines (Genealogy 6). Charlie was, therefore, third cousin to Ade's granddaughters, Delores and Nerissa. Leo's son Edgar was fathered by Joe-Joe Dobson from Maroon Town before Leo married Theopholous Little ('Mas T') – a deacon in the Seventh Day Adventist Church. When Edgar (whom Rebecca raised) died, Rebecca 'grew' his young son, Charlie, and then passed him on to his grandmother, Leo, and her husband, Mas T, who (as Charlie explained) 'grow me up like a grandson' and in the Adventist tradition. In 1999, by then aged 53, Charlie became my main guide around Maroon Town where he introduced me to his wide kinship network (which weaved through the Hines, Walker, Currie, Clarke and Reid clans) – including his cousins Alfonso, Annette, Nerissa and Delores, and the elders, Ade Hall and Mortimer Reid.[2]

Between 1999 and 2007, by which time he was 61 years old (figure 9.2), Charlie recounted narratives in which he repeatedly asserted his maroon ancestry. His story began with his childhood in St Elizabeth (where he was nicknamed 'Charlie') and St James (where he was also nicknamed 'Deacon' in Maroon Town, after his paternal step-grandfather, the Adventist deacon). Charlie was born, in 1946, in his mother's village, Kilmarnoch, St Elizabeth, not far from Accompong. At that time, in the 1940s, Charlie's father, Edgar, was a seasonal migrant labourer from Maroon Town to the United States on the Farm Work Scheme.

Around 1955, at the age of nine, Charlie came to live in Maroon Town with his father, Edgar and Edgar's family, including Leo (Charlie's paternal grandmother) and Rebecca Hines/Hilton (whose mother was from the Clarke clan) – whom he repeatedly described as 'Kongos and blooded Maroons' or 'people of maroon blood'. Charlie narrated that Leo, Rebecca and Ade were related, as Leo 'is Hines through her generation, blooded family, relatives of Walker breed too' and also related to the Clarkes. Charlie, who was Leo's 'giant [eldest] grandson' (and, therefore, Ade's first cousin twice removed), described Leo as 'a real Maroon, a

Figure 9.2. Charlie Dobson of Maroon Town and Montego Bay.

Kongo, eyes red and skin jet-black'.³ He asserted that he was, therefore, descended from 'the Kongo tribe' though he was 'not jet-black but mixed', adding that the 'Coromantee tribe' of Maroons are, however, 'not so black [as the Kongos], not jet-black'.⁴

Charlie narrated that the lands in and around Maroon Town were first owned by the Native Indians, then, under European rule, African slaves were imported through Falmouth to work the plantations. He said that runaway slaves from these estates came to Maroon Town through caves, via Flagstaff. He explained that the Maroons were chased by the planters' hunting dogs (a parallel with historical accounts of the Second Maroon War [chapter 2]) and that many Maroons went to Accompong and Moore Town. He said that his Kongo maroon grandmother, Leo, who taught him 'everything' he knew, told him of these 'maroon tribes' and it is with this maroon ancestry that Charlie identified (Genealogy 6). Rebecca Hines/Hilton, who fostered him, likewise symbolized to Charlie his maroon heritage (Genealogy 5), and he narrated that she had walked an extensive distance from Oracabessa in St Mary⁵ to Maroon Town where she had lived to the age of 108; for, as he reiterated concerning his paternal family, 'the whole a them are Maroons'.⁶

From Maroon Town, as a young man in the 1960s, Charlie made several visits to Myal Plays in Accompong. He described these celebrations as being 'like a picnic', with visits to 'the dead Maroons' graves and caves'; that is, the pilgrimages to the reputed ancestral graves at Old Town and the Peace Cave.

A further dimension of Charlie's maroon identity was that he had rights to lands in Maroon Town that are linked to narratives of marronage. One such piece of land, around five to six acres of family land with ancestral tombs passed down the generations and associated with Miss Leo and Mas T Little (Charlie's paternal grandmother and step-grandfather), is (as Charlie narrated) near 'Cudjoe River, same part of Maroon Town but more wilderness, named after Cudjoe – one of the maroon warriors'. That is where, he continued, 'First-Time people farm'.

Reflecting on his childhood in Maroon Town (after his father, Edgar, died when Charlie was ten years old), Charlie recalled how he moved freely among his various foster parents with relative autonomy as he would chose where to eat and sleep. In addition to Rebecca Hines/Hilton and Leo Little, these foster parents included Mortimer Reid (chapter 8) and Charlie would often 'eat, drink and play' in Mortimer's yard. Charlie, likewise, 'grew' at the house-yard of Baron McGhie of Maroon Town's central clan (chapter 10). Charlie's first employment was also with Baron and Mortimer, as well as with 'Farmer' Sutherland (below). Charlie had 'carried bananas' for Baron (who was one of the largest banana farmers in Maroon Town) between his banana plant and the depot, for export. Charlie also sometimes did a 'day's work' for Mortimer, farming bananas and yams. In addition, Mortimer, who as Councillor, was in charge locally of the Farm Work Scheme, supervised Charlie's successful test for the Scheme and gave him the 'card' to go overseas.

Having obtained his card, at the age of 26, Charlie (following in his father's migrant-labour tradition) migrated in 1973 and 1974 to Ontario, Canada, for two three-month trips, to harvest apples and tobacco. He described these migrations as 'a big experience – miles and miles of farming'. These migrations enabled him to 'make some money, able to send money home, able to shop, that was good.' On his return from Canada, Charlie obtained a job, in 1975, as a maintenance man in a condominium hotel in Montego Bay. For a while, he also had a taxi – which is how my husband and I first got to know him in the 1990s. By 2008, Charlie had held his hotel job for more than 30 years. From there, in his spare time, he often drove us to Maroon Town – where his maroon identity was embedded in his network of kin with their narratives of maroon ancestry and marronage.

When Charlie died suddenly, after a short illness, in Montego Bay, in 2008, he left four children (a son in Maroon Town, a daughter in Cayman and another daughter and young son, Kevin, in Montego Bay) and six grandchildren. A bus-load of friends and relatives from Maroon Town attended his funeral at the Montego Bay Adventist Church. Some of Charlie's kin in Maroon Town hoped he would be buried there on the Walker family land. However, he was interred in the Montego Bay Cemetery where his youngest children could more easily visit his grave. I visited his tomb with them in 2009 and, as mentioned in chapter 1, this book, with which he had helped so much, is partly dedicated to him.

A Flagstaff Narrative

Mr Moffat was born in Flagstaff in 1948 and still lived there when I interviewed him in 1999. He claims partial Trelawny Maroon descent from his maternal grandfather, who was likewise from Maroon Town. Mr Moffat provided a narrative on maroon warfare with the 'English' at Flagstaff (Trelawny Town), which included the widespread mythical theme in Maroon Town narratives that the Maroons had migrated from Flagstaff to Accompong after the war (rather than being deported to Nova Scotia by the colonists). As with other Maroon Town narratives of maroon ancestry and marronage, Mr Moffat's narrative, therefore, conflates the First and Second Maroon Wars, thereby repairing the ruptures that occurred within the Leeward Maroon polity after the Second Maroon War. Also, as in many other Maroon Town narratives, the historical theme of the British dragoons features in his account, as does the partly mythical point of the predominance of Nanny over Cudjoe, among the Leeward Maroons. His narrative combines both mythical and factual events to account for the transformation from Trelawny Town maroon society to non-maroon Maroon Town:

> This Maroon Town – the Maroons leave a place in St Ann, Runaway Bay, and migrated from there to Flagstaff [Trelawny Town]. There the biggest war was fought, in Flagstaff, with the English – before my time. We have a cemetery in Flagstaff, 99 English soldier buried there. Some is tombed, some is not. After the war the Maroon[s] migrated again to the place now called Accompong Town in St Elizabeth, that's where they reside at this time. They say Nanny was buried in St Elizabeth [but] I'm not sure. Most people not sure where Nanny buried. Dragoon is buried in Flagstaff, something to do with Cudjoe.

Mr Moffat emphasized the diverse mixed population in Maroon Town today, resulting from in-migration in the mid-twentieth century related to prosperous banana farming for the world market which has now declined and been partially replaced by escalating overseas migration:

> Sixty to 70 per cent of the people here in Maroon Town is *mixed* with Maroons (not completely Maroons) and other Africans. Most of the people in Maroon Town migrate from different places in the island – Manchester and especially Westmoreland and plenty of them is related. Trying to find better live [a better living]. Most of the *younger* generation drawn here. Maroon Town/Flagstaff is a booming community, especially in the 1950s – the farm era. Most of the farming fade out and marketing drop off and people migrate, for example to England, America, Canada.

Mr Moffat had migrated to the United States, where he worked for over 20 years. In 1999, he was farming bananas, fruit and yams on his late father's land at Flagstaff and selling produce there to higglers who came by van and resold, in markets, in Westmoreland, Montego Bay and Falmouth. However, in 2009 I was told that he had returned to the USA.

'Maroons' Pride'

In 2009, I met Robert Chambers who owns the banana chip factory, which was built a few years before on his bought land between Maroon Town Square and Vaughansfield (figure 7.5). Robert belongs to the Coote clan of Maroon Town (after whom Coote Bush near Flagstaff is named) through his mother, claims maroon ancestry 'down the blood line' and explained that this is why he named the factory and its products, 'Maroons' Pride'. He buys bananas from 'small farmers' in Maroon Town, who are 'the mainstay' of the local banana industry, but explained that bananas were now scarce because of the recent hurricane.

Robert went on to emphasize that the site of Maroon Town (Trelawny Town, including Petty River Bottom) was more significant than Accompong in maroon history:

> The real history not at Accompong, real history is here: fighting is here, the treaty was signed at Petty River Bottom. They [the Maroons] moved the kids and ladies to Accompong, a safe haven, and the war lasted 50 years, two treaties.

This narrative combination of myth and history repairs the rupture that occurred between the two Leeward Maroon villages in the Second Maroon War and, as in other Maroon Town narratives, symbolically accounts for the ascendancy of Accompong today.

Afro-Creole Narratives of Black Marronage

In addition to the above narratives asserting Afro-Creole maroon descent in Maroon Town, are narratives of black marronage to Cudjoe's Town/Trelawny Town told by Maroon Town villagers who do not themselves assert maroon ancestry. The narratives of two elderly men, 'Farmer' Sutherland and Asta 'Bada' Williams, both born in Maroon Town, illustrate this theme as do the narratives of the Newcomers, Cleopatra Jolly and Clinton McBean. Stories by two of Farmer's friends (one from Vaughansfield, the other a Newcomer) are likewise variations on this theme. In contrast to narratives of black marronage by Meso-Creoles asserting 'slave master' pickni' descent (chapter 8), these narrators regarded themselves as Afro-Creoles – though Farmer made a passing reference to some British ancestry.

'Campong Nanny and the Pumpkin Vine

'Farmer' Sutherland was born in Maldon in 1918. He was 81 years old when I interviewed him, in 1999, and he continued to farm into the new millennium. He died in 2007 and was buried in his yard near Maroon Town Square. In 1999, it had taken me some time to locate him for, as he explained, 'I'm a farmer, I'm hard to find'. I eventually found him selling cabbages outside the banana chip factory and later interviewed him at his house. His mother and maternal grandmother were from Maroon Town; his father (a Newcomer from the parish of Manchester) was of 'foreign' (British) descent: 'One set of Sutherland come to Jamaica'.

'Farmer', as Mr Sutherland was widely known, had four pieces of land (inherited and bought) comprising 11 acres in Maroon Town, including his yard near the Square and land at Woodlands, Pembroke Mountain and Bottom Pasture. On his dispersed landholdings he planted bananas, yams and cabbages and used to grow sugar cane for Hampden Estates. However, his banana-growing had declined, as he explained: 'Used to ship them from MoBay to England. Stopped ten years ago. Man who run the country don't know how to. Jamaica fasten [is paralyzed]. Rates of exchange. So we can't move at all.' But he described himself as 'a forward man' and his cabbages were thriving. In addition to selling cabbages outside the chip factory, he took them to marketplaces in Montego Bay, Wakefield, Falmouth and Savanna-la-Mar or sent them by his wife to market.

In addition to farming and marketing, Farmer and his household were supported by his 15 children, most of whom were in the United States. He also had countless grandchildren: 'grand-pickni, me can't count them'. He went to the USA for nine months, in 1943, on the Farm Work Scheme. His savings from this migration enabled him to purchase his yard and build the house, which was later extended by his children.

When I asked Farmer how Maroon Town got its name, he provided a detailed narrative that included 'Campong Nanny. In this narrative, 'Campong Nanny (though initially referred to in the masculine gender of Creole) is sister to Cudjoe – as asserted in Accompong (chapter 3) and in the narratives of Betsy Currie's descendants in Maroon Town (who claim that Betsy was 'Campong Nanny). But, in contrast to the narratives of Betsy's descendants, Farmer's 'Campong Nanny was childless.

Farmer's narrative asserts that, 'Campong Nanny was brought from West Africa in a slave ship to Jamaica but escaped. Farmer portrayed Nanny's marronage in detail, highlighting her strategies of guerrilla warfare and the related significance of self-sufficient maroon provision ground cultivation in the mountains and the butchering of plantation livestock, in addition to Nanny's role as an Obeah-woman or 'scientist'. As in the narratives of the descendants of Betsy Currie, in Farmer's account, Nanny's warrior skills included her reputed magical ability to deflect the colonists' bullets with her bottom. Farmer's narrative also portrays Nanny as travelling between the parishes of Portland and Trelawny/St James. These elements of the narrative, which have parallels with historical and oral accounts of Nanny of the Windwards, in Portland, in the First Maroon War (e.g., Bilby 2006, 204–207, 253–60), are, however, partially shifted into the context of the Second Maroon War in St James and Trelawny, including references to the maroon ambush of Dragoons and the use of Cuban bloodhounds by the colonists (chapter 2). Farmer's narrative also includes a mythical account of a visit from the Queen of England to Jamaica during Nanny's marronage, including a 'phone call' from the Queen to Nanny offering her land. Nanny is narrated as choosing that land, in St Elizabeth, and naming it Accompong after her brother, a deal reinforced by a blood oath and a treaty. As in other Maroon Town narratives, Farmer's narrative thereby accounts for the persistence of the Accompong maroon society today.

Farmer's narrative, which concludes with an account of the 1831–32 slave rebellion that started at Kensington, is given below, beginning with the reason for the name Maroon Town.

> Because it was the Maroon[s]. – Send them from Africa as slaves. Call them the Maroons 'cause they live ina bush. They came to Jamaica on slave ship. 'Campong Nanny came to Jamaica on a slave ship but wasn't bought as a slave. When him [she] come to Jamaica wouldn't in slave. Him go round the country, pick up potato and cassava. Slip [escape] and plant him own ground. And white man sen' chop down him cultivation, so when him can't get nothing to eat him will haffe come in as slave. [But] him *nah* go in as slave. 'Campong Nanny went down in Trelawny, six or seven o'clock in the evening, and hide in standing wood [the forest] and nine o'clock jump into cow pen, cut off him [the cow's] neck, quarter him off, skin him and only belly and gut dash 'way. They couldn't manage [cope with] 'Campong Nanny as she was a scientist.

> Right up there they have Garrison, soldier ground, burying ground at Flagstaff – same Maroon Town. One mile and three-quarter from the Square. Them did-deh deh fight [fought there], the African slaves. At that time, no road at Schaw Castle, only road from Pembroke Mountain just there from Spring Vale to Flagstaff. And Maroons dress up and in a green bush [camouflage] and sit roadside with machete, stick and sword. And the soldiers come with a gun-broke, no cartridge, only drive to Spring Vale and have to walk up. And they [the Maroons] start to chop and they kill about 250 of them [the soldiers] and bury them a Dragoon Hole. And the soldiers hunt them down and went to Packitik Wood between St James and Trelawny. And soldiers pull out de way and when they hear dog [when the Maroons heard the dog-hounds] start to walk. 'Campong Nanny people walk ina water five chains and dog can't tek dem scent again. And them [the Maroons] come out back and gaan [gone], so them [the soldiers] nuh capture them.

> Them [the soldiers] learn that 'Campong Nanny [was] under one cotton tree between Vaughansfield, this property [part of Maroon Town], and Kenmure. And when them go there, pick up gun and fire, 'Campong Nanny give them this [her bottom]! No bullets harm [her]. They couldn't manage 'Campong Nanny – she came from West Africa, scientist, 'Campong Nanny. Couldn't shoot him. They go 'way and lef' him.

> He [she/'Campong Nanny] was the manager [leader] in Portland. Divide him troop [she divided her troops], 'nough troop, [she deployed] some [in] Westmoreland, some Hanover. Live in the hill [the mountains], not on level [the lowlands]. Them search and search and can't find 'Campong Nanny. And one time in Portland find where them cook – but [she] nuh live there – and trace them till find where she live on hill and kill (with bullet) some of her men. But can't kill 'Campong Nanny. But after, she get sick. And him [she] have a brother, Cudjoe, living in Trelawny. And go a Cudjoe who seh him

can't fight again, him tired, he out fe stop. 'Campong Nanny march through standing wood to Portland, cut and plant pumpkin stem.

A history [this is history]. Anything me tell you, a [is] history. [If] pumpkin stem grow, [the Maroons] will win the war. Soldier back a them, [Nanny] stab the first one, drop [and killed him]. Run with meat him carry. One a 'Campong Nanny people sit down with spear. By time come up a shop at crossroads right here [Maroon Town Crossroads], 'Campong Nanny jump on soldier and kill him. 'Campong Nanny keep Nine Night and Forty Night [Myal/Revival mortuary rituals] fe the great man that him lost [one of her troops]. Keep to the river, white man and dog – every soldier – gone in a river. A right suh (here in Maroon Town) end the war.

['Campong Nanny was a] scientist, come from West Africa. White man seh can't fight them [the Maroons] and send fe Mrs Queen from England. When Mrs Queen come, she call up 'Campong Nanny and talk to him and said she must pattern [patent] the spot she want in Jamaica. So him [Nanny] choose a place in St Elizabeth, up 'Campong Town – that is the name. 'Campong Nanny have no children [so she] give it him brother's name, Accompong.

Them sign a blood oath, throw rum in a glass, cut the English blood and the maroon blood and throw in a glass and drink it. And after, 'Campong Nanny seh 'would you like to see likkle science [a little Obeah]?' Fifty soldier load up them gun and she [Nanny] seh 'I ready now, shoot me!' 'Campong Nanny catch 50 bullets [with her bottom] and Mrs Queen faint! And seh she ['Campong Nanny] must try him own case, but must send the death sentence to him. 'Campong Nanny went high [achieved a high status]!

Maroon Town now? The word 'Maroon' is people who live in standing wood, but were Africans. (Christopher Columbus found Jamaica in 1494, [there] was Arawak Indians.) They came by – some is here – from African slave, but speak English and belong to Mrs Queen. (People here [in Maroon Town] buy land from the government from the wartime.) Mrs Queen beat and took over from King Ferdinand and Queen Isabella [of Spain]. William Knibb, the parson-man from Falmouth, go a England and tell Mrs Queen [she] still have slave. Mrs Queen faint. [About] Sam Sharpe, [the slaves] wouldn't get a long weekend at Christmas and burn down cane-piece at Kessington [Kensington] and buckra house [the slave master's great house] and [the colonists] catch Sam Sharpe and hang him.

As seen in chapter 8, where Melvin Pearson's grandson amended Melvin's narrative, including some details derived from Farmer Sutherland concerning 'Campong Nanny and the pumpkin vine, Farmer's narrative has influenced the oral traditions of the younger generation in Maroon Town. This influence was also reflected in the narratives of Farmer's grandchildren who were visiting him at his yard. For example, his eight-year old granddaughter (a student at Maldon Primary School) narrated that Maroon Town is so named 'Because one woman who come from Africa did live here, Nanny, fought for us, provide for the country' and explained that she had learnt this from Farmer. Her cousin, aged seven, who likewise attended Maldon Primary, added that Nanny is buried 'up a Coote Bush hill-top' – in Browns' Town on the way to Flagstaff. (I was later shown 'Nanny Mountain' there.)

Two visitors at Farmer's home also joined in his discussion with their own versions of Maroon Town's history. One of them was a young man from Vaughansfield, a relative of Farmer's wife, who gave his own account of Accompong Town, Nanny and Flagstaff. Like Farmer's account, this narrative situates Nanny in Maroon Town and asserts her subsequent migration to Accompong. The narrative also refers to Nanny's reputed magical powers, as in Farmer's account and in the narratives of Betsy Currie's descendants. Like Betsy's descendants, the narrator refers to the image of Nanny on the Jamaican $500 note (which is, however, no longer the highest denomination banknote in circulation in Jamaica):

> Nanny drop [killed] two white men up Flagstaff, that is the right Maroon Town. Nanny was from Africa and she study science and she tek her batty [bottom] catch 50 bullets fired from Falmouth and she tek it at Maroon Town. Her headquarters at 'Campong Town. Walk through bushes to 'Campong Town, no tek no road. Now her money [the Jamaican five-hundred dollar note] is the highest.

The other visitor at Farmer's yard was an older man, a Newcomer, Edmund, who came from Westmoreland to Maroon Town, in 1936, because his late brother migrated there in the 1920s to farm in the government land settlement 'back a Flagstaff', where, like many others, he rented and then purchased land (chapter 7). That land purchase (two acres) was made in 1943 from the land settlement in the Camperdown/Schaw Castle area of Maroon Town that had been purchased by the government, in 1942, from Tommy Reid (chapter 8). Edmund leases this land from his brother's widow and built his house there in 1974. In 1985, Edmund purchased eight acres in the government land settlement at Georges Valley, near Flagstaff, where he cultivated coffee, coconuts, breadfruit and bananas. He used to sell boxed bananas to West Ban for export, but this 'now mash up' (beginning in 1997 and finally closing in 1999). He was now selling bananas to the chip factory and food at the Montego Bay marketplace.

Edmund narrated the following account of Maroon Town (which he defined as now including Maroon Town Square, Vaughansfield, Schaw Castle and Georges Valley in addition to the core area of Flagstaff) and Accompong, referring to a combination of historical and mythical themes in the maroon wars:

> Flagstaff is Maroon Town. Maroons had dem home, old building, on Camperdown. Georges Valley align [adjoins] and that's where the white people killed the maroon soldiers. Go to Flagstaff and see the white people' burying ground. You have Gun Hill, where the maroon guns are. The maroon burying ground down a Dragoon Hole from Georges Valley, the maroon burying ground. Nanny and Cudjoe lived at Maroon Town and when enemy 'pon dem they go through bush back a Flagstaff, and go right to 'Campong Town – at 'Campong Town where them live. They bury at 'Campong Town, where we go 6th of January to the sport [Myal Play] up there. They cook pork, chicken, anything Nanny seh she want, they cook, if a pork, mutton, fowl, beef. Mix-up sugar-water beverage.

Like the previous narratives in this chapter (as well as in chapter 8), Edmund's account asserts that Nanny (and Cudjoe) migrated from Maroon Town (Trelawny Town) to Accompong following maroon warfare. As in other Maroon Town narratives, Edmund's account conflates events from the First and Second Maroon Wars and, thereby, symbolically repairs the ruptures that occurred within the Leeward Maroon polity in the Second Maroon War. The next narrative likewise reiterates some of these themes.

Maroon Town, Accompong Town and 'Campong Nanny

Asta 'Bada' Williams, a Seventh Day Adventist (chapter 7), was born in Maroon Town on his father's family land. When I interviewed him, in 1999, he thought he was about 80 years old, so he was born around 1919. (He died about 2003.) As a young man, he migrated to the United States for farm work for six months in 1945, just after the Second World War. With the savings from that migration, he bought two square chains of hillside land above Maroon Town Square. There, he built a wooden cottage, where he settled. His son, who built a concrete house, lived beside him. Asta's paternal grandparents are buried on this land. His wife, from Maroon Town, and four of their eight children were in the United States.

On his return from the USA in 1945, Asta first worked as an agricultural labourer. In 1947, he started farming for himself and, on rented land, grew sugar cane which he sold to Hampden Estates. By 1999, he was only cultivating a provision ground. He appreciated the independence that his own house-yard provided; for, as he remarked, he could do what he wants and behave as he liked: 'When me sit down yah-so [here] nobody can tell me fe get up. And me can chat loud and boast!'

In his autonomous yard, Asta provided a detailed account of black marronage, with reference to Maroon Town, Accompong Town and 'Campong Nanny. The narrative includes a description of Nanny's reputed magical powers and of a maroon migration from Maroon Town to Accompong (and a related exchange of lands between the colonists and Maroons), where Nanny is said to be buried. These themes have parallels with other Maroon Town narratives of marronage which combine historical and mythical elements and conflate events or reputed events from the two maroon wars, thereby symbolically repairing the ruptures that occurred within the Leeward Maroon polity following the Second Maroon War. Asta also highlighted a contrast between Maroon Town and Accompong in relation to land tax. His account of Maroon Town's history included the Flagstaff barracks, which, after its desertion by the colonial troops in the mid-nineteenth century became an overgrown wilderness that the colonial government cleared in the early twentieth century when Asta was a boy. Asta's father was one of those who helped to clear the wilderness and as a child Asta himself explored the site and collected lead-shot bullets.

Asta's narrative, which also refers to the wider context of plantation slavery (including the legend of Mrs Annie Palmer, the slave mistress of Rose Hall Estate in St James, who reputedly took slave lovers and then killed them), is presented below:

> The Maroons did beat up the Spaniard. One woman, them call him 'Campong Nanny, ah up deh him dead. Under the cave dem [the colonial troops] shoot him in a de War. Up Ball Ground [at Flagstaff] is a cave call Nanny Cave. A deh in a de War dem kill him. In a de War him [Nanny] dress up ina wool clothes and pack him baggy [pants] so when they ah shoot she catch the bullets [with her bottom, as he demonstrated]. And they move

him and carry him a 'Campong Town. So the government did give them [the Maroons] that piece a land fe themselves. Pay no tax. [Nanny] bury in cave at 'Campong Town. They worship the cave where him bury. Me come up and see where the camp was, at Ball Ground. When the government clean out the wilderness [at Flagstaff], me see the Ball Ground and where the soldier camp. They when have [the soldiers had] no fridge. They built a foundation for a dripping jar.

A yah-so [here at Maroon Town] was the real maroon town, the natural maroon town. Because a Flagstaff, a deh the flag was put up. One hill dem call Gun Hill, a deh the gun was. One a the soldiers' gun point to Falmouth, one point to Lucea, one point to Kingston against the enemy. Me come up now come see where the kitchen was, the jail was, the hospital [at the barracks]. From me a boy, me father when work up there and we pick up all the lead ball, the bullet under the cave. And the marble the children played with. We find all dem thing. And the [water-] well.

JB: Are there still Maroons in Maroon Town?

Asta: No. All the Maroons they [the colonial government] put them up so – they call it 'Campong Town.

JB: So who are the people in Maroon Town today?

Asta: Those people them come here as a slave, the old generation come here as a slave. The Maroon fight with the Spaniard. The older generation come from Africa as slave and they fight with the Spaniard, who carry them here, and beat them out. The Maroons win the war and took this place [Maroon Town] but the government move them to 'Campong Town. Listen to me good! Like [how] Churchhill win the war [Second World War]. Them [the Maroons] have all this land around [Maroon Town] and the government tek it from them and put them in 'Campong Town. A when [it was during] Miss Palmer's days – slave master. Miss Palmer needed companions but then she killed them as she no want them to say they is friend.

Who they have here now [the present population of Maroon Town], they no mix up with 'Campong Town. For they [in Accompong] wasn't paying no tax. They have their own church, their own school, their own courthouse. The Headman is [was] Colonel Rowe, but when they vote they change him. Me never go [to Accompong], but every year they take truck [from Maroon Town] for the 6th of January [Myal Play] and go up and cook at the cave, worship the cave.

Yes, we in Maroon Town pay tax. Me grow come hear that me grandfather pay tax and all who here pay tax. Fe dem grandparents some give them [family land], some buy land.

A visitor added: 'Every First of April pay tax, every first Tuesday and last Tuesday pay tax'. Asta continued: 'And if you nuh pay, surcharge and pay more'.

Newcomers' Narratives of Marronage

Cleopatra Jolly was a Pentecostal Pastor and infant school teacher in Browns' Town, where she settled, in 1945, after working in her natal parish, Hanover and Montego Bay (chapter 7 and figure 7.7). She was born in 1911 and was 87 years old when I interviewed her, in 1999. She died around 2006 and was buried in Browns' Town.

Although a Newcomer to Maroon Town, Pastor Jolly provided a narrative of black marronage (portrayed as being from Annie Palmer's coastal Rose Hall Estate, which likewise featured in Asta's narrative above and Melvin Pearson's in chapter 8) to Trelawny Town/Maroon Town that included Nanny (said to be Cudjoe's sister, with reputed magical powers) and a subsequent maroon migration to Accompong – recurring themes in Maroon Town narratives. As in Asta's account, Pastor Jolly highlighted that Accompong maroon land is tax-free. Like Asta too, she referred to the colonial government's clearing of the Flagstaff site (and repairing the cemetery there) in the mid-twentieth century. The repairs were done by 'white men' who boarded with her:

> The Maroons don't really here [in Maroon Town]. They escape from Miss [Annie] Palmer down on the seacoast through the bush, after they killed Miss Palmer – Cudjoe. The white soldiers (living in Falmouth) followed them through the bush. They killed most a the Maroons in the bush and [the survivors] went to Dragoon Hole. They had a battle there with the white soldiers. In 1945, white men came to repair the tombs of the white soldiers and stay with me. They dig up a chillum pipe out a the earth, some jars and bones. I used to have some treasures and their monies that they used but I gave them to white people. [After Dragoon Hole] the Maroons escaped to 'Compong Town in St Elizabeth.

Pastor Jolly regularly visited Accompong, staying for a week at a time and holding Pentecostal meetings in the central square.

Of the Maroon Town population today, Pastor Jolly highlighted the dimension of in-migration from other parishes into the non-maroon community: 'Not altogether Maroons, we are just ordinary black people, from different parishes we come'.

Clinton McBean is another Newcomer who narrated an account of black marronage. Clinton keeps a grocery and rum shop with his wife (from Schaw Castle) next to their house-yard at Maroon Town Square (chapter 7). His father, from Adelphi, bought this land in the 1960s from Richard McGhie of Maroon Town's central clan, and built the house and shop. Clinton's parents' had seven children, some of whom migrated to Canada and the United States (but return to visit) and some of whom now have affinal and kinship ties in Maroon Town with the Reid and McIntyre clans. Clinton has six children, some of whom are in the USA. Clinton went to school in the United States, having been chosen to go there by the Maldon Baptist minister, and lived and worked there (on the railways and in the Army overseas) for 18 years, until 1975, when he returned to settle in Maroon Town, where his shop is at the heart of the community.

Clinton narrated an account of Maroon Town and its history, first explaining that the present-day population are not Maroons:

> No relation at all [to the Maroons]. The Maroons never stay in Maroon Town, only pass through – during the time of the Rebellion. Just stop for a while. Came from Cockpit Mountains in Trelawny, came to Flagstaff[7] where they had rebellion with the British soldiers – cemetery up there. Came down from Flagstaff to Maroon Town [Square], running away. Then they went to Accompong, where they settled with their own chief. They still live there in the same tradition. They have their celebration 6th of January. I went there once, 1978.

Like Pastor Jolly's account, Clinton's narrative demonstrates how the central themes of Maroon Town's oral traditions are transmitted to and by Newcomers. These themes include the fusion of the First and Second Maroon Wars and the mythical migration from TrelawnyTown/Maroon Town to Accompong, which repair the disjunctures of the aftermath of the Second Maroon War within the Leeward Maroon polity; namely, the deportation of the Trelawny Maroons and the ascendancy of Accompong from the secondary to the primary and sole surviving Leeward Maroon village.

The Felsenkopf Mulatto Maroons and the Rockhead Clan

In Maroon Town, in addition to narratives asserting Afro-Creole maroon ancestry and other oral traditions of black marronage, some Meso-Creoles who claim 'slave master' pickni' descent also assert mulatto maroon ancestry. Such narratives especially typify the Rockhead Old Family, whose enslaved ancestors are said to have escaped into the rocky landscape of the Cockpit Country to join the Second Maroon War.

Members of the Rockhead clan (traced through both genders) are now dispersed in the Cayman Islands, the British Virgin Islands, Cuba, the United States, England and Jamaica (Maroon Town, Montego Bay, Falmouth and Kingston). As the Rockheads have intermarried with other Old Families in Maroon Town, including the Waites, Fennels and Hedleys, the Rockhead clan overlaps with other such clans.

I interviewed older members of the Rockhead clan at Maroon Town Square, Browns' Town and Flagstaff and in Montego Bay, from 1999 to 2009. I combined their oral histories with other dimensions of my anthropological research, such as genealogies and data on landholdings, and with historical and Internet sources. Drawing these perspectives together, my research indicates that the Rockhead clan does indeed trace descent from mulatto Maroons who came to the Trelawny Town area in the Second Maroon War. This conclusion is consistent with historical evidence that some slaves deserted the plantations during the Second Maroon War (Campbell 1990, 223, in chapter 2).

According to the oral accounts and genealogies that I collected, the Rockhead clan comprises seven generations and is traced six ascending generations from the youngest generation to a slave woman in the parish of Trelawny who (as Willard Rockhead narrated), is said to have had six mulatto sons (born enslaved) fathered by 'two white bosses on the slave plantation' (Genealogy 7). Willard, born in 1935 in Browns' Town (who was 64 years old when I interviewed him in Montego Bay, in 1999, and 73 when we discussed it again in 2008) told me that the oral tradition of the Rockheads had been passed on to him by his father and paternal uncles.

Willard narrated that the slave ancestress (described as a beautiful house slave who worked in the kitchen as a housekeeper and cook) and her six mulatto sons were enslaved at Sherwood Content[8] in Trelawny. Sherwood Content is just a few miles inland from the former Trelawny slave-trading ports of Martha Brae and Falmouth (Besson 2002), near the foothills of the Cockpit Country and not far from the parish boundary between Trelawny and St James. Willard recounted that three of the slave woman's sons were fathered by a British slave master surnamed Stirling and that her other three sons (Robert, Ezekiel and John) had a white German father ('one of the bosses' on the plantation) surnamed Felsenkopf.

All six mulatto sons are said to have joined the Second Maroon War. As Willard (one of John Felsenkopf's great-grandsons) put it: They participated in 'the maroon rebellion, the second one, when the people strayed from the plantation and join the rebellion, particularly the "half-breed" – they would have been the most bitter – fighting for their mothers against their fathers'. The three Stirling Maroons are said to have escaped to the Somerton area of the Montego Bay Valley (south-west of Hampden Estate and a few miles north of Trelawny Town). The three Felsenkopf Maroons 'went to the Maroon Town area', at that time Trelawny Town, and are said to have rejected their German surname and assumed the surname Rockhead – a translation of Felsenkopf (and symbolizing the rocky Cockpit landscape).[9]

Documentary sources reinforce the Rockhead oral tradition of mulatto slave children born on the Stirling slave plantation(s) in Trelawny. My historical research reveals that the owners and managers of the Hampden slave plantation (on the boundary between Trelawny and St James) were a Scottish family surnamed Stirling, from 1757 to 1852; this includes the period of the Second Maroon War from 1795 to 1796. At least one of these Stirlings, Patrick Stirling, referred, in his will of 1776, to his mulatto slave children on Hampden Estate (Besson 2002, 64–65). This Scottish Stirling planter family (which comprised two branches) also owned the nearby slave plantation of Content in Trelawny (formerly in Old St James before the parish was subdivided),[10] as well as Frontier and Keir Estates in St James.[11] An Internet article by Jude Skurray, a descendant of the Stirling planter family (personal communication August 27, 2007), likewise refers to children born to this Stirling planter family in Trelawny/St James during slavery by a 'Creole woman' who was a 'Common Law Wife'.[12] Further Internet sources clarify that the name of today's village of 'Sherwood Content' should be hyphenated, as the name 'Sherwood-Content' actually refers to 'two separate places: "Sherwood" and "Content"',[13] derived from two livestock pens during slavery, Sherwood Pen and Content Pen.

The documentary evidence strongly indicates that the Rockhead oral tradition accurately refers to the birth of mulatto sons surnamed Stirling to a woman enslaved on the Content plantation in Trelawny around the time of the Second Maroon War. In the Rockheads' oral history, the white German, who fathered the slave woman's Felsenkopf sons, is said to have been the Stirlings' plantation 'Farm Manager' (overseer).

My anthropological data on landholdings in Maroon Town further reinforce the Rockhead oral tradition of descent from mulatto Maroons. According to this oral tradition, the Felsenkopf/Rockhead Maroons who escaped into the Trelawny Town area occupied and cleared forested state land, some of which has been passed down the generations of their descendants as family land. Some of this family land can be identified among the Rockheads today. For example, one of the Rockhead Maroon brothers, John Rockhead, is said to have transmitted some of this land as family land in Browns' Town. This land, with its extensive family burial ground, can still be seen there, near Flagstaff (the site of

Genealogy 7. Partial Genealogy of the Felsenkopf Maroons and the Rockhead Clan

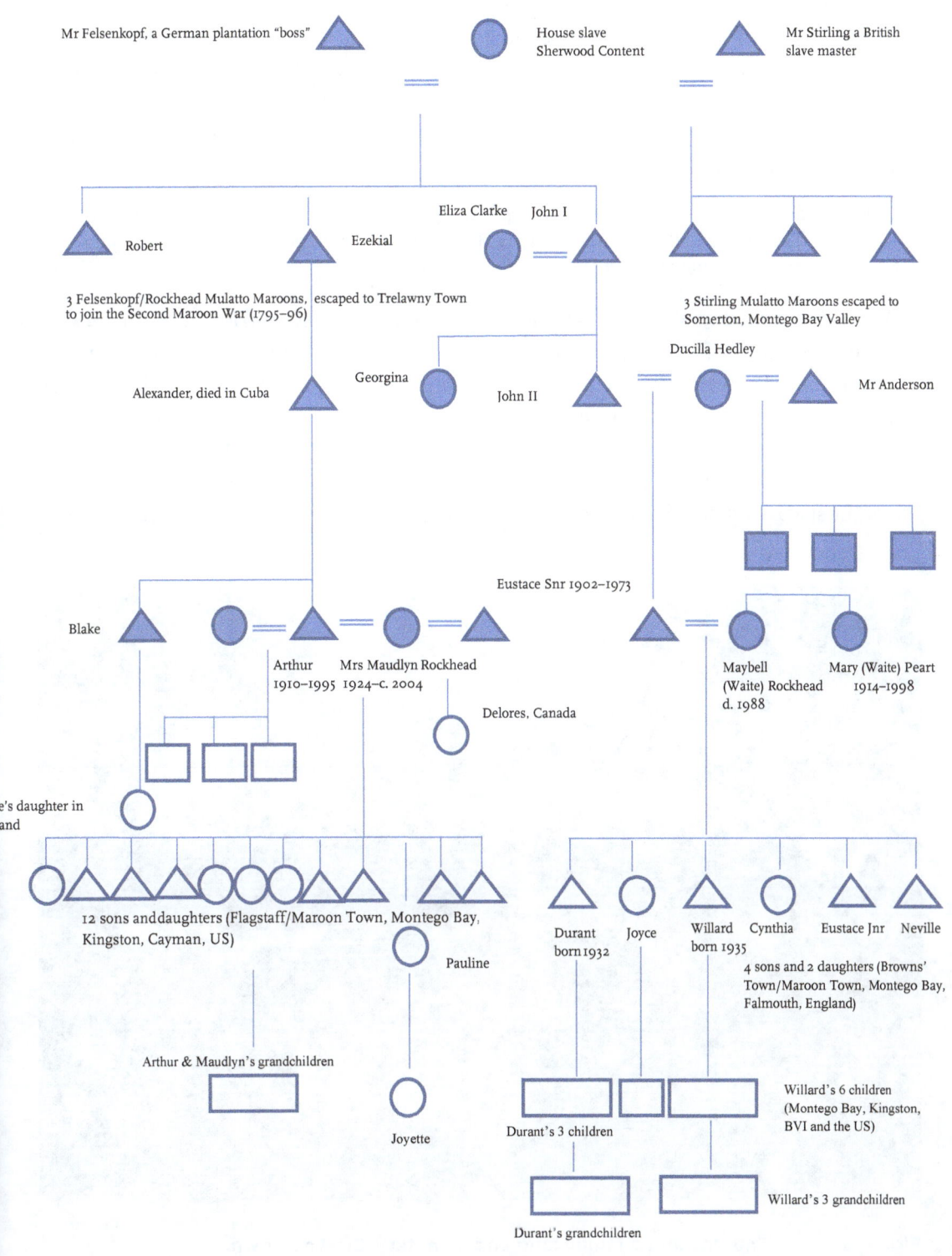

Trelawny Town and the Second Maroon War) where it remains among his Meso-Creole great-grandchildren and great-great-grandchildren today (figure 9.3).

Willard (one of John's great-grandsons) was born on this Rockhead family land at Browns' Town (in 1935) and narrated a history of this land. By way of background, he stressed that such mountainous land, held since the days of slavery and marronage, was not purchased but was cleared and occupied by rebel slaves such as his ancestors who fought in the Second Maroon War:

> The lands on the hills were never bought. They [the escaped slaves] cleared the land and settled. That was a battle-ground up there. Rebels [Maroons] came down from the hills and sabotage the sugar industry.

Willard narrated that his great-grandfather, John Felsenkopf/Rockhead (whom I refer to as John the First or John I), had various pieces of land that he transmitted to his children, who were sons. The name of the great-grandfather, John, had also been transmitted: 'there's a John Rockhead down all the generations'. For example, Willard's paternal grandfather was also named John (I refer to him as John II). John II, in turn, subdivided and transmitted his share of family land to his children. For example, Willard's father, Eustace Augustus Rockhead (1902–73), received the 25-acre piece at Browns' Town.

Figure 9.3. The Rockhead family land and cemetery, Browns' Town.

Eustace had eight children. Six of them were alive when I interviewed Willard, two daughters and four sons, most of whom now live beyond Maroon Town in Montego Bay, Falmouth and England. However, the eldest of these siblings, Durant (who has three daughters and grandchildren), is (as Willard put it) 'the man on the spot' who resides on and looks after the family land and sometimes conducts funerals there. I would meet Durant (aged 77, in 2009) several times in Browns' Town. Eustace's descendants all retain rights to this family land (for example, when Willard visits he 'plants two breadfruit trees', asserting his rights of occupancy) and any member of this lineage may be buried there.

This Rockhead family cemetery, which is beside the road from Browns' Town to Flagstaff and had about 30 tombs by 2009, was established by Willard's grandparents, including John II who died in 1920, and whose tomb can be identified there (figures 9.3 and 9.4). As I was told when I visited this cemetery, 'We're surrounded by Rockhead lands, as far as you can see, a big family'. Here Durant explained that:

> You are in Trelawny Town now. This is the border of Trelawny Town – over that side [Flagstaff] is Trelawny Town...Maroon die all about here, put flowers here, put flowers dere [referring to the symbolic plants at Dragoon Hole]. Black man [men] buried with whites at Flagstaff.

Figure 9.4. John Rockhead II's tombstone in the Rockhead family-land cemetery at Browns' Town.

This narrative of a white and black burial ground reflects the creolization process and parallels Accompong maroon narratives of the graves of white soldiers and black Maroons at the 'Peace Cave' in Accompong (chapter 3).

A young man from Browns' Town, who joined our tour of the Rockhead cemetery, pointed out 'Nanny Rock', a nearby mountain, and remarked that, 'Nanny used to live right over there'. But he asserted that, 'Maroon Town Square is the bloody square', where the Maroons were murdered in the maroon war. However, Durant reasserted: 'No man, up Flagstaff'.

In 1999, Willard had told me that there is another family cemetery in a bushy area (Coote Bush) of the land, off the main road at Browns' Town, where his great-grandparents (including the mulatto Maroon, John Rockhead I) are buried. In 2008, I set out to find this burial ground and in a cell-phone conversation from Montego Bay with me and Durant (who was unaware of these graves) at Browns' Town, Willard guided us there. He sent us up a rocky path, explaining to his amazed older brother that, 'the old man' (their father Eustace) had told him 'the spot' where his grandfather, the mulatto Maroon, John I is buried.

The untombed grave of the mulatto Maroon, John Rockhead The First, which we found overgrown by bush (figure 9.5), is on Hedley family land at Coote Bush, where members of the Hedley clan ('cousins' to the Rockheads and also interrelated with the Anderson and Hamilton clans) were subsequently tombed, in various styles, including old stone and tiles (figure 9.6). Willard narrated (by cell phone) that his paternal grandmother, Ducilla Hedley, had first married an Anderson, by whom she had three children, and then married his grandfather John Rockhead II, with whom she had five children, including Willard and Durant's father, Eustace (Genealogy 7). Willard explained that this is why the mulatto Maroon (John Rockhead I), who was Ducilla Hedley's father-in-law, was buried on Hedley family land, with Ducilla's parents (Hedleys) also being subsequently buried there.

In 2009, we revisited the mulatto Maroon's grave at Coote Bush, where we were shown around the graveyard (which had recently been cleared of bush [figure 9.6]) by Willis Smith, another member of the Hedley clan (born in 1929 and nearly 80) who had been a cane and banana farmer before 'breeze mashed them up'. Willis, who lives on bought land next to this family land, took us to the Maroon's grave (which he said used to be marked by stones) and told us that his 'old people' had said 'someone old bury here'. Another elderly farmer with us, Willis's cousin and neighbour, Winston Minto (born 1932), who likewise belonged to the

Figure 9.5. The burial place of the mulatto Maroon John Rockhead I, Coote Bush, Maroon Town.

Figure 9.6. The Hedley family-land cemetery (below the mulatto Maroon's grave), Coote Bush.

Hedley clan, remarked that, 'in dark days, slave days, no tombs'.[14] Willis also explained that his mother, Adella Hedley (1907–83), who is tombed in this graveyard, was the daughter of Abraham Hedley and Georgina Rockhead who was the sister of 'Jonathan Rockhead' (Willard and Durant's grandfather, John II). Abraham's mother had acquired the land, either through purchase or 'from old people'. Willis further narrated that, 'Jonathan Rockhead's father' (Willis's great-grandfather, who was also Durant and Willard's great-grandfather, John Rockhead I) 'came from Trelawny'; a narrative consistent with Willard's account of the origin of this mulatto Maroon, who escaped from Sherwood-Content to join the Second Maroon War. Willis added that this great-grandfather was married to Eliza Clarke. (As seen from the narrative of Ade Hall, who died, in 2007, aged 103, and her relatives, earlier in this chapter, Maroon Town's Clarke clan likewise claim maroon ancestry.)

When I met Willard in 1999, he further narrated that, in addition to the Rockhead family land at Browns' Town, transmitted from his great-grandfather, John Rockhead I (who captured the land but was buried on the Hedley family land as the Rockhead cemetery was only established by John Rockhead II), his great-grandfather's mulatto maroon brothers, Robert and Ezekiel Felsenkopf/Rockhead, likewise cleared and occupied adjacent land in the hills, some of which was passed down to their descendants. Willard said that, for example, his father's second cousins Blake and Arthur are descended from Ezekiel, though he did not know their father's name. However, Willard's third cousin, Pauline Rockhead (whom I often visited near Maroon Town Square), did know the name of her father Arthur's, father: Alexander Rockhead, who migrated to Cuba and died there. Pauline visits Blake's daughter in England who, likewise, visits Maroon Town.

In addition to interviewing Pauline early in my fieldwork and again in 2009, I interviewed her mother, the late Mrs Maudlyn Rockhead, Arthur's widow, at Flagstaff. Maudlyn (who was born in 1924 and was a member of Pastor Jolly's Pentecostal church at Browns' Town), narrated that the land that she resided on at Flagstaff was her late husband Arthur's family land, which he used to farm and that she now cultivated. She and Arthur (1910-1995) had 12 daughters and sons. They are now scattered in the United States, Cayman, Kingston, Maroon Town and Montego Bay, but they return to visit and some of their children lived with Maudlyn at Flagstaff. Arthur is buried on this family land and, as Maudlyn put it, 'there I'm going when time come' (she died around 2004). Pauline added that when Arthur died, all of his children who were overseas returned for 'some of the Revival practices', including a 'set-up at the dead-house' (eating, drinking and playing dominoes) for seven nights before the funeral. Of Flagstaff, Maudlyn narrated:

> Up here is the Maroon Town [Trelawny Town] and down there [Maroon Town Square] is the Crossroad. Is up here all the Maroons buried – Dragoon Hole – and white soldiers in the cemetery. Gun was up there [on Gun Hill].

Pauline now resides near Maroon Town Square on land bought by her father's second cousin, Eustace Rockhead, and his wife, Maybell (née Waite). These were Willard's parents (Eustace, who was born in 1902 on the family land at Browns' Town, being the son of

John Rockhead II). Willard (though born on the family land at Browns' Town) had grown up on this land near the Square, which now has three tombs in front of the house: those of Eustace (died 1973), Maybell (died 1988) and Maybell's sister, Mary Perte (née Waite, 1914–98) – though the Waite Old Family have a large burial ground elsewhere in Maroon Town. In 1999, a Revival 'tombing' memorial was held at this yard for Mary and her son returned from England for this ritual.

Willard narrated that his father, Eustace, and paternal grandfather, John Rockhead II, had travelled overseas to Nicaragua, Cuba, Colombia and Panama. Willard and Pauline gave further information on Eustace (1902–73), who was a prominent Maroon Town citizen and had received an award from the St James Parish Council for his voluntary social services and his contribution to agriculture in the island, parish and community. The citation for this award (given posthumously in 1978) reinforced this information. Born in Maroon Town and educated at the Mount Edmonson Methodist School before migrating (and then becoming a seaman on a ship), Eustace returned to Jamaica, settling back in Maroon Town in 1930 and marrying in 1934. In Maroon Town, he farmed bananas and sugar cane, exporting bananas to England. He became a leading banana grower in the community, extending his landholdings, was instrumental in setting up the first banana boxing plant in Maroon Town and eventually owned his own boxing plant. He became Chairman of the Maroon Town branch of the Jamaica Agricultural Society, representative of the St James branch of the All Island Banana Growers' Association and Secretary of its Maroon Town branch. Eustace was also Vice-Chairman of the Maldon Peoples' Co-operative Bank, President of the Maroon Town Citizens' Association, Chairman of the Maroon Town Library and Basic School and Chairman of the Maroon Town County Council. He was also a steward of the Mount Edmonson Methodist Church.

Like his father, Eustace, and paternal grandfather, John Rockhead II, Willard had likewise migrated, when he was 18 years old. However, Willard went to England. There, he worked in Birmingham as a driver and in a machine shop for ten years, from 1954 to 1965, at the height of Jamaican migration to Britain: 'I had relatives and friends there and the travelling fever was passing at the time'. When Willard returned, he went into trucking, transporting building materials from Kingston to Montego Bay. When I interviewed him, he was 'retired' and keeping a guesthouse in Montego Bay with his wife, who is a member of Maroon Town's Fennel Old Family (chapter 8). They have six children (daughters and sons in Montego Bay, Kingston, the British Virgin Islands and the USA) and three grandchildren who all belong to Maroon Town's overlapping Rockhead, Hedley, Waite and Fennel transnational clans.

Willard asserted that the Maroons had won the Second Maroon War (a recurring theme in Maroon Town narratives) and had defeated slavery, but that the English used religion to control the ex-slaves and masqueraded as Scots (who in some Maroon Town narratives are regarded as being less harsh than the English). Willard also referred to the English returning some of the former slaves to Sierra Leone, which coincides with historical accounts of the eventual return of the deported Trelawny Maroons from Nova Scotia to Freetown:

Slavery was never abolished, it was defeated. Of course the Maroons won the war! The second bout they defeated the English and the English used their cunning – the church, all the churches – Baptist, Methodist, Anglican, to conquer them. The English came back as a Scottish man-wolf in sheep's clothing. There were people who wanted to go back to Africa and the English saw fit to take some of them back – to Sierra Leone in West Africa. And up to today, they speak with Jamaican accent.

Willard further narrated that today the Maroons are 'all over the island' and 'are a set of people who believe they should be prominent, at all times, and seek to be at the top and in the civil service and teaching'. In addition to this portrayal of maroon tenacity, confidence and pride, Willard outlined changes within Maroon Town since his childhood, resulting especially from the overseas (and circulatory) migration of Maroon Town villagers and the in-migration there of sugar-plantation labourers from the lowlands to become banana farmers in the Cockpits:

> With the migration of the original people [of Maroon Town], they moved and hardly any of the original [inhabitants] of the Maroon Town area remain today. We all go there [to visit] and our sentiments are there. But in the 1970s, it was so fruitful, and before. People came in to work and settle there from every parish, especially from the cane-belt, sugar-belt, as up there [in Maroon Town] we produce bananas. The cane-cutters drifted up there from the flat-lands, arable lands. And the people from Maroon Town migrated, in search of prosperity, to England, Canada and the United States. England, from the 1950s mass migration started. Drift to the USA and Canada from the 1940s, during the [Second World] War.

Willard observed that emigration from Maroon Town is still 'unabated today' but that such migrants 'return on visits'.

Willard's wide-ranging narrative on Maroon Town, including his assertion of mulatto maroon ancestry, and the related accounts by other members of the Rockhead clan, added a significant theme to the narratives of the transformation from Trelawny Town to Maroon Town (chapters 8–9). Reinforced by my fieldwork and documentary research, the Rockhead oral tradition likewise adds to the history of Jamaican marronage. The mulatto maroon Rockhead clan also provided an important clue for my research on the link between the Meso-Creole transnational McGhie Old Family of Maroon Town (its central clan) and the historic mulatto 'McGhie Maroons', near Trelawny Town, whose neglected history I discovered in documentary records and whose descendants become visible through oral histories and other data uncovered in my fieldwork (chapter 10).

Notes

1. Currie is also a prominent surname in Accompong, including the surname of Melvin Currie who is guardian of the Kindah grove and who was Deputy Colonel during much of my fieldwork (chapters 3–6). Betsy may have married into this Accompong family.
2. As Charlie's third cousin, Delores (of the Currie, Clarke, Walker and Hines clans), had a child by Mortimer Reid's brother's son, Charlie considered the Reids to be his relatives too, especially as he had 'grown' with Mortimer.

3. Charlie's reference to the red eyes of the Kongo Maroons parallels, in part, the stereotypical description of the Leeward Maroons by Dallas: 'Their eyes were quick, wild, and fiery, the white of them appearing a little reddened; owing, perhaps, to the greenness of the wood they burned in their houses, with the smoke of which it must have been affected' (Dallas 1803, vol. 1, 88).
4. As seen in chapter 3, 'Kongo' and 'Coromantee' ethnicities are likewise significant in Accompong.
5. Some Windward Maroons live in the parish of St Mary, adjacent to Portland.
6. Charlie's claim of maroon descent seems clearest through the Walker clan and may, therefore, be rooted in the Windward Maroons as (in Alfred Walker's daughter, Ade's narrative) Alfred (Leo's maternal uncle) was from Moore Town in Portland. However, the Walker clan's overlap (through Ade's mother) with the descendants of Betsy Currie/'Campong Nanny and with Rebecca Hines (who like Ade's mother was descended from the Clarke clan who assert Trelawny Maroon descent) reinforced Charlie's Leeward Maroon identity, as did the sibling link between his paternal grandmother, Leo, and her sister, Elmazeen Hines, wife of Henry Hines.
7. This coincides with the route of the McGhie Maroons and the Felsenkopf/Rockhead Maroons in the Second Maroon War, as well as with a more general maroon route to Trelawny Town described by Melvin Pearson (chapters 7–10).
8. As mentioned previously, Sherwood-Content is the natal village of the Olympic and World gold medallist sprinter Usain Bolt.
9. Other spellings of this surname, such as Felzenkopf, were provided in the narrative. However, a German language teacher whom I consulted clarified that the spelling that translates to 'rockhead' is *Felsenkopf*; I am grateful to Elaine Knöerich for this information. This translation is reinforced by an Internet source that states in relation to the spelling *Felzenkopf*: 'There is no such word. You probably mean *Felsenkopf* (literally, 'rockhead'), which exists as a geographical name in various places...The *s* in *Felsenkopf* is voiced, which may have caused your misspelling.' Michael Hemmer, http://www.tonews.com/thread/1581112/alt/usage/german/felzenkopf.
10. Before the subdivision of the parish of Old St James in 1771, to create the new parish of Trelawny out of the eastern part of Old St James, Martha Brae, Hampden and Sherwood-Content were in Old St James.
11. http://www.cockpitcountry.com/TrelEstates.html.
12. http://www.clanstirling.org/Main/bios/EdwardStirlingbyJudeSkurray.pdf.
13. http://www.cockpitcountry.com/sherwoodcontent.html.
14. Winston Minto's mother was Martha Hedley, sister to Willis's maternal grandfather, Abraham Hedley. Winston is from Salt Marsh in Trelawny and had come to Coote Bush to reside on his maternal Hedley family land next to his cousin, Willis. As Winston remarked, in understatement, 'we are all family here'. He added that the 'old people' named Coote Bush after the Coote clan of Maroon Town. Consistent with Willis's narrative, Winston narrated that his maternal family land at Coote Bush 'comes from way back', from his mother Martha's mother, who had five children: Ketura, Martha, Dorcas, Tom and Abraham Hedley who 'all got it as family land'. Martha is buried in the Mount Edmonson Church Cemetery. I was amazed to discover that on his father's side, Winston belongs to the Minto Old Family, the central clan in post-slavery Martha Brae in Trelawny that I had previously studied. Winston's paternal great-grandfather was William Shakespeare Minto, one of the emancipated slaves who established the free village of Martha Brae (Besson 2002).

10 ▪ THE MCGHIE MAROONS AND THE MAROON TOWN MCGHIES

The McGhies are the central Old Family or cognatic clan (traced through both genders) in Maroon Town. They trace their Afro-Scots ancestry through seven generations to the earliest known McGhie in the community (Genealogy 8), dating back to the mid-nineteenth century – around the time of emancipation (1838) and just a few decades after the Second Maroon War (1795–96). Members of the McGhie clan, which includes hundreds of individuals traced through both women and men, are scattered in various parts of Maroon Town (including Flagstaff, Browns' Town, Maldon, Woodlands, Vaughansfield and Maroon Town Square) and dispersed through migration to other parts of St James, other parishes in Jamaica and elsewhere in the Caribbean as well as England, Canada and the United States.

However, the corporate identity of the McGhie clan remains rooted in Maroon Town, where their family lands and kin-based cemeteries are located. Indeed, during my fieldwork, I was told that, 'there is only one McGhie Family in Jamaica and they spring from Maroon Town'. Members of the McGhie clan residing elsewhere in the island and overseas, frequently return to Maroon Town to settle or visit; for example, for funerals, wakes and memorials, when the corporate identity of the transnational clan becomes highly visible. The McGhie clan also overlaps and interweaves with most other Old Families in Maroon Town (such as the Reids, Hamiltons, Andersons, Fennels, Peterkins, Waites, Hines, Walkers and Clarkes) due to intermarriage, kinship ties and common descent (chapters 7–10).

Despite the various surnames of the members of the McGhie clan (as many are the descendants of McGhie women but take their fathers' surnames) the McGhie clan is referred to, in and around Maroon Town, by its corporate title, 'The McGhie Family' or 'The McGhies'. However, in Maroon Town and throughout St James and Jamaica, the pronunciation of this Scottish surname has been creolized to 'Meggie' and many McGhies themselves pronounce their clan title and/or surname in this way.

During my fieldwork in and around Maroon Town from 1999 to 2009, I interviewed numerous McGhies and, with their permission, draw on their knowledge in this chapter, combined with my anthropological and historical research. None of those McGhies whom I met asserted maroon ancestry. Instead, they frequently referred to their partial Scottish origins from slavery and/or to their mixed 'slave master' pickni' descent (compare chapter 8).

However, my research (including historical records, genealogies, naming, family-land data and some aspects of oral tradition) indicates that the Maroon Town McGhies are not only of Afro-Scots descent, from slave masters and

Genealogy 8. The Early Afro-Scots McGhies of Maroon Town and their Descending Generations

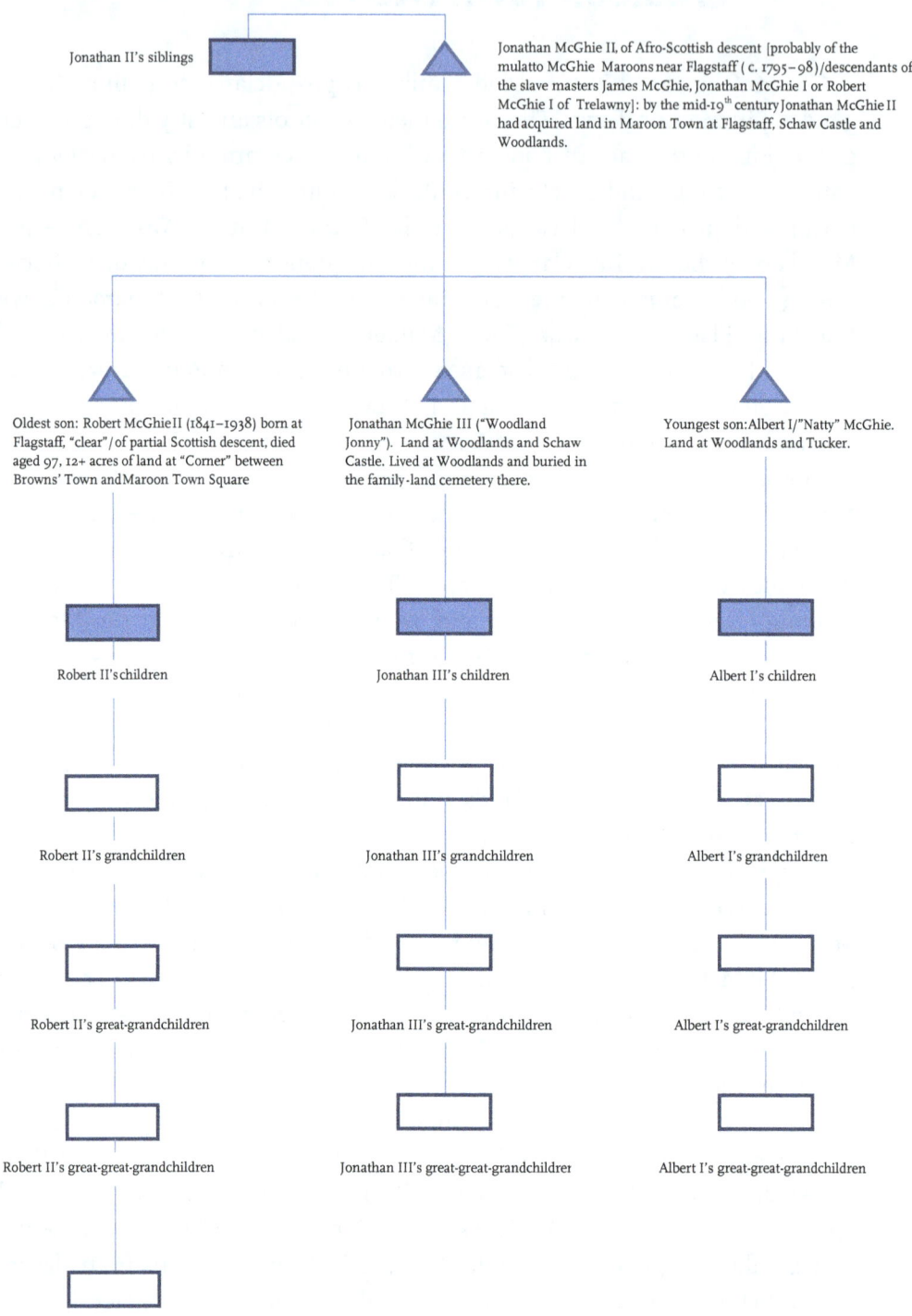

slaves, but also have mulatto maroon ancestry. More specifically, my findings strongly suggest that the Maroon Town McGhies are descended not only from the McGhie slave-owning planter family and a slave woman on Greenside Estate in the neighbouring parish of Trelawny, but also from the mulatto 'McGhie Maroons', who escaped from Greenside and resettled the historic maroon village of Congo Town/Highwindward/Me No Sen You No Come, in Trelawny, just a few miles from Trelawny Town (now Flagstaff/Maroon Town) in St James, around the time of the Second Maroon War. My conclusions are reinforced by the oral traditions of the Rockhead clan, who not only claim 'slave master' pickni' descent from a planter and slave from Sherwood-Content near Greenside Estate, but also assert maroon ancestry from mulatto slaves who escaped from that Trelawny plantation (Sherwood-Content) to join the Second Maroon War (chapter 9). In addition, some of the Rockhead family land is directly opposite a part of the McGhie family land in Browns' Town and both these clans have historical links with Flagstaff (the core of the former site of Trelawny Town).

In this chapter, I first outline the historical information that I found on the McGhie slave-owning planter family and the McGhie Maroons of Trelawny Parish. I then link this to the genealogies, names, oral histories and landholdings that I explored with the McGhie clan in Maroon Town. I also include reflections on the history of Maroon Town, by various McGhie generations, which reflect a strong awareness of marronage. I then discuss the widespread oral traditions in and around Maroon Town of the late Leonard Lambert McGhie (1902–73), known as 'Papa Meggie' or 'Pappy Meg' who, I was told in the plantation lowlands of St James and Trelawny, *did* assert maroon descent.

Overall, this chapter indicates that the Maroon Town McGhies have a significant history, reaching back more than 200 years to the Second Maroon War, which has played a major role in transforming the historic maroon site of Trelawny Town to modern Maroon Town. My findings, therefore, not only uncover an important dimension of the hidden history of the transformation of Trelawny Town to Maroon Town, but also further illuminate the internal differentiation of Jamaican Maroons who included Meso-Creoles as well as Africans and Afro-Creoles (chapters 3–10), thereby widening the more usual focus on black marronage (e.g., Bilby 2006; Price 1996, 2008; Zips 1999, 2011). In so doing, this chapter also throws further light on the process of creolization at the maroon/non-maroon interface.

Historical Records: The McGhie Planters and the McGhie Maroons

At least two historical sources refer to the McGhie slave-owning planter family of Greenside Estate in Trelawny Parish (originally the eastern part of the parish of Old St James until 1771) in the eighteenth century at the zenith of Jamaican plantation slavery (Mullin 1994; Lovejoy, Shepherd and Trotman 2003). My own research situates the eighteenth-century Greenside plantation near the British transatlantic slaving port of Martha Brae (the first town in eastern Old St James and Trelawny's first capital), in an area of intensive Scottish settlement in Jamaica's plantation heartlands (Besson 2002, 45,

54–72). I also have personal knowledge of Greenside, as that plantation (and the adjoining Maxfield Estate) was owned by my father, Ken McFarlane, in the late twentieth century. I grew up a few miles from Greenside on the former slave-and-sugar estates of Southfield, Merrywood, Holland and Irving Tower which surround both Greenside and the free village of Martha Brae (xxi–xxxi).

Michael Mullin, in his book, *Africa in America: Slave Acculturation and Resistance in the American South and the British Caribbean 1736-1831*, discussing 'a disturbance in 1798', in western Jamaica, two years after the Second Maroon War, refers to James McGhie as 'one of the wealthiest planters in the northside area of conflict' (Mullin 1994, 58). In a footnote, Mullin states that, 'James McGhie in Trelawny Parish returns, 1799, is listed with two other McGhies, Robert and Jonathan, at Greenside', where James McGhie 'owned 202 slaves', and that, 'at another unspecified estate, perhaps Hampstead, he owned 833' (321–22 n77). Paul Lovejoy, Verene Shepherd and David Trotman, in a footnote (2003, 40 n41) to their 'Introduction' to Cyrus Francis Perkins's historical novel, set at Greenside during slavery (written in 1854–55 and first published in 1911), state that 'Information in the Island Records Office indicates that 615 acres of Greenside estate were transferred from Robert McGhie to William Tynmore in the eighteenth century'.[1] In addition, a map dated 1800 (four years after the Second Maroon War) in the National Library of Jamaica shows Greenside in the ownership of a 'Robert McGhie Esquire' (map 11).[2]

In Mullin's account, the exact relationship among the three members of the McGhie planter family – James, Robert and Jonathan – is not mentioned. However, in a Deed, dated 20 April 1780, in the Island Record Office of Jamaica, regarding the will of the planter Hugh Barnett[3], these three names again occur together as the 'nephews' of Hugh Barnett and the 'heirs' of William Barnett (Hugh Barnett's son, William Hugh Barnett) of Trelawny.[4] It is, therefore, likely that James, Robert and Jonathan McGhie were brothers (and probably Hugh Barnett I's sister's sons).[5] The archives further indicate that at least one of these sons, Robert, had mulatto children (Thomas McGhie and Mary McGhie) by the time of the Second Maroon War.[6] The names James, Jonathan, Robert and Thomas McGhie (including the heirs of Robert McGhie of the Hampstead, Retreat and Coxheath plantations, in Trelawny, and the heirs of James McGhie) recur in the archives, in relation to the ownership and inheritance of slaves and stock in Trelawny and St James, in the Almanacs of the early decades of the nineteenth century.[7] The names Robert, Jonathan and Thomas McGhie likewise recur in the McGhie clan of Maroon Town. In subsequent discussion, I, therefore, refer to the slave-owning McGhies with these names as Robert I, Jonathan I and Thomas I to distinguish them from the later Maroon Town McGhies.

Michael Mullin, in his discussion of gendered slave resistance in the Americas, also refers to the McGhie Maroons of the settlement of Congo Town/Highwindward/Me No Sen You No Come in western Jamaica, a village that was repeatedly dismantled by the colonial militia and reoccupied by Maroons throughout its recorded history from the 1770s to the 1820s (Mullin 1994, 58–61). Mullin's map (55) situates this village in the parish of St Elizabeth. However, this community was actually deep in the south-western Cockpits of Trelawny Parish, some miles directly inland from Greenside Estate and between the

Map 11. *A Plan of the Parish of Trelawny ... performed AD 1800 (Estate Map Trelawny 496). Courtesy of National Library of Jamaica.*

maroon treaty towns of Cudjoe's Town/Trelawny Town, in St James, and Accompong in St Elizabeth (see, e.g., Patterson 1973, 264; Macmillan Shell Road Map 1999 [map 4]; compare Mullin 1994, 322 n87). Congo Town/Highwindward/Me No Sen You No Come was only a few miles from each of these Leeward Maroon treaty towns and was especially close to the Trelawny Town/Flagstaff area, which is now part of Maroon Town (map 4). This geographical proximity between the McGhie Maroon settlement of Congo Town/Highwindward/Me No Sen You No Come and Trelawny Town is an important point for my analysis linking the McGhie Maroons to Maroon Town.

Mullin states that about 200 plantation slaves escaped and joined the Trelawny Town Maroons, in the Second Maroon War, including 86 slaves from 29 estates in the parish of Trelawny; some of these runaways were mulattos and some were women (Mullin 1994, 293–94, 297). These escaped plantation slaves:

> joined and served the Maroons as either fighters or foragers. The latter, comprising the far greater number, lived with the Maroon women and children in a remote retreat [Congo Town/Highwindward/Me No Sen You No Come]. These foragers, who had to keep themselves and more than a hundred and fifty fighting men in food while on the run, literally worked around the clock. Two parties went out with armed escorts during a twenty-four hour period, one leaving in the morning as the other returned (Mullin 1994, 293).

Historical sources cited in Mullin (1994, 58–59, 321–22) indicate that the McGhie Maroons were runaway slaves of the McGhie planter family of Trelawny's Greenside Estate, who lived in Congo Town/Highwindward around the time of the Second Maroon War. By 1798, two years after the deportation of the Trelawny Town Maroons, McGhie runaway slaves had resettled the historic maroon site of Congo Town and had become 'the McGhie maroons', grouped around 'Old Quaco, an elderly obeah figure' (Mullin 1994, 58–59). Mullin notes that, 'by the Second Maroon War, it [the maroon settlement] was already more than twenty years old and known as Congo Town to the Trelawny Maroons' and that Congo Town, 'dismantled during that war', was 'quickly reoccupied' and 'renamed Highwindward, "the place of greatest safety"', by 1798 after the McGhie resettlement (58).

Mullin (who does not link the McGhie Maroons to Maroon Town) notes that Congo Town/Highwindward was not a treaty town, but a more remote and independent maroon settlement that had been used by the maroon leader, 'Cuffee as one of a string of march camps' in 'a disturbance in 1798' (1994, 58–59). By that year, McGhie runaway slaves had been settled there for some time (probably initially as foragers for the fighting Maroons), as a militia officer who found the camp 'said the McGhie maroons had "lived quietly there" and "grievously complained" about Cuffee's risky intrusion' (59). One such McGhie Maroon was Juba, 'a [female] McGhie slave who had lived for three years at Highwindward' (59).

According to the deposition of another female slave, Patty, Cuffee's band of male Maroons had taken plantation slave women, including herself (seized while at her provision ground) to Congo Town/Highwindward (Mullin 1994, 58). Patty reported that, after a two-day march, they had reached:

a town where authority was ethnic and vascillated in form between headman leadership and an informal equality. In the settlement, some spoke Coromantee, 'tribes' lived in their own districts, and Cuffee was 'stiled Headman, but on occasion all were headmen, as they all talk one word' (58).

The field commander who discovered Cuffee's camp described it as 'a home capable of holding more than 100 people' and as a 'little town of Huts [with]...well beaten paths in various directions', supported by gathering wild fruit and by two provision grounds (59).

The 'disturbance' by Cuffee, whom Juba reported had deserted the McGhie settlement ahead of the militia 'when trouble started' (taking the best weapons) on the pretext of foraging for wild yams (Mullin 1994, 59), was focused on the McGhie planter family of Greenside Estate.[8] Drawing on a letter, dated May 15, 1798, from William Green of the nearby Good Hope plantation in Trelawny, Mullin states that Cuffee was 'motivated by revenge' against the slave-plantation owner, James McGhie of Greenside (58, 321–22 n77):

> This maroon leader [Cuffee] would burn Peru, Fontibelle, and all back settlements in order 'to get room,' he said, 'to kill James McGhie...[and] once they got him they will be done' (Mullin 1994, 58).

The contrast in attitude between warlike Cuffee and the relatively peaceful McGhie Maroons towards the McGhie planters may have been due to the kinship ties between the McGhie Maroons and their former McGhie owners, as discussed in the next section below.

Congo Town/Highwindward was rediscovered in 1823 at which time it 'was described as sizeable' and was renamed again (Mullin 1994, 59):

> It had 14 buildings, some with shingle roofs and wood floors, none less than 25 feet in length; one, probably communal, was seventy feet long, rectangular and open in the middle. The maroons, who in the 1820s raised poultry, hogs, and 200 acres of 'very fine' provisions (among the most extensive on record including those of the treaty towns), this time bestowed a name denoting their self-contained stance: Me No Sen You No Com [I haven't sent for you, don't come after me] (Mullin 1994, 59, [my translation]).

Mullin suggests that the reason this place was recurrently resettled by Maroons, despite 'innumerable alternate locations' in the Cockpits, was because it was a sacred maroon ancestral burial ground:

> A persuasive answer [for the resettlements] is that maroons returned periodically for more than fifty years because the site was deemed sacred: inhabited by dead maroons, all of whom – in an African sense of time-reckoning – would be, as the recently deceased, hardly dead at all. As shades the dead watched until living kin returned (in each of the three phases caught in the records) to renew the rites that linked the two worlds at this particular spot: Congo Town/Highwindward/Me No Sen.

> In contrast to maroons who lived by raiding, women of the remote settlements conceived, raised, and buried their people in potent territory as far removed as possible from the sources of ritual contamination emanating from the coastal estates. And Maroons who employed the self-contained strategy fulfilled a primary aim of the first resistance by new Negroes regardless of where they were brought ashore in Anglo-America – to find a

way home. Once at the water's edge, however, they were forced to turn inward, where in a few plantation societies some developed a sane and remote space to recreate families that, in the African manner, included the dead as well as the living (Mullin 1994, 61).

However, such maroon families – whom Mullin (1994, 293–94) argues were, by the 1790s, often comprised of three generations and led by women, including mulattos – were being re-created through Caribbean creolization. Many Maroons, including some of the McGhie Maroons, had lived (and been born) enslaved on Jamaican plantations, such as those of Trelawny Parish, where their proto-peasant culture-building was pronounced in slave villages and on provision grounds at the edges of plantations (Mintz 1989; Trouillot 1998; Besson 1995b, 1995d, 2002). Such creolization included the transformation of African unilineal descent groups into cognatic landholding lineages, traced through both women and men (Besson 2002; Mintz 1994, 330; and chapter 2). Such creole lineages, with their sacred burial grounds, consolidated and burgeoned into larger cognatic clans in the Jamaican maroon treaty towns and later in non-maroon free villages – linking generations of kin through time and space and maximizing, in the Caribbean context, these kin groups and their scarce land rights among descendants of chattel slaves (Besson 1984b, 1995b, 1995d, 2002, 2005, and chapters 2–10). Today, as we have seen, such creole clans, with their component lineages, family lands and cemeteries, form the core of Maroon Town at the maroon/non-maroon interface. Many of these clans are Meso-Creole, highlighting Caribbean miscegenation and creolization (chapters 8–9). The Afro-Scots McGhies are the most extensive of these Meso-Creole clans, with the largest landholdings. Their periodic family reunions, including the return of migrants for mortuary rituals, parallel the periodic resettlements and mortuary rites of the McGhie Maroons' sacred site of Congo Town/Highwindward/Me No Sen You No Come, nearby.

After Congo Town/Highwindward/Me No Sen You No Come was rediscovered in 1823, it was destroyed in 1824 by 'a Shooting Excursion on the Mountains near Dromilly Estate, in the Parish of Trelawny' (Mullin 1994, 58–61, 322 n87; see also Patterson 1973, 264). Combining the historical sources with my anthropological fieldwork, it seems likely that, after the destruction of the maroon settlement in 1823–24 (if not before), the McGhie Maroons migrated the few miles from Me No Sen You No Come to re-settle the former site of Trelawny Town (now Maroon Town including Flagstaff) in the aftermath of the colonial deportation of the Trelawny Maroons and the confiscation of their lands, possibly through an initial period of informal occupation or 'squatting'. It is also probable that the McGhie Maroons purchased former Trelawny Town lands when they were subdivided and sold by the colonial government after emancipation (chapter 7); a hypothesis reinforced by my fieldwork and by McGhie oral traditions (below).

Anthropological Fieldwork: The Afro-Scots McGhie Clan of Maroon Town

My anthropological fieldwork in and around Maroon Town from 1999 to 2009 revealed that, at the turn of the millennium, the Maroon Town McGhie clan traced its genealogy seven ascending generations (including the youngest living generation) to a Jonathan

McGhie who owned land in the mid-nineteenth century in the Flagstaff area of Maroon Town (Genealogy 8). Flagstaff (situated on the former core site of Trelawny Town) was just a few miles from the maroon village of Congo Town/Highwindward/Me No Sen You No Come, which had been settled by the McGhie Maroons, around the time of the Second Maroon War of 1795–96 and was disbanded by colonial troops in 1824. Jonathan McGhie is said by his elderly great-grandsons, whom I interviewed, to have had siblings (names unknown) and three sons: Robert (the eldest), Jonathan and Albert/'Natty' (the youngest) McGhie. These three sons (now deceased) were known to their elderly grandsons and grandnephews who helped me with my research.

These early McGhie ancestors in Maroon Town are said to have been of partial Scottish descent and to have had links with the parish of Trelawny. In light of the parallels between this oral tradition and the historical references to the slave-owning planters James, Robert and Jonathan McGhie (who were listed as owners of Greenside Estate in the Trelawny Parish records of 1799) and to the McGhie Maroons around the time of the Second Maroon War (and the related 'disturbance' of 1798 at Congo Town/Highwindward/Me No Sen You No Come), it is likely that Jonathan McGhie of Flagstaff and his sons were direct descendants of both the McGhie planter family and the mulatto McGhie Maroons. I, therefore, hereafter refer to Jonathan McGhie of Flagstaff as Jonathan II and to his sons, Jonathan and Robert, as Jonathan III and Robert II. The names Jonathan and Robert continue further down the generations. Albert also became a family name, so I refer to Jonathan II's son as Albert I (Genealogy 8).

Through interviews, including the collection of genealogies from numerous members of the McGhie clan, I traced hundreds of descendants of Jonathan McGhie II in and around Maroon Town, elsewhere in Jamaica and overseas (Genealogies 8–11). I also identified their family lands and cemeteries. The following subsections unravel some of these themes and include extracts from McGhie narratives. References to skin colour and the distinction between 'lawful' and 'bastard' children featured prominently in these narratives, being much more pronounced among slave master pickni Meso-Creoles in Maroon Town than in the Afro-Creole villages that I studied (Besson 2002, and chapters 3–5). I have omitted many of these references in the extracts that follow but they were recurring themes.

Jonathan McGhie II of Flagstaff and His Sons

One of the most knowledgeable McGhie oral historians whom I interviewed was the late Vincent McGhie (Genealogy 9), an elderly great-grandson of Jonathan II and a grandson of Robert II, who lived in Browns' Town[9] (between Flagstaff and Maroon Town Square). Vincent, a retired farmer and shopkeeper, was born in Browns' Town in 1908. He was aged 91 when I first interviewed him in 1999 and, by then, was the oldest person in Browns' Town. He was 95 years old when I talked with him again in the summer of 2003, shortly before his death later that year. On that occasion, he was being cared for and visited by members of the Rockhead clan (who claim descent from mulatto Maroons in the Second Maroon War and some of whose family land is opposite Vincent's house-yard [chapter 9]), and by a member of the Rowe clan from Accompong. Vincent's late wife (of the Peterkin clan, born in Browns' Town in 1915), whom I met in 1999, died in 2001 and is 'tombed' in their front yard (figure 10.1).

Vincent narrated that his great-grandfather, Jonathan McGhie II, had a big property[10] at Flagstaff (acquired in the mid-nineteenth century), that he had other land in Woodlands and Schaw Castle and that he had siblings and three sons (Genealogy 8). Vincent could not recall knowing his great-grandfather, Jonathan II, or his great-grandfather's siblings as he (Vincent) was 'very small'. However, Vincent remembered his grandfather, Robert II, very well and also his granduncles, Jonathan III and Albert I, who both had family land in Woodlands; Jonathan III also having land at Schaw Castle, which he inherited from Jonathan II. Some of this land had since been rented out or sold, but some remains among Jonathan II's descendants. For example, many McGhies (and other villagers in Maroon Town) told me that Jonathan III had lived on the family land at Woodlands and I found his tomb there in the family-land cemetery.

Jonathan II's son, Robert McGhie II, had also been well-known to some of the other older McGhies whom I interviewed, including his other elderly grandsons. Robert II is said (by his grandson Vincent) to have been born in Flagstaff around 1841 (17 years after the disbanding of the maroon village Me No Sen You No Come near Flagstaff in 1824 and three years after emancipation in 1838). His 'forefathers' are said to have been Scottish and Robert II is described by his descendants as light-skinned or 'clear' (perhaps a mulatto or a quadroon).

Figure 10.1. Vincent McGhie's house-yard at Browns' Town.

Vincent used to live with his paternal grandfather, Robert II, who died in 1938, aged 97. Robert II had '12-plus' acres of land, described by Vincent as an 'old ancestral home', at 'Corner', between Flagstaff/Browns' Town and Maroon Town Square, near Vincent's father's land (discussed later). Robert II was a farmer: first cultivating sugar cane that he sold to Hampden Estates. He also made sugar head (wet sugar fudge), which he sold at the Wakefield marketplace in Trelawny.[11] He then farmed bananas, which he sold to the (American) United Fruit Company's John's Hall banana depot near Kensington, for export. In those days, transport to the depot was by mule-cart. The United Fruit Company would then truck the bananas to the wharf in Montego Bay. Robert II's brothers, Jonathan III and Albert I, had also been farmers, as Vincent narrated:

> Yam ground, banana, plantain, Irish potato, and make sugar and sell it to the market, Trelawny at Wakefield. My grandfather and him brothers had [sugar] mill of their own, make sugar [head] Monday to Friday and sell it Saturday at Wakefield. Sometime six shillings, 15 shillings a tin and try and live off that. Then we did farming in banana and started to ship banana to Canada and England. And grew ginger in those days...Robert [II] rent land to people to help them and lent them money...All we Meggies [McGhies] tried to help, [we] was living a little better than plenty [other people].

Below, I trace further descendants of Jonathan McGhie II of Flagstaff through his three sons Robert II, Jonathan III and Albert I (Genealogies 9–11) and identify many of their family lands, some of which dominate Maroon Town Square as well as Woodlands, Browns' Town and Flagstaff.

Robert II's Lineage

I learned from various McGhies that Robert McGhie II (c.1841–1938) had seven children (now all deceased): Richard/'Dick' (the eldest), 'Tattee', William, Jacob, Robert III, Walter and Edna (the two youngest) (Genealogy 9). Richard was a cane farmer and also had a shop at Maroon Town Square (which was later sold) and a rum-bar in Montego Bay. He fathered 11 sons and daughters, some of whom migrated to the US, and many of his descendants are now overseas. Tattee migrated to the United States and never returned. William had been a migrant labourer to Cuba but returned to live as a farmer in Browns' Town. His many descendants (including some of his 13 daughters and sons) are scattered in Maroon Town, Montego Bay, Kingston, Bermuda, England and the US. Jacob had lived on his own land near Maroon Town Square and farmed land in Browns' Town and Flagstaff. He had six children (daughters and sons), all now deceased, who have left many descendants, some of whom live in Maroon Town. Robert III, who took over farming in Maroon Town from his father, Robert II, had six sons and daughters, five of whom were still alive and in Maroon Town, Montego Bay, and the United States. Walter (who married into Maroon Town's Harris clan) had a daughter and son. Edna had children too. Regarding these numerous children and transnational descendants of Robert II, I was given most information on the branches of his sons, William, Jacob and Robert III (Genealogy 9).

Genealogy 9. Partial Genealogy of the Descendants of Robert McGhie II

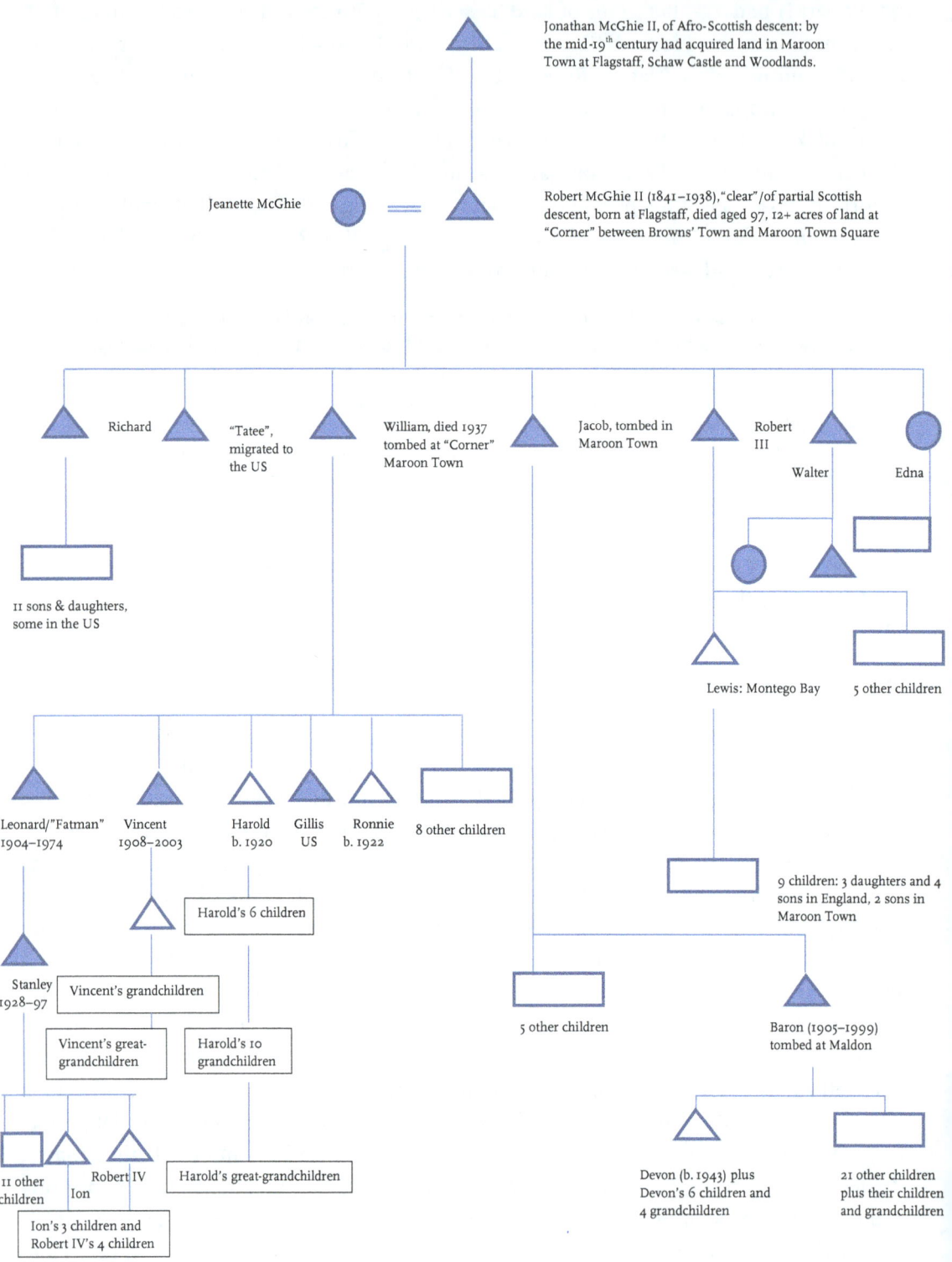

William's Branch

I was able to interview three of William's elderly sons: the above-mentioned Vincent McGhie (1908–2003), in Browns' Town, and Harold (born 1920) and Ronnie (born 1922) in Montego Bay. According to Vincent, William fathered eleven children (Ronnie added two more) and his many descendants include great-great-grandchildren. William is 'tombed' on his own land, 'Big Yard': five acres near 'Corner' (between Flagstaff/Browns' Town and Maroon Town Square), next to land owned by the Peterkin clan ('all farmers') into which Vincent (and other McGhies) married. I visited William's tomb. Vincent did not know the origin of this land and it may have been a part of the land of William's father, Robert II. William also had 'a lovely land here', 17 and a half acres at Browns' Town, origin unknown. In addition, he had '16 acres over the back' at Flagstaff, bought from his father-in-law, Joseph Waite. Vincent explained that, in 1929, the land at the government's Flagstaff barracks had been subdivided and sold.

William had migrated to Cuba to cut cane on sugar estates. Vincent remarked that many people from Maroon Town had established themselves (for example, as landholders) in this way: 'plenty a them start like this' – though William himself had some land before he migrated. William returned to Maroon Town where he died, in 1937, a year before his father Robert II.

Vincent himself had an acre of land at Browns' Town, given to him by his father, William. Vincent had built a 'wooden house' there ('no wall house here' except the 'old ancestral home' of his grandfather, Robert II, at Corner, now burnt down). Vincent used to have a grocery shop on the land where he lives (and was nicknamed 'Mr Pence'). He had also farmed 30 acres of bananas on William's property and on rented land. Like other Maroon Town villagers, Vincent explained that the banana industry was now dying out. However when I first met him in 1999, he was still farming bananas. For 12 years (1959–71), in addition to farming, Vincent used to transport market women and men to sell their produce at the Santa Cruz marketplace in St Elizabeth. He bought a car and sometimes had two. From 1959 to 1962, he also transported cane in his truck to Hampden Estates and bought/drew sleepers for/to the railway in Montego Bay, buying the sleepers from men who cut them in the woodland. In 1943, he had been a migrant farm labourer to the United States, reaping corn and potatoes but (unlike his father William), never sugar cane (the symbol of slavery): 'Never go to the cane farm. I was so lucky'. Vincent had one child, a son in Montego Bay, several grandchildren and great-grandchildren and belonged to the Mount Edmonson Methodist Church.

Of William's 11 children, whom Vincent identified, ten were still alive. In addition to Vincent, these included five sons (in Montego Bay, Bermuda and the United States) and four daughters (in Kingston, the USA and England). Vincent explained that they all 'come and go' between these locations and Maroon Town. Regarding these siblings and their father William's family land, Vincent explained that, 'We all live together – no fuss with any of us. Everybody out [who has migrated] can come and build, not cut up [the land is not divided], not selling – me Daddy's land', which has become family land. All these siblings have children, grandchildren and great-grandchildren who, like Vincent's descendants, are members of the transnational McGhie landholding clan. This Old Family, including William's large branch, has gained social mobility primarily through banana farming and/or return/circulatory migration. Providing transport for villagers in this mountainous community has also been a significant theme.

In 2004, shortly after Vincent's death, I met two more of William's sons, Harold and Ronnie, who lived in Montego Bay and learned more about William and his descendants. Harold (then aged 84) is Vincent's full sibling and Ronnie (aged 82, in 2004) is their paternal half-brother. Both were still alive in 2009, when I spoke with Harold again. Ronnie explained that his father, William, had 'two sets' of children: 'nine in, four out'. Ronnie (of the 'inside' set) showed me a photo of his father, William, and his wife (Ronnie's mother, of Maroon Town's Waite clan). William was very light-skinned and Ronnie referred to William's partial Scottish ancestry, explaining that he had visited Scotland two years previously, with his daughter from London, 'Because of the ancestry, always heard that the ancestry was from Scotland'.

Ronnie narrated that he had left Maroon Town at the age of 19 (around 1941), working in Panama for three years as a truck driver before returning to Jamaica and migrating again (around 1944) to the United States to work for 16 months on the Farm Work Scheme. He then returned to Jamaica, where he again worked as a truck driver until he took up a white-collar occupation in Montego Bay in 1952. By 2004, he was 'semi-retired' in a suburb of the city, but still visited his mother in Maroon Town. Like his half-brother Vincent, Ronnie had known his paternal grandfather, Robert II. He also recalled his paternal grandmother, Jeannette McGhie.

Harold provided further information on William's branch and the two preceding generations. Harold gave the fullest information on the children of his grandfather, Robert II, identifying a daughter and six sons (previously discussed). According to Harold, William's four 'outside' children were Vincent, Leonard/'Fatman' and Harold (full siblings) and Gillis, their half-brother, who died two years previously in the US. Like Vincent, Harold also knew his grandfather, Robert II, and his two brothers, Jonathan III, known as 'Woodland Jonny', and another brother whom Vincent had identified as Albert I, but who Harold called 'Natty' (Genealogy 8). The oldest of these brothers was Robert II, followed by Jonathan III then Albert I/Natty. They lived in Maroon Town but Albert I also lived at Tucker (between Maroon Town and Montego Bay). Woodland Jonny had several daughters and sons. Albert I/Natty had at least two sons.

Like Vincent, Harold was born (in 1920) in Browns' Town on their father William's land. Harold 'grew there' and from 1943 to 1945, during and after the Second World War, he travelled for Farm Work to the United States. In 1946, back in Jamaica, he worked renovating old buildings in Falmouth. He then took up banana farming on his father's land at Browns' Town and on more remote Crown Land. He then migrated again to the United States, returning to settle in Jamaica in 1954. In 1957, he left Maroon Town to live in Montego Bay, where he drove a taxi and a city bus until his retirement in 1975, when he bought a piece of land in the hills above Montego Bay. Harold has four sons and two daughters (scattered in the United States and Jamaica), ten grandchildren and some great-grandchildren.

According to Harold (like other McGhies), 'all the Meggies are related' and he had heard that 'Meggie [McGhie] is a Scottish name and they were on the plantations, that's how they come [to Jamaica]'. He continued his narrative by highlighting a link with 'fair-skinned' McGhie relatives in Trelawny, where the name Jonathan McGhie (IV and V) recurs again twice, who visited Maroon Town: 'They were family, as Meggies [McGhies]'.

Leonard's Segment

William's eldest child, Leonard (Vincent and Harold's brother and Ronnie's half-brother), was born in 1904 and died in 1974, aged 70. Known throughout Maroon Town as 'Fatman' (a nickname denoting success), he was an outstanding example of the entrepreneurship and social mobility that characterizes the McGhie clan – in Leonard's case by cultivating bananas and consolidating landholdings. Leonard, who was a Mount Edmonson Methodist, is buried in his house-yard at Flagstaff where he had farmed bananas on about 60 acres of land. The first time that I visited Leonard's yard, one of his great-grandsons showed me his vault. There are three other vaults there, those of Leonard's wife, their only son Stanley/'Baboo' (1928–97) and one of Stanley's children. Another of Stanley's children, Robert McGhie IV, lives with his family in Leonard's house. Robert IV follows in his grandfather's footsteps as a successful banana farmer, whose business includes selling ripe bananas to a tourist hotel in Montego Bay. I would meet Robert IV in 2009.

Meanwhile, one of Robert IV's brothers, Ion McGhie (in his 30s when I first interviewed him in 1999), a returned migrant from Canada who resides at Maroon Town Square, gave me more information about his grandfather, Leonard's segment (Genealogy 9). In contrast to Leonard's first cousin, the late Baron McGhie (1905–99, below) who became socially mobile partly through migration (and in contrast to Ion himself), Leonard never left Jamaica. Ion, in beginning his narrative, outlined how his grandfather, Leonard, had become a successful landholder and banana farmer in Maroon Town, partly through providing transport from this mountainous village, and a patron to those in the community less successful than himself:

> My grandfather worked very hard in his days. He was the only man who owned a Chevrolet [car] and a couple of Leyland trucks. He was a big guy. Respectable. People look up to him. Large landowner and farmer. And 'saviour' to the people. He helped people.

Before Ion was born, his late father, Stanley, drove Leonard's trucks: taking market women and men to the marketplaces in Montego Bay and Santa Cruz, and bananas to Montego Bay for export. Leonard's 60-plus acres of land included 50 acres of bought land at Flagstaff, Hines Mountain (near Flagstaff) and Ball Ground (where the barracks had been), nine acres at Browns' Town, three pieces in Montego Bay and a property at Maroon

Town Square with a large upstairs building (a residence and shop) where Ion now works and lives.

After driving Leonard's trucks, Stanley migrated many times to the United States, often returning to Maroon Town (where he died). Ion narrated that Stanley had 13 children ('eight sets'). His 12 living sons and daughters were residing in Maroon Town, the United States and England. Those who have migrated return home to visit.

Ion (who said he is 'looking forward' to this book), was born in 1965 at his granduncles' land in Browns' Town (where Vincent lived). Ion is a cabinet maker and works in the large shop at Maroon Town Square, having developed a pattern of circulatory migration between Maroon Town and Canada (where he renovates basements). He lives with his wife above the shop, has three children and had a computer by 1999. When I met him again (goat farming at Flagstaff) in 2009, he was still one of only a few people with a computer, in Maroon Town.

Ion explained that the land with the large upstairs building where he lives and works at Maroon Town Square is McGhie family land. One of his sisters also lives upstairs and works at the barber's shop below. Ion narrated that some of his grandfather, Leonard's lands 'hand down from generation to generation, all the way down'. This land is 'for nobody special [no particular individual]: for generation to generation, everybody have a lot of space' on Leonard's various landholdings; for example, at Flagstaff where Ion's brother, Robert IV, farms and lives.

In 2009, I finally found Robert IV – a busy banana farmer, aged 44 – near his home at Flagstaff. He generously stopped his farming to grant me an interview, gave me photographs (e.g., figure 10.2) and said he is looking forward to my account of the McGhie family tree. He was born near Santa Cruz but grew up at Flagstaff in 'an old house further down the road', 'just a couple of chains' from Dragoon Hole. Of his grandfather Leonard, Robert IV said: 'He couldn't read but he had *vision*, good common sense' and 'in his time' farmed about 60 acres of bananas which he used to export to England. At that time, Robert IV 'was around' as a child and developed 'a passion' for farming bananas. He later started his own banana farming for export on 18 acres of land.

Figure 10.2. Robert McGhie IV, Flagstaff. Courtesy of Robert McGhie IV.

In his narrative, Robert IV shrewdly assessed the impact of globalization and environmental disasters on the Jamaican banana industry and his own banana farming. About ten years previously, he was exporting bananas and this was 'thriving', West Ban was in control of the industry and one could make a living from it. But, as he explained, 'a couple of years after, banana took a nose-dive due to the export market and the local market can't take it and the price goes down and the import/input of fertilizer goes up'. Then around 2007 Moko disease destroyed six acres of his bananas and, in 2008, Hurricane Gustav further damaged the crop, so he now only farms about ten acres and no one is exporting bananas. Instead, he supplies ripe bananas two to three times a week to a Sandals Hotel in Montego Bay. He also sells to the Maroon Town banana chip factory. In 2009, he observed: 'with the price, can hardly keep things floating but this year the European Market and the [Jamaican] government gives us a good imput'.

Robert IV has four children. A son and a daughter work in St James. Another son and daughter are in the US: the daughter is at school and the son (named Leonard after his great-grandfather) is 'a computer genius' at College.

Jacob's Branch and Baron's Segment

While Leonard/'Fatman' McGhie (Robert II's grandson through William) achieved his success mainly through banana farming, Leonard's first cousin, the late Baron McGhie (Robert II's grandson through Jacob), had combined banana farming with migrant labour to Cuba. Both Leonard (1904–74) and Baron (1905–99) achieved community-wide reputations as Maroon Town's largest landholders. In addition to the narrative of elderly Vincent (Leonard's brother), I was given information on Baron and his descendants by his son, Devon and widow, Lola (of the Reid clan). Devon also provided information on Baron's father, Jacob (Genealogy 9).

Devon was born in Maroon Town in 1943 and was 56 when I interviewed him in his extensive hillside yard, near Maroon Town Square in 1999, a week after his father, Baron's death. Devon narrated that his grandfather, Jacob, had lived in Maroon Town in an 'old family house' on this same land where Devon now lives, between the Square and Calder Hill (the Reids' property, which stretches to Vaughansfield). Jacob is buried on this land where Devon resides, which was initially eight acres (five acres had since been donated by Baron for a Health Centre) and adjoined other land that Jacob owned stretching to the banana boxing station at Calder Hill. Both Vincent and Devon thought that Jacob purchased this land. Jacob's wife was Honour Peterkin (Baron's 'stepmother'), of the 'light-coloured' Peterkin clan, who is buried on the Peterkins' property in Maldon. Jacob (who also had children with Annie Anderson) had two daughters and four sons, some of whom went to the US and England. He left land to his children and Baron inherited the land where Devon now lived.

Devon outlined Baron's life history. Born in 1905 at Maldon, Baron went to Cuba, at the age of 13, with his mother, around 1918, where he later worked as a plumber and blacksmith. Baron then returned to Maroon Town 'pretty young'. He saved to buy land by working on the Peterkins' land and by 'rearing cow and one goat'. He sold the livestock and made his first land purchase, cheap. He planted yams and cane, boiled sugar and sold wet sugar in Adelphi and Wakefield markets, travelling by donkey or mule. He was soon able to supply cane to Hampden Estates. Baron 'then plants bananas and exports to England, and rears pigs and cows. After certain years, sickness, and lived off his earnings and children'.

Devon narrated that Baron had 22 children, including 'two lawful sets', and described his own status as Baron's 'lawful heir, first wife's [only] son'. Baron's various children, who now have children and grandchildren, are scattered throughout Maroon Town, elsewhere in Jamaica, Cuba, the United States, Canada and England. Baron had visited his children overseas several times and when he fell ill and died (aged 94), many of his children and descendants returned to Maroon Town for his Revival-Baptist mortuary rituals. Devon had wanted him buried in his (Devon's) front yard but Baron had chosen the Maldon Baptist Church cemetery, where he was interred in a vault near the church. I met some of his relatives at the Maldon Baptist Church, preparing the vault.

In 2002, I learned more about Baron's mortuary rituals when I met his widow, Lola McGhie, through her uncle, Mortimer Reid. At her shop, Lola narrated that as well as the Baptist funeral, there had been a Revival 'set-up', at Baron's home in Maldon the night before the burial.[12] In addition, a year after Baron's funeral, about 50 of his children and descendants, including those from Canada, the United States and England, had re-gathered in Maroon Town for his memorial. This included a reception at the Maldon Baptist Church Hall, where an organ was donated in his honour, to the church.

By the time of Baron's death in 1999, he had accumulated about 34 acres of land in various parts of Maroon Town. Most of his land (except the five acres donated for the Health Centre) was passed on to his children and descendants. There were, however, in the distribution of the land, variations on the theme of family-land transmission: drawing on the principles of legal marriage and 'lawful' children as well as the distinction among various 'sets' of offspring.

Devon himself, who farms, now 'controls 13 squares [square chains]' of Baron's land, between Maroon Town Square and Calder Hill. One of Baron's former spouses lives next door to Devon with some of Baron's other children and grandchildren. Devon has 'two sets' of children – a daughter and five sons (one of whom is buried in his yard) – and four grandchildren, some of whom also belong to the overlapping Hines, Clarke and Walker clans.

Robert III's Branch

In 2004, I met Lewis McGhie, a son of Robert III (brother of William and Jacob), in Montego Bay, and spoke with him again in 2009. Early in his narrative, Lewis 'corrected' the widespread creolized pronunciation of his paternal clan's surname from 'Meggie' to 'McGhie' and said that one of his ancestors was 'a white man from Scotland'.

Lewis explained that he was born in Browns' Town and 'is to call Vincent cousin, two brothers' children'. He is, therefore, a first cousin to Vincent, Leonard ('Fatman'), Harold and Ronnie and also to Baron McGhie. Like these cousins, Lewis knew his grandfather, Robert McGhie II, and narrated a similar account to Vincent's of Robert II as a sugar manufacturer at 'Corner', between Flagstaff and Maroon Town Square. According to Lewis, Robert II:

> ...build a small sugar factory there just up the hill from Maroon Town Square, first right at Corner, on the way to Flagstaff. Had a factory there, make quite a lot of sugar. That was their business.

Lewis's father, Robert III, was one of the younger of Robert II's seven children (Genealogy 9). Robert III had six children, five of whom were alive in 2004. Lewis is the eldest, two of his siblings are in Maroon Town and two are in the US.

In 1955, Lewis had migrated from Maroon Town to England, where he first worked in London driving buses and on the Underground. He then worked as a truck driver in London and Cardiff. Next, he obtained employment in Manchester where he also bought old houses for renovation, rental and sale. He then drove coaches with Manchester Transport, all over Europe, for 14 years. However, he became tired of the cold, damp climate, so in 1987 he built a house in Montego Bay and settled there in 1992. There, he joined Jamaica Co-operative Automobile and Limousine Tours (JCAL) in the tourism industry and 'picks up jobs' with his mini-bus – for example, at the Ritz-Carlton (now Hyatt Ziva/Zilara) Hotel. Like his first cousins, Fatman and Vincent, and his uncle, Jacob, Lewis married into the Peterkin clan. Lewis and his wife have nine children, three daughters and six sons, who belong to both the McGhie and Peterkin clans. Two of the sons reside in Maroon Town. The other seven children are in England.

In addition to the numerous descendants of Robert II over five descending generations, are the parallel lineages of his two younger brothers: Jonathan III and Albert I/'Natty', who had lived at Woodlands and Tucker (Genealogies 8, 10 and 11). I look next at the lineage of Jonathan III (Genealogy 10).

Jonathan III's Lineage

Several members of the McGhie clan, as well as elderly Maroon Town villagers such as Ade (Walker) Hall (born 1903) and Mortimer Reid (born 1910), had known Jonathan McGhie III who was nicknamed 'Woodland Jonny'. Jonathan III was much older than these elderly villagers; as Mortimer put it, 'I born and see him'. I saw Jonathan III's tomb and that of his wife, Margaret (mother of 12 of his children), and those of some of his children and grandchildren in one of the McGhie family-land cemeteries at Woodlands, which is situated at the side of a steep road down a mountainside from Maroon Town Square.

I was told that Jonathan III had 13 children, including the late Albert II ('Bertie', the youngest), who themselves had children and other descendants. Jonathan III's other children included his sons, Henry (who is buried on his own land at Vaughansfield), George, Joseph, Rufus and Shandy, and daughters, Isobel, Rowena, Mary, Amy and Sue.

Genealogy 10. Partial Genealogy of the Descendants of Jonathan McGhie III

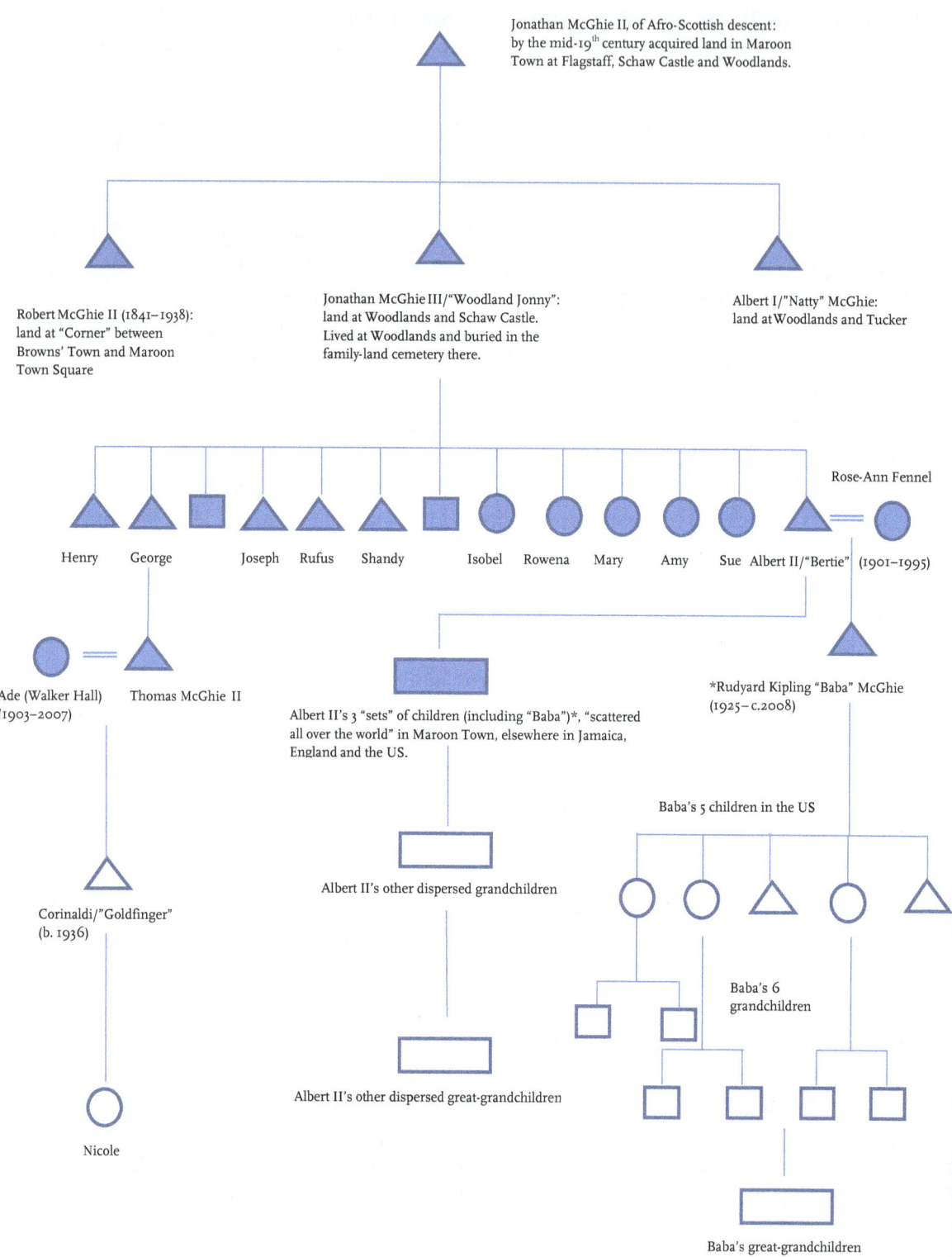

According to Ade Hall (who died in 2007, aged 103), George was the father of Thomas McGhie II and the grandfather of her son, Corinaldi McGhie. Ade narrated that Thomas, whom she described as 'a brown man', 'born and grow at Maroon Town' and then migrated to Portland. Ade explained that Thomas was 'family' to Baron and Vincent. Vincent's brother, Harold, also knew Thomas, who had returned from Portland to Maroon Town to stay with Harold's grandfather, Robert II (Thomas's granduncle) at Corner. Harold described Thomas as 'a good singer, an Adventist' (a musical talent that was passed on to his son, Corinaldi).[13]

In 2003, I met Corinaldi, nicknamed 'Goldfinger', and his daughter, Nicole, in Montego Bay and kept in touch with him up to 2011, by which time he was 75. Goldfinger narrated that he grew up in Portland, Maroon Town and Kingston. He now lived in Montego Bay where he works as a mini-bus driver for tourists. He is also a Baptist and disk jockey – composing, singing and recording Revivalist songs in a calypsonian style (he gave me a CD), richly elaborated with references to social issues such as race, ethnicity, migration and tourism. Through his mother Ade, Goldfinger traces his ancestry four ascending generations to Betsy Currie (said to be 'Campong Nanny, chapter 9), whom he stated was 'sister to Cudjoe and Quaco'. He, therefore, claimed that the Accompong Maroons are 'my relatives'. However, on his father's side, Goldfinger claims Afro-Scots McGhie descent.

Jonathan III's youngest child, Albert II (whose widow I interviewed), who was a banana farmer, had remained in Woodlands until his death, on a part of the family land there. This land has the house-yard and cemetery where Jonathan III is buried. Albert II was described by the late Mortimer Reid as 'a front line citizen' of Maroon Town, who had recently died in his 90s. Albert II's widow confirmed that he was born in 1901 and died, aged 94, in 1995. I was told that Albert II, who is buried in the Woodlands family-land cemetery, had 'three sets of children' that are 'scattered all over the world'. I spoke with two of their mothers. These children (daughters and sons), who live in Maroon Town, elsewhere in Jamaica, England and the United States have children and other descendants too.

In 2006, I met Albert II's son, Rudyard Kipling ('Baba') McGhie, who had recently returned to Maroon Town after migrations to the United States, England and Canada. Baba was born in Maldon around 1925 and was 81 years old when I interviewed him. As mentioned in chapter 8 (where I include Baba's narrative of his mother's Afro-Irish Fennel Family and his paternal grandmother's Meso-Creole Anderson clan), Baba explained that he was the son of the late Albert 'Bertie' McGhie of Woodlands and Rose-Ann Fennel. He also narrated that 'the McGhies came from Scotland, some spell it "McGhie" and some spell it "McGhee", came way back, in slave days'.

Baba could not trace his McGhie ancestry any further back than his paternal grandfather, Jonathan III, who died before Baba was born. However, Baba had some information from his father on his (Baba's) grandfather, Jonathan's siblings: 'Two different set. One from Woodland [Albert I], one from Flagstaff [Robert II]. Me father said is his first cousin up there [Flagstaff]. But they are related, as Jacob [was] from Flagstaff.' He also recalled Jacob's brother, William, these being sons of Robert II, and knew their children (including

Genealogy 11. Partial Genealogy of the Descendants of Albert McGhie I

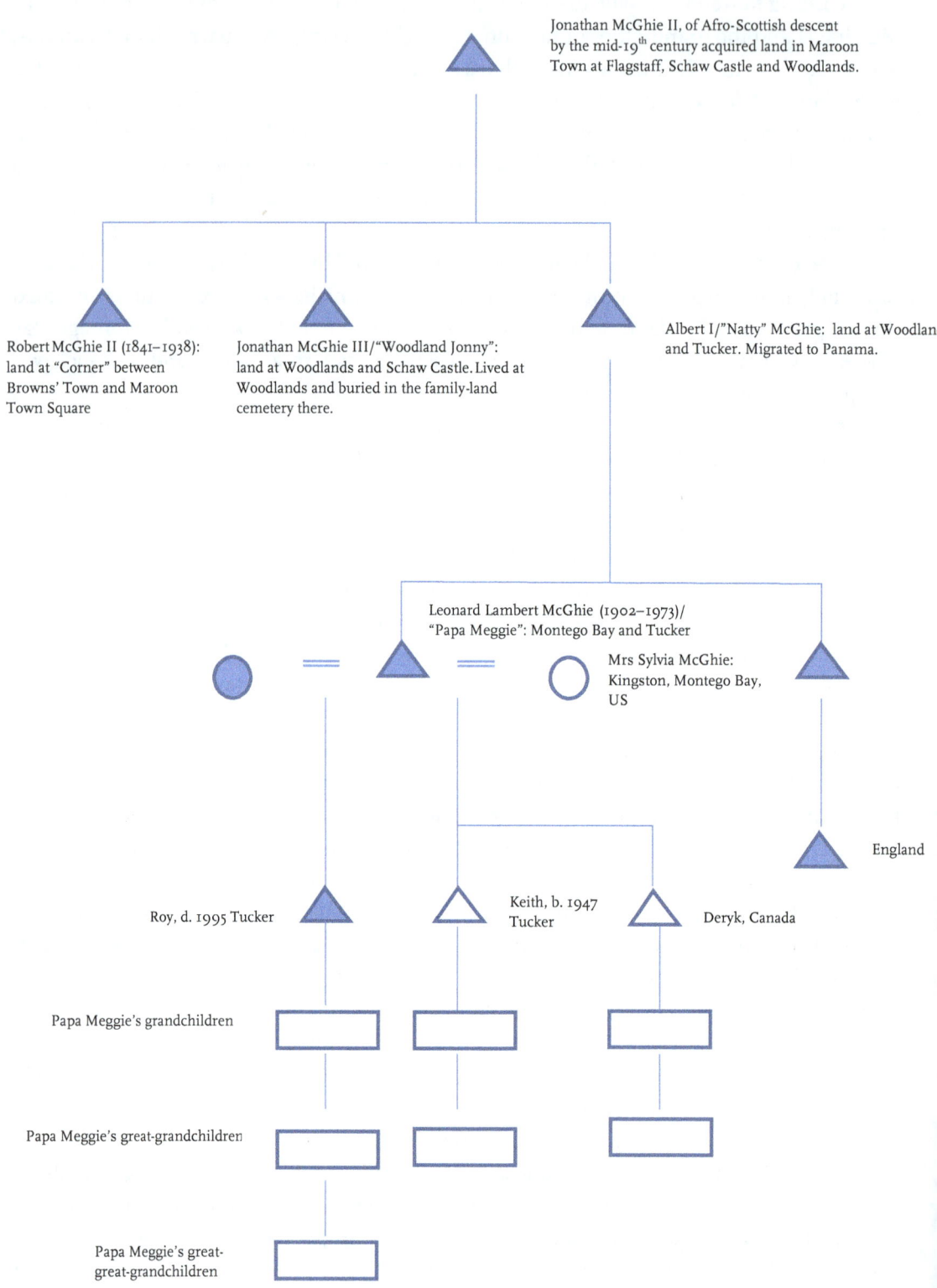

Leonard/Fatman, Vincent, Ronnie and Harold) as his 'second cousins'.

Baba had inherited land rights from his father, Albert II, in Woodlands but was living in Vaughansfield. He had five children, all in the United States, six grandchildren and also great-grandchildren.

Albert I's Lineage and Leonard Lambert's Branch

While several McGhies spoke of the ancestral brothers, 'Woodland Jonny' (Jonathan III) and Robert II (sons of Jonathan II), their brother, Albert I, seems a more shadowy figure. Nevertheless, a third brother (said to be the youngest of Jonathan II's sons) was remembered by four of his grandnephews: Robert II's grandsons Vincent, Harold and Lewis and by Jonathan III's grandson Baba McGhie. Vincent (1908–2003), the oldest man in Browns' Town, said this granduncle was named Albert and lived at Woodlands. Baba also referred to this granduncle as living at Woodlands. Harold recalls this granduncle as nicknamed 'Natty', as living at Tucker and as having at least two sons and also a grandson in England. Vincent, likewise, indicated that Albert I had at least two sons. Lewis said this granduncle migrated to Panama and never returned.

Vincent narrated that Albert I's eldest son was the legendary 'Papa' McGhie, whom I subsequently learned was Leonard Lambert McGhie (1902–73) who was born in Montego Bay. According to several sources, Leonard Lambert had a mechanic's workshop – first in downtown Montego Bay and then on land that he bought at Tucker. Through two spouses he had three sons. The eldest (Roy) lived near Tucker and died in 1995, leaving children, grandchildren and great-grandchildren. Leonard's second son Keith (born in 1947), whom I interviewed, continues his father's work at the mechanic's yard at Tucker. Leonard's youngest son Deryk lives in Canada. Both these younger sons have children and grandchildren (Genealogy 11). I return to the oral traditions surrounding Papa McGhie later in this chapter.

The McGhie Genealogy

The genealogy of the transnational McGhie clan of Maroon Town is undoubtedly even wider than the descendants of Jonathan II (the father of Robert II, Jonathan III and Albert I) identified through my fieldwork; for Vincent's narrative states that his great-grandfather, Jonathan II, had siblings – who would have produced generations of descendants. Many of the McGhie clan are scattered elsewhere in St James and Jamaica or live overseas. The branch of Jonathan II alone, traced through both women and men, now numbers hundreds of descendants. As seen above, my research reveals that many of these individuals, and the Old Family itself, have played a central role in the transformation of the historic maroon site of Trelawny Town to Maroon Town.

Reflections by the McGhie Generations

Those McGhies whom I met did not claim maroon ancestry but rather stressed their partial Scottish origins from the McGhie planters and their mixed Afro-Scots descent.

However, as explored above, my research strongly suggests that the McGhie clan of Maroon Town is descended not only from the McGhie slave-owning planter family of Greenside Estate in Trelawny but also from the mulatto McGhie Maroons. These Maroons included the '1798 generation' who resettled Congo Town in the south-western Cockpits of Trelawny Parish, a few miles from Trelawny Town (now Flagstaff/Maroon Town) in St James, and renamed it Highwindward, "'the place of greatest safety'" and later creolized its name to Me No Sen You No Come (Mullin 1994, 58–59).

Nevertheless, although the links between the McGhie Maroons and the Maroon Town McGhies indicated by my research do not feature in the oral traditions of the McGhies whom I met, not only is the theme of mulatto ancestry prominent in their narratives but also the various McGhie generations whom I interviewed contributed a range of reflections on marronage and Maroon Town, some of which are consistent with the links I have made. In this section, I present extracts from some of these narratives.

Reflections by McGhie Elders

The late Vincent McGhie (1908–2003, the oldest man in Browns' Town), reflected on Maroon Town's name and history. His narratives referred to marronage from the parish of Trelawny (where the McGhie planter family lived and the McGhie Maroons originated), as well as to events and names of places from the Second Maroon War (the historical context of the McGhie Maroons). Vincent also referred to the 'capturing' by Maroons, after the Second Maroon War, of former Trelawny Town land (which had been confiscated by the colonial state) at Flagstaff, and the resettlement of Trelawny Town as Maroon Town through the subdivision and sale of Trelawny Maroon lands. This is significant, for (as previously discussed) it is likely that the McGhie Maroons migrated the few miles from Me No Sen You No Come, after c. 1824, to resettle the former site of Trelawny Town, through a combination of squatting and land purchase – paralleling the historic resettlements through squatting of the sacred site of Congo Town/Highwindward/Me No Sen You No Come. In addition, Vincent had narrated that his great-grandfather, Jonathan II, had extensive lands at Flagstaff (which had been the core site of Trelawny Town) in the mid-nineteenth century.

However, in addition to these similarities with my historical-anthropological research, Vincent's narratives included a partly mythical account of 'Campong Nanny and conflated elements of the First and Second Maroon Wars,[14] recurring themes in many Maroon Town oral traditions which symbolically re-order the ruptures of slavery and marronage (chapters 8–9). Here is an extract of Vincent's narratives from 1999:

> JB: *What is the reason for the name Maroon Town?*
>
> VM: Because the Maroons was here...The Maroons fight all around. The battle [in the Second Maroon War] win at Waterloo. The white soldiers win it. Was government land – cut up to poor people now, buy it. Battle of Waterloo. A river and a big cave, that's where the maroon soldiers buried and they call that place 'Distress' and a whole heap of red flowers grow there [symbolizing the blood of warriors who fell in the War].

Dragoon Hole round the other road. The black soldiers ... used to dig out the dirt and hide underneath. The lady them called Nanny was in Trelawny. When him running [she ran] from battle him gallop through the woodland day and night, because they were after her to kill her, until him land up in Accompong Town in St Elizabeth. Call him 'Campong Nanny. A woman.

In 2003, Vincent (by then aged 95) volunteered the following narrative which has similarities with some of his earlier themes:

When the war over between the white man [planters] and the black man [the Trelawny Maroons], at Waterloo, Battle of Waterloo, the white and the black meet together at Waterloo, near Silver Grove, that's where the war end. And the citizens around took up water from a spring at a rock and that was the place the war over. When the war over, the black them capture the place and say they is the owner of Maroon Town and they took Flagstaff as their own and they settle there.

There are also some significant parallels between Vincent's accounts and narratives that I collected from elderly Melvin Pearson (chapter 8). Like Vincent, Melvin referred to marronage from the parish of Trelawny, specifically via the Green Park slave plantation – which adjoined the McGhies' Greenside Estate (Lovejoy, Shepherd and Trotman 2003, 25; and map 11). Moreover, Melvin outlined a specific route taken by the Maroons (the McGhie Maroons?) from Trelawny Parish, through Green Park and Wakefield, which is near Dromilly Estate, the base for the colonial routing of the McGhie Maroon settlement of Me No Sen You No Come in 1824 (see Patterson 1973, 264; and map 4): 'they *come through* Green Park [from neighbouring Greenside?], Wakesfield and Dundee, and up Long Hill and a shortcut to Flagstaff' (my emphasis and queries). Like Vincent, Melvin also referred to Waterloo ('a property near Flagstaff'), a place with a spring coming out of a rock where Maroons gathered to drink after the war was over. In addition, Melvin's narrative made references to mulatto 'slave master' pickni'.

There are also parallels between Vincent and Melvin's accounts on the one hand and the Rockhead clan's oral tradition on the other, which refers to marronage by mulattos from a Trelawny slave plantation (Content) owned by the Scottish Stirling Family (who also owned Hampden, near Greenside), into the Cockpits, to support the Second Maroon War (chapter 9). It is possible that the Felsenkopf/Rockhead runaways joined the McGhie Maroons at Congo Town, which was directly inland from the Greenside, Green Park and Hampden plantations. Reinforcing this possibility is the fact that some of the Rockheads' family land is directly opposite a part of the McGhie family lands in Browns' Town and that both clans also had family land at Flagstaff.

Vincent's brother, Harold, likewise, narrated his view of the Maroons – including reference to Nanny and to some of the sacred sites of the Cockpit Country landscape associated with the maroon wars, such as Accompong and Flagstaff, and to Maroon Town:

The Maroons, as far as I gather, they have one them call Nanny. They have Dragoon Hole, when you go up to Flagstaff and going to Georges Valley, where they [the colonial troops] capture one of the Maroons, don't know if it's Nanny. They have [there is] a burial ground on the main [road] before you go up to Flagstaff Square. They had a playground, we call it 'Ball Ground' now where they play cricket and so. They have a tank where they do swimming. And a hill, they call 'Gun Hill', always had a gun up there, the Maroons, and you can stan' on the top and see the lights of Falmouth. That's right beside the Square at Flagstaff.

They don't have any Maroons in Maroon Town now. But Maroons in Accompong Town, in St Elizabeth. When the Maroon War in the eighteenth or seventeenth century was on, some of them [Maroons] had to flee and went to Accompong. They claims a portion of land up there now and [the colonists] have to give them. Some [Maroons] were also fighting in Portland.

When I asked Harold how the land at Maroon Town had been acquired, he referred to the subdivision of the land of the government barracks at Flagstaff in the early twentieth century:

In the early 1920s, or after that, government cut up that land in lots. Call that Flagstaff area 'Maroon Town Barracks', place where they had hospital and so on. Some get five acres, some ten acres, some three acres – depending on what they could manage.

Reflections by Younger McGhies

In the next descending generation of the McGhie clan, Devon (aged 56, when I first met him in 1999), reiterated the Afro-Scots theme of McGhie 'slave master' pickni' descent:

I am not a Maroon: [I am] a mix between the white and the black of African descent. The foreparents of my father [Baron McGhie] was from Scotland – Meggies [McGhies], in slavery. My father was high-colour brown [light brown], like you [the author, JB]. My mother was darker.

Devon situated the acquisition of lands in Maroon Town by the McGhies and other Old Families, and the transmission of such lands as family lands, within the wider context of Jamaican post-slavery peasantization:

After the Buckie-Master [*buckra*/white slave master] sell out [land] to the slaves. After the people [slaves, including mulattos] rebel, say they want their land. That's how people got the land at Maroon Town and elsewhere in Jamaica. A lot of it [the Maroon Town land] is handed down from the foreparents over many years [family land]. Some after was bought and sold, and rented, but most lands are handed down.

Devon's narrative, therefore, situates the transformation from Trelawny Town to Maroon Town by Meso-Creoles in relation to the post-emancipation land market and related free village movement (around 1838–60, see chapters 2 and 7). This coincides with the historical period that my research indicates was the context in which the mulatto McGhie Maroons consolidated their acquisition of former Trelawny Town land and with the desertion of the Flagstaff Barracks around the 1850s.

While Devon does not claim maroon ancestry, he has a strong awareness of the history of slave rebellion in the area, including the Trelawny Maroon wars and the 1831 slave rebellion at Kensington. Devon also narrated that, when he was younger, he participated in the January 6 Accompong maroon celebrations.

In the generation below Devon's, Ion McGhie, reflecting on the name Maroon Town, remarked that, 'the English and the Maroons fight here and the English bury in Flagstaff'.[15] However, when I asked him whether there were any Maroons in Maroon Town today, he answered, 'I don't think so. Most a the Maroons in 'Campong Town [Accompong]. The people here migrate. Come here.'

Even children in the McGhie clan have some awareness of the history of marronage. For example, in 1999, one young McGhie, aged 15, narrated a story of Nanny the Maroon who 'fought'. Another, aged 12, asserted an association between Maroon Town and Maroons. Both were granddaughters, but in different lines, of Baron McGhie.

The transnational McGhie clan of Maroon Town has perhaps yet to discover their likely links to the McGhie Maroons, with whom they share a remarkable talent for shaping their own history. Meanwhile, however, oral traditions of marronage are being passed down the McGhie generations. Moreover, in 2003, I would discover, from various sources beyond Maroon Town, that the legendary 'Papa' McGhie (Leonard Lambert McGhie, 1902–73), who was older than all of the McGhies and other Maroon Town villagers whom I interviewed, *had* asserted maroon descent when he was in the plantation lowlands of St James and Trelawny; an assertion that reinforces my research linking the McGhie Maroons and the Maroon Town McGhies.

The Oral Tradition of 'Papa' McGhie

When I began my fieldwork in Maroon Town, I was unaware that the McGhies were its central clan. On my first visit (in 1999), I stopped at Maroon Town Square to ask directions to Vaughansfield and a man (whom I would subsequently get to know) helpfully came to the car and introduced himself as Devon 'Meggie'. Immediately I recalled the many times in my childhood (in the 1940s–'50s), in the lowlands of St James and Trelawny, that my late father had told me about his friend 'Meggie' – the dark-skinned 'genius' who had a mechanic's workshop in Montego Bay and who (in 1939) built a seaplane that successfully ran out to sea but 'wouldn't lift'. I was often told this story, especially when I walked with my father, on summer holidays, along the Montego Bay sea wall overlooking the bay where the seaplane had failed to take off, or when I was the only member of the family who would go out with him in his little fishing boat that wouldn't float.

My father's friendship with 'Meggie' cross-cut colour and class. My father Ken McFarlane (1910–86), born in Montego Bay, was a fair-skinned planter and lawyer (Besson 2002, xxv–xxvi). In his schooldays (at Munro College in St Elizabeth), he had been a boxer and footballer, interests he continued as a young solicitor in the 1930s, in Montego Bay, before moving to Trelawny where he became a planter as well. It was my father's sporting interests that were the basis of his friendship with 'Meggie', who was his regular companion for weight-lifting at the Montego Bay gym.

So when, decades later, I met Devon 'Meggie' at Maroon Town Square, I asked him whether he was related to my father's friend and he said that he was. My mother, Margaret ('Meggie') McFarlane (1914–2004), who on that occasion was with me, pointed out to me that in Jamaica the surname 'Meggie' is a creolized pronunciation of the Scottish 'McGhie'. I then realized that my father and his friend had called each other by their surnames, McFarlane and McGhie, with both of them using the creolized 'Meggie'. I would later learn through my research that my father's friend was Leonard Lambert McGhie (1902–73), who in his older years was nicknamed 'Papa Meggie' or 'Pappy Meg'.

As my fieldwork in Maroon Town progressed and I kept meeting more and more 'Meggies' (McGhies), I often asked them whether they had known my father's friend. Many of the older ones replied that they had and several younger ones said they had heard of him – generally in relation to the seaplane. All those McGhies who knew or had heard of him said they were related to him.[16]

For example, when I first met elderly Vincent McGhie (born 1908, the oldest man in Browns' Town), he said he not only knew my father's friend but also that he (Vincent) was 'same Family as Papa Meggie'. On another occasion, Vincent told me (as mentioned above) that Papa was the eldest son of Albert I (Genealogy 11), the youngest brother of Vincent's grandfather Robert II (who was said to be light-skinned or 'clear'), adding of Papa 'but he was dark'. Vincent (who also told me he had known my father 'through business') elaborated his account of Papa – whom, he said, had been unable to obtain parts for the seaplane that he built due to his dark skin (a view that Papa's former apprentice would later reiterate):

> He built a plane and was trying to buy parts [in Kingston] to lift it, but because he was a black man they [the white elite in Kingston] refuse and *turn* him down…He had the experience [to build the seaplane] and was the first Jamaican to build a plane. But because he was a dark man, the white man wouldn't sell him the parts [needed to make the plane 'lift']. It did the run but wouldn't lift.

Likewise, two generations below Vincent, Ion McGhie at Maroon Town Square said he had heard of 'Pappy Meg' who 'had built the seaplane that wouldn't lift'. At Ion's workshop, another villager, Mr Moffat (born in 1948 at Flagstaff, chapter 9), contributed his memories of Papa whom he had known in his childhood and who he said was related to the Maroon Town McGhies:

> I knew Papa Meggie. I was a little boy when he was around. He used to work on my father's truck in MoBay, that's how I know him. Papa – same Meggie [McGhie], same line of family. Baron, Fatman, Pappy Meg, Mr Pence [Vincent], Jarman [Harold] McGhie one Family – like brothers' kids, same generation. Pappy Meg was the first man from this area of Jamaica to engineer a plane but it didn't fly.

Vincent's younger brother, Harold (born 1920) told me that he too had known 'Pappy Meg', whose 'name was Leonard, like my brother [Fatman]' and Pappy's brother, Eustace St Vincent McGhie, who spent most of the time at sea. According to Harold, these two brothers were from Montego Bay and, although he did not know the exact connection, he knew these brothers were related to the Maroon Town McGhies.

Vincent and Harold's first cousin, Lewis, in Montego Bay had likewise known 'Papa Meggie as cousin, second cousin, my father and his father were cousins as well'. Lewis (who strongly resembles Papa's photograph that I would see later and who said the likeness is often remarked on), then qualified this statement in light of the fact that he was much younger than Leonard Lambert: 'But as Papa was doing his [mechanic's] business here when I was a boy at school, I could be second line of cousin', in other words, a first cousin once removed. In 2009, I asked Lewis again about his relationship to Papa and he restated the relationship, adding that Papa's father was the brother of his (Lewis's) grandfather, Robert II, and that this granduncle was either Jonathan III of Woodlands or Albert I of Somerton/Tucker (consistent with Vincent's account).

In Montego Bay also, Goldfinger McGhie (born 1936) explained that, 'I am to call Papa Meggie's father granduncle'. He added (as others had told me), that his paternal McGhie Family is the only McGhie clan of Afro-Scots descent in Jamaica and 'they all spring from Maroon Town'. Likewise, in Maroon Town, the late Baba McGhie (born 1926), said, 'Pappy Meg' was a relative, that 'he had the biggest mechanic shop in MoBay' and that, 'Pappy Meg mek airplane you know! I never see it but everybody tell me. The propeller [is on display] in Mazouca's shop in the window beside the [Montego Bay] courthouse'.

In the course of contacting Papa's son, Keith, at Tucker through Goldfinger in 2003, I was first taken to meet Papa's former apprentice, Will McKenzie, in his mechanic's yard on the outskirts of Montego Bay. On the way there, Goldfinger told me that Will (born 1932) who had been taught his trade by 'Papa Meggie', had worked and lived with him, and would give me 'solid information' about my father's friend that would also help my research. As we drove up the rocky road to Will's yard, Goldfinger narrated his own memories of Papa – focusing on his strength and physique as a bodybuilder and his talent as a musician, in addition to his mechanical skill:

> He [Papa Meggie] was six feet tall and one of the strongest men, even shortly before his death [aged 71]. He was a quiet man, no talk much, him hand them [his arms] longer than a normal person's. And if someone trouble him, he fling them so! Papa was one of the most skilful engineers, and self-taught. And a very good musician, saxophone and drum. The engine [of the seaplane he built] wasn't fast enough to gather momentum, needed more thrust. Later he used to fly a Cessna aircraft and flew to Kingston. My grandfather (from Maroon Town) was Papa's father brother. I called Papa's father 'granduncle'.

After we arrived at Will's workshop, Will did indeed provide 'solid information' about his late mentor – including Papa's initials and full name ('L.L. McGhie, Leonard Lambert'), an account of his mechanical genius within the context of the Jamaican colour-class system and of his physical strength and musical ability, as well as the illuminating observation that Papa claimed to be a Maroon from Maroon Town:

> He [Papa Meggie] was a genius. Worked on anything mechanical and electrical. They wouldn't sell him the right parts [to lift the seaplane] because he was a negro. *Papa Meg was a Maroon from Maroon Town.* And he had a saxophone in a band, played at Holy Trinity Episcopalian Church in MoBay. Everybody said Mr Meggie couldn't read. But he had the books [catalogues] upstairs and could say how next year's cars would be built. He owned a plane before he die. Papa was strong. He had his own weights [for bodybuilding] (my emphasis).

I double-checked with Will, the unexpected information that Papa had claimed maroon ancestry. Will, who told me that he had worked and lived with him for around 17 years, assured me that Papa had indeed said he was a Maroon (and reiterated in 2007 that he was from Maroon Town). Goldfinger reinforced this assertion of maroon ancestry by commenting: 'Papa looked like a Maroon, dark, flat nose, straight hair'. I would later see that this description (which highlighted both Papa's Afro-Creole phenotype and Meso-Creole descent) fitted Papa's photograph. Continuing his own narrative of Papa, Goldfinger observed that: 'Nobody teach him to fly plane [the Cessna]. Licence to fly plane. Flew it to Kingston and right around the island. And when it need repair, he'd fix it himself.'

Will narrated that he had worked with Papa at his first workshop in downtown Montego Bay, that they had resided together in Montego Bay and that Papa later moved his residence and workshop to land that he bought at Tucker. This is where I found Papa's second son, Keith, whom Goldfinger described as 'one of the most remarkable drivers in Montego Bay and six feet tall' like his father.

Keith (born in 1947 and aged 56 when I met him in 2003) inherited his father's mechanic's yard. Here, he continues Papa's work, specializing in fixing wrecked trucks. Keith also sometimes trucks sugar cane. Surrounded by trailers and trucks, and assisted by a maternal cousin, Keith kindly stopped work to discuss his late father. He narrated that Papa had sent him to secondary school in the parish of Hanover so, as Papa had been busy in his workshop, Keith had not spent as much time with him as Will had done. However, Keith recalled that Papa had said he was from Maroon Town and had relatives there (though Keith could not trace the genealogy beyond Papa). Keith also knew the story of the seaplane. However, rather than attributing the difficulty of obtaining the parts needed to lift the plane to the Jamaican colour-class system (as both Vincent and Will did), Keith explained this with reference to the Second World War: 'it was war time [1939] and he couldn't get the right engine, the right specification'.

Keith narrated that Papa had later flown his own Cessna plane, which was sold when he died. He added (like Goldfinger and Will) that his father was a fine musician, who played the saxophone. Keith then arranged for his cousin to take us to a beach house outside Montego Bay owned by Papa's youngest son, who now lives in Canada, telling us that we would find there a framed photograph of Papa standing by his Cessna plane, which we did. We also saw Papa's saxophone hanging on the wall (figures 10.3 and 10.4).

Keith also gave me the phone number of his mother, Sylvia McGhie (Papa's widow), in Washington, DC. I phoned her and explained my research. She generously agreed to help with details of her late husband (who she referred to as 'Pops') and told me that she is from Kingston but had lived with Pops in Montego Bay. In a second phone call, Sylvia gave me the dates of his birth (August 14, 1902) and death (December 4, 1973, aged 71), both in Montego Bay.[17] She narrated that Pops was born in downtown Montego Bay, where he was raised by his maternal grandparents. Sylvia also told me that his maternal grandfather was a cooper and that Pops had a brother, who was a blacksmith, and a sister, both now deceased, but Sylvia could not trace the genealogy further than this.[18] She also referred to some of Pops's McGhie relatives from Maroon Town and had accompanied him there many years ago to attend the funeral of old Charlie McGhie.[19]

Figure 10.3. Leonard Lambert McGhie (Papa Meggie, left), with friends by his Cessna plane, Montego Bay. Courtesy of Keith McGhie.

Figure 10.4. Leonard Lambert McGhie's saxophone.

Papa's widow said his seaplane was before her time with him, but she had heard about it and recalled how he loved to fly his Cessna plane. She remarked that he was a good flyer and had often invited her to 'come and fly [over the Cockpit Country] and *see where the Maroons live*' (my emphasis). However, he never managed to persuade her to fly, so instead he used to fly low over their house. She narrated (as my father had) that Papa also used to lift weights and swim every morning in the sea.

Like many others who had known Papa McGhie, his widow reflected on his mechanical genius – recalling how members of the Montego Bay elite would send for him to drive their new cars and would fly with him in his Cessna plane (figure 10.3). Will had likewise remarked that if machinery at sugar factories broke down the planters would send for Papa to fix it.

From the narratives of Papa's widow, Sylvia, and his former apprentice, Will, combined with those of my father and many McGhies (and reinforced by Papa's photo and saxophone), a portrait emerges of Leonard Lambert McGhie as a dark-skinned musical mechanical genius from an Afro-Scots clan at the heart of Maroon Town who, despite experiencing the constraints of the Jamaican colour-class system, moved easily among the elite, especially on the lowlands of his native St James. For example, both Sylvia and Will told me they had known my paternal grandfather, 'Mas Georgie' McFarlane (1870–1957), a fair-skinned planter who resided near Montego Bay, through Papa McGhie. Will recalled that my grandfather 'smoked a pipe and had a Prefect car, you could walk past it [he drove so slowly]! Papa Meg was good friend with him, that's how I knew him'.

The narratives of both Will and Sylvia, likewise, reinforced each other on the theme of Papa's strong maroon identification (a point also referred to by Goldfinger). This theme of Papa's maroon identity was further highlighted from an unexpected source. During my fieldwork, my mother reminded me that, as a child, I had met 'Meggie' at the Southfield plantation (where we lived in Trelawny), when he came from Montego Bay to fix our first fridge that wouldn't freeze. To my surprise (I had not yet met Papa's apprentice or spoken with Papa's widow), my mother remarked that 'Meggie' had told her that he was 'a Maroon' from Maroon Town. I asked whether 'Meggie' had actually said he was a Maroon and she confirmed that he definitely did.

These narratives by people who knew Leonard Lambert McGhie outside Maroon Town suggest that he was aware of, and proudly proclaimed, his McGhie Maroon heritage in the context of the plantation lowlands of St James and Trelawny, where the McGhie Maroons originated. As one of the oldest McGhies (born 1902) in the living memory of the McGhies of Maroon Town, this maroon identification is likely to have been passed down to him from the early McGhie ancestors who settled in Flagstaff, the heart of the former site of Trelawny Town. Leonard Lambert's lifestyle, with its emphasis on physical fitness and intrepid adventure, complementing his mental agility and the ability to shape his own destiny, was certainly consistent with the McGhie Maroons' way of life. Historical sources indicate that the McGhie Maroons assisted the Trelawny Maroons in the Second Maroon War, led by brave and athletic men such as Leonard Parkinson (chapters 2 and 10) – after whom Leonard Lambert McGhie (as well as Leonard 'Fatman' McGhie, born 1904) may have been named. Indeed, in Goldfinger's narrative, Leonard Lambert's father is said to have been named Leonard too (possibly Albert I's middle name) and my research revealed that Leonard was a recurring name elsewhere in the Maroon Town McGhie clan.

In summation, my research – combining historical sources, anthropological fieldwork on kinship, landholdings and naming, and the narratives of the McGhie Old Family, Maroon Town's central clan – indicates that these Meso-Creole Maroon Town McGhies of Afro-Scots ancestry are descendants of the mulatto McGhie Maroons of Trelawny Parish near Trelawny Town/Flagstaff, St James. However, paradoxically, it seems that the knowledge of this historic link was lost after Leonard Lambert McGhie's death through the continuing process of creolization.

Notes

1. The footnote continues: 'Tynmore appears to have later sold the estate to Samuel Barrett, who in turn sold it to George Cunningham. According to legal records, Samuel Barrett sold 600 acres of Greenside to George Cunningham on October 17th 1817 for £2,422....' (Lovejoy, Shepherd and Trotman 2003, 40 n41). For further discussion of the Barrett and Cunningham slave-owning planter families in Trelawny see Besson (2002, chapter 2). The Barretts were of English origin, the Cunninghams were of Scottish descent (66).
2. The map is headed, 'Trelawny 496 – Plan of the parish of Trelawny in the county of Cornwall' and the surviving portion of the map focuses on north-western Trelawny. I am grateful to John Fowler for drawing my attention to this map (personal communication, December 19, 2012).
3. Hugh Barnett was a slave-owning planter of slave descent. As I wrote in my earlier book on Trelawny: 'Hugh Barnett, a quadroon with one-quarter Negro ancestry, [was] the son of Captain Jonathan Barnett (the founder of Montego Bay) and his mulatto mistress, Jane Stone. Hugh Barnett inherited what is now the eastern two-thirds of Montego Bay and, at his death in 1779, controlled five plantations, including Sportsman's Hall, Biddeford, and Hopewell in Trelawny. After his death, most of the Barnett real estate was inherited by his son, Hugh II, who, along with his father's sister's children [his cousins, probably the three McGhie brothers], now controlled six plantations: Catherine Hall and Catherine Mount in Montego Bay and four in Trelawny' (Besson 2002, 66).
4. I am grateful to Jackie Ranston for locating this information on my behalf and for the quote from her personal communication to me 18 July 2006: 'Caribbeana, Volume 3, Deeds. In Chancery: Charles Mitchell, Esq., administrator of Wm. Innes, Merchant, decd, App., and Hugh Barnett, Esq., Wm Hugh B. and Mary Ann B., infants, by the Executors of Rd Brissett, Esq., decd. On Dec 13, 1786 the Creditr of H.B. filed a Bill v. the Ex'ors of H.B. – H.B. son of testr. H.B.'s will, April 20, 1780. Sportsmans Hall and 100 slaves to his son Hugh B. at 25, remr to his nephews Rob. McGhie, James McG and Jonath. MCG., heirs of Wm B., Jr, of Trelawney –Hopewell and Bidiford for said son at 30. Rd Brissett proved the will 1783. Personal estate £23,792 c. H.B. att. 25 on 1 Jan. 1785 and took possession of Sportsm. Hall 1787. Arthur Boyer and Rob. Kenyon, surv. cop. of Peter Holme, bkrupts. H.B. in 1779 owed them £20,000 c. and d. on h. passage to Gt B. On 8 Novr 1800 total debts were £76,000 c. Receivers now appointed and £300 a yr. c. allowed to H.B.'

5. See note 3 above. Moreover, the Cunningham planter family of Trelawny later owned the Hopewell and Biddeford plantations as well as becoming owner of at least part of the McGhies' Greenside Estate (see Besson 2002, 66 and note 1 above). This indicates further links among the Barnett, McGhie and Cunningham planter families.
6. In 1790 (five years before the Second Maroon War), Thomas and Mary McGhie are referred to in the archives as follows (I quote from Ranston's personal communication of 18 July 2006, see note 3 above): 'National Archives, Kew, UK. Acts of Assembly Giving Rights to People of Colour: CO/139/47 (776) December 10, 1790: Thomas McGhie, Mary McGhie, free mulattoes, the reputed children of Robert McGhie of the parish of Trelawney by Sarah McGhie a free negro woman to all rights and privileges under certain restrictions.' While these free mulattos are unlikely to have been among the McGhie Maroons discussed later in this section, their mulatto descent indicates the practice of miscegenation within the McGhie planter family – as was widespread in the Jamaican planter class including that of Trelawny (see, e.g., Besson 2002, 63–66; Petley 2005; Green 2006). The archives also indicate a transfer of property (one-third of the Retreat and Hampstead plantations in Trelawny and one-third of slaves, all formerly belonging to Jane Stone deceased, Hugh Barnett I's mulatto mother) from Robert McGhie to Thomas McGhie (Caribbeana, Volume 3, Deeds, 26 December, 1781, cited in Ranston's personal communication of July 18, 2006).
7. From the *Returns of Givings In* in the Almanacs, researched by Ranston (personal communication 18 July 2006): '1833 (for March Quarter 1832): St James: Thomas McGhie, proprietor, Williamsfield, 2 slaves. 1832 (for March Quarter 1831) St James: Thomas McGhie, proprietor of Williamsfield, 2 slaves. 1831 (for March Quarter 1830): St James: James McGhie, heirs of, 10 slaves. Thomas McGhie, Williamsfield, 2 slaves. 1831 (for March Quarter 1830): Trelawny: Robert McGhie, heirs of, Hampstead, 215 slaves. 1828 (for March Quarter 1827): St James: Jonathan McGhie, 6 slaves. 1826 (for March Quarter 1825): St James: Jonathan McGhie, 6 slaves. 1824 (for March Quarter 1823): St James: Jonathan McGhie, 6 slaves. 1822 (for March Quarter 1821): Trelawny: Jonathan McGhie, 3 slaves. 1822 (for March Quarter 1821): Trelawny: Robert McGhie, heirs of, Coxheath 26 slaves, 122 stock. 1820 (for March Quarter 1819): Trelawny: Jonathan McGhie, 3 slaves. 1820 (for March Quarter 1819): Trelawny: Robert McGhie, heirs of, Coxheath, 29 slaves, 180 stock. 1818 (for March Quarter 1817): St James: Patrick McGhie, Mount Union, 10 slaves. 1818 (for March Quarter 1817): Trelawny: Robert McGhie, heirs of, Retreat, 211 slaves, 151 stock. 1818 (for March Quarter 1817): Trelawny: Robert McGhie, heirs of, Hampstead, 260 slaves, 191 stock.'
8. In an interesting parallel, Cyrus Francis Perkins (1813–67), in his historical novel set at Greenside Estate in the days of slavery, refers to 'a small body of men [which] was seen moving stealthily towards the [estate] works. *By a peculiar foraging cap, this party was identified as Maroons*' (Lovejoy, Shepherd and Trotman 2003, 118, emphasis mine). In the same paragraph, the novel also states that, 'it appeared that the Maroons had urged on the slaves to aid them in the plot' and refers to a slave Quamin, who had 'been working for the Maroons since "duppy frightened him off Greenside"' (118). In their Introduction to the novel, the editors comment that, 'the reference to Maroon activity...reflects Trelawny's preoccupation with runaway slaves, especially after the first Maroon War' (33).

9. It seems likely that Browns' Town was so named after the brown-skinned descendants of the mulatto Maroons and of other 'slave master' pickni'.
10. Said to have been named Stewart Castle, this was also the name of a Scottish-owned slave plantation in Trelawny (Besson 2002, 66, 112).
11. Vincent recalled that one kerosene tin of sugar cost 1/9 – one shilling and nine pence – at that time.
12. There were not, however, further set-ups nor a 'nine night' until the memorial a year later, reflecting changing mortuary ritual in the context of transnational re-gatherings, described more fully for Trelawny's free villages (Besson 2002).
13. In addition to the names Jonathan, Robert, Albert and Leonard that recur in the McGhie clan (for as Lewis put it, 'they take the names of the old people'), Thomas is a recurring name too. As seen above (note 6), the archives show that in 1790, a free mulatto named Thomas McGhie was the reputed son of the Trelawny planter, Robert McGhie. The name Thomas McGhie then recurs three times in the archives of 1831, 1832 and 1833 (just before emancipation) as the slave-owning 'proprietor' of Williamsfield, St James (see note 7 above).
14. For example, historically 'Nanny' was from the Windward Maroons in the parish of Portland – not from either Trelawny Parish or the Leeward Maroon Accompong community in St Elizabeth, as narrated. Likewise, historically, Nanny was in the First, rather than the Second Maroon War. Also, the Leeward Maroon acquisition of land (e.g., at Accompong) occurred during and after the First War, not the Second.
15. The presence of this cemetery might contribute to the tradition that the Maroons won the Second Maroon War.
16. However, the genealogical details of the narrators were not always consistent, see note 18 below.
17. Sylvia McGhie's information, which included consulting Leonard Lambert McGhie's passport, is consistent with other documentary sources (his birth certificate obtained from Jamaica's *Family Search* website and the birth and death records for St James). I thank Sylvia McGhie, Jackie Ranston and Stephen Porter for their help with this documentary research.
18. As seen above, in constructing the McGhie geneaology, I have used Vincent McGhie's information that Papa McGhie was the son of Albert I. Other McGhie narratives were not always consistent with this, sometimes indicating that Papa could have been the son of either Jonathan III (Albert I's brother) or of Richard, Jacob or Henry (Jonathan II's grandsons). However, as Vincent was the oldest McGhie in Maroon Town, I took his account to be the most knowledgeable. In addition, on this point, Vincent's information was reinforced by that of Lewis McGhie (above).
19. In Montego Bay in 2004, Lewis McGhie also told me about Charlie McGhie, whom he said had been an elderly relative of his 'from Scotland' who was both a farmer and a preacher ('he had books') at the Mount Edmonson Methodist Church in the Dundee area of Maroon Town. In 2004, Ade Hall (then aged 98, the mother of Goldfinger McGhie) likewise told me about 'old man Charlie Meggie', whom she had known since they were school-children: 'Me and Charlie go to school together at Dundee'. She described Charlie (who she said had children) as 'a brown man who preached at Mount Edmonson all the time', as well as being a farmer who 'plant plenty food'. In 2009, Harold McGhie said Charlie was one of his uncle's sons.

11 ▪ MAROON TOWN AND ACCOMPONG: RITUAL, TOURISM AND NATIONHOOD

Earlier chapters have explored creolization in Accompong, Aberdeen and Maroon Town, at the maroon/non-maroon interface. This chapter extends these perspectives by highlighting variations between the Accompong maroon community and non-maroon Maroon Town (the two original sites of the Leeward Maroon polity) in relation to the wider post-colonial Jamaican society through the themes of ritual, tourism and nationhood as they evolved in the later stages of my research.

I first discuss Emancipation Day festivals at Flagstaff in Maroon Town against the background of the revival of such celebrations in the Caribbean and Jamaica. My research reveals that Flagstaff is a highly symbolic and contested site in Jamaican history and that the Flagstaff festivals represent a complex statement of the place of Maroon Town in the Jamaican nation state.

By contrast, such celebrations are not generally held in Accompong as the Maroons secured their freedom in 1738/39, a century before emancipation in 1838. Instead, Accompong Maroons hold an annual Myal Play on January 6 to celebrate both the treaty and Cudjoe's birthday (chapters 3–5). However, Emancipation Day celebrations were held in Accompong on August 1, 2003 (but have not been held there since that date). I illuminate this short-lived innovation by relating it to the internal political factions of the maroon polity and their relationship with the Jamaican nation state, which continued to evolve, up to the time of writing, in 2012–15. I then discuss transformations of the Myal Play in the new millennium within the contexts of the ambiguous alliance between Accompong and the Jamaican state with its national and global tourist industry.

In conclusion, I look at recent innovations to revive maroon history and culture in Maroon Town, especially at Flagstaff, in the context of Jamaican heritage tourism. These transformations include the reconstitution and opening of maroon trails through the Cockpits, linking Maroon Town and Accompong, the two sites of the historic Leeward Maroon polity.

Emancipation Day Festivals at Flagstaff

To contextualize the significance of the Emancipation Day festivals in the Flagstaff area of Maroon Town, I first outline such celebrations in the Caribbean and Jamaica, including the reconstitution of Emancipation Day. I then focus on Emancipation Day festivals at Flagstaff, including the Jonkonnu masquerade at the turn of the millennium.

Emancipation Day Celebrations in the Caribbean and Jamaica

The celebration of the anniversary of Emancipation Day in Caribbean societies has recently become the focus of attention among historians (Brereton 1996, 2010; Higman 1998; Van Stipriaan 2004). Bridget Brereton (1996) analyses variations in the social history of this celebration among different British West Indian colonies during the first 54 years after slavery, including the first celebrations on August 1, 1834 and 1838 (the dates of the abolition of slavery and the end of Apprenticeship) and the Jubilee of Emancipation on August 1, 1888. Brereton explores the attitudes and involvement of the traditional elites, the Christian clergy, the black and coloured middle class, and the ex-slaves and their descendants (1996, 79–80). Through the celebration and related discourses, the elites and churches exerted social control over labour forces and congregations; the middle class negotiated socio-racial identities; and the ex-slaves and their descendants commemorated slavery and emancipation. Brereton shows that the importance of the celebrations for the black and coloured middle-class was greatest in Trinidad; white elite control was most pronounced in Barbados; and commemoration of slavery and emancipation by the ex-slaves and their descendants was most significant in rural Jamaica, where such celebrations continued until the 1920s.[1]

Barry Higman argues that, 'The memory of slavery, and the changing role of that memory in contemporary thought, has commonly found its most complete expression in the celebration of the anniversary of emancipation' (1998, 90). He charts the rise, decline and revival of Emancipation Day in the English-speaking Caribbean from 1834/1838 to 1997. Initially, the rise of the celebration in the British West Indies focused on the blessing of abolition and gratitude to God and the British monarchy, rather than on the history of enslavement (Higman 1998, 90–91). But by the 1880s, August 1 had become 'the site for competing interpretations of slavery and attitudes to the past' (91). However, the 1888 Jubilee (which was declared a public holiday in some but not all of these colonies) saw a shift from focusing on the past to looking to the future (91–92).

In Jamaica, where the Jubilee had not been a public holiday, August 1 was commercialized and established as a holiday in 1893. However, in the 1890s, the significance of Emancipation Day in the island was strengthened by the lectures of Dr Robert Love (1835–1914), an Afro-Bahamian doctor, who expressed gratitude to the anti-slavery Baptist Church (Higman 1998, 92). In the first part of the twentieth century, attempts were made to heighten the significance of Emancipation Day throughout the British West Indies but there were also counter-currents to dismiss its relevance. In Jamaica, from 1928 to 1934 (the centenary of abolition), Marcus Garvey stimulated the commemoration of Emancipation Day (Higman 1998, 93–94).

For around the next 50 years, Emancipation Day celebrations declined, though the public holiday was retained in several British West Indian colonies (Higman 1998, 95). In Jamaica, Garvey's perspective had middle-class opponents; universal suffrage in 1944 generated the new public holiday of Constitution Day on November 20;[2] and, with political independence in 1962, Independence Day on the first Monday of August replaced Emancipation Day (94–95). However, increasing global discourses on black empowerment in the 1960s and 1970s (reinforced by Garveyism and the Jamaican Rastafarian movement), the 150th anniversaries of abolition and emancipation in the 1980s, and Quincentenary anniversaries in 1992 contributed to refocusing attention on Emancipation Day. For example, this anniversary was restored in Trinidad and Tobago in 1984, and in Jamaica, in 1997.³ Nevertheless, debate continued on a national, regional and global scale, concerning the interpretation of slavery and freedom, and the celebration of emancipation (Higman 1998, 96–103).

Alex Van Stipriaan (2004) examines the significance of the July 1, Emancipation Day, as a contested *lieu de mémoire* or realm of memory from emancipation, in 1863, in Dutch Guiana to 2003 in independent Suriname. He notes that since the late 1980s, historians have focused on *lieux de mémoire* as 'historical icons in nation-states', but argues that in globalized diasporas the realms of memory of the powerless may 'belong to shared identities or ideologies that undermine, and even exceed, the nation-state', making these sites of memory 'heavily contested areas of history' (Van Stipriaan 2004, 269). In addition, Van Stipriaan contends that most *lieux de mémoire* are imposed or censored by those in power and may, therefore, also serve as '*lieux d'amnésie* (realms of amnesia or forgetting)', but that this imposed interpretation of history may be challenged and transformed 'from below' (269–70).

Van Stipriaan reveals this contestation in Suriname with respect to the anniversary of emancipation. From the early post-emancipation years, Emancipation Day was used by the state and the Catholic and Moravian Churches to control the ex-slaves and their descendants. Around the end of the nineteenth century, however, Emancipation Day became 'a symbol of and forum for Afro-Surinamese identity' (Van Stipriaan 2004, 281). But this African-American identification excluded the Maroons and continued to be linked to the Christian churches and Dutch monarchy (284). With burgeoning nationalism in the twentieth century and since independence in 1975, Emancipation Day in Suriname became increasingly secularized. However, its celebration still reflects inter-ethnic conflicts and African-American non-maroon identity. Even in the twenty-first century, the emancipation anniversary is rejected by the Surinamese Maroons, who 'have always considered themselves as having been responsible for their own emancipation, as opposed to the plantation slaves who, in their view, were only granted their freedom by the whites' (Van Stipriaan 2004, 294). These themes in Suriname find similarities and differences with the maroon/non-maroon interface in the Jamaican Cockpit Country, especially in Flagstaff/Maroon Town and Accompong.

Emancipation Festivals at Flagstaff

At the beginning of my fieldwork in Maroon Town in 1999, I learned that the newly improved road from Maroon Town Square to Flagstaff was expected to facilitate the Emancipation Day celebrations at Flagstaff in 2000, by encouraging members of the Jamaican government as well as visitors and returned residents to attend. I myself was returning from London to Jamaica that summer and after my arrival in Montego Bay in late July 2000, received details of the Flagstaff Emancipation Day programme for August 1 from the St James Parish Councillor for Maroon Town, Glendon Harris, at his office in Montego Bay. The celebrations would begin at 10:00 a.m., with speeches at 2:00 p.m., and the election of 'Miss Flagstaff Emancipation' at 9:00 p.m. There would be a tent and portable toilets sent from Montego Bay, traditional Jamaican food, Mento (Jamaican folk music), May Pole and Quadrille dancing, and a Jonkunnu masquerade. Jamaica's Minister of Local Government and Community Development would be attending, underlining the national significance of the millennial Emancipation Day festival at Flagstaff – a site of symbolic significance (as the former site of Trelawny Town) in the nation's history.

Therefore it was with much anticipation that I set off with my companions, early on the morning of August 1, 2000, to Flagstaff. We arrived for 10:00 a.m. at the historic site, now 'Ball Ground' (figure 7.2). However, many years in Britain had dulled my appreciation of 'Jamaican Time', and our arrival was well ahead of the commencement of the event at 2:00 p.m. Nevertheless, I was able to see the preparations for the festival, as the Maroon Town villagers gradually gathered to set up food stalls under blue tarpaulins, to protect them from the sun or rain. A platform for performances was also erected, in front of the single (uncompleted) concrete building, and the 'portables' were in place.

As the morning wore on and the crowds increased, radio music (transmitted by the national radio station) from the little Flagstaff cottages nestling at the foot of the surrounding mountains competed with the deafening 'sound system' – an oppositional Afro-Jamaican creation (cf. Henry 2005) – set up for Emancipation Day. The sound system was organized by 'DJs', including several dreadlocked Rastafarians (whose ideology is a critique of slavery), and reggae music (such as Bob Marley's 'Come We Go Burn Down Babylon') blasted through the Cockpits, highlighting resistance to enslavement and opposition to oppression. Delicious cooking smells drifted from the food-stalls: frying fish and chicken, roasting breadfruit and corn, and bubbling pork stew and soup. All of these traditional foods are part of the creole cuisine created by the enslaved (Mintz 1996c). At the subsequent Emancipation Day festivals at Flagstaff that I attended, the emphasis on Jamaican food was a recurring theme, with the addition of drum barbeques for jerk pork – a recipe from the fighting Maroons that has now become a national and tourist dish.

On August 1, 2000, as on the 2001 and 2002 emancipation anniversaries that I attended,[4] the ages of the crowds from Maroon Town, its neighbouring villages and Montego Bay, ranged from babies to the elderly. For example, on two occasions, I met Melvin Pearson of 'Zambia' (the land settlement above Flagstaff) there, who was by then in his 80s (chapter 8). The emphasis, however, was on the 'youth', such as the schoolboys and -girls who played in music bands and the young men playing football. This focus was underlined by the presence of the 'Youth and Community Committee' (as well as the 'Flagstaff Community Development Committee'), as advertised on their tee-shirts. Whatever their age, however, participants dressed to impress and celebrate, and such attire was complemented by the decorated hairstyles of the female babies, girls and women. The Councillor, when he arrived for the 2000 celebration, likewise looked impressive in an Afro-Creole batik suit and cap (figure 11.1).

Figure 11.1. Councillor Glendon Harris at the Emancipation Day festival, Flagstaff, 2000.

At 2:00 p.m., the celebration started with a loud-speaker instruction to 'Clear the field of cars to the perimeter', and the subsequent announcement of the 'Cambridge Junior Boys and Girls Marching Band on parade performing for you on Emancipation Day'. This teenage band from the village of Cambridge, in St James, marched onto the Ball Ground, playing brass horns, cymbals and drums. Other musical performances followed, including a Mento Band, whose members were dressed in the green, gold and black colours of the Jamaican flag, playing traditional Jamaican tunes. There was also a band representing Sam Sharpe Teachers' College, from the village of Granville in St James, playing trumpets, drums and cymbals. The presence of the Sam Sharpe band was highly symbolic, as Sam Sharpe was the leader of the 1831–32 slave rebellion at nearby Kensington. The band first played British folk songs, followed by Afro-Creole folk music; a musical paradox, reflecting creolization, which also characterized Jamaican slave festivals (Patterson 1973, 231–59; Burton 1997, 67, 70, 72).

I spoke with many people at the Flagstaff emancipation celebrations that year, as well as at the festivals on August 1 in 2001 and 2002 (and kept in touch with the festivals up to 2010). In 2000, these interviews included a Member of Parliament, who stressed the significance of Emancipation Day in contrast to Independence Day. He also referred to the national reinstatement of the emancipation anniversary, in 1997, and the annual celebrations since that date – including the national Emancipation Vigil at Kensington the previous night (compare figure 1.5).

Other interviews at the 2000 Flagstaff festival included young adult male Rastafarians. Our discussions ranged from the history of the Leeward Maroons to the significance of emancipation. One of these Rastafarians (a DJ) also told me that he had recently returned from music tours in Europe and the US. On August 1, 2002, the Rastafarian presence at the Flagstaff festival was even more pronounced, with Rasta tee-shirts advertised for sale (figures 11.2a and 11.2b).[5] I purchased one of the shirts and had further discussions with the Rastafarians on the history of resistance to enslavement. These Rastafarians at Flagstaff were skilfully highlighting their role in Jamaican national history as well as participating in transnational migration and the global music and tourist industries.

Figure 11.2a. A Rastafarian stall at the Emancipation Day festival, Flagstaff, 2002.

Figure 11.2b. Rastafarian tee-shirts at the Emancipation Day festival, Flagstaff, 2002.

Figure 11.3a. Jonkonnu masqueraders at Flagstaff, Emancipation Day festival, 2000.

Figure 11.3b. Jonkonnu Cow-Whip masquerader, Flagstaff, 2000.

Jonkonnu at Flagstaff

A highlight of the Emancipation Day 2000 festival at Flagstaff was the Jonkonnu masquerade, originating in West African secret societies and evolving through the slaves' oppositional Afro-Creole culture-building, and, which by the late eighteenth century, had especially become part of the Jamaican festival of Christmas (Patterson 1973, 231–48; Bettelheim 1988; Bilby 1999; Mullin 1994, 70, 100, 208; Craton 1995; Moore and Johnson 2002).

As described for the slavery era (Patterson 1973, 243–46; Burton 1997, 65–83; Bilby 1999; Moore and Johnson 2002), and as in my childhood when I watched Jonkonnu in Falmouth, Trelawny, around 1950, the Jonkonnu costumes at Flagstaff were very colourful and the masqueraders wore masks (figure 11.3a). Some carried agricultural tools (machetes and a hoe) reminiscent of plantation labour. The characters portrayed included a male 'Captain' of the procession, a 'Tom Boy' with a cow whip who 'cleared the way' (figure 11.3b), and an elaborately painted and decorated 'Cow head' with horns and teeth – a character that is a continuity from the slavery past (Bilby 1999, 64; Burton 1997, 67, 73; Moore and Johnson 2002, 145). Some of the masked dancers were decorated with Christmas tinsel, symbolizing the historical significance of Jonkonnu at Christmas, during slavery. The masqueraders were accompanied by a small music band, whose instruments included a flute/fife and drum, instruments that were used by Creole slaves (Burton 1997, 67). There was a repeat Jonkonnu performance (as well as a range of speeches and the beauty contest for 'Miss Flagstaff Emancipation').

How do we interpret the Jonkonnu masquerade – originally part of a Christmas festival during slavery – at Flagstaff on August 1 at the turn of the millennium? Richard Burton, in an exploration of Jonkonnu during slavery, including its ambiguous symbolization of the slaves' 'self-assertion' of both 'plantation unity' and 'otherness' or autonomous identification (1997, 71), sums up this masquerade as follows:

> An African cultural form rapidly indigenized in Jamaica and only belatedly subject to surface creolization, Jonkonnu functioned as the core of the oppositional culture of Jamaican slaves, at first in isolation then increasingly as part of a much wider cultural phenomenon: the extraordinary 'Negro Carnival'...that was Christmas in Jamaica during the last thirty or forty years of slavery (Burton 1997, 66).

Burton also links the 'subversive potential' of Jonkonnu to the 'Christmas Rebellion' of 1831–32, the great slave uprising (originating at Kensington, near Maroon Town) that began in the aftermath of Christmas 1831 (1997, 82–83).

Christmas celebrations, including Jonkonnu, were restricted in Jamaica by the colonial authorities after the Morant Bay Rebellion of 1865, especially in towns. Nevertheless, Jonkonnu masquerades continued into the late nineteenth and early twentieth centuries, particularly in the rural areas – including Lacovia (near Accompong) in St Elizabeth (Moore and Johnson 2002, 157–58). These authors identify the continuation of Jonkonnu bands up to the 1920s (158). However, Jonkonnu was still being performed in the streets of Falmouth around 1950 – when, as a child, I watched the masquerade. Burton notes that, despite its retreat 'into rural fastnesses, during the second half of the nineteenth century', Jonkonnu returned 'somewhat as a folkloric remnant of "old-time Jamaica", to national visibility after 1950' (1997, 65). Fifty years later, however, in 2000, Jonkonnu at Flagstaff would mean much more than this.

In 1999, Kenneth Bilby had noted that:

> The forms of masked dance and street celebration known as *Jonkonnu*...represent the closest equivalent in the former British plantation colonies to the better known Afro-Catholic carnivals of the francophone, hispanophone, and lusophone American territories. Perhaps for this reason, Jonkonnu – despite the comparatively modest scale on which the surviving folk festival traditions that go by this name are practiced today – has been elevated to a position of high visibility in several postcolonial anglophone Caribbean nations (Bilbly 1999, 47).

Bilby quotes Judith Bettelheim's conclusion in the 1980s that, 'Jonkonnu is today *the* Jamaican national festival, the image of an island' (Bettelheim 1985, 85, quoted in Bilby 1999, 47). However, Bilby argues that the interpretation of Jonkonnu masquerades has been largely based on the observations of European writers during slavery and questions the adequacy of interpreting them as temporary 'rituals of rebellion' by the enslaved at Christmas (66).

Based especially on his ethnographic fieldwork in the rural hill community of Nassau in St Elizabeth in the late twentieth century, Bilby offers an alternative explanation. In Nassau, he found that the 'Jangkunu' house head-dress and dance associated with the Christmas Jonkonnu masquerade during slavery persisted as a seasonal focus, but is part of a year-round religious drumming ceremony, Gumbay Play, which is believed to harness the spiritual power of the ancestors through Myal or ancestral spirit possession. Following Bettelheim (1985), Bilby notes that the Jangkunu house head-dress was possibly of African origin but became creolized to symbolize the power of the slave plantation Great House. In Nassau, the Jangkunu house head-dress is created by a myal-man in honour of the ancestors who are buried in family-land cemeteries, where the dance is held. The dance culminates in the destruction of the house head-dress, symbolizing both the satisfaction of the ancestral spirits and the destruction of the power of the plantation. Bilby, therefore, concludes that the Jonkonnu masquerade was a public expression of a hidden religious complex among the slaves and is today part of a wider creolized Afro-Jamaican worldview that includes Myal and Gumbay drumming in Nassau, Lacovia and Accompong in St Elizabeth and among the Windward Maroons, as well as Revival in free villages (Bilby 1999, 66). However, the seasonal Jonkunnu masquerade with its 'masking and parading' that featured 'fife and drum bands' reflected the increasing impact of European cultural influences on African traditions – including the African-derived 'cow-head' mask – in the process of creolization (64; see also Burton 1997, 67).

On the basis of his Nassau ethnography, Bilby (1999, 64–65) argues that the religious Jangkunu house head-dress rituals and the secular Jonkonnu masquerade have always been two distinct things. However, his analysis in fact suggests that they were interrelated through transformations of African and European influences in the process of Caribbean creolization.[6] This interpretation is reinforced by other sources. Drawing on Cynric Williams's (1826, 21–26) account of Christmas and Boxing Day on a Jamaican slave plantation, which, Richard Burton (1997, 73) notes coincides with accounts by Stewart (1808, 262–64) and the anonymous author of *Marly* (Anon. 1828, 288–89), Burton describes the house head-dress (and gumbay drum) ritual as taking place on the plantation (and on neighbouring plantations) on Boxing Day with a more aggressive Jonkonnu masquerade being performed in the towns (Burton 1997, 25–26, 73). For Burton, the slaves' Jonkonnu performance on the plantations, with the house head-dress symbolizing their harnessing of the power of the planters' Great House, and the urban Jonkonnu masquerade (including the horned cow-head mask) portraying the slaves' power over the animal world, temporarily symbolically reversed the powerlessness of the enslaved (80–82).

These oppositional rituals paralleled the protective function of the Myal Dance in Jamaican slave society, which Schuler (1979, 1980) shows aimed to eradicate the 'sorcery' of slavery. This interpretation is consistent with Bilby's (1999, 58) ethnography in which the builder of the Jangkunu head-dress in Nassau is a myal-man. It is also reinforced by Patterson's point that the term, 'John-Canoe' derives from 'the Ewe word meaning sorcerer-man' (1973, 246). This perspective is likewise consistent with Mullin's observation on the slaves' Christmas celebrations or Plays in the Caribbean, especially Jamaica, where the masks and head-dresses of Jonkonnu were seen as representing the spirit world (1994, 70).

These insights, combined with my own research on Myal in Accompong (chapters 3–5), and on Revival in the Trelawny free villages that were the vanguard of Myalism during and after slavery (Besson 2002, 2009), as well as on Revival in Maroon Town (chapter 7), illuminate the Jonkonnu masquerade at Flagstaff. The Flagstaff masquerade may be seen not only as highly symbolic of the opposition and resistance to slavery in the history of both the nation state and the locality of Maroon Town, a symbolization reflected in the enthusiasm of the crowds as the masqueraders appeared at Ball Ground. Jonkonnu at Flagstaff, performed on August 1, 2000 (rather than at Christmas) at the maroon/non-maroon interface, may also be interpreted as a part of the wider year-round religious Myal complex from Jamaican slave society that both persisted and became transformed through marronage and emancipation. This creolized religious complex not only continues in Accompong (where gumbay drums are played and also made for tourists) but also, as the core of Revival in free villages, including Maroon Town. Myal in Accompong, Revival in Maroon Town and Aberdeen, and Jonkonnu at Flagstaff, therefore, all reflect Caribbean creolization and maroon and non-maroon variations on this theme. At the turn of the millennium, Jonkonnu at Flagstaff included further transformations as an attraction for tourists and a statement of Jamaican nationhood.

Interpreting Emancipation Festivals at Flagstaff

The Emancipation Day celebrations at Flagstaff, since Jamaica's revival of this anniversary in 1997 (and which have continued into the new millennium), may be seen as an annual statement by Maroon Town villagers of the significance of their community in the nation's history of resistance to enslavement and related transformations of freedom.

The choice of Flagstaff (the core of the former site of Trelawny Town) as the setting for Maroon Town's Emancipation Day celebrations is highly symbolic of Jamaican struggles for freedom. However, Flagstaff may also be interpreted as a contested site of memory in Jamaican national history. The site symbolizes the resistance of the Trelawny Maroons to the colonial state in the Second Maroon War of 1795–96, which was the culmination of a longer history of marronage including the First Maroon War (1725–38) and the treaty of March 1738/39 that defeated the colonial state and consolidated the Leeward Maroon polity. However, the colonial treaty can also be seen as confining the Maroons to a marginal reservation (Kopytoff 1979). Flagstaff also symbolizes the betrayal and deportation of the Trelawny Maroons to Nova Scotia in 1796 by the colonial government (who were supported by the Accompong Maroons) in the aftermath of the Second Maroon War, as well as the British barracks at Garrison, the related confiscation of Trelawny Maroon territory and the fracturing of the Leeward Maroon polity.

However, all of the former Trelawny Town site (now Maroon Town, including Flagstaff) is near Kensington, where the great slave revolt took place in 1831–32; a rebellion that led to the abolition of slavery throughout the British Empire in 1834. In addition, the subdivision and sale of former Trelawny Maroon lands at Flagstaff by the colonial government to ex-slaves were part of the evolution of Maroon Town in the aftermath of emancipation in 1838 and the desertion of the barracks around the 1850s. This process of post-slavery peasantization was itself an integral dimension of the history of opposition and resistance by enslaved Africans and their Creole descendants to European colonialism, slavery and plantations (cf. Besson 1992a, 1995b, 2002).

Flagstaff, therefore, also symbolizes the disjunctures and continuities between Trelawny Town and Maroon Town, whose inhabitants variously claim descent from slaves, colonists and Maroons. Their complex history of resistance, opposition and creolization mirrors, in microcosm, wider themes in the memory of slavery and freedom in Jamaica. The Emancipation Day festivals at Flagstaff, which draw on and elaborate a strong and long tradition of such celebrations in rural Jamaica, crystallize these themes and their continuities and transformations in the island today. The building of the new road to Flagstaff (overseen by the St James Parish Council) for Emancipation festivals and the political organization of these Flagstaff celebrations (the prominent role of Maroon Town's Parish Councillor and representatives of the Jamaican government) further highlight the links between the local community and the post-colonial nation state.

The Paradox of Emancipation Day in Accompong

I had planned to again attend the Emancipation Day festival at Flagstaff on August 1, 2003. However, in July 2003, I was puzzled to learn from the Jamaican newspapers that Emancipation Day would also be celebrated in Accompong. Intrigued by this new development among the Maroons, who stress their history of marronage in contrast to emancipation, I decided to instead spend Emancipation Day in Accompong.

On the morning of August 1, 2003, I travelled with my companions from Montego Bay through Sam Sharpe Square (where emancipation celebrations would be held), and on through Maroon Town to Accompong. The journey was slower than usual, due to a particularly heavy deluge of rain. However, eventually the sun came out and brightened the brooding Cockpit landscape.

On arrival in Accompong, we first stopped at Ex-Colonel Cawley's house. This busy Ex-Colonel, who was often out elsewhere in the community or transporting higglers to market, was conspicuously at home today, despite the celebrations. In response to my mystified questions, he confirmed that the Maroons do not normally observe Emancipation Day.

We were directed to the emancipation celebrations at the 'Bickle Village' area of Accompong. The Bickle Village had been built about a year before (in time for the 2002 Myal Play) with funding from the Tourism Product Development Co. Ltd (TPDCo), an Agency of the Jamaican government's Ministry of Tourism and Sport.[7] The development began with the building of two small tourist 'villas', combining traditional and modern architectural styles (small round concrete structures with thatched roofs, furniture and running water), at the top of a mountainside offering spectacular views. The villas were reached by a path off one of the village streets, with a sign 'Mystic Pass mountain villas', pointing the way (figures 11.4a and 11.4b). As the development progressed, a thatched meeting house, public toilets, a stage for musical performances and food stalls were erected behind the villas.

Figure 11.4a. Sign to the tourist villas at the Bickle Village, Accompong.

Figure 11.4b. Tourist villa at the Bickle Village, Accompong.

As we approached the Bickle Village, it became apparent from banners in the streets that the Emancipation Day celebrations (which continued well into the evening) were being supported by the TPDCo. To enter the Bickle Village, each visitor had to pay an entrance fee of J$300. There was a large crowd at and around the Bickle Village but attendance at the event was dampened by the deluge of rain which, we were told, was the heaviest for the year. As a result, the Bickle Village was flooded and muddy with the red earth of the sodden Cockpits. However, the fresh Cockpit air was heavy with delicious cooking smells of traditional maroon recipes, especially jerk chicken and jerk pork. There had been drumming but there was now sound-system music from the stage. There were maroon tour guides available, some of whom had been trained by the Maroon Town Councillor's senior tour guide (Kenneth Watson), who conducted the Councillor's tourist tours from Montego Bay to Maroon Town and Accompong.

What was the meaning of these Emancipation Day celebrations in Accompong, which was consolidated through victory in the First Maroon War a century before emancipation in 1838? I discovered that these celebrations were being contested by political factions relating to the impending elections of Colonel. These factions were grounded not only in individual personalities and the issues that each candidate represented, but were also elaborated by a discourse concerning knowledge of maroon history and culture.

As I discussed the matter with Maroons, I learned that the celebrations were the innovation of the most recent Ex-Colonel at that time, Meredie Rowe, who was standing for re-election a few months later. Near the meeting-house at the Bickle Village, I spoke with Ex-Colonel Rowe (who was a member of the island's police force in Montego Bay). He confirmed that the Emancipation Day celebrations in Accompong were his innovation, which (as he put it) was playing to a 'national audience'. In addition to arranging for the presence of the Jamaican government's TDPCo, he had invited the national radio and television broadcasters to the celebrations. The Ex-Colonel informed me that he had also 'masterminded' several articles for the national newspapers, in addition to some pieces that he had written himself. He explained that all of these strategies were part of his campaign for re-election in October 2003, at which time (he asserted), he would definitely be returned to office with Ex-Colonel Cawley as his Deputy. He outlined that, when he returned to office, he would give up his job in the Jamaican police force to concentrate on being a full-time Colonel, focusing on maroon history and culture. He explained that he would still be interested in national politics, as he felt the Jamaican government was 'trying to come in through the back door' to run the trans-island highway (Highway 2000) through maroon territory. The same situation, he claimed, applied to the government's plans for a National Park and World Heritage Site on maroon lands in the Cockpits. However, he added, the Maroons had held some meetings with the government on these issues.

Some of the national newspaper articles that were either masterminded or written by this Ex-Colonel dealt with contentious national issues such as the alleged growth and international trade of marijuana in Accompong, which the former Colonel as an employee of the Jamaican police force, had vowed to stamp out, and the boundaries and status of Leeward Maroon treaty land. The trans-island highway and the proposed National Park and World Heritage Site were other issues that he had addressed.

While the boundaries and status of Leeward Maroon lands are of common concern in Accompong, there are diverse opinions on these issues among these Maroons (chapters 3–6). Membership by Accompong Maroons of the national police force is another contentious issue, being a continuation of the ambiguous historical relationship between the maroon polity and the colonial/post-colonial state (including the role of the Accompongs as allies of the colonists against the Trelawnys in the Second Maroon War [chapter 2]). The varying views on the celebration of Emancipation Day in Accompong were both a part of this internal factionalism and a dimension of the ambiguous relationship between the maroon polity and the Jamaican state.

The elections for Accompong's Maroon Colonel scheduled for October 2003 were subsequently postponed to 2004 due to conflicts over election lists. When the elections were held, the then current Colonel, Sydney Peddie, was re-elected for a second term with Melvin Currie as his Deputy. Since then, Emancipation Day celebrations have not been held in Accompong. As Colonel Peddie put it, when I raised the issue of Emancipation Day celebrations with him, in March 2009, 'I couldn't see the reason for that – most unusual!' Peddie himself would stand again for re-election in 2009, the elections would again be postponed (due to disagreement over how the elections would be organized in relation to both the Maroon Council and the Jamaican government),[8] and when the elections were held in August 2009, a new candidate, Ferron Williams (a member of the Jamaican police force in the parish of Westmoreland) was successful (chapter 3).

The Transformation of the Myal Play: Tourism and Nationhood

Like the short-lived Emancipation Day celebrations in Accompong, the transformation of its enduring annual Myal Play in the new millennium (touched on in chapters 3–5) highlights the ambiguous relationship between the maroon polity and the Jamaican nation state and various views on this relationship, in Accompong. This transformation of the Myal Play (a transformation that I first observed in 2002, in comparison with Plays in the 1980s and 1990s, and which has continued up to 2015) also manifests the increasing involvement of the Accompong Maroons in Jamaica's global tourist industry. In addition, my research reveals a growing relationship between Maroon Town and Accompong within the context of heritage tourism. In this section, I elaborate on the transformation of the relationship between Accompong and the Jamaican nation state as manifested in the Myal Play and on the related internal factionalism in Accompong, both of which reflect ongoing creolization.

The factionalism within Accompong that crystallized in relation to the planning of the 2002 Myal Play was publicized through the national media. On Thursday, January 3, 2002, the *Gleaner* published a front page article (by the Western Bureau) entitled, 'Turmoil among Accompong Maroons' that opened with the following statement:

> With just days to go for the Annual Celebration of the Signing of the Maroon Peace Treaty, the relationship between the serving Colonel Sidney Peddie and his predecessor Meredie Rowe, is far from being cordial.

Based on a press release from Ex-Colonel Rowe, the article argued that Colonel Peddie's plan to hold the celebration on Sunday, January 6 (instead of on the Monday) went against maroon tradition, was due to external influences, and would have dire political consequences for the Colonel in the next elections (due in 2003).[9]

I had learned from the Maroons that Monday was their day of rest and recreation, due to the commitments of attending church on Sundays. This contrasts with the wider Jamaican society, where Sunday is the day of both church and rest. The internal political issue then, in Accompong, regarding the relationship between the maroon polity and the Jamaican nation state was expressed in a discourse over the place of Sunday church and Monday Myal ritual.

Shortly before reading the above article, I had heard that an elderly woman in Accompong was, likewise, opposing Peddie's plan to hold the Play on Sunday as this was a day for *church*. I had also been told that there would be road blocks to prevent the event being held that day. I discussed this rumour with the Maroon Town Councillor in Montego Bay, as he was transporting us to Accompong. However, as Councillor Harris observed, 'How can they be blocking roads if they are in church?' He confidently continued: 'The Colonel and Deputy have assured me it's going ahead on Sunday'.

The Councillor, who was arranging tourist tours in two mini-buses from his guesthouse office in Montego Bay to his family-land home in Maroon Town and on to Accompong, proved to be right about the day for the Play. Clearly, there was an efficient line of communication between the Councillor and the Colonel. It would emerge that both these leaders had a strong interest in attracting tourism to their communities. It would also become apparent that the Councillor's schedule for January 6 was to arrive in Accompong for an official ceremony involving national dignitaries with its 'Civic Function Program', at 3:00 p.m. rather than for what was now being called the 'Traditional Ceremony' at the Kindah Tree at 10:00 a.m. (see chapter 3). This schedule was because, along with guests from Montego Bay hotels, we would spend the morning being tourists in Maroon Town. This agenda was consistent with his role as Parish Councillor and his aim to draw Maroon Town into the tourist industry (chapter 7).

We arrived at Maroon Town at about 11:00 a.m., noting a new road-retaining wall that had been built by the Urban Development Corporation (UDC) at the mountainous entrance to the village. We stopped at the Councillor's family-land home, just beyond the Square. In the yard, in the recently built thatched tourist meeting house, we were invited to eat and drink from a 'Taste of Jamaica Snack' that the Councillor had brought and to sit on rows of chairs. Afterwards, the tourists wandered around, visited the small museum and took photographs. The museum, set up by the Councillor's tour guide, includes documents and artefacts relating to marronage – such as bullets found at Gun Hill, Flagstaff, from the Second Maroon War. At noon we resumed our journey to Accompong. The Councillor, however, remained in Maroon Town and would join us later.

We arrived at Accompong at 1:30 p.m., via a one-way system set up for the day's event. A Pentecostal church congregation was singing lustily at the crossroads entrance to the village, highlighting the contentious issue of whether the Myal Play should be held on Sunday. However, it was not only immediately apparent that the Sunday Play was receiving much support but also that the whole atmosphere and scale of this event had been transformed. In contrast to the modest scale of previous Plays, there was a large amount of traffic ascending onto this mountainous village, where at that time vehicles were few. There were also several hundred people already thronging through the streets. The crowds included many non-maroon Jamaicans and some foreign tourists. (The Councillor's mini-buses, for example, included Austrian and American tourists and non-Maroons from Kingston and Montego Bay, as well as the drivers from Maroon Town.)

The advance national newspaper coverage had indicated this impending transformation of the Myal Play. On Friday, January 4, 2002, the *Gleaner* broadsheet carried a full page 'Special Advertising Feature', by the Western Bureau, on the 'Accompong Maroon Celebrations' that coming weekend. The articles included, 'A proud history' and 'The abeng shall sound'. However, more than half of the main article, which was entitled, 'Maroons celebrate in fine style', comprised a section headed, 'TPDCo trains Accompong Maroons'. Beside this, was a large advertisement of the 'Tourism Product Development Co. Ltd – TPDCo', identified as 'An Agency of the Ministry of Tourism and Sport' with the role of 'Developing and Sustaining Jamaica's Tourism Product'. The section of the main article that focused on the TPDCo opened with the statement that:

> Some 40 Accompong Maroons graduated from training programmes conducted by the Tourism Product Development Company (TPDCo) as the organisation moves ahead with plans to foster social and economic development in the community through tourism.

The following information was added:

> TPDCo signed an agreement with the Council of the Accompong Maroons earlier this year in which the organisation committed to undertaking human resource development and certain infrastructural improvements to enhance standards in safety, security and aesthetics, as well as the identification and development of products and services related to tourism.

At a later point in the article, one of the trained Maroons was quoted as explaining that funds had been given to the community by TPDCo in advance of the celebration, for constructing a gate and a 'Bickle Village' (discussed above), refurbishing the Community Centre and erecting signs for a tour route through Accompong.[10]

After our arrival in Accompong on January 6, 2002, we were given printed programmes of the day's events and numbered identity wristbands. The cover of the programme, decorated with two pictures of the abeng, read:

> Welcome to the 264th Annual Accompong Maroon Festival January 6, 2002. Featuring: Traditional Ceremony, drumming, dance, music, food, craft, and herbs. Cost $200.00 [Ja] Adult, $100.00 Children, Maroons a minimum donation of $50.00.

Inside the programme, two pages listed the details of the 'January 6, 2002 Acitvities' and the items of the 'Civic Function programme January 6, 2002'. The Activities included: the 'Traditional Ceremony' at the Kindah Tree, scheduled for 10:00 a.m., at which visitors were welcome; the 'Traditional Street March' at 2:00 p.m.; drumming all day at the Monument (erected during my fieldwork to commemorate Captain Cudjoe) and 'Wreath laying in honor of the Ancestors' at 2:30 p.m.; the 'Civic Function and Cultural Show' at the Parade Ground at 3:30 p.m.; a 'Maroon Exhibition' and the 'First Aid Station' at the Community Centre; and 'Traditional Foods', 'Mento Band', 'Drumming' and 'Dub Poetry' at the Bickle Village.

The 'Civic Function Program' was scheduled to start at 3:00 p.m. with (national) 'Dignitaries to the VIP area', followed at 3:15 p.m by 'Blowing of the Abeng', 'Opening Prayer', 'Welcome by Chairman', and 'African Drum Welcome'. There would be the 'Official Welcome' at 3:25 p.m. by Colonel Sydney Peddie. Other items, scheduled at intervals up to 4:50 p.m., included a 'Traditional Choir', 'DJ Jeff; Peter, Gospel DJ; I am Nanny – Poem; Dub Poem'; 'Greetings from other communities'; 'Ancestral Roots Culture group'; 'Gospel Choir' and a 'Skit'; 'Greetings From Other Guests; Vote of Thanks – Dpt. Colonel; Accompong Culture group'; and a 'Finale – All Drummers on stage'.

On the back of the programme was a detailed advertisement of the 'Accompong Community Development Committee'.[11] In addition to the programmes and wristbands, we noted the TDPCo publicity signs and colour photocopies of the 'Accompong Town Guided Tour Map' available in the Community Centre. The TDPCo sign to the 'Peace Cave', stating that this was where Cudjoe signed the peace treaty near 'Old Town', reflected the Accompong Maroons' symbolic shifting of this sacred site on the Cockpit Country landscape and the creolization of the commons (chapters 3–5).

After receiving the programme we went immediately to the Kindah grove. I was pleased to find that we had not missed the 'Traditional Ceremony' scheduled for 10:00 a.m., as the Myal Play was only now in full swing at 2:00 p.m. However, the Austrian tourists from the Councillor's mini-bus, who seemed especially interested in the traditional choir in the Civic Function Program were mystified by the discrepancy between the published schedule and the actual events: 'But it says it [the Civic Program] starts at 3:00 p.m!' I explained 'Jamaican Time' to them.

Those who gathered at Kindah were partaking of the traditional Myal feast, for example, eating pork, on leaves, from a large pot boiling on the rocks near the Kindah Tree. Like ourselves, those present at Kindah were mainly non-Maroons as many Maroons had gone on the Myal pilgrimage to 'feed the spirits' at Old Town (as we were told at Kindah). From Kindah, we could hear the sound of gunshots or squibs from Old Town, symbolizing the gunshots of the First Maroon War. About half an hour later, the pilgrimage returned to Kindah in cacoon-vine battle-camouflage (see chapter 3).

The Play continued with gumbay drumming and the blowing of the abeng. From Kindah, I noticed the recent innovations of a herbal garden and a thatched meeting house nearby. As I learned from Maroons and the media, the establishment of the herbal garden had been assisted by the Canadian International Development Agency (CIDA), which was also involved with 'a marketing assistance programme' in the community.[12]

After the conclusion of the Play at Kindah, those attending marched to join the larger crowds that were now clustering at the Monument for the drumming and wreath-laying to the ancestors, and at Parade for the Civic Function and Cultural Show. By now, the crowds had reached an estimated 4,000 to 5,000 people – some of whom were at the Community Centre – and vendors had set up their stalls along the village streets. In fact, as we saw on our journeys to and from Accompong that day, vendors lined the entire route to the village through maroon territory from both Jointwood and Cedar Spring.

As the crowds teemed through the village and clustered at Monument and Parade, tantalizing cooking smells and the heavy smoke of barbeques from vendors' stalls drifted over the proceedings. The street food included jerk pork, jerk chicken and curry goat. Some vendors' stalls sold brightly coloured artificial flowers, crafts and clothes. Mingling with the cooking smells and smoke was the sweet scent of marijuana, the Rastafarian sacred 'herb'.

The craft vendors included Rastafarians and many other Rastafarian visitors (mainly male) were prominent in the crowds. These included a vehicle of Rastafarians from Nine

Miles, Bull Bay (in the parish of St Thomas, in the east), which was formerly Prince Immanuel's Rastafarian camp (Chevannes 1994), who had travelled across the island to attend the celebration. One of them told me that he was the Prince's 'Deputy', Prince Immanuel having (he explained) 'dropped [dead] from stroke' in 1994. As we continued along the village streets, talking to old maroon friends (including a Rastafarian carving gumbay drums for maroon festivals and the tourist industry) and making new non-maroon acquaintances, numerous competing sound systems blared out across the crowds. This music included Bob Marley's Rastafarian songs, Pentecostalist church-singing, gumbay drumming and the blowing of the abeng at the Myal Play.

We visited the Community Centre, where representatives of the TDPCo were highly visible at desks. Another new dimension of the celebration was the cultural exhibition at the Centre. This exhibition (by a historian from the University of the West Indies in Kingston) included an Islamic theme, focusing on Islamic slaves and Maroons. In light of my earlier fieldwork, there seemed to be an ongoing negotiation of maroon identity, in Accompong, in relation to African ethnicities. Throughout most of my research, maroon descent from 'Coromantees'/'Ashantis' and 'Kongos' from West and Central Africa was highlighted. At the Play that I attended in 1991, a representative from the Nigerian embassy in Jamaica was prominent. Some years later, I learned of Colonel Meredie Rowe's visit to Ghana. Now, in 2002, links with Islamic African slaves (and African-Jamaican Maroons) were being stressed.

These 2002 celebrations were broadcast on the Jamaican national television news at least twice that Sunday evening. In subsequent years (up to the time of writing in 2012–15), the significance of these annual maroon celebrations to the Jamaican nation continued to be highlighted in the island's media. This included two articles in the *Gleaner* on January 6, 2005 and another on January 11, 2005. The media coverage launching the annual celebrations in Accompong on Thursday, January 6, 2005 was shaped by Colonel Peddie, who was re-elected in 2004. In 2005, Peddie's national media publicity highlighted the continuing role of the TDPCo and the establishment of the Accompong Town Maroon Foundation, linked to a 20-year development plan for the maroon polity, relating to both its economy and cultural heritage, and to Caribbean regional tourism.

The scene was set by a short article, 'Maroons gear up for annual celebration' (the *Gleaner*, January 6, 2005), based on an interview with Colonel Peddie, which heralded the change that he planned for the celebrations. The article outlined Peddie's plans to secure funding for development projects, which, he envisaged, would both protect the maroon polity's environment and cultural history and transform Accompong into 'the most sought-after tourist destination in the West Indies'. Plans for the next five years included the continuation of improvements of roads, telecommunications and water supply for the community.

Commentary on these issues was elaborated in a more prominent article by *Gleaner* writer, Melville Harris, entitled, 'Maroon Foundation set for Accompong' (the *Gleaner*, January 6, 2005), likewise based on the press conference with Peddie. This article again linked the Foundation's development plan to the enhancement of Accompong's maroon cultural heritage and economy, and its links with the tourist industry, 'as part of efforts to create sustainable development within the community' and to transform it 'into a major tourist attraction'. The article also informed the national public that the Jamaican government's Minister of Tourism and Industry would be the guest speaker at the annual celebration, and pointed to the 'tremendous role' of the TPDCo in training maroon tour guides. Peddie's plans for a 'cultural awareness initiative' offering 'educational tours... for primary and high schools' included 'development of a tour itinerary, production of a Maroon booklet, marketing of tours...and the acquisition of a tour bus'. The Colonel was, however, less enthusiastic about the vendors who in recent years had thronged into Accompong for the event and warned that there would be 'sweeping changes' from 2006: 'Starting next year and beyond, the flea market atmosphere, which now prevails on the January 6 celebrations, would be significantly reduced' and replaced by an increased display of the maroon cultural heritage. This theme would resurface under a new Colonel in 2010 and 2011.

Following the celebration on January 6, 2005, another newspaper article on January 11[13] confirmed that Colonel Peddie had launched the Foundation by an announcement at the anniversary in Accompong, which outlined the role of the Foundation and its 20-year development plan as raising funds for preserving maroon culture and developing its tourism potential. The article also carried a short report of the celebration:

> Thousands of Maroons and visitors descended on Accompong Town, St Elizabeth for the festivities, which ran from Thursday until the early hours of Friday morning. 'I have been given the mandate twice by my people, but I do not intend to rest on my laurels,' said Colonel Peddie. 'My dream is that Accompong will become the most sought-after tourist attraction in the Caribbean.'

Figure 11.5. A Rastafarian street stall at the Myal Play, Accompong, 2006.

The Myal Plays and Civic Functions continued to feature at a national and even international level up to 2015. For example, the celebrations that I attended in 2006 drew a crowd of around 6,000, including Jamaican government officials, market vendors, Rastafarians, tourists, non-maroon Jamaicans and Maroons from elsewhere in the island and overseas. The Jamaican police force was also visible as were representatives from the national media. In 2006, the street stalls included Rastafarian flags, crafts and 'Ital' food as was likewise the case in 2007 (figure 11.5). A few days before the Myal Play in 2006, the Council of Overseas Maroons (based in New York) held their first Accompong Maroon Homecoming and International Conference in Accompong and, at the Civic Function that year, I began to meet more overseas Maroons there visiting from North America and Britain.

At the celebrations in Accompong on January 6, 2007, in the year of the bicentenary of the abolition of the British transatlantic slave trade, the crowd was even larger and a BBC film crew from England and various educational groups from Jamaica and the United States attended as well as Maroons and Colonels from the Windward Maroon communities and numerous overseas Maroons. The celebrations were again covered in the national media.[14]

Figure 11.6. The Overseas Maroons' Conference, Accompong, 2007. Photo by Johnny McFarlane.

Two days earlier, on January 4, 2007, the Council of Overseas Maroons held their Second Annual Accompong Maroon Homecoming and International Conference, in Accompong, which included non-maroon environmentalists and NGOs concerned about potential bauxite mining in the Cockpits. The Council of Overseas Maroons, which is based in North America but was planning to expand to Britain, acted (as described on the conference programme) 'In Collaboration with Colonel Sidney Peddie & the Maroon People of the Sovereign State of Accompong'. The conference theme was 'Preserving, Protecting, Promoting Our Rich History and Cultural Heritage'. The environmentalist issue in the Cockpits, which had been ongoing for some years, was escalating and overseas Maroons were active in launching an international petition opposing it on the Internet.

I was invited to speak on maroon cultural history at this conference and did so (figure 11.6), and with other invited speakers, received a 'Special Citation' from the Council of Overseas Maroons who (on the citation) described themselves as 'The Descendants of the Trelawny Town Maroons of the Sovereign State of Accompong, Jamaica, West Indies – 1738' (thereby, by symbolically relocating Trelawny Town to St Elizabeth, repairing the fractured Leeward Maroon polity and reinforcing the creolization of the commons). The inscriptions on the citations stated that they were being awarded 'For Your Support and Interest In Irreversibly Drawing The Battle Lines To Prevent the Destruction of The Sovereign State Of Accompong And the Pristine Cockpit Country'. The Keynote Speaker at the conference was the late John Maxwell, a well-known Jamaican writer, described as a 'Veteran Journalist and Environmentalist' and guest speakers included other environmentalists. The Prime Minister and some Members of Parliament were also listed as speakers on the programme but did not attend. Several Accompong Maroons, including Colonel Peddie, his Deputy, Melvin Currie and Ex-Colonel Cawley spoke eloquently against the threat of bauxite mining in the Cockpits. Young Maroons also spoke on issues concerning maroon youth. Along with the call for reparations for enslavement, the environmentalist theme likewise featured in the speeches at the Civic Function on January 6, 2007 (for example, by the Colonel and his Deputy) and were reported in the national press.[15]

By 2009, Colonel Peddie advised me that the January 6 celebrations were drawing several thousand people; for, as he explained to me (in March 2009): 'Plenty Maroons [came that year] from Canada, America, England, Kingston, Montego Bay, plus local people and tourists'. He also mentioned that he was considering turning the Play into a three-day event. However, a new Colonel (Ferron Williams) was elected in August 2009, along with a new Deputy (Norma Rowe-Edwards, a returned migrant from the USA, chapter 3). The national media coverage of January 6, 2010 in Accompong (described as the 272nd annual event) included a newspaper article which, in addition to reporting the attendance 'as usual' of 'persons from England, Canada, the United States and even Kenya' at this 'major calendar event in St Elizabeth', set out the new Colonel's policy for January 6, 2011 as being a 'return to traditional customs', including the sale of maroon crafts rather than the sale of goods by non-maroon market vendors on the streets of Accompong.[16] The article also remarked that the 'downtown market layout...is taking away from the authenticity of the festivities, and [the] community-tourism thrust Maroons are pushing for'. This theme was reiterated by Colonel Williams for the 273rd annual celebration on January 6, 2011,[17] which was advertised on the Internet by the Jamaica Tourist Board in London, England.[18] Paradoxically, then, the Accompong maroon society, born out of resistance to globalization, is now negotiating a significant role in Jamaica's global tourist industry.

Another paradoxical transformation is that Accompong, a virtually autonomous state within a state (compare Price 1996, 293), has become a symbol of Jamaican nationhood. As discussed in chapter 3, this development was highlighted at Accompong's January 6, 2012 Civic Function, which was defined by the Jamaican government (whose Director of Culture in the Ministry of Youth and Culture attended the ceremony), the national media and the Maroons themselves as the start of Jamaica's 50th Anniversary of Independence celebrations.

It remains to be seen how the relationship between Accompong Town and the Jamaican government will evolve if Jamaica pursues its 50th Anniversary plan to become a Republic without the British monarchy; for the Accompong Maroons not only continue to assert their autonomy from the Jamaican post-colonial state, but also regard themselves as having a special relationship with the British monarch resulting from the treaty of 1738/39 (chapters 2–4; compare Bilby 1997).

Figure 11.7. Flagstaff Maroons United Youth Club sign at Ball Ground, Flagstaff, 2008.

Maroon Trails from Flagstaff: Repairing the Leeward Maroon Polity

In the later years of my research, the Flagstaff area of Maroon Town attracted support from local, national and international organizations for its emerging heritage tourism which has also become a focus for youth in the community. By 2008, a youth club 'Flagstaff Maroons United', had put up a sign at Ball Ground indicating that this was the site of Trelawny Town (figure 11.7). Another sign was erected in 2008 by the Jamaica National Heritage Trust at Flagstaff Square indicating a 'community tourism' (history, culture and biodiversity) development project to commemorate the sacred sites of the Second Maroon War at Trelawny Town by cutting trails through the Cockpits for a 'Flagstaff Heritage Tour and Trails Project Site' (figures

11.8a and 11.8b). The sign indicates support by the United States Agency for International Development (USAID) through its Protected Areas and Rural Enterprise (PARE) Project in partnership with The Nature Conservancy to support the Jamaican government's Forestry Department's Local Forest Management Committee to develop the project. When I revisited Flagstaff Square in March 2009, I was told by residents that 'Dignitaries' from USAID, the Cockpit Country Preservation Association and the Forestry Department had held a 'big meeting' there the previous day at the Flagstaff New Testament (Pentecostal) Church. In addition, Robert McGhie IV, by then Maroon Town's most prominent banana farmer (chapter 10), who lives next to the church, informed me that he had leased the developers the upstairs of a large building at the Square.

In March 2009, Robert Chambers, the owner of the 'Maroons' Pride' banana chip factory, who is from Flagstaff, gave me a five-page typescript from the Flagstaff community history project. Robert explained that the project had developed two trails to Dragoon Hole and Petty River Bottom (sites of the maroon wars, chapters 2, 8 and 9). He mentioned that a leader of the project was from near Maroon Town and is 'mixed with the McGhies and the Reids' (two of Maroon Town's Meso-Creole clans).

In Montego Bay, the Maroon Town Councillor shed further light on this development project, explaining that:

> The Cockpit Country Preservation Association is working with an organisation up there [in Flagstaff] with a view to establishing trails to

Figure 11.8a. The Jamaica National Heritage Trust sign at Flagstaff Square, 2008.

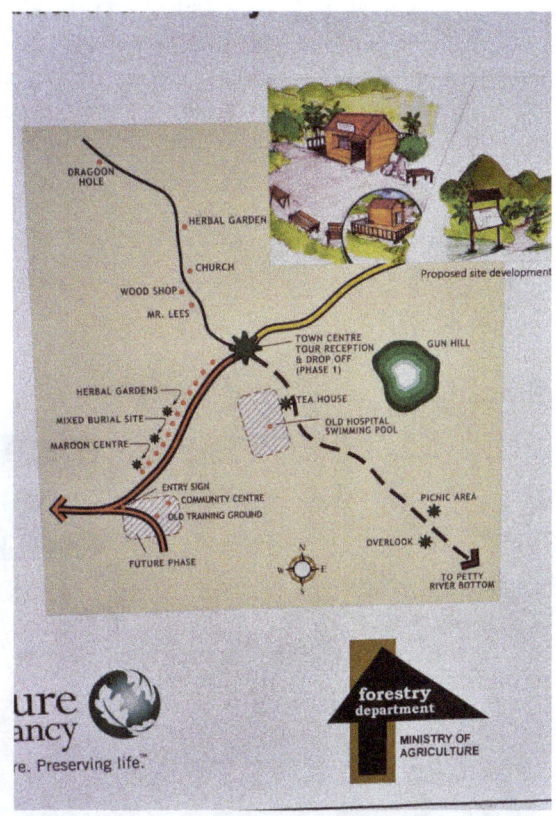

Figure 11.8b. Maroon Trails on the Jamaica National Heritage Trust sign at Flagstaff Square, 2008.

Petty River and other places of maroon interest, with a view to making it a Heritage Community Eco-Tourism Site.

In addition, Councillor Harris elaborated, as well as American aid, there is European support for the heritage-tourism development of Flagstaff, focusing on sites from the aftermath of the Second Maroon War, including the water tank that was part of the colonial barracks and military cemetery:

> The European Union has signed a contract with the Parish Council to enhance community tourism there [at Flagstaff]. The project is to include restoring the pool and access to the pool [figure 7.3], plus a memorial park at the cemetery – the cemetery is to be developed into a memorial park. And the establishment of story-boards.

Then the Councillor reflected: 'There was a hospital there [at the barracks] as well. Flagstaff and Maroon Town Crossroads was all Trelawny Town/Cudjoe Town. Flagstaff was just a point [for the colonists] to hoist their flag.'

When I revisited Accompong in March 2009, Colonel Peddie likewise commented on the Flagstaff heritage-tourism development in which the Accompong Maroons are also involved:

> We are in close contact with the Maroons up in Flagstaff to set up trails...We are in dialogue with the government and with the Forest Management Committee and are a part of it [the Committee]...It concerns [bauxite] mining issues. We are setting up trails right across the Cockpits. We the Maroons and the Flagstaff Maroons, they are cutting [trails] from both ends to meet up (figures 11.9a, 11.9b and 11.9c).

Figure 11.9a. The Accompong Development Centre and Rastafarian craft shop, 2009.

Maroon Town and Accompong: Ritual, Tourism and Nationhood • 329

Figure 11.9b. The Accompong Development Centre with the Maroon Trails sign, 2009.

Figure 11.9c. The Maroon Trails sign, Accompong Development Centre, 2009.

I expressed surprise that he had referred to the Flagstaff population as Maroons. He explained that: 'There used to be Maroons up there' as 'Trelawny Town was at Flagstaff. Anferry Town is here, Accompong Old Town' (see chapters 3–4). However, he continued, the Maroon Town villagers are 'now so integrated' with non-maroon society, that the Flagstaff population are non-Maroons. Nevertheless, he explained, the inhabitants of Flagstaff had recently expressed the wish to be included as Maroons, despite their tax-paying status:

> They do not have the privilege we do. They are taxed by the government. They [the British colonists] took them [the Trelawnys] to Sierra Leone. But recently they [the villagers at Flagstaff] want to be part of the maroon community.[19]

As Colonel, Peddie was on the Forest Management Committee, as was the Deputy Colonel, Melvin Currie, and Ex-Colonel Cawley who was Vice-President. Colonel Peddie said that the 'President is from Flagstaff, St James, Michael Grizzle'. Peddie explained there was also a member of the American Peace Corps recently stationed in Accompong (since June 2008) on this Eco-Tourism Project cutting trails and putting up signs, for example, to Old Town and the Peace Cave (in St Elizabeth), to Flagstaff (St James) and towards Quick-Step in southern Trelawny. A trail had been made from Accompong to Quick-Step and a trail was planned from Flagstaff to Quick-Step to link Flagstaff and Accompong. However, there seemed to be some disagreement on this issue between the two communities in relation to the sacred sites of Leeward Maroon history (compare chapters 3–6).

Later that year, a *Gleaner* article, 'Maroon heritage resurrected in Flagstaff, St James' by Paul H. Williams, published November 1, 2009, announced the opening of the first phase of this heritage tourism project at Flagstaff including 'three trails, an interpretive centre, gift shop, local food and craft[s]', with the building of a museum (backed by the Minister of Tourism) planned as the second stage. While highlighting the significance of Flagstaff in maroon history and underlining its neglect, the article elides the deportation of the Trelawny Maroons after the Second Maroon War, portraying the history of the community as being one where the post-treaty Maroons 'were subsequently left alone to carry on their lives in that rocky place' with only in- and out-migration diluting the maroon community and its culture. This media coverage of Flagstaff parallels aspects of some Maroon Town narratives that likewise suppress the trauma of the aftermath of the Second Maroon War and the related fracturing of the Leeward polity (chapters 8–9).[20]

The *Gleaner* article was nevertheless very informative on the national and international stake-holders in this heritage-tourism project and their alliance with the Flagstaff community and the leader of the project, Michael Grizzle:

> This dream is now a reality for Michael Grizzle, chairman of the Cockpit Country Local Forest Management Committee, and the residents of Flagstaff. Conceived as an eco-tourism project which also exposes visitors and locals to Maroon history and heritage, it was spearheaded by The Nature Conservancy, The United States Agency for International Development through its Protected Areas and Rural Enterprise Project and The Forestry Department...

> 'The need to preserve the Maroon heritage in Flagstaff arose from the community, who saw the need to rekindle the historical factors of the area as Flagstaff was little known to readers of history,' Grizzle told the *Sunday Gleaner*.
>
> Also, 'with the inception of the Cockpit Country Local Forest Management Committee in March 2007, the vision of establishing an anchor heritage tourism project in the community of Flagstaff, as an example of how natural resources in an area can be used for community development, came about.'
>
> It took much work to get the project off the ground, but with great contribution from other partners such as the Jamaica Business Development Centre, HEART Trust, Institute of Jamaica, Tourism Product Development Company and the Jamaica National Heritage Trust, the Cockpit Country Local Forest Management Committee: Flagstaff Heritage Tours and Trails are now up and running.

This heritage-tourism project at Flagstaff reflects the negotiation of identities and the on-going transformations of freedom among descendants of slaves, Maroons and colonists at the maroon/non-maroon interface. In addition, in contrast to the low-key awareness of Maroon Town in Accompong, reflected in narratives collected there around 1999 (chapter 6), Accompong's participation in this project in the new millennium highlights a heightened recognition of Maroon Town and its historical links with Trelawny Town. In Maroon Town (especially Flagstaff), the project makes a strong statement of the community's links with the maroon past and its role in relation to both the Leeward Maroon polity and Jamaican non-maroon society. Combined with the Emancipation Day festivals at Flagstaff, this maroon-heritage project also highlights the complexity of identification in and about Maroon Town both in the Cockpits and in the Jamaican nation state.

On October 26–27, 2012, an international conference 'The African in Jamaica – Safeguarding Intangible Cultural Heritage of the Maroons for Democracy, Governance & Development' was hosted in Accompong to launch 'The Quick Step 7 Mile Maroon Trail', linking Flagstaff and Accompong.[21] The Jamaican Prime Minister, the Honourable Portia Simpson Miller, delivered the Keynote Address.[22] The conference had been launched on October 4, 2012 at the Spanish Court Hotel in Kingston, where the Minister of Youth and Culture, Hon. Lisa Hannah, 'announced the full support of her Ministry for the conference'.[23] At the hotel conference launch, Ferron Williams, Colonel of Accompong, highlighted the link between the conference, the United Nations' focus on intangible culture and peoples of African descent, Jamaica's 50th Anniversary of Independence and Accompong's 274th treaty anniversary:

> On October 17, 2003, the United Nations adopted a Convention for the safeguarding of intangible culture and later declared 2011 as the year for the recognition of people of African descent. These actions, along with Jamaica's 50th Anniversary celebration and Accompong's 274th treaty anniversary, propelled us to host this important conference.[24]

As with the narratives in Accompong and Maroon Town that symbolically repair the disjunctures of Leeward Maroon history (chapters 3–10), including the rupture resulting from the deportation of the Trelawnys following the Second Maroon War (chapter 2), the development of maroon trails from the Flagstaff area of Maroon Town to Accompong launched by the conference and the participation of both these communities in this project represent a symbolic repairing of the fractured Leeward Maroon polity. The project also represents the symbolic reclamation of some of the Trelawny Town territory.

Yet, simultaneously, the strengthening relationship between the Accompong Maroons and the Jamaican government and the focus on maroon trails between Flagstaff and Accompong reflected in the conference highlight the growing role of maroon culture and history in the identity of the non-maroon Jamaican nation state and of Accompong as a symbol of Jamaican nationhood. Such developments further highlight and reinforce the ongoing creolization of the Leeward Maroon polity and its commons (chapters 3–5). These symbolic reparations also situate creolization in the Cockpits within the wider context of Jamaica and its global tourist industry.

Notes

1. An early illustration of the significance of such emancipation celebrations in Jamaica was the celebration of August 1, 1843 (five years after 'full freedom') in the Trelawny free village of Martha Brae and the nearby town of Falmouth, as described by the Baptist missionary, William Knibb (Besson 2002, 130).
2. Up to the 1950s, however, Emancipation Day continued to be celebrated in Jamaica in association with both the Anglican and Baptist Churches. As a child in Jamaica, in the late 1940s and 1950s, I regularly participated with my family in the August 1st Anglican Church Fair in Falmouth, Trelawny.
3. Significant in this re-establishment of Emancipation Day in Jamaica, in 1997, was a national vigil on the eve of Emancipation Day in Jamaica's former capital of Spanish Town, St Catherine, in association with the Phillippo Baptist Church. Participants in the vigil included villagers from nearby Sligoville, the island's first Baptist-founded free village (Davis-Palmer 2010). On Friday, August 1, 1997, the main Jamaican newspaper, the *Gleaner*, carried an 'Emancipation Feature', which included extracts from the *Falmouth Post* of August 1, 1838. With the reinstitution of Emancipation Day celebrations, similar vigils would be held at other significant national sites of memory elsewhere in the island. These included the Emancipation Vigil in Falmouth's 'Market Square' in Trelawny, on the evening of July 31, 2001, following the Ben' Down Market earlier that day (Besson 2002, 208). The market and the vigil both underlined the strategies of opposition and resistance employed by the enslaved to challenge slavery. Annual national vigils have also been held at historic Kensington in St James (a few miles from Maroon Town), the site of the start of the great slave rebellion of 1831–32.
4. As discussed later, my plan to attend the 2003 Emancipation Day celebrations at Flagstaff were changed due to the intriguing celebration of this event that I attended in Accompong. As I was not always in Jamaica in August, Councillor Harris of Maroon Town kindly kept me up to date with the Flagstaff celebrations, up to 2010, while I was in London.
5. As seen in figure 11.2b, the central motif on the white and yellow tee-shirts was a red flag framing a globe coloured green, gold and black, thereby combining the colours of the Jamaican

national flag (black, gold and green) with those of the Rastafarian movement (red, green and gold). Above the flag were printed the words: 'Emancipation Day 2002'. Below the flag were the manufacturers' postal agency address and e-mail and telephone details: 'Flagstaff, P.A., Jamaica, W. I., @ right needles int., Pro L.T.D. 912 5261'.

6. This conclusion is reinforced by Kenneth Bilby's (2010) later analysis of 'Jankunu (John Canoe)' festivals throughout the Anglophone Caribbean, where he argues that despite the secularization of Jankunu in the Caribbean these festivals represent an African-derived spiritual/religious worldview focused on the ancestors.

7. *Gleaner*, 'Accompong Maroon Celebrations', January 4, 2002.

8. Paul H. Williams, 'Maroon power vacuum – Battle lines drawn in Accompong as leadership squabble stirs debate', *Gleaner*, July 1, 2009. See also chapter 3.

9. Rowe's argument against 'this piece of administrative blunder [that] has caused severe confusion among the rank and file of the Maroons as well as well-wishers who always support us in this our rich cultural heritage', was outlined at some length in the article. Its essence was that 'The celebration is normally held on a Monday', especially if January 6 falls on the preceding Sunday, and the plan for 'this Sunday's reveling cannot spare his [Peddie's] back', was influenced by outsiders and supported by only '15 per cent of the Maroons'. According to Rowe, 'who claims that during his tenure as Colonel, no outsider could have dared influence him to hold the celebration on a Sunday', and who had 'chided Colonel Peddie for making such a decision', there had never been such a Sunday celebration 'in the 264-history of the Peace Treaty'.

10. In addition to the extensive coverage of the impending Accompong maroon celebrations, including the role of the TDPCo, the *Gleaner* feature included two other advertisements. One of these was for the 'Accompong Maroon Festival' itself, where '264 Years of Tradition will be rekindled'. This advertisement invited the national and international public to 'Come Be a Part of the Culture', and 'Enjoy the traditional ceremony, food, craft, dance, music, drumming and herbs', at the cost of J$200 for adults and J$100 for children. This advert also included a 'Vendors Notice', stating that: 'Vendors of Traditional Foods & Craft Items are being invited to participate in the Celebrations. All Food Vendors must have a food handler's permit and be pre-registered'. The other advertisement, 'Visit Maroon Country in the Cockpit Mountains', decorated with small symbols of the mountains and the maroon abeng, publicized the 'Maroon Attraction Tours, Co', based in Montego Bay, which I knew to be the Councillor's tours to Maroon Town. However, in the wider context of the full-page newspaper feature of the 'Accompong Maroon Celebrations', the advert implicitly linked Maroon Town to Accompong's maroon cultural heritage. Readers were advised to dress casually and wear comfortable shoes for this 'all inclusive bus tour', which was an 'all day excursion' to Maroon Town available on Tuesdays, Thursdays and Saturdays, on which further information could be obtained from the Hotel Tour Desks where reservations could be made. Our trip with the Councillor, which continued to Accompong, was an elaboration of these tours.

11. This included the Committee's mission statement (dated October 31, 2001): 'To develop the community of Accompong, to improve and sustain the quality of life of all its citizens; socially, culturally and economically and to preserve the heritage of the Maroons for future generations'. The advertisement continued with a list of projects that would benefit from the gate fees (and

additional donations) for the day's event: upgrading sanitation facilities, a literacy programme, completing the Community Centre, care of the elderly and a skills training programme.

12. 'Accompong Maroon Celebrations', Special Advertising Feature, *Gleaner*, January 4, 2002.
13. Monique Hepburn, 'Accompong Town Maroon Foundation established', *Gleaner*, January 11, 2005.
14. The island's main newspaper even included a photo of me and some of my companions from Montego Bay talking at Kindah with a Windward Maroon Colonel.
15. See, e.g., Garfield Myers, 'Maroons unite in defence of Cockpit Country', *Jamaica Observer* January 8, 2007.
16. Sheena Gayle, 'Tradition rules! – Maroon chief signals return to traditional customs', *Jamaica Gleaner*, January 13, 2010. The article also reported that the Colonel's innovations included charging an admission fee and that some of the proceeds 'would be used to fund a new education initiative, and some to partially finance the education of students preparing for the Grade Six and Nine Achievment Tests'. However, the charging of admissions fees had in fact already been the case in recent years.
17. Sheena Gayle, 'Maroon celebration is not downtown market – Colonel Williams', *Gleaner*, January 6, 2011.
18. 'Accompong Maroon Festival', http://www.whatsonwhen.com/sisp/index.htm?fx= event&event_ id =18141, accessed 1/4/2011.
19. Consistent with this recent development, the programme of the Charles Town 5th Annual International Maroon Conference in the Windward Maroon polity on June 21–23, 2013 included a speaker (Gloria 'Mau Mau G' Simms) from the 'Trelawny Maroons'. Gloria Simms is founder and director (since 2007–2008) of the Maroon Women's Indigenous Circle and has been previously described as 'from the Trelawny Town Maroons in St James' (see chapter 3, note 12); that is, from Maroon Town/Flagstaff. The Simms surname is the title of the Ex-Councillor Mortimer Reid's maternal clan in Maroon Town (chapter 8).
20. See also note 19 above.
21. 'Accompong Maroon Conference 2012', http://www.facebook.com/events/478882435479702/; 'Accompong Maroon Conference 2012 – Pre-Conference Day', http://www.facebook.com.events/194439960690864/
22. '2012 Accompong Maroon Conference', http://www.facebook.com/media/set/?set =a.10151114326053021.43.
23. Calving Brown, 'JAMAICA – Accompong to Host Maroon Conference', Wednesday, October 17, 2012, http://www.caricomnewsnetwork.com/index.php?option=com_conte.
24. Ibid.

12 ■ CREOLIZATION AT THE MAROON/NON-MAROON INTERFACE

This comparative ethnography of Accompong, Aberdeen and Maroon Town reveals significant variations in creolization among the descendants of slaves and Maroons at the heart of African-America. This chapter draws together these themes by highlighting the similarities and differences in peasantization, descent and land transmission, and ritual and politics in these Cockpit Country communities. I then reflect on the wider contributions of this ethnography at the maroon/non-maroon interface, including its relevance to the comparative study of creolization in maroon and non-maroon derivations of African-American slave cultures.

Transformations of Freedom

My research on Accompong, Aberdeen and Maroon Town highlights the varying transformations of freedom that have occurred through peasantization in the Cockpits. Since the colonial deportation of the Trelawny Town Maroons, following the Second Maroon War of 1795–96, Accompong has been transformed from the secondary community of the Jamaican Leeward Maroon polity, established by rebel slaves through squatting and treaty in the First Maroon War (1725–38), to become its sole surviving village and the oldest African-American corporate maroon society. This peasantization has involved the transformation of a colonial reservation into a sacred landscape, reinforced by narratives and Myal rituals. Since the building of the rocky road to the village in the 1940s (Barker and Spence 1988), Accompong has participated in the burgeoning and declining Jamaican banana industry as well as becoming a transnational community through overseas labour migration. This transnationalism is now reflected in the Council of Overseas Maroons which, since 2006, has held annual Homecoming and International Conferences in Accompong a few days before the Myal Play.

Maroon Town, on the former site of Cudjoe's Town/Trelawny Town, reflects the transformations of freedom that have occurred on this historic site of African-American marronage. Trelawny Town was the primary treaty town of the Leeward Maroon polity, established by rebel slaves through the First Maroon War, but became a ghost town after the Second Maroon War, following the deportation of the Trelawnys and the confiscation of their territory. Further transformations occurred in the contexts of miscegenation between colonists and slaves, continuing marronage, post-slavery peasantization, the consolidation of a banana peasantry and the incorporation of Maldon, the first Baptist free village in St James. This peasantization, combined with pronounced international circulatory migration since emancipation, has created another new site of Jamaican transnational identity.

Aberdeen was transformed from a proto-peasant slave community on the Aberdeen plantation, bordering the Accompong commons, to a post-emancipation free village in the foothills of the Cockpits in association with the Moravian church. As in Maroon Town, this Aberdonian post-slavery peasantry claims descent from slaves, colonists and Maroons. With overseas labour migration since emancipation, Aberdeen too has become a transnational community, whose global networks span the Caribbean, the Americas and Britain. Like Maroon Town and Accompong, Aberdeen has also been impacted by the global and national banana industry.

Caribbean Cognatic Clans and Creole Tenures

A central theme of peasantization in the Cockpit Country communities is the transformation of lands formerly held in European legal tenures (by either planters or the colonial/post-colonial state) into lands held through Caribbean creole tenures based on kinship and community (see also Besson 2000). Such transformations have occurred as a result of the appropriation and creolization of land rights (through squatting, treaty, purchase and customary transmission) by Maroons and slaves and their descendants. Similarities and variations on this theme have occurred in the three Cockpit communities studied, including the consolidation of landholding clans and lineages, the creolization of the commons in Accompong and the creation of family lands in Maroon Town and Aberdeen.

In all three villages, transnational cognatic landholding clans and their component lineages are the core of the community (as in the Trelawny free villages descended from emancipated slaves [Besson 2002]). This gendered mode of descent and land transmission, traced through both women and men and now including migrants overseas, originated on the Caribbean slave plantations as a creole transformation of both European primogeniture and West and Central African unilineal landholding. This creole system maximized, in the Caribbean context, scarce land rights and formerly forbidden family lines among the descendants of enslaved Africans, who were not only legally landless and kinless but also property themselves (Besson 1995b, 1995d, 1997, 2002, 2005 and chapters 2–10).

In Accompong, overlapping cognatic clans and lineages are embedded in the corporate maroon community that especially claims descent from Cudjoe and/or his 'sister', Nanny, who is sometimes said to have been Matilda Rowe, the ancestress of the Rowe Family, Accompong's central clan. In Aberdeen and Maroon Town, many cognatic clans claim 'slave master' pickni' descent from colonists and slaves and in some cases from African, Afro-Creole or Meso-Creole Maroons. In Maroon Town, these maroon ancestors are said to include 'Accompong Nanny', who is sometimes said to have been Betsy Currie (an ancestress of the Currie, Clarke, Walker and Hines Old Families). In Aberdeen, cognatic clans include the descendants of the African-Prince Maroon.

In all three villages, burial practices embed the identities of communities and kin groups in the land. However, there are differences between Aberdeen and Maroon Town, on the one hand, and Accompong on the other. In both Aberdeen and Maroon Town (as in the non-maroon Trelawny villages), the landscape is embroidered with family-land burial grounds. These cemeteries provide sites of identity for cognatic kin groups, including overseas migrants who return for mortuary ritual especially in intensely transnational Maroon Town.

By contrast, in Accompong, the entire common treaty land has been transformed through actual or symbolic burial grounds into a sacred landscape that reflects and reinforces the Leeward Maroon polity. These cemeteries also symbolize the process of creolization within the maroon society, charting the transformation from reputed early African ethnic groups to an Afro-Creole community. However, house-yard burial is also emerging there, as cognatic clans and lineages consolidate usufructuary rights to house-yards within the commons. As in Aberdeen and Maroon Town, the evolving architecture of vaults and sepulchres reflects the impact of migrant savings and remittances.

In addition, in all these communities, cognatic clans and lineages are perceived as transmitting and transforming ancestral African substance to construct new Creole ethnicities: maximizing its transmission among Afro-Creoles in Accompong, Aberdeen and Maroon Town (as in Trelawny's free villages) and diluting it in various degrees among 'slave master' pickni' ('mulattos', 'sambos', 'quadroons', 'mustees', 'musteffinos' and 'high-colour browns') in Maroon Town and Aberdeen (see also Besson 1999b, 2003a). Among Afro-Creoles and Meso-Creoles in Aberdeen and Maroon Town, both maroon and non-maroon ethnicities have been created. In Accompong, the explicit transformation from African ethnicities to Afro-Creole maroon identity is reflected in the creolization of the commons.

Ritual and Politics

Like peasantization, land, descent groups, narratives and ethnicities, ritual reflects the similarities and differences in creolization among the three Cockpit Country communities and their varying political relationships with the Jamaican post-colonial state. In Accompong, the annual Myal Play reinforces the identity of the Leeward Maroon polity and highlights its ambiguous alliance with the Jamaican nation state. The Myal Play derives from the Myal slave religion, which was the first creolized African-Jamaican worldview, in which a morally neutral magical/spiritual power (Obeah) was believed to be accessed from the ancestors through spirit possession (Myal) and used for protection and healing during enslavement (Bilby 1993; Handler and Bilby 2001; Schuler 1979, 1980; Besson 2002). Myalism was transformed in marronage, through further creolization, to focus on the ancestral spirits of the First-Time Maroons (chapters 3–4).

My research reveals a continuing process of creolization in the Myal Play, when compared with Barbara Kopytoff's (1987) earlier study which described the ascendance of the Christian God over Accompong Town's traditional cosmology. My ethnography shows the re-emergence, strengthening and further transformation of Myalism in Accompong, with a shifting focus from Captain Accompong to his leader, Captain Cudjoe. This shift has elaborated the sacred landscape and reinforced the creolization of the commons. This re-ascendancy of Myalism, including the recent focus on Cudjoe, the creation of Kindah, and the symbolic relocation of Old Town and the Peace Cave, encapsulates the continuities and disjunctures in Leeward Maroon history and symbolically repairs and strengthens the shrunken Leeward Maroon polity.

The Myal Play has now further creolized, becoming a symbol of the Jamaican nation, a magnet for overseas maroons and an attraction in the island's tourist industry. The coexistence of Myalism in Accompong with the Presbyterian/United Church and the Revival, Pentecostal and Rastafarian religions likewise reflects continuing creolization.

Aberdonians who claim Accompong maroon ancestry participate in the Myal Play, as well as in their own Moravian/Revival/Pentecostal rituals, indicating both Aberdeen's close relationship with the Leeward Maroon polity and its integration into the Jamaican nation state.

Some Maroon Town villagers likewise attend the Myal Play, as well as belonging to their own Baptist/Revival/Adventist religions, highlighting the complexities of creolization at the maroon/non-maroon interface. In addition, national Emancipation Day rituals are held at Flagstaff (the former site of Trelawny Town), which is both a symbolic and contested site in Jamaican history – being a sacred place from both maroon wars, the location of the colonial barracks following the Second Maroon War and an area of subsequent peasantization. The Flagstaff festivals, which are becoming a tourist attraction and which, at the turn of the millennium, included a Jonkonnu masquerade deriving from the Myal slave religion and relating to the Revival worldview, symbolize the complex role of Maroon Town in Jamaican nationhood. These celebrations, organized by the Parish Councillor for Maroon Town, likewise reflect the incorporation of this former maroon site of Trelawny Town into the Jamaican political system. The recent heritage-tourism project focusing on maroon trails from Flagstaff to Accompong both elaborates this relationship and symbolizes the reparation of the Leeward Maroon polity. In addition, Accompong's growing recognition of the significance of Maroon Town, resulting from the re-creation of maroon trails between the two communities and the support from the Jamaican government to this project, highlights the symbolic reparation of the historic Leeward Maroon polity in the context of Jamaican nationhood.

Emancipation Day celebrations are not usually held in Accompong, as the Leeward Maroon polity secured its freedom a century before emancipation. However, in 2003 emancipation celebrations were held in Accompong. I related this short-lived innovation to internal political factions in Accompong and their varying relationships with the Jamaican nation state, revealing further nuances of creolization. However, in Accompong, this process of localization is more fully reflected in the ongoing transformations of the enduring Myal Play which reinforces the continuing creolization of the commons.

Ethnography at the Maroon/Non-Maroon Interface

As seen above, this ethnography of Accompong, Aberdeen and Maroon Town reveals significant similarities and differences in creolization among the descendants of slaves and Maroons. Within this comparative context, the book also provides an ethnography of the fractured but enduring Jamaican Leeward Maroon polity, the oldest African-American corporate maroon society. This ethnography complements Kenneth Bilby's (2006) study of the Jamaican Windward Maroons (figure 12.1) and provides an alternative interpretation to Werner Zips's (2011, 9; 2012) dismissal of creolization in Accompong.

My ethnography of Accompong is enhanced by comparative perspectives from Maroon Town and Aberdeen and by my previous Trelawny free village study (Besson 2002). This wider perspective contrasts with the narrower focus on maroon societies by maroon specialists, including Barbara Kopytoff (1973, 1976a, 1976b, 1979, 1987), Mavis Campbell (1990), Carey Robinson (1969) and Bev Carey (1997) on the Jamaican Maroons, Kenneth Bilby (1996, 2006) on the Guianese and Windward Maroons, Richard Price (e.g., 1983, 1990, 2008, 2011) and Sally Price (e.g., 1993) on the Maroons of Suriname and French Guiana, and Werner Zips's (1999, 2011) Accompong study.[1]

This book also revises some of the interpretations of maroon specialists on the Leeward Maroon polity, including Kopytoff's (1987) conclusion on the demise of Myalism in Accompong and Campbell's (1990) view of so-called confusion among the Accompong Maroons regarding Nanny's burial place. It also revises interpretations of Accompong maroon society and its common land in terms of passive African retentions and static legal pluralism (Barker and Spence 1988; Campbell 1990; Zips 1996, 1998, 1999, 2011), revealing instead the dynamic process of Caribbean creolization that engages with the wider racialized class-based society and which has enabled the Leeward Maroon polity to endure.

Figure 12.1. The author (left) and Ken Bilby discussing research at Kindah, Accompong, c. 2002.

Further, by situating the study of the Leeward Maroon polity in a wider comparative canvas including the descendants of plantation slaves, colonists and rebel slaves, the book highlights that maroon societies like Accompong are a variation on the Caribbean peasantization process that began soon after the European Conquest and which includes squatters, proto-peasants, post-emancipation peasantries and Maroons (Mintz 1989, 1996a; Besson 2002, 2007, 2012a). This comparative perspective on peasantization, embedded in the process of creolization, in turn, reveals the significance of the creole tenures of common land, family land and informal occupation or 'squatting'[2] as modes of sustainable development among both Maroons and non-Maroons (see also Besson 1984a, 1987a, 2000, 2003c; Besson and Momsen 1987, 2007).

In addition to such transformations from European to Caribbean creole tenures, the comparative study of the three Cockpit Country communities reveals other related transformations of freedom through peasantization. These include the ascendance of Accompong from the secondary to the primary village of the Leeward Maroon polity; the transformation of the historic maroon site of Cudjoe's Town/Trelawny Town to the non-maroon village of Maroon Town; and the evolution of the Aberdonian proto-peasant slave community into the free village of Aberdeen. These transformations have both similarities and differences with the Trelawny free villages forged from proto-peasant slave communities, including the appropriation and transformation of Martha Brae, a former slave-trading planter town (Besson 2002). The ongoing consolidation of the Trelawny squatter-peasant community of Zion, on a former slave plantation, is a further variation on this theme (Besson 2002, 2007, 2012a).

The scope of this comparative study in the Cockpits, which includes an in-depth ethnography of Maroon Town and its evolution on the historic site of the former Leeward Maroon village of Cudjoe's Town/Trelawny Town, also uncovers the hidden story of this transformation and its importance for Jamaican national history. In so doing, it sheds light on the internal differentiation of the category 'Maroons' who included mulattos, foragers and women, as well as the black male warriors who have been the focus of attention in most studies of marronage (e.g., Zips 1999, 2011; R. Price 1983, 1996, 2011), and whose descendants blur the boundaries of 'true-born maroons' (Bilby 2006). In this context, this book especially highlights the significance of the mulatto McGhie Maroons of the non-treaty maroon village of Congo Town/Highwindward/Me No Sen You No Come in Trelawny and their legacy in Maroon Town, where the Meso-Creole McGhie Old Family is the central clan.

In addition, this comparative ethnography in the Cockpits shows that the narratives in both Accompong and Aberdeen of military and conjugal alliances between the Accompong Maroons and the Aberdonian proto-peasant slaves, which bridged the divide between those who fought for freedom and those who created some autonomy on the backlands of the Aberdeen plantation, contrast with the oral traditions of opposition between the Windward Maroons and the descendants of plantation slaves (Bilby 1984b). My identification of these oral traditions in Accompong and Aberdeen, and my exploration of the ambiguous relationship between these communities, also illuminates the still-neglected historical 'relationships between proto-peasantries and maroon bands', which, as Sidney Mintz noted, 'though hardly known at all, could prove of immense significance for our understanding of slave resistance' (Mintz 1989, 153, in Besson 1995a, 311 n6).

Likewise, the theme of 'slave master' pickni' descent in Maroon Town oral traditions (as well as in some Aberdonian narratives), combined with historical sources and other aspects of my anthropological fieldwork, illustrates from an ethnographic perspective the legacy of miscegenation in African-America between slave masters and slaves that has only recently received the attention it deserves (Petley 2005; Green 2006).

This ethnography at the Jamaican maroon/non-maroon interface also contributes to the neglected comparative study of creolization in maroon and non-maroon transformations of African-American slave cultures, as discussed more fully below.[3]

Maroon and Non-Maroon Transformations of African-American Slave Cultures

In their classic discussion of African-American creolization, Sidney Mintz and Richard Price (1992, 2, 8) observed that Africans brought to the New World came from diverse ethnic groups, preventing the conveyance of a generalized African cultural heritage to any single plantation colony. They concluded that the African heritage is, therefore, not reflected in retentions of surface form, as Herskovits (1941) contended, but in underlying meanings or 'cognitive orientations' (Mintz and Price 1992, 10). They argued that, 'the organizational task of enslaved Africans in the New World was that of creating institutions – institutions that would prove responsive to the needs of everyday life under the limiting conditions that slavery imposed upon them' (19). They posited rapid institution-building, examples being creole language and religion and the fictive-kinship shipmate bond. They contended that such institutions were created '*within* the parameters of the masters' monopoly of power, but *separate from* the masters' institutions' (39).

From these perspectives, Mintz and Price pointed to the 'mysteries' of Caribbean peasant kin-based land-tenure institutions, especially in Haiti and Jamaica (Price 1967, 47–48; Mintz 1989, 242). In addition, they asserted that, in contrast to the matrilineal descent groups of the Saramaka Maroons in the Surinamese interior, the non-exclusive cognatic ancestral-ritual groups of the plantation slaves of the Para coastal region of Suriname 'would not function efficiently to hold land in common' after emancipation as such groups would overlap and escalate in size, and that, therefore, 'the plantation communities themselves became the land-holding corporations' (Mintz and Price 1992, 70). Despite evidence of unrestricted cognatic landholding corporations among the Para ex-slaves and their descendants, as individuals gained 'rights to land use through their genealogical connections to ancestors who had lived there' (70),[4] Mintz and Price called for clarification on 'the precise nature' of similar landholding kin groups among the descendants of plantation slaves 'in both the Haitian and Jamaican cases' (75).

Elsewhere, in relation to maroon societies, Price (1996, 28) argued that, 'Maroons indeed drew on their diverse African heritages in building their cultures', but observed that, 'We still know almost nothing about the actual culture-building processes that took place'. He posited that, rather than stressing isolated African retentions, as Bastide (1972) had done, we should focus on deeper African principles, including the 'internal dynamism' of 'West African cultural systems' with 'their ability to grow and change' (Price 1996, 30). Price further suggested that, in contrast to the isolated Saramaka, this process of creolization has gone furthest among the Maroons of Jamaica who have had 'increasing contact with the rest of Jamaican society' (228). However, as noted in chapter 5, he concluded that,

> Exactly how much of the [Jamaican] Maroons' distinctive cultural heritage, and which particular aspects of it remain alive beneath the surface is a question that only sensitive in-depth field work, carried out in the immediate future, can answer (229).

My interpretation of the creolization of the commons in Accompong, based on in-depth fieldwork and combined with the comparative study of Aberdeen and Maroon Town (as well as my earlier Trelawny free-village study), builds on, modifies and advances these perspectives in five main ways that are significant for the comparative exploration of creolization in maroon and non-maroon derivations of African-American slave cultures.

First, rather than displaying African retentions of form (Barker and Spence 1988; Campbell 1990; Zips 1996, 1998, 1999, 2011), my ethnography shows that Accompong common tenure reflects pronounced Caribbean creolization, manifesting the 'internal dynamism' of African cultures with 'their ability to grow and change' (Price 1996, 30). This culture-building is due in part to 'increasing contact with the rest of Jamaican society' as Price (228) hypothesized, and partly derives from Accompong's history as the oldest African-American corporate maroon polity.

Second, my research highlights that institution-building among African-American slaves was not entirely *'separate from* the masters' institutions' as Mintz and Price (1992, 39) contended, even in marronage. Instead, like the Jamaican proto-peasantry who appropriated plantation yards and provision grounds and reversed or overturned colonial primogeniture to create the gendered institution of family land (Besson 2002, and chapters 6–10), the rebel slaves and their descendants in Accompong *appropriated, negotiated and transformed* the masters' European agrarian-capitalist institutions (a colonial legal-freehold treaty and a marginal reservation) to create a sacred Caribbean landscape through the creolization of the commons (chapters 3–5).

Third, in this process of creative transformation and place-making, unrestricted cognatic landholding clans and lineages have crystallized in Accompong within the wider context of the commons; a variation on a wider Caribbean-peasant theme of creole tenures rooted in kinship and community. Such creole tenures include the family lands of Maroon Town and Aberdeen (as well as the Trelawny free villages), where cognatic landholding kin groups maximize family lines and scarce land rights as well as creating cultural sites of identity, facilitating return- and circulatory-migration and remittances, and generating new laws for Jamaican nationhood (Besson 2002, 2012a and chapters 7–11). This interpretation not only offers an alternative to Mintz and Price's (1992, 70) conclusion that non-exclusive descent groups 'would not function efficiently' for landholding in the Caribbean after slavery but also advances their creolization theory by revealing a culture-building process more creative than even they envisaged.

Fourth, this conclusion underlines Price's (1996, 30) assertion that, 'With a rare freedom to extrapolate African ideas and adapt them to changing circumstance, maroon groups include what are in many respects both the most meaningfully African and the most truly "alive" of all Afro-American cultures'. The symbolic landscape of the Accompong Maroons, forged through Caribbean creolization, highlights the significance of Price's thesis in the oldest enduring African-American corporate maroon society.

However, fifth, as I have shown, non-maroon post-slavery peasantries have likewise created cognatic landholding institutions with similarities to Accompong's tenurial system. Moreover, this institution-building began even within the constraints of plantation-slave communities, as proto-peasants established customary cognatic land transmission systems that consolidated after emancipation. In addition to the non-maroon Trelawny villages on the plantation lowlands, such culture-building is evident in Aberdeen and Maroon Town in the Cockpits, which are both non-maroon villages despite their links with the Leeward Maroons.

The mode of unrestricted cognatic descent and land transmission found in all the Jamaican communities that I studied, was long considered inoperable by anthropologists and is still regarded as ethnographically rare, being documented primarily for East Africa and the Pacific. However, as I have further shown, such cognatic landholding kin groups are widely found among non-maroon communities throughout the Antilles and also characterize the Black Caribs of the Caribbean coastlands of Central America and the post-slavery peasantries of the plantation coastlands of Guyana and Suriname, as well as Jamaican free villagers and Maroons (Besson 1995d, 1997, 2000, 2001, 2002, and chapter 5). This mode of descent and land transmission has similarities with the matrilineal landholding systems of the Maroons in the interiors of French Guiana and Dutch Guiana/Suriname (e.g., R. Price 1975; 2011; S. Price 1993; Bilby 1996). However, in the Antilles and on the circum-Caribbean coastal plains where land is scarce, cognatic kin groups maximize land rights, whereas the Guianese Maroons have had greater autonomy and more extensive territories that have enabled them to retain or forge anew, African-type unilineal landholding systems (Besson 1997; 2002, 313–15, and chapter 5).

The ethnography of Accompong, Aberdeen and Maroon Town, therefore, advances this comparative exploration of landholding kin groups among descendants of African-American plantation slaves and Maroons, as well as throwing into sharp relief other similarities and differences in creolization at the maroon/non-maroon interface.

In addition, the identification of cognatic landholding kin groups in the Cockpits, reinforced by my previous Trelawny study and my ethnographic reviews identifying such descent groups in other Caribbean societies (Besson 1984a, 1995b, 1997, 2000, 2001, 2002, 2005), has significant implications for the understanding of kinship, temporality and cultural memory among the descendants of slaves and Maroons in African-America's Caribbean core.

Kinship, Temporality and Cultural Memory

In episode 4 of *Britain's Slave Trade*, 'A Message From Our Ancestors' (Channel 4 Television, London, Black History Month, October 1999), Trevor Phillips argued that, 'some of the worst aspects of slavery are that memories are broken, chains of memory are broken' and that, 'the graveyards of the Caribbean are a record of the personal history of a few privileged families'. The Caribbean *oikoumenê* was indeed forged through catastrophic ruptures resulting from the European Conquest, the swift extirpation of indigenous Caribs and Tainos, the transatlantic trade in Africans, the plantation system and slavery, slave revolts and marronage, the flight of freed slaves from the plantations, and post-slavery migrations to the Americas and Europe. These ruptures have been central to the history of Accompong, Aberdeen and Maroon Town and the Trelawny free villages.

However, in all these communities, metaphors of these ruptures – such as narratives of ancestral displacement and oral traditions of marronage and the post-slavery exodus from the estates – have been created by the descendants of slaves and Maroons and embedded in cognatic clans and lineages, with their graveyards, to represent and maximize continuity in the reconstruction of kinship as memory of the past relating persons, places and relations over time, and as reflecting hidden histories of the African diaspora in Jamaica (Besson 1999b, 2002 and chapters 3–12). The transmission in these now transnational descent groups of ancestral land, trees, houses, names, blood, substance and cemeteries (with their continuity, change[5] and symbolic regeneration of life [compare Bloch and Parry 1982]) further reflects the conveyance of memories across time and space. Descent group mortuary ritual is also a route for regeneration, re-gathering and continuity; while reputed spirit possession, from the Myal and Revival spirit pantheons, is perceived as a transmission of messages and spiritual substance from ancestors to their cognatic descendants traced through both women and men.

Other transmitting symbols linked to these cognatic descent groups include the abeng, drums, and phones. During slavery, drums were forbidden and played in secret among the enslaved, transmitting messages and facilitating perceived ancestral spirit possession, and drumming remains central to Myal, Revival and Rastafarian rituals. In Accompong, at the Myal Play and related mortuary rites, the abeng is likewise blown. In other contexts too, the abeng's melodious tones still drift over the Cockpits carrying messages within the kin-based community, as among the First-Time Maroons.

On my return visits to Accompong, from 1998 to 2002, I found that the abeng had been reinforced by two mobile 'cell phones' (introduced by Dolphie Rowe, a returned migrant Maroon of Accompong's central clan), one of which was often taken into the provision grounds and forest to 'receive incoming calls' (I was told). At that time, in contrast to the near absence of phones in remote Accompong and their scarcity in most of the other communities that I studied, was the ubiquitous telephone network in Maroon Town (installed on the initiative of Councillor Harris in 1997). The landline network in this mountainous community is amazing: even precarious chattel cottages have multiple phones. This reflects not only the strong integration of Maroon Town into the national political system, but also the intense transnational nature of that village where the landlines were installed to receive incoming messages from cognatic clan folks abroad and other overseas kin. For a similar purpose, by the turn of the millennium, Ion McGhie, a returned migrant from Toronto in Maroon Town's central clan, had set up his computer online and intended to demonstrate email to even the youngest schoolchildren (though he told me in 2009 that the introduction of the Internet there has been slow).

When I revisited Accompong from 2006 to 2009, cell phones had become widespread – for receiving incoming calls from North America and Britain – and a cell phone mast now rises into the sky just behind Kindah, where Maroons perceive that they receive spiritual messages from their ancestors. There is also a second cell phone mast near the school.[6] By 2011, there was a similar mast in the Trelawny free village of Martha Brae (compare Horst and Miller 2005, 2006) and Accompong had an Internet café,[7] with the potential of not only enhancing education in the community but also linking transnational kin.

In all these ways, in all the Jamaican communities that I studied, chains of memory, routed through transnational and trans-generational kinship and rooted in kin-based lands and their cemeteries, will undoubtedly endure within creole cognatic clans and lineages that are also transmitting messages and memories through abengs, drums, narratives, landlines, radio-frequency waves and cyberspace.

These findings have further implications for the understanding of kinship, temporality and cultural memory among the descendants of African-American slaves and Maroons in the Caribbean core. African-American kinship has traditionally been regarded as 'disorganized' and attributed to either anachronistic African survivals or deviations from European norms (e.g., Frazier 1939; Herskovits 1941; Henriques 1968; R.T. Smith 1956). This was especially so in relation to the so-called 'matrifocal' family, particularly in Jamaica which has been described as having the world's highest rate of so-called 'illegitimacy' (Hartley 1980; Laslett 1980, xi).

More recently in the study of African-American and Caribbean kinship, attention has focused on horizontal ego-focused bilateral kinship networks; that is, the relatives surrounding each individual traced through both parental sides (Davenport 1961b; Olwig 1981; R T Smith 1988; Stack 1970, 1974). However, such studies only highlight a dimension of kinship that does not persist over time[8] and overlook the enduring vertical ancestor-focused cognatic clans and lineages that I have identified in the Cockpit Country communities, Trelawny's free villages and throughout the Antilles and African-American coastlands of the Caribbean Sea (Besson 1997, 2000, 2002, 2005 and this book). These gendered descent groups link dead ancestors, living kin and their unborn descendants through time (compare Gutman 1987). These temporal continuities are often projected onto family land and common land and their cemeteries, and these lands and graveyards with their oral traditions, likewise, link kin through time and space.[9]

In all the Cockpit Country communities that I studied, as well as in the Trelawny free villages, such dispersed but enduring vertical transnational cognatic descent groups transmitting and transforming cultural memories co-exist with short-term horizontal bilateral kinship networks, serial polygamy,[10] and either 'complex' or 'elementary' marriage exchange (compare Lévi-Strauss 1969);[11] variations resulting from similarities and differences in creolization among descendants of Maroons and slaves. Some Accompong Maroons practise endogamous cousin-conjugality, a creolized form of 'elementary' marriage exchange, which they say originates in a marital alliance between the African 'tribes' of the early Maroons. Aberdeen and Maroon Town, like the Trelawny free villages, have an open or 'complex' marriage system with marriage prohibitions (including the prohibition of cousin-conjugality) but no preferential marriage rules.[12] These ordered systems of descent, kinship and marriage, manifesting elaborate creativity and both short-term and long-term temporality, have not been fully recognized before. These family systems are neither European nor African, but rather reflect Caribbean creolization and maroon and non-maroon variations on this theme.

The Wider Contributions of the Book

By exploring the neglected comparative study of creolization in maroon and non-maroon derivations of African-American slave cultures through this ethnography at the maroon/non-maroon interface in the Cockpits, reinforced by my earlier study of Trelawny free villages (Besson 2002), this book contributes to a range of issues in social anthropology which traditionally marginalized the Caribbean heart of African-America but has now begun to recognize its centrality to the discipline (Mintz 1996a; Besson 2002; Martin 2012). These issues include the cross-cultural study of globalization, post-colonialism, transnationalism, identity histories, new ethnicities, kinship and temporality,[13] cognatic descent and land-transmission, gender, religion, narratives and place-making (e.g., Maurer 1997; Rapport and Dawson 1998; Lovell 1998; Stone 2000; Besson and Olwig 2005; Mayo 2005).

This comparative ethnography in the Cockpits likewise illuminates global debates on land and development in the twenty-first century (Besson 2003c; Williams 2003; Home and Lim 2004; Besson and Momsen 2007), highlighting the creativity of customary land tenures embedded in kinship and community and their potential for sustainable development in the face of an escalating Eurocentric focus on land markets in the capitalist world system (e.g., de Soto 2000). Within that wider canvas, this book challenges Garrett Hardin's (1968) classic theory of 'the tragedy of the commons', revealing instead the sustainability of common landholding and the creative Caribbean culture-building in the creolization of the commons in Accompong, the oldest corporate maroon society in African-America enduring on common land.[14]

Notes

1. See, however, chapter 1 note 1 on Kenneth Bilby (1984b) and Sidney Mintz and Richard Price (1992).
2. As in the Trelawny squatter settlement of Zion (and in the early history of post-slavery Martha Brae), 'squatting' or informal occupation was a significant mode of land acquisition in the history of all three of the Cockpit Country communities that I studied: in Cudjoe's Town (Trelawny Town/Maroon Town) and Accompong during pre-treaty marronage, and in Aberdeen and Maroon Town after emancipation, before land purchases were made. Such informal occupation, therefore, provided the foundation for these communities. In addition, as in Trelawny, the expansion of Aberdeen and part of Maroon Town occurred through the peasantization of former plantation lands.
3. This section of this chapter draws on and develops my earlier analysis in Besson (1997, 228–32). I thank the editors of *Plantation Society in the Americas* for permission to reproduce and expand those conclusions here.
4. Since Sidney Mintz and Richard Price (1992, 69) point out that this was not a unilineal system, such ancestral genealogical connections could only be cognatic. Moreover, 'the principles of descent and ancestry' are still 'richly particularized and anchored in the land' (70).
5. From boulders, cairns and old stone tombs to modern concrete tombs, vaults and sepulchres.
6. Cable and Wireless (now known as LIME Jamaica) near Kindah and Digicel near the school.
7. 'Accompong Town gets Internet café', *Jamaica Observer*, Thursday, March 24, 2011. This Internet café is funded by the Universal Access Fund (UAF).
8. As individual kin networks dissolve after each person's death.
9. A few other analyses have acknowledged the importance of cognatic descent groups in African-America, but have asserted that they are restricted by residence and exclude absent members (Solien 1959; Davenport 1961a; Otterbein 1964; Espeut 1992); an approach that obscures the transnational nature of the transgenerational dimension of such kinship that persists through both time and space – linking not only the dead and the living, but also both migrant and resident kin. Evidence of enduring unrestricted cognatic descent groups was implicit in Edith Clarke's groundbreaking study of Jamaican family land in the non-maroon communities of Sugartown, Orange Grove and Mocca. However, Clarke mistakenly characterized the landholding group as the bilateral 'kindred' (a short-term ego-oriented kin group). Nevertheless, she indicated the enduring ancestor-focus of the landholding kin group, arguing that land rights and descent are transmitted '*either* "through the blood" *or* "by the name"' (Clarke 1966, 48, my emphasis, see also 68, and 1953, 83, 112). Clarke argued that this dictum derived from the Ashanti concepts of *abusua* (glossed as clan; blood; derived from the female parent; matrilineal descent) and *ntoro* (spirit; semen; derived from the male parent; patrilineally transmitted). However, Clarke's interpretation does not seem accurate as the Ashanti have a system of *unilineal* descent with 'complementary filiation': they have primary *matrilineal* corporate descent groups, traced through women, that hold and transmit rights to land; and secondary *patrilineal* non-corporate groups, which stress father-son spiritual ties (Fox 1967, 101–102, 132; Goody 1969; Besson 2002, 308–309). In contrast, in the Cockpit Country communities that I studied in St James and St Elizabeth, as well as in the Trelawny free villages (Besson 2002) – and I suggest in Clarke's communities as well – ancestral substance and related land rights and graveyards are

traced and transmitted through *both genders* within the *same* family line: that is, through the 'blood' *and* by the 'name'; namely a creole system of unrestricted cognatic descent, which also includes migrants as well as residents. See also chapter 5 note 2.
10. The concept of 'serial polygamy' (or sometimes 'serial monogamy') is used by anthropologists of the Caribbean region to refer to sequential multiple conjugal unions.
11. See chapter 1 note 31.
12. This system is more 'complex' than even Claude Lévi-Strauss envisaged, as it interrelates with both serial polygamy and multiple marital forms (extra-residential relations, consensual cohabitation and late legal marriage, chapters 3–10 and Besson 2002).
13. This theme was the focus of an international conference on 'Kinship and Temporality' at Goldsmiths, University of London organised by Olivia Harris and Monica Conrad on the eve of the new millennium in December 1999 (e.g. Besson 1999b).
14. My interpretation is reinforced by David Lowenthal's and Colin Clarke's essay on 'the triumph of the commons' in Barbuda (Lowenthal and Clarke 2007). See also Besson (1997) and Olwig (1997).

References

Aarons, John A. 1981. The Maroon Town Cantonment. *Jamaican Historical Society Bulletin* 8, no. 2:28–31.

Agorsah, E. Kofi. 1994. Archaeology of Maroon Settlements in Jamaica. In *Maroon Heritage*, edited by E. Kofi Agorsah, 163–87. Kingston: Canoe Press.

Ahmed, Belal. 2004. The Impact of Globalisation on the Caribbean Sugar and Banana Industries. In *Beyond the Blood, the Beach and the Banana*, edited by Sandra Courtman, 256–72. Kingston and Miami: Ian Randle Publishers.

Alleyne, Mervyn. 1996. *Africa: Roots of Jamaican Culture*. Chicago: Research Associates School Times Publications (Orig. pub. 1988).

Anonymous. 1828. *Marly, or the Life of a Planter in Jamaica*. Glasgow: Richard Griffin.

Austin-Broos, Diane J. 1997. *Jamaica Genesis*. Chicago and London: University of Chicago Press.

Barker, David, and David J. Miller. 1995. Farming on the Fringe: Small-Scale Agriculture on the Edge of the Cockpit Country. In *Environment and Development in the Caribbean*, edited by David Barker and Duncan F.M. McGregor, 271–92. Kingston, Jamaica: University of the West Indies Press.

Barker, David and Balfour Spence. 1988. Afro-Caribbean Agriculture: A Jamaican Maroon Community in Transition. *The Geographical Journal* 154, no. 2:198–208.

Barker, Robert B. 2000. Mid-Eighteenth Century Jamaican House Design. Paper presented to the Friends of the Georgian Society of Jamaica, London.

Barnard, Alan, and Jonathan Spencer. 2002. Glossary. In *Encyclopedia of Social and Cultural Anthropology*, edited by Alan Barnard and Jonathan Spencer, 594–628. 2nd ed. London and New York: Routledge (Orig. pub. 1996).

Bastide, Roger. 1972. *African Civilizations in the New World*. New York: Harper and Row.

Bauer, Elaine, and Paul Thompson. 2006. *Jamaican Hands Across the Atlantic*. Kingston: Ian Randle Publishers.

Beckford, George L. 1972. *Persistent Poverty*. London: Oxford University Press.

Beckwith, Martha. 1929. *Black Roadways*. Chapel Hill: University of North Carolina Press.

Berleant-Schiller, Riva. 1977. Production and Division of Labor in a West Indian Peasant Community. *American Ethnologist* 4:253–72.

———. 1978. The Failure of Agricultural Development in Post-Emancipation Barbuda. *Boletin de Estudios Latinoamericanos y del Caribe* 25:21–36.

———. 1987. Ecology and Politics in Barbudan Land Tenure. In *Land and Development in the Caribbean*, edited by Jean Besson and Janet Momsen, 116–31. London: Macmillan.

Besson, Jean. 1974. Land Tenure and Kinship in a Jamaican Village. 2 vols. PhD diss., University of Edinburgh.

———. 1984a. Family Land and Caribbean Society: Toward an Ethnography of Afro-Caribbean Peasantries. In *Perspectives on Caribbean Regional Identity*, edited by Elizabeth M. Thomas-Hope, 57–83. Liverpool: Liverpool University Press.

———. 1984b. Land Tenure in the Free Villages of Trelawny, Jamaica. *Slavery & Abolition* 5, no.1: 3–23.

———. 1987a. A Paradox in Caribbean Attitudes to Land. In *Land and Development in the Caribbean*, edited by Jean Besson and Janet Momsen, 13–45. London: Macmillan.

———. 1987b. Family Land as a Model for Martha Brae's New History. In *Afro-Caribbean Villages in Historical Perspective*, edited by Charles V. Carnegie, 100–132. Kingston, Jamaica: African-Caribbean Institute of Jamaica.

———. 1988. Agrarian Relations and Perceptions of Land in a Jamaican Peasant Village. In *Small Farming and Peasant Resources in the Caribbean*, edited by John S. Brierley and Hymie Rubenstein, 39–61. Winnipeg: University of Manitoba.

———. 1992a. Freedom and Community: The British West Indies. In *The Meaning of Freedom*, edited by Frank McGlynn and Seymour Drescher, 183–219. Pittsburgh, Pa.: University of Pittsburgh Press.

———. 1992b. Review of Veront M. Satchell, *From Plots to Plantations*. Mona, Jamaica: Institute of Social and Economic Research, University of the West Indies, 1990. In *The Journal of Peasant Studies* 19, no. 2:358–61.

———. 1993. Reputation and Respectability Reconsidered: A New Perspective on Afro-Caribbean Peasant Women. In *Women and Change in the Caribbean*, edited by Janet H. Momsen, 15–37. London: James Currey.

———. 1995a. Free Villagers, Rastafarians and Modern Maroons: From Resistance to Identity. In *Born out of Resistance*, edited by Wim Hoogbergen, 301–314. Utrecht: ISOR Press.

———. 1995b. Land, Kinship and Community in the Post-Emancipation Caribbean: A Regional View of the Leewards. In *Small Islands, Large Questions*, edited by Karen Fog Olwig, 73–99. London: Frank Cass.

———. 1995c. Religion as Resistance in Jamaican Peasant Life: The Baptist Church, Revival Worldview and Rastafarian Movement. In *Rastafari and Other African-Caribbean Worldviews*, edited by Barry Chevannes, 43–76. London: Macmillan.

———. 1995d. The Creolization of African-American Slave Kinship in Jamaican Free Village and Maroon Communities. In *Slave Cultures and the Cultures of Slavery*, edited by Stephan Palmié, 187–209. Knoxville: University of Tennessee Press.

———. 1997. Caribbean Common Tenures and Capitalism: The Accompong Maroons of Jamaica. In *Common Land in the Caribbean and Mesoamerica*, edited by Bill Maurer, Special Issue, *Plantation Society in the Americas* IV, nos. 2 and 3:201–232.

———. 1998a. Changing Perceptions of Gender in the Caribbean Region: The Case of the Jamaican Peasantry. In *Caribbean Portraits*, edited by Christine Barrow, 133–55. Kingston: Ian Randle Publishers.

———. 1998b. Folk Law and Legal Pluralism in Jamaica. In the *Commission on Folk Law and Legal Pluralism,* Proceedings of the 14th International Congress of Anthropological and Ethnological Sciences, 311–38. Williamsburg, Virginia.

———. 1999a. Folk Law and Legal Pluralism in Jamaica: A View from the Plantation-Peasant Interface. *Journal of Legal Pluralism and Unofficial Law* 43:31–56.

———. 1999b. Hidden Histories of the African Diaspora: Kinship and Temporality in Transnational Jamaica. Paper presented to the *Kinship and Temporality Workshop,* Goldsmiths College, University of London, December 16–18.

———. 2000. The Appropriation of Lands of Law by Lands of Myth in the Caribbean Region. In *Land, Law and Environment,* edited by Allen Abramson and Dimitris Theodossopoulos, 116–35. London: Pluto Press.

———. 2001. Empowering and Engendering Hidden Histories in Caribbean Peasant Communities. In *History and Histories in the Caribbean,* edited by Thomas Bremer and Ulrich Fleischmann, 69–113. Madrid: Iberoamericana; Frankfurt am Main: Vervuert.

———. 2002. *Martha Brae's Two Histories: European Expansion and Caribbean Culture-Building in Jamaica.* Chapel Hill: University of North Carolina Press.

———. 2003a. Euro-Creole, Afro-Creole, Meso-Creole: Creolization and Ethnic Identity in West-Central Jamaica. In *A Pepper-Pot of Cultures,* edited by Gordon Collier and Ulrich Fleischmann, 169–88. New York, NY and Amsterdam: Rodopi.

———. 2003b. Gender and Development in the Jamaican Small-Scale Marketing System: From the 1660s to the Millennium and Beyond. In *Resources, Planning and Environmental Management in a Changing Caribbean,* edited by David Barker and Duncan McGregor, 11–35. Kingston, Jamaica: University of the West Indies Press.

———. 2003c. History, Culture and Land in the English-speaking Caribbean. In *Land in the Caribbean,* edited by Allan N. Williams, 31–60. Land Tenure Center, University of Wisconsin-Madison.

———. 2005. Sacred Sites, Shifting Histories: Narratives of Belonging, Land and Globalisation in the Cockpit Country, Jamaica. In *Caribbean Narratives of Belonging,* edited by Jean Besson and Karen Fog Olwig, 17–43. Oxford: Macmillan.

———. 2007. 'Squatting' as a Strategy for Land Settlement and Sustainable Development. In *Caribbean Land and Development Revisited,* edited by Jean Besson and Janet Momsen, 135–46. New York: Palgrave.

———. 2009. Myal, Revival and Rastafari in the Making of Western Jamaica: Dialogues with Chevannes. In *The African-Caribbean Worldview and the Making of Caribbean Society,* edited by Horace Levy, 26–45. Kingston, Jamaica: University of the West Indies Press.

———. 2011a. M.G. Smith's Plural Society Theory and the Challenge of Caribbean Creolization. In *Caribbean Reasonings. M.G. Smith: Social Theory and Anthropology in the Caribbean and Beyond,* edited by Brian Meeks, 22–42. Kingston, Jamaica: Ian Randle Publishers.

———. 2011b. Missionaries, Planters and Slaves in the Age of Abolition. In *The Caribbean: A History of the Region and Its Peoples,* edited by Stephan Palmié and Francisco A. Scarano, 317–29. Chicago and London: The University of Chicago Press.

———. 2012a. Maroons, Free Villagers and 'Squatters' in the Development of Independent Jamaica. Paper presented at the conference *Fifty Years of Jamaican Independence: Developments and Impacts*. Institute for the Study of the Americas, University of London, February 10.

———. 2012b. Transformations of Freedom in the Land of the Maroons: Creolization in the Cockpits. Lecture to the Jamaican Historical Society, Kingston, University of the West Indies, December 11.

———. 2013. Unpublished Notes on the Jamaican McFarlanes.

Besson, Jean, and Barry Chevannes. 1996. The Continuity-Creativity Debate: The Case of Revival. *New West Indian Guide* 70, nos. 3 and 4:209–228.

Besson, Jean, and Ian McFarlane. 1995/2005/2009. The Jamaican McFarlanes and Related Families. Unpublished papers, London.

Besson, Jean, and Janet Momsen. 1987. Introduction. In *Land and Development in the Caribbean*, edited by Jean Besson and Janet Momsen, 1–9. London: Macmillan.

Bettelheim, Judith. 1985. The Jonkonnu Festival in Jamaica. *Journal of Ethnic Studies* 13, no. 3: 85–105.

———. 1988. Jonkonnu and other Christmas Masquerades. In *Caribbean Festival Arts*, edited by John W. Nunley and Judith Bettelheim, 39–83. Seattle: University of Washington Press.

Bilby, Kenneth M. 1984a. The Treacherous Feast: A Jamaican Maroon Historical Myth. *Bijdragen tot de Taal, Land- en Volkenkunde* 140:1–31.

———. 1984b. 'Two Sister Pickni': A Historical Tradition of Dual Ethnogenesis in Eastern Jamaica. *Caribbean Quarterly* 30, nos. 3 and 4:10–25.

———. 1993. The Strange Career of 'Obeah': Defining Magical Power in the West Indies. Paper presented to the General Seminar, Institute for Global Studies in Culture, Power & History, Johns Hopkins University, Fall.

———. 1996. Ethnogenesis in the Guianas and Jamaica: Two Maroon Cases. In *History, Power, and Identity*, edited by Jonathan D. Hill, 119–41. Iowa City: University of Iowa Press.

———. 1997. Swearing by the Past, Swearing to the Future: Sacred Oaths, Alliances, and Treaties among the Guianese and Jamaican Maroons. *Ethnohistory* 44, no. 4:655–89.

———. 1999. Gumbay, Myal, and the Great House: New Evidence on the Religious Background of Jonkonnu in Jamaica. In *ACIJ Research Review* 4:47–70. Kingston, Jamaica: African-Caribbean Institute of Jamaica.

———. 2006. *True-Born Maroons*. Kingston and Miami: Ian Randle Publishers.

———. 2010. Surviving Secularization: Masking the Spirit in the Jankunu (John Canoe) Festivals of the Caribbean. *New West Indian Guide* 84, nos. 3 and 4:179–223.

Blackburn, Robin. 1997. *The Making of New World Slavery*. London: Verso.

Bloch, Maurice, and Jonathan Parry. 1982. Introduction. In *Death and the Regeneration of Life*, edited by Maurice Bloch and Jonathan Parry, 1–44. Cambridge: Cambridge University Press.

Blustain, Harvey S. 1981. Customary Land Tenure in Rural Jamaica: Implications for Development. In *Strategies for Organization of Small-Farm Agriculture in Jamaica*, edited by Harvey S. Blustain and Elsie LeFranc, 47–65. Mona: Institute for Social and Economic Research, University of the West Indies and Ithaca: Center for International Studies, Cornell University.

Bohannan, Paul. 1967. Africa's Land. In *Tribal and Peasant Economies*, edited by George Dalton, 51–60. Garden City, New York: Natural History Press.

Bolland, O. Nigel. 2002. Creolisation and Creole Societies: A Cultural Nationalist View of Caribbean Social History. In *Questioning Creole*, edited by Verene A. Shepherd and Glen L. Richards, 15–39. Kingston, Jamaica: Ian Randle Publishers.

Braithwaite, Lloyd. 1953. Social Stratification in Trinidad. *Social and Economic Studies* 2:5–175.

Brathwaite, Edward Kamau. 1968. Jamaican Slave Society, A Review. *Race* IX, no. 3:331–42.

———. 1971. *The Development of Creole Society in Jamaica, 1770-1820*. Oxford: Clarendon Press.

———. 1982. The Slave Rebellion in the Great River Valley of St. James – 1831/32. *The Jamaican Historical Review* XIII:11–30.

Brereton, Bridget. 1996. A Social History of Emancipation Day in the British Caribbean: The First Fifty Years. In *Inside Slavery*, edited by Hilary McD Beckles. Mona, Jamaica: Canoe Press.

———. 2010. National Narratives in Post-Independence Trinidad and Tobago. Paper presented to the 34th Annual Conference of the Society for Caribbean Studies, University of Southampton.

———. 2011. Jubilees: How Trinidad Remembered Emancipation, the Centenary of British Rule and Victoria's Jubilees. Paper presented to the 35th Annual Conference of the Society for Caribbean Studies, Liverpool.

Burton, Richard D.E. 1997. *Afro-Creole*. Ithaca: Cornell University Press.

Campbell, Mavis C. 1990. *The Maroons of Jamaica 1655–1796*. Trenton: Africa World Press.

Caplan, Patricia. 1969. Cognatic Descent Groups on Mafia Island, Tanzania. *Man* 4, no. 3:419–31.

Carey, Bev. 1997. *The Maroon Story*. St Andrew, Jamaica: Agouti Press.

Carnegie, Charles V. 1987. Introduction. In *Afro-Caribbean Villages in Historical Perspective*, edited by Charles V. Carnegie, iv–x. Kingston: African-Caribbean Institute of Jamaica, Research Review No. 2.

Cassidy, Frederic C. 1971. *Jamaica Talk*. 2nd ed. Basingstoke and London: Macmillan (Orig. pub. 1961).

Chevannes, Barry. 1978. Revivalism: A Disappearing Religion. *Caribbean Quarterly* 24, nos. 3 and 4:1–17.

———. 1994. *Rastafari: Roots and Ideology*. Syracuse: Syracuse University Press.

———. 1995a. Introducing the Native Religions of Jamaica. In *Rastafari and Other African-Caribbean Worldviews*, edited by Barry Chevannes, 1–19. London: Macmillan.

———. 1995b. New Approach to Rastafari. In *Rastafari and Other African-Caribbean Worldviews*, edited by Barry Chevannes, 20–42. London: Macmillan.

Clarke, Edith. 1966. *My Mother Who Fathered Me*. 2nd ed. London: George Allen & Unwin (Orig. pub. 1957).

Clegg, Peter. 2004. The Transatlantic Banana War and the Marginalisation of Caribbean Trading Interests. In *Beyond the Blood, the Beach and the Banana*, edited by Sandra Courtman, 242–55. Kingston and Miami: Ian Randle Publishers.

Comitas, Lambros. 1962. Fishermen and Co-operation in Rural Jamaica. PhD diss., Columbia University.

———. 1973. Occupational Multiplicity in Rural Jamaica. In *Work and Family Life*, edited by Lambros Comitas and David Lowenthal, 157–73. Garden City: Anchor Press/Doubleday.

Conolley, Ivor, and James Parrent. 2005. Land Deeds that Tell the Story of the Birth of Falmouth. *Jamaican Historical Society Bulletin* 11, no. 15:383–409.

Cooper, Arch. 1939. Letters, Notes and Diaries. Kingston, Jamaica: University of the West Indies Library.

Craton, Michael J. 1982. *Testing the Chains*. Ithaca: Cornell University Press.

———. 1987. White Law and Black Custom: The Evolution of Bahamian Land Tenures. In *Land and Development in the Caribbean*, edited by Jean Besson and Janet Momsen, 88–114. London: Macmillan.

———. 1995. Decoding Pitchy-Patchy: The Roots, Branches and Essence of Junkanoo. *Slavery and Abolition* 16:14–44.

Crichlow, Michaeline A. 2005. *Negotiating Caribbean Freedom*. Lanham, MD: Lexington Books.

Cross, Malcolm. 1979. *Urbanization and Urban Growth in the Caribbean*. Cambridge: Cambridge University Press.

Cundall, Frank. 1915. *Historic Jamaica*. London: published for the Institute of Jamaica by the West India Committee.

———. 1937. *The Governors of Jamaica in the First Half of the Eighteenth Century*. London: The West India Committee.

Dallas, R.C. 1803. *The History of the Maroons*. 2 vols. London: T.N. Longman and O. Rees.

Davenport, William. 1961a. Introduction. *Social and Economic Studies* 10, no. 4:380–85.

———. 1961b. The Family System of Jamaica. *Social and Economic Studies* 10, no. 4:420–54.

Davis-Palmer, Yvonne. 2005. Narratives and the Cultural Construction of Belonging in Sligoville, Jamaica's First Free Village. In *Caribbean Narratives of Belonging*, edited by Jean Besson and Karen Fog Olwig, 44–62. Oxford: Macmillan.

———. 2010. *Cultural Identity and Creolized Religion in Sligoville, Jamaica's First Baptist Free Village*. Saarbrücken, Germany: Lambert Academic Publishing.

Desai, Vandana, and Robert B. Potter, eds. 2002. *The Companion to Development Studies.* London: Arnold.

De Certeau, Michael. 1980. On the Oppositional Practices of Everyday Life. *Social Text* 3:3–43.

De Friedemann, Nina S., and Jaime Arocha. 1995. Colombia. In *No Longer Invisible*, edited by Minority Rights Group, 47–76. London: Minority Rights Publications.

De Soto, Hernando. 2000. *The Mystery of Capital.* London: Black Swan.

Douglas, Mary. 1966. *Purity and Danger.* London: Routledge and Kegan Paul.

Dunn, Richard S. 2000. *Sugar and Slaves.* Reprint. Kingston, Jamaica: University of the West Indies Press (Orig. pub. 1973).

Durkheim, Emile, and Marcel Mauss. *Primitive Classification.* 1903. London. 1963.

Edwards, Bryan. 1796. *The Proceedings of the Governor and Assembly of Jamaica in Regard to the Maroon Negroes.* London: John Stockdale.

———. 1801. *The History, Civil and Commercial, of the British Colonies in the West Indies*, vol. 1. London: John Stockdale.

Eltis, David. 2000. *The Rise of African Slavery in the Americas.* Cambridge: Cambridge University Press.

Espeut, Peter. 1992. Land Reform and the Family Land Debate. In *Plantation Economy, Land Reform and the Peasantry in a Historical Perspective,* edited by Claus Stolberg and Swithin Wilmot, 69–84. Kingston: Friedrich Ebert Stiftung.

Eyre, L. Alan. 1980. The Maroon Wars in Jamaica – a Geographical Appraisal. *The Jamaican Historical Review* 12:5–19.

———. 1995. The Cockpit Country: A World Heritage Site? In *Environment and Development in the Caribbean,* edited by David Barker and Duncan F.M. McGregor, 259–70. Kingston, Jamaica: University of the West Indies Press.

Fox, Robin. 1967. *Kinship and Marriage.* Harmondsworth, Middlesex: Penguin Books.

Frazier, Franklin E. 1939. *The Negro Family in the United States.* Chicago: University of Chicago Press.

Genevose, Eugene D. 1981. *From Rebellion to Revolution.* Reprint. Baton Rouge, Louisiana: Louisiana State University Press (Orig. pub. 1979).

Goodenough, Ward H. 1955. A Problem in Malayo-Polynesian Social Organization. *American Anthropologist* 57, no. 1:71–83.

Goody, Jack. 1969. The Classification of Double Descent Systems. In *Comparative Studies in Kinship,* edited by Jack Goody. London: Routledge and Kegan Paul.

Green, Cecilia A. 2006. Hierarchies of Whiteness in the Geographies of Empire: Thomas Thistlewood and the Barretts of Jamaica. *New West Indian Guide* 80, nos. 1 and 2:5–43.

Gutman, Herbert G. 1987. The Black Family in Slavery and Freedom: A Revised Perspective. In *Power and Culture,* edited by Ira Berlin, 357–79. New York: The New Press.

Hall, Douglas. 1989. *In Miserable Slavery.* London: Macmillan.

Hall, Stuart. 1991. Iron in the Soul. *Redemption Song.* BBC 2 Television Series Redemption Song (sung by Bob Marley), presented by Professor Stuart Hall.

Hamilton, Douglas J. 2005. *Scotland, the Caribbean and the Atlantic World, 1750–1820*. Manchester: University of Manchester Press.

Handler, Jerome S., and Kenneth M. Bilby. 2001. On the Early Use and Origin of the Term 'Obeah' in Barbados and the Anglophone Caribbean. *Slavery and Abolition* 22, no. 2:87–100.

Hanson, F. Allan. 1971. Nonexclusive Cognatic Descent Systems. In *Polynesia: Readings on a Culture Area*, edited by A. Howard, 109–32. Scranton: Chandler.

Hardin, Garrett. 1968. The Tragedy of the Commons. *Science* 162:1243–48.

Hart, Richard. 1985. *Slaves Who Abolished Slavery: Volume 2 Blacks in Rebellion*. Mona: Institute of Social and Economic Research, University of the West Indies, Jamaica.

Hartley, Shirley Foster. 1980. Illegitimacy in Jamaica. In *Bastardy and its Comparative History*, edited by Peter Laslett, Karla Oosterveen and Richard M. Smith, 379–96. London: Edward Arnold.

Hastings, S.U., and B.L. MacLeavy. 1979. *Seedtime and Harvest*. Bridgetown, Barbados: Cedar Press.

Hennessy, Alistair. 1993. Introduction. In *The Autobiography of a Runaway Slave Esteban Montejo*, Miguel Barnet, 1–12. London: Macmillan.

Henriques, Fernando. 1968. *Family and Colour in Jamaica*. 2nd ed. London: MacGibbon and Kee (Orig. pub. 1953).

Henry, William (Lez). 2005. Projecting the 'Natural': Language, Citizenship and Representation in Outernational Culture! In *Caribbean Narratives of Belonging*, edited by Jean Besson and Karen Fog Olwig, 280–97. Oxford: Macmillan.

Herskovits, Melville J. 1941. *The Myth of the Negro Past*. New York: Harper & Brothers.

Heuman, Gad, ed. 1985. *Out of the House of Bondage*. Special Issue *Slavery and Abolition* 6, no. 3.

———. 1994. *The Killing Time*. London: Macmillan.

Higman, Barry W. 1998. *Montpelier, Jamaica*. Kingston: University of the West Indies Press.

———. 1999. *Writing West Indian Histories*. London: Macmillan.

Hinds, Allister. 2002. 'Deportees in Nova Scotia': The Jamaican Maroons, 1796–1800. In *Working Slavery, Pricing Freedom*, edited by Verene A. Shepherd, 206–22. Kingston: Ian Randle Publishers.

Hoben, Alan. 1973. *Land Tenure among the Amhara of Ethiopia*. Chicago: University of Chicago Press.

Hoetink, H. 1985. 'Race' and Color in the Caribbean. In *Caribbean Contours*, edited by Sidney W. Mintz and Sally Price, 55–84. Baltimore: The Johns Hopkins University Press.

Home, Robert, and Hilary Lim, eds. 2004. *Demystifying the Mystery of Capital*. London: Glasshouse Press.

Hope, Kempe R. 1989. Internal Migration and Urbanization in the Caribbean. *Canadian Journal of Latin American and Caribbean Studies* 14, no. 27:5–21.

Horowitz, Michael M. 1992. *Morne-Paysan*. Revised ed. Prospect Heights, Illinois: Waveland Press (Orig. pub. 1969).

Horst, Heather A., and Daniel Miller. 2005. From Kinship to Link-up: The Cell Phone and Social Networking in Jamaica. *Current Anthropology* 46, no. 5:755–78.

———. 2006. *The Cell Phone*. Oxford: Berg.

Karasch, Mary. 1979. Commentary One on M. Schuler, Afro-American Slave Culture. In *Roots and Branches*, edited by Michael Craton, 138–41. Toronto: Pergamon Press.

Karras, Alan L. 1992. *Sojourners in the Sun*. Ithaca: Cornell University Press.

Knight, James. n.d. The Naturall, Morall and Political History of Jamaica...From the Earlist [sic] Account of Time to the Year 1742. B.M. Ms. 12415.

Kopytoff, Barbara Klamon. 1973. *The Maroons of Jamaica*. PhD Thesis, University of Pennsylvania.

———. 1976a. Jamaican Maroon Political Organization: The Effects of the Treaties. *Social and Economic Studies* 25, no. 2:87–105.

———. 1976b. The Development of Jamaican Maroon Ethnicity. *Caribbean Quarterly* 22, nos. 2 and 3:33–50.

———. 1978. The Early Political Development of Jamaican Maroon Societies. *The William and Mary Quarterly* 35:301–304.

———. 1979. Colonial Treaty as Sacred Charter of the Jamaican Maroons. *Ethnohistory* 26, no. 1:45–64.

———. 1987. Religious Change among the Jamaican Maroons: The Ascendance of the Christian God within a Traditional Cosmology. *Journal of Social History*, 20, no. 3:463–84.

Kroeber, Alfred K. 1946. The Ancient *Oikoumenê* as a Historic Culture Aggregate. *Journal of the Royal Anthropological Institute* 75:9–20.

Laslett, Peter. 1980. Preface. In *Bastardy and Its Comparative History*, edited by Peter Laslett, Karla Oosterveen and Richard M. Smith, ix–xv. London: Edward Arnold.

Leach, Edmund R. 1965. Anthropological Aspects of Language: Animal Categories and Verbal Abuse. In *New Directions in the Study of Language*, edited by E. Lenneberg. Cambridge, Mass: M.I.T. Press.

Lévi-Strauss, Claude. 1964. *Totemism*. London: Merlin Press.

———. 1966. *The Savage Mind*. Reprint ed. Chicago: University of Chicago Press (Orig. pub. 1962).

———. 1969. *The Elementary Structures of Kinship*. Reprint ed. Boston: Beacon Press (Orig. pub. 1949).

Long, Edward. 1774. *The History of Jamaica*. 3 vols. London: T. Lowndes. (Republished 2002).

Lovejoy, Paul E., Verene A. Shepherd and David V. Trotman. 2003. Introduction. In *Busha's Mistress or Catherine the Fugitive*, by Cyrus Francis Perkins, 9–42. Kingston and Miami: Ian Randle Publishers.

Lovell, Nadia, ed. 1998. *Locality and Belonging*. London: Routledge.

Lowenthal, David. 1972. *West Indian Societies*. London: Oxford University Press.

Lowenthal, David, and Colin Clarke. 2007. The Triumph of the Commons: Barbuda Belongs to All Barbudans Together. In *Caribbean Land and Development Revisited*, edited by Jean Besson and Janet Momsen, 147–58. New York: Palgrave Macmillan.

Marshall, Woodville K. 1985. Peasant Development in the West Indies since 1838. In *Rural Development in the Caribbean*, edited by P. I. Gomes 1–14. Reprint ed. Kingston, Jamaica: Heinemann (Orig. pub. 1968).

Martin, Emily. 2012. Turning Points: The Cambridge Anthropological Expedition to the Torres Straits (1898), Malinowski's Fieldwork in Kiriwina (1914–18), and the Puerto Rico Project (1947–49). The 19th Annual Sidney W. Mintz Lecture in Anthropology, Johns Hopkins University, November 7.

Mathurin, D.C. Emerson. 1967. An Unfavourable System of Land Tenure. Paper presented at the Second West Indian Agricultural Economics Conference, St. Augustine, Trinidad.

Maurer, Bill. 1997. *Recharting the Caribbean*, Ann Arbor: University of Michigan Press.

Mayo, Marjorie. 2005. *Global Citizens*. London: Zed Books.

Meeks, Brian, ed. 2011. *Caribbean Reasonings: M.G. Smith: Social Theory and Anthropology in the Caribbean and Beyond*. Kingston: Ian Randle Publishers.

Miller, Learie A., and David Barker. 2007. Land Policy in Jamaica in the Decade after Agenda 21. In *Caribbean Land and Development Revisited*, edited by Jean Besson and Janet Momsen, 119–32. New York: Palgrave Macmillan.

Mintz, Sidney W. 1973. A Note on the Definition of Peasantries. *Journal of Peasant Studies* 1: 91–106.

———. 1989. *Caribbean Transformations*. Morningside Edition, New York: Columbia University Press (Orig. pub. 1974).

———. 1994. Review of *Africa in America* by Michael Mullin, Urbana: University of Illinois Press. *New West Indian Guide* 68, nos. 3 and 4:327–33.

———. 1996a. Enduring Substances, Trying Theories: The Caribbean Region as Oikoumenê. *Journal of the Royal Anthropological Institute* 2, no. 2:289–311.

———. 1996b. Ethnic Difference, Plantation Sameness. In *Ethnicity in the Caribbean*, edited by Gert Oostindie, 39–52. London: Macmillan.

———. 1996c. Tasting Food, Tasting Freedom. In *Tasting Food, Tasting Freedom*, Sidney W. Mintz, 33–49. Boston: Beacon Press.

———. 2010. *Three Ancient Colonies*. Cambridge, Massachusetts: Harvard University Press.

Mintz, Sidney W., and Richard Price. 1992. *The Birth of African-American Culture*. Reprint ed. Boston: Beacon Press (Orig. pub. 1976).

Momsen, Janet. 1987. Land Settlement as an Imposed Solution. In *Land and Development in the Caribbean*, edited by Jean Besson and Janet Momsen, 46–69. London: Macmillan.

Moore, Brian L., and Michelle A. Johnson. 2002. Celebrating Christmas in Jamaica, 1865–1920: From Creole Carnival to 'Civilized' Convention. In *Jamaica in Slavery and Freedom*, edited by Kathleen E.A. Monteith and Glen Richards, 144–78. Kingston, Jamaica: University of the West Indies Press.

Mullin, Michael. 1994. *Africa in America*. Urbana: University of Illinois Press.

Mutabaruka. 2011. Epilogue: The 'Maroon' Struggle as Part of an African Freedom Struggle. In *Nanny's Asafo Warriors* by Werner Zips, 219–27. Kingston and Miami: Ian Randle Publishers.

McDonald, Roderick A. 1993. *The Economy and Material Culture of Slaves*. Baton Rouge: Louisiana State University Press.

McFarlane, Anthony. 1985. *Cimarrones* and *Palenques*: Runaways and Resistance in Colonial Colombia. In *Out of the House of Bondage*, edited by Gad Heuman. Special Issue, *Slavery and Abolition* 6, no. 3:131–51.

Olwig, Karen Fog. 1981. Women, 'Matrifocality,' and Systems of Exchange: An Ethnohistorical Study of the Afro-American Family on St John, Danish West Indies. *Ethnohistory* 28:59–78.

———. 1993. *Global Culture, Island Identity*. Philadelphia: Harwood.

———. 1995. Cultural Complexity after Freedom: Nevis and Beyond. In *Small Islands, Large Questions*, edited by Karen Fog Olwig, 100–120. London: Frank Cass.

———. 1997. Caribbean Family Land: A Modern Commons. In *Common Land in the Caribbean and Mesoamerica*, edited by Bill Maurer, Special Issue, *Plantation Society in the Americas* IV, nos. 2 and 3:135–58.

Otterbein, Keith F. 1964. A Comparison of the Land Tenure Systems of the Bahamas, Jamaica, and Barbados: The Implications It Has for the Study of Social Systems Shifting from Bilateral to Ambilineal Descent. *International Archives of Ethnography* 50:31–42.

Paget, Hugh. 1964. The Free Village System of Jamaica. *Caribbean Quarterly* 10:38–51.

Palmer, Geoff. 2007. *The Enlightenment Abolished*. Penicuik, Midlothian: Henry Publishing.

Patterson, Orlando. 1973. *The Sociology of Slavery*. Reprint ed. London: Granada (Orig. pub. 1967).

Perkins, Cyrus Francis. 2003. *Busha's Mistress or Catherine the Fugitive*. Kingston: Ian Randle Publishers (Orig. pub 1911).

Petley, Crister. 2005. 'Legitimacy' and Social Boundaries: Free People of Colour and the Social Order in Jamaican Slave Society. *Social History* 30, no. 4:481–98.

Pocock, David. 1975. *Understanding Social Anthropology*. London: Hodder and Stoughton.

Price, Richard. 1967. Studies of Caribbean Family Organization: Problems and Prospects. Manuscript, Dept. of Anthropology, Johns Hopkins University, Baltimore, Md.

———. 1975. *Saramaka Social Structure*. Rio Piedra: Institute of Caribbean Studies.

———. 1990. *Alabi's World*. Baltimore: The Johns Hopkins University Press.

———. 2001. The Miracle of Creolization: A Retrospective. *New West Indian Guide* 75, nos. 1 and 2:35–64.

———. 2002. *First-Time*. 2nd ed. Chicago: University of Chicago Press (Orig. pub. 1983).

———. 2006. On the Miracle of Creolization. In *Afro-Atlantic Dialogues*, edited by Kevin A. Yelvington, 115–47. Sante Fe, New Mexico: School of American Research Press.

———. 2008. *Travels with Tooy*. Chicago and London: University of Chicago Press.

———. 2011. *Rainforest Warriors*. Philadelphia, PA: University of Pennsylvania Press.

———, ed. 1996. *Maroon Societies*. 3rd ed. Baltimore: The Johns Hopkins University Press (Orig. pub. 1973).

Price, Richard, and Sally Price. 1991. *Two Evenings in Saramaka*. Chicago: Chicago University Press.

Price, Sally. 1993. *Co-wives and Calabashes*. 2nd ed. Ann Arbor: University of Michigan Press (Orig. pub. 1984).

———. 2006. Seaming Connections: Artworlds of the African Diaspora. In *Afro-Atlantic Dialogues*, edited by Kevin A. Yelvington, 83–114. Sante Fe, New Mexico: School of American Research Press.

Rapport, Nigel. 2000. The Narrative as Fieldwork Technique: Processual Ethnography for a World in Motion. In *Constructing the Field*, edited by Vered Amit, 71–95. London: Routledge.

Rapport, Nigel, and Andrew Dawson, eds. 1998. *Migrants of Identity*. Oxford: Berg.

Reid, Ahmed, and Verene Shepherd. 2007. Abolition Watch: Massacre on the 'Zong' – Outrage Against Humanity. *Jamaica Gleaner*, Sunday July 1.

Robinson, Carey. 1969. *The Fighting Maroons of Jamaica*. Jamaica: William Collins and Sangster.

Robotham, Don. 1980. Pluralism as an Ideology. *Social and Economic Studies* 29, no. 1:69–89.

Rodman, Hyman. 1971. *Lower-Class Families*. London: Oxford University Press.

Romberg, Raquel. 2005. Ritual Piracy or Creolization with an Attitude. *New West Indian Guide* 79, nos. 3 and 4:175–218.

Rosaldo, Renato. 1993. *Culture and Truth*. London: Routledge.

Satchell, Veront M. 1990. *From Plots to Plantations*. Mona: University of the West Indies.

———. 1999. Government Land-Lease Programs and the Expansion of the Jamaican Peasantry, 1866–1900. *Plantation Society in the Americas* VI, no. 1:47–64.

Satterthwaite, David. 2002. Urbanization in Developing Countries. In *The Companion to Development Studies*, edited by Vandana Desai and Robert B Potter, 243–47. London: Arnold.

Schuler, Monica. 1979. Afro-American Slave Culture. In *Roots and Branches*, edited by Michael Craton, 121–55. Toronto: Pergamon Press.

———. 1980. *'Alas, Alas, Kongo'*. Baltimore: The Johns Hopkins University Press.

Seaga, Edward. 1969. Revival Cults in Jamaica: Notes towards a Sociology of Religion. Reprinted in *Jamaica Journal* 3, no. 2 (1982): 3–20.

Seymour-Smith, Charlotte. 1986. *Macmillan Dictionary of Anthropology*. London: Macmillan.

Sheller, Mimi. 2003. *Consuming the Caribbean*. London: Routledge.

———. 2012. *Citizenship from Below*. Durham and London: Duke University Press.

Sheridan, Richard B. 1977. The Role of the Scots in the Economy and Society of the West Indies. In *Comparative Perspectives on Slavery in New World Plantation Societies*, edited by Vera Rubin and Arthur Tuden, 94–106. New York: New York Academy of Sciences.

Sibley, Inez Knibb. 1978. *Dictionary of Place-Names in Jamaica*. Kingston: The Institute of Jamaica.

Smith, M.G. 1960. The African Heritage in the Caribbean. In *Caribbean Studies: A Symposium*, edited by Vera Rubin, 34–46. 2nd ed. Seattle: University of Washington Press (Orig. pub. 1957).

———. 1962a. *Kinship and Community in Carriacou*. New Haven: Yale University Press.

———. 1962b. *West Indian Family Structure*. Seattle: University of Washington Press.

———. 1965a. *The Plural Society in the British West Indies*. Berkeley: University of California Press.

———. 1965b. *Stratification in Grenada*. Berkeley: University of California Press.

———. 1983. Robotham's Ideology and Pluralism: A Reply. *Social and Economic Studies* 32, no. 2:103–139.

———. 1998. *The Study of Social Structure*. New York: Research institute for the Study of Man.

Smith, Raymond T. 1956. *The Negro Family in British Guiana*. London: Routledge and Kegan Paul.

———. 1975. Review of R. Price (ed.), *Maroon Societies*. *Man* 10:149.

———. 1988. *Kinship and Class in the West Indies*. Cambridge: Cambridge University Press.

———. 1996. *The Matrifocal Family*. London: Routledge.

Solien, Nancie L. 1959. The Nonunilineal Descent Group in the Caribbean and Central America. *American Anthropologist* 61:578–83.

Stack, Carol B. 1970. The Kindred of Viola Jackson: Residence and Family Organization of an Urban Black American Family. In *Afro-American Anthropology*, edited by Norman E. Whitten, Jr. and John F. Szwed, 303–312. New York: The Free Press.

———. 1974. *All Our Kin*. New York: Harper and Row.

Stewart, John. 1808. *An Account of Jamaica and Its Inhabitants*. London: Longman, Hurst, Rees & Orme.

Stone, Linda. 2000. *Kinship and Gender*. 2nd ed. Boulder, Colorado: Westview Press (Orig. pub. 1997).

Tanna, Laura. 1984. *Jamaican Folk Tales and Oral Histories*. Kingston, Jamaica: Institute of Jamaica Publications.

Trouillot, Michel-Rolph. 1988. *Peasants and Capital*. Baltimore: Johns Hopkins University Press.

———. 1992. The Caribbean Region: An Open Frontier in Anthropological Theory. *Annual Review of Anthropology* 21:19–42.

———. 1998. Culture on the Edges: Creolization in the Plantation Context. *Plantation Society in the Americas* 5:8–28.

Turner, Mary. 1982. *Slaves and Missionaries*. Urbana: University of Illinois Press.

Turner, Victor. 1962. Three Symbols of Passage in Ndembu Circumcision Ritual. In *Essays on the Ritual of Social Relations*, edited by Max Gluckman. Manchester: Manchester University Press.

———. 1966. Colour Classification in Ndembu Ritual. In *Anthropological Approaches to the Study of Religion*, edited by Michael Banton. London: Tavistock.

Van Gennep, Arnold. 1960. *The Rites of Passage*. London: Routledge and Kegan Paul (Orig. pub. 1909).

Van Stipriaan, Alex. 2004. July 1, Emancipation Day in Suriname: A Contested *Lieu de Mémoire*, 1863–2003. *New West Indian Guide* 78, nos. 3 and 4:269–304.

Wallerstein, Immanuel. 1974. *The Modern World-System I*. San Diego: Academic Press.

Wardle, Huon. 2011. The Double Life of M.G. Smith? Rethinking Caribbean Citizenship Beyond, Between and Within the National Frame. In *Caribbean Reasonings. M.G. Smith: Social Theory and Anthropology in the Caribbean and Beyond*, edited by Brian Meeks, 270–89. Kingston: Ian Randle Publishers.

Warner-Lewis, Maureen. 2002. The Character of African-Jamaican Culture. In *Jamaica in Slavery and Freedom*, edited by Kathleen E.A. Monteith and Glen Richards, 89–114. Kingston, Jamaica: University of the West Indies Press.

———. 2003. *Central Africa in the Caribbean*. Kingston, Jamaica: University of the West Indies Press.

Watson, James L. 1980. Slavery as an Institution, Open and Closed Systems. In *Asian and African Systems of Slavery*, edited by James L. Watson, Berkeley, Calif.: University of California Press.

Webster, Steven. 1975. Cognatic Descent Groups and the Contemporary Maori: A Preliminary Reassessment. *Journal of the Polynesian Society* 84, no. 2:121–52.

Williams, Alan N., ed. 2003. *Land in the Caribbean*. Land Tenure Center, University of Wisconsin-Madison.

Williams, Cynric. 1826. *Tour through the Island of Jamaica*. London: Hunt and Clarke.

Wilson, Peter J. 1973. *Crab Antics*. New Haven: Yale University Press.

Young, Virgina Heyer. 1993. *Becoming West Indian*. Washington: Smithsonian Institution Press.

Zips, Werner. 1996. Laws in Competition: Traditional Maroon Authorities within Legal Pluralism in Jamaica. *Journal of Legal Pluralism and Unofficial Law*, 37–38:279–305.

———. 1998. 'We Are Landowners': Territorial Autonomy and Land Tenure in the Jamaican Maroon Community of Accompong. *Journal of Legal Pluralism* 40:89–121.

———. 1999. *Black Rebels*. Princeton, NJ: Markus Wiener.

———. 2011. *Nanny's Asafo Warriors*. Kingston: Ian Randle Publishers.

———. 2012. Review of *Caribbean Reasonings. M.G. Smith: Social Theory and Anthropology in the Caribbean and Beyond*, edited by Brian Meeks. Kingston: Ian Randle Publishers, 2011. *Journal of the Royal Anthropological Institute* 18, no. 4:902–903.

Index

Aberdeen, xvii; Accompong narrative on lands of, 146–48; African-Prince Maroon lineage in, 17; community formation, 15, 32, 38; creolization in, xviii; estate, 148–50, 152–53; great house, 147; maroon and non-maroon ethnicities in, 156–62; migration and, 18; Moravian missionaries and, 153–56; Old Families in, 16; perception of, by Accompong Maroons, 66–67; revivalism in, 17

Accompong (Town), xvii; Afro-Creole identity, 15–16; burial grounds, 86–90; cognatic clans and lineages, 336; commons, xix, 16, 337; community formation, 14–15, 41; creolization in, xviii, 94; Emancipation Day at, 338; established, 37; Myal in, xx, 17, 18, 21; Overseas Association of Accompong Maroons, 18; peasant economy of, 71; Presbyterian Church in, 135; relationship between Maroon Town and, 164–72; sacred groves, 81, 83–84; as sole surviving village of the Leeward polity, 48; as symbol of Jamaican nation-state, 91; war cemeteries, 85

African-Prince Maroon, 17, 157; Charles Wint's relationship to, 157–58

Afro-Creole maroon ethnicity: in Accompong, 15–16

Agrarian structure: Jamaica, 6

Austin-Broos, Diane, xix

Baptist Church, 51
Baptist War. See Christmas Rebellion
Besson, Jean: ancestry of, 22–23; *Transformations of Freedom in the Land of the Maroons*, 346

Brown, Roberta: narrative of, 219–220
Bye-Maroon, 26, 30 n.39

'Campong Nanny: and Maroon Town and Accompong Town, 256–57; and the pumpkin vine, 252–56
Caribbeanization, 2
Cawley, Harris: on Aberdeen lands, 146–48; on Myal play, 111–13; narrative on Maroon Town, 169–72
Cellular telephones: in Accompong, 344, 345
Chambers, Robert: narrative of, 251
Christmas Rebellion, 49–50
Clarke, Edith, xix
Cockpit Country, 1; in the global economy, 7; in Jamaica's social system, 54–56; land transformation in, 336; and Maroon Wars, xvii; research area described, 8, 10–14
Cognatic clans, Caribbean: and creole tenures, 336–337
Commons: Caribbean origins of the, 61–63; in Caribbean creole tenures, 127–31
Commons (Accompong), xix, 16; as creolization and peasantization, 60, 94; described, 72–75; the maroon polity, 64–71; sacred landscapes of, 63–93
Congo Town, 20. See also Highwindward, Me No Sen You No Come
Cooks, ritual, 97 n.20, 108–11
Creolization, xvii, xviii; and Accompong maroon commons, 16, 342–43; cognatic landholding clans and, 89–90, 336–37, 343; comparative study of, 1; critique of Zips's argument on,

135–42; defined, 2–3; and globalization, 1–2; in Myal Play, 337–38; and primogeniture, 4; slave rebellions and, 32
Cudjoe, Captain, 34–35
Cudjoe's Town, established, 37; shifted, 63, 133. *See also* Trelawny Town
Cultural negotiations, xix, xx
Currie, Betsy: partial genealogy of descendants of, 241
Currie, Melvin: on relationship between Maroon Town and Accompong, 165–66

De Bolas, Juan, 34
Dobson, Orville (Charlie), 8, 27; narrative of, 246, 248–50, partial genealogy of, 247
Dragoon Hole, 41
Drummond, Bishop: revivalist worldview of, in Maroon Town, 191–94
Dunstan, Jonathan: narrative of, 189–91

Emancipation: Day, xx, 21; at Accompong, 314–18, 338; in the Caribbean, 305–306; celebration in Maroon Town, 177; at Flagstaff, 306–308; re-establishment of, in Jamaica, 332 n.3
Emancipation War, 51. *See also* Christmas Rebellion

Family land, 15, 33
Felsenkopf mulatto maroons, 259–67
Fennel, Edgar: narrative of, 236–37
Finnigan, Caleb: narrative of, 231–33
First Maroon War, 14; and consolidation of Leeward Maroon polity, 34–41
First-Time Maroons, 16, 29 n.27, 70
Flagstaff, 15, 46, 47; Ball Ground at, 212; Emancipation Day celebrations at, 306–308; Emancipation festivals interpreted, 313–314; heritage tourism at, 330–332; Jonkonnu at, 311–13; white soldiers' cemetery, 212
Foster, William, 153
Foster-Barham, Joseph, 153
Free villages, 32; and the peasantry, 53–54
Freedom: transformations of, 335–36

Gender: in Myal rituals, 78–79, 111–12
Globalization, 2; and creolization, 1–2; impact in Jamaica, 7

Hall, Adeline: narrative of, 240, 242, 244–45
Harris, Glendon: narrative of, 226–29; partial genealogy of the McIntyre, Stennett and Harris clans, 222
Highwindward, 20, 47, 61
Hines clan: partial genealogy of, 243
Honour Rock, 13

Jamaica: agrarian structure, 6; impact of globalization on, 7
James, Alfonso: narrative of, 245–46
Johnson, Bunny: narrative of, 229–31

Kensington: 10–11
Kindah, 70; Grove, 75–80, 81, 137–41
Kinship: in Maroon Town, 199–201; implications of the research for understanding of, 345–46

Land boundaries: Accompong, 65
Landholding clans, cognatic: and creolization process, 89–90
Land transmission: among proto-peasants, 33. *See also* Family land
Lawrence, Caroline (Ena), ancestry of, 99–101; narrative of the Myal worldview, 101–103

Leeward Maroons, xvii; Accompong as sole surviving village of the polity, 48; consolidation of the polity, 34–41; impact of Second Maroon War on, 41–48; polity, 14; trails, 21, 326–32

Maldon Baptist Church, 188–91
Maroon Council, 67, 69–70
Maroon descent: narratives of Afro-Creole, 240–51
Maroon Town, xvii, Aberdonian narrative on, 163–64; absence of Myalism in, 165; Accompong Maroon narratives on, 164–72; boundaries and political integration into the nation-state, 177–79; community formation, 15, 176–77; creolization in, xviii; crossroads, 11, 13; education in, 196–99; gender and class in economy of, 184–87; hidden history, 19; kinship and ethnicity in, 199–201; McGhie Maroons, 17, 269–301; McGhie Old Family, 17, 269–301; Meso-Creole cognatic clans in, 16–17; migration and, 18, 187–88; mortuary rituals in, 213–15; narratives of maroon descent and marronage, 239–68; Old Families in, 16; oral traditions in, 203–205; peasant economy of, 184–87; in post-slavery peasantization, 184; religion in, 188–96; revival worldview in, 17, 191–94; telephones in, 344; transformation of Trelawny Town into, 20, 179, 181–84; transport in, 187
Maroon/Non-Maroon interface: Aberdeen, Accompong and Maroon Town, 146–72; ethnography at the, 338–41
Maroon Wars, xvii, 3; Cockpit Country landscape and, 33–34; and treaties, 32, 39
Maroons Land Allotment Act (1842), 48, 61–62, 114, 147

Marronage: Afro-Creole narratives of, 251–58; in the Americas, 32; newcomers' narratives of, 257–59
McFarlane family, 26, 30 n.35
McFarlane, Margaret, 25
McGhie, Albert I, partial genealogy of descendants, 290; Devon, 295; Jonathan II, 277–79; Jonathan III, partial genealogy of, 288; Leonard Lambert, 296–98, 300–301; Robert II, partial genealogy of descendants, 279, 280; William, descendants, 281–85; Rudyard, narrative of, 234–36
McGhie Maroons, 17, 269–301; and the McGhie Old Family, 20
McGhie Old Family, 17, 269–301; and the McGhie Maroons, 20
McGhie generations: reflections of, 292–95
McGhies: partial genealogy, Afro-Scot McGhies, 270, 276–77; planters and maroons in historical records, 271–76
McIntyre, Gaby: narrative of, 221, 223–24; partial genealogy of the McIntyre, Stennett and Harris clans, 222
Me No Sen You No Come, 20, 47, 61
Meso-Creole ethnicities: in Maroon Town, 203–37
Meso-Creole non-maroon ethnicities, 16–17, 161–62
Migration: impact on Jamaica, 7; in Aberdeen and Maroon Town, 18
Mintz, Sidney, xix
Missionaries: activity in Aberdeen, Accompong and Maroon Town, 48–53; Moravians in Aberdeen, 153–56
Moffatt, Mr.: narrative of, 250–51
Mortuary rituals: in Maroon Town, 213–15
Mundy, William, 161–162
Mundy Old Family: mixed British and African ancestry, 161–62

Myal: absence of, in Maroon Town, 165; in Accompong, xx, 15–16, 17; continued creolization of, 131–35, 337–38; Dance/Play, 78; paradox of transformation of, 318–26; and Rastafari, 134–35; worldview, 99–123

Nanny, 36; Nanny Town, 36
Nanny Rock, 263
Nanny's Asafo Warriors: The Jamaican Maroons' African Experience (Zips): critiqued, 135–42
Nedham, Colonel, 57 n.7

Ockbrook, 15. *See also* Aberdeen
Oikoumenê, 2, 27 n.3
Old Families: in Aberdeen and Maroon Town, 16, 159
Old Town, 83
Oral history narratives, xvii–xviii, xix
Overseas Association of Accompong Maroons, 18

Parkinson, Leonard, 43, 45
Pearson, Melvin; narrative of, 215–19
Peasant economy: of Accompong, 71
Peasantry: and free villages, 53–54
Peddie, Sydney: on Myal worldview, 121–24
Peterkin, Walter: narrative of, 233–34
Politics: in Aberdeen, 17; in Accompong, 17; in Maroon Town, 17
Pentecostalists: in Maroon Town, 195–96
Presbyterian Church: in Accompong, 135
Primogeniture: effect of creolization on, 4, 33
Proto-peasantry, 32; and land transmission, 33

Rastafarians: in Accompong, 134; in Maroon Town, 17

Reid, Gladys: on pilgrimage to Old Town, 104; on public nature of the Myal Play, 104
Reid, Mortimer: narratives of, 205–15
Reid, Rupie: as abeng blower, 105–107
Reid clan (Maroon Town): in Afro-Scots Old Families, 208; partial genealogy of, 209, 210, 215–16
Revivalism, 8; in Aberdeen and Maroon Town, 17
Rockhead Old Family, 259–67; partial genealogy of Felsenkopf maroons and Rockhead clan, 261
Rockhead, Willard: narrative of, 259–67
Rowe clan (Accompong), 124; narratives on Maroon Town from, 166–69; partial genealogy of, 100
Rowe, Mann O., 113–21; on the Myal Play, 116–18
Rowe-Edwards, Norma: first female Deputy Colonel, Accompong, 125, 126 n.6

Salter's Hill Baptist Church, 8, 49
Sam Sharpe, 50
Scottish settlement: in Jamaica, 3
Seal Grounds (Revival): in Accompong, 121–22, 134
Second Maroon War: causes, 41–42; course of, 43–45; impact on the Leeward Maroon polity, 41–48
Serial polygamy, 348 n.10
Seventh Day Adventists: in Maroon Town, 194–95
'Slave master' pickni', 203
Slave rebellions: in the Americas, 31–32; in the creolization process, 32
Smith, R.T., xix, 1
Stennett, Vicky: ancestry of, 225–26; narrative of, 224–26; partial genealogy of the McIntyre, Stennett and Harris clans, 222

Sugar estates, corporate, 6

Taylor, Lucien: narrative of, 162
Transformations of Freedom in the Land of the Maroons (Besson): and comparative anthropology, 346
Trelawny Maroons: deportation of, 45–46, 47
Trelawny Town, 15, 46; transformation into Maroon Town, 20. *See also* Maroon Town

Wardle, Huon, xix
Williams, Alan: ancestry of, 159–61; ties to Aberdeen and Accompong, 159–61
Williams, Asta: on Seventh Day Adventists in Maroon Town, 194–95
Williams, Aubrey: narrative of, 108–11
Williams, Lucal: narrative of, 108–11
Windward Maroons, 3
Wint, Charles: ancestry of, 156–59; relationship to African-Prince Maroon, 157–58

Zips, Werner: *Nanny's Asafo Warriors: The Jamaican Maroons' African Experience*, 135–42
Zong massacre, 4